Economic Issues For Consumers

Seventh Edition

Economic Issues
For Consumers

Seventh Edition

Roger LeRoy Miller
University of Texas at Arlington

Alan D. Stafford
Niagara County Community College

West Publishing Company
St. Paul/Minneapolis   New York   Los Angeles   San Francisco

Production Credits

Copyediting Maggie Jarpey
Interior Design Hespenheide Design
Composition Parkwood Composition
Index Terry Casey

Production, Prepress, Printing and Binding by West Publishing Company.

A Student Study Guide

A study guide has been developed to assist students in mastering the concepts presented in this text. It reinforces chapter material by presenting it in a concise format with review questions. An examination copy is available to instructors by contacting West Publishing Company. Students can purchase the study guide from the local bookstore under the title *Study Guide to Accompany Economic Issues for Consumers,* Seventh Edition, prepared by M. Barbara Killen.

WEST'S COMMITMENT TO THE ENVIRONMENT

In 1906, West Publishing Company began recycling materials left over from the production of books. This began a tradition of efficient and responsible use of resources. Today, up to 95 percent of our legal books and 70 percent of our college and school texts are printed on recycled, acid-free stock. West also recycles nearly 22 million pounds of scrap paper annually—the equivalent of 181,717 trees. Since the 1960s, West has devised ways to capture and recycle waste inks, solvents, oils, and vapors created in the printing process. We also recycle plastics of all kinds, wood, glass, corrugated cardboard, and batteries, and have eliminated the use of styrofoam book packaging. We at West are proud of the longevity and the scope of our commitment to the environment.

COPYRIGHT ©1975,
1978, 1981, 1984,
1987, 1990 By WEST PUBLISHING COMPANY
COPYRIGHT ©1994 By WEST PUBLISHING COMPANY
610 Opperman Drive
P.O. Box 64526
St. Paul, MN 55164-0526

Printed in the United States of America

01 00 99 98 97 96 95 94   8 7 6 5 4 3 2 1 0

Library of Congress Cataloging-in-Publication Data

Miller, Roger LeRoy,
    Economic issues for consumers / Roger LeRoy Miller, Alan D.
Stafford.—7th ed.
        p.   cm.
    Includes index.
    ISBN 0-314-02261-9 (hard)
    1. Finance, Personal.   2. Consumer education.   I. Stafford, Alan
D. II. Title.
HG179.M48   1994
332.024—dc20   93-8170
                                                          CIP

PRINTED ON 10% POST CONSUMER RECYCLED PAPER

To Michelle Webb,

who has extended the
meaning of courage.
Thanks for your cheeerfulness.

R.L.M.

To Barbara,

who allowed me to disappear
into the abyss of my computer
and pulled me back from time to time.

A.D.S.

Contents in Brief

Contents

Chapter 12   Putting a Roof over Your Head   245

Chapter 13   The Appliance Society   273

Preface

As the end of the twentieth century draws near, we can look back over the past hundred years and realize how much the lives of American consumers have changed. At the beginning of this century our society was primarily rural. We were still using horses and buggies. Women had not yet obtained the vote in federal elections. Heavier-than-air flight was only a dream in the minds of the Wright brothers. Taking spaceships to the moon was the topic of science-fiction novels. Although the telephone existed, there were fewer than 20 for every thousand people in 1900. Electricity had found its way into less than 5 percent of all houses. Radio, television, VCRs, tape recorders, and even movies had yet to be invented. Today we take these products and many more for granted. It is safe to say that no other hundred-year period in the history of civilization has witnessed such profound and socially transforming technological change.

What does this mean to our nation's consumers? It means we face a more complex world and more difficult consumer decisions every day. In at least one important aspect, however, consumer decision making is the same today as it was a hundred years ago. All consumers, everywhere on earth, and at all times, are, have been, and will be, faced with limited resources. Regardless of the point in time, consumers have to make choices in how to spend their limited income. We assume throughout this text that all consumers have the common goal of achieving a higher quality of life through the choices they make.

In the seventh edition of *Economic Issues for Consumers,* major topics have been added or expanded because they are more important today than they were in the past. Ethical questions are arising more often, and they are given prominent discussion in the pages that follow. The global nature of our economy is causing rapid changes in the types of decisions consumers must make. Accordingly, an entire new chapter is devoted to consumerism and environmental problems. The ongoing crisis in banking is examined in another chapter. Another directs attention to choosing medical care and obtaining affordable medical insurance. The process of selecting a lawyer and the ethical question of what type of advertising is appropriate for children are among other new topics in this edition. Actually, the list of new areas of concern that are examined in this text would go on for pages. It is fair to say that the most important consumer issues of our day are covered.

The Format of the Book—Chapters and Issues

You will notice the format of this book lends itself to easy use and understanding. It presents major topics of consumer economics in chapter form. Most of these chapters are followed by one or more Consumer Issues. To a large extent, the Consumer Issues offer more practical advice than do the chapters. For example, after discussing fraud in the marketplace in Chapter 6, Consumer Issue E outlines measures individuals can take to protect themselves against fraud in a specific area of the marketplace—auto-repair services. As another example, following the chapter on health care, an issue suggests specific steps consumers can take to choose doctors and other health-care providers.

Key Changes For The Seventh Edition

So much has happened since the publication of the sixth edition that a large number of changes were necessary to provide the most up-to-date information possible in a usable format for students who want to be rational consumers.

New and Significantly Revised Chapters

The first chapter, **"The Consumer in Our Global Economy,"** has been significantly revised to provide a more extensive foundation in basic economic understanding. It also explains how our economic system is related to events in other countries. It begins a discussion of the global nature of our economy which is a recurring theme throughout the seventh edition.

Chapter 4, **"Environmentally Responsible Consumer Behavior,"** has been added because of our growing awareness of the need to protect the environment we live in. It includes discussions of the following topics:

▶ The scope of our environmental problems.
▶ How advancements in technology have contributed to the growth of environmental problems.
▶ The global nature of most of our environmental problems.
▶ The choices that individual consumers can make to help limit damage to our environment and protect it for the benefit of present and future generations.

Chapter 7, **"The Consumer as a Wage Earner,"** includes a new section on inflation that emphasizes how price increases change what consumers' wages will buy. It explains how the consumer price index is determined, and how it can be used to measure consumers' real income and purchasing power. This chapter also presents information that concerns the impact of the Civil Rights Act of 1991 on American workers and employers.

Chapter 9, **"Paying for Government,"** is now followed by a consumer issue that discusses how taxpayers may choose appropriate forms to use when filing federal income taxes. It explains the differences between forms 1040 EZ, 1040 A, and 1040. Although this issue cannot provide a comprehensive explanation of how to complete tax returns, it does help students build a foundation of understanding that will allow them to ask informed questions and know where to look for further information.

Chapter 23, **"Consumers in a Changing World,"** presents topics related to the many ways that new technology is changing our lives. It is similar to the chapter on technology in the sixth edition but has a new focus. This focus is on the continuing need of consumers to learn and stay aware of changes in technology. Consumers must stay up-to-date to maintain their standard of living, and to continue to be able to make rational consumer decisions. The point is made that students should not regard consumer economics as a body of knowledge one acquires, but as an ongoing process that never ends in our changing world.

Updated Chapters and Consumer Issues

Other chapters and Consumer Issues in *Economic Issues for Consumers* have been updated to make sure that the text, tables, graphs, charts, and references are as current as possible. Important changes and additions include the following:

Chapter 3, **"Rational Consumer Decision Making,"** includes a section on time management to help students learn how to budget their time.

Chapter 8, **"You Have to Live .with What You Have,"** discusses special budgeting problems faced by college students.

Chapter 10, **"The $600+ Billion American Diet,"** reports on costs and benefits of new food labeling regulations that were mandated by the Food and Drug Administration in 1992 to be effective in 1994.

Chapter 13, **"The Appliance Society,"** has been expanded to include useful information on choosing furniture.

Chapter 14, **"Getting There Is Half the Worry,"** provides suggestions for how consumers may benefit from using public transportation when available instead of private automobiles.

Chapter 15, **"Banks and the Banking System,"** has a new section that describes the savings and loan disaster and how it has affected choices American consumers make.

Chapter 19, **"The Health-Care Dilemma,"** discusses the concept of shared risk and how the rising costs of medical care have increased this risk and also, therefore, medical insurance premiums.

Chapter 21, **"Life Insurance and Social Security,"** explains methods consumers can use to determine the financial stability of companies from which they might purchase life insurance.

Chapter 22, **"Your Retirement Years,"** includes a new section devoted to enhancing the quality of retirement years by achieving financial security and participating in activities that add meaning to older consumers' lives.

New Consumer Issues

Four new Consumer Issues have been added. The Issue, **"Children's Advertising,"** following Chapter 5, **"A Flood of Advertising,"** discusses business and ethical considerations of advertising directed at children. It also shows how parents can use these advertisements as a vehicle for teaching consumer skills to their children.

"Budgeting Time for Recreation and Leisure" now follows Chapter 8, **"You Have to Live with What You Have."** This issue considers the tradeoff consumers make when they use their time and earnings for recreation. It emphasizes the importance of planning ahead to make the best use of leisure time.

"Purchasing Medical Care," follows Chapter 19, **"The Health-Care Dilemma."** This issue provides extensive information and advice on choosing health-care providers, hospitals, or nursing homes. This issue is likely to be particularly useful to students in light of the rapid increase in the cost of medical care and the growing difficulty of obtaining affordable medical insurance.

The final new issue is **"Choosing a Lawyer,"** which follows Chapter 22, **"Planning for Your Retirement Years."** This issue deals with many of the situations in which consumers need legal advice. It emphasizes the fact that not every such situation requires the services of a lawyer, and it suggests other sources of legal assistance. The issue provides advice on ways to select a lawyer when necessary, and on how to develop a relationship with a lawyer that is beneficial and no more expensive than need be.

Two New Features

New "boxed" features have been added to many of the chapters. **"The Global Consumer"** shows how consumers are affected by international trade and events in other nations. **"The Ethical Consumer"** demonstrates how personal ethics influences decisions consumers make. These boxed features are similar to the **"Consumer Close-Ups"** that were introduced in the sixth edition, and which have been revised and expanded in the seventh edition.

Pedagogical Aids

Students will find a number of pedagogical aids in both the chapters and Consumer Issues. Each chapter begins with a "Preview," a set of questions that indicate to the reader that will be covered. To introduce new terminology and to allow the reader to follow the text more meaningfully, **"Key Terms"** appear in boldface type when they are first used. They are then defined in the margin of that page. In the seventh edition, these terms are again listed and defined in a **"Glossary of Terms"** at the end of the text.

At the end of each chapter, there is a point-by-point **"Summary"** that can be used for review. The **"Questions for Thought and Discussion"** that follow the summary may be used as the basis for class discussion or as the basis for individual thought or even group work without the direct aid of the instructor. **"Things to Do"** lists projects that a class can do as a group or that individuals can do on their own at the request of the professor. The **"Application"** allows students to take concepts they have studied in each chapter and apply them in their own lives or in their communities. These activities are intended to demonstrate practical applications for knowledge gained in this course. Finally, **"Selected Readings"** presents additional sources of reading for those who wish further information on subjects covered within the chapter or issue.

The Consumer Issues have basically the same pedagogical devices, except that the glossary terms are presented and defined at the opening of the issue instead of in the margins of the pages on which they first appear, and there is no chapter preview or application activity.

Other Useful Changes or Additions to the Seventh Edition

You will notice a wide use of illustrative materials—photographs, charts, and tables. Visualization of certain ideas not only aids students in understanding the material but also makes the task of reading the text more enjoyable. All illustrations are referred to directly in the text, or they have captions that include critical-thinking questions to relate them to the topics being discussed in the text.

Supplementary Materials

A practical and easy-to-understand *Student Study Guide* has been provided by M. Barbara Killen. Students using it will find the material interesting and well presented. The workbook will also allow students to apply the principles of rational decision making to practical problems.

The *Instructor's Manual* by Judy Farris includes a summary for each chapter and Consumer Issue, an increased number of test items, and a current list of resource ideas.

Acknowledgments

Major reviewers who offered detailed criticism for the first, second, third, fourth, fifth and sixth editions were as follows:

Judy L. Allen
Southwest Texas State University

Howard Alsey
Arkansas State University

Joseph E. Barr
Farmingham State College

Phillis B. Basile
Orange Coast College

Carolyn Bednar
Peru State College

Margarita Blackwell
Eastern Kentucky University

Harold R. Boadway
Moraine Valley Community College

Jean S. Bowers
Ohio State University

Margaret Jane Brennan
Western Michigan University

Kay P. Edwards
Brigham Young University

Judy Farris
South Dakota State University

Barbara Follosco
Los Angeles Valley College

David G. Garraty
Thomas Nelson Community College

Linda Graham
Wichita State University

Joyce S. Harrison
Middle Tennessee State University

Ron Hartje
Souk Valley College

Ann R. Hiatt
University of North Carolina
at Greensboro

James O. Hill
Vincennes University

Hilda Jo Hennings
Northern Arizona University

Thomas A. Johnson
William Rainey Harper College

William L. Johnston
Oklahoma State University

Jane Buchwald Kerr
Cameron University

Hazel Kirk
Brevard Community College,
Cocoa Campus

Ann Lawson
Thomas Nelson Community College

John R. Lindbeck
Western Michigan University

Dr. Merlene Lyman
Fort Hays State University

Esther McCabe
The University of Connecticut

Michael L. Oliphant
Southwest Virginia Community

Geraldine Olson
Oregon State University

Claudia J. Peck
Oklahoma State University

James Poley
City College of San Francisco

Rose Reha
St. Cloud State University

Shirley Schecter
Queens College

Jolene Scriven
Northern Illinois University

Eugene Silberberg
University of Washington

Rueben Slesinger
University of Pittsburgh

Nancy Z. Spillman
Los Angeles Trade-Technical
College

Barbara L. Stewart
University of Houston

Faye Taylor
University of Utah

Louise Wesswick
University of Wyoming

Merle E. Taylor
Santa Barbara City College

Mari S. Wilhelm
University of Arizona

Margil Vanderhoff
Indiana University

Joseph Wurmli
Hillsborough Community College

Mary Ann Van Slyke
North Central Technical Institute

Prudence Zalewski
California State Polytechnic
University
San Luis Obispo

Frank A. Viggiano, Jr.
Indiana University of Pennsylvania

Roberta W. Walsh
University of Vermont

Reviewers for the seventh edition were:

Judy L. Allen
Southwest Texas State University

Reuben E. Slesinger
University of Pittsburgh

Patricia A. Daly
Framington State College

Alden W. Smith
Anne Arundel Community College

Michael Magura
University of Toledo

Patti Wooten Swanson
Bethel College

Thomas J. Porebski
Triton College

It goes without saying that we are extremely appreciative of the tremendous help that the above reviewers provided to us. Without them, this seventh edition would not be as complete and accurate as we believe it now is.

We have found through the years that the best way we can improve on what we write is by soliciting the comments of those who use our texts. We therefore stand ready to answer any and all comments, criticisms, or questions relating to what follows in this book. It is with the help of those who want the best for their students that we can find out what is best for the ultimate reader of *Economic Issues for Consumers*.

To The Student

Your text, *Economic Issues for Consumers,* provides you with a foundation of information that will help you gain valuable and useful knowledge from the course you are taking. Although this text contains substantial factual data and describes many specific law and consumer protection regulations, its greatest value lies in the practical advice it offers to help make your own consumer choices. Much of what you learn from this text will have immediate and beneficial application to your personal life.

To use this text to best advantage, you should read the "Preview" questions that are found at the beginning of each chapter. These provide a general idea of the content of the chapter. You should then read the assigned material, taking notes of topics that you would like more information about, that you do not understand, or that have particular significance for you. Use these notes as study aids and as the basis for participating in classroom discussions. Your professor is well qualified to provide you with additional information, but he or she needs you to identify the areas that you find most interesting or challenging.

Economic Issues for Consumers is a tool that will help you gain useful knowledge and skills, but it is only a tool. The value you receive from this text, and from your class, to a large extent depends on you and the amount of effort you put into your study of consumer economics.

ADS
Lewiston, NY, 1993

The Consumer in Today's World

The Consumer in Our Global Economy

PREVIEW

▶ What is scarcity, and why does it necessitate choices?

▶ What are tradeoffs and opportunity costs, and how are they involved in consumer decisions?

▶ How do the laws of demand and supply affect the consumer?

▶ What are some of the different roles governments play in various types of economic systems?

▶ How has the American economy been affected by the increasingly global nature of the world's economies?

▶ How can American consumers make responsible choices in our global economy?

This is a book about consumer economics. That means it has to do both with economics and with you, the consumer. The goal is to help you apply economic principles when making consumer decisions—such as whether to buy a house, how to buy it, what kind of insurance to purchase, whether a new or a used car is a better deal, what type of checkable and savings accounts to use, and so on. The list of such decisions is virtually endless, since we are all consumers, and will be all our lives. An understanding of economics helps us to be more rational consumers, able to analyze alternatives and base our decision making on facts relevant to us.

Accountants, lawyers, and other professionals who work in specialized fields must acquire the unique knowledge that enables them to provide the **services** of their chosen occupation. Unlike these professionals who have special training, American consumers often make buying decisions before they have had any formal instruction in the basic principles that determine economic behavior in the world around them. The task of this chapter is to put the horse back before the cart, so to speak, by presenting some of the fundamental economic concepts that apply to you as a consumer. The finer points of economic theory do not concern us here. We leave that kind of instruction for a course in either microeconomics—the study of individual and business decision-making behavior—or macroeconomics—the study of economy-wide problems such as inflation and unemployment.

SCARCITY AND THE CONSUMER

We begin our discussion of economics with the problem of **scarcity** because it is the heart of economic analysis. Would you like to have more time to study and still have time for all the other things you want to do like going to the student union with your friends? Would you like to have a bigger house or apartment, or a bigger room in your dorm or fraternity or sorority house? Would you like to have more clothes without giving up buying other products you enjoy? Indeed, why can't we all have more of everything? The answer is that individually and collectively we face the problem of scarcity.

Scarcity exists because we have unlimited wants and only a limited supply of resources to produce products that satisfy our wants. Scarcity is a relative term. For someone who has no food, a crust of bread is a scarce product, while others may experience scarcity in their inability to afford steak or lobster every night. As long as we are not able to have everything we want, scarcity exists. This means that scarcity and poverty are not the same thing. Scarcity can exist in an environment of affluence and abundance.

Imagine you were the richest person in the world. You still could not have everything you want. The most obvious example of scarcity in this case would be your scarcity of time. With only one life to lead, you would be unable to enjoy all the things you owned.

Usually people perceive scarcity in terms of having a limited amount of money to spend. Although from their personal point of view they are correct, from the perspective of the entire economy there is a different cause of scarcity. Remember, scarcity is the result of our limited ability to produce **goods** and services to satisfy our wants. If our government printed enough money to give every person $1 million, the food, clothing, houses, swimming pools, yachts, and other products they wanted to buy with that money would not be available in sufficient amounts for everyone; more of these products would

Services
Intangible actions that have the ability to satisfy human wants.

Scarcity
A term used to describe the condition in which we are unable to provide enough products to satisfy all people's needs and wants because of our limited resources.

Goods
Tangible objects that have the ability to satisfy human wants.

not magically come into existence. There would be no more oil in the ground, factories, workers, or other **productive resources** than previously existed, so it would not be possible to create enough products to satisfy everyone's wants. We would all have more money, but we would not have solved the problem of scarcity. Thus, scarcity is an unavoidable fact of everyone's life.

UNIVERSAL SCARCITY

The problem of scarcity is not unique to consumers, it is faced by businesses, the government, and by all nations in the world. Successful businesses in the United States earn a **profit** when they receive more income from sales than the costs they pay to produce and offer products for sale. When a firm uses its profits to buy resources to produce a television set, it cannot use those same resources to produce a VCR or tape recorder. A business that buys machines to automatically assemble electric mixers cannot use that money to hire more workers. Businesses must make these types of choices because the supply of resources they may use to produce products to offer consumers are scarce regardless of how much profit they earn.

We all receive valuable services from our government. The roads we drive on, the schools we attend, and the fire and police protection are only a few of the many government services we all need but that most individuals could not afford to purchase for themselves. Our government pays for the resources it uses by taxing or borrowing money. When our government buys resources to provide services, it faces the problem of scarcity because it cannot use the same money to accomplish more than one objective. Money used to pay for road repairs, for example, may not be used to pay schoolteachers. The government may also be seen as contributing to the problem of scarcity for other parts of society. The resources it uses are not available to people and businesses to buy and use for other purposes. Within our country, consumers, businesses, and the government compete for use of the scarce resources we have.

Just as Americans must deal with scarcity, all nations in the world face this problem. Resources that are used to build automobiles in Japan cannot be used to reduce the shortage of affordable housing in that country. Land that is used for growing sugarcane in Cuba may not be used to raise other crops. Oil that is pumped from the ground in Saudi Arabia today will not be available for use in the future. Although the way in which economic decisions are made will vary from one nation to another, all nations face this problem. Differences in the way resources are distributed in the world and how decisions are made to use scarce resources form the basis for international trade that affects all our lives. More will be said about the global nature of our economy later in this chapter.

THE NECESSITY OF CHOICE

Scarcity forces us, as consumers, to make choices all the time. We must choose how we spend our time, how we spend our labor power (that is, what kind of work we do), and how we spend our income (our purchasing power). Life would be simple without scarcity. You and I would not have to bother much about consumer economics. In a world without scarcity, choices would not

Productive resources
Raw materials, tools, and labor that may be used to produce other goods or services that have the ability to satisfy human wants.

Profit
The difference between the total amount of money income received from selling a good or a service and the total cost of providing that good or service.

have to be made because everyone would possess every good or service they want. But we never will achieve such total satisfaction. That is why a knowledge of consumer economics is essential for maximizing the value we can derive from the consumer decisions we make.

For example, in making a budget, you need to decide whether you would receive more satisfaction from the purchase of new clothing or from taking a relaxing vacation. Or you may decide to save your money to buy a new car in the future instead. You can think of consumer decision making as a rational way of determining how to allocate your scarce time and money resources. Later in this chapter we will consider how consumer decisions in our country help determine the way our productive resources are allocated.

CHOICE AND OPPORTUNITY COST

Opportunity cost

The value of a second-best choice that is given up when a first choice is taken.

Every choice you make requires you to give something up. When you sit down to read this book, you have chosen not to do at least a thousand other things with your time. You could have read your English text, you could have watched television, you could have slept, you could have gone to the movies, and so on. Thus, scarcity of time has led you to choose to read this book rather than do something else that is presumably of less value. The something else that you chose not to do is the cost associated with spending time reading this book. Economists call it **opportunity cost.**

Let's assume that of all the other things you could have done instead of reading this book, the thing you most wanted to do, but didn't do, was watch television. If that's the case, then the value of the enjoyment you would have received from watching television is your opportunity cost of reading this book. Opportunity cost is defined as the value of a second-best choice that is given up when a first choice is taken. Opportunity cost is an unavoidable part of all decisions consumers make. It helps us place a value on the scarce resources that are used to produce products that satisfy our wants.

THE TRADEOFFS FACING YOU

Tradeoff

A term relating to opportunity cost. To get a desired economic good, it is necessary to trade off some other desired economic good whenever we are in a world of scarcity. A tradeoff involves a sacrifice, then, that must be made to obtain something.

Whatever you do, you are "trading off" one use of a resource for one or more alternative uses. The value of a **tradeoff** is represented by the opportunity cost just discussed. Let's go back to the opportunity cost of reading this book. Assume that you have a maximum of ten hours per week to spend studying just two subjects—consumer economics and accounting. The more time you study consumer economics, the higher you believe your grade will be in this subject. The same is true for accounting. There is a tradeoff, then, between spending an hour reading this book and spending that time studying accounting. A better grade you could earn in consumer economics must be purchased at the expense of a lower grade in accounting.

Similar tradeoffs occur for every choice you make. If you decide to join your school's basketball team, you must trade the value of other uses of your time for the value of the enjoyment received from participating in that sport. Whenever businesses, the government, or people in other nations make choices, they also make tradeoffs in which an opportunity cost is paid for the choice that is made.

AN IMPLICIT ASSUMPTION

Economic analysis rests upon an assumption that we should make clear at this time: Most people generally make choices that are intended to make themselves better off. Making oneself better off can take many forms depending on each person's individual values. For the purpose of economic analysis, however, we may assume that people attempt to make themselves better off in such things as their opportunity for leisure time and their ability to buy goods and services that satisfy their wants.

MARKETS

In economics, a **market** is the sum of all transactions that take place between buyers and sellers of a particular type of product. Therefore, if we talk about the "used car market," we are referring to the transactions between people who buy and sell used cars. The "labor market" is made up of the agreements between workers and their employers. There is even an "education market" in which students pay tuition to receive instruction and academic guidance.

Markets exist between and among people, businesses, governments, and other nations in the world. To demonstrate the importance of international markets, consider the fact that in 1992 roughly $1 out of every $10 spent in this country was used to buy a product that was manufactured in a different nation. At the same time, millions of Americans relied on our ability to sell American-made products in other nations for their employment. Despite its importance, however, the American economy is only a part of the larger world economy. To understand markets in that international economy, as well as local and national markets, we need to learn more about the way transactions are carried out.

Market
The sum of all transactions that take place between buyers and sellers of a particular type of product.

VOLUNTARY EXCHANGE IN U.S. ECONOMY

In the United States, consumers and producers are generally free to use their resources to buy and sell products as they choose. This means that we enjoy the right to **voluntary exchange** in most situations. You can spend your income collecting stamps while I buy an expensive boat if we wish. Other people are free to start businesses that offer rare stamps or expensive boats for sale. Although limitations do exist on the types of products Americans may legally buy or offer for sale (drugs, for example) individual people in the United States are free to make most economic choices.

Whenever a voluntary exchange takes place, it is reasonable to assume that both the buyer and the seller will benefit. Imagine you paid $10 for gasoline for your car. You must have felt that the gasoline had greater value than the $10 you spent. The owner of the filling station, in contrast, must have valued the $10 more than the gasoline. When the transaction was completed, both parties gained, because they valued the money and the gasoline differently. The same must be true of all other voluntary exchanges, because people would not choose to complete a transaction that they did not feel benefited them.

Voluntary exchange
Transactions completed through the free will of those involved.

DEMAND AND SUPPLY ANALYSIS—A BRIEF INTRODUCTION

In the U.S. economy the forces of demand and supply most often work together to determine which products will be produced and the quantity of each type of product that will be offered for sale. Later in this text you will discover how these same forces help consumers make many other economic decisions.

LAW OF DEMAND

Demand
The quantity of a product that will be sold at each possible price.

Law of demand
A basic economic principle that states that as the price of goods or services rises, the quantity of those goods and services demanded will fall. Conversely, as the price falls, the quantity demanded will rise.

The term **demand** refers to the quantity of a product consumers are willing and able to buy at each possible price. The **law of demand** states that if nothing else changes, consumers will buy a greater quantity of a product at a lower price than at a higher price. Therefore, if the price of a product falls, the quantity demanded will grow, and if the price increases, the quantity demanded will fall. Imagine that you and several of your friends have made a habit of going to the movies together every Friday night after work. If the price of a movie ticket increased by $2, some of the people in your group might not be able to afford it, while others might prefer to spend their money on some other product. In either case, the quantity of movie tickets demanded would be less because of the increase in price.

The quantity of a product consumers demand at any price depends on many factors other than price. These factors include tastes, income, the price of other related products, and expectations of what may happen in the future. For example, if your friends all chose to wear a particular brand of clothing, your demand for this brand of clothing might increase even if the price remained unchanged. If you were offered a new job that paid you more than you earn now, you could afford to demand a greater quantity of products like new cars or vacations. An increase in the price of gasoline, however, could cause you to drive fewer miles. This would reduce your demand for replacement tires for your car. As a final example, suppose your boss tells you that you will be laid off in two weeks. At the present you still have an income, but you know you won't in just 14 days. Your demand for many products would be less because you expect your income to be smaller in the near future. Each of these examples demonstrates one of many possible reasons why consumers might demand more or less of a product when there is no change in its price.

LAW OF SUPPLY

Supply
The quantity of a product businesses are willing to offer for sale at each possible price.

Law of supply
A basic economic principle that states that as the price of goods or services rises, the quantity of those goods and services supplied will increase. Conversely, as the price falls the quantity supplied will also decline.

Supply refers to the quantity of a product businesses are willing to offer for sale at each possible price. Businesses in the United States intend to earn a profit. The more consumers are willing to pay for a product, the more likely firms are to earn a profit by supplying it. Therefore, consumer acceptance of higher prices often causes existing firms to increase their production, as well as encouraging the creation of new firms that produce this type of good (or service).

The **law of supply** states that if nothing else changes, a greater quantity of a product will be supplied at a higher price than at a lower price. Therefore, if the price of a product increases, the quantity of the product that is supplied should also increase, and if the price falls, the quantity supplied should decline. You may see the law of supply in your own life. Ask yourself how many hours you would be willing to work at $1 an hour? $5 an hour? $100 an hour? Isn't it true that you would be willing to supply more of your labor as the wage (price) you receive grows?

Other factors that affect the profit a firm earns will also change its willingness to supply products. For example, a firm that produced bread might choose to go out of business if a 50-percent increase in the cost of flour eliminated its profit. A firm that found a way to produce carpet with fewer workers would be encouraged to supply more of its product because of its reduced labor costs and increased profits. Generally, an increase in a firm's costs of production will reduce the quantity of products it will supply at each possible price, while a decrease in its costs will cause it to supply greater quantities.

EQUILIBRIUM PRICE

The price you pay for most goods and services you buy is determined by the forces of demand and supply. There is a price for every product at which the quantity demanded would be exactly equal to the quantity supplied. Natural forces exist within markets that tend to force prices toward this **equilibrium price.**

Suppose that lettuce farmers were selling their products for $2 a head. This high price would encourage many farmers to grow more lettuce. However, it would discourage consumers from buying the product. As a result, there would be a surplus of lettuce, which would force the price down until it reached the equilibrium price (let us say 90 cents) where the quantity supplied and the quantity demanded were the same.

In a similar fashion, prices below the equilibrium price tend to be forced up by demand and supply. If farmers can get only 50 cents for a head of lettuce, they will be discouraged from supplying many units of this product. The low price, however, will cause consumers to demand more lettuce. The result will be a shortage of lettuce that will encourage farmers to increase their price to the equilibrium price (90 cents) where the quantity they are willing to supply is equal to the quantity consumers are willing to buy.

Although prices may be set in our economy that are not equilibrium prices, the forces of demand and supply still tend to push prices to this level. Prices may remain at other levels for extended periods of time only when there is imperfect competition. This condition will be discussed later in this chapter.

RELATIVE PRICE

The **relative price** of any product is its price compared with the prices of other goods in the economy. The price we pay in dollars and cents for a product at any point in time is called its **money price** (also known as *absolute, nominal,* or *current* price). Consumer buying decisions, however, depend on relative, not money prices. Consider the hypothetical example of prices of compact discs (CDs) and cassettes in Exhibit 1–1. Note that the money prices of CDs and cassettes have risen during the year. That means consumers have to pay more for both of them in today's dollars and cents. If we look at the relative prices, however, we find that last year CDs were twice

Equilibrium price
A price at which the quantity of a good or service demanded is exactly equal to the quantity that is supplied.

Relative price
The price of a commodity expressed in terms of the price of another commodity or the (weighted) average price of all other commodities.

Money price
The price that we observe today in terms of today's dollars. Also called the absolute, nominal, *or* current price.

▶ Exhibit 1–1 Money Price versus Relative Price

The money price of both compact discs (CDs) and cassettes has risen. But the relative price of CDs has fallen (or conversely, the relative price of cassettes has risen).

	MONEY PRICE		RELATIVE PRICE	
	Price Last Year	Price This Year	Price Last Year	Price This Year
CDs	$12	$14	$\frac{\$12}{\$6} = 2$	$\frac{\$14}{\$8} = 1.75$
Cassettes	$6	$8	$\frac{\$6}{\$12} = 0.5$	$\frac{\$8}{\$14} = 0.57$

as expensive as cassettes, whereas this year they are only one and three-fourths as expensive. Conversely, cassettes cost only half as much as CDs last year, whereas today they cost 57 percent as much. In the one-year period, the prices of both products have gone up in money terms, but the price of cassettes has gone up more rapidly. Therefore, the relative price of CDs has fallen while the relative price of cassettes has risen. If the law of demand holds true, then over this one-year period a relatively larger quantity of CDs will have been demanded, while a relatively smaller quantity of cassettes will have been sold, other things being equal.

Once the distinction between money prices and relative prices is made, there is less chance of confusion about the effect of price increases on the quantities of different products that are demanded during a period of time when all money prices are increasing. Products whose money prices increase more rapidly than most will be demanded less, while those whose money prices increase less rapidly will be demanded more.

Someone not familiar with this distinction might believe that the increased demand for CDs despite their higher price violates the law of demand. But, as we can see, the price of CDs must be considered in relation to the prices of other products, in this case the price of cassettes. Although this example involves only two products, in our economy the prices of all products must be considered. The demand should grow for any product that experiences lower rates of price increase than the average for most goods, while it should fall for goods that experience price increases greater than the average.

CONSUMER SOVEREIGNTY IN A MARKET ECONOMY

Market economy
An economy that is characterized by exchanges in markets that are controlled by the forces of demand and supply.

Perfect competition
A market condition in which many businesses offer the same product for sale to many customers at the same price.

Consumer sovereignty
A situation in which consumers ultimately decide which products and styles will survive in the marketplace; that is, producers do not dictate consumer tastes.

The American economy is a type of **market economy** because it is characterized by transactions that are free exchanges based on the laws of demand and supply. In a market economy individuals are free to use resources as they see fit to produce goods and services that are then offered for sale to consumers, who are free to buy or not buy them. In an ideal market economy there would be **perfect competition** and **consumer sovereignty.** In such a world no firm would be large or powerful enough to set prices for its products higher than those charged by other firms that offered similar goods or services for sale. Consumers would buy products they desired at the lowest possible prices. The most successful firms would be those that produced goods and services most efficiently. Their success would allow them to expand their own production and encourage others to open similar businesses. Money and resources would flow to the types of production that consumers demanded. Therefore, consumers would determine how scarce resources would be used to produce goods and services that were best able to satisfy their wants. If perfect competition existed in our economy, consumers would control production through the way they spend their money. They would be sovereign.

THE REAL WORLD OF IMPERFECT COMPETITION

In the real world, **imperfect competition** keeps consumers from always controlling production decisions and the allocation of scarce resources. There may be a limited number of producers, or other suppliers may be prevented from offering a similar product for sale by various barriers. In this event, a high price and large profits will not necessarily increase the quantity of the product that is supplied in the market, or of the resources allocated to that type of production.

Imperfect competition
A market condition in which individual businesses have some power to set the price and quality of their products.

Suppose you produce a medical device that doctors have found very useful in surgery. Suppose also that you have patented your device and have not sold the patent rights to any other producer. You have restricted entry into the market for this device because no other firm may legally produce it or offer it for sale while you hold your patent. Although you might charge a high price for your device and earn a large profit, other individuals may not use their resources to produce an alternative product to compete with your product. Even if other firms could make the product more efficiently and offer better quality, they would not be allowed to do so. In this situation you would have a **monopoly.** This is a simplistic example, of course, but it illustrates how the principle of consumer sovereignty can be invalidated by an economy made up of firms that hold some degree of monopoly power.

Monopoly
The only producer of a product that has no substitutes.

Businesses that hold monopoly-like powers are sovereign because they do not need to respond to the demands of consumers. Not that many are sovereign, however. Most small firms are quite competitive, and there is a limit to what even the largest firms are able to do with their economic power. Consider the difficult times experienced by American automobile manufacturers that once had significant monopoly-like powers in our economy. Even when large firms use sophisticated marketing techniques, they often lose the battle for sovereignty to consumers. It has been estimated that nine out of every ten new products offered to American consumers fail within one year. Essentially, such failures are due to the unwillingness of consumers to demand these products at a price that would allow the producing firms to earn a profit.

Even where consumer choice exists, individuals may be forced by law to buy some products. For example, in many states, it is illegal to drive a car without also purchasing automobile liability insurance. To be sure, some people ignore the law, but if they are apprehended they may pay a heavy penalty.

As shown in Exhibit 1–2, consumers confront a range of purchasing situations. In some cases they have almost total control over production through their purchasing decisions. In others they may be faced with government regulations or with the power of firms that possess monopoly-like power. Even advertising may reduce their control over the types of products offered in the market. It is safe to say that we generally are in the middle of the range of purchasing decisions, somewhere between being forced to purchase and being able to make independent choices.

At one extreme, no one forces us to buy anything; at the other, we are required to purchase an item whether we like it or not. Generally, depending on the situation, we are somewhere in between.

Perfect Consumer Sovereignty — We are not forced to buy.

No Consumer Sovereignty — We must buy.

Given our imperfectly competitive economy, neither complete producer sovereignty nor complete consumer sovereignty can exist. As a result, from an early time in our nation's history the government has imposed regulations on various markets to protect both business and consumer interests.

ROLE OF GOVERNMENT

Economic system
A set of understandings that governs the production and distribution of goods and services that satisfy human wants.

Socialist economic system
An economic system in which there is group (most often government) ownership of productive resources and control over the distribution of goods and services.

Capitalism
An economic system based on private ownership of the means of production and on a demand and supply market. This system emphasizes the absence of government restraints on ownership, production and trade.

Everyone in the world is a consumer of goods and services when he or she uses products to fill basic needs for food, shelter, and clothing. The role and economic power of consumers varies from country to country because each nation has its own unique **economic system.** In some countries resources have been owned, controlled, and allocated by an agency of the government. Individual consumers were given little power to determine what products would be produced or how resources would be used. Many nations with these **socialist economic systems,** after experiencing great economic difficulties and individual hardship, have changed their economic systems to rely more on the forces of demand and supply.

In nations such as the United States, an economic system known as **capitalism** has dominated production. Capitalism is an economic system in which the ownership and control of resources and businesses are held largely by private individuals, and the forces of demand and supply are relied upon to control the production of goods and services and the allocation of resources.

A strong theme in the American economic experience has always been "the less government, the better." This view holds that we should not hamper the functioning of the laws of demand and supply in our markets with unnecessary government regulation and intervention. Individuals willing to take the risk of establishing businesses to reap profits or suffer losses should be allowed to do so. During the 1800s and early 1900s, this "hands-off" attitude prevailed. But beginning around the turn of the century, and accelerating during the Great Depression of the 1930s, some economists began to advocate government intervention in the marketplace to aid economic stability and to prevent the catastrophe of recurring depressions. A deepening involvement of government in our economic system was characterized by the New Deal legislation of President Franklin Roosevelt during the Great Depression.

This does not mean that the government had nothing to do with the economic life of the nation before this century. From the beginning of our nation's history the government has been active in many economic areas—developing railroads, building canals, establishing tariffs to promote domestic industrial growth, and, to a limited extent, regulating business activities to protect both businesses and consumers. Indeed, although most people think of government involvement in our economic system as a relatively recent development, in fact, it has a long history. Much more will be said of this involvement in later chapters of this book.

AMERICAN CONSUMERS IN THE GLOBAL ECONOMY

In 1945, the last year of World War II, less than 2 percent of the products sold in the United States were imported from other nations. American consumers had little choice in where the products they bought had been made. Most other industrialized nations were involved in the war, and the productive capacity of many had been largely destroyed. They were in no position to export goods or services to the United States.

Almost half a century later, in 1992, the situation had changed dramatically. In that year nearly $530 billion worth, or more than 9 percent, of the goods and services purchased in America were produced in foreign countries. This trend toward more purchases of foreign-made products by American consumers is even more apparent when specific products are considered. For example, roughly 20 percent of the automobiles sold in the United States were produced in other countries. Almost all of the televisions, VCRs, tennis shoes, and a large share of the microwave ovens we purchased were imported. The list of foreign-made products we buy goes on and on.

In a similar way, many American consumers earn their living by producing products that are exported to other nations. In 1992 foreigners purchased almost $450 billion worth of American-made goods. It was estimated that sales

Money spent by American consumers to purchase imported products, like Japanese cars, provides income in foreign nations that may be used to purchase American-made goods and services.

of these goods and services created nearly 14 million jobs in this nation. By examining Exhibit 1–3 you can see the growing importance of international trade in the American economy. There are many indications that this trend will continue into the future.

A recent demonstration of the growing importance of trade can be seen in the December 1992 signing of the North American Free Trade Agreement (NAFTA) by President Bush. This treaty was designed to eliminate trade barriers between the United States, Canada, and Mexico over the following 15 years. Although NAFTA had to be ratified by the U.S. Senate and by the governments of the other signatory nations to go into effect, it clearly demonstrated the growing international nature of our economy. American consumers are faced with a growing need to understand and evaluate the costs and benefits of buying imported goods when they make consumer decisions.

Benefits of Trade

Not all nations are equally well suited to produce all types of goods and services. Since countries have different types and qualities of raw materials, climates, workers, transportation systems, and technology, they can be more efficient when they **specialize** in producing certain goods and then trade them for other goods. By specializing and trading this way, countries are able to increase their standard of living.

The United States, for example, is well suited to the efficient production of food and other agricultural products. We have vast areas of fertile land with sufficient rainfall to grow far more food than we need for ourselves in most years. We also have an extensive interstate highway system, many navigable rivers, and railroads that allow bulky agricultural products to be shipped quickly and at relatively low costs. It makes good sense for the United States to specialize in the production of farm products that can be purchased by nations that are less well suited to this type of production. In return we can buy products we are not able to produce as efficiently from them.

Specialization

The concentration of efforts on one area of production with the aim of having a comparative advantage in the marketplace. Students specialize when they major in a certain subject at college, thus allowing them to have a comparative advantage in the job market later—assuming there is a demand for their specialized knowledge.

▶ Exhibit 1–3 **Value of U.S. Merchandise Exports and Imports, 1983–1992 (values in billions of dollars)**

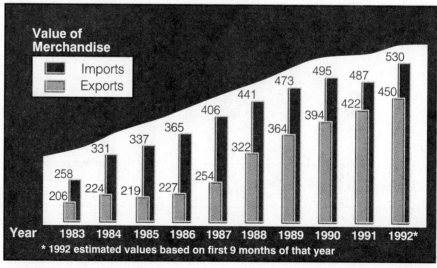

Source: *Economic Indicators*, November 1992, p. 35.

UNIT 1   THE CONSUMER IN TODAY'S WORLD

American consumers often choose to buy foreign-made products because these goods are less expensive than similar American-made products. In some cases consumers may believe imported goods have higher quality or superior design. And some of the goods Americans want to own are made only in foreign nations. In 1992, for example, no television picture tubes were manufactured in this country. It was therefore impossible for an American consumer to buy a truly American-made television set regardless of the label, or trademark, that it might have been sold under.

We should remember that selling American-made products in other countries provides many benefits to our economy and to American consumers. Products we export provide employment and income for American workers. They generate profits for U.S. firms, and tend to increase growth in the U.S. economy. When Americans are working at making products for export, there is more income for the government to tax. There is also less need for government social programs. Finally, selling products to other countries provides income that allows American consumers to buy the products we need from other nations.

Costs of Trade

Although many individual Americans benefit from international trade, there are clearly some who do not. When American consumers choose to buy imported goods, they provide income for foreign workers and their employers. Although this money may eventually be returned to the United States if foreigners use it to buy our products, it is nevertheless income that is not immediately going to American workers or their employers. Many businesses in this country have been forced to close by competition from imported products. It has been estimated, for example, that roughly half of the jobs that existed in the U.S. textile industry in 1960 have been lost due to foreign competition. Certainly the individual workers who lost their jobs, and the owners of the firms that were forced out of business, are not better off because of international trade.

When a country imports a greater value of goods than it exports, it has a negative **balance of trade.** Countries that have a negative balance of trade tend to have more unemployment, lower business profits, and slower growth than they otherwise might expect to have. The United States has had a negative balance in the value of goods it trades in each year since 1975. Study Exhibit 1–4 to see how this balance has changed over the years.

Being a Responsible Consumer in the Global Economy

"Buy American" slogans are intended to help create more jobs, production, and income in this country. But although many American consumers recognize a need to achieve these goals, they continue to buy imported goods in large quantities. Some people even argue that buying American-made goods when imports offer lower prices or better quality is not necessarily good for the American economy in the long run.

Foreign competition has helped bring about technological advancements that have benefited many American firms. The U.S. steel industry, for example, is much more efficient today than it was 20 years ago. The number of worker-hours required to produce a ton of steel was cut roughly in half between 1970 and 1990. Some of this improvement was made necessary because of competition from lower-cost foreign steel.

> Although many individual Americans benefit from international trade, there are clearly some who do not.

Balance of trade
The relationship between the value of a country's imports and exports: if exports have a greater value it has a positive balance of trade: if its imports have a greater value it has a negative balance of trade.

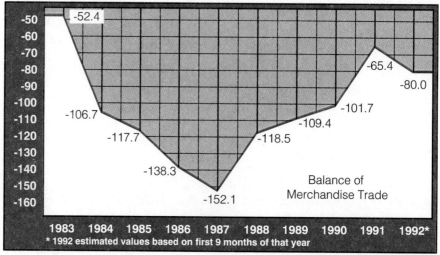

▶ Exhibit 1–4 **U.S. Balance of Merchandise Trade, 1983–1992 (values in billions of dollars)**

Source: *Economic Indicators*, November 1992, p. 35.

In some cases U.S. firms have surpassed foreign competition in their own markets. In the 1980s the Motorola Corporation undertook investments in research and development that have made it the largest producer of cellular telephones in the world. In the early 1990s it exported millions of dollars worth of this product to Japan each year.

The prices American consumers pay for many products are lower because of imported goods. It has been estimated that in the decade of the 1980s Americans would have paid as much as $400 billion more for the automobiles they purchased if they had not been able to buy less expensive imported cars. The same argument can be made for imported textiles, shoes, and garments. Although some Americans have lost their jobs because of these imports, most Americans benefited from lower prices and in some cases higher quality. In other words, most Americans have been able to enjoy a higher standard of living because of international trade.

When consumers choose whether or not to buy imported goods and services, they are choosing whether to (1) help save some American jobs by buying products made in this country, or (2), by buying imported goods, possibly encourage greater efficiency and different types of growth in our own economy. The continuing loss of jobs in types of production where this country is not the most efficient probably cannot be stopped. It may make more sense to concentrate our resources in types of production that take advantage of our unique abilities to create growth in the future. Ultimately, the decision to "buy American" is an individual choice that all American consumers must make for themselves. This choice, and the growing importance of our global economy, will be recurring themes throughout this text.

▶ SUMMARY

1. Consumer economics is the study of how consumers can apply economic principles in their decision making. Some consumers make buying decisions without understanding the basic principles that guide economic behavior in the world around them.

2. Scarcity is an age-old problem faced by consumers, businesses, and the government in all nations. Because of scarcity, choices and tradeoffs must be made. As consumers, we must choose how we spend our time and effort, as well as our income. A knowledge of consumer economics can help us maximize the satisfaction we obtain from the choices we make.

3. Because time, money, and productive resources are scarce—that is, limited—whenever we use any of these resources, we must forgo some other option that we could have used the resources for. The forgone option is the opportunity cost of our first choice. That is, the opportunity cost is the value of the second-best choice that is given up in favor of the first choice. If we work one hour longer, for example, we give up one hour of leisure time to do so. The opportunity cost of working that one additional hour is the value that we place on our second-best choice of using the hour for leisure time.

4. A tradeoff is the process of giving up one alternative for another. Tradeoffs must be made because scarcity exists. An opportunity cost is involved in every tradeoff.

5. A basic assumption in consumer economics is that people generally attempt to make themselves better off in their standard of living—that is, in their command over leisure time and their ability to buy goods and services that will satisfy their wants.

6. In economics a market is the sum of all transactions that take place between the buyers and sellers of a particular type of product. Markets exist between and among people, businesses, governments, and other nations in the world. In the American economy most transactions in markets are voluntary exchanges that benefit both buyers and sellers.

7. The law of demand states that if nothing else changes, consumers will buy a greater quantity of a product at a lower price than at a higher price. The quantity of a product that consumers will buy at any particular price may change as the result of a change in consumer tastes, income, the price of related products, or in their expectations of the future.

8. The law of supply states that if nothing else changes, a greater quantity of a product will be offered for sale at a higher price than at a lower price. The quantity of a product that is supplied at any particular price may change as the result of a change in the cost of supplying that product.

9. Prices are determined in competitive markets by the forces of demand and supply. The price that we pay for a good or service at any point in time is its money price. The price of an item relative to other items in the marketplace is its relative price. Consumer buying decisions depend on relative, not money, prices.

10. In a world of perfect competition many businesses would make the same products and offer them for sale to many customers. Consumers would control what is produced through their spending decisions. The result would be complete consumer sovereignty. To earn a profit businesses would allocate more resources to the production of products that sell well, and fewer to the production of goods or services that are less in demand.

11. In the real world there are many cases of imperfect competition where businesses have more control than consumers over the products they produce and the prices they are able to charge. In such situations the businesses have a degree of sovereignty over production. The most extreme case of imperfect competition is a monopoly, where there is no competition.

12. Our government has often intervened in our economic system in an attempt to make it work better or to protect the rights of consumers or business owners. Although the amount of government intervention has increased in recent years, it has been manifested to some degree since the United States was first created in the 1700s.

13. International trade has become a larger part of the American economic system in recent years. Almost one-tenth of the products purchased in the United States in 1992 were imported. Roughly 14 million Americans depend on trade for their employment.

14. American consumers have benefited and paid costs as a result of the increasingly global nature of our economy. Trade has made it possible for us to buy better quality products at lower prices. It has encouraged American businesses to become more efficient and to offer a wider selection of goods and services for sale.

15. Competition from imported goods has cost many individual Americans their jobs and has caused some businesses to fail. When American consumers choose to buy, or not buy, imported products they may weigh the costs and benefits of their decision both in terms of their own values and in relation to the impact their choice may have on the American economy.

▶ QUESTIONS FOR THOUGHT AND DISCUSSION

1. If you were a millionaire, why would you still be faced with the problem of scarcity?

2. What is your opportunity cost for taking a course in consumer economics?

3. Describe a tradeoff that you have recently made.

4. How do the forces of demand and supply result in an equilibrium price for most products?

5. If the prices charged by all fast-food restaurants increased, but at a lower rate than most other prices, what would happen to the demand for their products? Explain the reasons for your answer.

6. How would consumers control the production of goods and services in a world of perfect competition?

7. How many firms in imperfect competition harm consumers?

8. Why has the need for government involvement in our economic system increased in recent years?

9. Describe several situations in the United States that demonstrate the increasingly global nature of our economy.

10. What benefits and costs to our economy might American consumers consider when they choose whether or not to buy imported goods?

▶ THINGS TO DO

1. Analyze a recent consumer decision you have made. Explain how scarcity forced you to make this decision. Identify the opportunity cost of making this choice. Describe how government regulations affected your decision.

2. Describe and contrast the characteristics of two markets you buy products in. One should be essentially competitive and the other should demonstrate a degree of imperfect competition. Which market do you believe serves your consumer interests best? Explain the reasons for your choice.

3. Research the history of a specific type of legislation that has influenced the way American consumers make decisions. Possible topics could include laws that limit the powers of firms with monopoly-like powers or that regulate labeling of consumer products. Include a discussion of the benefits and costs to consumers as a result of these laws.

4. Choose a type of consumer product you use that is both produced in this country and imported from other nations. Investigate the price and quality of these alternative products. Write a report that identifies and explains the benefits and costs American consumers may consider when they choose whether to buy imported or domestically produced brands of this product.

▶ APPLICATION

In the summer of 1990 the military forces of Iraq invaded Kuwait, sending economic shock waves through the global economy. Within weeks, the price of crude oil in the world market doubled from roughly $17 for a 40-gallon barrel to nearly $34. Write an essay that explains how this situation in the global economy forced consumers to make decisions that demonstrated the economic concepts of scarcity, tradeoffs, demand, supply, and equilibrium prices.

▶ SELECTED READINGS

▶ Angevine, Erma, ed. *Consumer Activists: They Made a Difference*. Mt. Vernon, NY: Consumers Union Foundation, 1982.

▶ Ambry, Margaret. *Consumer Power: How Americans Spend Their Money*. Ithaca, NY: New Strategists Publications, 1991.

▶ Becker, Gary S. "Working Woman's Staunchest Allies: Supply and Demand." *Business Week*, December 2, 1991, p. 18.

▶ Berke, Richard L. "Deregulation Has Gone Too Far, Many Telling Administration." *New York Times*, December 11, 1988, pp. 1, 23.

▶ Caplan, Marc. *Ralph Nader Presents a Citizens' Guide to Lobbying*. New York: Norton, 1983.

▶ Dolbeare, Kenneth M. *American Public Policy: A Citizen's Guide*. New York: McGraw-Hill, 1982.

▶ "Fifty Years Ago." *Consumer Reports*, January and February 1986.

▶ Harbrecht, Douglas A. "The Second Coming of Ralph Nader." *Business Week*, March 6, 1989, p. 28.

▶ Miller, Roger LeRoy. *Economics Today*, 7th ed. New York: Harper & Row, 1991.

▶ Miller, T. J. "Can America Compete in the Global Economy?" *Kiplinger's Personal Finance Magazine*, November 1991, pp. 81–83.

▶ Pertschuk, Michael. *Revolt against Regulation: The Rise and Pause of the Consumer Movement*. Berkeley: University of California Press, 1982.

▶ Remington, R. H. "Eastern Europe after the Revolution." *Current History*, November 1991, pp. 379–383.

▶ Zuckerman, M. B. "How to Help the Russians." *U.S. News & World Report*, December 23, 1991, p. 72.

Ethics and the Consumer

The United States is not a country in which the Latin maxim, *caveat emptor*—"let the buyer beware"—reigns supreme. Rather, the age of consumerism has established numerous rights for consumers that were never even dreamed of a mere 50 years ago. The course in consumer or family economics that you are now taking focuses on the rights that consumers have and on how consumers can seek redress for their grievances concerning shoddy products and improper services rendered.

You must be aware, however, that we are not living in a world that is 100 percent *caveat venditor*—"let the seller beware." You, in your role as a consumer, have duties and responsibilities. These duties and responsibilities can be summarized in one sentence: The consumer has a duty to act honestly and ethically when purchasing products and services. An age-old aphorism holds that "what goes around comes around." In the context of consumer dealings, this means that if enough consumers act dishonestly, prices of consumer products and services will rise.

▶ WHAT IS ETHICAL BEHAVIOR?

Ethical behavior essentially means acting in accordance with one's moral and ethical convictions as to what is right and what is wrong. Many commonly held ethical convictions are written into our laws. But ethical behavior sometimes requires us to do more than just comply with laws in order to avoid the penalty of breaking them. In some circum-

stances, one can break the law and be fairly certain that no one will ever find out about it.

Imagine, for example, that you withdrew $50 from your savings account one night at an **automated teller machine (ATM).** You punched in your **personal identification number (PIN)** and drove home with your money. The next day you read about a runaway truck smashing into the bank where you made your withdrawal. You are relieved that the accident happened after you left the bank and think nothing more about it. A few weeks later, when you receive your monthly statement from the bank, you discover that your $50 withdrawal has not been recorded. You put two and two together and assume that the record of your transaction was destroyed in the accident. If you keep the money without telling the bank what happened, you will be breaking the law, but your lawbreaking is unlikely to be detected. What would your ethical choice be in such a situation?

Let's turn now to a situation that occurs a little more frequently than the $50 surprise windfall in the above example. What if you purchased a number of items from your local Kmart and discovered when you got home that the cashier had failed to charge you for a $50 cooler. What is your obligation? Obviously, the cooler does not legally belong to you—you have not paid for it. But why should you have to take the time and trouble to return to the store to pay for the item? After all, it wasn't your fault that the cashier did not ring up the purchase price of the item. What would your decision be? Would the price of the item be a factor in your decision?

It's Not Always Easy

These examples illustrate that it's not always easy to do the "right thing"—or even to know what the right thing to do is in a given set of circumstances. You can be pretty certain that in the ATM example the bank would never have any proof that you kept $50 of its money. (You can't be too sure, though, because some banks keep a video record of all such transactions.) In the case of the $50 cooler from Kmart, most likely, such a big store will never find out that you were not charged. And, if it did, you could always plead ignorance and say that you assumed that you had paid for it. In fact, the simplest alternative in each example would be to keep the "gift" and say nothing to anybody about it. Who wouldn't be tempted to do this? In addition to having more money in your pocket or a free cooler for your next vacation, you would be spared the time and trouble of returning the cooler or the money. And your sterling reputation in the community as an ethical person would not be marred in the slightest, because no one else would ever know what you had done. But you would. And this is what ethics is all about. At the heart of ethical decision making is *determining whether you personally feel that a given action is right or wrong and acting accordingly*. After all, you're the one who has to live with your conscience.

Somebody Has to Pay

When trying to determine the rightness or wrongness of a given action, it is helpful to consider the consequences of each alternative. Keep in mind that if you don't pay for benefits you receive, someone else will have to. As economists are wont to emphasize, there is no such thing as a "free lunch." In other words, somebody, somewhere, has to pay for all that is produced and consumed. And that somebody is another consumer—or, rather, other consumers. This is because sellers who absorb these added costs will pass them on eventually to all purchasers in the form of higher prices.

EXAMPLES OF UNETHICAL CONSUMER BEHAVIOR

While most consumers act responsibly in their purchase transactions, they are obviously not saints any more than businesspersons are. And examples are plentiful of consumers who give in to the temptation to evade the letter of the law in order to get "something for nothing." Consider, for example, the following scenario: Jeannie orders by mail a new Nikon camera from Flash Electronics, a discount house in a distant city. The camera arrives by mail, and Jeannie immediately uses it to take photographs to be included in the consumer textbook she is writing. A few days later, she drops the camera and breaks the casing. She decides to "pass the buck" to the seller and returns the camera to Flash Electronics, claiming that the camera was broken when it arrived and demanding a replacement. Jeannie, who eventually receives the replacement camera, has just saved herself the cost of repairing the broken camera—at the expense of the discount firm, of course, or the manufacturer.

But she suffers few pangs of conscience about her dishonesty. After all, she reasons, Flash Electronics and Nikon are huge and profitable businesses. Whereas the repair bill would be but a drop in the bucket for Flash Electronics or Nikon, it would represent Jeannie's entire food budget for a week.

What Jeannie overlooks in her reasoning is the long-run consequences of her behavior. In the short run, yes, the discount house or the manufacturer will pay for the repairs. But, ultimately, who pays? Other consumers, like Jeannie, who buy cameras or other products from the discount house and Nikon and who have to pay more because of Jeannie's fraud. But Jeannie might still rationalize that the cost of the camera repair—when spread out over thousands of consumers—would represent no real burden to each individual consumer, which is true. But, if all—or even a substantial number of—consumers acted similarly to Jeannie, what then?

It takes little effort to imagine dozens of other ways in which consumers have behaved dishonestly or unethically to gain a personal benefit at the expense or inconvenience of others. We look here at just a few variations of this theme.

So Sue Me

Most consumers periodically receive in the mail invitations to subscribe to certain magazines, or to "sign here" and receive a product to try out for 30 days, and so on. A typical offer is to sign up for membership in a book club. All you have to do is sign and send a card to receive, say, four books for which you will be billed $1 at some future date. Of course, having signed up for membership in the club, you will be obligated to purchase a given number of books per year—or at least notify the club each month if you don't want a particular book or books. You receive the four books and, after a few months, have received several more. You haven't had time to read the books, don't really want them, and don't really want to be a member of the club. But you're busy and fail to do anything about it. Eventually, the book club begins to send stern demands for payment—you owe them $69. You are a struggling student, short of money, and you ignore the bill. It certainly does not take priority in your budget. If they want to sue you for collection, fine. You are not worried about it because you know that the amount is too trivial to justify any legal action against you by the book club. Eventually, to your relief, they stop sending you any bills at all—your account has been written off as a "bad debt"—along with hundreds of others. And you have acquired six "free" books.

▶ Me First, Please

Many consumers have been inconvenienced by delays and other travel complications because of overbooked flights. They could not board their designated flight—for which they had reservations—because the plane was full. Airlines overbook flights because they can predict, based on past flight records, that a certain number of passengers will cancel or change their reservations at the last minute or simply not show. Some passengers pay higher fares for the privilege of changing flights at the last minute, if necessary. Other passengers cancel their planned trips owing to unforeseen

circumstances that arise. But part of airline overbooking is due to consumers who make multiple reservations. Although airlines, by requiring advance ticketing, have curbed the problems caused by multiple reservations somewhat, it is still estimated that between one-third to one-half of overbooking is done because of multiple reservations made by consumers.

▶ More "Me First"

Toni buys an expensive new dress for a special party she has been invited to attend. She wears the dress to the party, receives many compliments on it, but decides it was really far too expensive a purchase. She returns it to the store for a refund. The sales clerk does not inspect the dress closely and fails to notice the ginger ale stains on the front. Toni gets her refund. The result? Either the next purchaser gets a slightly soiled dress instead of the brand-new garment she paid for, or the store must discount the price of the dress heavily to sell it if the stain is discovered.

▶ Make the Manufacturer Pay

In the past two decades American courts and consumer-protection statutes have increasingly sought to protect the "little person" against the powerful corporate entity or business firm. This has been a boon to consumers who are injured by faulty products that they have purchased. It allows them to sue sellers and manufacturers for compensation, in the form of money damages, for injuries caused by carelessness in product design or production. But now and then a consumer will take advantage of these laws, and the court system, to seek damages from the product manufacturer or retailer.

Assume, for example, that John, a minibike enthusiast, purchases minibikes for his two sons, ages 9 and 11. In the instruction manual, and clearly indicated in large letters on the bikes themselves, are instructions not to use the bikes on city streets and to always wear a helmet while riding them. Nonetheless, John allows his sons to ride on the city streets without helmets. One day, while racing with another friend on a minibike, the oldest son, Chad, carelessly runs three stop signs and then enters a fourth intersection while looking backward toward his friend. Chad is hit by a truck and injured. John sues the manufacturer of the minibike for damages, claiming that the minibike is a dangerous product and should not have been placed on the market.

▶ The Nuisance Suit

Sellers are also often faced with so-called nuisance lawsuits. A typical one might involve the following series of events: Jerry, in a daze about his latest girlfriend, walks through a hardware store, carelessly trips over a stepladder being displayed very close to a wall (and definitely not a hazard), falls, and falsely claims that he injured his back. Alleging that the owner was negligent by having the stepladder displayed as it was, he sues the owner for damages. Similarly, Zane sues the owner of a national chain store for $10,000, alleging that a can of paint displayed on a shelf in the owner's store fell on his toe and injured it. And so on and on. Such suits are often settled by the store owners out of court, because it would cost them more to defend themselves in court than to settle. Even though most store owners carry liability insurance, out of which such claims are paid, the insurance is not free to the store—and the premiums will rise (and they have risen dramatically in recent years) as more claims have to be paid by insurance firms.

▶ ETHICS IN AN IMPERSONAL MARKETPLACE

In the increasingly impersonal and mechanized marketplace of today it is much easier to lose sight of our responsibilities toward others than it once was. This is because in today's consumer world, the "others" are usually abstract entities and not people we know personally. In the past, when stores were smaller and most transactions were conducted face to face, consumers were more motivated to act honestly and ethically because they also faced the consequences of their actions directly. Imagine, for example, that Jeannie in the camera example had lived in 1900 instead of the 1990s. After breaking her camera, she returned it to her local camera store, claiming that it was already broken when she purchased it from the seller. Very likely, the seller would remember the transaction, would know that the camera had been in good condition, and would know that Jeannie was acting dishonestly—regardless of whether he could prove it. Jeannie might be deprived of—or at least face a reduced quality in—the services of that store, and her reputation in the community could be affected. Because of these possible negative consequences, it might not even occur to Jeannie to defraud the seller. Moreover, if she knew the merchant quite well, she might have some strong ethical reservations about requiring the merchant to pay for the broken casing for which she alone was responsible.

Now let's return to the present and to a much different marketplace. When Jeannie returned the camera

to the discount house, she knew that she was being dishonest, but she would not lose sleep at night over the "victim" of her fraud—who was not a real person but an X quantity of "others." Moreover, and perhaps most significantly, Jeannie was quite sure that she would never be "caught." No one would ever know of her dishonesty, and she would face no negative consequences. The worst that could happen is that the discount store would refuse to repair or replace her camera. In short, Jeannie felt little incentive to be ethical.

Because there are fewer *external* constraints to guide us toward ethical consumer behavior, an understanding of one's responsibilities in the marketplace is even more important today than it was in the past. Huge chain-store operations and computerized networks are increasingly hiding the identities—and the behavior—of individual buyers and sellers in the marketplace. And if we are slightly dishonest or violate our own ethical standards occasionally, who will know?

▶ ONLY YOU CAN DECIDE

Obviously, there is no exact formula for ethical behavior. Every individual has his or her own set of values and moral principles, and every situation is different. But it is important to remember that, although moral and ethical convictions are necessarily very personal qualities, our individual behavior always, in one way or another, affects others around us. This is true in all of our activities— as family members, as citizens, as employers or employees, and as consumers. Ethical decision making involves becoming aware of how our behavior affects others and evaluating whether these consequences

are desirable. And this is something only you can decide.

▶ ETHICAL SHOPPING

Although consumers may not be sovereign, there is no doubt that they can and do affect, by their choices, the financial well-being of business firms. This means that, if you have doubts about the ethical behavior of a certain corporation, you can cast your "ethical vote" by not purchasing that firm's products. The major block to such ethical shopping is, of course, the time it requires to investigate the ethical or not-so-ethical practices of the numerous corporations that produce the products we frequently use.

To assist those consumers who wish to engage in **ethical shopping,** the Council on Economic Priorities (CEP) has created a guide for ethical shopping entitled *Shopping for a Better World*. This 126-page booklet rates the producers of over 1,300 brand-name products on their performance relative to ten current social issues. These issues and the ranking criteria used by the CEP in determining the social responsibility of each corporation are listed in Exhibit A–1.

If you are interested in purchasing this guide or in membership in the CEP—which is a nonprofit organization formed to promote corporate responsibility—you can write to CEP, 30 Irving Place, New York, NY 10003, or call toll-free (800) 822-6435. In New York, call (212) 420-1133.

▶ ETHICAL USE OF GOVERNMENT SERVICES

Our government provides many services that are intended to benefit specific groups of citizens who are disadvantaged or who have special needs. Some people make unethical

▶ Exhibit A–1 **Corporate Social Responsibility—Assessment Criteria Used by the Council on Economic Priorities**

SOCIAL ISSUE	CRITERIA FOR RANKING SOCIAL RESPONSIBILITY
Charity	Percentage of pretax earnings given to charity.
Women's Advancement	Number of women on board of directors or at vice presidential (or higher) level.
Minority Advancement	Number of minority members on board of directors or at vice presidential (or higher) level.
Military Contracts	Number of contracts with Department of Defense to make weapons, supply fuel, etc., to military.
Animal Testing	Use of animals in research and testing; extent of contribution, if any, to alternative methods of research.
Disclosure of Information	Willingness to disclose corporate information to CEP and type of information disclosed.
Community Outreach	Involvement in community education, housing, and other projects benefiting community.
Nuclear Power	Involvement in construction and maintenance of nuclear plants or providing consulting services.
South Africa	Investment in, or business licenses with, South Africa.

▶ Exhibit A–2 **"Ethical" Funds With 1990–1991 and 1991–1992 Returns**

Fund Name & Telephone	Sales Charge	1990–1991 Return*	1991–1992 Return*	Portfolio
Pax World 800-767-1729	None	22.4%	2.4%	Avoids liquor, tobacco, gambling industries; Department of Defense contractors
New Alternatives 516-466-0808	5.66%	12.4%	–4.0%	Purchases stock in firms involved in conservation and recycling
Calvert-Ariel Appreciation 800-368-2748	4.75%	21.6%	10.9%	Avoids investments in South Africa
Dreyfus Third Century 800-645-6561	None	21.5%	0.8%	Invests in companies with policies on the environment, employment, and consumer protection
Parnassus 800-999-3505	3.50%	17.3%	3.2%	Invests in companies sensitive to employees, customers, and communities

*Returns are from July 1 to June 31 of each year.
Source: *Working Woman,* December 1992, pp. 62, 63.

use of such benefits. An obvious example is the able-bodied person who parks in a handicapped parking space. Other people take advantage of social programs like welfare, food stamps, or Medicaid by providing false information to government administrators. Some health care providers have been convicted of billing the government for Medicaid or Medicare services that were unnecessary or never performed. These practices add to the cost taxpayers must bear.

On a simpler level, people may abuse or purposefully destroy public property—breaking up picnic tables in parks to build fires, stealing road signs to be sold as scrap aluminum, and charging government accounts for private travel. Such behavior adds to the cost of government and may also reduce the quantity of goods and services that government is able to provide to those who truly need them.

▶ ETHICAL INVESTING

Ethical investing consists of making investments only in those companies that engage in socially responsible behavior. In recent years, ethical investment funds have been on the increase, climbing from $40 billion in 1984 to $600 billion in 1992. The money managers of these ethical funds scan the universe of over 8,500 publicly held companies to determine which ones meet their ethical standards. In the past several years, companies that have direct or indirect dealings with South Africa have headed the list of firms to be avoided by ethical investors. The funds vary widely, however, in what they will or won't invest in, as you can see from Exhibit A–2. In some cases, the determining factor may be a firm's involvement in defense contracts or in nuclear power plants; in others, it may be the extent to which a firm is concerned with environmental preservation or consumer protection.

The performance of ethical funds varies. A study comparing 1990 returns on ethical investments to the Dow Jones Industrial Average (DJIA) showed that, while some funds gained higher returns than the DJIA, overall the ethical funds lagged behind in rate of return. More recently, however, Ritchie Lowry, who publishes an investment newsletter called *Good Money,* has reported that the ethical funds he monitors have a return of 484.7 percent, compared with the DJIA return of 114.2 percent. According to Lowry, "The companies that are socially aware tend to be the best managed, too," and thus investments in such firms pay off. Although Lowry is right overall in his assessment, some ethical funds have not done well (see Exhibit A–2).

If you are interested in investing "morally," Co-op America publishes a *Socially Responsible Financial Planning Guide* that lists numerous brokers, financial planners, insurers, bankers, and credit unions that engage in ethical investing. For a copy, send $5 to Co-op America, 2100 M St., N.W., Suite 310, Washington, DC 20063.

▶ QUESTIONS FOR THOUGHT AND DISCUSSION

1. Assume that you have a part-time job at a local office supply store.

You have noticed that your supervisor frequently takes home various supplies—a ream of paper, a carton of file folders, an electric pencil sharpener, and so on—for her own use, and you are quite sure that she is not paying for them. You like the supervisor and you like your job. What should you do?

2. Have you ever been dishonest or unethical as a consumer? How did you rationalize your behavior—if you did?

3. Why is it that, although we read of business fraud daily, we only rarely hear about consumer fraud?

▶ THINGS TO DO

1. Visit three stores in your area and ask their managers about consumer fraud or dishonesty. Although they will be reluctant to release specific data concerning their businesses, they will probably give you a general idea of what their experiences have been in this area.

List several ways—in addition to those discussed in the issue—in which consumers defraud sellers or behave unethically in their transactions.

3. Ask six friends or family members what they would do if they received a $50 overpayment from an ATM machine and the money could not be traced to them. Tally the results.

▶ SELECTED READINGS

▶ Allman, William F. "Planet Earth." *U.S. News & World Report,* October 31, 1988, pp. 61–68.
▶ Borowsky, Larry. "The Consummate Recycler." Environmental Action, March–April 1989, pp. 22–24.
▶ Council on Economic Priorities. *Rating America's Corporate Conscience.* Reading: Addison-Wesley, 1987.
▶ Griswald, C. L. "Conscience of Capitalism." *The Wilson Quarterly,* Summer 1991, pp. 53–56.
▶ Loeb, Marshall. "Humanistic Funds." *Marshall Loeb's 1992 Money Guide,"* Boston: Little, Brown, 1992, pp. 124–126.
▶ Miller, Roger L., and Gaylord A. Jentz. "Ethics and Social Responsibility." *Business Law Today.* St. Paul: West, 1988, Ch. 37.
▶ Nemethy, Andrew. "Ecologically Correct Products for a Household of the 90's." *New York Times,* February 23, 1989, p. 3.
▶ "People Who Make a Difference." *National Wildlife,* October–December, 1991, pp. 40–46.
▶ Queenan, Joe. "Ethical Shopping." *Forbes,* April 17, 1989, pp. 80–84.

CHAPTER 2

Protection for the Consumer

PREVIEW

▶ How has the government's role in consumer protection grown in this century?

▶ What major federal agencies monitor and enforce consumer protection legislation?

▶ What are the basic functions and powers of the Federal Trade Commission and Consumer Products Safety Commission?

▶ What sources of consumer assis-tance and protection exist in the private sector?

▶ What is the difference between express and implied warranties?

Students of consumer economics will benefit from a basic knowledge of the history of consumer protection. The earliest forms of consumer protection in the United States were really attempts to make sure that markets functioned efficiently. In competitive markets there are many buyers and sellers, so no single individual is able to influence the price or quality of a particular good. Even if consumers are familiar with the products they are bargaining for, it can be difficult for them to be sure they receive the amount of a product for which payment has been made. Therefore, from the earliest recorded times, governments have been involved in setting uniform standards for weights or measurements. The quality of products has also been regulated by many governments. The quality of flour exported from American colonies, for example, was regulated by governments in North America before the United States became a nation. Even earlier, in ancient Greece, it was a crime for a merchant to add water to wine that was offered for sale.

After standards of weights and measures, and quality are established, the next problem is enforcement. This second responsibility of consumer protection, policing standards, has caused the courts and other administrative bodies of our government to become involved in the consumer protection system. For consumer protection to work, standards must be set, they must be defended, and those who violate them must be apprehended and punished.

SOURCES OF CONSUMER PROTECTION

There are several important and distinct sources of consumer protection. Exhibit 2–1 lists the most significant laws passed specifically to protect consumers. In addition to federal legislation, each state has a consumer protection bureau, either as a separate state office or as a division of the state attorney general's office. County and municipal governments also often have consumer affairs offices, and numerous private groups—such as the Better Business Bureau—exist to help consumers solve problems relating to product sales and services. Most major industries in the United States have also established consumer divisions to deal with complaints about their products. Indeed, today's consumer, with just a telephone and a few basic consumer reference materials, including the telephone book, can get nearly instant help with almost any consumer problem.

Effective consumer protection helps businesses as well as consumers. Businesses are protected from unfair competition by those who would cheat, or commit **fraud** against consumers. After all, money that consumers give to fraudulent businesses, and resources that are used creating inferior products, are money and resources that cannot be used by honest businesses. Remember, businesses buy resources in markets, too. Standards established by the government protect businesses from being taken advantage of in those markets. Businesses, then, have two reasons to support the enforcement of uniform standards:

1. To protect themselves when they go into the market to buy resources.
2. To protect themselves against competition from fraudulent businesses.

Antitrust Laws

Further regulation of the marketplace occurred in the late 1800s when **antitrust laws** were established to limit monopoly-like powers held by some businesses. The rights of buyers and other competitors had long been protected

Fraud
Making a false statement of a past or existing fact with knowledge of its falsity, or with reckless indifference as to its truth, with the intent to cause someone to give up property or a right that has value.

Antitrust laws
Laws designed to prevent business monopolies. Antitrust laws are part of government antitrust policies that are aimed at establishing and maintaining competition in the business world to assure consumers of fair prices and goods of adequate quality.

Statute or Agency Rule	Purpose
ADVERTISING	
Federal Trade Commission Act (1914/1938)	Prohibits deceptive and unfair trade practices
Public Health Cigarette Smoking Act (1970)	Prohibits radio and TV cigarette advertising
FTC Rules of Negative Options (1973)	Federal Trade Commission rules regulating advertising of book and record clubs
Smokeless Tobacco Act (1986)	Prohibits radio and TV advertising of smokeless tobacco products; requires special labeling to warn consumers of potential health hazards associated with smokeless tobacco
Children's Advertising Act (1990)	Directed FCC to establish rules to limit TV advertising directed toward children
CREDIT	
Consumer Credit Protection Act (Truth-in-Lending Act) (1968)	Offers comprehensive protection covering all phases of credit transactions
Fair Credit Reporting Act (1970)	Protects consumers' credit reputations
Equal Credit Opportunity Act (1974)	Prohibits discrimination in the extending of credit
Fair Credit Billing Act (1974)	Protects consumers in credit-card billing errors and other disputes
Fair Debt Collection Practices Act (1977)	Prohibits debt collectors' abuses
Counterfeit Access Device and Computer Fraud and Abuse Act (1984)	Prohibits the production, use, and sale of counterfeit credit cards or other access devices used to obtain money, goods, services, or other things of value
Home Equity Loan Consumer Protection Act (1988)	Prohibits lenders from changing the terms of a loan after the contract has been signed; requires fuller disclosure in home equity loans of interest-rate formulas and repayment terms
HEALTH AND SAFETY	
Pure Food and Drug Act (1906)	Prohibits adulteration and mislabeling of food and drugs sold in interstate commerce
Meat Inspection Act (1906)	Provides for inspection of meat
Federal Food, Drug, and Cosmetic Act (1938)	Protects consumers from unsafe food products and from unsafe and/or ineffective drugs (superceded Pure Food and Drug Act of 1906)
Flammable Fabrics Act (1953)	Prohibits the sale of highly flammable clothing
Poultry Products Inspection Act (1957)	Provides for inspection of poultry
Child Protection and Toy Safety Act (1966)	Requires child-proof devices and special labeling
National Traffic and Motor Vehicle Safety Act (1966)	Requires manufacturers to inform new car dealers of any safety defects found after manufacture and sale of auto
Wholesome Meat Act (1967)	Updated Meat Inspection Act of 1906 to provide for stricter standards for slaughtering plants of red-meat animals
Consumer Product Safety Act (1972)	Established the Consumer Product Safety Commission to regulate all potentially hazardous consumer products
Department of Transportation Rule on Passive Restraints in Automobiles (1984)	Requires automatic restraint systems in all new cars sold after September 1, 1990
Toy Safety Act (1984)	Allows the Consumer Product Safety Commission to quickly recall toys and other articles intended for use by children that present a substantial risk of injury
Drug-Price Competition and Patent-Term Restoration Act (Generic Drug Act) (1984)	Speeds up and simplifies Food and Drug Administration approval of generic versions of drugs on which patents have expired
Clean Air Act (1990)	Revised act of 1970 to establish new pollution limitations that include standards for automobile, power plant, and cancer-causing substance emissions that will be phased in by 1995
LABELING AND PACKAGING	
Wool Products Labeling Act (1939)	Requires accurate labeling of wool products
Fur Products Labeling Act (1951)	Prohibits misbranding of fur products
Textile Fiber Products Identification Act (1958)	Prohibits false labeling and advertising of all textile products not covered under Wool and Fur Products Labeling Acts
Hazardous Substances Labeling Act (1960)	Requires warning labels on all items containing dangerous chemicals
Cigarette Labeling and Advertising Act (1965)	Requires labels warning of possible health hazards
Child Protection and Toy Safety Act (1966)	Requires child-proof devices and special labeling

(Continued)

Statute or Agency Rule	Purpose
LABELING AND PACKAGING	
Fair Packaging and Labeling Act (1966)	Requires that accurate names, quantitites, and weights be given on product labels
Smokeless Tobacco Act (1986)	Requires labels disclosing possible health hazards of smokeless tobacco; prohibits radio and TV advertising of smokeless tobacco products
Food Labeling Act (1990)	Directed FDA to establish new lableing standards for food products that would be more meaningful to consumers
SALES AND WARRANTIES	
Interstate Land Sales Full Disclosure Act (1968)	Requires disclosure in interstate land sales
Odometer Act (1972)	Protects consumers against odometer fraud in used-car sales
FTC Door-to-Door Sales Rule (1973)	Federal Trade Commission rule regulating door-to-door sales contracts
Real Estate Settlement Procedures Act (1974)	Requires disclosure of home-buying costs
Magnuson-Moss Warranty Act (1975)	Provides rules governing content of warranties
FTC Vocational and Correspondence School Rule	Federal Trade Commission rule regulating contracts with these types of schools
FTC Used-Car Rule (1981)	Federal Trade Commission rule requiring dealers in used-car sales to disclose specified types of information in "Buyer's Guide" affixed to auto
FTC Funeral Home Rule (1984)	Federal Trade Commission rule requiring disclosure by funeral homes regarding prices and services

Common law

The unwritten system of law governing people's rights and duties, based on custom and fixed principles of justice. Common law is the foundation of both the English and U.S. legal systems (excluding Louisiana, where law is based on the Napoleonic Code).

by **common law** based on traditions because courts refused to enforce monopolistic contracts. But before the Sherman Antitrust Act was passed in 1890, there had been no federal law that specifically made monopoly and price fixing illegal in the American economy. Although the original intent of this legislation was to protect the interests of competing producers in the market, it had consumer implications as well. By preventing firms from unfairly harming their competition, the Sherman Act and other antitrust laws protected consumers' access to a wider selection of products that were offered at lower prices.

At the turn of the century, consumer protection, as it is understood today, did not exist. It was during the years between 1900 and World War I, that today's concept of consumer protection evolved. This was the time of the "muckrakers": politicians who fought against corruption and the abuse of power in the economy and the government. Their efforts led to the passage of the first wage-and-hour laws, the first women's and minors' protective legislation, and the first federal laws designed specifically to protect consumers. Possibly the most important of these early laws was the Food and Drug Act of 1906, which dealt with the production, transportation, and sale of foods and drugs in this country.

Food and Drug Act

Although the federal government made fraud through the mails illegal in the 1870s, it emphasized consumer protection only in terms of transactions at the retail level of the marketplace. Upton Sinclair's book *The Jungle* awoke the general public to the fact that consumer protection meant more than making sure that accurate information was provided at the point of sale. In his book, Sinclair graphically described the squalor and unsanitary practices that existed in the meat-packing industry. In response, groups began seeking some form of "consumer protection" in the processing of products before they arrived at the marketplace. Eventually, the government reacted by passing the Food and Drug Act of 1906, as well as the Meat Inspection Act of the same year.

More progress in consumer protection came about 10 years later when the Federal Trade Commission Act was passed in 1914. Administrative machinery to enforce antitrust laws and to spell out unfair methods of competition, including deceptive advertising, was provided by this act. It was not until 32 years later, however, that the 1938 Food, Drug, and Cosmetic Act was passed to strengthen the protective features of the 1906 legislation. This act required manufacturers to prove, for the first time, that their drugs were safe before marketing them. Also, with the 1938 act, the Food and Drug Administration no longer had to prove that a firm manufacturing a harmful product had intentionally committed a violation before it could take action against that company.

The passage of the 1938 legislation was the last significant federal activity on the consumer protection front until the 1960s and 1970s, when a flood of legislative activity occurred at federal, state, and local levels. Between 1965 and 1975, more than twice as many consumer protection laws were passed than had been passed in the previous 90 years.

A Renewed Interest in the Consumer

What happened to rekindle the interest in consumer protection in the 1960s and 1970s? Some people attribute the renewed interest to Ralph Nader, whose 1965 book *Unsafe at Any Speed* brought public attention to focus on the issue of automobile safety. But other books, like Upton Sinclair's *The Jungle* and Stuart Chase's *Your Money's Worth* of the 1930s, did not lead to a sustained consumer protection movement. So apparently something else was operating in the 1960s and 1970s that had not been in U.S. society before. This something else may have been the growing complexity of modern economic life. By the early 1960s, the American public had felt the impact of the technology explosion as it affected production, transportation, and information systems. The development of plastics, frozen foods, and freeze-dried foods had made pre-processing and prepackaging an everyday fact of American life. The automobile had become a complex, accessory-loaded machine that many buyers could no longer understand. Consumers found themselves having to cope with ever increasing amounts of information. Accompanying this expansion of the need for knowledge was a depersonalization of the American marketplace. Many American consumers came to feel that they did not understand the products they bought and that the businesses they dealt with no longer cared about them as individuals.

In making buyer decisions today, consumers often spend much time seeking and evaluating information. In a more simple economic system, one might know enough about the products and their producers to feel comfortable about making a good decision. But with our complex technology, no one can possibly know enough about every product bought to feel confident of making the best or even satisfactory consumer decisions in every field. Furthermore, many of the businesses consumers buy from are so large that they have taken on the characteristics of a huge, uncaring machine in the consumer's mind. Consequently, consumers in the 1960s began to feel the need of more government protection. Government regulations multiplied for standards of packaging and for disclosure of information that would enable consumers to compare manufacturers' claims more easily. In addition, many consumers began to agitate for government-enforced standards of safety.

Individual consumers have little control over producers because the few dollars they might withhold from a large corporation will have no significant

> Many American consumers came to feel that they did not understand the products they bought and that the businesses they dealt with no longer cared about them as individuals.

impact on the firm's profits. Moreover, until the significant changes of the 1960s, the legal system was not suited to handle the problems of millions of individuals with small sums of money at stake, each sum important to the individual but no one amount large enough to pay for the costs of taking a firm to court. The legal concept of *caveat emptor,* "let the buyer beware," therefore seemed to rule the economy.

A mounting sense of helplessness and frustration led consumers to look to the government for a new form of consumer protection: protection after the fact. The new emphasis in consumer protection became **consumer redress:** the right of every consumer to air legitimate grievances and to seek satisfaction for damages incurred through the use of a product or service. This was not the same as the earlier consumer protection against fraud. Consumers could now ask for redress, not because they had been deliberately defrauded, but because the complexity of the marketplace had made it impossible, in their eyes, for them to protect themselves adequately before the fact of purchase.

Consumer redress
The right of consumers to seek and obtain satisfaction for damages incurred through the use of a product or a service: protection after the fact.

The Presidents Speak Up

In the early 1960s, the government responded to consumer needs. In 1962 President John F. Kennedy sent a consumer protection program to Congress calling for the recognition of four fundamental consumer rights:

1. *The right to safety*—protection against goods that are dangerous to life or health.
2. *The right to be informed*—disclosure laws to allow consumers not only to discover fraud but also to make rational choices.
3. *The right to choose*—a restatement of the need for there to be many firms in a competitive market and for protection by government where such competition no longer exists.
4. *The right to be heard*—the right of consumers to have their interests heard when government policy decisions are made.

To these four rights, subsequent presidents have added others:

5. *The right to a decent environment*—assurance that consumers' health, property, and quality of life will not be harmed by actions that damage the environment.
6. *The right to consumer education*—through government programs specifically created for that purpose.
7. *The right to reasonable redress for physical damages suffered when using a product*—the right to receive just compensation for losses that result from the use of defective or dangerous products.

During the 1960s and 1970s, these rights were supported by a host of consumer protection laws passed by Congress and by the creation of federal agencies to administer and enforce them. The election of Ronald Reagan to the presidency in 1980, heralded a change in the executive attitude toward the consumer movement. According to the school of economic thought guiding the Reagan administration, if the government stepped back and gave businesses a freer hand to operate as they saw fit, competition and the marketplace would eventually eliminate many market imperfections. Although President Reagan stressed the importance of the consumer in the health of the economy, agencies involved in the administration and enforcement of consumer protection legislation faced significant reductions in their powers and budgets.

To an extent, the Reagan administration's approach to consumer protection was a response to the growing resentment on the part of many Americans against increased regulation by government agencies. It is also possible that the success of consumer protection legislation in the 1960s and 1970s reduced the need for greater government action in this time. In any case, the level of federal government involvement in consumer protection began to grow again under the Bush administration. For example, in October of 1990, the Consumer Products Safety Commission (CPSC), which oversees the safety of consumer products sold in the United states, was reauthorized, and its funding was increased by $42 million. The powers of the CPSC to keep track of businesses that were found guilty of producing or selling hazardous products were expanded. At the same time, the CPSC's power to suspend its own rules to benefit manufacturers was severely limited. It is not clear how far the trend toward greater government involvement in consumer protection will go under the new administration of President Clinton, but in the early 1990s the federal government was taking a larger responsibility in this area.

> The passage of consumer legislation is only the first step in consumer protection. Legislation must be administered effectively.

CONSUMER RESPONSIBILITIES

No president has yet produced a list of consumer responsibilities to accompany the consumer rights listed earlier, but some obvious ones exist:

1. *The responsibility to give correct information*—when, for example, filling out an application for a loan or trading in a used car. To put it bluntly, consumers, like salespeople, shouldn't lie.

2. *The responsibility to report defective goods*—both to the seller and to the manufacturer. This way the seller and manufacturer can warn other consumers of defective and dangerous products, stop selling them, and perhaps recall them. This is a particularly important responsibility with respect to automobiles and electrical equipment. The consumer has a responsibility to society in this area.

3. *The responsibility to report wrongs incurred in consumer dealings*—either to the appropriate government agencies and to private organizations responsible for monitoring various aspects of the marketplace. Again, this is for the protection of other consumers.

4. *The responsibility to keep within the law when protesting*—a fundamental responsibility addressed in Consumer Issue B.

ENFORCEMENT OF FEDERAL CONSUMER PROTECTION LAWS

The passage of consumer legislation is only the first step in consumer protection. Legislation must be administered, and administered effectively. In 1964 President Lyndon Johnson made a gesture in this direction when he appointed the first special presidential assistant for consumer affairs. Although this person, a member of the staff of the Office of the President, had no direct authority, the fact that such a position existed made certain that consumer interests would have some representation at the federal policy level. The office was continued by President Nixon in 1973, when it was transferred to the Department of Health, Education, and Welfare, now the Department of Health and Human Services.

Consumer Affairs Council and Coordination of Consumer Programs

The Consumer Affairs Council is composed of representatives of the 13 cabinet-level departments and is chaired by the president's special assistant for consumer affairs. The Consumer Affairs Council was established by an executive order signed by President Carter on September 26, 1979. That order established a comprehensive federal policy to guide agencies in responding to consumer issues. It was also meant to stimulate the growth of a more effective group of federal employees by giving them additional tools with which to serve consumers. In addition to establishing the Consumer Affairs Council, the executive order required that, by June 9, 1980, each agency would have to have a consumer program designed to satisfy the needs and interests of consumers. The order required that each agency create a consumer staff and educate its staff in the principles underlying the executive order. Not every agency was made subject to the executive order; for example, independent agencies were exempt.

Two of the most important agencies regulating consumer protection legislation are the Federal Trade Commission (FTC) and the Consumer Product Safety Commission (CPSC).

Federal Trade Commission

The Federal Trade Commission is foremost in federal consumer protection activities. Created in 1914 as a result of the Federal Trade Commission Act of that year, the FTC has five commissioners appointed by the president for terms of seven years. The commissioners have extensive enforcement responsibilities for a number of federal statutes.

The FTC's activities are divided among three bureaus—the Bureau of Consumer Protection, the Bureau of Competition, and the Bureau of Economics. Through its Bureau of Consumer Protection, the FTC can stop any "unfair or deceptive acts or practices" that are used to influence, inhibit, or restrict consumers unfairly in their purchasing decisions. Violations are punishable by law. For example, the FTC might issue a **cease-and-desist order** that prohibits General Motors from advertising fuel-economy levels achieved by professional drivers without disclosing the drivers' professional status. If General Motors fails to obey the order, the company may be fined $10,000 for each subsequent illegal advertisement. Then the FTC can impose legal penalties against Ford and Chrysler as well if they advertise similar mileage tests without the disclosure that professional drivers have been used.

The Bureau of Competition is the arm of the FTC that, in conjunction with the Justice Department, enforces antitrust laws, such as price discrimination legislation that makes it illegal for one seller to sell the same product or service to two different buyers at two different prices (unless this difference can be justified in terms of different costs). The FTC Bureau of Economics provides economic advice to the other two bureaus and conducts economic studies concerning government regulations and their effect on consumers and the American economy generally.

Regional offices of the FTC are located in major cities across the country. These offices, the locations of which are given in Consumer Issue B, act as "mini-FTCs" and assist consumers whose complaints or problems fall under FTC jurisdiction.

Consumer Product Safety Commission

As a result of 1970 recommendations of the National Commission on Product Safety, the Consumer Product Safety Act was passed in 1972, creating the Consumer Product Safety Commission to regulate all potentially hazardous consumer products. The Consumer Product Safety Act was the outcome of product safety legislation that had begun in 1953 with the enactment of the Flammable Fabrics Act. In the 20 years that followed, Congress continued to enact legislation regulating specific classes of products or product design or

Cease-and-desist order
An administrative or judicial order commanding a business firm to cease conducting the activities that the agency or a court has deemed to be "unfair or deceptive acts or practices."

An example of the government's role in consumer protection is the inspection and grading of meat by the United States Department of Agriculture (USDA).

Product	Projected Total Accidents
1. Stairs, ramps, landings, & floors	1,450,421
2. Bicycles	514,738
3. Knives	335,083
4. Playground equipment	210,236
5. Cans & other metal containers	179,484
6. Toys	147,898
7. Bathtubs & shower stalls	125,829
8. Manual shop tools	88,813
9. Power saws	71,074
10. Glass containers	71,058
11. Lawn mowers	61,864
12. Chain saws	37,278
13. Cleaning agents (non-soap)	35,673
14. Paints and solvents	17,649

Source: *Statistical Abstract of the United States,* 1992, p. 121.

composition. The Consumer Product Safety Act, however, is concerned with the overall safety of all consumer products.

The 1972 act states that "any article, or component part thereof produced or distributed for sale to a consumer for use in or around a permanent or temporary household or residence, a school, in recreation or otherwise, or for the personal use, consumption or enjoyment of a consumer" shall be subject to regulation by the CPSC. The CPSC can set safety standards for consumer products as well as ban the manufacture and sale of any product deemed hazardous to consumers. The commission has the authority to remove from the market products that are deemed imminently hazardous and can require manufacturers to report information about any products already sold or intended for sale that have proved to be hazardous.

By using data obtained from hospital emergency rooms, the CPSC annually determines which products are the most hazardous—that is, which products are related to the most injuries (those treated in emergency rooms). Exhibit 2–2 shows the results of the most recent study.

Many other government agencies contribute to the effort to protect consumers. These include the Food and Drug Administration, which administers federal laws that regulate the quality of foods and drugs offered for sale, and the Securities and Exchange Commission, which is charged with protecting consumer rights in many financial markets.

STATE AND LOCAL GOVERNMENTS AND CONSUMER PROTECTION

While federal action clearly illustrates the national importance of an issue, the adoption of a federal policy is often the result of prolonged activity at the state and local government levels or in the private sector of the economy. This has been especially true of consumer protection policy. In fact, some states, localities, and private groups have gone far beyond the limits now set by federal policy.

State and local governments have always been involved in setting standards of weights and measures and marketing standards, as well as standards that define the term *fraud.* Even today, enforcement of consumer fraud statutes is left largely to state and local governments. Many areas of fraud are commonly dealt with under state and local criminal fraud statutes arising out of the criminal fraud case decisions of earlier years. Furthermore, in the areas of credit, insurance, health and sanitation, and all issues concerning contract rights, it has been mainly the state governments that have enacted legislation dealing with consumer problems. In fact, state response has sometimes come much earlier than federal response. For example, as early as 1959, both New York and California had legislation on the books to protect the rights of consumers in credit transactions. And not until Massachusetts passed the first truth-in-lending law was federal action on this important issue likely to succeed. When the federal Consumer Credit Protection Act was passed in 1968, Massachusetts became, in effect, a pilot case for the national legislation.

SOURCES OF PRIVATE-SECTOR CONSUMER PROTECTION

How does the private sector of the economy fit in with the public activities for consumer protection? As you might expect, activity in the private sector has been highly variable and, in many cases, short-lived. But in some specific areas, private activities have been significant.

Organizations that Report on Consumer Products

One of the most successful private forms of consumer protection has been in the area of product testing and reporting by not-for-profit organizations. Although the federal government has only recently begun to test products and to reveal test results in a form that aids consumers in their purchasing decisions, private product-testing and reporting groups have been active for a long time. Consumers Union and Consumers' Research, Inc., are two examples.

Consumers Union

Consumers Union, the publisher of *Consumer Reports,* is a nonprofit organization chartered in 1936 under the laws of the state of New York. The object of Consumers Union has been to bring more useful information into the seller/buyer relationship so that consumers can buy rationally. The first issue of *Consumer Reports,* in May 1936, went to 3,000 charter subscribers, who were told about the relative costs and nutritional values of breakfast cereals, the fanciful claims made for Alka Seltzer, the hazards of lead toys, and the best buys in women's stockings, toilet soaps, and toothbrushes. Consumers Union's policy has always been to buy goods in the open market and bring them to the lab for objective testing.

Approximately 3½ million subscribers and newsstand buyers now read *Consumer Reports* every month to receive advice on purchasing credit, insurance, and drugs. A priority of Consumers Union's testing is automobiles: which are the best buys, which are safe, which have good brakes, which have safety defects, and so on. Consumers Union has also published articles on such ecological topics as pesticides, phosphates in detergents, and lead in gasolines. (It also strongly criticizes government agencies when they act against consumer interests.) Consumers Union accepts no advertising in its magazine to avoid possible financial pressure by the advertisers.

Consumers' Research, Inc.

Consumers' Research, Inc., founded in 1929, publishes *Consumers' Research* magazine, with a monthly readership of several hundred thousand. It contains product ratings, ratings of motion pictures and phonograph records, and short editorials. In its reports on consumer goods, *Consumers' Research* strives to use only results from products that were selected at random rather than ones that were specifically prepared for test purposes by manufacturers. Consumers' Research, Inc., often restricts its reporting to brands or goods that are nationally distributed, while Consumers Union sometimes tests brands that are distributed only in specific high-population-density localities. It is the policy of Consumers' Research to service its national and international audience rather than give any special attention to products or brands sold in specific geographic areas. Further, the *Consumers' Research* magazine does not give brand names as "best buys" as does *Consumer Reports*. Both publications pride themselves on stressing safety and efficiency in products, and both have identified potentially unsafe products that escaped the government's detection.

Other Product-Testing Groups

Other product-testing groups provide information that consumers can use even though they were formed for other purposes. The American Standards Association (ASA), for example, is a private agency that was organized in 1918 to develop standards and testing methods to be used by manufacturers. By setting a uniform level of performance, these standards and testing methods can protect manufacturers against unfair competition. But they also provide protection to the consumers who buy products by ensuring their safety. Using the standards developed by the ASA, other private laboratories or testing groups may certify the efficiency and/or safety of such items as electrical and gas appliances, textiles, and many other products. In addition to product testing at the manufacturing level, there is a wide range of product testing by retailers who are eager to perform a consumer service and to provide themselves with a competitive advantage. We mustn't place too much stock, however, in the "seals of approval" that appear on numerous products. Their value depends on the organization that issues them.

Better Business Bureaus

Local private agencies are also active participants in the public area of consumer protection. Probably the best known of such private agencies is the Better Business Bureau, which is business-supported. The National Better Business Bureau has been in existence since 1916 and has local affiliates in all major cities and counties. Its purposes are

1. To provide information to consumers on the products and selling practices of businesses.
2. To provide businesspeople with a source of localized standards for acceptable business practices.

3. To provide a technique for mediating grievances between consumers and sellers.

Because the Better Business Bureau has no enforcement powers, all actions must be voluntary. And because the Better Business Bureau is dependent on the business community for its membership, it cannot afford to antagonize that community. The weaknesses in the voluntary system were felt most strongly when the consumer movement began to press for protection not only against the fly-by-night, illegal, fraudulent firm, but also against marketing practices that were generally accepted by the business community. Once consumers began to seek redress for damages suffered from exaggerated advertising, ineffective warranties and guarantees, safety hazards, and poor consumer choices due to market structure, the private business organization was unable to police its members effectively. But the Better Business Bureau continues to survive and to thrive as it seeks to improve communication with the consumer. For example, the Better Business Bureau's arbitration program has been expanding in an attempt to deal more formally with the issue of consumer redress for grievances against sellers and producers of goods and services.

Don't get the impression, though, that the Better Business Bureau in your community is a truly effective consumer agency. In many communities, the Better Business Bureau simply keeps files on businesses regarding consumer complaints.

Role of the Media

Although the Better Business Bureau is the oldest of the private agencies that seek to mediate grievances, it is by no means the only one. Newspapers, radio stations, and TV stations have all been in the forefront of the movement to help consumers who have legitimate complaints by providing column space or air time for consumer action, and they have been highly successful in obtaining results for consumers able to make use of them. Affiliates of commercial networks have run regular consumer reports and consumer-action series, as have public television stations. These programs typically use publicity as a powerful weapon to resolve consumer grievances.

PRIVATE INDUSTRY'S SELF-REGULATION

Self-regulation involves the creation of a set of standards for an industry's products or services, publication of those standards, and their subsequent enforcement. We are observing an increase in the willingness of industry to regulate itself, which is partly due to industry's desire to avoid government regulation.

Many industry associations now help resolve problems between their member companies and consumers. Depending on the industry, responsibility for dispute resolution may rest with a trade association, a service council, or a consumer action program. For example, the Automotive Consumer Action Program (AUTOCAP) is a consumer-action group created by the National Automotive Dealer Association to resolve disputes between consumers and automobile dealers. Similarly, the Major Appliance Consumer Action Panel (MACAP) offers dispute-resolution services between consumers and business firms in the appliance industry. These are only two of the more than forty or so major trade association consumer-assistance programs that have arisen in

> We are observing an increase in the willingness of industry to regulate itself, which is partly due to industry's desire to avoid government regulation.

the past two decades. Most major corporations today also have a consumer-relations department and often a hotline that consumers can call when they have a complaint or wish to obtain information. Corporate consumer offices normally provide the most direct, and least expensive, method for resolving problems you may have with products or services. You will find further information concerning these programs in Consumer Issue B.

WARRANTIES AND CONSUMER PROTECTION

Many times consumers buy equipment that turns out to be defective and needs repairs or replacement. Of course, we are all used to buying products bearing labels that promise a "money back guarantee" or "full satisfaction guaranteed." But such guarantees may not be worth the paper they are printed on. In the early 1970s a survey by the Major Appliance Consumer Action Panel revealed that many warranties did not state the name and address of the warrantor, did not mention the product or part covered, did not indicate the length of the warranty, and did not indicate what the warrantor would actually do and who would pay for it. Instead, they presented the coverage in "legalese" that would be difficult for the average consumer to understand.

Magnuson-Moss Warranty Act

The Magnuson-Moss Warranty–Federal Trade Commission Improvement Act of 1975 closed many of the loopholes that manufacturers had included in their warranties. The act does not require that a manufacturer provide a written warranty or a guarantee, but if a warranty is offered, it has to comply with the following legal provisions.

1. Any warranty on a product that costs $15 or more must include a simple, complete, and conspicuous statement of the name and address of the warrantor, a description of what is covered and for how much, a step-by-step procedure for placing warranty claims, an explanation of how disputes between the parties will be settled, and the warranty's duration. This must be available to the consumer as prepurchase information.

2. Manufacturers cannot require as a condition of the warranty that the buyer of the product use it only in connection with other products or services that are identified by brand or corporate name. In other words, the maker of a flashlight cannot require that the purchaser use only Duracell batteries in that flashlight for the warranty to be effective.

Full versus Limited Warranties

If a warranty meets minimum federal standards, it can be designated a *full warranty*. If it doesn't, it must be explicitly designated a *limited warranty* and state how it is limited. An example of a limited warranty is given in Exhibit 2–3. Under a full warranty, the consumer merely informs the warrantor that the product is defective, does not work properly, or doesn't conform to the written warranty. The warrantor must then fix the product within a reasonable time and without charge. In fact, in order to obtain the designation "full warranty," the warrantor must pay the consumer for all incidental expenses if there are unreasonable delays or other problems in getting the warranty honored.

Further, the Federal Trade Commission now has the power to set a limit on the number of unsuccessful repair attempts possible under a full warranty. If, after a reasonable number of repairs, the product is still defective, the customer

▶ Exhibit 2–3 **Example of Limited Warranty**

Limited Warranty

MPH COMPUTER PRODUCTS (MPH) warrants to the original retail purchaser of this MACBCOOL that MPH will repair or replace, at its option, this product if defective in material or workmanship, without charge for parts or labor, for a period of one (1) year from the date of original retail purchase. Parts used for replacement are warranted for the remainder of the one-year period.

TO OBTAIN WARRANTY SERVICE, DELIVER OR MAIL THE PRODUCT, USING THE ORIGINAL PACKAGING OR OTHER OFFERING A SIMILAR DEGREE OF PROTECTION, PREPAID, TO MPH COMPUTER PRODUCTS.

This warranty does not cover defects or failures of this product caused by damage (not resulting from a defect in material or workmanship) while in the possession of the owner, including defects or failures caused by accident, neglect, or unauthorized alterations, or from misuse of or operation of this product in any manner contrary to the instructions set forth in the instruction manual accompanying the product, or from repairs made or attempted by persons other than MPH.

MPH makes no other warranties, express or implied, aside from those made in this warranty.

MPH MAKES NO IMPLIED WARRANTY OF MERCHANTABILITY OR OF FITNESS FOR PARTICULAR PURPOSE. SOME STATES DO NOT ALLOW LIMITATIONS ON HOW LONG AN IMPLIED WARRANTY LASTS, SO THE ABOVE LIMITATIONS MAY NOT APPLY TO YOU.

UNDER NO CIRCUMSTANCES SHALL MPH BE LIABLE TO THE OWNER OF THIS PRODUCT OR ANY OTHER PERSON FOR ANY SPECIAL, INCIDENTAL OR CONSEQUENTIAL DAMAGES RESULTING FROM ANY DEFECT OF MATERIAL OR WORKMANSHIP, BREACH OF WARRANTY OR BREACH OF CONTRACT, OR OTHERWISE. SOME STATES DO NOT ALLOW THE EXCLUSION OR LIMITATION OF INCIDENTAL OR CONSEQUENTIAL DAMAGES, SO THE ABOVE LIMITATION OR EXCLUSION MAY NOT APPLY TO YOU.

The enforceability of this warranty is limited to the original retail purchaser of this product.

As a condition to the enforceability of this warranty, the attached registration card must be completed and mailed to MPH within fifteen (15) days after the date of purchase. Failure to do so will void this warranty.

This warranty gives you specific legal rights, and you may also have other rights which vary from state to state.

can choose between a refund or a replacement. The replacement must be made free of charge. If the refund option is chosen, the warrantor can deduct an amount for "reasonable depreciation based on actual use."

Full warranties apply to both initial purchasers and to those who buy the product secondhand during the warranty period.

Settling Disputes

Under the new law, consumers who are dissatisfied with what the warrantor has done for them must try an informal settlement procedure first. Then, if still dissatisfied, the consumer may sue and is entitled to the recovery of purchase costs, damages, and attorneys' fees if the suit is won.

If many consumers feel they have been victimized by a fraudulent warranty, they may engage in a federal class action suit. At least 100 consumers with a minimum claim of $25 each must be involved, and the total amount in controversy must be at lest $50,000.

Implied Warranties

Up to this point, we have been discussing what are considered *express warranties* because they are *expressly* pointed out in some written document, such as on a label or a card enclosed with an instruction booklet for a consumer durable. There are also several types of *implied warranties* that the law derives by implication or inference from the nature of the transaction. No implied warranties are covered under the Magnuson-Moss Warranty Act. They are created according to the Uniform Commercial Code, which is the code of law governing sales of products in the United States. There are basically two types of implied warranties: one of merchantability, the other of fitness.

Implied Warranty of Merchantability   An **implied warranty of merchantability** arises in every sale of goods made by a merchant who deals in goods of the kind sold. Thus, a retailer of ski equipment makes an implied warranty of merchantability every time he or she sells a pair of skis, but a neighbor selling skis at a garage sale does not.

Goods that are merchantable are "reasonably fit for the ordinary purposes for which such goods are used." They must be of at least average, fair, or medium-grade quality—not the finest quality and not the worst. The quality must be comparable to quality that will pass without objection in the trade or market for goods of the same description. Some examples of nonmerchantable goods include light bulbs that explode when switched on, pajamas that burst into flames upon slight contact with a stove burner, high-heeled shoes that break under normal use, or shotgun shells that explode prematurely.

The implied warranty of merchantability imposes *absolute* liability for the safe performance of their products on merchants when dealing in their line of goods. It makes no difference that the merchant might not have known of a defect or could not have discovered it.

Implied warranty of merchantability
An implicit promise by the seller that an item is reasonably fit for the general purpose for which it is sold.

Implied Warranty of Fitness   There is an **implied warranty of fitness** for a particular purpose whenever any seller (merchant or nonmerchant) knows the particular purpose for which a buyer will use the goods and knows that the buyer has relied on the seller's skill and judgment to select suitable goods.

A "particular purpose of the buyer" differs from the concept of merchantability. Goods can be *merchantable* but still not fit the buyer's particular pur-

Implied warranty of fitness
An implicit warranty of fitness for a particular purpose, meaning that the seller guarantees the product for the specific purpose for which a buyer will use the goods, when the seller is offering his or her skill and judgment as to suitable selection of the right products.

pose. For example, house paints suitable for ordinary walls are not suitable for painting stucco walls. A contract can include both a warranty of merchantability and a warranty of fitness for a particular purpose that relates to the specific use or special situation in which a buyer intends to use the goods. For example, a seller recommends a particular pair of shoes, *knowing* that a customer is looking for mountain-climbing shoes. The buyer purchases the shoes *relying* on the seller's judgment. If the shoes are found to be suitable only for walking and not for mountain climbing, the seller has breached the warranty of fitness for a particular purpose.

A seller does not need "actual knowledge" of the buyer's particular purpose. It is sufficient if a seller "has reason to know" the purpose. The buyer, however, must have relied on the seller's skill or judgment in selecting or furnishing suitable goods for an implied warranty to be created. For example, Judy Josephs buys a shortwave radio from Sam's Electronics, telling the salesperson that she wants a set strong enough to pick up Radio Luxembourg. Sam's Electronics sells Judy Josephs a Model XYZ set. The set works, but it will not pick up Radio Luxembourg. Judy Josephs wants her money back. Here, since Sam's Electronics is guilty of a breach of implied warranty of fitness for the buyer's particular purpose, Judy Josephs will be able to get her money back. The salesperson knew specifically that she wanted a set that would pick up Radio Luxembourg. Furthermore, Judy Josephs relied on the salesperson to furnish a radio that would fulfill this purpose. Sam's Electronics did not do so. Therefore, the warranty was breached.

CONSUMER PROTECTION TODAY

During the 1930s consumer groups sprang up all over the country as many people found it necessary to stretch a precious few dollars to cover basic living needs. But the big burst of consumerism occurred in the 1960s, and, by the early 1970s, organizations existed at state and local levels throughout the country. In 1967 the Consumer Federation of America was formed to coordinate the efforts of such groups at the national level. Consumer activist groups have aggressively pressed for legislation on credit, packaging, no-fault insurance, and adequate labeling of food and drugs. More recently, consumer advocate groups have been calling for reform and offering legal self-help to consumers.

While seeking redress for consumers who feel they have been harmed in private transactions, these consumer groups also have worked to provide education and representation to consumers in hearings before government legislative and administrative bodies. The ultimate goal of these groups is consumer participation in government policy decisions, both directly and indirectly. Thus, at least some consumers seek to participate in the functioning of the marketplace in the same way that large corporations and major trade unions do.

This kind of consumer activism is significant because it gives consumers a voice in government. On any issue, there may now be a business interest, a labor interest, and a consumer interest.

▶ SUMMARY

1. Consumer protection is not new. Standards of weights and measures and standards for quality have long existed to benefit both consumers and businesses in the marketplace. By 1900 antitrust laws had been created that were aimed at preventing firms from using monopoly-like powers to harm consumers or other businesses by fixing prices or controlling the allocation of resources and production and services.

2. The first federal law passed specifically to aid consumers was the Food and Drug Act of 1906. Other federal legislation such as the Federal Trade Commission Act of 1914 followed. After the passage of the Food, Drug, and Cosmetic Act of 1938, however, there was little significant federal activity in the area of consumer protection until the 1960s.

3. In the 1960s and 1970s, starting with the administration of President Kennedy and extending through that of President Carter, the rights of consumers and the need for increased consumer protection were popular causes for our chief executives.

4. The election of Ronald Reagan in 1980 brought about a change in favor of less government involvement in business. Although the Bush administration took some steps to increase the government's efforts in consumer protection, it maintained President Reagan's objective of limiting government involvement in the economy to the greatest extent possible. The impact of the Clinton administration on consumer protection remains to be seen, but it appears to favor increased government intervention.

5. Sources of consumer protection include federal and state legislation, agencies, and bureaus protecting consumers' rights; county and municipal government consumer offices; and private groups.

6. President Carter established the Consumer Affairs Council by executive order on September 26, 1979. The Council's purpose was to coordinate consumer protection programs at the federal level. The executive order also required each federal agency (except independent agencies) to have a consumer staff educated in consumer protection legislation by June 9, 1980.

7. Two important federal agencies in monitoring and enforcing consumer protection legislation are the Federal Trade Commission and the Consumer Product Safety Commission.

8. State and local agencies have introduced means to help consumers recover damages for fraudulent business activities. At the very minimum, local government mediators act in disputes between consumers and sellers and often refer both parties to an appropriate agency if specific laws have, in fact, been violated.

9. The best-known private agencies are Consumers Union and Consumers' Research, Inc., both established chiefly to provide information to consumers. In addition, branches of the Better Business Bureau attempt to help consumers as well as businesspeople, but they are not effective consumer protection agencies. There are also private testing agencies, such as the American Standards Association.

10. Many industry associations now help resolve problems between their member companies and consumers. Depending on the industry, responsibility for dispute resolution may rest with a trade association, a service, a council, or a consumer action program such as the Automotive Consumer Action Program (AUTOCAP).

11. The media—newspapers, television, and radio—often assist consumers who have legitimate complaints by providing column space or air time for consumer action.

12. Legislation passed in 1975 tightened the definition of warranty that manufacturers can use.

13. The Uniform Commercial Code stipulates that every good sold by a merchant (when dealing in his or her line of goods) has an implied warranty of merchantability. Additionally, any person who sells a good for a specific purpose gives an implied warranty of fitness for that specific purpose.

14. Consumer activists seek to participate in the functioning of the marketplace in the same way that large corporations and major trade unions do. This kind of consumer activism is significant because it gives consumers a voice in government.

▶ QUESTIONS FOR THOUGHT AND DISCUSSION

1. What is the current administration's stand on consumer protection?
2. What private sources of consumer information do you use in making your decisions about what to buy?
3. What tradeoffs between price and quality would be likely to result from laws that required manufacturers to provide better warranties for their products?
4. What are the benefits to industry of self-regulation?
5. What is the difference between an implied warranty of merchantability and an implied warranty of fitness for a particular purpose? Give some examples.

▶ THINGS TO DO

1. Call your local Better Business Bureau and ask for its booklet describing the bureau and all of the areas in which it is active. If there is no Better Business Bureau in your area, contact the local chamber of commerce.
2. Call your local television and radio stations and newspaper office or offices to find out if any of them devote time or space to consumer-action services.
3. Look at the warranties of any consumer products you have recently purchased or are about to purchase. Do any of them give full warranties? If they are limited warranties, under what conditions can you have the product repaired or replaced?

▶ APPLICATION

Identify a particular good or service that you believe should be more closely regulated by the government to protect consumers. Investigate this product, and use the information you find to write an essay that explains why consumers need protection in their use of the product. Suggest the type of protection or regulation that you believe would be appropriate. In your essay you should explain the benefits consumers would receive and any costs they would pay as the result of your proposal.

▶ SELECTED READINGS

▶ *Antitrust Enforcement and the Consumer*. Available free from the Department of Justice, 666 11th St., N.W., Room 910, Washington, DC 20530.
▶ Clarkson, Kenneth W., et al. *West's Business Law,* 4th ed. St. Paul: West, 1989, Ch. 20.
▶ *Compliance and Enforcement*. Available free from the Federal Trade Commission, 6th St. and Pennsylvania Ave., N.W., Washington, DC 20580.
▶ Dolbeare, Kenneth M. *American Public Policy: A Citizen's Guide*. New York: McGraw-Hill, 1982.

▶ Gest, Ted. "Product Paranoia." *U.S. News & World Report,* February 24, 1992, pp. 67–69.

▶ "Getting Warranty Protection." Facts for Consumers, Winter 1986, pp. 11–13. Available free from the Federal Trade Commission, 6th St. and Pennsylvania Ave., N.W., Washington, DC 20580.

▶ Merline, J. W. "Consumers' Past." *Consumers' Research Magazine,* October 1991, p. 38.

▶ "A Pyramid Topples at the USDA." *Consumer Reports,* October 1991, pp. 663–666.

▶ Shapiro, L. "Labels We Can Live By." *Newsweek,* November 18, 1991. p. 90.

▶ Steorts, N. H. "The United States' Viewpoint on Product Safety and Quality." *Vital Speeches of the Day,* December 15, 1991, pp. 133–138.

▶ *Warranties.* Available free from the Federal Trade Commission, 6th St. and Pennsylvania Ave., N.W., Washington, DC 20580.

▶ Wilson, James Q., ed. *The Politics of Regulation.* New York: Basic Books, 1980.

How to Get Help for Consumer Problems

GLOSSARY

INJUNCTION   A legal order requiring that an activity be stopped, corrected, or undertaken.

Knowing what kinds of services are available is the first step toward taking advantage of consumer service agencies. Generally, government agencies and private voluntary and business groups provide the following four consumer services.

1. Information to consumers before a purchase is made. This service includes standard setting, inspection, investigation of marketing techniques, product testing, labeling and other disclosure legislation, publication of results, and formal teaching.

2. Aid to consumers after a purchase is made, generally through the enforcement of public policy to prevent repeated unsatisfactory or fraudulent practices. This service includes accepting complaints, investigating the complaints, possibly instituting legal proceedings followed by a judgment, and imposing either an **injunction** against the action or a penalty for breaking the law. This kind of action does not help individual consumers make up their own losses.

3. Redress to individual consumers for their individual losses as a result of purchases. This involves a complaint, an investigation, possibly publicity or mediation, sometimes a settlement, or a legal action followed by a judgment and enforcement of it.

4. Representation of consumers in issues with a consumer interest before a legislative body, government administrative agencies, and private business leadership. Here again, this generally concerns the complaint, investigation and research regarding the complaint and the problem it reflects, and the subsequent development and publication of plans for its remedy. Often this results in changes in legislation.

▶ BE PREPARED

Obviously, the best way to deal with consumer problems is not to have them in the first place. While this may be an impossible goal, you can take a large step toward it by having the following consumer resources immediately available in your home:

1. *Consumer Reports.* The dollars you pay for a subscription to this publication, which was discussed in the preceding chapter, will be well spent.

2. *Consumer's Resource Handbook.* This booklet, which is published annually and continually updated, lists addresses, phone numbers, and names of staff members of hundreds of federal and state organizations, corporate consumer-relations agencies, private consumer action organizations, and arbitration and dispute-settling groups. It is an invaluable guide to the resources available to anyone who wishes information about consumer assistance of any kind. For example, if you wish to call a local Better Business Bureau to check on the reputation of a firm you may want to do business with, this *Handbook* has a complete listing of the addresses and phone numbers for the more than 170 bureaus throughout the United States. And if you need help in solving a dispute with a seller, you can locate the appropriate agency or organization to call within seconds. This publication is available free from the government. Write to the Consumer Information Center, Department 532-G, Pueblo, CO 81009, for a current copy.

3. *Consumer Information Catalog.* This catalog, which is also available free from the above Pueblo address, lists hundreds of free or next-to-free federal publications of interest to consumers. Food, nutrition, health, quackery, mortgages, credit, automobiles, travel, education—these are some of the areas covered by these federal publications.

By having this small, but effective, library at your fingertips—in addition to a telephone book—you will find it much easier to be an "informed consumer" and to avoid many potential pitfalls when purchasing consumer goods or services.

▶ WHEN YOU DO HAVE A PROBLEM

Thirty-seven states have one or more federal information centers (listed at the end of this Consumer Issue feature) to help consumers when problems in the marketplace arise, and there are even more state, local, and private agencies or organizations that offer consumer assistance services.

Whenever you have a complaint about a product or service you have purchased, though, the logical person to contact first is the seller from whom you bought it. And for this you must be prepared.

▶ A STRATEGY

First, you should always try to figure out a strategy for settling your grievances without going to an outside party. After all, it takes additional time and effort to get a third party involved in your disputes with a seller. Thus, whenever you buy anything, *keep a receipt* if you are worried that there may be problems later. But even before you make the purchase, be certain to *have everything put in writing* about any take-back provisions, warranties, or guarantees.

Exhibit B–1 shows the chain of complaint. Imagine, for example, that you buy something, and it falls apart a week later. A friendly, polite call to the store and a talk with the salesperson will tell you immediately whether you will have problems. Many times, reputable stores will either give you an identical article that is in good working condition, repair the one you have, or refund your money. If the salesperson does not agree, then seek out the manager or the owner. If you still do not get satisfaction and if you are dealing with a nationally advertised product or with a large chain store, you may want to write the president or the chairperson of the board directly to complain.[1]

Exhibit B–2 shows a sample copy of an appropriate letter of complaint. Personal letters to the presidents of large companies get quick responses surprisingly often. But sometimes they do not. If your letter-writing effort fails, what is your next recourse?

▶ CALLING FOR HELP

When you need consumer assistance, it is best to work first at the local level. Is there a consumer affairs agency or office in your local government? The telephone book is probably your nearest source of this information; in most major cities today, there is a Yellow Pages listing under "Consumers" of the major public agencies that provide consumer services. A call to the administrative officer of your county or

---

▶ Exhibit B–1 Chain of Complaint

1. Purchase a product and save the sales receipt. Write down the salesperson's name.
2. The product proves to be defective.
3. Visit or call the store and talk to the salesperson.
4. If unsuccessful in dealing with the salesperson to obtain a refund, repair, or new article, find out the manager's name and either call or visit him or her.
5. If unsuccessful with the manager, do the following three things simultaneously:

   a. When dealing with a nationally advertised product or a large retail chain, obtain from your local library the name and address of the president or chairperson of the board and write to him or her directly, enclosing a copy of the letter shown in Exhibit B–2.
   b. Write to local and state consumer groups about your problem, enclosing a copy of the letter you sent to the president or chairperson of the board.
   c. Contact national consumer-help agencies and consumer-action panels, such as the Major Appliance Consumer Action Panel (MACAP) or the Automobile Consumer Action Program (AUTOCAP) discussed in Chapter 2.

6. If you still receive no satisfaction, lodge your complaint with the state attorney general's office.

▶ Exhibit B–2 How to Lodge a Complaint

Your address
Date

Addressee
Company Name
Street Address
City, State Zip Code

Dear Sir or Madam:

I am writing this letter to inform you of my dissatisfaction with [name of product with serial number or the service performed], which I purchased [the date and location of purchase].

My complaint concerns [the reason(s) for your complaint]. I believe that in all fairness you should [the specific action you desire for satisfaction] in order to resolve this problem.

I sincerely look forward to your reply and a speedy resolution to my complaint. I will allow two weeks before referring this complaint to the appropriate consumer agency.

Yours truly,

Your Name

Enclosures (include copies, not originals, of all related records)

---

1. In your local library, you can consult the *Consumer's Register of American Business* and *The Directory of Foreign Manufacturers in the United States.*

city should also give you information on the availability of public consumer services.

If you find no local consumer agency, look under the state listings; if no listing there looks promising, call the state attorney general's office. That office works closely with consumer agencies because much of the consumer fraud uncovered by consumer agencies is prosecuted through the attorney general's office. Exhibit B–3 lists the addresses of state consumer-protection agencies.

▶ Private Organizations

You might also want to contact a private consumer-action group at the local level. Many local newspapers and radio and television stations in the United States today have an "action line" or "hotline" service to help consumers. These groups often can be extremely effective in bringing about a rapid and satisfactory resolution to consumer problems. To locate such services, check with your local newspapers, radio and TV stations, or local library. There may be other local organizations available also. You doubtless will have heard of any successful ones, which probably will be listed in the telephone book. You might even consider joining one of these groups if you want to prevent a recurrence of your problem.

▶ Legal Assistance

Getting your money back may depend on private legal action. If you have to go beyond the small claims court—which we discuss in Consumer Issue C—to a higher court, you must be prepared to pay legal fees. But even if you can't pay them, don't give up; in many cities, the traditional legal-aid society has been augmented by special legal services

for low-income families, and these services often place strong emphasis on consumer problems. In some states, too, group legal practices have been approved, and you might obtain help through your union or some other organization that has contracted with such a service. Some college governments have made available to students legal services that permit students to pursue solutions to their consumer problems.

A number of legal self-help and consumer-advocacy groups exist that may be able to help you. For information relating to self-help, shopping for attorneys, and court procedures and requirements, you can write to HALT, 201 Massachusetts Avenue, N.E., Suite 319, Washington, DC 20002.

▶ SPECIFIC INDUSTRY AGENCIES: THIRD-PARTY INTERVENTION

An increasingly popular way to resolve consumer problems is to allow third parties to settle a dispute between you and the seller of a product or service. Local agencies, trade associations, and individual companies are setting up mediation procedures, most of which are free to consumers. There are basically three types of third-party interveners:

1. **A conciliator,** who simply brings together the parties in a dispute to get them to resolve their differences.
2. **A mediator,** who is in a stronger position and can make nonbinding recommendations and proposals.
3. **An arbitrator,** who makes a decision that can be binding on some or all of the parties. A binding decision can be enforced in a court of law.

Obviously, from the consumer's point of view, the best of all possi-

ble worlds is a dispute-settling process that is binding on the business but not on the consumer. This may sound unrealistic, but the arbitration procedures of Ford Motor Company's Consumer Appeals Board and the Homeowners Warranty Corporation (HOW), which provides guarantees on new home construction, operate that way; we will discuss HOW further in Chapter 20.

▶ Where to Go

Where you go depends on the kind of problem you have. If it is a dispute between you and a local company, going to a local agency makes sense. Approximately one hundred and seventy local Better Business Bureaus across the country provide arbitration. Your county Office of Consumer Affairs will also be able to help. If it is a dispute between you and a manufacturer of a product, then you should find out if there is an arbitration panel for that industry. The names and addresses of such services are given in the chapters of this text as we discuss specific products and services. There are arbitration panels for new automobiles, automobile-repair services, new-home construction, major appliances, and so on.

▶ American Arbitration Association

The American Arbitration Association has been remarkably successful in settling disputes before they reach the courts. If there is a branch of this organization in your area, you may find it useful. For information or assistance, write to Public Relations Director, American Arbitration Association, 140 West 51st Street, New York, NY 10020, or call (212) 484-4006.

Alabama

Director
Consumer Protection Division
Office of Attorney General
11 South Union Street
Montgomery, Alabama 36130
(205) 242-7335
800-392-5658 (toll free—Alabama only)

Alaska

Chief
Consumer Protection Section
Office of Attorney General
1031 West Fourth Avenue, Suite 200
Anchorage, Alaska 99501
(907) 269-5100

Arizona

Chief Counsel
Financial Fraud Division
Office of Attorney General
1275 West Washington Street
Phoenix, Arizona 85007
(602) 542-5763 (fraud only)
800-352-8431 (toll free—Arizona only)

Arkansas

Director
Consumer Protection Division
Office of Attorney General
Justice Building
323 Center St., Suite 200
Little Rock, Arkansas 72201
(501) 682-2341
800-482-8982 (toll free—Arkansas only)

California

Director
Public Inquiry Unit
Office of Attorney General
1515 K Street, Suite 511
Sacramento, California 94244
(916) 322-3360
800-952-5225 (toll free—California only)

Colorado

Director
Antitrust and Consumer Protection
Enforcement Unit
Office of Attorney General
1525 Sherman Street, Third Floor
Denver, Colorado 80203
(303) 866-5167

Connecticut

Director
Department of Consumer Protection
State Office Building
165 Capitol Avenue
Hartford, Connecticut 06106
(203) 566-4999
800-842-2649 (toll free—Connecticut only)

Delaware

Director
Division of Consumer Affairs
Department of Community Affairs
820 North French Street, 4th Floor
Wilmington, Delaware 19801
(302) 571-3250

District of Columbia

Director
District of Columbia Department of
Consumer and Regulatory Affairs
614 H Street, N.W.
Washington, D.C. 20001
(202) 727-7000

Florida

Assistant Director
Division of Consumer Services
508 Mayo Building
Tallahassee, Florida 32399
(904) 488-2221
800-342-2176 (toll free—Florida only)

Georgia

Administrator
Governor's Office of Consumer Affairs
2 Martin Luther King, Jr. Drive, S.E.
Plaza Level—East Tower
Atlanta, Georgia 30334
(404) 656-3790
800-869-1123 (toll free—Georgia only)

Hawaii

Director
Office of Consumer Protection
Department of Commerce and Consumer
Affairs
250 South King Street, Room 520
P.O. Box 3767
Honolulu, Hawaii 96812
(808) 548-2540 (complaints and
investigations—Hawaii only)
Out of state (808) 587-3222

Illinois

Director
Governor's Office of Citizens Assistance
222 S. College St.
Springfield, Illinois 62706
(217) 782-0244

Indiana

Chief Counsel and Director
Consumer Protection Division
Office of Attorney General
402 W. Washington St., 5th Floor
Indianapolis, Indiana 46204
(317) 232-6330
800-382-5516 (toll free—Indiana only)

Iowa

Iowa Citizens' Aide/Ombudsman
215 East 7th St.
Des Moines, Iowa, 50319
(515) 281-3592
800-358-5510 (toll free—Iowa only)

Kansas

Chief
Consumer Protection Division
Office of Attorney General
Kansas Judicial Center, 2nd Floor
Topeka, Kansas 66612
(913) 296-3751
800-432-2310 (toll free—Kansas only)

Kentucky

Director
Consumer Protection Division
Office of Attorney General
209 Saint Clair Street
Frankfort, Kentucky 40601
(502) 564-2200
800-432-9257 (toll free—Kentucky only)

Louisiana

Chief
Consumer Protection Section
Office of Attorney General
P.O. Box 94005
Baton Rouge, Louisiana 70804
(504) 342-7013

Maine

Chief, Consumer and Antitrust Div.
Office of Attorney General

(Continued)

▶ **Exhibit B–3 State Consumer Protection Agencies,** *Continued*

State House Station No. Six
Augusta, Maine 04333
(207) 289-3716 (9:00–10:00 a.m.)

Maryland
Chief
Consumer and Investor Affairs and
Consumer Protection Division
Office of Attorney General
200 St. Paul Place
Baltimore, Maryland 21202
(410) 528-8662 (9:00–1:00)

Massachusetts
Director
Executive Office of Consumer Affairs and
Business Regulation
One Ashburton Place, Room 1411
Boston, Massachusetts 02108
(617) 727-7780

Michigan
Assistant Attorney General
Consumer Protection Division
Office of Attorney General
670 Law Building
Lansing, Michigan 48913
(517) 373-1140

Minnesota
Director
Office of Consumer Services
Office of Attorney General
117 University Avenue
St. Paul, Minnesota 55155
(612) 296-2331

Mississippi
Assistant Attorney General and Chief
Consumer Protection Division
Office of Attorney General
High and President Streets
P.O. Box 220
Jackson, Mississippi 39205
(601) 359-3680

Missouri
Chief Counsel
Trade Offense Division
Office of Attorney General
P.O. Box 899
Jefferson City, Missouri 65102
(314) 751-2616
800-392-8222 (toll free—Missouri only)

Montana
Consumer Affairs Unit
Department of Commerce
1424 Ninth Avenue
P.O. Box 200501
Helena, Montana 59620-0501
(406) 444-4312

Nebraska
Assistant Attorney General
Consumer Protection Division
Department of Justice
2115 State Capitol
P.O. Box 94906
Lincoln, Nebraska 68509
(402) 471-2682

Nevada
Commissioner of Consumer Affairs
Department of Commerce
State Mail Room Complex
Las Vegas, Nevada 89158
(702) 486-7355

New Hampshire
Chief
Consumer Protection and Antitrust Division
Office of Attorney General
State House Annex, 25 Capitol St.
Concord, New Hampshire 03301
(603) 271-3641

New Jersey
Director
Division of Consumer Affairs
124 Halsey St.
Newark, New Jersey 07102
(201) 504-6200

New Mexico
Director
Consumer and Economic Crime Division
Office of Attorney General
P.O. Drawer 1508
Santa Fe, New Mexico 87504
(505) 827-6000
800-432-2070 (toll free—New Mexico only)

New York
Assistant Attorney General
Bureau of Consumer Frauds and Protection
Office of Attorney General
State Capitol
Albany, New York 12224
(518) 474-5481

North Carolina
Special Deputy Attorney General and Chief
Consumer Protection Division
Office of Attorney General
Department of Justice Building
P.O. Box 629
Raleigh, North Carolina 27602-0629
(919) 733-7741

North Dakota
Director
Consumer Fraud Division
Office of Attorney General
State Capitol Building, 600 East Blvd.
Bismarck, North Dakota 58505
(701) 224-3404
800-472-2600 (toll free—North Dakota only)

Ohio
Consumers' Counsel
77 S. High St., 15th Floor
Columbus, Ohio 43266-0550
(614) 466-9605
800-282-9448 (toll free—Ohio only)

Oklahoma
Assistant Attorney General for Consumer Affairs
Office of Attorney General
112 State Capitol Building
Oklahoma City, Oklahoma 73105
(405) 521-3921

Oregon
Attorney in Charge
Financial Fraud Section
Department of Justice
Justice Building
Salem, Oregon 97310
(503) 378-4320

Pennsylvania
Director
Bureau of Consumer Protection
Office of Attorney General
Strawberry Square—14th Floor
Harrisburg, Pennsylvania 17120
(717) 787-9707
800-441-2555 (toll free—Pennsylvania only)

Rhode Island
Director

(Continued)

Assistant Attorney General and Chief
Consumer Protection Division
Department of Attorney General
72 Pine Street
Providence, Rhode Island 02903
(401) 277-2104

South Carolina
Administrator
Department of Consumer Affairs
P.O. Box 5757
Columbia, South Carolina 29250
(803) 734-9452
800-922-1594 (toll free—South Carolina only)

South Dakota
Assistant Attorney General
Division of Consumer Affairs
Office of Attorney General
500 E. Capitol
Pierre, South Dakota 57501
(605) 773-4400

Tennessee
Deputy Attorney General
Antitrust and Consumer Protection Division
Office of Attorney General
450 James Robertson Parkway
Nashville, Tennessee 37219
(615) 741-2672

Texas
Assistant Attorney General and Chief
Consumer Protection Division

Office of Attorney General
Capitol Station
P.O. Box 12548
Austin, Texas 78711
(512) 463-2070

Utah
Director
Division of Consumer Protection
Department of Business Regulation
160 East 300 South
P.O. Box 45804
Salt Lake City, Utah 84145-0804
(801) 530-6601

Vermont
Assistant Attorney General and Chief
Public Protection Division
Office of Attorney General
109 State Street
Montpelier, Vermont 09602
(802) 828-3171
800-642-5149 (toll free—Vermont only)

Virginia
Assistant Attorney General
Division of Consumer Counsel
Office of Attorney General
Supreme Court Building
101 North Eighth Street
Richmond, Virginia 23219
(804) 786-2115

Washington
Assistant Attorney General and Chief

Consumer and Business Fair Practices
Division
Office of Attorney General
2000 Bank of California Bldg.
900 4th Avenue
Seattle, Washington 98164-0112
(206) 464-7744
800-551-4636 (toll free—Washington only)

West Virginia
Director
Consumer Protection Division
Office of Attorney General
812 Quarrier Street, 6th Floor
Charleston, West Virginia 25301
(304) 558-8986
800-368-8808 (toll free—West Virginia only)

Wisconsin
Assistant Attorney General
Office of Consumer Protection
Department of Justice
P.O. Box 7856
Madison, Wisconsin 53707
(608) 266-1852
800-362-8189 (toll free—Wisconsin only)

Wyoming
Assistant Attorney General
Office of Attorney General
123 State Capitol Building
Cheyenne, Wyoming 82002
(307) 777-7841 or 6286

▶ CONSUMER HOTLINES

For a specific complaint, you may wish to call the consumer hotline that deals with consumer complaints concerning a particular industry or problem. Following is a list of hotline numbers that have been established by industry associations or the government to assist consumers.

1. **Advertising:** Federal Trade Commission, Marketing Practices Division, (202) 326-3128; Council of Better Business Bureaus, National

Advertising Division, (212) 754-1320.
2. **Air safety:** Federal Aviation Administration, 800-FAA-SURE.
3. **Airline passenger complaints:** Department of Transportation, (202) 366-2220.
4. **Appliances:** Major Appliance Consumer Action Panel (MACAP), 800-621-0477.
5. **Auto problems:** Automotive Consumer Action Program (AUTO-CAP), (703) 821-7000; Ford, 800-241-8450; Chrysler, (313) 956-5970.
6. **Auto safety:** National Highway

Traffic Safety Administration, 800-424-9393.
7. **Bus travel:** Interstate Commerce Commission, (202) 275-7844.
8. **Counterfeit goods:** Department of the Treasury, 800-USA-FAKE.
9. **Credit:** Office of Consumer Affairs, (202) 634-4140.
10. **Fraud:** Federal Trade Commission, Marketing Practices Division, (202) 326-3128.
11. **Insurance:** Health Insurance Association of America (life and health insurance), 800-635-1271; In-

surance Information Institute (property and liability insurance), 800-221-4954.

12. Mail fraud: Postal Service Inspector, U.S. Postal Service, (202) 268-4267.

13. Mail-order problems: Federal Trade Commission, Marketing Practices Division, (202) 326-3128.

14. Movers: Interstate Commerce Commission (202) 275-7844.

15. Product safety: Consumer Product Safety Commission, 800-638-CPSC.

16. Safety at work: Occupational Safety and Health Administration, (202) 523-8151.

17. Stocks and Bonds: Office of Consumer Affairs, Securities and Exchange Commission, (202) 272-7440.

18. Surgery: Department of Health and Human Services, 800-638-6833.

19. Travel: American Society of Travel Agents, (703) 739-2782.

20. Unwanted mail: Direct Marketing Association, (212) 689-4977.

21. Warranties: Federal Trade Commission, Marketing Practices Division, (202) 326-3128.

▶ FEDERAL GOVERNMENT

If your problem concerns a product sold nationally or if it affects a large number of people nationwide, you should appeal to a federal agency.

▶ Office of Consumer Affairs (1009 Premier Building, 1725 "I" St., N.W., Washington, DC 20201)

The Office of Consumer Affairs once advised the president directly but is now part of the Department of Health and Human Services. For a while, it coordinated all federal activities on behalf of consumers. Although it is still involved in consumer programs, many consumer specialists believe that this office has

little power today. In any event, if you have complaints about products or services, you can write directly to the Federal Complaint Referral Center in the Office of Consumer Affairs or call (202) 634-4140.

▶ Food and Drug Administration (500 Fishers Lane, Rockville, MD 20857)

The Food and Drug Administration has regional offices in many cities, and on each office staff is a person specifically charged with consumer services. Many of the FDA's employees are technical experts working in specific fields under FDA jurisdiction. Any complaint about a food, drug, or cosmetic that you purchase should be made either to your regional office or to the above address. The agency will ask you for complete information, and its staff is particularly interested in examining the questionable food or drug about which you are complaining or the container in which it was sold. If they believe your complaint is justified, a member of the staff will visit the firm in question to observe its production and packaging procedures. If you do not have the product, you still may complain. The FDA is always interested in receiving consumer reports, even though the complaints may have no legal consequence. Through such reports, the FDA often discovers new problems or new incidences of old problems. In those areas in which the FDA sets and/or enforces standards, consumers can play a very important role. But unless the agency hears from consumers, it may be making avoidable mistakes.

▶ Federal Trade Commission (Washington, DC 20580)

The FDA largely enforces standards of products and performance, but

the Federal Trade Commission's standards are essentially those that are established for normal competitive businesses. In addition, the FTC handles complaints that are subject to federal credit and federal warranty legislation.

The FTC has regional offices and consumer-service representatives in major U.S. cities. It has established a special office to serve consumers, and it provides a wide range of informative pamphlets for them. If you have a complaint for the FTC, you may address it to a regional office or to the Washington, D.C., headquarters. If it believes you have a valid complaint, the FTC will send an investigator out to check with both you and the firm. Typically, the FTC works in two ways. First, it investigates whether or not a particular seller or advertiser has violated a particular law that the agency enforces; if its findings are positive, it takes actions, which may include seeking an **injunction** against the firm, to stop the practice by the single firm. Second, the agency looks for new patterns of practice that may mislead consumers; if it finds such patterns, the FTC may attempt to act against an entire industry, rather than a single firm, to stop the practice altogether.

▶ U.S. Department of Agriculture (Washington, DC 20250)

Although the U.S. Department of Agriculture primarily provides services to farmers, it also protects consumers in very important ways, notably by inspecting and grading meat, poultry, and fish. In recent years, the agency has also become a primary source of information for consumers on the best ways to spend their food dollars. The USDA does this through its Cooperative Extension Service, operated in conjunction with land-grant universities throughout the United States. Any complaint you have about the grades of meat you buy or the quality of poultry that is shipped interstate should be reported to your local health department or your local department of agriculture.

The Department of Agriculture provides other services, including the Agricultural Research Service, the Animal and Plant Health Inspection Service, the Economic Research Service, the Food and Nutrition Service, the Forest Service, and the Rural Development Service. If you are interested in any of these services, you can get the appropriate telephone numbers and addresses from the Office of Information, USDA, Washington, DC 20250.

▶ U.S. Postal Service (Washington, DC 20260)

This agency is responsible for investigating mail fraud, unordered merchandise, obscenity in the mails, and other mail-related problems.

▶ U.S. Department of Housing and Urban Development (Washington, DC 20410)

This department is responsible for numerous federally subsidized housing programs. If you are experiencing problems relating to fair housing, you can call 800-424-8590 toll free for assistance. This department also regulates interstate land sales. You can contact the department's consumer-affairs coordinator if you have any relevant problem.

▶ Interstate Commerce Commission (Washington, DC 20423)

Any complaints you have regarding moving companies, truck shipments, or railroads can be addressed specifically to this agency.

▶ Consumer Product Safety Commission (Washington, DC 20207)

If you think there is an unsafe product on the market, or if you have any questions about product hazards and safety, you may want to get in touch directly with the CPSC. The number, toll-free from anywhere in the United States, is 800-638-2772. You can also write to the Consumer Product Safety Commission, Washington, DC 20207, and explain your concern about a particular product or products.

▶ Obtaining More Information on Federal Consumer Services

To obtain more information on the availability of federal consumer services, send for the *Guide to Federal Consumer Services,* publication number (OS) 76-512, available from the Superintendent of Documents, Government Printing Office, Washington, DC 20402. You may also wish to call the Federal Information Center and request information about the vast number of federal agencies and programs. Exhibit B–4 is a list of the Federal Information Center toll-free phone numbers.

▶ SUMMARY

1. Generally, government agencies and other consumer-oriented groups provide four types of consumer services: (1) information to consumers before a purchase is made; (2) aid to consumers after a purchase is made; (3) redress to consumers for losses that result from their purchases; and (4) representation of consumers in issues with a consumer interest before a legislative body, government agencies, and private business leadership.

2. By keeping a few consumer references in your home, you can help to prevent consumer problems and know where to turn when a problem does arise.

3. Thirty-seven states have one or more federal agencies to help the consumer and even more state, local, and private organizations that offer consumer services.

4. Develop a strategy to use when buying products you think you may have problems with. The chain of complaint begins with the salesperson who sold the product, then moves on to the manager of the store, and ends at the manufacturer's headquarters. If your appeals to those sources fail, turn to federal, state, or local consumer groups for assistance.

5. Properly written complaint letters, with copies to the Better Business Bureau and state attorney general's office, are an essential part of the consumer-complaint process.

6. Local consumer action groups are often the most effective in helping consumers get their money back or in solving problems. Such groups are often listed in the Yellow Pages or can be reached through local radio, newspaper, and television action lines or hotlines.

7. If you have to go to court—other than small claims court—it will involve the payment of legal fees. Several legal-aid and legal self-help groups may be available to lend assistance, however.

8. Third-party intervention agencies can be very helpful in settling disputes between consumers and manufacturers. There are many such groups at the national level for many industries—such as Ford Motor Company's Consumer Appeals Board and the Homeowners Warranty Corporation (HOW).

9. The Better Business Bureau has more than 170 offices across the country to help consumers at the lo-

▶ Exhibit B–4 Federal Information Center

Have you ever tried to find an answer to a simple question about the federal government and ended up on a merry-go-round of referrals? Or, have you ever had a question about the federal government that was so difficult that you didn't even know where to begin?

The Federal Information Center is one office that has specially selected and trained its staff to answer your questions or help you find the right person with the answer.

Simply call the telephone number listed below for your metropolitan area or state. If your area is not listed, please call (301) 722-9098. If you would prefer to write, please mail your inquiry to the Federal Information Center, P.O. Box 600, Cumberland, MD 21502. Users of Telecommunications Devices for the Deaf (TDD/TTY) may call toll-free from any point in the United States by dialing (800) 326-2996.

Alabama
Birmingham, Mobile
(800) 366-2998

Alaska
Anchorage
(800) 729-8003

Arizona
Phoenix
(800) 359-3997

Arkansas
Little Rock
(800) 366-2998

California
Los Angeles, San Diego,
San Francisco, Santa Ana
(800) 726-4995
Sacramento
(916) 973-1695

Colorado
Colorado Springs,
Denver, Pueblo
(800) 359-3997

Connecticut
Hartford, New Haven
(800) 347-1997

Florida
Fort Lauderdale,
Jacksonville, Miami,
Orlando, St. Petersburg,
Tampa, West Palm Beach
(800) 347-1997

Georgia
Atlanta
(800) 347-1997

Hawaii
Honolulu
(800) 733-5996

Illinois
Chicago
(800) 366-2998

Indiana
Gary
(800) 366-2998
Indianapolis
(800) 347-1997

Iowa
All locations
(800) 735-8004

Kansas
All locations
(800) 735-8004

Kentucky
Louisville
(800) 347-1997

Louisiana
New Orleans
(800) 366-2998

Maryland
Baltimore
(800) 347-1997

Massachusetts
Boston
(800) 347-1997

Michigan
Detroit, Grand Rapids
(800) 347-1997

Minnesota
Minneapolis
(800) 366-2998

Missouri
St. Louis
(800) 366-2998
All other locations
(800) 735-8004

Nebraska
Omaha
(800) 366-2998
All other locations
(800) 735-8004

New Jersey
Newark, Trenton
(800) 347-1997

New Mexico
Albuquerque
(800) 359-3997

New York
Albany, Buffalo,
New York, Rochester,
Syracuse
(800) 347-1997

North Carolina
Charlotte
(800) 347-1997

Ohio
Akron, Cincinnati,
Cleveland, Columbus,
Dayton, Toledo
(800) 347-1997

Oklahoma
Oklahoma City, Tulsa
(800) 366-2998

Oregon
Portland
(800) 726-4995

Pennsylvania
Philadelphia, Pittsburgh
(800) 347-1997

Rhode Island
Providence
(800) 347-1997

Tennessee
Chattanooga
(800) 347-1997
Memphis, Nashville
(800) 366-2998

Texas
Austin, Dallas,
Fort Worth, Houston,
San Antonio
(800) 366-2998

Utah
Salt Lake City
(800) 359-3997

Virginia	**Washington**	**Wisconsin**
Norfolk, Richmond,	Seattle, Tacoma	Milwaukee
Roanoke	(800) 726-4995	(800) 366-2998
(800) 347-1997		

cal level. The Office of Consumer Affairs at the county level can also aid in settling disputes. Another alternative is the American Arbitration Association.

10. Many government agencies and private consumer or business groups have hotlines to call when consumer complaints arise. These provide immediate information and, often, effective help.

11. A variety of federal government departments and agencies can be contacted for help with consumer complaints. Among them are the Office of Consumer Affairs, the Food and Drug Administration, the Federal Trade Commission, the Department of Agriculture, the U.S. Postal Service, the Department of Housing and Urban Development, the Interstate Commerce Commission, and the Consumer Product Safety Commission.

12. Consumers are free to call any of the Federal Information Centers throughout the United States for information and assistance.

▶ QUESTIONS FOR THOUGHT AND DISCUSSION

1. Who do you think benefits most from consumer protection agencies?

2. What would an ideal organizational plan for the coordination of consumer agencies and groups look like?

3. How do you decide when it is time to seek help for a consumer grievance?

4. If you purchase a harmful product—such as a food item—but are not harmed yourself by it, is it your responsibility to report it to the appropriate consumer agency?

▶ THINGS TO DO

1. Call one or more of the toll-free hotlines given in this Consumer Issue. Ask them for information on their services. Evaluate their helpfulness to you, the consumer.

2. Call your local Better Business Bureau. Ask them how many complaints they receive per month concerning faulty services or products sold in the area.

3. Draw up a list of consumer affairs agencies in your area. First look in the Yellow Pages under "Consumer" to see what is listed there. Then contact the district attorney's office. Next contact the state attorney general's office.

4. Write or call (or visit in person, if possible) your state's consumer services division (see Exhibit B–3). Ask them to send or give to you as much information as possible relating to their services.

▶ SELECTED READINGS

▶ American Association of Retired Persons. *How to Write a Wrong: Complain Effectively and Get Results.* Available for 50¢ from AARP, Consumer Affairs Section, Program Dept., 1901 K St., N.W., Washington, DC 20049.

▶ Ashton, Betty. "Complaints That Get Action." *Guide to Living on Your Own.* Boston: Little, Brown, 1988, pp. 260–266.

▶ Bowker, Michael. "Paying Less for Legal Help." *Consumers Digest,* July–August 1987, pp. 41–43.

▶ *Consumer Information Catalog.* Available free from the Consumer Information Center, Pueblo, CO 81009.

▶ Consumers Union. *Consumer Reports Annual Buying Guide.* Published annually in December.

▶ *Consumer's Resource Handbook.* Available free from the Consumer Information Center, Department 532-G, Pueblo, CO 81009.

▶ Dingle, D. T. "The Traveler's Bill of Rights." *Money,* October 1991, pp. 171–172.

▶ Federal Financial Institutions Examination Council. *Important Consumer Information.* Available from FFI, 1776 G St., N.W., Suite 701, Washington, DC 20006.

▶ *How to Complain and Get Results.* Available free from the Federal Trade Commission, Room 270, 6th St. and Pennsylvania Ave., N.W., Washington, DC 20580.

▶ Nassar, Sylvia. "Best Ways to Get Your Money Back." *Money,* April 1989, pp. 149–158.

▶ Rowse, Arthur E., and the staff of Consumer News, Inc. *Help: The Indispensable Almanac of Consumer Information.* New York: Everest House. Published annually.

▶ Wall, Edward C. *Consumer's Index to Product Evaluations and Information Sources.* New York: Pierian Press. Published annually.

▶ *What's Going on at the FTC?* Available free from the Federal Trade Commission, Room 270, 6th St. and Pennsylvania Ave., N.W., Washington, DC 20580.

How to Use a Small Claims Court

Did you think that your former landlord cheated you by keeping your security deposit when you moved out? Did a dry cleaner ruin or lose your clothes? Did you make a claim to your insurance company that it refused to pay? Did a company issue you a warranty on one of its products and then charge you for a repair job while the product was still covered?

If you've ever felt helpless in these or similar situations, you needn't have. To right such wrongs, you could have used the small claims court in your area.[1] But because it may take some time, effort, and patience to get on a court calendar, first you should examine some of the possible alternatives outlined in Consumer Issue B, including the use of consumer hotlines available in many states and cities; consumer advocates, who will take up your gripes with the appropriate people and see that the results are publicized; and, in some cities, radio and TV newscasters who narrate complaints over the air. In Consumer Issue B, we discussed still other ways you can complain and get redress for your consumer grievances. If you still feel you need judicial help, then you might want to use a small claims court.

▶ WHY WERE THEY FOUNDED?

In 1913 Roscoe Pound, a noted professor of the Harvard Law School, gave a justification for small claims courts: "It is a *denial of justice* in small causes to drive **litigants** to employ lawyers, and it is a shame to drive them to legal-aid societies to get as charity what the state should give as a right." In most states today, you have the right to use the services of small claims courts to litigate claims of, usually, less than $2,500; most small claims (approximately 85 percent) are less than $500. Because citizens who elect to take the time and trouble to go to small claims courts usually have valid complaints, decisions in these courts are in favor of the consumer about 75 percent of the time.

▶ BUT YOU HAVE TO WATCH OUT

Complications can arise in small claims court proceedings. In many states, the defendant can automatically and routinely have a case transferred to a regular civil court. In most civil courts, your efforts are useless unless you have an attorney; if a case in which you are the **plaintiff** is transferred to the civil court, you must incur the expense of an attorney or drop the suit.

Further, a small claims judgment in your favor does not mean you will get full satisfaction for your loss. The judge may order the defendant to pay you $100 on a $150 claim (which, of course, is still $100 more than you started with). *But no matter what the defendant is ordered to pay you, the small claims court does not act as a collection agency.* The judgment merely gives you the legal right to your claim. You may be able to obtain what is called a *writ of execution* from the small claims court if you can show that the defendant is not paying you, but this writ against the defendant's property, bank account, or wages is often ineffective.[2]

Additionally, you must realize that you probably will have to make several trips to the courthouse, and, if the court has no evening session in your area, you may miss time from work. Plaintiffs—those bringing the lawsuits—spend between 10 and 30 hours on court-related activities, such as filing papers, preparing the case, and so on. Going to court—even small claims court—takes time and energy.

▶ DOES YOUR CASE MAKE SENSE?

Before you go to the cost and bother of filing an application for a grievance to be heard in a small claims court you should ask yourself if pursuing your case makes sense. From a strictly logical point of view, having suffered a loss is not enough cause, by itself, to file. You need documentary evidence to support your claim. To be successful you must be able to prove that a legal

---

1. Called a *magistrate's court* in some areas and a *court not of record* or *conciliation court* in others.

---

2. Even if a debt is not collectible now, however, it stays on the records. Thus, if the person who lost the judgment in small claims court and who owes you money comes into some assets in the future, you can activate the judgment at that later time.

contract has been broken, that your property or person has been harmed by the other party's negligence, that a legal right you are entitled to has been violated, or that you have purchased a defective good or service. Even when one of these situations exists, there is little reason to sue someone who clearly has no assets and no income with which to pay you. If you have purchased a defective product for cash from someone who sells goods from the trunk of his or her car, there is little reason to sue. You almost certainly will not be paid, even if the court rules in your favor. Judgments made by small claims courts are most likely to be paid only by individuals or firms with a reputation worth defending in the community.

▶ HOW THESE COURTS WORK

The first thing you do is ask the clerk of the small claims court in your area whether the court can handle your kind of case. For example, some large cities have special courts to handle problems between renters and landlords. While you're at the courthouse, it might prove helpful to sit in on a few cases; that will give you an idea of what to expect when your day in court arrives. Then make sure that the court has jurisdiction over the person or business you wish to sue. Usually, the defendant must live, work, or do business in the court's territory. If you're trying to sue an out-of-town firm, you may run into problems. You probably should go to the state government, usually the secretary of state, to find out where the summons should be sent. Remember that the small claims court does not act as a collection agency; if you're filing suit against a firm that no longer is in business, you'll have a very difficult time collecting.

Make absolutely certain that you have the correct business name and address of the company being sued. Frequently courts require strict accuracy; if you don't abide by that requirement, the suit is thrown out.

Once you file suit, a summons goes out to the defending party, either by registered mail or in the hands of a sheriff, bailiff, marshal, constable, or sometimes a private citizen. When a company receives the summons, it may decide to resolve the issue out of court; about one-quarter of all cases for which summonses are issued are settled this way. Many times, however, the defendant company may not even show up for the trial, in which case you stand a good chance of winning by default. (But no-shows are usually hard to collect from.)

▶ PREPARING FOR TRIAL

How should you prepare for trial? Obviously, if you know a lawyer, seek advice from him or her. In any event, you should have on hand all necessary and pertinent receipts, canceled checks, written estimates, contracts, and any other form of documentary evidence that you can show the judge. Set the entire affair down in chronological order with supporting evidence so you can show the judge exactly what happened. Make sure that your dates are accurate; inaccuracies could prejudice your case against you. Make sure you have a copy of the "demand letter"—similar to the one shown in Exhibit B–2 in Consumer Issue B—that you sent to the offending party. This document should be no more than two double-spaced, typewritten pages and should clearly summarize the facts, as well as your demands of the other party. It is important that you be able to hand this letter to the judge on trial day. It will

not only present your version of the story but also will demonstrate your reasonable approach to the situation.

If you are disputing something such as a repair job, you may have to get a third party—generally someone in the same trade—to testify as an "expert." It is often difficult to get persons to testify against others in their own profession, but they may be willing to give written statements (notarized), which sometimes are considered acceptable evidence. If possible, when you are suing over disputed performance or repairs, bring the physical evidence of your claim into court. If, for example, your neighborhood dry cleaner shrank a wool sweater of yours to a size 3, be sure to show it to the judge.

▶ WHAT HAPPENS IN COURT

The judge generally will let you present your case in simple language without the help of a lawyer. In fact, in some states neither the plaintiff nor the defendant may have a lawyer present. You may receive the judge's decision immediately or by notice within a few weeks. In some states, you can appeal the case, but in many situations the small claims court plaintiff does not have that right. Remember, whatever action you decide to take after the judgment should be weighed against the costs of that action. Your time is not free, and the worry that may be involved in pursuing a lost case further might detract from the potential reward of eventually winning.

If your opponent tries to settle the case out of court, make sure everything is written down so that it can be upheld if the offer is withdrawn. You should sign all written documents and file them with the court so that the agreement can be enforced by the court. It is best to have your opponent appear with you before the judge to outline the settlement terms. Generally, if you win or if you settle out of court, you should be able to get your opponent to pay for the court costs, which range from zero to $85, or more, depending on the state.

▶ WHERE, WHAT, AND HOW MUCH?

Exhibit C–1 briefly summarizes the characteristics of small claims courts in selected states. To be a truly rational consumer decision maker, you must weigh the potential benefits of going to court against the potential costs. If the potential gain to you means less than the value you place on saving your time and energies, it may be best to forget the whole thing. On the other hand, if you are convinced that your case is just and that you have indeed been cheated out of a significant sum of money, by all means take advantage of the information presented in this Consumer Issue and start the proceedings.

▶ SUMMARY OF HOW TO HANDLE YOUR CASE

1. Identify your opponent properly.
2. Send a warning letter.
3. Find the correct court.
4. File a claim.
5. Notify the defendant.
6. Assemble the evidence.
7. Consider settling out of court, if possible.

8. Present your case.
9. Stand up when you make your first statements to the judge.
10. Don't read your statements; rather, present them conversationally.
11. Be brief.
12. Don't interrupt your opponent or any of the witnesses.
13. If part of your case is difficult to express in words, bring the necessary physical materials, such as a diagram, a faded rug, a battered bicycle tire, and so on.
14. Remember that a judgment in your favor does not guarantee payment of the claim.

▶ QUESTIONS FOR THOUGHT AND DISCUSSION

1. In your opinion, who makes the most use of small claims courts?
2. Why should you decide in some cases not to go to a small claims court?
3. Do you think that small claims courts should take on bigger cases? That is, do you think that the maximum amount of money at issue in a suit should be raised in many states? Why or why not?

▶ THINGS TO DO

1. Find out the current maximum amount of money for which you may enter a suit in the small claims court in your state. Are lawyers allowed in small claims courts in your state today? Can both plaintiff and defendant appeal? What does it now cost to sue?

2. Go to a local small claims court and observe some of the action. Do you think that all the cases should have been brought into court? What would determine whether some of them should not have been brought into court?

3. Talk to a lawyer about the advisability of using the small claims court in your area.

▶ SELECTED READINGS

▶ Ashton, Betty. "When All Else Fails." *Guide to Living on Your Own.* Boston: Little, Brown, 1988, pp. 267–268.
▶ Biggs, Don. "Taking Your Case to Small Claims Court." *How to Avoid Lawyers.* New York: Garland, 1985, Ch. 39.
▶ Decker, Russell. "You Don't Need a Lawyer to Sue in Small Claims Court." *Purchasing,* August 16, 1984, pp. 85–86.
▶ Elias, Steve. "After You Win a Lawsuit: Collecting Your Money." *Nolo News,* Summer 1988, p. 7.
▶ Englander, Barbara. "Small Claims Court: Winning Is Just the Beginning." *Money,* April 1989, pp. 150–151.
▶ Vetzner, Stephen. "See You in Court." *Changing Times,* March 1987, pp. 65–70.
▶ Warner, Ralph. *Everybody's Guide to Small Claims Court.* 2d ed. Berkeley: Nolo Press, 1985.

> ▶ **Exhibit C–1** **Characteristics of Small Claims Courts in Selected States**

State	Maximum Amount of Suit	Lawyers Allowed?	Who Can Appeal?		Filing Cost*
			Plaintiff	Defendant	
Alabama	$ 1,500	yes	yes	yes	$22
Arizona	$ 1,500	no	yes	yes	$18.50
California	$ 5,000	no	no	yes	$ 8
Colorado	$ 3,500	no	yes	yes	$0–$2,000, $17 $2,001–$3,500, $26
Connecticut	$ 2,000	yes	no	no	$25
Washington, D.C.	$ 2,000	yes	yes	yes	$ 1
Florida	$ 2,500	yes	yes	yes	$69
Georgia	$ 5,000	yes	yes	yes	$40
Illinois	$15,000	no	yes	yes	$0–$250, $20 $251–$500, $30 $501–$2,500, $40 $2,501–$15,000, $85
Indiana	$ 6,000	yes	yes	yes	$31
Iowa	$ 2,000	yes	yes	yes	$30
Kansas	$ 1,000	no	yes	yes	$0–$500, $15 $500–$1,000, $35
Kentucky	$ 1,500	yes	yes	yes	$23.90
Louisiana	$ 2,000	yes	no	no	$55
Maine	$ 1,400	yes	yes	yes	$20 per defendant
Maryland	$ 2,500	yes	yes	yes	$5
Massachusetts	$ 1,500	yes	no	yes	$9
Michigan	$ 1,500	no	no	no	$33.50
Minnesota	$ 4,000	yes	yes	yes	$16
Mississippi	$ 1,000	yes	yes	yes	$32.50
Missouri	$ 1,500	yes	yes	yes	$36
New Jersey	$ 1,000	yes	yes	yes	$12
New York	$ 2,000	yes	judge, yes arbitrator, no	yes no	$19
North Carolina	$ 1,500	yes	yes	yes	$19
Ohio	$ 1,000	yes	yes	yes	$21
Oklahoma	$ 1,000	yes	yes	yes	$37
Oregon	$ 2,500	no	no	no	$20
Pennsylvania	$ 5,000	yes	yes	yes	$1–$500, $16 $501–$2,000, $22 $2,001–$5,000, $42
South Carolina	$ 2,500	yes	yes	yes	$30
Tennessee	$10,000	yes	yes	yes	$42.75
Texas	$ 5,000	yes	yes	yes	$50
Virginia	$ 7,000	yes	yes	yes	$10 per defendant
Wisconsin	$ 2,000	yes	yes	yes	$18
Wyoming	$ 2,000	yes	yes	yes	$13

*In most states a serving fee is added to the filing fee. This amount will generally be charged for each defendant served with legal papers. In Mississippi, for example, an extra $8 is charged for each person who is being sued.

Rational Consumer Decision Making

PREVIEW

▶ What is rational consumer decision making?

▶ Why is value clarification important in decision making?

▶ How do your values and goals affect your consumer choices?

▶ How can you use a decision-making process to make better choices?

▶ What are some common pitfalls in consumer decision making?

▶ How can you manage your time to make the best use of the money and resources you have?

Individuals who purchase (or are given), use, maintain, and dispose of products and services in their final form in an attempt to achieve the highest level of satisfaction possible with their income limitation.

You consume; I consume; we all consume—in one way or another. Thus, we are all **consumers.** And the dollar value of what we consume is staggering. The estimate for 1993 is close to $4.0 trillion.

What do we buy as consumers? In a word, everything. Our purchases include goods as varied as eighteen-karat gold wristwatches, toothpicks, racehorses, microcomputers, four-bedroom houses, televisions, hamburgers, filet mignon, and goldfish bowls. Exhibit 3–1 lists some of the broad categories of goods and services for which we spend our money each year.

DECISIONS, DECISIONS

Behind these consumption figures lies a process of continual decision making on the part of individuals and households. For every dollar spent, a decision has been made to spend it. Some decisions are more or less automatic—such as the decision to buy food. But the question of what kind of food to buy, and how much, involves a whole host of other decisions. Should we buy national brands or generic foods? Should we buy fresh or frozen broccoli? Should we cook at home or go out for dinner? Should we have a Big Mac or lower-calorie fare? We make hundreds of these kinds of decisions each day, implicitly or explicitly.

When we shop, we are faced with an increasing number of products to choose from and with increasingly high-tech items to learn about. Each new product that comes to our attention requires our decision on whether or not to buy it. How many of us, for example, have had the experience of walking by a store window, seeing something we like, and then deciding whether we like it enough to buy it? Ten minutes earlier, there was no decision to be made—because we didn't know that particular product existed. Advertisements on television, in the newspapers, and in magazines likewise acquaint

▶ **Exhibit 3–1   Personal Consumption Expenditures by Major Type, 1992**

This tabulation of the billions of dollars spent in 1992 is expressed in 1987 dollars, meaning the amounts have been adjusted for inflation. You can check the latest issue of the *Survey of Current Business* to find out how much personal consumption expenditures have grown since 1992.

Type of Expense	Total Spent (in billions)	Percentage of Total Spent
Total spending in 1987 dollars	$3,184.0	100.0%
Automobiles and parts	179.2	5.6
Furniture and household equipment	181.4	5.7
Food	514.5	16.2
Clothing and shoes	191.0	6.0
Gasoline and oil	96.7	3.0
Housing services	485.8	15.3
Household operation services	205.8	6.5
Transportation	124.1	3.9
Medical care	457.9	14.4
All others	747.6	23.4

Source: *Survey of Current Business*, November 1992, p. 2.

us with new, sometimes very tempting products—and, of course, with still more decisions to make.

We face far more consumer decisions today—and more complexity in decision making—than our parents or grandparents did. We can reap the greatest rewards for our dollars by making rational consumer decisions.

RATIONAL CONSUMER DECISION MAKING

Consumer decision making occurs in both the product market (households as demanders of goods and services) and in the productive resources market (households as suppliers of labor, raw materials, tools, and managerial ability). In both markets, **rational consumer decision making** requires allocating time and money resources economically. To make a rational decision when purchasing a VCR, for example, you will want information about what VCRs are available and at what prices. But information is costly to obtain. You will have to use your time and sometimes a portion of your income to obtain an *optimum* (as opposed to an *infinite)* amount of information about alternatives; the optimum amount of information is not too much and not too little, just the ideal amount. You will find out how to determine this amount later in this chapter.

There are often other costs consumers should consider when they decide how to use their scarce money and time. For example, if you drive to a store on the other side of town to buy a pair of shoes that are on sale for $10 off the regular price, you need to weigh the value of using your time and the costs of driving your car against the value of the $10 you save. Or, if you buy 100 shares of stock in a corporation for $20 a share through a stockbroker, you may pay a commission of $100 or more. Costs of obtaining information and completing exchanges that are additional to the price of the product are called **transaction costs** and are a consideration in rational decision making.

Perhaps the most important part of rational consumer decision making is the initial decision on whether or not to even consider buying a particular type of good or service. You might ask yourself, "Do I really need a VCR at all, or should I save my money to buy a better car I know I will soon need?" The "cost" you are considering here is an example of an opportunity cost. You are comparing the value you believe you would receive from the best possible deal you could find for a VCR with the value you believe you would receive from buying a better car in the future.

Remember, cost and value are not always measured in terms of money. When you decided to read this book you gave up the value of other possible uses of your time. How do you quantify the benefits of reading a book one more hour? Those benefits could be the value you place on the knowledge you expect to gain, or on the higher grade you hope to receive. To make the best possible choice, you weigh the value of these benefits against the value of alternative uses of your time.

Rational decision making, whether it involves the use of time or money, is completed through a series of **cost/benefit analyses** in which choices are made that yield the highest net benefits within the constraints of limited time and income. A *net benefit* is the value of all the benefits of a decision totaled together minus all of its costs totaled together.

Using cost/benefit analysis to determine your most beneficial choices may seem difficult. Whenever your personal values or feelings enter into your de-

Rational consumer decision making
Making consumer decisions that maximize the satisfaction you can obtain from your time and money resources and that assist you in attaining life-long, as well as short-term, goals.

Transaction costs
All the costs associated with completing an exchange beyond the price of the product that is purchased.

Cost/benefit analysis
A way to reach decisions in which all the costs are added up, as well as all the benefits. If benefits minus costs are greater than zero, then a net benefit exists and the decision should be positive. Alternatively, if benefits minus costs are less than zero, then a net cost exists and the decision should be positive.

cision making, you will have a difficult time quantifying them. Nonetheless, you are always implicitly making choices on the basis of what is best for you, given the alternatives and the opportunity cost of each alternative. Such an analysis requires that you have a clear understanding of your priorities and the importance that you attach to different wants you may have. By clarifying your priorities, which are determined by the values you hold as an individual, you can make choices and purchases that accord with your overall goals in life.

VALUES AND RATIONAL DECISION MAKING

When you were a child, people probably asked you what you wanted to be in life. You might have said a musician, an artist, a scientist, a doctor, a lawyer, a flight attendant, a firefighter, or any number of other roles and occupations you might have been aware of at that time. Later on, however, you had to consider which occupational choices were consistent with your particular resources—that is, which ones were realistic given your abilities and opportunities for training.

For many, the decisions involved in this choice begin in high school. Should you drop out or stay in? Should you be a vocational-education major or a precollege major? Should you take more or less math? Once you have decided to stay in high school, you face another choice: Should you go on to college after high school or get a job? In either case, you must decide what you really want to do. If you go to college, you will have to decide on a major. When you graduate (if you do), you must decide where you want to work and how, the amount of free time you want to have, what kinds of risks you want to take, what kinds of people you want to be with, and so on.

It's very easy to make the wrong decision or to fail to make a decision at the right time. Often, in retrospect, we decide we have made a mistake. As consumers, too, we may decide in retrospect that a choice we made was a mistake. It could have been the result of a failure to clarify values and goals, or to gather enough information. In fact, one reason young people should take advantage of opportunities they have to gain education and guidance from others is to reduce their likelihood of making bad choices for these reasons.

What Are Values?

Values
Fundamental concepts or high-level preferences that regulate our behavior. High-level values determine lower-level tastes and preferences that affect our everyday lives.

Values can be defined as concepts or high-level preferences that regulate or in some way affect our behavior. For example, if a person places a high value on the simple life, that individual's preference for simplicity will determine to a great extent the decisions he or she makes as a consumer. That individual will very likely not purchase a Ferrari or an enormous, showy mansion. Another person, for religious or humanitarian reasons, may place a high value on service toward others. That value would very likely affect his or her career decisions and other choices.

How Are Values Formed?

Values stem from numerous sources, some external and some internal. One source of our values or general beliefs relating to life is custom. In the United States, custom plays a smaller role in consumer decision making than it does in many other nations. Nonetheless, if you examine your own behavior as a consumer, you may be surprised at the extent to which your decisions depend on established customs. Here are just a few areas of our lives that are dictated more or less by custom:

1. The types and combinations of food that we eat.
2. The holidays that we celebrate.
3. The style of clothes that we wear.
4. The way we dispose of the dead.
5. The types of ceremonies by which we marry.
6. The types of leisure activities that we choose.

Customs serve a useful purpose. Without them, we could not predict behavior, and the result would be considerable confusion. By following customs that are in line with our values, we reduce both time and search costs in determining what our behavior should be. Consider the example of Thanksgiving; since custom says that we will have a turkey on Thanksgiving, the decision about what to fix for Thanksgiving dinner has been made for most of us.

Another source of our values is, of course, our family and our friends. If your parents, for example, place a high value on hard work and frugal spending habits, you may—consciously or unconsciously—do the same. Similarly, the attitudes and beliefs of close friends may exert a strong influence on the values that you hold.

> By following customs we reduce both time and search costs in determining what our behavior should be. Since custom says that we will have a turkey on Thanksgiving, the decision about what to fix for Thanksgiving dinner has been made for most of us.

Value Clarification

We are often unaware of certain values that we hold, even though they affect our decisions. You might say to yourself, for example, that you are buying a car because you need transportation to and from your part-time job after school. On closer inspection, however, it might turn out that you really don't "need" the car for transportation—you could easily ride to work with another student who works at the same firm. If you examine your motives closely, you might discover that what you really want is more than just transportation. Perhaps you want the freedom that having your own car allows you. Perhaps you don't want to encroach on your friend's independence—by obligating him or her to drive you to work each day. Further, you might be seeking the prestige that having an auto would gain for you. Such motives are indicative of certain values you hold—values relating to freedom, to independence, and to prestige and the respect of others.

There is nothing wrong with any of the values in the preceding example, of course. The point is that, when making the decision to purchase the automobile, you did not consciously take these values or preferences into consideration. You therefore could not weigh these particular values against other values you may hold and determine their relative priorities. If a high-level priority in your life is to become a successful lawyer, for example, you will want to save money for law school and not spend it on a car unless it's absolutely necessary to do so. *Value clarification* entails not only learning what your values are but also ranking them in terms of their relative priority in your hierarchy of values.

How do you learn what your values are? One way is to ask yourself "why" whenever you make a decision. Don't stop with just one "why" but continue the process—querying each answer you give until you have related the decision to a high-level value.

Another way to clarify your own values is to compare your beliefs, tastes, and preferences with those of your friends and closest associates. Be candid

> For all of us, the ultimate goal is happiness, which, of course, means different things to different people. How we get there is another matter.

in your appraisal. Remember that values are highly personal in nature; each individual has his or her own set of beliefs. You may be surprised at what you learn about yourself by these comparisons.

Clarifying our values is an ongoing process. All of us change throughout our lives (or at least we think we do). You're probably not the same person you were five years ago in terms of your values and your view of the world. Sometimes, a discussion with your family or friends or even a career-guidance counselor helps clarify the extent of change you have experienced as you mature. When you make decisions, you are weighing values; you are asking yourself, "What is important to me *now?*"

For all of us, the ultimate goal is happiness, which, of course, means different things to different people. How we get there is another matter, but one way to assure that we at least approach our goal is to clarify our values on a regular basis. Change is inevitable, and, as our life situations change, so will our values. Gradual change is generally less painful and less costly than abrupt change. Suppose a computer operator of many years suddenly realized that she couldn't bear the tedium of typing another set of data into her machine's memory. This person might become so unhappy in her job that she would simply quit without any consideration of the future. Such hasty decisions based on newly found values may have disastrous results. If, on the other hand, this individual had consistently clarified her values and related them to her employment situation, she could have made and carried out plans to change her life gradually and without disastrous results. Perhaps she would have attended night school to learn a more interesting skill, let's say computer programming, and then transferred to a new position, possibly with her employer's blessing within the same company!

The importance of knowing what you want out of life—and what you don't—is central to making rational consumer decisions. Once you have a fairly clear idea of what you wish to achieve, you then have a framework for establishing concrete goals and for evaluating the alternatives implicit in the decisions you make.

Goals and Values

Goals are linked to our values: A set of values leads to a set of goals. For example, if you place a high value on educational success, your goal may be to graduate from college with honors.

Everybody has goals, whether or not they are well defined. To attain that ultimate and universal goal of happiness, we set numerous subgoals. Yours may be to finish college or to get a good job or to play the guitar well; you may set goals for your children, if and when you have them; you may have set a goal in your job or your business. These goals will often determine your consumption behavior. If one of your goals is to be relatively well off by the time you are 50, you may then decide to work hard, spend little, and save a lot. That means you will not be tempted to take long vacations or buy costly housing, at least not in the earlier stages of your career. If, on the other hand, your goal is different, you may take these longer vacations, even knowing you will pay for them later because your savings will be smaller.

Goals and planning go hand in hand. Consumer decision making is sometimes based on plans that are themselves based on goals. Planning can at times be a difficult procedure, particularly when a family is involved and numerous, diverse interests must be considered. Compromise is always part of making and following plans. People who tend to "want the stars" invariably have to compromise and face the reality of scarcity.

Consumers who plan in a rational manner may appear to lack spontaneity, and that certainly is one of the costs of planning. But one of the benefits is that goals can often be met—on schedule and to the satisfaction of the planner. If you decide to become a consumer who plans, then you may be able to satisfy many of your desires and needs. But if spontaneity is important in your life, you'll probably chafe at the prospect of making plans and following them.

DECISION-MAKING PROCESS

Up to this point, we have been looking at two of the essential requirements for rational consumer decision making: cost/benefit analysis and values clarification. Now let's examine the decision-making process itself. Basically, the process includes the following five steps:

1. Deciding to act.
2. Determining the alternatives.
3. Evaluating the alternatives.
4. Committing yourself to the decision.
5. Evaluating the results.

Deciding to Act

The first step in the decision-making process is simply recognizing when a decision needs to be made. This may sound obvious, but how many times have we all let the force of inertia, or habit, make decisions for us? How many times have we delayed making a decision until it's too late? If, for example, you are "thinking about" taking a vacation during spring break but fail to make any airline reservations, you won't go. Later you may regret your inaction, but by then it will be too late. In this case, it wasn't that you made a wrong decision, but that you failed to make a decision at all. This type of choice may be called decision by default.

Maximizing our satisfaction in life—the purpose of all rational consumer decision making—means controlling our decisions to the greatest possible extent. One of the ways we can control our decisions is to realize when decisions should be made and when we should take action.

Determining the Alternatives

The next step in decision making—and a very important one—is to determine all of the possible alternatives. Assume, for example, that you have decided to visit Hawaii for a vacation. The price you will pay for your travel will vary depending on when you are willing to travel and the type of accommodations you wish to have. By paying an extra $40 a day you might be able to have a studio apartment with a kitchenette that would allow you to save money on meals. If you are willing to travel in the middle of the week instead of on weekends, you may be able to pay less for your flight. Other choices you could make include whether to buy cancellation insurance and whether to rent a car or rely on public transportation. For each possible choice you consider, there will be tradeoffs between costs you will pay and benefits you will receive.

This is the stage in which it is easy to slip up by failing to consider alternative possibilities. Perhaps you find a description of a hotel that takes your fancy.

It seems to have many of the features you want, so you immediately book reservations without investigating other possible locations where you could stay. Later, when you are actually in Hawaii, you find that the hotel is not conveniently located and that its prices are higher than those of competing establishments. Too late, you realize that you could have made a better choice if you had taken more time to find other alternatives.

Evaluating the Alternatives

In this step of the decision-making process, you weigh the costs and benefits associated with each alternative you have identified. You consider costs not only in terms of money but in terms of the opportunity cost of other choices you will have to give up. If, for example, you choose to spend an extra $500 to stay in an especially nice hotel on your vacation, you should also consider the value of other goods or services you could have used this money to buy. Many people find it helpful to write these costs and benefits down on paper because, as Benjamin Franklin once said, it is hard "to keep all the pros and cons in mind at one time."

In evaluating alternatives you may call into question even relatively high-level values you hold. In this case you should consider the value of alternative uses you might have for the several thousand dollars you would spend on a trip to Hawaii. If your trip would take so much of your money that you would not be able to pay your tuition and attend college, it could interfere with your high-priority goal of completing your education and pursuing the career of your choice. You would need to ask yourself what you really want most, a relaxing vacation now, or a rewarding career in the future? When you need to make important decisions like this, it is often worthwhile to discuss your alternatives with another person whose opinion you trust and respect. Generally, the more expensive the purchase or important the decision, the more time you will want to devote to evaluating each alternative.

Committing Yourself to the Decision

The next step in making a rational decision is choosing an alternative and committing yourself to it. Sometimes this commitment can be an ongoing process, as when you decide to save a certain amount of money every week. Or, it may require you to complete a series of steps, like making all the different reservations and plans necessary to take a trip. Part of making a good decision may involve persevering in its implementation—which is not always easy to do. If, for example, you have decided to spend no more than $50 a day on food while you are on vacation, you may be tempted to go over your budget, causing the total cost of your vacation to grow beyond the amount you can afford.

Evaluating the Results

The final step in the decision-making process is to evaluate the results of your choice. There are at least two good reasons to do this. In many cases it is possible to change your mind even after a choice has been made. If you buy a table for your living room and discover that it simply doesn't look right when you get it home, you can usually return it for a refund. In other cases you may not be able to change a decision you have made. Certainly you would not be flown back from Hawaii for free if you found you were not having a good time. However, even in such cases, an evaluation of the results of your choice should provide you with information that will help you make better choices in the future.

PITFALLS IN RATIONAL CONSUMER DECISION MAKING

There are a number of pitfalls in decision making that the wise consumer will be aware of. A few of the most common ones involve impulse buying, habit buying, failing to read the fine print, using credit unwisely, and engaging in conspicuous consumption.

Impulse Buying

To buy impulsively is to walk into a store, see something we like, and purchase it without taking time for cost/benefit analysis, value clarification, or any of the steps in the rational decision-making process just described. Merchants exploit impulse buying by displaying whimsical and relatively inexpensive items at the checkout counter. Obviously, impulse buying cannot explain all our buying habits because we have certain needs that must be met if we are to survive, the most obvious being minimum amounts of food and shelter, and these purchases must be planned for. Many others, however, can be purchased solely on the basis of spur-of-the-moment decisions.

Sometimes, impulse buying is a wise choice—when the purchase is truly a bargain and will help increase income or when it makes you feel good but will not compromise more important goals. Nonetheless, there is a limit—our income plus our available credit—to acceptable impulse buying. Most consumer economists argue against impulse buying because it can undermine a budget and may lead to financial difficulties. The best way to control impulse buying is to ask yourself: Why am I buying this? Do I need it? Will I use it? Can I afford it? Will it keep me from buying something I want more later? Remember, for every purchase you make, you forgo some other alternative.

Habit Buying

Many purchases are made as a result of habits acquired through the years. No plans are involved and no impulses either, just the force of habit. A person might stop at a tavern on the way home from work every Friday night. An individual might continue subscribing to, say, a photography magazine even though he or she gave up the hobby long ago and doesn't even own a camera anymore. Consider, also, that habit buying may be necessary in order to free up time for other buying that requires time and thought. In other words, habit buying isn't necessarily bad (as long as you don't make a habit of it).

The Fine Print

If there is one major, consistent failing on the part of consumers, it is signing contracts or purchase agreements without verifying their contents. One has only to spend a brief amount of time reviewing the records of court cases to realize how often problems arise because a consumer was not familiar with the written terms of a contract. To avoid this pitfall, the wise consumer will make sure that whatever a seller has promised is included in the written purchase agreement.

The Seductiveness of Credit

We all know how seductive credit can be. It is very tempting to buy now and pay later, especially when you have a steady income and feel you can afford

> If there is one major, consistent failing on the part of consumers, it is signing contracts or purchase agreements without verifying their contents.

to take on a debt. But, even though you have a steady income now and your budget can tolerate additional debt, are you sure this will be the case in the future? Assuming that one's spendable income will remain the same over time is a common pitfall for consumers. What if an emergency arises? What if you have an accident and are unable to work? What if one of your parents should become seriously ill and you have to spend money on expensive, long-term nursing care? Unless such contingencies are provided for by a savings cushion, any one of these developments could spell disaster for your household.

Conspicuous Consumption

Conspicuous consumption
Consumption of goods more for their ability to impress others than for the inherent satisfaction they yield.

Many people buy products more to impress other people than because they expect to receive value from their use. Such **conspicuous consumption** demonstrates a person's wealth and economic power. It is, however, often wasteful of our scarce resources and may cause people to receive less satisfaction than they could from their time and income. A person who buys a very expensive and powerful automobile, for example, might impress his or her neighbors but not have enough money left over to pay bills or buy the basic necessities of life. Driving such a car would also be wasteful of our energy resources. Conspicuous consumption is a pitfall that consumers can easily avoid if they evaluate the true value of their alternative choices.

TIME MANAGEMENT

In every alternative lifestyle, at least one element is constant: the limited amount of time we all have available. In other words, scarcity rears its head again. We all suffer a scarcity of time. We must each answer the question of how to spend our time to best satisfy our individual needs. Consider the differences in the lives that would be led by a woman who owns and manages a restaurant and a different person who is employed to wash dishes in that restaurant's kitchen. The owner probably earns more money but also bears more responsibility. She may spend 60 or 70 hours each week working at the restaurant and keeping its financial records. Even when she is at home or on vacation, problems of her business may occupy her mind. The dishwasher, on the other hand, works 40 hours a week and goes home to other interests. He is able to use his free time to satisfy his needs in ways that are truly free. Each lifestyle involves a different set of values and goals and different choices that have been made in how these people manage their time.

To manage time, people need to consider time as if it were a commodity like food or clothing, or as if it were money that could be used to buy something of value. If your employer asks you to work an extra 12 hours next weekend, you know you will be paid overtime and may earn as much as several hundred dollars in extra income. Working these extra hours, however, could prevent you from spending time with your friends or family. You might not be able to complete household tasks or finish necessary repairs on your car. To make a rational choice, you should weigh the value of the benefits of the extra income against the costs of the alternative uses of your time that you would have to give up. You should remember that earning extra income is pointless if you have no time left to enjoy the products it may buy. It is quite possible that a rational choice for you would be to forgo the extra work and income so you can spend your time doing something else of greater value to you.

When parents spend time with their children they make tradeoffs for other uses of their time. What opportunity costs do you pay when you use your time to be with your family?

If you live with another person or persons, then another important part of managing time is to divide responsibilities and work in an efficient way. It may make more sense for all members of a family to share household chores equitably than to expect one person to do more than others. Or, if one member of a family has a job that pays a large hourly wage, it may be a better choice for this person to work more hours outside the home while others complete household tasks. It is easiest to make decisions that involve time management when you have a clear idea of your goals and values. When decisions involve different members of a family group, the interests of all members need to be considered, and each individual should have a voice in the decision-making process.

Breaking Parkinson's Law

Whatever our values may be and whatever our lifestyles become, most of us share a certain psychological trait commonly known as **Parkinson's Law.** C. Northcote Parkinson, a management expert, made an observation that unfortunately seems to have universal validity: *Work expands to fit the time allotted for it.* If you're aware of Parkinson's Law, you can fight it. If you're not, it may overwhelm you. Say you have allotted yourself four hours to write a report. You had better believe that the report will take you *at least* four hours. Had you allotted yourself, say, three hours, however, it would probably have taken only three hours and probably would not have been any better or worse. In fact, it might have been better because you would have started in earnest immediately instead of twiddling your thumbs, sharpening pencils, and looking at additional reference materials for the first hour.

One way to avoid falling victim to Parkinson's Law is to plan and draw up lists of things to do. The more specialized and specific the lists are, the more

Parkinson's Law
Work will expand to fit the time allotted for it.

helpful them seem to be. For many people, list making is beneficial to accomplishing all types of goals. For example, instead of just telling yourself that you really ought to read more books, you can schedule in some reading time every day when you make a list of the day's activities. Don't set an unrealistic goal, such as five hours at a sitting, but shoot for something you know you can manage—say, fifteen minutes at a time, four times during the day. You will be surprised at how many books you can read that way. If you really would like to keep up correspondence with old friends, stop putting it off: Set up a specific time and note it in your list of weekly or monthly tasks.

Another way to make sure you accomplish tasks and use your time efficiently is to reward yourself. One writer used the reward system and increased his output significantly. Because he was an avid stamp collector, he decided to reward himself with one new stamp after finishing each chapter. Once his plan was in place, he never missed his deadlines. When he completed the entire book, he rewarded himself with a rare stamp that he had wanted for a long time. Your own choice of rewards will likely be quite different, but equally effective.

Such a technique can be extended to lifetime planning. You can set goals for each day, each week, each month, each five-year period, and you can keep redefining these goals. Some extremely efficient people always list more goals every day than they know they can achieve. But sometimes they actually accomplish more than they thought they could because listing their goals provides such a strong impetus.

BUYING AND SEARCHING

Most consumer decision making depends on information that must be acquired through some searching procedure. The best search procedure is, of course, different for each person, but a general rule for rational consumer decision making can be made: *The larger the expected payoff is from searching for better information in the marketplace, the greater the cost that should be incurred to acquire the information.* In plain language, this means we probably will spend considerably less time trying to get the best deal on a tube of toothpaste than we will spend trying to get the best deal on a new car. The expected gains from a good deal on toothpaste may be at most a few cents, but on a car the gains may be several hundred dollars. The major difference between rational and so-called irrational buying habits is that the former includes looking at the expected costs and benefits in order to determine the best deal.

Some people, such as doctors, lawyers, and top executives, consider their time so valuable that they seek out very little information. For example, they may purchase many products from an expensive store in their neighborhood. They are willing to pay higher prices because they have found that the store carries relatively higher-quality brand names, and they aren't willing to spend additional time searching for alternative sources. For them, the transaction cost, or the value of the time they would spend looking for additional information, is greater than the value they place on finding alternative choices.

For any one of us, it is not *always* beneficial to spend more time searching for lower price or higher quality in a product. At some point, we have to stop our search. We won't search every store in our city for the lowest toothpaste price, even though we know that the next store might offer that lower price.

The point at which we stop searching is determined by the information we already have and a comparison of what it will cost to acquire new information against what we expect the benefits to be from that new information.

▶ SUMMARY

1. We are all consumers who purchase a variety of goods and services.

2. Rational consumer decision making requires allocating our time and money resources in such a way as to maximize our satisfaction.

3. A cost/benefit analysis helps us look more objectively at the potential consequences of our decisions and can therefore assist us in making more rational decisions.

4. Values are fundamental concepts or preferences that regulate or in some way affect our behavior. High-level values give rise to tastes and preferences that affect our everyday lives.

5. Through the process of value clarification, we not only learn what our values are but also establish the relative priority in our lives of various values that we hold. The resulting hierarchy of values provides a framework for directed, rational decisions that are harmonious with our basic goals in life.

6. Goals are closely linked to our values. Once we are aware of what we value most, we can establish goals and subgoals that are consistent with our values. If we place a high value on education, for example, we may establish the goal of going to graduate school. A subgoal might be getting straight A's next term to ensure our acceptance at the graduate school of our choice.

7. The decision-making process involves five steps: (1) knowing when a decision is called for, (2) determining the possible alternatives, (3) evaluating each alternative through cost/benefit analyses, (4) committing oneself to a particular alternative, and (5) evaluating the results of the decision.

8. There are numerous pitfalls in consumer decision making. Some of the most common are (1) impulse buying, (2) habit buying, (3) failing to read the fine print of purchase agreements, (4) using credit unwisely, on the assumption that one's spendable income will remain the same in the future, and (5) engaging in conspicuous consumption.

9. The amount of time that one has available is constant and unchangeable. A major choice for every consumer is how to spend it.

10. Even if you have decided to accomplish certain goals because they fit in with your values, you may not succeed if you fall prey to Parkinson's Law, which says that work will expand to fit the time allotted for it. It is your responsibility to manage your personal time most efficiently.

11. Information must be acquired before purchases can be made. It is, however, useful to acquire information only up to the point at which the expected payoff from searching for more information is not as great as the expected costs of that additional search. The larger the purchase contemplated, the more time you should spend seeking information on the best product and the best financial deal.

▶ QUESTIONS FOR THOUGHT AND DISCUSSION

1. What are some of the customs of your family or your community that influence your expenditures? How do they differ from the customs of other groups that you have observed?

2. How is it possible that what is rational for one individual may not be

rational for another? What, really, does "rational" mean in the context of rational consumer decision making?

3. What psychological factors are involved in impulse buying? Are there benefits attached to impulse buying that offset the costs (such as the effect such behavior has on one's budget)?

▶ THINGS TO DO

1. Think back to a recent decision you made. Examine carefully the decision-making process you undertook. Write on a sheet of paper the costs and benefits of that decision. On another sheet of paper, list the personal values that were operative in the decision-making process.

2. Create a form on which there is a space for every hour of every day of the week, including the weekends. Blacken those spaces during which you are engaged in some activity—classes, work, personal grooming, eating, and so on. Remember, if you are a student, to allow approximately two hours of study time for every hour in class. Fill in the white space remaining with a plan for spending that time—reading a few pages of a book, practicing the guitar, planning your future, and so on. Follow through on your plan for a week and write up the results.

3. Make a list of your goals in life. Separate them into financial and nonfinancial goals. Analyze the decisions you have made to date in light of these goals.

4. Make a list of ten or fifteen activities that you most enjoy. Then note beside each entry the last time you engaged in that activity. Finally, relate these preferences to the decisions you have made over the last year.

5. Write down a set of short-term, intermediate, and long-term goals. Are these the same goals you had last year, the year before, or the year before that? Do you think you will have the same long-term goals five years from now? If not, why will your goals change? Is there any way you can predict how they will change?

▶ APPLICATION

Keep a record of how you use your time over a typical weekend. Use this record as the basis of an essay that discusses the value of managing your time. What did you do that was wasteful of your time? What steps could you take to make better use of your time in the future? What tradeoffs would be involved?

▶ SELECTED READINGS

▶ Albin, Francis M. "Planning, Organizing, Controlling." *Consumer Economics & Personal Money Management,* 2d ed. Englewood Cliffs: Prentice-Hall, 1989, pp. 1–80.

▶ David, Morton. *The Art of Decision-Making.* New York: Springer-Verlag, 1986.

▶ Earl, Peter E. *Lifestyle Economics: Consumer Behavior in a Turbulent World.* New York: St. Martin's Press, 1986.

▶ Karni, Edi. *Organizational Behavior and Human Decision Processes.* New York: Academic Press, 1985.

▶ Lee, Stewart M., and Mel J. Zwlenak. *Personal Finance for Consumers.* Columbus: Publishing Horizons, 1987 (chapters on decision making).

▶ Maynes, E. Scott. *Decision Making for Consumers.* New York: Macmillan, 1976.

▶ Warner, Stephanie. *Getting Organized.* New York: Warner Books, 1988.

Environmentally Responsible Consumer Behavior

▶ How extensive is the damage consumers do to the environment?

▶ In what ways may damage to the environment affect consumers?

▶ What steps have been taken by the government to try to control damage to the environment?

▶ How are the costs of environ-mental protection paid?

▶ What can consumers do to help protect the environment?

In recent years an awareness has been growing that irresponsible acts are damaging our environment—the physical surroundings in which we live, work, and play—possibly to the point of endangering our future existence. Consumers' decisions can encourage or discourage business's efforts to preserve our environment. In addition, our personal lifestyles either contribute to environmental problems or ameliorate them.

SCOPE OF THE PROBLEM

If you are a typical American consumer, you will create 3.5 pounds of trash today. Do you wonder where your trash goes? The problem of disposing of household waste is, of course, only the tip of the environmental iceberg, so to speak. It is easy to recognize that space for discarded trash in our landfills is running out. Other environmental problems are less obvious, but no less important. Consider the following facts.

▶ In 1992 Americans produced over 800 million pounds of trash each day, of which 90 percent were discarded into the environment.
▶ Roughly 90 percent of the pesticides in use in 1992 were not tested for health hazards. Almost none were tested for dangers that could result from interactions among them.
▶ About 1.5 billion tons of carbon dioxide gas are released into the atmosphere annually by Americans. This contributes to the problem of global warming.
▶ About 16 tons of sewage are dumped into our nation's waterways every minute of every day.
▶ It has been estimated that the depletion of the earth's ozone layer will cause an additional million cases of skin cancer in the United States by the year 2000, and will have an unknown but detrimental impact on food crops and animal life.
▶ Each year enough rain forest is being burned or cut to cover the state of California.

Dangers at Home

Many everyday products you use at home pose dangers to your health and create problems in the environment when they are discarded. For example, when you put on a new piece of clothing that is made of permanent-press fabric, the chances are good that some of its new smell is formaldehyde. Formaldehyde is used by manufacturers to give permanent-press garments body. Fumes from formaldehyde have been found to cause cancer in laboratory animals. Although the amount released from garments is so small that it creates little danger, the same may not be said of many building products that were used in construction before the mid 1980s. People who live in prefabricated homes, house trailers, or in homes that were insulated with a foam product in the 1970s may well breathe air that contains a dangerous level of formaldehyde. Unfortunately, there is little that can be done about this problem short of tearing these homes apart to remove the offending products, a process that would be far too costly for most affected people.

Our problems are not limited to the structures in which we live. Even something as basic and necessary as water cannot be trusted to be pure. Recent surveys have shown that there are areas in every state where drinking water is contaminated with either organic or chemical pollutants. In some states, like

New Jersey, every major aquifer contains contaminants of one type or another. The filtration and chlorination processes that are commonly used to clean water are not able to remove many of these contaminants. Living in sparsely populated, non-industrialized areas offers no guarantee of water purity, either. Chemicals used by our nation's farmers have resulted in contamination rates for well water that are as high as 97 percent in some rural communities.

Dangers at School and Workplace

Schools contain a significant number of health hazards for our children. Although the lead-based paints and asbestos insulation that were common 30 years ago are no longer used in construction of new schools, many older schools still contain these products and must be monitored to reduce the risk of a release that could harm our children. Also, substances such as cleaning products and duplicating fluid in use today represent potential hazards in our schools.

Our places of employment are often dangerous to our health. For example, workers subjected to breathing vinyl chloride fumes during the process of making products like plastic pipe or floor tiles were found to be 2,000 percent more likely to develop liver cancer than the population at large. Coal miners often suffer from emphysema and black lung disease. People who work near strong electric fields are more likely to develop leukemia. Workers and employers may be unaware of potential hazards in the workplace until people begin to fall ill—at which time it is too late to protect those who have been exposed. Even when dangers are known, the cost of eliminating them may leave workers and employers only two realistic alternatives: shutting down, or working with the hazards.

CONSUMER-CREATED POLLUTION

It is impossible to discuss all the ways that consumers can damage our environment in the space available in this book. We will therefore focus on some major issues, exploring opposing points of view to illustrate the environmental choices responsible consumers must make.

Diaper Debate

In the 1980s Americans used an average of 18 billion paper diapers every year. Wood pulp from roughly 10 million trees was necessary to produce these products. Moreover, their production required 67,500 tons of plastic film each year—a material that will not degrade in the environment for hundreds of years. Buried diapers contain viruses that can leach into the groundwater people drink. For these and other reasons many people believe that the use of disposable diapers is detrimental to the environment and our health and therefore support the use of reusable cotton diapers.

Important environmental problems are associated with the use of cotton diapers, though, as well. Growing cotton depletes nutrients in the soil, making necessary the use of artificial chemical fertilizers. Fertilizers used by cotton farmers often run off into bodies of water, causing pollution. Delivery trucks for cotton-diaper services use scarce energy resources. More energy is used washing diapers in water heated sufficiently to kill bacteria. And some diaper services do not heat the water enough to kill organisms before it is dumped into sewer systems, from which it may find its way into our lakes and rivers.

In addition, the water used for washing diapers creates greater demand on the limited supplies of fresh water in many areas of the country.

Diapers represent an environmental danger regardless of what they are made from or how they are used. Consumers are left with no clear best choice that will protect the environment. They may do the least harm by using no more diapers of any type than is necessary.

Tradeoff between Automobile Size and Safety

Driving an automobile is a risky proposition even under the best of conditions. Automotive accidents are the leading cause of death for our nation's teenagers. Consumers are able to limit the risk they take in driving a car by choosing vehicles that are strong and well constructed. There is usually a direct relation between a car's weight and the safety it offers drivers and passengers. The risk of being killed in an automobile accident is roughly 30 percent greater for people who drive subcompact cars than for those who use full-size automobiles.

Another consideration consumers need to keep in mind, however, is that large, often safer cars are less fuel-efficient and more damaging to the environment than smaller cars. Drivers are faced with the choice of using a car that is safer or one that creates less pollution and uses less fuel. There is no easy solution to this tradeoff. Perhaps the best choice is to limit your driving to the absolute minimum necessary and to try to share rides or use public transportation whenever possible.

Convenience in Packaging

One of the most popular innovations in food packaging in recent years has been the drink box. Introduced in the United States in 1983, sales of drink-box products exceeded 3 billion units in 1992. Light, leak-resistant, and easy to discard, they have become a standard item in lunchbox menus. Their manufacturers claim that drink boxes are better for the environment than alternatives because when compacted, they take up less space than other types of disposable drink containers. Critics of the product point out that the six layers of plastic, paper, and aluminum foil making up the product will not degrade in the environment under normal conditions. They also argue that the use of drink boxes is sending the wrong message to our children. Since the boxes are meant to be discarded, they reinforce the "throw-away" mentality that we should be trying to counteract. These critics would encourage parents and children to carry less expensive, reusable containers even if they are less convenient. In 1991 Maine banned the sale of most drink-box products, and similar legislation has been considered in other states.

ECONOMIC CAUSES OF POLLUTION

Much of the damage done to our environment takes place during the production of goods and services that satisfy our needs. Indeed, pollution, production, and profit are three concepts that are often related to each other. In the United States most businesses exist to earn a profit for their owners. Steps toward pollution abatement add to the costs of production and tend to reduce a firm's profit. The money spent by a paper factory, for example, to remove chemicals and other residues before it returns water to the environment, could increase the firm's costs to the point where it would be forced out of business.

Among the functions of the Environmental Protection Agency is the monitoring of radioactive materials to be sure that they are used and disposed of in a manner that is environmentally sound.

ENVIRONMENTAL LEGISLATION

Many people believe the government should encourage environmental protection by heavily taxing firms that release pollution into the environment. This policy could cause the businesses that damage the environment the least to be the most profitable, making pollution-abatement equipment cost-effective. Of course, increased costs businesses would pay to protect the environment would probably be passed on to consumers in the form of higher prices. Nevertheless, consumers have in fact pressured federal, state, and local governments to create agencies and pass laws to protect the environment.

Environmental Protection Agency

The federal Environmental Protection Agency (EPA) is responsible for administering laws that protect the nation's land, air, and water. Included under its mandate are standards for water quality, solid and hazardous waste disposal, radiation, and air pollution. The EPA also regulates the use of pesticides and fertilizers for home, landscaping, and farm use.

In addition to enforcing regulations, the EPA provides technical assistance to firms that need help in meeting pollution-control standards. It has offices in most cities across the United States. Its objective is to strike a balance between our need to protect the environment and to produce goods and services that provide employment.

Clean Air Act of 1990

In 1990 Congress concluded 16 months of deliberation by passing a major revision of the original 1970 Clean Air Act. This legislation is designed to have the greatest impact in urban areas, where the problems of air pollution are most profound. It establishes controls on car emissions that significantly exceed those of the 1970 law, and will require the use of cleaner-burning fuels

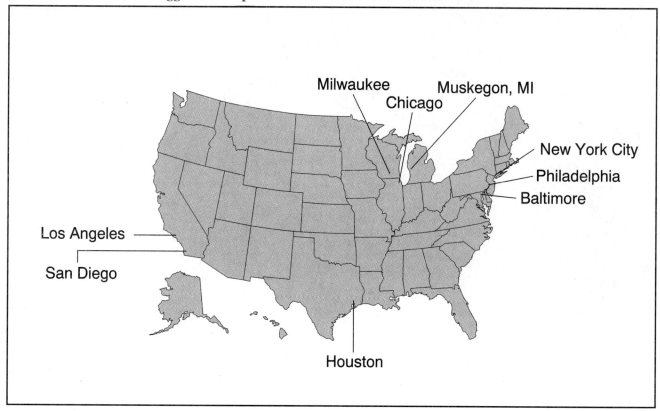

Milwaukee
Chicago
Muskegon, MI
New York City
Philadelphia
Baltimore
Los Angeles
San Diego
Houston

in many urban areas. It attacks the problem of acid rain by forcing utilities to reduce smokestack emissions and requires other industries to reduce the amount of cancer-causing compounds they release into the atmosphere.

Under this law, 1994-model cars must reduce nitrogen oxide emissions by 60 percent and hydrocarbons by 40 percent from 1990 standards. The emission control equipment installed on cars must last a minimum of 100,000 miles or ten years. The EPA was also given the power to tighten these requirements in 2003 depending on the conditions that exist at that time. By 1995 oil companies will be required to sell only cleaner-burning types of gasoline in the nation's nine smoggiest metropolitan areas. Businesses that operate fleets of vehicles will be encouraged to use cleaner-burning fuels like natural gas in 20 smoggier areas. In the mid 1990s, gasoline stations in roughly two dozen cities will be required to install devices that will trap fumes that would otherwise be released when consumers fill their cars. The EPA was given the power to ease many of these requirements temporarily if it determined that they were impossible to meet or would create unreasonable hardships.

In addition to the new automobile regulations, standards were established for electric utilities that would require smokestack emissions of sulfur dioxide and nitrogen oxide to be reduced by 50 percent. These regulations will not be applied uniformly. The 111 dirtiest coal-fired plants in 21 midwestern states will first be required to reduce their sulfur dioxide emissions by 1995, because they are thought to be responsible for the largest part of the acid rain that falls in the Northeast. The plan allows plants that exceed required emission reductions to sell these amounts to other utilities that do not meet standards.

In a final section of the law, restrictions were placed on businesses that release cancer-causing substances into the atmosphere. They will be required to reduce their emissions of 189 chemicals by 90 percent or more, using the best available technology by the year 2003. The EPA was given the power to set safety standards at plants where combinations of the toxic chemicals are used according to appropriate safety needs.

Some business and political leaders believe the costs of this law will exceed its benefits. They point out that it is impossible to eliminate pollution totally. The higher we set our standards, the more achieving them will cost. Meeting abatement standards set by the Clean Air Act may force prices up to a point that many people won't be able to afford to own or drive automobiles, and electrical appliances may become very expensive to operate.[1]

State and Local Government Efforts

In many cases state and local governments have been in the front lines of the environmental protection effort. In a number of cases their laws and regulations have set standards that were eventually adopted by the federal government for the nation.

California's 1991 Car Emission Standards In 1991 the state of California passed laws to set standards for automobile emissions that were even more stringent than the ones in the federal Clean Air Act. By 1994, 10 to 20 percent of new cars sold in California must product less than half the federal standard for hydrocarbon emissions. By the year 2003 these hydrocarbon emissions must be cut in half again and will apply to up to 75 percent of new cars sold in California. Standards for nitrogen oxide emissions will also be phased in. Up to 10 percent of new cars will be electric-powered by 2003 and will therefore create no direct emissions.

Automobile manufacturers have shown a willingness to try to meet these standards, not only because of the 1.7 million cars and trucks sold in California each year, but because there is an assumption that the rest of the nation will follow California's lead over time. California, in effect, is becoming a giant laboratory for testing new methods of automobile pollution control.[2]

New York's Solid Waste Disposal and Recycling Regulations On September 1, 1988, the New York State Commissioner of Environmental Conservation announced a new set of regulations for the disposal of solid waste regarded as the most sweeping and toughest in the United States at that time. The regulations included special rules for the proper disposal of the often toxic ash that results from burning trash. A significant effect of meeting these regulations was an estimated 30-percent increase in the cost of operating solid waste disposal sites. Powers were also given to the New York State Department of Environmental Conservation to penalize local governments that failed to implement recycling programs by 1991.

A few months earlier the government of Suffolk County, New York, passed a law that made it illegal to sell or distribute plastic grocery bags and many

---

1. *Facts on File* (Facts on File, Inc., New York, NY), p. 814.
2. *Wall Street Journal,* "Auto Makers Strive to Get Up to Speed on Clean Cars for the California Market," March 26, 1991, p. B-1.

other types of plastic containers in that county even if they could be recycled. The intent of the law was to encourage the use of biodegradable materials and reusable containers that would have less impact on the environment.

Although individual consumers do not have the power to pass laws, they have the power, as voters and citizens, to influence the actions of their elected representatives. New laws don't just happen. Usually they are in response to consumer pressure.

WHO PAYS THE COST OF ENVIRONMENTAL PROTECTION?

Many people believe that businesses should be forced to pay the costs of environmental protection made necessary by their production of goods or services. Although firms often make direct payments for pollution-control devices, we can be sure that most try to pass these costs on to consumers in higher prices. When automobile manufacturers like Ford and General Motors began to install catalytic converters made from platinum in car exhaust systems, they raised the price of their products roughly $400 apiece. Utilities that produce electricity will ask regulatory agencies for permission to pass the added cost of required pollution-abatement equipment on to their customers. When firms that manufacture solvents and plastics are forced to reduce the amount of cancer-causing fumes they release into the atmosphere, the price of paint, plastic products, and other goods made from these compounds increases.

Ultimately, then, people pay for pollution abatement. It is important for consumers to weigh the benefits they will receive from a particular piece of legislation against its costs to see if the benefits are great enough to make it worthwhile.

Environmental Cleanups

It is unfortunate that many environmental problems today are the result of weak or nonexistent regulation in the past. Dumps can be found in every state that contain toxic chemicals, and in some cases radioactive waste. Many of these sites were used and abandoned many years ago. The materials in them were dangerous when they were discarded and may be even more of a threat today. Over the years these materials have often seeped into the groundwater and migrated to areas where people live and from which they take their drinking water. Names like Love Canal and Times Beach (both locations that were contaminated with discarded chemicals that contained dioxin) raise a specter of undiagnosed sickness and painful death.

Estimates of the cost of cleaning up existing dumps that contain dangerous materials run into the hundreds of billions of dollars. Many of the firms that originally used these dumps no longer exist, or if they do, their assets could not possibly pay the cost of cleaning up the waste. When, or if, these dumps are cleaned up, the bulk of the cost is likely to be paid by American consumers through their taxes. The largest part of the costs of the clean-up effort at Love Canal and Times Beach were indeed paid by taxpayers.

"Not in My Backyard"

When businesses produce goods and services that satisfy consumer needs they often create by-products that are harmful and dangerous as well. Although the day may come when it is possible to recycle these materials or turn them into harmless compounds, it is not here now. Regardless of any efforts we make to conserve our resources, to limit the production of radioactive or toxic waste, or to degrade such waste into safe materials, we still end up with a significant amount of dangerous materials that must be put somewhere. Most people define this "somewhere" as anywhere but in their own community.

In 1992 only one site had been granted approval to accept toxic chemical wastes in a large section of the northeastern part of the United States. The firm that operated this dump in Model City, New York, received permission from the state of New York to double the amount of waste it could accept in 1991 over the protests of local citizens and governments. To many residents it appeared that because a toxic dump already existed in their community they were singled out to have the only toxic dump site. When other locations were suggested for new dumps, demonstrations, letterwriting campaigns, and legal maneuvering prevented them from being established. Similar problems have occurred when sites for the storage of radioactive waste were chosen in the late 1980s.

Americans need to recognize that part of the tradeoff they must make for the lifestyle they enjoy is the cost of disposing of waste materials. If we are not responsible in how we choose to deal with this problem, we will harm ourselves, and leave a legacy of environmental destruction to our children as well.

> Americans need to recognize that part of the tradeoff they must make for the lifestyle they enjoy is the cost of disposing of waste materials.

ENVIRONMENT AS GLOBAL CONCERN

Although there are steps individual nations, states, and communities may take to protect the environment, many situations require global action. We do not live in isolation. Acts that are destructive to the environment hurt us all no matter where we live.

Damage to Ozone Layer

In 1991 the EPA announced that studies indicated the level of ozone over the United States had fallen by an average of 4 percent to 5 percent in the years between 1978 and 1990. It predicted that the total loss could reach as high as 20 percent by the year 2000 if the rate of loss remained unchanged.

Scientists theorize that a natural layer of ozone (three atoms of oxygen bonded together) developed over millions of years in the atmosphere at a height from 30 to 60 miles. This ozone layer shields the earth from most harmful ultraviolet rays from the sun. You might ask yourself, "How important is the ozone layer to me?" The answer is, "Very!" If the ozone layer was depleted by 20 percent, scientists estimate that the number of cases of skin cancer in the United States would increase by as many as 100,000 a year. It is likely, too, that climatic changes would result that would have an unknown impact on our ability to produce food and other crops. Experiments have shown that grain production drops by as much as 20 percent when plants are exposed to elevated levels of ultraviolet light. Higher concentrations of smog might occur because of chemical reactions brought on by ultraviolet light. The ozone layer makes life as we know it possible. Its importance cannot be overestimated.

Most of the destruction of the ozone layer is the result of reactions between ozone molecules and chemicals released into the atmosphere by man-made products. The most important is a family of chemicals called **chlorofluorocarbons (CFCs)** that has been used in aerosol sprays, plastic foam, refriger-

Chlorofluorocarbons (CFCs)
A family of chemicals that are associated with the depletion of ozone in the earth's upper atmosphere.

ation units, and in many other ways for many years. As we became aware of the danger posed by CFCs, steps were taken to reduce and eventually eliminate their use. In 1986 DuPont, the largest producer of CFCs in this country, announced it would produce a substitute for them by 1991. In 1989 a tax was placed on the production of CFCs to discourage their use. Many businesses, including McDonald's, reduced their use of plastic foam products that are made with CFCs. In 1992 the U.S. government announced that its ban on the production of CFCs would become effective in 1995 rather than 2000 because of the rapidly growing problem. These steps, although useful, are not able to solve the problem for a number of reasons, including the following:

▶ It is estimated that CFCs already released into the atmosphere may take as many as ten years to rise to the ozone level and cause destruction of ozone molecules. Reduction of CFC use now, therefore, will do nothing to stop the effect of CFCs that have already been released.

▶ A vast reservoir of CFCs exists in millions of refrigerators, freezers, and air conditioning units that will probably be discarded and leak the chemical into the atmosphere.

▶ Many nations have not taken steps to eliminate the production and use of CFCs, probably because alternative products are more expensive.

The destruction of the earth's ozone layer is a global problem. Even if the American people and the leaders of our businesses and government act to protect the ozone layer, the problem cannot be solved without the cooperation of other nations. Although a treaty to limit the production and use of CFCs was signed by 27 developed nations in 1987, this did nothing to reduce the use of these chemicals in less-developed nations. To try to remedy this situation, an agreement among developed nations was suggested in 1990 that would have paid less-developed nations to reduce their use of CFCs. The total cost of the program was estimated to be roughly $40 billion over five years. The first U.S. share was to be $20 million in 1991. In May of 1990, representatives of the Bush administration refused to participate in the program and suggested that the reduction of CFCs in less-developed nations be financed through loans from the World Bank. There is little reason to believe that this will happen.

CFCs released into the air in India, China, or other places do not stay there. They destroy the ozone layer over your home as much as over the cities of New Delhi or Peking. The time is rapidly approaching when something must be done on a global level if we are to avoid an environmental disaster of truly epic proportion.

Greenhouse Effect

It has been suggested that global warming, also known as the **greenhouse effect,** represents as much of a problem to our environment in the long run as the depletion of the ozone layer. Measurements indicate that average temperatures increased at a rate between .05 and .10 degrees per year during the decade of the 1980s. This may seem like a trivial amount, but if this rate of increase continues for the next 50 years, the earth's average temperature will be 2.5 to 5 degrees higher in the 2040s.

Scientists believe dire consequences would result from such an increase in average temperatures. It is possible that as much as 15 percent of the earth's land area could be covered by water as higher temperatures melt the polar ice caps. Large numbers of plant and animals species that need cold weather

Greenhouse effect
The gradual warming of the earth's atmosphere, primarily as a result of the release of carbon dioxide from the burning of fossil fuels.

You might find it surprising to learn that many American businesses have benefited from their experience in dealing with environmental contamination and toxic chemical problems—by selling what they have learned to Europe and the former Soviet Union. Obviously, the United States is not the only nation in the world with toxic dumps. However, we are farther along in developing technology for cleaning up these wastes than many. Probably the world's most serious environmental problems now exist in the former Soviet Union and in Eastern Europe. For years untreated waste of every imaginable type was simply discarded into their environment. Vast areas in these countries are in desperate need of cleanup, and at least some money is there to do it. Much of the aid from the European Community to the former communist countries requires clean-up efforts. To be sure, there are European firms that are also involved, but they tend to have much higher prices than many American firms. U.S. firms have been in the waste management business longer and are often more efficient than their European counterparts. For example, International Waste Management Systems, of Knoxville, Tennessee, made a deal to supply pollution-monitoring equipment to Czechoslovakia. Lakes and rivers in Poland are being revived by Clean-Flo Laboratories of Minneapolis. American waste disposal services have also been purchased by West Germany, Australia, and even Japan. The list goes on and on. Our ability to export waste management technology helps American firms and workers and demonstrates the global nature of the world economy.

could become extinct, including many varieties of freshwater fish that are an important source of food. Droughts could become common, reducing our ability to grow food and causing world deserts to grow in size by as much as 100 percent.

There are several causes for global warming. The one that Americans and people in other developed nations are most responsible for is the release of carbon dioxide into the atmosphere from burning fossil fuels in automobiles and at power plants. Other causes include the burning of vast areas of the world's rain forests. This not only produces smoke and carbon dioxide, but destroys the plant life that is able to take carbon dioxide from the atmosphere and convert it into oxygen and other carbon compounds. There is also evidence that pollution of the world's oceans is killing the plankton that produces the largest part of the oxygen in our air. Again, steps by individual countries to reduce their production of carbon dioxide are helpful, but a comprehensive, worldwide program is needed.

WHAT CONSUMERS CAN DO

Many consumers feel powerless to help protect the world's environment. They need to realize that although the actions of any one individual will have a limited effect on the problem, when combined with efforts of millions of other individuals, they can make an important difference.

The Green Consumer

Consumers who make choices that protect the environment are sometimes called "green" consumers. These are people who attempt to encourage businesses to produce environmentally responsible products through their buying choices. For example, some consumers are convinced that using plastic containers is bad for the environment. They refuse to purchase laundry detergents in plastic bottles. They believe that detergent manufacturers will respond to their reduced sales by finding another type of container to use that is safer for the environment.

Businesses operate to earn a profit and are therefore responsive to changes in consumer demand and other types of public pressure. Part of the reason McDonald's and other fast-food restaurants reduced their use of plastic foam boxes was the pressure from environmental groups that was damaging to their public image and sales.

There are many publications that identify businesses and their products according to the degree of effort they make to be socially and environmentally responsible. One of the best known is the Council on Economic Priorities' book, *Shopping for a Better World*. This book rates most large firms by their environmental policies in a way that is easy to understand and use. In 1991 it could be ordered from CEP, 30 Irving Pl., New York, N.Y. 10003. Another such book is *Save Our Planet,* written by Diane MacEachern. It contains helpful suggestions for recycling and conservation and is published by Dell. Two editions of *50 Simple Things You Can Do to Save the Earth* have been published by the Earth Works Group that provide ideas for easy methods of conservation and recycling. This publication can be purchased in most larger book stores.

Conservation, Reuse, and Recycling

The best tool for protecting the environment is conservation, because resources that are never used do not need to be recycled or reused. Consumers can conserve energy by using car pools, driving slower, buying smaller cars, using public transportation, and heating or air-conditioning their homes less. They can put less strain on the environment by using less fertilizer and by watering less. People do not need to buy more newspapers than they will actually read; they could even share with a neighbor or friend.

An alternative to conservation is the reuse of products. If we make the effort, we can reuse many products. Taking a lunch to school or work packed in plastic boxes and glass containers is less convenient than using plastic bags and drink boxes, but it is good for the environment. We could take canvas bags when we go shopping instead of accepting the throw-away bags supplied by stores. The reuse of products requires extra effort, but it is environmentally responsible.

When neither conservation nor the reuse of products is possible, recycling used products is a better choice than simply discarding them into the environment. It has been estimated that as much as 80 percent of the 200 million tons of trash Americans discarded in 1992 could have been recycled and used again. Until recently, recycling saw limited use in the United States because it was often less expensive to use new resources than recycle old ones. Economic forces are rapidly changing this situation. Recycling not only offers a large supply of resources but will eventually reduce the cost of discarding old products as our landfills are used up and the cost of opening new ones grows.

To operate a successful recycling program, methods of collection and sorting must be developed and a market must be found for the products that are gathered. This takes time and costs money but will result in long-term savings. Many state governments have passed laws that either encourage or require local governments to establish recycling programs.

American consumers should remember that they enjoy the benefits of a representative form of government. If they want more environmental protection, they can pressure their government to provide it. Of course, they must realize that there are costs associated with every government regulation and the benefit-cost tradeoff should be recognized. However, if we as citizens are willing to make responsible decisions, we will improve our current situation and also leave a decent environment for our descendants.

▶ SUMMARY

1. Damage to the environment threatens the quality of our lives where we live, attend school, and are employed. Much of the damage is the result of decisions consumers make when they chose how to live, what products to buy, and the type of transportation to use.

2. American businesses are responsible for a large part of the damage to our environment when they use resources to produce goods and services consumers buy. Our competitive economic system may discourage businesses from protecting the environment when the cost of doing so decreases their profits.

3. The federal, state, and local governments have passed laws and created agencies that are intended to regulate production and reduce the damage to the environment. The Environmental Protection Agency is the most important federal agency with this responsibility. It is responsible for administering the Clean Air Act of 1990 and other federal laws.

4. The costs of most environmental protection and clean-up efforts are eventually paid by consumers. Businesses pass most of the cost of required environmental protection on to their customers in higher prices, and clean-up actions are primarily paid for by taxpayers.

5. The production of some toxic chemicals is unavoidable if we are to maintain our standard of living, yet people in many communities have resisted attempts to place toxic waste facilities near their homes. Locating and managing such facilities remains a major problem.

6. Most environmental issues are global problems in one way or another. The depletion of the earth's ozone layer by CFCs and other chemicals is a good example. Although the United States and other developed nations have taken steps to reduce the use of these chemicals, little has been accomplished in less-developed countries. CFCs released into the air anywhere will have a detrimental effect on life throughout the world.

7. Global warming is another example of a global environmental problem. The release of carbon dioxide from burning fossil fuels appears to be causing a gradual but steady increase in the earth's temperature. This may result in serious environmental consequences over the next 50 years.

8. Consumers can take steps as individuals to protect the environment. They can buy products from firms that have demonstrated a concern for the environment, and they can choose to buy products that are least damaging to the environment. They can become involved in recycling, reuse, and conservation programs. They can also use their political power to pressure governments to take actions that will protect the environment.

9. Consumers must remember that there is a tradeoff when choices are made to protect the environment. Decisions that are environmentally sound may be very costly and may involve a change in our material standard of living.

▶ QUESTIONS FOR THOUGHT AND DISCUSSION

1. What are three changes you could make in your life that would help protect the environment? Why haven't you chosen to take these steps?

2. Do you believe that it is possible to have too much environmental protection? Explain your answer.

3. The Clean Air Act of 1990 will allow people who live in rural areas to pay less of the cost for environmental protection than those who live in more polluted urban areas. Do you believe this is fair? What, if anything, would you do to change the way the law distributes this cost?

4. How is the depletion of the ozone layer likely to affect your life? Would you be willing to give up air-conditioning in your home or car to protect the ozone layer?

5. What responsibility do you believe the United States and other developed nations have to help the former communist countries and less-developed nations to solve their environmental problems? Explain your answer.

6. Which of the government steps described in this chapter do you believe will be most effective in encouraging people or businesses to protect the environment? Explain your answer.

▶ THINGS TO DO

1. Identify and describe at least three situations in your community that you believe represent a threat to the environment. Choose the one you believe is most serious, and write an essay that explains a method for reducing or eliminating this problem.

2. Describe how the Clean Air Act of 1990 is likely to affect life in your community. Do you believe that people in your community will be better or worse off as a result? Explain the reasons for your answer.

3. Would you support a law to increase the amount of everyone's income taxes by 5 percent if the money would be used to clean up toxic chemicals that have been dumped across the nation? Explain your answer.

4. Identify a national environmental problem that you believe represents a significant danger to future generations. Describe the scope of this problem. Write and explain a proposal for a law that would reduce or eliminate it.

▶ APPLICATION

Attend a meeting of a local government body that has an environmental issue on its agenda. Investigate this issue before the meeting and try to form an opinion about what should be done. When you attend the meeting, take notes on what is said and participate in the discussion if the public is invited to do so. Write an essay that describes what happened and what you learned about the issue.

▶ SELECTED READINGS

▶ Begley, Sharon. "A Bigger Hole in the Ozone." *Newsweek,* April 15, 1991, p. 64.

▶ Commoner, Barry. *Making Peace with the Planet.* New York: Pantheon Books, 1990.

▶ Elkington, John. *The Green Consumer.* New York: Penguin Books, 1990.

▶ "Environmental Shopper's Guide." *Changing Times,* February 1990, special section.

▶ Gutfeld, Rose. "Eight of 10 Americans Are Environmentalists, At Least So They Say." *Wall Street Journal,* August 2, 1991, p. A1.

▶ Henry, Ed. "Sorry, That's Out of Warranty." *Changing Times,* March 1990, pp. 53–57.

▶ Hollander, Jeffery. *How to Make the World a Better Place.* New York: Quill, 1990.

▶ Manes, Christopher. *Green Rage: Radical Environmentalism and the Unmaking of Civilization.* Boston: Little, Brown, 1990.

▶ McPhee, John A. *The Control of Nature.* New York: Farrar, Straus & Giroux, 1989.

▶ McKibben, William. *The End of Nature.* New York: Random House, 1989.

▶ Mills, Stephanie, ed. *In Praise of Nature.* Washington, D.C.: Island Press, 1990.

▶ Piasecki, Bruce. *In Search of Environmental Excellence: Moving Beyond Blame.* New York: Simon and Schuster, 1990.

▶ Silver, Mark. "Doing Your Bit to Save the Earth." *U.S. News & World Report,* April 2, 1990, pp. 61–63.

▶ Skow, John. "Can Lawns Be Justified?" *Time,* June 3, 1991, pp. 63–65.

▶ Smith, Emily T. "The Greening of Corporate America." *Business Week,* April 23, 1990, pp. 96–103.

▶ Sprigen, Karen, and Annetta Miller. "Doing the Right Thing." *Newsweek,* January 7, 1991.

▶ Taylor, Paul W. *Respect for Nature: A Theory of Environmental Ethics.* Princeton: Princeton University Press, 1986.

▶ Templin, Neal. "Auto Makers Strive to Get Up to Speed on Clean Cars for the California Market." *Wall Street Journal,* March 26, 1991, p. B1.

▶ Young, John. *Sustaining the Earth.* Cambridge: Harvard University Press, 1990.

A Flood of
Advertising

> Since businesses are out to make money they are not going to lose money by advertising, at least not intentionally.

Whether you like it or not, this year more than $130 billion worth of producer-generated information about products and services will be aimed at you and other consumers. We call this advertising. When you turn on a commercial radio station, the sounds of advertising strike your ears at least every five minutes. When you watch a commercial television station, you will usually be treated to some sort of ad at least every fifteen minutes. Whenever you open your local newspaper or leaf through a magazine, advertisements cross your field of vision. When you receive your daily mail, a good proportion of it is likely to consist of eye-catching ads, mail-order catalogs, or product samples. When you answer your phone or door, you might hear about even more products that may or may not interest you.

And if that's not enough, you can purchase more information about every good or service you might want to buy. You can buy books on how to invest money in the stock market, how to buy a house or a car or a computer, how to keep fit and trim, or how to avoid being defrauded. Information is all around us, bombarding us every second of every waking hour—or so it seems.

Obviously, some of this information is useful, and some of it is not. Some of it can even deceive you into making a purchase you may regret. This chapter first examines the world of advertising and how it affects us as consumers. It then looks at sources of consumer information that are available for private purchase and discusses how we, as consumers, can benefit from the abundance of information at our fingertips.

COSTS AND BENEFITS OF ADVERTISING

Information in the form of advertisements relating to products in our economy has been on the upswing, as is shown in Exhibit 5–1, which details the expansion of U.S. advertising in its various forms. On average, advertisers pay over $500 per person each year in the United States.

There must be a fairly good reason why we are subjected to so much advertising and why it is increasing each year. Let's look at it from the advertiser's point of view. Most businesspeople are in business for one reason and one reason only—to make money. Obviously, they wouldn't advertise if they didn't think that advertising could help increase their profits or at least help maintain their current sales and level of profits. Thus, we can assume that businesspeople believe the additional sales they will make through advertising will at least cover the costs of that advertising. So the advertising explosion can be attributed partly to the realization by businesses that increased advertising yields more than enough additional sales to justify the expenditure. Of course, when you look at it this way, you also realize who ultimately pays for advertising.

Who Pays?

Since businesses are out to make money for themselves and are not necessarily altruistic, we can be certain that they are not going to lose money by advertising, at least not intentionally. Only when they make a mistake about the profitability of a particular advertising campaign do they pay for it themselves—by taking a loss on that particular expenditure. In general, however, the cost of advertising is built in to the prices of the products we buy. After all, the cost of labor is built in to the prices of the products we buy and so are the costs of buildings and machines. There is very little we can do about

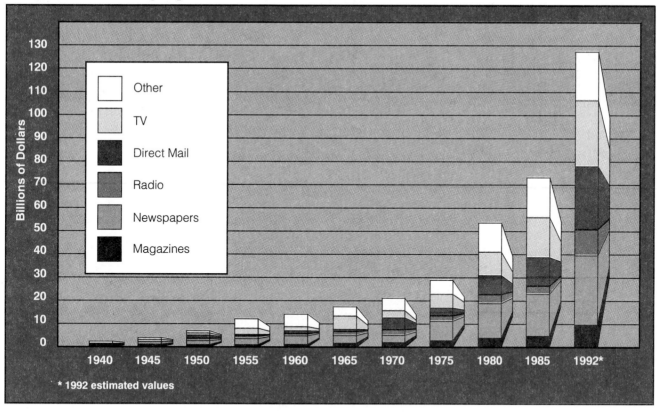

it, except, of course, to purchase nonadvertised items that are similar in quality to advertised ones and lower in price. Consumers may do this by shopping at supermarkets that sell nonnational brands of food and other products.

In all fairness, it should be pointed out that the advertising industry claims that the increased sales due to advertising can motivate some industries to use more efficient mass-production techniques, which lower per unit costs. Hence, the consumer benefits when these lower unit costs are passed on.

BRAND-NAME ADVERTISING

Many consumers look for particular brands of products to buy when they shop. Producers, therefore, often market goods or services they produce with brand names because they believe it will increase their profits. And it does, if consumers buy more of, or are willing to pay higher prices for, a brand-name product they recognize and trust. Consumers do this because they are convinced the brand-name product is superior to alternative goods or services. They may feel this way even when there is little evidence for that conviction. The most common method producers use to create brand-name recognition among consumers is advertising.

Promoting Brand-Name Loyalty

A common way to develop consumer recognition for a particular brand-name product is **persuasive advertising.** The objective of this type of advertising

Persuasive advertising
Advertising intended to associate a specific product with a certain lifestyle or image in the minds of consumers.

> Persuasive advertising provides virtually no factual information. It is intended to change consumer tastes by appealing to their psychological needs.

is to associate a specific brand of product with a certain lifestyle or image in the minds of consumers. Persuasive advertisements imply that if you use a particular brand-name product, you're "cool," or you'll look young, seductive, competent, or upwardly mobile. If you drink a particular brand of beer, gorgeous women in outrageously skimpy swimming suits will suddenly find you irresistible. Or by choosing to wear a particular brand of perfume, you will find your dull, mundane life filled with mysterious men who are helpless to resist your charms. Persuasive advertising provides virtually no factual information. It is intended to change consumer tastes by appealing to their psychological needs. Persuasive advertising is sometimes referred to as *puffery* because it often is little more than hot air.

Although brand-name recognition is fostered by advertising, a large dent has been made in consumer loyalty to specific products in recent years because of the proliferation of similar but unbranded products that are offered to consumers at substantially lower prices. Informed consumers have learned to save money by purchasing these unbranded products. To combat this trend, businesses have resorted to new techniques of advertising.

One such technique is *market segmentation*—dividing the market according to age group, lifestyle, ethnic background, and so on, and advertising accordingly. Brand-name jeans, for example, are advertised during TV programs that predictably attract teenagers and young adults who most often purchase such products. Selective audiences for advertising materials are also targeted through direct-mail lists that advertisers purchase from mail-marketing firms.

The Value of Brand Names

It is often possible to purchase products that do not have advertised brand names at lower prices than similar products that do. Why, then, do many consumers choose to buy more expensive brand-name goods and services? There are at least three reasons that can provide an answer to this question.

1. *Brand names may mean less variance in quality.* If we have learned that brand-name products generally vary less in quality than other products, then the brand name has value, for it tells us to anticipate fewer problems. This may be true, for example, with electronic equipment. You may decide to purchase, say, Sony stereo components because you have found out, or have heard from your friends, that the brand name Sony means less likelihood of breakage and repair. Therefore, if you go to a stereo shop and see two amplifiers next to each other, one by an unknown company and the other by Sony, you may be willing to pay a higher price for the nationally advertised brand item.

The same is true for other products and services. People sometimes prefer to pay slightly more for nationally advertised products because they have more confidence in them. Whether or not national brand names and quality are always related is a moot point. Advertisers have been selling brand-name reliability for years, but only recently has such reliability been questioned. Although many consumers have concluded that brand name and reliability are not associated, many others are still willing to pay more for brand-name products.

2. *Brand-name products may offer better warranties.* When something goes wrong with the national-brand product you bought, it may have a superior warranty, and the service you can get for it may be quicker and easier to obtain than service for a nonnational brand. For that reason, you may decide to pay more for the national brand.

3. *National-brand products may be repaired at a larger number of facilities*. It may be more difficult to get nonnational-brand products repaired. This is especially true for automobiles. How many gas stations can help out when a Maserati refuses to start? And even if a mechanic knows how to fix it, how quickly would he or she be able to get the parts?

Benefits of Brand Names to Producers

Brand-name loyalty is designed specifically to benefit producers. When brand-name loyalty occurs on a wide scale, producers gain **market power,** the ability to change price and/or quality without substantially losing sales. Every producer has as its goal some degree of market power. In a perfectly competitive environment, no producer has any market power; that is, each producer must take the price of its product as given in the marketplace. In a perfectly competitive world, any producer that raises its prices will lose virtually all sales. But, as was pointed out in Chapter 1, for the most part we do not live in a perfectly competitive economy. Rather, producers have various degrees of market power. Brand-name loyalty is just one attempt by those producers to obtain more market power and to make higher profits.

Market power
The ability of producers to change price and/or quality without substantially losing sales.

OTHER TYPES OF ADVERTISING

Much of the advertising we see can be placed into two broad categories, which sometimes overlap: *informative advertising* and *defensive* (or *competitive*) *advertising*.

Informative Advertising

Informative advertising is self-explanatory: It simply informs. Consumers see a tremendous amount of informative advertising: Supermarkets advertise their prices; stereo shops advertise the brands they sell and their prices; producers advertise new products that were not previously available. In other words, you, the consumer, are constantly being informed about prices, products, and availability. You can take that information for what it is worth and use it any way you want. You are not asked to believe that a product is better or worse than another one or that a company does a good or a bad job. Rather, you are simply given the relevant information about the key aspects—price and availability—of a good or service.

Informative advertising
Advertising that simply informs.

In the United States, informative advertising is particularly heavy. There are some very unusual products you would never expect to be advertised because the market is so specialized. Did you know, for example, that the producers of multimillion-dollar steam-electricity generators send salespeople around to various electric utilities to inform them about the availability and the costs of different types of steam generators? Did you know there are hundreds of specialized trade magazines that treat very narrow fields of interest and that companies in those fields subscribe to them just to find out what is happening and what products are available? There are journals published exclusively for the fields of printing, publishing, electric utilities, leatherworks, paper production, flour milling, and so on. In fact, most industries have a trade magazine or two in which very specialized informative ads can be found.

More recently, it has become possible to "rent an ad"—a videotaped, informative commercial. In the United states, more than 4,000 stores now carry such items for consumers who want specialized information about everything from hot tubs to skiing equipment to exotic vacation possibilities. These commercials are longer and more informative than 30-second or 60-second TV ads, and consumers can watch them on their VCRs at their own convenience.

As more and more traditionally unadvertised services—such as health care, accounting and legal services, and financial services—enter the promotional and marketing fields, more informative advertising about these areas will be available as well.

Comparative and Defensive Advertising

Comparative advertising
Advertising that makes comparisons between a product and specific competing products.

Until the last few years, there was very little **comparative advertising**—that is, advertising that actually named competitive brands (not merely Brand X) when comparing them with the advertised brand. Although many people had thought that such advertising was illegal, it never actually was; but in the past, radio and television stations were either reluctant to broadcast it or refused it altogether. When properly and honestly done, comparative advertising is obviously beneficial to consumers because it saves us the time of doing the comparisons ourselves. Consumers must be careful, however, because comparative advertising is bound to be selective and show only what the advertiser wants us to know.

Defensive advertising
Advertising intended to rebut claims made by competing firms about a firm's product or business practices.

Another kind of advertising is called **defensive advertising,** and, again, it is just what the name implies. Defensive advertising fosters—and is fostered by—brand-name competition. Cold remedies are a good example. Each of the large companies manufacturing these products advertises extensively, but no single company gets an edge on the others through this advertising. If any one company stopped advertising, it would lose sales, but it gains no more by advertising than it would if *no* company advertised at all. This is what defensive advertising is all about.

THE UGLY SIDE OF ADVERTISING

Advertising, particularly informative advertising, is an important source of information for consumers. But advertising has its ugly side, too. One of the major criticisms of the advertising industry from the consumer's point of view is that some ads are designed to appeal not to our reason but rather to our emotions and psychological needs—our guilts or fears or our need to be accepted socially. Obviously, sellers want us to spend our money, and they are not particularly concerned whether we spend it rationally or foolishly.

In addition to this general concern of consumers are some specific problems relating to advertising. Let's turn now to two such problems: (1) deceptive advertising; and (2) the intrusive nature of certain forms of advertising on our privacy (perceived as a problem by some consumers).

DECEPTIVE ADVERTISING

Numerous government agencies, both federal and state, are empowered to protect consumers from deceptive advertising. At the federal level, the most important agency regulating advertising is the Federal Trade Commission (FTC). Under a 1938 amendment to the 1914 Federal Trade Commission Act, the FTC is authorized to prohibit "unfair or deceptive acts or practices" in the marketplace. Under this authority, one of the important functions of the FTC is to ensure that consumers are not misled by deceptive or fraudulent advertising techniques.

What Kinds of Ads Are Deceptive?

The terms *unfair* and *deceptive* are very broad, and the FTC has a difficult task in defining exactly what types of advertising are illegal under these broad guidelines. Advertising may be deemed deceptive if it is scientifically untrue. In an early case, for example, a claim that a cosmetic cream would "rejuvenate" skin was held to be misleading because there was no scientific basis for the claim. Recently, the FTC has alleged that the makers of Campbell soups have made deceptive claims in one of their ads. The ad claimed that "most" of Campbell soups were low in fat and cholesterol and thus helpful in fighting heart disease. What the ad didn't say was that Campbell soups are high in sodium content, and high-sodium diets may increase the risk of heart disease.

An ad may also be deceptive even though it is literally true. For example, you see an ad for "Teak Dining Tables" at only $69.95 each. It sounds like an incredible bargain, so you go to the store to purchase one. You learn at the store that the tables are in fact plastic, but the manufacturer is a company called "Teak." In all likelihood, this ad would be considered deceptive because most consumers would be led to assume that the ad referred to teak wood. As a general rule, the test for whether an ad is deceptive is *if a reasonable consumer would be deceived by the ad*.

False or deceptive advertising comes in many forms. The following example of one of the many types of false advertising should give you an idea of what you have to watch out for.

Bait and Switch: The Case of the Obsolete Video Camera

Let's assume that you read in the newspaper that Joe's Electronics Emporium is having a tremendous sale on hand-held video cameras for only $449. As you walk into the store, you are greeted by a friendly salesperson named Hank. You are holding a copy of the ad and ask to see the video camera that is on sale. Hank shows you the camera, packed in a box that is yellow with age and covered with dust. The camera weighs about 12 pounds and requires a battery pack that weighs another 15 pounds or more. It appears to have

What Constitutes Bait and Switch?

How would you feel if you responded to an advertisement that promised low-interest-rate car loans and special low prices on specific automobile models only to learn that you did not qualify for the loans or that the cars were "out of stock" when you arrived at the dealership? Further, how would you react to then being pressured to buy a different, more expensive automobile with a finance plan that involved higher interest rates? Would you feel that you were being victimized by a bait-and-switch ploy? In 1991 many consumers in the area of New York City thought this was exactly what was happening when they responded to newspaper advertisements placed by Potamkin car dealerships.

New York State Attorney General Robert Abrams brought suit against the Potamkin organization (in 1991 roughly 50 dealerships were owned in the New York City area by Potamkin) on December 4, 1991, charging regular use of bait-and-switch tactics. Mr. Abrams stated his office had received 115 complaints against the dealerships from consumers between 1989 and 1991. The dealerships were accused of refusing to return customer deposits when cars were unavailable and breaking promises of low-interest-rate financing, among other things. Several customers charged they had made deposits on cars that were never delivered and later they were told they could not have their deposits refunded but could only apply them to the purchase of different automobiles from the dealerships.

Stanley S. Arkin, a lawyer who represented the Potamkin organization, charged Attorney General Abrams of using the case for political ends. He said the 115 cases represented less than .04 percent of the firm's customers in the two-year period of time. Of course, this small percentage represented only the customers who chose to complain. There may have been other dissatisfied customers who said nothing. Anyway, even if these 115 customers were the only ones hurt by the firm's advertising, would that make you feel any better if you were one of the 115? What do you believe the role of the government should be in protecting consumers from bait-and-switch tactics?

Source: Dennis Hevest. "State Sues Potamkin, Citing Tactics in Car Sales." *New York Times*, December 5, 1991, pp. B10–B11.

Bait and switch
A selling technique that involves advertising a product at a very attractive price (the "bait"); then informing the consumer, once he or she is in the store, that the advertised product either is not available, is of poor quality, or is not what the consumer "really wants"; and, finally, promoting a more expensive item (the "switch").

been manufactured at least ten years ago and is scratched and dented in several places. Hank starts by telling you that he is sure a person of your obvious intelligence and worth would not want such an inferior product and leads you on a tour of the store in which he shows you many other video cameras that list from $899 to $1,299 in price. Hank eventually convinces you to purchase a model that has a zoom lens, can be used as a VCR, and has a built-in memory to record programs off your television. When you get your camera home, you realize that you had never intended to buy such an expensive model and that you really can't afford to pay for it.

You have become the victim of a **bait-and-switch** ploy by the electronics store. The bait was the unrealistically low-priced camera. The switch was to the much higher-priced machine. The key to avoiding being tricked by this type of ploy is learning how to recognize the pattern of a bait-and-switch scheme and to walk out of a store when you think you're being duped. No one forces you to take the bait or accept the switch. You may also report stores that make these offers to your state's legal authorities, because bait-and-switch ploys are against the law. The accompanying Consumer Close-Up describes a firm that was taken to court after being accused of using bait-and-switch tactics.

Other Deceptions

The Federal Trade Commission puts bait and switch at the top of the list of common fraudulent advertising practices or deceptions. Other deceptions that often involve advertising include the following.

1. *Contest winner.* You are told you have won a contest that you didn't enter, but it turns out you must buy something to receive your prize.
2. *Free goods.* You presumably will get something free if you buy something else, but you may be paying a higher price for that "something else" than you would have otherwise. For example, in one case, a paint retailer advertised that it would sell two cans of paint for the price of one but then set a very high price for a single can of paint. This was held to be deceptive advertising.
3. *Merchandise substitution.* In place of what you thought you were buying, the seller substitutes an item of a different variety, make, model, or quality.
4. *Rebates.* A consumer will pay a lower price if he or she takes advantage of an advertised "manufacturer's rebate." Often, however, it is inconvenient for the consumer to collect the rebate because of (unadvertised) time-consuming or costly requirements.

What the FTC Can Do

The FTC receives letters and other communications complaining of violations from many sources, including competitors of alleged violators, consumers, consumer organizations, trade associations, Better Business Bureaus, government organizations, and state and local officials. If enough consumers complain and the complaints are widespread, the FTC will investigate the problem and perhaps take action.

Cease-and-Desist Orders If, after its own investigations, the FTC believes that a given advertisement is unfair or deceptive, it can conduct a hearing—which is similar to a trial—in which the company that has allegedly violated FTC rules on advertising can present its defense. If the FTC succeeds in proving that an advertisement is unfair or deceptive, it usually issues a cease-and-desist order (defined earlier in this book) requiring that the challenged advertising be stopped. A company that fails to obey such an order may be fined $10,000 for each consequent illegal advertisement.

Counteradvertising A controversial type of sanction imposed by the FTC is known as **counteradvertising** (also called *corrective advertising*). When a firm has been found liable for deceptive advertising, a counteradvertising order by the FTC requires the company to advertise anew—in print, on radio, and on television—giving information to correct the earlier misinformation. For example, Listerine advertised that its mouthwash could prevent or cure colds and sore throats. This claim was found to be unsupported, and the FTC required Listerine to state in future advertisements that its product did not prevent colds or sore throats. In another case, the makers of Profile breads advertised the weight-reducing quality of its product by stating that Profile bread had fewer calories per slice than other breads. It turned out that this was true—but only because Profile bread had thinner slices than other breads. The FTC required the corporation selling Profile bread to spend a specific amount of money to explain, via advertising, that they had indeed presented misleading

Counteradvertising
New advertising that is undertaken pursuant to a Federal Trade Commission order for the purpose of correcting earlier false claims made about a product.

information. Interestingly, although counteradvertising has been carried out for a number of years, there is little evidence that it has had a significant impact on consumer buying habits.

What You Can Do

If you feel that you have been victimized by fraudulent or deceptive advertising techniques, there are a variety of things you can do. If you have bought a product as a result of false advertising and want to get your money back, follow the procedures described in Consumer Issue B (and possibly Consumer Issue C, if you want to take the matter to a small claims court). In any case, you should let government authorities know about the problem. You can notify the FTC by writing directly to the national headquarters (6th St. and Pennsylvania Ave., N.W., Washington, DC 20580) or contacting one of its regional branches (call your nearest Federal Information Center, listed in Exhibit B–4). You may also wish to notify your state attorney general's office about your problem. In recent years, state attorneys general have been among the most aggressive forces in curbing deceptive advertising practices. Other government agencies that may help you are the Food and Drug Administration (FDA), the U.S. Postal Service, the Federal Communications Commission (FCC), and the Securities and Exchange Commission (SEC). Depending on the nature of your complaint, you may wish to contact one of these agencies.

ADVERTISING AND YOUR PRIVACY

If you don't want to hear television ads, you have several choices: You can "zap" the ad by muting the sound or turning to a different channel; you can watch noncommercial and pay TV channels; or you can simply turn off your TV. Similarly, you can turn off your radio or listen to a public broadcasting

How often has your mailbox looked like this? What benefits do consumers receive from direct mail advertising and what costs do they pay?

station if you want to avoid advertising. And you can skip over the ad sections in newspapers and magazines. But some forms of advertising are more difficult to control—namely, direct-mail advertising and telephone promotions.

As you can see in Exhibit 5–1, direct-mail marketing now accounts for a good deal of total advertising expenditures in the nation; next to newspaper and TV ads, it attracts the most dollars. It is estimated that, during 1991, roughly 40 billion pieces of this type of mail were processed by the postal system. Commercial supporters of direct mail contend that it permits more informative advertising than radio or television because written ads can deal with the subject in more detail than can those that are broadcast for 30 or 60 seconds. With the high cost of TV commercials (currently about $180,000 for a national commercial ad), it's not surprising that advertisers turn to the less expensive alternative.

Once you subscribe to any magazine or request a catalog, your name will soon be on numerous lists that are rented or exchanged for other lists. If you apply for a credit card, your name will appear on yet other lists. In a short time, your mailbox may be stuffed with unrequested information from direct-mail promoters. Even if you do none of the above, your name will still be on numerous lists that are compiled by marketing agencies from U.S. government data, such as that available from the Census Bureau.

Many consumers feel that direct-mail and telephone advertising represents an invasion of their privacy. Even those with unlisted telephone numbers cannot completely avoid the sales tactics of energetic marketers who dial every number within a certain area code.

If you want to avoid the problem of unsolicited mail or wish to have your name removed from a current mailing or telephone list, you can do the following:

1. Whenever you subscribe to a magazine or request a catalog, request in writing that your name not be rented or sold to others as part of a direct-mail list.

2. Write to any organization that uses your name and ask that it be removed from its list.

3. Fill out Form 2150 ("Notice for Prohibitory Order Against Sender of Pandering Advertisement in the Mail") at the post office; by law, any mailer listed on that form must drop your name from its mailing list. Incidentally, there is no universally accepted definition of exactly what *pandering* materials are. The dictionary defines *pander* as providing gratification for others and exploiting their weaknesses. To many, the word also has a sexual connotation, but, strictly speaking, mail that panders is not necessarily salacious.

4. Write to Consumer Services, Direct Marketing Association, Inc., 6 East 43rd St., New York, NY 10017, and request a Mail Preference Service form. After you have completed and returned it, the Direct Marketing Association will notify its member companies of your wish to be removed from all direct-mail lists. The DMA also has a telephone preference service and will remove your name from telephone soliciters' lists if you so request.

BUYING PRIVATELY PRODUCED INFORMATION

If you want to buy a product but are not quite sure which brand to purchase, you need not rely solely on manufacturers' advertisements. You can purchase

THE ETHICAL CONSUMER

Whitewashed Advertising

Imagine you are a parent (maybe you are), and that your seven-year-old child sees a billboard directly outside his schoolroom window depicting scantily clad women and strong athletic men playing on a beach while drinking a particular brand of beer. Do you believe such advertising might affect your child's values, or cause him to be more likely to drink beer now or in the future? Do you think laws should restrict where, or if, such types of advertising may be used? What would you do if the government did not take action to stop this type of advertising when you personally felt such actions were needed?

In 1990, someone in Chicago, Illinois, took matters into his own hands. This person, rumored to be a middle-aged African-American professional, spent nights painting billboards white and signing them "Mandrake." Mandrake was selective in his work. He painted over only those billboards that promoted cigarettes or liquor in inner-city neighborhoods. His message was mirrored in the actions of others in minority urban communities. Reverend Jesse Brown of Philadelphia led a protest against advertising for a new brand of cigarettes, Uptown, that was allegedly targeted by R. J. Reynolds Tobacco Co. at young urban African Americans. His efforts

were supported by Dr. Louis Sullivan, the Secretary of Health and Human Services, and Dr. Harold Freeman, the director of surgery at Harlem Hospital, who said the cigarette amounted to "corporate violence" against black youth. In this case RJR chose to withdraw Uptown cigarettes from the market, although it continues to produce and promote other brands of cigarettes in minority communities. Indeed, almost 60 percent of its advertising in these areas is spent on billboards that may be seen by young and old alike. Do you believe Mandrake's solution is ethical? What would you do to protect your children's present or future health?

brand-name product information in the form of such publications as *Consumer Reports* and *Consumers' Research Magazine*. These two important sources of consumer information were discussed in Chapter 2. Consumers Union and Consumers' Research, Inc., the respective publishers of these magazines, both report information about consumer products for the benefit of consumers.

If you decide to rely on the recommendations of these consumer groups, you have to realize that it is difficult for their researchers always to present purely objective results. This is not to say that you will get misinformation, but the researchers may sometimes emphasize certain aspects of products that are consistent with their interests and preferences but not with your own. For example, recommendations about cars may give more weight to safety, gas mileage, or comfort than you personally want to give. You may opt for a different car because you prefer styling or low cost as opposed to safety. Even though the occupants of subcompact cars face a higher probability of serious injury in an accident than do occupants of bigger cars, people continue to buy small cars because they are more economical. Obviously, you will face this problem of evaluating any information you obtain, either free or at a price.

In the last analysis, only you can make your own decisions, and they must be based in part upon your personal value judgments. If you are not a tireless shopper, you may be content simply to look at *Consumer Reports* for whatever you want to buy, pick either the "best buy" or the top of the line, call your local dealer, and have your selection delivered. You may get some products you dislike, but, on average, if your tastes correspond with those of the product testers, you will save considerable time and probably will avoid seriously defective products.

Consumer Reports publishes an annual *Buying Guide* in December; the *Consumers' Research* annual buying guide appears in October. Both contain a wealth of information on such things as food and nutrition, energy-saving ideas, and the like. Unfortunately, they both suffer from a problem that is impossible to avoid in a dynamic economy: Certain models that are listed may no longer be available by the time you decide to make a purchase.

At any one time, you can choose from at least a half-dozen other buying guides, such as the *Consumers' Handbook,* edited by Paul Fargas; *Better Times,* edited by Francis Cerra; and the Department of Agriculture's *Shoppers' Guide.* All are uneven in coverage, and none can be recommended without reservation.

There are an increasingly large number of privately produced information sources in addition to those just described. For example, *Money,* a monthly magazine published by Time-Life, is aimed at families of middle income and above. This publication emphasizes financial management—stocks, bonds, retirement, real-estate investments, and commodities. It also provides valuable information about making better consumer choices in other areas as well.

Kiplinger's Personal Finance Magazine, published monthly, provides information on such items as weight-reduction gimmicks, insurance plans, new tax rulings that might affect you, tips on how to get interest on your checking account, or warnings against long-term car loans.

Newsweek magazine carries a regular series of articles by Jane Bryant Quinn that concern various consumer issues. Similar features appear in other monthly magazines like *Time* and *U.S. News & World Report. Better Homes and Gardens, Sunset, Family Circle, Woman's Day,* and other homemaker-oriented magazines give helpful consumer information. Even less traditional publications like *Mother Earth* may be used by consumers to investigate many products offered for sale. A final source of information that should never be ignored is the first-hand experience of your friends and relatives. Knowledge of products gained through personal use may be the most valuable information a consumer can find, although it should be evaluated in light of the values and knowledge of the consumer making the recommendation.

HOW MUCH INFORMATION SHOULD WE ACQUIRE?

What we want is reliable information at the "right" price. In our daily lives, we *acquire information up to the point where the cost of acquiring any more would outweigh the benefits of that additional information.* In other words, we engage in rational decision making, which we have defined and discussed in a previous chapter. When we decide to go shopping for goods, we may look at advertisements for only a few supermarkets instead of trying to find out the price of specials at all 46 stores in the city. Why do we look at only a few? Because we have found that it does not pay to look at any more than those few pieces of information. When we go shopping for a new car, we may go to only a few dealers within the immediate area. Why go to only a few and not all? Because, again, we have found that it does not pay to go to all of them.

This is because the *time* that we spend in **comparison shopping** has a cost, too—the opportunity cost of our time, which was discussed in Chapter 1. This cost varies from consumer to consumer. Whereas one individual might be content to spend five hours comparing prices of toasters to save $5, another

Comparison shopping
Comparison shopping is acquiring and comparing information about different sellers and different products in order to find the best price for products of substantially the same quality.

person would not spend five hours in such comparison shopping even if the savings might be $50 on the item being purchased.

Indeed, some of us may not even bother to read advertisements or to seek any additional information about the goods and services we wish to purchase. Instead, we may decide to shop at a store where only the most expensive brands are carried on the assumption that high price means high quality, or because we are "status-seeking." If we shop this way, we may have decided that it is not worth our while to acquire quantities of information, and we are, therefore, essentially nonshoppers.

The most that can be said here is that you have an abundance of information available to you, both through advertising and through private consumer publications. By making use of these information sources and comparison shopping, it is possible to save many of your consumer dollars. How much you save depends on the value you place on your available time, and that's a decision that only you can make.

▶ SUMMARY

1. Advertising expenditures in the United States have climbed to more than $127 billion a year.

2. Sellers advertise for one reason only—to make more profits. Ultimately, however, it is normally the consumer who pays for advertising, because producers include the cost of advertising in the prices of their products.

3. Individuals often associate brand names with (a) less variance in quality, (b) better warranties, and (c) a larger number of repair facilities.

4. A large dent has been made in brand-name loyalty by the proliferation in recent years of similar competing products that are priced substantially lower. Brand-name producers have responded to this development by inventing effective new marketing strategies, including market segmentation and psychologically linking a brand-name product to a given image or lifestyle.

5. There are several basic types of advertising. These include informative advertising that provides specific information about products, persuasive advertising that is intended to change consumer tastes by appealing to the psychological needs, comparative advertising that makes a direct comparison between competing products, and defensive advertising that is intended to rebut claims made by competing firms in comparative advertisements.

6. Advertising has its ugly side, too. A major complaint from the consumer's point of view is that advertising appeals not to our reason but to our emotions, and may cause us to bypass the rational decision-making process.

7. Advertisers occasionally engage in unfair or deceptive advertising practices, such as bait-and-switch advertising. Generally, any ad that could mislead a reasonable consumer will be considered deceptive.

8. Both state and federal agencies are empowered to protect consumers from deceptive or fraudulent advertising practices. At the federal level, the Federal Trade Commission can issue a cease-and-desist order to prevent a company from continuing a specific ad that has been deemed deceptive. The FTC can also direct the company to correct the misinformation given to consumers by counteradvertising ("corrective" advertising).

9. Telephone sales and direct-mail advertising are considered by some consumers to be an invasion of their privacy. You can request to have your name removed from direct-mail lists and telephone lists.

10. You can obtain privately produced information about products and services by purchasing *Consumer Reports, Consumers' Research Magazine, Money, Kiplinger's Personal Finance Magazine,* and other consumer publications.

11. Comparison shopping is acquiring information about alternative sources for a particular product. Because comparison shopping requires time and perhaps other resources, there is a limit to how much you will want to do. This limit will vary with each consumer—depending on the opportunity cost of his or her time.

▶ **QUESTIONS FOR THOUGHT AND DISCUSSION**

1. Do you think it is really possible to "correct" (through counteradvertising) misinformation given in an advertisement?

2. What are some of the ways in which defensive (competitive) ads can mislead consumers?

3. What kind of an effect do ads featuring a celebrity have on you? Do they affect your view of the merits of the product?

4. To what extent do you feel advertisers have succeeded in linking products to certain lifestyles or images? Do you think that consumers have reason to be concerned about this kind of advertising technique?

5. Think of the last consumer purchase you made that cost more than $100. To what extent, if any, did the advertising affect your purchase decision?

▶ **THINGS TO DO**

1. Examine three marketing publications, such as the *Journal of Marketing,* the *Journal of Advertising Research,* and *Advertising Age.* According to the authors who write for those magazines: (1) What are the most successful techniques used by advertisers? (2) What percentage of advertising is ineffective? (3) Which medium—television, print, or radio—is likely to be most used by advertisers in the future?

2. Watch the ads in your local newspaper carefully for a week. See if you find any that are likely to mislead consumers.

3. Watch closely all TV commercials that you are exposed to during a given week. Keep a record of which ones succeeded in catching your attention and maintaining it. Then analyze the advertising technique used.

4. Compare the various informative consumer magazines, such as *Consumer Reports, Consumers' Research Magazine, Money,* and *Kiplinger's Personal Finance Magazine.* If you had a limited amount of time, which one or ones would you read most often? Why?

▶ **APPLICATION**

Investigate the quality of competing brands of a particular type of household product that you and many of your friends and relatives own. You may survey individuals about their personal experiences and look up information published in various sources identified in this chapter. Use the information you find as the basis for writing an article about this product that could appear in a weekly news magazine. Your essay should be informative, concise, helpful, and interesting to the reader.

▶ **SELECTED READINGS**

▶ *Advertising Age* (various issues).
▶ Allman, William F. "Science 1, Advertizers 0." *U.S. News & World Report,* May 1, 1989, pp. 60–61.

▶ Altheide, David L. *Media Power*. Beverly Hills: Sage, 1985.

▶ *The Book of Inside Information*. New York: Boardroom Books, 1987.

▶ *Consumer Reports* (various issues, "The Docket" section).

▶ Edel, Richard. "American Dream Vendors." *Advertising Age,* November 9, 1988, pp. 152–156.

▶ Galbraith, John Kenneth. "Economics and Advertising: Exercise in Denial." *Advertising Age,* November 9, 1988, pp. 80–87.

▶ Giltenan, Edward F. "The Sheer Catalogs." *Forbes,* October 17, 1988, p. 164.

▶ Kolenda, K. "Honesty in Advertising." *The Humanist,* November–December 1991, pp. 37–38.

▶ Lesco, Matthew, ed. *Information USA*. New York: Penguin, 1986.

▶ Lipman, Joanne. "Television Ads Ring Up No Sale in Study." *The Wall Street Journal,* February 15, 1989, p. B6.

▶ Loeb, Marshall. *Marshall Loeb's 1992 Money Guide*. Boston: Little, Brown, 1992.

▶ Packard, Vance. *The Hidden Persuaders*. New York: McKay, 1957.

▶ Samuelson, R. J. "The End of Advertising?" *Newsweek,* August 19, 1991, p. 40.

▶ *Shopping by Phone and Mail*. Available free from the Federal Trade Commission, 6th St. and Pennsylvania Ave., N.W., Washington, DC 20580.

▶ *What's Going On at the FTC?* Available free from the Federal Trade Commission, 6th St. and Pennsylvania Ave., N.W., Washington, DC 20580.

▶ *The World in Your Mailbox*. Available free from the Consumer Services Department, Direct Marketing Association, 6 East 43rd St., New York, NY 10017.

Children's Advertising

GLOSSARY

BRAND LOYALTY A willingness by consumers to purchase a particular brand of product without seriously considering alternative brands.
DISCRETIONARY SPENDING Spending for goods and services that are not necessities.

Studies show that the role children play in consumer decision making in our economy is rapidly expanding. A 1990 estimate put the **discretionary spending** (spending for products that are not necessities) of the 37 million children from ages 4 through 12 at $9 billion a year. Another $30 billion was spent by adults for *nondurable* (defined as having an expected useful life of less than one year) toys that were given to children. Bicycles, sporting equipment, and electronic games added another $50 billion. When the costs of children's furniture, clothing, toiletries, and special food products are added in, total spending for children's products reached well over $350 billion dollars in 1990 and was growing at a rate of roughly 8% a year.

It is hard to say exactly why spending on products intended for children is growing so rapidly. Take-home pay for many consumers actually fell in the recession of 1990–1991. It has been suggested that part of the explanation may be that parents are trying to make up for time they can't spend with their children while they are working or looking for a job. Another possible reason is the growth in advertising that is directed toward children.

Although most purchase decisions for children's products are made by adults, children almost always influence these choices. How often have you heard children demand particular brands of breakfast cereal or soft drinks in a grocery store? How often do their parents give in to these demands? The impact of children on consumer spending far exceeds the few billion dollars they spend themselves.

The fact that children are an important force in our economy has not been lost on businesses that manufacture and market products. In 1990 expenditures for advertising directed to children exceeded a total of $450 million. These advertisements presented American consumers with important economic and ethical choices to make.

▶ WHY BUSINESSES ADVERTISE TO CHILDREN

The most apparent reason for directing advertising to children is the influence they have over their parents' spending. For example, the average American consumed 11.4 pounds of ready-to-eat breakfast cereal in 1991. By assuming that each child from 4 to 12 years old ate this average amount of cereal we can estimate that these 37 million children consumed over 400 million pounds of cereal. The market value of this cereal alone was close to $1 billion. It is not surprising that cereal producers direct much of their advertising to children.

Other businesses direct advertising to children in an attempt to establish **brand loyalty** that they hope will last as the children mature. Their reasoning is that children who become accustomed to drinking a particular type of soda, or to wearing a special brand of shoes when they are young, will continue to purchase and use these products as adults. This is probably one reason why such a large portion of McDonald's advertising is directed toward young people. Ronald McDonald may appeal only to children, but people who become used to eating McDonald's food as children are likely to continue to purchase these products as adults.

There are even some firms that sell no products intended for use by children but still buy advertising directed to children. This may seem to be a contradiction, but marketing experts believe it will pay off in the long run. Delta Air Lines, for example, has purchased advertising that is oriented to children's interests even though few children will purchase airline tickets until they are adults. The firm hopes to create an awareness of its business and products in children that will cause them to fly Delta when they are adults. Hyatt Hotels also advertise to children, apparently for the same reason. Both IBM and Apple Computers have provided free equipment to schools and directed advertising to children. Although few children are in a position to purchase the computers IBM and Apple manufacture, children often influence their parent's spending decisions and may develop a lasting desire to use these brands of computers when they become adults.

▶ SELLING CHILDREN ADULT PRODUCTS

The most rapid growth in children's advertising in the late 1980s and early 1990s was for children's versions of products that are most often consumed by adults. For example, Gregory's "boy's cologne" was marketed for $15.50 an ounce using an advertisement that showed a four-year-old splashing the product on his neck. Other brands of children's toiletries that have been marketed include "Radical Hair Stuff" (for $3.50), "Environmental Protection Cream" (for $16.50), and "Fun and Fresh" deodorant (for $2.50). There is doubt that children need any of these products.

Marketing some types of clothing products to children is an area of concern. Many people question the wisdom of buying a camisole marketed in 1990 by Christian Dior that looked strangely like a bra for four-year-olds. Land's End has advertised children's button-down Oxford shirts that look like "Dad's dress shirts." Talbot's Kids has advertised children's Ralph Lauren designer down-filled expedition jackets for $300.

Another class of goods frequently promoted to children is electronic products. Sanyo markets a child-sized "mini-vac" so kids can "clean up your mess by yourself." The Little Operator Easy Dialer Picture Phone sells for $50 and may be programmed to dial numbers by pushing the picture of a person children want to call. This product allows even two- or three-year-olds to use a telephone. Digital watches and hand-held electronic games add to the list of products children are encouraged to demand.

Advertisements often encourage children to demand products that are unnecessary or too expensive for their family's budgets. This raises an ethical question for society: Since children lack the knowledge and critical thinking skills to analyze advertisements and make rational consumer choices, should limitations be placed on the content or form of advertising that is directed toward them?

▶ INCREASED PRESSURE AND ADULT RESPONSIBILITIES

Many adults have expressed resentment to marketers and the government for the impact children's advertising has had on their lives. The more products that are advertised to children, the more often the parents are forced to say "no." Many adults believe that children's advertising encourages children to grow up too rapidly, to become materialistic, and to develop lifestyles and relationships better suited to adults. These are some of the reasons why some parents have pressured the government to limit the advertising that may be directed to children or placed on television shows primarily watched by young people.

Other people support children's advertising by saying it provides parents an opportunity to teach their children values and how to use buying strategies. Some people have gone so far as to suggest that parents should provide children with control over a share of their family's food or clothing budget so they may learn how to be responsible consumers. Although there is a value to teaching children good spending habits, many people believe these ideas are little more than rationalization by advertisers to justify their current practices.

In 1991 the typical American child watched 26 hours of TV programming a week. During this time that child was exposed to an average of 520 commercials, or a total of 4 hours and 20 minutes of advertising. This amount of advertising certainly affected the desires and judgment of many children. It probably made them want more products, and many of the products they were encouraged to want probably did not represent a good use for their family's limited incomes.

Parents faced with their children's demands for more, and often expensive, products of questionable value are left with essentially three choices. They may choose to give in and buy as many of the products as they can afford. They may simply ignore their children's demands and spend their money as they see fit. Or they can take the time to explain to their children why certain products are not the best ways to spend the family income. Obviously, the last alternative involves the most time and effort.

Even young children can be taught to distinguish between reality and advertising hype. When questioned, a three-year-old will usually be able to explain that the plastic model that flies unaided through the air to destroy the invading slime people in a TV advertisement will need to be held in their hands when they use it at home. Children can be taught that terms like "each part sold separately," "some assembly required," or "batteries not included," mean that what they see is not what they get. Sometimes it is worthwhile to show children how much of their favorite type of food could be purchased with the price of a single toy that they will use for a day and then discard. Many children can understand simple cost-benefit problems.

Consumers Union has produced a videotape called "Buy Me That: A Kid's Survival Guide to TV Advertising" that may be borrowed from many libraries. This entertaining tape shows how TV commercials use double meanings and special photography to mislead young consumers. *Zillions* is a worthwhile consumer magazine for children that is also published by the Consumers Union. At $14 a year it is not cheap, but if it saves a child from making one bad purchase a year it may pay for itself. A final strategy parents can use to help their children make better consumer decisions is to require them to give three logical reasons for buying a product they want. Statements like "I want it" would not be acceptable; the child would have to explain the product's value.

▶ GOVERNMENT INTERVENTION

Although federal government regulations do not satisfy many critics, steps have been taken to put some limitations on the amount of advertising directed to children. Congress passed a law in 1990 that directed the Federal Communications Commission (FCC) to draw up regulations for this type of advertising. In 1991, to comply with this law, the FCC announced that TV programming directed to children could contain no more than 12 minutes of advertising per hour on weekdays, and 10½ minutes on weekends. In addition, TV stations were required to summarize the advertising they aired directed to children in the applications for license renewals. At this time, members of the community served by the TV stations would have the right to make complaints. Although this law limited the amount of advertising that could be directed to children, it did nothing to control advertising content or the type of products that could be promoted.

Many people feel the time limits established under this law are inadequate. Other regulations that have

been suggested but not implemented include eliminating advertisements for food products that contain large amounts of sugar or fats. Many people would stop programming that features commercial products based on characters like GI Joe and Teenage Mutant Ninja Turtles. There is even pressure from some organizations to adopt a policy similar to that of the French government which outlaws the use of children in any television advertising. It is likely, however, that for the foreseeable future, American children and their parents will be subjected to a continuing barrage of advertising that they will need to evaluate for themselves.

▶ SUMMARY

1. Children are playing a growing role in consumer decisions. Spending on products intended for children's use exceeded $350 billion in 1991 and was rapidly growing. Part of this growth may have been the result of advertising directed toward children.

2. Although the amounts of money children spend themselves are not enormous, many advertisements are directed toward children because they often influence their parents' spending. Businesses also direct advertising toward children to try to establish product and brand loyalty that they hope will be carried over into adulthood.

3. Many advertisements are apparently intended to encourage children to demand products that are better suited to adult use—such as deodorant. Some people believe these advertisements encourage children to grow up too rapidly.

4. Advertising heightens the need of teaching children to make responsible consumer decisions. Some peo-

ple have suggested that the best way to deal with the need is to allow children to have a meaningful voice in how their family's spending decisions are made.

5. There are published materials that can help children make responsible consumer decisions, including *Zillions,* published by the Consumers Union.

6. Federal regulation of advertising has essentially been limited to setting maximum amounts of advertising that may be aired per hour on TV programming directed to children. Many people feel the government should take a more active role in controlling the content and techniques used in children's advertising.

▶ QUESTIONS FOR THOUGHT AND DISCUSSION

1. Although TV may provide the most obvious examples of advertising that is directed toward children, it is not the only type. What are three other ways businesses attempt to influence the type of products children demand? Which of these do you believe is most significant? Explain the reasons for your answer.

2. Do you believe changes have taken place in American society in recent years that have made children and their parents more vulnerable to advertising? Provide a logical explanation to support your answer.

3. What do you believe the government's role should be in limiting advertising directed toward children? Explain the reasons for your answer.

▶ THINGS TO DO

1. Watch Saturday morning children's TV programming for one hour. Keep a list of the products advertised and write a brief description of each advertisement. Identify the one you believe is most helpful and

the one you find most misleading. Explain the reasons for your choices.

2. Business owners also have rights in a competitive market economy. Write an essay that evaluates the idea of limiting advertising rights as you believe it would be written by the owners of a major toy manufacturer.

3. Interview three or more children about their reactions to advertisements they see on TV. Write an essay that summarizes what they say and explains why their statements tend either to support or to contradict the idea that we need more government regulation of advertisements directed toward children.

The Many Faces of Fraud

PREVIEW

▶ How can you avoid being victimized by deceptive practices of sellers?

▶ How are fraudulent claims sometimes used to sell personal-care products?

▶ How can you protect yourself from door-to-door salespersons, telemarketing ploys, or direct-mail frauds?

▶ What can you do to avoid being defrauded by repair services?

▶ What are some common financial-services frauds?

The formal, legal definition of fraud is

> Making a false statement of a past or existing fact with knowledge of its falsity, or with reckless indifference as to its truth, with the intent to cause someone to rely upon such a statement and therefore give up property or a right that has value.

Quite a mouthful, isn't it? The essence of this legal definition is that fraud occurs when an individual or company knowingly misrepresents or fails to reveal an important fact to the consumer, with the ultimate result that the consumer is somehow cheated. In our judicial system, fraud is limited to deliberate deceit. In other words, it must be proved that the seller intended deceit, not just that the customer was deceived. Such proof is often difficult to obtain. Consequently, the best consumer protection is to be aware of and on guard against the numerous fraudulent schemes that some sellers in the marketplace have devised.

Many businesspeople contend that fraud must be short-lived, since businesses rely on repeat customers (continuous dealing) to stay in business. The reasoning goes that the use of fraud will therefore eventually cause a business to lose money. In our complex and multidimensional economy, however, information is not always reliable or easily available. Furthermore, the population being serviced is huge, and this increases the possibility of sellers using unscrupulous marketing techniques on many different people throughout the country. In other words, many businesses can survive without repeat customers. This is particularly true in the sale of products through the mails or over the phone.

Deceptive or fraudulent advertising was discussed in the previous chapter. Here we look at additional fraudulent or semifraudulent sales schemes.

PERSONAL-CARE AND HEALTH-CARE FRAUD

Many consumers are dissatisfied with their appearance, concerned about their health, or disappointed in their physical condition. Such people are often vulnerable to offers promising a way to become the healthy, robust, energetic person they would like to be.

Heading the list of fraudulent practices in the area of health care is the marketing of food products and "nutritives" that claim to cure various physical ailments. Legally, any product making such health claims falls into the "drug" category and therefore under the jurisdiction of the Food and Drug Administration (FDA). To avoid FDA drug-testing and labeling requirements, however, manufacturers of many of these products market them as "food," with instructions on the labels to "take one or two a day as a dietary supplement." No curative claims are included on the container label itself; instead, they accompany the product on flyers or other literature given to the retail dealer (often a health-food store). Many shrewd entrepreneurs, seeing fertile ground for a fast dollar, have become millionaires in this industry at the consumer's expense (and sometimes to the detriment of his or her health). Firms that produce goods labeled as food products are required to meet sanitary standards but face fewer types of regulation than firms that produce drugs. Some producers of food products—but, unfortunately, only some—have been served with injunctions and had their products seized by the FDA.

Surgeon General C. Everett Koop reported in 1989 that food quackery costs the American public at least $10 billion a year. Frequently, the victims of this kind of fraud are elderly people who are afflicted with health problems. More than 30 million Americans, many of them elderly, suffer from arthritis, for example, and they spend at least $2 billion a year on ineffective "miracle cures" containing anything from snake venom to lemon juice for this malady.

Sometimes American consumers risk their health and even their lives by using unproven and often dangerous remedies. Examples of these products include compounds claimed to cure cancer that are derived from apricot pits, treatments purported to cure AIDS that are made from the bark of Brazilian trees, and treatment for sexual impotence made from body parts of crocodiles.

False remedies pose at least two problems: First, they may do harm. Many have produced side effects that include kidney failure, bone-marrow depression, and convulsions. Second, their existence may encourage consumers to neglect proven medical treatments. The FDA published the following list of the ten most common health frauds in 1990.

Sometimes American consumers risk their health and even their lives by using unproven and often dangerous remedies.

1. Fraudulent arthritis products
2. Spurious cancer clinics
3. Bogus AIDS cures
4. Instant weight-loss schemes
5. Fraudulent sexual aids
6. Quack baldness remedies and appearance modifiers
7. False nutritional schemes
8. Chelation therapy (supposed to remove fat deposits in arteries)
9. Unproven use of muscle stimulators (supposed to reduce skin wrinkles)
10. Candidiasis hypersensitivity (supposed to kill body fungus)

Weight Reduction

Consumers spend millions of dollars each year on miracle weight-reduction products—pills or potions that "melt away fat even while you sleep," or that promise other impossible results. Many of these products achieve temporary weight reduction through water loss (dehydration). At the present, the only effective drugs for appetite suppression are those sold by prescription only. Doctors are recommending these drugs (usually amphetamines) less often because of their possible effects on the heart and central nervous system and their addictive properties.

Most over-the-counter dietary weight-loss products exploit wishful thinking. Every year new products are introduced that promise weight loss with little effort or appetite restraint. Many of these products are marketed in misleading ways. In October of 1991, for example, the FTC warned three liquid-diet programs to revise their advertising claims to eliminate promises of "rapid and permanent weight loss" and guarantees of "no serious health risks" to users. The programs, Optefast Diet Program, National Centers for Nutrition, and Medifast 70, agreed to follow the FTC's ruling and avoided fines that could have reached amounts in the millions of dollars.

Unless a person has a true physiological imbalance, the problem of being overweight can only be "cured" by burning more calories per day than are consumed. To lose one pound of weight, a body must burn 3,500 calories in excess of those consumed. For most consumers this simple fact points to the only realistic path to weight reduction: eating less and/or exercising more. The subject of weight control and low-calorie diets is explored further in Consumer Issue I.

The High Price of Beauty

All people want to look attractive. Consequently, Americans are willing to spend hundreds of millions of dollars a year on cosmetic products, many of which do little, if anything, to enhance physical attractiveness. Cosmetics fall under the jurisdiction of the FDA, but—unlike drugs—cosmetics do not have to be proved to be safe and effective, just safe. If the label on a cosmetic product reads "anti-aging," who can tell if it's mislabeled? Such a description is so ambiguous and difficult to measure that legally it is not considered fraudulent labeling. As a result, creams and lotions that boast of a "new discovery" among their ingredients that will "reduce wrinkling" are freely marketed, often at exorbitant prices.

Health-Insurance Scams

In 1992 *U.S. News & World Report* placed the cost of health-care fraud in the United States between $50 billion and $80 billion a year. Patients who are involved when fraudulent claims are made are often poor or elderly and unaware of their rights or of the cost of medical fraud to the government and private insurance companies. The increased use of electronic billing and record keeping has made it easier to commit medical fraud because fewer people check claims.

The perpetrators of health-insurance fraud are doctors and dentists who inflate their bills to insurance companies for services they have performed for patients, who file claims for services or tests that were never performed at all or that were unnecessary. Sometimes this type of fraud takes place with the patient's knowledge and permission in return for not having to pay for any part of the bill that the insurance company won't cover.

Who is the victim here? At the first stage, the insurance company is the victim, forced to pay out a higher dollar amount in claims. But the ultimate victim is the consumer, who has to pay a higher insurance premium to cover the insurance company's added expenses.

CONSUMER GOODS FRAUD

The increasing range and complexity of consumer goods we buy has contributed to the opportunities for dishonest individuals to take advantage of people by offering products or services for sale that are not what they appear to be.

Many such fraudulent practices occur in door-to-door sales. Encyclopedias, home-improvement services, solar-heating equipment, screening or storm windows, and even Bibles have been pushed by quoting phony list prices of competitive products (to make the seller's price seem reasonable) and asking people to sign "questionnaires" that really are installment credit contracts. So many techniques have been used that it is impossible in this book to go into detail about how dishonest door-to-door salespeople ply their trade.

Being an Assertive Consumer

Assertive consumers rarely fall prey to bait-and-switch techniques or the high-pressure pitches of door-to-door salespeople. Being assertive, of course, does not mean being rude. If you don't want to deal with a door-to-door salesperson simply ask the person, courteously, to leave. Salespeople are human, too, so remember your manners, as well as your rights. If the salesperson fails to

Suppose you were in your mid-fifties and received a call from a medical-care organization that promised to provide a complete physical examination at absolutely no charge to you. Would you be interested? This offer certainly interested Dr. William Marr when he received it in 1987. At that time, Dr. Marr worked for the Pacific Mutual Insurance Company and was involved in investigating health-care fraud.

The offer to Dr. Marr was made by a business operated by David and Michael Smushkevich. When Dr. Marr reported for his examination, he was asked to complete a personal health history that in-cluded no space for information about any current health problems. Indeed, Dr. Marr was in excellent health. As a result of his examination, however, his insurance company was billed for more than $7,500 for medical services suppos-edly provided by the Smushkevich brothers. Included with the bills was a list of ailments Dr. Marr did not suffer from, but which they claimed they treated him for, that included high blood pressure, diabetes, heart disease, and cancer.

Eight months of investigations followed, resulting in police raids on the offices of the Smushkevich organization. Data gathered by prosecutors asserted that more than $50 million was collected from private insurance companies and from government Medicare or Medicaid programs through fraudulent claims. Most of the firm's patients did not complain about billings because any amounts they would normally have been responsible for were waived by the Smushkevich organization.

In what ways do we all pay for health-care fraud? Would you turn in your doctor if you believed he or she was cheating on health-care bills?

Source: Gordon Witkin, "Health Care Fraud," *U.S. News & World Report*, February 24, 1992, pp. 34–43.

respond courteously and persists in pushing for a sale, you can always call the police.

Sometimes, of course, door-to-door salespeople may provide you with a product or service that is both useful and a bargain. In fact, certain products are most often sold door-to-door and may be difficult to obtain in other ways. Examples include specific brands of household cleaning aids, and certain cosmetics and toiletries, such as Amway and Avon products. These products are not sold in retail outlets. Because of the increasing costs of direct sales and growth in the number of people who work outside their homes (so there is often no one home to sell to) Avon Products, among others, now supplements its traditional door-to-door marketing with direct-mail brochures and catalogs. In these cases, you obviously are not dealing with someone trying to sign you to a 36-month installment contract for a set of 58 books at a total price of $1,150. Much smaller amounts of money are involved, and these companies have been in business for many years and have established a reputation for quality and reliability. Buying their products involves no more risk than making purchases of competing items at local retail stores.

Although there is now less door-to-door selling than in the past, there is a significant amount of consumer-solicited in-the-home sales. For example, many insurance salespeople, home decorators, and landscaping services ask consumers to invite them to their homes for a sales presentation. These are established firms that are responding to legitimate consumer interest and therefore are less likely to engage in fraudulent practices.

Cooling-off Periods

Cooling-off period
A specific amount of time in which a consumer has the right to reconsider and back out of a transaction.

Several states now have a *cooling-off law* that applies to many, if not all, installment contracts. For example, Ohio has a three-business-day **cooling-off period.** If a door-to-door salesperson gets a resident of Ohio to sign a contract to purchase a set of encyclopedias, to be paid for over a 36-month period, he or she has the legal right to back out of that contract within the next three business days. Thus, consumers have three days to reconsider their commitment and also to acquire information about alternative means of purchasing the product in question.

The Federal Trade Commission adopted a cooling-off provision for some types of contracts in 1973. This law makes it a violation for door-to-door sellers to fail to tell consumers that they have three business days to cancel any sale that uses their home as collateral for a credit agreement. The law does not interfere with previously mentioned state statutes. Consumers, therefore, benefit from the most favorable law, either the FTC rule or their own state statute. Additionally, the FTC rule requires that written notification of the cooling-off period be given in Spanish if the oral negotiation is in that language. Exhibit 6–1 is a typical "Notice of Cancellation" that should be available from any door-to-door salesperson.

▶ **Exhibit 6–1   Typical Notice of Cancellation for Door-to-Door Solicitation Sales**

(enter date of transaction)

_____
(date)

You may cancel this transaction, without any penalty or obligation, within 3 business days from the above date.

If you cancel, any property traded in, any payments made by you under the contract or sale, and any negotiable instrument executed by you will be returned within 10 business days following receipt by the seller of your cancellation notice, and any security interest arising out of the transaction will be cancelled.

If you cancel, you must make available to the seller at your residence, in substantially as good condition as when received, any goods delivered to you under this contract or sale; or you may, if you wish, comply with the instructions of the seller regarding the return shipment of the goods at the seller's expense and risk.

If you do make the goods available to the seller and the seller does not pick them up within 40 days of the date of your notice of cancellation, you may retain or dispose of the goods without any further obligation. If you fail to make the goods available to the seller, or if you agree to return the goods to the seller and fail to do so, then you remain liable for performance of all obligations under the contract.

To cancel this transaction, mail or deliver a signed and dated copy of this cancellation notice or any other written notice, or send a telegram to

_____
(name of seller)

at _____ not later than midnight of _____
(address of seller's place of business)   (date)

I hereby cancel this transaction.

_____   _____
(date)   (buyer's signature)

Telemarketing and Mail-Order Madness

Come-ons advertised by telephone and direct-mail, or placed in printed advertisements in magazines and newspapers, constitute a significant percentage of all advertising dollars. Certainly, ordering products by telephone or by mail has simplified life for many consumers by saving them hours spent shopping in malls or department stores. Mail-order shopping, however, can involve significant risks. Telemarketers and direct-mail advertisers are notorious perpetrators of fraud. They head the list of consumer complaints registered by the Council of Better Business Bureaus (see Exhibit 6–2). Here is just a partial list of telemarketing and mail-order scams to which you might be (or perhaps already have been) exposed:

1. Home-improvement schemes (read the fine print carefully).
2. Get-rich-quick investments (request written information).
3. Charitable causes (check them out with the Better Business Bureau).
4. Fake contests (if you have to buy something to "win" a prize, it's illegal).
5. Official-looking envelopes (letters sent in envelopes that look official, like they came from the IRS or Social Security Administration, for example).
6. Chain-letter schemes (don't even think about it).

Consider a telemarketing scheme that's becoming increasingly popular among (and profitable for) scam artists—a vacation club or travel certificate that sounds like a dream but in fact is a nightmare. A common variety of this scheme goes as follows: You get a postcard in the mail announcing that you have been chosen to receive a luxury vacation. For details about your "free" trip, all you have to do is call a certain telephone number, usually toll-free. When you call, you are told that you must join a travel club to be eligible for the trip (sometimes, a credit card number is also requested for billing purposes). After you pay the membership fee, you are sent a vacation package with further instructions. First, you must submit the reservation request form (and send the accompanying fee). Then, you will be introduced to still further hard-to-meet conditions or fees that must be complied with or paid before your reservations will be confirmed. At some point, you may decide to unpack your dreams and take a loss; or continue the process and take a very expensive vacation; or continue the process and take no vacation at all, because the "Travel Club" doesn't really exist.

Federal Trade Commission Rules

The Federal Trade Commission has established the following rules to protect you when you shop by mail:

1. If a catalog or ad indicates that the goods will be sent within a certain period, such as a week, they must be sent within that time. When no date is mentioned, the items must be shipped within 30 days.
2. If the item can't be shipped within the specified time or within 30 days, you must be notified and be given a free means of stating what you want to do about the delay; the supplier must provide a toll-free telephone number or a postage-paid postcard.
3. You can cancel an order or agree to the new shipment date. If you cancel, you must receive your refund within 7 business days. If you fail to reply, and if the delay will be less than 30 days, the company can assume that you agree to the delay. For any delays over 30 days, your money must be refunded if you have not given your consent to the delay.

▶ **Exhibit 6–2 Top Ten Categories of Consumer Complaints**

1. Ordered product sales by telephone or mail
2. Retail sales
3. Service firms (except auto)
4. Home-improvement remodeling companies
5. Auto repair and services
6. Auto/truck dealers
7. Financial services
8. Vacation-certificate companies
9. Health/medical services
10. Travel-related services

SOURCE: Council of Better Business Bureaus, 1989.

The preceding rules do not apply to magazine subscriptions, photofinishing services, plants and seeds, COD orders, and credit orders that aren't charged until the goods are shipped.

Hints to Catalog Shoppers

Following are some guidelines for shopping by mail.

1. Keep a record of your order by writing the company's name and address on your check stub or record.
2. Do not send cash; use only checks, money orders, or credit cards.
3. Keep a copy of the catalog pictures of the items you selected.
4. Mark on your calendar the date you mailed the order and the date you expect it to arrive.
5. Print your full name and address on the order form.
6. Send your order in immediately, or order it by phone if there is a toll-free number to call. This will reduce the chance of the item you want being out of stock when your order is received.
7. Whenever you suspect fraud, contact your nearest postal inspector.

Automobile Sales

Automobile sales personnel have dubious reputations, which may or may not be justified in individual cases. Nonetheless, it pays to be aware of three common techniques used to sell cars—and to extract more money from the gullible customer.

High-balling
When an artificially high value offered for a product that is traded in is made up for by inflating the price of the new product.

High-Balling The salesperson offers you an unreasonably high trade-in value on your car, far more than competitive dealers are willing to pay. The wily practitioner of such **high-balling** hopes the unwary consumer will think he or she is getting a bargain, but actually the additional price the consumer

It is relatively easy for a dealer to make a new car look attractive. What factors other than appearance should a consumer consider before choosing to purchase any vehicle?

receives for the trade-in will be included elsewhere in the price of the new car. To avoid being high-balled, assume that you can get only the wholesale or "blue book" value of your car as a trade-in, even if it is in good condition.

Low-Balling   Over the phone, you are told that a particular car can be sold to you at a very low price; that is, you are given a **low-ball** estimate. When you come to the dealer's showroom, however, the salesperson tells you that he or she made a mistake and that the car actually will cost you a few hundred dollars more. Or the salesperson will *pack* the transaction by adding on a number of unreasonable extra charges to make up the difference so that he or she obtains the normal profit of the sale.

Low-balling
Offering to sell a product at a low price in a telephone conversation and then increasing the price when the consumer visits the firm to purchase the product.

Bushing   In **bushing,** the salesperson adds on unordered accessories. When you go to pick up your car, you find that it is costing you more than you bargained for because of these accessories, which the salesperson simply claims he or she thought you wanted.

Bushing
Adding unordered accessories to a product to increase its price.

Guidelines for Automobile Purchases   Once you reach an agreement with the salesperson, make sure that the exact car and optional equipment that you've selected are listed plainly on the order. Make sure, too, that the order is countersigned by someone in authority, such as the sales manager of the dealership. At minimum, the following four assurances should be listed on the order.

1. There will be no increase in price; the price shown at the bottom of the order is the total price to be paid on delivery.
2. There will be no reappraisal of your trade-in.
3. There will be no substitutions of nonfactory equipment for anything that you ordered on the car.
4. The car will be delivered within a reasonably specific time period.

Finally, don't fall for the "switch" that a salesperson might try to pull. For example, a few days after you place your order, a salesperson might call and tell you that the factory has a backlog of orders and that it will take longer than anticipated to get your car. The salesperson then might say that the identical car has been located at another wholesale source—but with a few unordered options for about $500 more.

Automobile Repair Services

Some unscrupulous mechanics try to gyp customers who bring their cars in for normal services like oil changes or tire rotation. They say they just "happened to notice" that the car is in need of a certain expensive repair. The ball joints in the front suspension are often said to need replacement. An unscrupulous mechanic may put your car on a hoist, turn the wheels to the side, and wiggle them to make it appear that the ball joint is about to jump from the socket. True, these and other parts do wear out, but ball joints are fairly sturdy, and some movement is acceptable. Before you have any expensive repair completed, get the opinion of another mechanic; you may not need to have the work done at all.

Because fraudulent auto repairs rank high on the list of consumer complaints, that problem is the subject of Consumer Issue E.

TV Repair Services

Since most consumers know little, if anything, about the inner working of a television set, dishonest repair personnel can easily take advantage of such ignorance. They may use the low-ball technique to get their "foot in the door," advertising a relatively low price for a complete TV overhaul and then, once in the customer's house, claiming that major repairs are necessary. A good rule of thumb is to avoid patronizing shops that advertise ridiculously low prices. A good TV technician earns well over $30 an hour, and you can't expect a decent job for less than that.

One method retail establishments often promote as a way to avoid costly TV repairs is to purchase a *service contract* for the product. Although there may be value to such agreements, most consumer groups recommend against making such purchases because they most often cost far more than they are worth. Today most TV sets, and other types of electronic equipment, have fewer problems than did earlier models. Your set probably uses solid-state technology, so when something goes wrong, a simple exchange of a circuit board may be all that is necessary. Given the relatively low price of modern TV sets, it is often better to buy a new one when a major repair is actually needed.

Buying Education

Most of us want to improve our position in life. That's why billions of dollars are spent for home-study education programs each year in this country. Although most of these programs are legitimate, offered by accredited schools and have realistic requirements, some teach very little and promise the impossible. Their advertisements may appear to guarantee that anyone passing their home-study course will find a high-paying job in a specific industry. Even though the Federal Trade Commission prohibits false representation of job-placement abilities, many of these scams succeed.

If you are seriously considering investing in a home-study program, investigate those offered by a major college or university in your area. If you are convinced that a for-profit institution offers a better home-study course, check out exactly what you will be getting for your money. Get names of graduates and talk to them to find out if the job-placement claims of the home-study institution are valid.

Financia Services Fraud

Many people would like to find a way to earn money with little effort. People who believe this is possible may be easy marks for people who offer dishonest, get-rich-quick schemes.

One scam, which seems to come in cycles, rather like locusts, is the **pyramid scheme.** Often pyramid schemes use multilevel marketing endeavors. For example, Glenn W. Turner had a firm called "Dare to Be Great" that sold motivational self-improvement materials. When a person sold one of Turner's courses, she kept some of the money and forwarded the rest up the pyramid, with each person at a higher level taking a cut. The seller would, in turn, work her way up the pyramid by recruiting others into the scheme; they would purchase the materials through her, and the recruiter would also take a cut when new people sold the materials. Money went to the top of the pyramid, where people no longer had to recruit or to sell the courses through their own efforts. They only needed to sit back and collect income generated from other people's efforts.

Pyramid scheme
An illegal sales plan through which people collect fees and a share of income earned from sales made by other individuals they recruit into the program.

When people get in at the beginning of a pyramid scheme they can make lots of money, as Turner did—he earned millions of dollars before he was tried and convicted for his activities. But the majority of people involved in pyramids don't make much at all. In fact, the average individual who participates in such schemes makes nothing at all. The problem with the pyramid schemes is that the only way they can work is for people to find others who are willing to participate in the effort. Pyramid schemes capitalize on the "greater-fool theory": that is there is always a greater fool than you out there to help you get richer.

> Many prospective real estate investors have, at one time or another, fallen victim to land scams.

Interstate Land Sales

Most of us would like to own a "piece of the country." Some people dream about having a second home. Others consider land one of the best investments available. Unfortunately, many prospective real estate investors have, at one time or another, fallen victim to land scams.

Land scams used to be fairly easy to carry out. A canny buyer would purchase, say, 10,000 acres of low-valued land in the middle of nowhere. The land might be partially under water, as in the Florida Everglades, or in a totally arid region of Arizona or New Mexico. The owner might develop a small section of the 10,000 acres and take photographs to show its apparent beauty. Those publicity pictures would form the basis of an advertising campaign with an alluring name, such as The Hills of Monte Cristo, or Terra Bella Villages, and the land would be sold at five, ten, or even a hundred times its actual cost. All sales would be transacted over the phone and through the mails. Only when the unsuspecting buyer actually visited the location or attempted to resell the land would he or she discover the fraud.

In 1968 Congress passed the Interstate Land Sales Act, which went into effect in 1969. This act requires anyone engaged in the interstate selling or leasing of land to register their offering with the Department of Housing and Urban Development (HUD). Unfortunately for consumers, that law was revised in 1979. Today only a limited amount of information on interstate land sales must be made available to HUD. Numerous land swindles still occur, evidence that the amended law isn't very effective. This was demonstrated by the arrest, trial, and conviction of Louis Rosen in 1990 for cheating over 2,200 investors out of more than $150 million in bogus real estate deals in Florida and other states.

The obvious way to protect yourself from land swindles is to investigate before you invest. A good rule of thumb is: Never purchase land sight unseen. If you are genuinely interested in property being sold by a land-development company, obtain the property report from HUD. Remember, though, HUD only provides information about a land offering. It does not pass judgment on the value of the offering.

Credit Card Fraud

There are numerous ploys that dishonest individuals use to swindle credit card holders, and credit card fraud is now a multimillion-dollar business in this country. According to John D. Perry of the Fraud Division of the Secret Service, credit card fraud losses in the United States total more than $700 million each year.

You can help protect yourself against many credit card frauds by observing the following precautions.

1. Whenever you hand a salesclerk your credit card, try not to let it out of your sight. Be alert to merchants who have their card machines in a back room or where you can't watch the transaction. A dishonest merchant could use your card to run off a blank sales slip, which could then be filled in later and your forged signature added to it.

2. Always ask for any carbon copies of credit card invoices and dispose of them safely to prevent your credit card number from falling into dishonest hands. For the same reason, never throw away your copy of the sales transaction if it's possible that it could be found and used fraudulently.

3. Keep the copies of your credit card transactions so that you can verify the accuracy of your billing statement when it arrives. This way, you will be able to tell if an unauthorized charge has been made to your account.

4. Be very careful about giving your credit card number to any telephone solicitor unless you are sure that the solicitation is not part of a fraudulent scheme.

True-name fraud

When a person uses another individual's identity to obtain and use credit cards issued in the other person's name.

5. Also be wary about giving your Social Security number to anyone over the phone. This will help to prevent what is known as **true-name fraud,** which occurs when an individual uses your identity to obtain a credit card in your name. Often, this kind of fraud takes the form of announcing that you have won a prize of some kind but must supply your Social Security number for verification purposes. Then the con artist applies for a credit card in your name and gives a post office box as an address. The rest is obvious: The con artist goes on a spending spree and you are stuck with the bill. True-name credit fraud is on the increase, and, as this chapter's Consumer Close-Up illustrates, it is an especially frustrating experience for victims.

6. Keep a list of all your credit card numbers in a safe place known only to you. That way, if you lose your cards or they are stolen, you can call in their numbers to the credit companies. Notification of theft or loss within two days will limit your liability to $50 for any unauthorized use of your cards.

WAYS TO AVOID BEING VICTIMIZED BY CONSUMER FRAUD

To avoid falling prey to dishonest merchandising and selling practices, you should first be aware of what the more common ploys are. The following guidelines will help you keep your pride and your pocketbook intact.

1. Beware of any free or bargain offers. Remember, there's no such thing as a free lunch.

2. Avoid any deal that must be made immediately—even if it sounds genuinely attractive. Allow yourself some time for at least minimal comparison shopping. Always wait two to three days before signing a contract.

3. Beware of any products, especially food supplements or drugs, that make unrealistic promises. Research them carefully before you risk your money or your health.

4. Be aware that an offer costing "pennies a day" or "less than the price of a daily newspaper" may add up to a significant total. After all, 75 pennies a day is almost $275 a year.

5. Avoid bait-and-switch sales practices; don't allow yourself to be "traded up."

A New Scam from Credit Card Crooks

Criminals are constantly finding new ways to find and use credit card numbers for their personal gain at the expense of consumers. One relatively new practice is to charge goods and services to the credit accounts of people who are on vacation. When crooks know a person will be out of town for several weeks, they also know that person won't be looking at his or her credit card bills during that time. Criminals have been known to break into rented cars, search through trash at travel agencies, or even videotape consumers as they shop at resorts in order to obtain their credit card numbers. This enables them to charge and receive goods before a vacationing card owner sees the bill.

For example, in 1992, Gary Orin, a kidney specialist from New York City, did not see his American Express bill for one month when he was on vacation. He later found that someone had used his card number to book and take a ski vacation in Vermont before Orin returned from his own trip. Orin's card issuer eventually paid the direct cost of this crime, but such crimes increase the costs of issuing credit cards to all consumers, which costs are passed on in higher prices and credit card fees.

If you ever find that your credit card number has been used by someone else, you must write the card issuer about it, being sure to say that "unauthorized" use of your card was made. It is important to use the word *unauthorized* because the issuer may treat the situation as a *billing error* if you don't. The difference between the two terms is important. Consumers have only 60 days to report billing errors, but there is no time limit for reporting the unauthorized use of a credit card number that does not involve the actual use of a lost card. Although card issuers may be slow to resolve individual cases, when credit card numbers are used to place unauthorized telephone orders, card holders are not responsible for any part of the cost. Still, the best way to avoid credit card problems is to try to be sure no one else has access to your credit card number.

Source: "Credit Card Crooks Devise New Scams." *The Wall Street Journal*, July 17, 1992, p. C-1.

---

6. Politely, but firmly, get rid of fast-talking salespeople who come to your home unannounced or contact you by phone.

7. Don't give your credit card number to any telemarketing or direct-mail firm unless you know the firm is legitimate.

8. Buy defensively. Keep a file of advertisements for products you are thinking of buying. These ads are legal documents in the eyes of the courts, and you will do well to have them on hand—just in case.

9. Deal with local and/or reputable firms whenever possible.

10. Stay informed. Check with the Food and Drug Administration, the Federal Trade Commission, and other government agencies for information on current fraudulent schemes and practices. The government generates a great deal of information on this topic, much of which is available free to the public.

The existence of fraud is a fact of life. Although the government and private organizations try to protect American consumers from unscrupulous businesses, it is impossible for them to oversee every transaction. The best protection consumers have is their own ability to evaluate carefully each purchase they make to be sure they understand what they are buying and under what terms they will be required to make payment.

▶ SUMMARY

1. Consumer fraud involves making a false statement of a past or existing fact with knowledge of its falsity, or with reckless indifference as to its truth, with the intent to cause someone to rely upon such a statement and therefore give up property or a right that has value.

2. Proof of fraud by sellers is often difficult to obtain. The best protection against fraud is to be aware of the various fraudulent schemes practiced by sellers in the marketplace.

3. Many consumers are dissatisfied with their appearance, concerned about their health, or disappointed in their physical condition. Such people are often vulnerable to firms that offer products or services that claim to offer ways they may become the healthy, robust, energetic, persons they would like to be.

4. The increasing range and complexity of consumer goods we buy has contributed to the opportunities for dishonest individuals to take advantage of people by offering products for sale that are not what they appear to be. Consumers may be subjected to fraudulent practices when they buy new products or when they have their possessions repaired.

5. Door-to-door salespeople may use questionable selling practices to persuade consumers to buy their products on an installment basis. It should be noted, however, that there are reputable firms that do business on a door-to-door basis.

6. Many people would like to find a way to earn money with little effort. People who believe this is possible may be easy marks for dishonest offers of get-rich-quick schemes.

▶ QUESTIONS FOR THOUGHT AND DISCUSSION

1. Do you think that fraud in the marketplace is a major problem? Have you or a member of your family ever been a victim of a fraudulent sales scheme? How did you or they handle the situation?

2. Do you think that businesses can continue to use fraudulent selling techniques indefinitely? Why or why not?

3. What are some of the benefits of shopping by mail or by telephone? What are some of the risks?

▶ THINGS TO DO

1. Check through several tabloid-type magazines. Make a list of the types of products advertised in these publications. Do many of them carry ads for products that promise amazing improvements in personal appearance, health, and so on? Do you believe any of these products can do what they advertise? Why or why not?

2. Assume that someone has contacted you by telephone and interested you in a legitimate-sounding investment. List the steps you would take and the sources you would contact to ensure that you would not be fair bait for a fraud shark.

3. The next time you or your parents receive a "you are a contest winner" letter in the mail, analyze it closely. Write down your version of what the offer is saying.

▶ APPLICATION

Visit a local health-food store and examine the labels on food supplements offered for sale. What claims are made? Choose one product and ask the clerk to explain the claims on the label and how these claims have been substantiated. Do not be rude or abusive. Investigate this type of product by looking up information in your school library. Use the information you gain to write an essay that explains what the product is, what it is claimed to do for consumers, and what you have been told the basis for these claims is. Evaluate the value of the product in light of what you have learned. Do you believe that producers and marketers of the product are guilty of consumer fraud? Explain the reasons for your answer.

▶ **SELECTED READINGS**

▶ Barrett, S. *Health Schemes, Scams and Frauds.* New York: Consumer Reports Books, 1991.

▶ Bianco, A. "Ah Mr. Levine, Your Usual Hot Seat?" *Business Week,* October 21, 1991, p. 126.

▶ Castro, Janice. "Reach Out and Rob Someone." *Time,* April 3, 1989, pp. 38–39.

▶ "Con Games That Target the Elderly." *Consumers' Research Magazine,* September 1991, pp. 30-32.

▶ *Contest Cons.* Available free from the Federal Trade Commission, 6th St. and Pennsylvania Ave., N.W., Washington, DC 20580.

▶ *Door-to-Door Sales.* Available free from the Federal Trade Commission, 6th St. and Pennsylvania Ave., N.W., Washington, DC 20580.

▶ *Handbook of Nonprescription Drugs.* Washington, DC. Published biannually by the American Pharmaceutical Association.

▶ *Health Claims: Separating Fact from Fiction.* Available free from the Federal Trade Commission, 6th St. and Pennsylvania Ave., N.W., Washington, DC 20580.

▶ *Investment Swindles: How They Work and How to Avoid Them.* Available free from the Consumer Information Center, 2033 K St., N.W., Washington, DC 20581.

▶ Keller, M. "The Educated Consumer." *Motor Trend,* December 1991, p. 134.

▶ "Mail Order Companies." *Consumer Reports,* October 1991, pp. 643-649.

▶ "Of Pyramids and Things." *Kiplinger's Personal Finance Magazine,* November 1991, pp. 70–71.

▶ Papazian, R. "Product Bans and Controversies." *FDA Consumer,* October 1991, p. 10.

▶ *Quackery.* Available free from the U.S. Department of Health and Human Services, Food and Drug Administration, 500 Fishers Lane, Rockville, MD 20857.

▶ *Questions Concerning Cosmetics.* Available free from the Consumer Information Center, P.O. Box 100, Pueblo, CO 81009.

▶ *Shopping by Phone and Mail.* Available free from the Federal Trade Commission, 6th St. and Pennsylvania Ave., N.W., Washington, DC 20580.

▶ Slomski, Anita, and Butler, Mary S. "Charities: Where Does Your Money Go?" *Consumers Digest,* March–April 1989, pp. 24–28, 83.

▶ *Telemarketing Travel Fraud.* Available free from the Federal Trade Commission, 6th St. and Pennsylvania Ave., N.W., Washington, DC 20580.

▶ *Telephone Investment Fraud.* Available free from the Federal Trade Commission, 6th St. and Pennsylvania Ave., N.W., Washington, DC 20580.

▶ Wiener, Daniel. "Behind Those Fast-Buck Ads." *U.S. News & World Report,* April 24, 1989, pp. 70–71.

How to Avoid Fraudulent Car-Repair Practices

GLOSSARY

LIEN A claim placed on the property of another as security for some debt or charge.

Since the inner workings of an automobile engine are a mystery to many consumers, the likelihood of fraud is high in this industry. It is estimated that perhaps half of the nearly $70 billion spent each year on car repairs is wasted—through incompetence or fraud. Even if you know nothing about car engines, though, you can avoid falling prey to unscrupulous mechanics by taking certain precautions. The following tips may help you avoid getting "taken for a ride" the next time you have car trouble.[1]

▶ WHEN SOMETHING GOES WRONG

If your car begins to sound strange or performs significantly differently in any way, have it checked immediately. Don't ignore the problem in the hope it may disappear. Chances are, if you don't check it out while it's still in running condition, you may face a breakdown at an inconvenient time or place.

Before taking your car to a repair shop, however, be sure to do the following:

1. **Check your owner's manual.** Sometimes you can diagnose the problem yourself by carefully reading your owner's manual. Such manuals often offer troubleshooting advice that may help you fix the problem yourself. If you don't have a manual for your model of car, try to obtain one from the nearest dealer.

2. **If the owner's manual can't help you, try to determine as closely as possible where the problem is located.** Don't take your car to a specialty shop if you think a local service station might be able to fix it.

3. **Before you take your car in for repairs, check your warranty, if you have one.** If some repairs and parts are covered by your warranty, you probably will be required to take it to an authorized franchised dealership for your make of car.

▶ WHERE TO GO?

Even if you don't have a warranty for repairs, you may consider taking your car to a dealership for service. Although a dealership is likely to charge more for services than some competing garages, it may be able to provide better quality service. Most mechanics at dealerships have received training in servicing the particular types of cars their employer sells. The dealer also has its reputation to consider. If you receive inferior service, you are unlikely to return to buy a new car in the future. Records show that consumer complaints about service received from dealerships is lower than for independent repair shops.

For reliable work at perhaps a lower price, however, you may want to shop around. The following suggestions may be helpful.

1. **Talk to your friends, family, and co-workers.** Find out where they take their cars for repairs. This is often the best way to obtain the name of a reputable mechanic. If a certain shop comes highly recommended, try it out—and let the owner know who recommended you. If the shop owner thinks you, or whoever recommended you, may return for future repairs, your chances of getting good service may increase.

2. **Call various local repair shops.** See if you can find a mechanic who is certified by the National Institute for Automotive Service Excellence (NIASE). This organization certifies auto mechanics on the basis of voluntarily taken competency tests in eight different repair specialties. Of course, this certification doesn't guarantee excellent repair service, but it does increase its likelihood.

3. **Call the American Automobile Association (AAA).** The AAA can refer you, whether or not you are a member, to mechanics in your area who are on its list of reputable car-service mechanics. Again, the AAA doesn't guarantee the quality of these mechanics' services, but it does base its recommendations on objective information, including dealership testing and certification by the National Institute for Automotive Service Excellence.

4. **You may also want to drive to an independent diagnostic center if one is located in your area.** These centers use electronic equip-

---

1. Many of the suggestions in this issue are based on an analysis of car-repair fraud complaints made by the Council of Better Business Bureaus, 1515 Wilson Blvd., Arlington, VA 22209, and published in their Consumer Information Series, Publication No. 311-03246.

ment to test your car thoroughly and diagnose any problems. Many of these centers, however, are affiliated with repair shops that may have a vested interest in the diagnostic results.

▶ AT THE REPAIR SHOP

Once you've located a repair service, you can take several steps to ensure yourself against possible fraud.

1. Have a list handy of the things you want done. If you're not sure what's wrong with your car, describe the problem as clearly as you can. And if you don't know the difference between a differential and a distributor, don't advertise your ignorance.

2. Get an estimate. This is probably the single most important step you can take to prevent being overcharged for your repairs. Have the mechanic specify clearly what he or she thinks is causing the malfunction and what it will cost to repair it. If you have to leave your car for a time—to go to school or work—leave your phone number so the mechanic can call you with the estimate prior to doing any repairs. If the required repairs are major, get your estimate in writing.

3. If you think the estimate is higher than it should be, or if you don't think the diagnosis is correct, get a second opinion. Be especially wary if the mechanic claims you need to have any of the following parts replaced: ball joints, batteries, shock absorbers, or brakes. It's relatively easy for consumers to be conned by mechanics who can be persuasive about why these need to be replaced—when, in fact, they really don't.

4. When you decide to go ahead with repairs, check the service order carefully. Make sure it includes either the specific repairs you

have requested or those recommended by the mechanic who gave you the estimate.

5. Stay with your car if possible. If you can't, leave a number where you can be reached by phone in case the mechanic needs to talk to you.

6. Check your odometer if you have to leave your car at a repair shop overnight—unless you know the mechanics well. It is possible for mechanics to "road test" a car for their own transportation purposes and at your expense.

7. Last, but not least, clarify with the mechanic or repair-shop manager the terms of payment. Must it be in cash, or do they take credit? Do they take personal checks? Many consumers have found themselves in the uncomfortable position of being refused possession of their car after repairs because they lacked the cash to pay for them. In such cases, if you can't produce the payment within a reasonable time, the repair shop can legally place a **lien** on the car, sell it, and collect the amount due from the price—returning the balance to you.

▶ BEFORE PAYING FOR REPAIRS

Before you write out your check or pull out your credit card, be sure to check your car thoroughly to make sure that everything was, in fact, repaired or that parts were really replaced. Don't be afraid to ask the mechanic to show you any replaced parts and explain specifically what he or she did. Ask questions until you understand what was done. After all, it's *your* car and *your* money. Check to make sure the actual charge is reasonably close to the estimate.

Also request an itemized bill listing all repairs that were done and all

parts that were replaced. If possible, get a written guarantee for the services performed. If certain kinds of repairs were made, such as installing brakes or a transmission, you may also want to roadtest your car before paying. Be sure to keep all of your receipts in case problems develop in the future.

▶ STATE REGULATION

Some states have passed legislation specifically to regulate auto repair shops. If you live in California, for example, you have a right to a written cost estimate for repairs before any repair work is undertaken. The final cost of the work cannot exceed this estimate—unless you have authorized the increase. You also have a right to the return (or at least the inspection) of all parts that have been replaced and to a written invoice itemizing parts and labor.

If you are unsure of whether your state has a comparable law, you can find out by calling the state consumer affairs division (see Exhibit B-3 in Consumer Issue B).

▶ REPAIRS ON THE ROAD

Having your car break down in the middle of nowhere or on a freeway in the middle of a city can be a very costly nightmare. If you are not a member of an auto club, such as the AAA, your only recourse may be to call a towing service listed in the Yellow Pages. Be wary of mechanics or repair services recommended by tow-truck drivers, however. The driver may be more interested in kickbacks from repair shops than in your pocketbook or the quality of service you get. If you are unfamiliar with the area, your best bet is to arrange to have your car towed to a local dealership for diagnosis and minimum repairing. Save the major repairs, if possible, until you return home.

▶ WHEN THOSE NEW-CAR REPAIRS GET STICKY

When the going gets sticky on a matter of warranty or car performance, you can turn for help to an organization called the Automotive Consumer Action Program (AUTOCAP). AUTOCAP was formed because of the numerous complaints consumers have made concerning car dealerships and repair services.

▶ How Does AUTOCAP Work?

If your new car isn't performing satisfactorily and if the dealer isn't giving you the repair service you feel you should have, check your local White Pages for the AUTOCAP nearest you. If you can't find one nearby, write its headquarters at 8400 Westpark Dr., McLean, VA 22102, or call (703) 821-7000. You will be sent a complaint form, and when you return it, AUTOCAP will contact the dealer and urge the dealer to work out the problem with you. If this fails, the matter goes before the AUTOCAP arbitrating panel, consisting of four dealers and three public members.

It is a painless job to arrive at a "just" settlement when a dealer and a customer can agree. Obviously, the panel is not a court of last resort; it has no enforcement powers and relies on dealer cooperation to handle complaints satisfactorily. So far, about 40 to 50 percent of the complaints coming before AUTOCAP each year have been settled in favor of car owners. If you feel you are not getting fair treatment from AUTOCAP, you can go to the state motor vehicle agency or take private legal action.

▶ SUMMARY

1. It is estimated that perhaps one-half of the nearly $70 billion spent each year in the United States on car repairs is wasted—through incompetence or fraud.

2. If your car is performing differently than usual and you suspect malfunction, have it checked immediately, while it's still running.

3. Before you take your car to a repair shop, check your owner's manual for troubleshooting advice, and check your warranty, if you have one, for coverage.

4. In searching for a reliable repair shop, first check with your friends and family. Other alternatives are (1) find a shop with mechanics certified by the National Institute for Automotive Service Excellence; (2) go to a dealer or repair service recommended by the American Automobile Association; or (3) go to an independent diagnostic center for an electronic evaluation of your car's condition.

5. When you go to the shop of your choice, give the mechanic a list of what you want repaired, or have the mechanic evaluate your car and provide an estimate before any repairs are done.

6. If the estimate sounds high, or if you are suspicious in any way concerning the diagnosis, get a second opinion.

7. Before repairs are done, check the service order to make sure all repairs you requested or the mechanic recommended are included clearly on the order.

8. Stay with your car, if possible, while repairs are made, or leave a phone number where you can be reached.

9. Clarify the terms of payment—cash, credit, or personal check—before repairs are undertaken.

10. Before paying for your repairs, make sure everything you requested, or the mechanic promised, has actually been done.

11. Some states have passed legislation to regulate auto repair shops. If the actual cost of repairing your car exceeds the estimated cost, or if you are unhappy with the service you've obtained, check with your state consumer affairs division to see if your state has an automotive consumer protection bureau that can help you.

12. If you're on the road and your car breaks down, arrange to have it towed to a nearby dealership that can service your make of car. Save major repairs for later, if possible.

13. If you have trouble getting warranty repairs on your new car, you can call the Automotive Consumer Action Program (AUTOCAP).

▶ QUESTIONS FOR THOUGHT AND DISCUSSION

1. Do you think that, even if you know a lot about cars, you still might become a victim of fraud? In what way or ways might this be possible?

2. Can you think of other ways—beyond those discussed in this issue—to avoid car-related fraud?

3. Do you think car-repair services and mechanics should be tested and regulated by the government?

4. When would mechanics consider it economically beneficial to themselves to render honest and reliable car-repair service?

▶ THINGS TO DO

1. Call your nearest AAA representative and ask how the AAA determines which car-repair services to include on their recommended list. Find out if any mechanics or service shops in your area are included on that list.

2. Check the White Pages of your telephone directory for an AUTOCAP listing. If none is there, write to AUTOCAP headquarters at the address given in this Consumer Issue

and ask for information.

3. Check with your local Better Business Bureau to see if any cases of car-repair fraud have been reported. Learn the names of the repair shops or mechanics to avoid.

4. Contact your state's attorney general's consumer protection office, as listed in Consumer Issue B. Ask the office representative to send you information on car-fraud complaints and any available tips on how to avoid being defrauded.

▶ SELECTED READINGS

▶ Ashton, Betty. "Getting Repairs Done Right." *Guide to Living on Your Own*. Boston: Little, Brown, 1988, pp. 213–17.

▶ *Auto Facts*. Available for 50 cents from the Consumer Information Center, P.O. Box 100, Pueblo, CO 81002.

▶ *Automatic Transmission Repair*. Available for 50 cents from the Consumer Information Center, P.O. Box 100, Pueblo, CO 81002.

▶ *The Backyard Mechanic*. Available free from the Consumer Information Center, P.O. Box 100, Pueblo, CO 81002.

▶ Center for the Study of Services. "Auto Repair Shops." *Bay Area Consumers Checkbook* 4, no. 2 (Spring 1988), pp. 2–13.

▶ Chandler, J. "How to Get Your Car Repaired Honestly." *Mechanics Illustrated*, December 1982, p. 49.

▶ "A Good Mechanic Is Hard to Find." *Changing Times*, July 1983, p. 24.

▶ *How to Deal with Motor Vehicle Emergencies*. Available free from the National Highway Traffic Safety Administration, 400 7th St., S.W., Washington, DC 20590.

▶ *Odometer Fraud*. Available free from the National Highway Traffic Safety Administration, 400 Seventh St., S.W., Washington, DC 20590.

▶ Whittemore, M. "Bumper to Bumper Auto Care." *Nation's Business*, October 1991, pp. 70–71.

Budgeting

The Consumer as Wage Earner

PREVIEW

▶ How can you invest in yourself?
▶ What factors determine the value of your labor and how much you earn?

▶ What rewards might you receive for going to school?
▶ Why do some workers earn more than others?

▶ How does inflation affect the purchasing power of our earnings?
▶ How do we measure the rate of inflation?

In the American economic system, the amount people earn depends largely on the value of their contribution to the production of goods and services. The value of this contribution depends in part on an individual's basic intelligence, competence, and aptitude, and in part on the demand for the type of labor that that individual can provide. To achieve the highest possible productivity and income, people need to develop their personal aptitudes into the more highly demanded skills through education, training, and job experience. What we are talking about here is **human capital,** or the ability of a person to produce goods and services from other productive resources. Developing human capital is the key to increasing income.

Human capital
The skills and abilities humans have that allow them to produce goods and services from other productive resources.

INVESTMENT IN HUMAN CAPITAL

Few would consider it unfair to pay a person with a college degree more than one with only a grade-school education. The value of the more educated person's labor to an employer is expected to be greater than that of the person with less education. This basic fact of life is probably one reason why you are making an investment in yourself by pursuing an education.

One way to define an **investment** is to say it is the act of giving up the use of something of value now so that you may receive something else of greater value in the future. When you invest in a business, for example, you could use your $10,000 to buy corporate stock in the hope that your stock will be worth more in the future. Thus, going to school is a type of investment in yourself—in your own human capital. By paying tuition, and giving up income you could be earning now, you hope to increase your future income. Usually, the longer you go to school, the more skills you will learn, the more knowledge you will obtain, and the better your thinking ability will become. You may find it easier to solve problems, to direct and motivate other people, to organize and to plan. Employers will be willing to pay you more because they assume your labor will have greater value to them than if you had not received those additional years of education. This is, at least, the theory of the labor market. Exceptions always exist.

Investment
Giving up something of value at the present to be able to receive something else of greater value in the future.

Of course, education in general does not automatically guarantee you a higher income. To be marketable, your skills must be in areas of high demand. No amount of obscure services you could supply would induce others to hire you at high wages; what determines the individual's wages or income is the supply and demand for different types of labor.

Ultimately, then, your investment in your human capital requires careful planning. It should increase your productive capacities in areas that the economy demands. For example, it appears that very few people will own and use manual typewriters in the future. Most people who have reason to type letters or reports will probably use computers or electronic typewriters. It makes more sense, then, to study computer maintenance and repair than the repair of manual typewriters.

So choosing the right occupation may require that you become informed not only about current marketable job skills but also about future demands for different types of jobs. Just as you want to be careful about investing cash that you have on hand, you also should be careful about investing time and effort in the development of your own human capital. You might want to seek the aid of a career-counseling service, either on or off campus, in order to make the best possible choices.

RATE OF RETURN FOR EDUCATION

Although the evidence is overwhelming that an education is valuable, the old saying "Get all the education you can" does not apply equally to everybody. Perennial students, after all, are not big earners. We can offer a general rule, though: Acquire more education as long as the expected benefits at least cover the costs.

Of course, our general rule has its limits because it is always more expensive to acquire more education. The main cost of going to college is not tuition and books, but forgone income—that is, the *opportunity cost* of not working. In other words, had you decided not to go to college, you could be working full time at some average salary during those four years. But even with the costs of forgone earnings, tuition, and books, the rate of return for investing in education (if you are successful at college) is at least as good as the rate of return for investing in the stock market and certainly higher than putting your savings into a savings account.

Exhibit 7–1 shows the annual mean earnings for workers with varying amounts of formal education. As you can see, there is a direct relationship between the amount of education you acquire and your future income prospects. The difference in earnings between a person with eight years of schooling and a person who has completed college is $25,366 for men and $15,689 for women. Exhibit 7–2 illustrates the relationship between education and income over time in an **age/earnings profile.**

Experts in the field of education now put much more emphasis on the nonmonetary benefits of going to college. There is, of course, no way to put a monetary value on "the educated person" or "the whole person" or on the fact that college introduces you to new people, new ideas, and new ways of thinking. But it does undoubtedly give you intellectual flexibility and fosters self-discovery. College grads do a lot of things differently than do those who have not graduated from college. For example, they read more books, vote more often, participate more in civic organizations, and are more satisfied with their jobs.

Age/earnings profile
The profile of how earnings change with your age. When you're young and just starting out, your earnings are low; as you get older, your earnings increase because you become more productive and work longer hours; finally, your earnings start to decrease.

THE CHANGING JOB SCENE

In the 1960s a college degree could almost guarantee its recipient a managerial job or a professional position. Unfortunately for those seeking college degrees,

▶ **Exhibit 7–1   Education and Annual Mean (Average) Earnings for Full-Time Male and Female Workers 25 Years Old and Over in 1990**

YEARS OF SCHOOL COMPLETED	MEAN EARNINGS	
8 or fewer	$19,188	$13,222
1–3 years of high school	22,564	15,381
Completed high school	28,043	18,954
1–3 years of college	34,188	22,654
4 years of college	44,554	28,911
More than 4 years of college	55,831	35,827

Source: *Statistical Abstract of the United States, 1992*, p. 454.

▶ Exhibit 7–2   Age/Earning Profile for Selected Levels of Educational Achievement and by Sex for 1990

Age group	Levels of Educational Achievement and Mean Income			
	8 years or less of elementary	4 years of high school	1-3 years of college	4 years of college
Men 25-34	$15,887	$24,043	$28,298	$35,534
35-44	$18,379	$28,927	$36,180	$47,401
45-54	$19,686	$32,862	$39,953	$50,718
55-64	$22,379	$30,779	$36,954	$55,518
65+	$17,028	$25,516	$34,323	$43,092
Women 25-34	$11,832	$17,076	$20,872	$27,210
35-44	$13,714	$19,886	$23,307	$31,631
45-54	$13,490	$19,986	$24,608	$29,242
55-64	$13,941	$19,382	$23,364	$27,975
65+	(*)	$18,285	(*)	(*)

(*) sample group too small to be statistically significant

THE GLOBAL CONSUMER

Preparing For a Career in the Global Economy

If there ever was a time when college students could expect to step into a good job right after graduating and then work for the same employer until retirement, it is clearly gone. The reason? Increased global competition. American firms and workers now compete vigorously with firms and workers from other nations and cannot afford to provide jobs to any workers who fail to contribute to productivity and efficiency.

American schools need to help students acquire the skills American businesses demand. A particularly valuable skill is the ability to communicate in foreign languages. We cannot expect to maintain our posi-

tion in the world's economy if our businesses market their products only in English. Unfortunately, though, relatively few college students have chosen to acquire the language skills that could help them to be our future leaders in the world economy. As our economic system has become more global in nature over the past ten years, the number of college students enrolled in foreign language classes has actually declined. Although the number of college students enrolled in Spanish and French fell only slightly through the 1980s, enrollment in German, Italian, and Chinese fell by as much as 25 percent. The only significant growth

was in the number of American students who studied Japanese. This figure went from 11,500 to 24,000—a very small number when we consider that virtually all Japanese college students study English.

The question arises, how can American businesses compete in foreign markets if we can't speak the languages of other nations? We can't reasonably expect foreign customers to learn English just to make it easier for us to sell them our products. Would you consider learning a foreign language to further your own career, and perhaps to help the American economy?

that is no longer the case. The reason for this change is, of course, the increase in the *supply* of college-degree holders between 1960 and 1990. As Exhibit 7–3 illustrates, in just the last decade and a half, the proportion of workers with a college background has nearly doubled.

Does this mean that you shouldn't bother about getting a college degree? No. Although a college degree no longer guarantees a good job, the lack of one may bar you from being considered for higher-paying, higher-status jobs. According to the Bureau of Labor Statistics, in the 1990s the fastest-growing jobs will be in executive, managerial, professional, and technical fields that require the highest levels of education and skill. To compete in the market-place for these kinds of jobs requires, at a minimum, a college degree. Those with only a high school education, or less, will face increasingly limited opportunities in the future.

Another advantage of having a college degree, according to Howard Brown, author of *Investment in Learning,* is that it keeps lifetime options open; it allows for more flexibility in the job market in response to changing economic conditions. This is an important consideration, especially in view of the fact that American workers change jobs, on average, six times during their lives.

> Although a college degree no longer guarantees a good job, the lack of one may bar you from being considered for higher-paying, higher-status jobs.

OCCUPATIONAL WAGE DIFFERENTIALS

At the top of the income ladder shown in Exhibit 7–4 are the so-called professions—medicine, dentistry, and law. Does that necessarily mean you should decide to study medicine, dentistry, or law? Obviously not. You could be wasting your time. For example, unless you're able to get into an accredited medical school (and, of course, graduate from it), you cannot legally practice medicine in the United States. The ratio of applicants to acceptances in most medical schools is astounding. Therefore, unless your father or mother is a doctor, or you are an extremely good student in an extremely good school, the odds are against your admission to medical training.

▶ **Exhibit 7–3 Proportion of Workers with a College Background, 1972 and 1991**

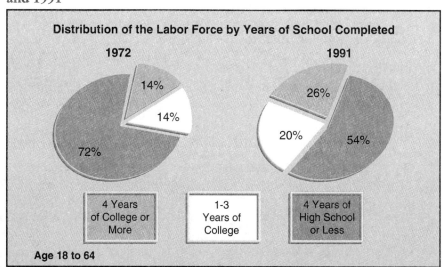

Distribution of the Labor Force by Years of School Completed

1972
- 14%
- 14%
- 72%

1991
- 26%
- 20%
- 54%

4 Years of College or More

1-3 Years of College

4 Years of High School or Less

Age 18 to 64

Occupation	Male	Female
Managerial and professional	$38,844	$27,716
Technical sales and administrative support	$26,312	$18,200
Service occupation	$17,160	$12,792
Precision production and repair	$25,740	$16,848
Operators, fabricators, and laborers	$19,812	$16,016
Farm, forestry, and fishery workers	$13,780	$11,232

Source: Bureau of Labor Statistics, *Employment and Earnings Report*, October 1991, p. 75.

The same is not true of law, however. There are numerous law schools you can attend; you can even learn law at home by mail in California. Of course, you should not look only at the high salaries in law. To obtain a law degree, you must take three additional years of training after college, and, if you attend during the day, that means three more years of not earning any income. This additional cost means that the rate of return on becoming a lawyer may be no higher than if you chose another career.

Moreover, you may receive a relatively low salary for a number of years before you become a junior partner in a law firm. Even doctors earn relatively low incomes when they start their practices. So even though the average salary for a particular occupation is very high, don't anticipate that your impressive amount of schooling will make you a nice sum of money right away. To see why this isn't necessarily unfair, we must look at the reasons behind the shape of the typical age/earnings profile, as represented in Exhibit 7–5.

Wages and Ages

When you first start a job, or return to the labor force after a long absence, you may lack the skills you need to carry out your job responsibilities. If you need a lot of on-the-job-training, your employer won't be inclined to pay you as much as a more experienced worker. Gradually, as you become better trained and more productive, your wage rate increases (even corrected for inflation). Your employer gets more and more information on your productivity and your reliability from your continuing work record.

Your earnings may peak at age 45 to 55 and then slowly decline until retirement, when you cease work altogether. The age/earnings profile eventually shows a downturn because older people generally work fewer hours per week and usually are less productive than middle-aged people.

Occupational Choice and Income

Not only are there vast differences among the wages for different occupations, as shown in Exhibits 7–4 and 7–6, there are also vast differences in the qual-

► Exhibit 7–5   **Typical Age/Earnings Profile**

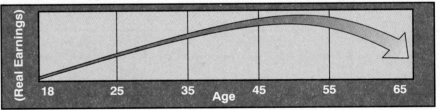

ifications, the amount of training, and the type of work required in each occupation. In an occupation with highly variable periods of employment, the average wage rate is relatively higher than in occupations that offer steadier employment; the higher wage rate compensates for the periods of unemployment.

Money income alone is not going to determine whether you make the right career choice. If you have a spirit of independence, you certainly won't be satisfied doing paperwork in a large insurance office, and if you have a spirit of adventure, you'll be restless as a salesclerk. Therefore, you may finally choose an occupation that promises you a lower wage rate than some others but a more acceptable work situation. After all, most of us work the better part of our lives; if we hate our work, we won't be very happy, even if we make quite a bit of income. In other words, the total income you make from an occupation includes more than just money income. It also includes **psychic income,** or the satisfaction derived from your work situation or occupation. And psychic rewards from a job can be more important for some people than monetary payment.

You also have to decide whether or not you want to live in one area for a long period of time. If you become a junior executive in a company that has a history of switching its executives around the country every 18 months, you'll be very unhappy if you dislike moving. On the other hand, you might be very happy with this transient lifestyle if you want to see the country while you're young.

In some ways, your choice of occupation depends on your values and your desired lifestyle. The occupation you choose may even determine the nature of your consumption—that is, the house you live in or the clothes you wear. Your choice of occupation will also determine how much leisure you will have. As you've already seen, very few things come free of charge. If you want a job with more leisure, you generally will have less income to spend than from a job that offers less leisure. If you want a job that is highly stable and risk-free, you will pay for it in the form of a lower income.

NONMONEY INCOME

In figuring out what your standard of living would be in different types of occupations, you also must look at the nonmoney income that might be available. Nonmoney income, as opposed to the nonmonetary psychic rewards just discussed, refers to goods and services that individuals can obtain without paying money for them. The following are several sources of nonmoney income that can make our lives more satisfactory and/or comfortable.

1. *Material goods produced at home.* Such goods include those that come from growing our own produce, sewing our own clothes, and cutting firewood from the family lot, for example.
2. *Income from services in the form of food, clothing, or housing.* For example, farm laborers may receive housing accommodations in addition to money income. Ministers are often given food and housing. In fact, the whole category of fringe benefits for wage earners is covered under nonmoney income.
3. *Services provided by family members.* Full-time homemakers provide services to other members of the family for which the latter do not pay di-

Money income
The total amount of actual dollars you receive per week, per month, or per year.

Psychic income
The satisfaction derived from a work situation or occupation; nonmonetary rewards from doing a particular job.

▶ **Exhibit 7–6   Average Starting Salary, by Degree, 1991**

Bachelor's Degree	
Mathematics	$27,370
Computer science	30,696
Engineering (civil)	29,658
Humanities	23,567
Social Sciences	21,357
Accounting	26,642
Marketing	23,713
Chemistry	26,836
Physics	29,227
Business (general)	24,019
Master's Degree	
Marketing	43,182
Engineering (civil)	34,551
Computer science	37,894
Accounting	30,996
Chemistry	33,575
Doctorate	
Mathematics	41,146
Computer science	58,300
Chemistry	47,911
Physics	39,913
Engineering (civil)	43,060

Source: *Statistical Abstract of the United States,* 1992, p. 172.

rectly. Certain members of the family may do auto repairs, chores around the house, and lawn mowing without pay, thus providing nonmoney income to other family members.

4. *The implicit income or pleasure received from owned items, such as a house, a car, or furniture.* Specifically, if you own a house, you receive considerable pleasure from living in it. You could approximate the value of that pleasure by seeing what it would cost to rent the house.

5. *Barter income.* If you are able to exchange goods for services, goods for goods, or services for goods without resorting to the use of money or the marketplace, this can constitute part of your nonmoney income. Farmers, for example, can grow crops on their land and then trade them with other people for, say, furniture or clothes.

6. *Social income.* Such income is available largely at public expense and includes public health clinics, libraries, parks, public education, roads, and fire and police protection.

To estimate your total income, it would be necessary to add up monetary income, the value of psychic income, and the value of all the nonmoney income you receive.

GENDER AND JOBS

In the 1950s a majority of Americans felt that the woman's place was in the home. And that's where most women were. Since 1960, however, the female work force has more than doubled. Today, three out of four women hold jobs, and more than 65 percent of all married women are in the labor force. The Bureau of Labor Statistics predicts that two out of every three entrants into the labor force during the 1990s will be women. This means that by the end of the decade women will constitute about 50 percent of the labor force.

The growing presence of women in our nation's labor force can be seen in the increasing number of women who choose to become professionals, such as lawyers or doctors.

Changing views on the role of women in society, as well as civil-rights legislation prohibiting discrimination against women in the workplace, have opened to women an increasing number of occupations once restricted to men. There are a growing number of women physicians, executives, airline pilots, construction workers, police officers, mechanical engineers, and fire-fighters—positions traditionally held by men. There are also a growing number of women who are establishing and managing their own business firms.

Lest we paint too rosy a picture, however, note that many women enter the labor force not out of choice but out of necessity—it is now an economic fact of life that, to meet living expenses, more households must have two incomes. In 1989, for example, only 15 percent of married couples with only one income could afford to purchase their first home. Also, the number of single-parent households headed by women has increased significantly in recent years.

In spite of their aggressive pursuit for equality in wages, women continue to earn less than men holding similar positions, as Exhibits 7–1 and 7–4 illustrate. In 1989 women earned approximately 72 cents for every dollar earned by men holding similar jobs. Although the gender gap in wages is closing, it is doing so at a very slow pace. In the past ten years, the gap has shrunk by approximately 1 cent per year. If this rate continues, it will take until the year 2017 before pay equity is achieved.

> Although the gender gap in wages is closing, it is doing so at a very slow pace. In the past ten years, the gap has shrunk by approximately 1 cent per year.

PROBLEMS IN THE WORKPLACE

Numerous federal and state laws exist to protect employees against job discrimination, hazardous or unsafe workplaces, sexual harassment, and other unfair employment practices. The Consumer Close-Up in this chapter describes the possible results of the Civil Rights Act of 1991 on the workplace. Some of the problems that consumers, as employees, might encounter in the course of employment are listed in Exhibit 7–7, along with the relevant federal legislation and the appropriate agency or agencies to contact. Since state laws relating to employment vary from state to state, only federal legislation is included.

JOBS THROUGH THE YEAR 2000

Forget for the moment the current economic situation, as it may have changed by the time you use this text. The current economic situation is not really that important in making your career choice. Rather, you must look to the future to determine where the greatest demand will be for different occupations. The U.S. Department of Labor has devised a way to help you. The results of its study of employment through the year 2000 are presented in Exhibit 7–8. Your choice of occupation may be influenced if you know where the jobs will be, but you still want to maximize the happiness factor in your work, so you should choose an occupation that you think you're going to enjoy from among those that are expected to be in demand.

THE PROBLEM OF INFLATION

Inflation is defined as a sustained rise in the weighted average of all prices. It must be considered whenever economic data are evaluated. For example,

Inflation
A sustained rise in the weighted average of all prices.

▶ Exhibit 7–7 **Federal Legislation Protecting Employees**

PROBLEM	LEGISLATION	AGENCY TO CONTACT[a]
Discrimination		
Hiring, promoting, assigning jobs, enforcing dress codes, disciplining employees, firing, awarding pensions, retirement, etc.	Civil Rights Acts of 1964 and 1991 Age Discrimination in Employment Act of 1967 Rehabilitation Act of 1973 Pregnancy Discrimination Act of 1978	Equal Employment Opportunity Commission or U.S. Department of Labor, Office of Federal Contract Compliance Programs
	Retirement Equity Act of 1984	U.S. Department of Labor, Pension and Welfare Benefits Administration
Health & Safety		
Workplace conditions	Occupational Safety and Health Act of 1970	Occupational Safety and Health Administration
Refusing dangerous work	National Labor Relations Act of 1935	National Labor Relations Board
Health care and insurance	Health Maintenance Act of 1973	U.S. Department of Health and Human Services, Social Security Administration
	Employee Retirement Income Security Act of 1974	U.S. Department of Labor, Pension and Welfare Benefits Administration
	Pregnancy Discrimination Act of 1978	Equal Employment Opportunity Commission
	Tax Equity and Fiscal Responsibility Act of 1982	Equal Employment Opportunity Commission
Disability and death	Social Security Act of 1935	U.S. Department of Health and Human Services, Social Security Administration
Hours & Wages		
Hours, minimum wages and overtime	Fair Labor Standards Act of 1938	U.S. Department of Labor, Wage and Hour Division
Payment of wages (including deductions, assignments, garnishment and collection)	Fair Labor Standards Act of 1938	U.S Department of Labor, Wage and Hour Division
	Equal Pay Act of 1963 Civil Rights Act of 1964 Age Discrimination in Employment Act of 1967	Equal Employment Opportunity Commission
	Consumer Credit Protection Act of 1968	U.S. Department of Labor, Wage and Hour Division
Retirement benefits	Social Security Act of 1935	U.S. Department of Health and Human Services, Social Security Administration
	Employee Retirement Income Security Act of 1974	U.S. Department of Labor, Pension and Welfare Benefits Administration
Unemployment compensation	Social Security Act of 1935 Federal Unemployment Tax Act of 1954	State Unemployment Compensation Agency
Termination		
Bankruptcy of employee	Bankruptcy Act of 1978	U.S. Department of Labor, Wage and Hour Division

PROBLEM	LEGISLATION	AGENCY TO CONTACT[a]
Garnishment of wages	Consumer Credit Protection Act of 1968	U.S. Department of Labor, Wage and Hour Division
Military service	Veterans' Reemployment Rights Act of 1974	U.S. Department of Veterans Affairs, Veterans Employment Rights Office
Union activity	Labor-Management Relations Act of 1947	National Labor Relations Board
Whistle-blowing	Fair Labor Standards Act of 1938 Federal Water Pollution Control Act of 1948 Clean Air Act of 1963	U.S. Department of Labor, Wage and Hour Division
	Civil Rights Act of 1964	Equal Employment Opportunity Commission
	Occupational Safety and Health Act of 1970 Energy Reorganization Act of 1974	U.S. Department of Labor, Wage and Hour Division
	Employee Retirement Income Security Act of 1974	U.S. Department of Labor, Pension and Welfare Benefits Administration
	Federal Railroad Safety Authorization Act of 1980	National Railroad Adjustment Board
Plant closing	Worker Adjustment and Retraining Notification Act of 1988	U.S. Department of Labor, Wage and Hour Division
Unions		
Organizing, collective bargaining and strikes	Railway Labor Act of 1926	National Mediation Board
	Norris-LaGuardia Act of 1932 National Labor Relations Act of 1935	National Labor Relations Board
	Labor-Management Relations Act of 1947	Federal Mediation and Conciliation Services
	Labor-Management Reporting and Disclosure Act of 1959	National Labor Relations Board
Other		
Credit reports	Fair Credit Reporting Act of 1971	U.S. Department of Labor, Wage and Hour Division
Employing minors	Walsh-Healey Act of 1936 Fair Labor Standards Act of 1938	U.S. Department of Labor, Wage and Hour Division
Polygraph testing	Employee Polygraph Protection Act of 1988	U.S. Department of Labor, Wage and Hour Division
Veterans' rights	Veterans' Reemployment Rights Act of 1974	U.S. Department of Veterans Affairs, Veterans Employment Rights Office

[a]The addresses and telephone numbers of the federal agencies nearest you are listed in the White Pages under "United States Government." If you are uncertain about which agency to contact, call the Federal Information Center nearest you (listed in Consumer Issue B).

the amount of money a person earns must be evaluated in terms of what that income is able to buy. If a person in 1992 said, "When I started to work in 1959 I earned only 75 cents an hour," his statement would have little meaning for those who had no idea what 75 cents could buy in 1959. Between 1959 and 1992 the average price level in the United States increased by a little more than 360 percent. The 75 cents earned in 1959 had about the same purchasing power as $3.50 in 1992. This information, regarding inflation, is necessary to understand the true value of the person's 75-cent wage in 1959.

How Inflation Is Measured

Although it is easy to recognize when prices are going up, it is much more difficult to measure inflation. The most common measurement of inflation is the **consumer price index (CPI)** that is prepared by the U.S. Bureau of Labor Statistics every month. This is a weighted average that measures price changes in what has been determined to be a "typical market basket" of goods and services American consumers buy. The government has identified roughly 400 products (both goods and services) that consumers typically buy. These include foods, clothing, automobiles, homes, rents, household supplies, medical care, sports equipment, legal services, transportation, utilities, and many other consumer products. The next step in completing the CPI is to determine what proportion of the typical consumer's income is spent on each type of product. If, for example, you buy a toothbrush every three months and 12 quarts of milk each week, a 10-cent increase in the price of the toothbrush would be

Consumer price index (CPI)
A price index based on a fixed representative market basket of about 400 goods and services purchased in 85 urban areas.

▶ **Exhibit 7–8   Percentage Change in Employment, 1986–2000**

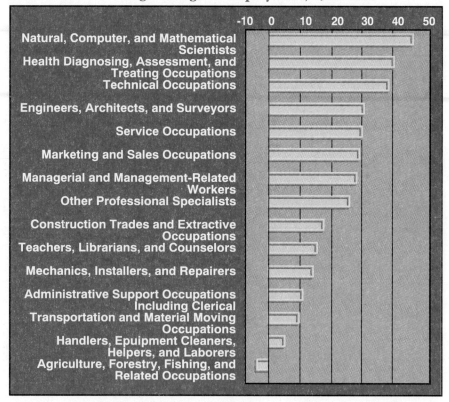

much less important to you than a 5-cent increase in the price of milk. Therefore, a change in the price of milk is counted as a larger part, or is weighted more, than a change in the price of a toothbrush. These weights allow the government to count price changes in the CPI according to the share of consumer spending each one represents.

Each month statisticians from the Bureau of Labor Statistics measure the price of the products in the typical market basket by collecting data from over 18,000 households, 24,000 retail stores, and 18,000 housing establishments, in 85 urban areas across the nation. The average price of each individual product is then multiplied times its weight, and the answers are added together to reach a total. This total is compared with the total at some earlier time that is called the *base year*. In 1992 the base year was the average for prices in 1982 through 1984. The base year is assigned the value of 100. Increases in this average appear as percentage changes in the index. For example, the CPI was 137.9 at the end of 1991, meaning that the average weighted price of the typical market basket of goods and services had increased 37.9 percent between 1982–1984 and 1991.

It is very easy to misunderstand the meaning of a change in the CPI. For example, if the CPI had increased to 142.2 by the end of 1992, you might think the rate of inflation between 1991 and 1992 was 4.3 percent (142.2 − 137.9 = 4.3). *But you would be wrong!* The 4.3 percent is based on prices as they were in 1982–1984, not as they were in 1991. To determine the percent of increase from one year to the next, you must divide the index from the first year into the index of the current year and then subtract 1, which represents prices as they were in the beginning year. Therefore, you find that the rate of inflation as measured by the CPI between 1991 and 1992 was 142.2/137.9 − 1 = .031, or 3.1 percent.

Problems with the CPI

Although the CPI is the best measure of inflation we have, it is not perfect, particularly when it is used to compare prices over a period of many years. The nature of many products we buy has changed dramatically over time. A 1992 automobile, for example, is substantially different from a 1972 model. It has safety features, pollution-control devices, and on-board computers that make our driving easier, safer, and less damaging to the environment. When the CPI is used to compare the prices of automobiles over time, it does not take these changes into account. We end up comparing apples to oranges, so to speak. This problem is made greater by the purchase of products that did not even exist at one time. For example, three out of every four American families own VCRs today, a product that was not available for home use 25 years ago.

Another problem in the CPI is caused by our different lifestyles and different spending patterns. People who are old or young, married or single, who live in the North or the South, or in urban or rural areas, are likely to spend their money in different ways. They will, therefore, be affected differently by changes in prices. For example, a person who lives in Idaho suffers from any increase in the cost of heating more than someone who lives in Florida. Housing prices have increased rapidly in recent years, so if you purchased your home in 1975, you were not affected by increased housing costs as much as if you are looking for a home to buy now. Differences like these cannot be completely accounted for in the CPI.

Varying Effects of Inflation

Not everyone is equally affected by inflation. An increase in prices of 10 percent will have a limited impact on your life if your wages also grow by 10 percent. Inflation has its greatest effect on those whose incomes remain the same from year to year. Many retired people receive fixed pensions from their former employers that have not changed since they retired. In 1975 a monthly pension payment of $1,000 could provide a comfortable life in most parts of the United States. By 1992 the same annual $12,000 had much less purchasing power because of inflation.

Inflation also harms people who have saved money that earns a return smaller than the rate of inflation. If inflation was 10 percent (as it was in 1979) and you had $1,000 deposited in a bank account that paid you 6 percent interest, your savings would lose 4 percent of their purchasing power each year—before taxes are considered. That 6 percent interest would be taxed down to an amount between 3 percent and 5 percent for most people. High rates of inflation obviously tend to discourage people from saving.

But sometimes inflation can be beneficial. If you borrowed $1,000 and were required to pay interest at a rate that is lower than the rate of increase in your income, the debt would be easier for you to pay off. Suppose you agreed to pay the lender $1,080 at the end of one year (you would be paying an 8 percent rate of interest). If at the same time your income and prices increase by 10 percent, you would find it easier to pay your debt, and the money you paid back would have less purchasing power than the money you borrowed. In effect, you would gain, while the lender would lose.

Inflation and Consumer Decisions

Inflation may affect consumer decisions in a number of ways. The rate of inflation, for example, is not likely to be the same for all individual products. Therefore, relative prices of different goods and services will certainly change. If the price of beef increases by 20 percent when chicken's price goes up only 5 percent, the relative price of chicken will go down. People, then, will buy more chicken and less beef.

Beliefs about inflation can either encourage or discourage people from spending. If you think the price of the type of car you want will increase $1,000 in the next few months, then you have an incentive to buy the car now before the price goes up. Even if you need to borrow more money now, the extra interest you would pay would almost certainly be less than the amount you would save by avoiding the price increase. On the other hand, if you believe that price increases will make it difficult for you to buy more than the basic necessities of life in the future, you will hesitate to take on debt to buy a car or other expensive consumer goods. Most economists believe the effect of inflation is more often to reduce the total amount of goods and services that are sold and therefore to reduce production and employment in the economy.

Increased inflation often contributes to increased rates of interest. There are at least two reasons for this relationship. Lenders do not want to be paid back with dollars that have less purchasing power than those that they lent. Therefore, they are likely to demand higher rates of interest to compensate them for expected inflation. In addition, an agency of the federal government, the *Federal Reserve System,* is likely to take steps that will force interest rates up to discourage borrowing and spending when there is inflation. The purpose of such a policy is to reduce spending and therefore the amount of inflation that actually does take place. In either case, consumers should not be surprised if inflation leads to higher interest rates that may affect the decisions they make.

Real and Money Values

In Chapter 1 you learned about money prices versus relative prices. Related to these terms are two others, money values and real values. *Money values* are expressed in terms of the number of dollars that are involved in a transaction at a particular time. Your wage may have a money value of $7 an hour. Or the money value of your tuition may be $150 per credit hour. Money values provide information about current costs, but they have little meaning when they are used to describe changes over time. Remember the example of the 75-cent wage rate paid in 1959.

Real values have been adjusted for inflation. When the 75-cent wage rate was adjusted for inflation, it became the equivalent of $3.50 in 1992. Real values provide more meaningful information than money values in most sit-

> Most economists believe the effect of inflation is to reduce the total amount of goods and services that are sold and therefore to reduce production and employment in the economy.

Real values
Dollar values that have been adjusted for inflation.

uations. If your uncle tells you he bought his first house for $38,000 in 1971, it tells you almost nothing. But if you know that $38,000 in 1971 dollars has a real value equal to $140,000 in 1992, you have a much clearer idea of the financial commitment he made. Consumers often need to consider the effect of inflation, and hence the real values, when they make decisions. Workers should be more concerned with the real value of their wages than the money value.

▶ **SUMMARY**

1. Many income differences are the result of inherent differences in human beings, but they also are determined by the amount of training and education an individual has obtained, the amount of on-the-job training, and the riskiness of the occupation.

2. Going to school is an investment in human capital because it makes you, the human, more productive in the future. Generally, your investment in human capital will pay off in the form of a higher wage later on.

3. You should specialize in an activity that is in demand and for which there is not a surplus supply. Hence, choosing your occupation requires predicting both the demand and the supply for that particular occupation in the future.

4. Usually individuals are paid according to their productivity. Therefore, anything that raises an individual's productivity may lead ultimately to a higher income.

5. The rate of return on education is as high as the rate of return on investing in other things. A college-degree holder may make two to three times as much income as a person who has graduated from grade school.

6. The greatest cost of going to college is not the money amount of books and tuition, but rather the opportunity cost of not being able to work and to make an income during those years.

7. An individual's wages (corrected for inflation) are usually lowest when he or she first enters the labor force. That's because people are least productive then.

8. In determining your standard of living, it is important to include non-money income, which includes, but is not limited to, goods produced at home, services produced at home, and social income from government-provided goods and services.

9. Women are entering the labor force in increasing numbers, and by the year 2000 will constitute approximately 50 percent of the labor force. In spite of aggressive pursuit of pay equity with men, women still make approximately 72 cents for every dollar earned by men holding similar positions. If current trends continue, pay equity will not be achieved until the year 2017.

10. Numerous federal and state laws protect employees against unfair or unhealthy employment situations.

11. Inflation is defined as a sustained rise in the weighted average of all prices. The most common measure of inflation in the United States is the consumer price index that is prepared by the Bureau of Labor Statistics every month. The CPI is determined by tabulating the weighted prices of a typical market basket of products and comparing the total to prices in a base year.

12. The CPI is the best measure of inflation we have, but it is not able to

account for all changes in products or all differences in the way people spend their money.

13. Inflation affects people in different ways. It may encourage some spending decisions and discourage others. It hurts people on fixed incomes and those who have saved or loaned money. It can help those who are in debt.

14. The difference between money values and real values is that real values have been adjusted for inflation. In most cases, real values are more useful in making consumer decisions.

▶ **QUESTIONS FOR THOUGHT AND DISCUSSION**

1. In your opinion, what are the most important nonmonetary benefits of investing in an education?

2. Why are physicians the most highly paid professionals in the United States?

3. In 1988 individuals with M.B.A. degrees received an average starting salary of over $36,000, while persons with Ph.D. degrees (which require more educational training) received an average starting salary of about $31,500. Why is this? Do you think it is fair?

4. What are some of the most important factors that contribute to differences in income?

5. Why does the government subsidize so much higher education?

6. If you felt your civil rights had been violated by your employer, would you be willing to sue? What benefits might you receive and what costs would you probably pay? What alternative actions might you take to try to resolve this type of problem?

7. If you knew that you would earn $50,000 a year in the year 2010, why would you have little knowledge of the standard of living you would be able to enjoy in that year?

8. Why are people who live in rural areas often less affected by inflation than would be indicated by the CPI?

9. Why have many labor unions attempted to negotiate cost-of-living adjustments into their wage rates?

▶ **THINGS TO DO**

1. Visit the career-guidance center of your college or university. Ask them to detail for you what testing, counseling, and other services they offer to students who are trying to choose a career.

2. Check the latest edition of the *Occupational Outlook Handbook* (issued annually by the Bureau of Labor Statistics, U.S. Department of Labor) for a forecast of your chosen career.

3. Estimate and make a list of the costs and benefits of your investment in education.

4. Identify and explain three different specific ways in which you or members of your family have been affected by inflation.

▶ **APPLICATION**

Prepare a simple example of a weighted price index by filling in the blanks in the accompanying table using current prices. Estimate the share of your total spending you devote to each product. If you spend 3 percent of your income on milk, for example, the weight in column 1 would be 3. Divide the current total weighted prices by the 1992 total weighted prices to obtain your index for these five products. Although this is a very simple demonstration, it is similar to the method used by the government to determine the CPI.

1	2	3	4	5	6
Product	Estimated Percent of Total Spending (weight)	1992 Price	1992 Weighted Value (column 2 × column 3 = column 4)	Current Price	Current Weighted Value (column 2 × column 5 = column 6)
Quart of milk	_____	$ .59	$ _____	$ _____	$ _____
Fast-food hamburger	_____	.69	_____	_____	_____
Gallon of gasoline	_____	1.13	_____	_____	_____
Pair of athletic shoes	_____	49.99	_____	_____	_____
Ticket to a movie	_____	6.00	_____	_____	_____
		Total	_____	Total	_____
		Index = (Current Total/1992 Total)			_____

▶ **SELECTED READINGS**

▶ Bolles, Richard N. *What Color Is Your Parachute?* Berkeley: Ten Speed Press. Published annually.

▶ Cohin, B. "A Turnabout on Civil Rights." *Newsweek,* November 4, 1991, p. 32.

▶ Ehrlich, Elizabeth. "The Mommy Track." *Business Week,* March 20, 1989, pp. 126–134.

▶ "How Imports Have Depressed U.S. Workers' Wages." *Business Week,* December 23, 1991, p. 20.

▶ Krantz, Les, ed. *The Jobs Rated Almanac.* New York: World Almanac, 1988.

▶ Mandel, M. J. "Mom, What's Inflation?" *Business Week,* August 26, 1991, pp. 20–22.

▶ McCormally, Keven, and Lindy Spellman. "Your Inflation Rate." *Changing Times,* January 1989, pp. 61–65.

▶ Quint, Michael. "Can a Kinder, Gentler Fed Tame Inflation?" *New York Times,* February 26, 1989, section 3, pp. 1, 10.

▶ Stein, Herbert. "Inflation Is Here, Still." *The Wall Street Journal,* March 6, 1989, p. A14.

▶ U.S. Department of Labor. *A Working Woman's Guide to Her Job Rights,* Washington, DC: U.S. Government Printing Office, 1988.

▶ U.S. Department of Labor. *Occupational Outlook Handbook,* Washington, DC: U.S. Government Printing Office. Published annually.

How to Choose and Start a Career

The choice of a career will determine, to a large extent, your future income, but the choice of a career is not based on money alone.

▶ APTITUDE MAY DETERMINE YOUR CAREER

Many individuals have special aptitudes and abilities that lend themselves to specific careers. It would be futile to choose a career as a concert violinist if you had no aptitude for music. Virtually all specialty occupations that might be labeled "glamorous" or "artistic" require special talents. This is also true for professional sports. Many individuals want careers in these areas but cannot and, indeed, should not seek them because they lack the appropriate abilities.

On the other hand, you can, with relatively little risk, try out a few of these areas. In effect, it is possible to test your aptitude when you are young. At this time, you can decide whether you should take the considerable risk of choosing a "glamorous" career.

You can also consider the possibility of choosing a less glamorous career in a glamorous field. If you would love to be in the theater but realize during your second year in college that you just don't have any natural acting talent, you can still enter that profession. You might train as a technician, an assistant producer, or a cameraperson.

In such careers as law, medicine, engineering, accounting, and others, aptitude is still crucial. The competition for good jobs (and even entrance to professional schools) is keen. If you are considering these careers, it would be appropriate to take aptitude tests well in advance. Most colleges and universities have services that can, either free or for a small fee, provide you with such tests.

▶ GETTING INFORMATION ABOUT AN OCCUPATION

There are several publications you can consult to get information concerning career outlooks.

1. *The Encyclopedia of Careers and Vocational Guidance* is a two-volume work published by J. G. Ferguson Company of Chicago and distributed by Doubleday & Company. These two volumes contain general information on vocational testing, interviewing, and the like. In addition, there is information on jobs and professions that do not require college training.

2. *The Occupational Outlook for College Graduates* is an annual publication of the U.S. Department of Labor. It surveys the job outlook for college graduates and describes each profession in terms of training required, salaries, working conditions, and the nature of work. This publication may help you avoid choosing a career for which there will be no demand in the future.

3. *The College Placement Annual* is published by the College Placement Council, Inc., 62 Highland Ave., Bethlehem, PA 18017. It gives job information for college graduates and alphabetically lists all major private employers in the United States, as well as government agencies. A unique employment index lists employers by occupations that are needed in the region the employer serves.

4. *Occupation in Demand,* another publication of the Department of Labor, is issued monthly and provides a summary of available jobs. Two extra editions are published in the spring and fall for students and recent graduates. It also includes job-search tips. Write to the Superintendent of Documents, Government Printing Office, Washington, DC 20402, for a copy.

5. *Occupational Outlook Quarterly,* another publication of the Department of Labor, has articles on labor research and trends in the labor market. The information it provides is often less directly applicable to individual job searches than that found in other publications of the Department of Labor, but it is helpful in learning about employment trends and other factors that affect the labor market.

The following are some places where you can obtain additional job information.

1. **College or university placement centers.** Virtually every college and university has some type of placement center. For college students, this might be the first place to look for job information. Placement centers have career consultants and vocational guidance counselors, as well as facilities for setting up interviews between prospective gradu-

ates and recruiters from major firms and government agencies.

2. State employment agencies. All 50 states have state employment offices. There are more than 1,800 employment offices operating in conjunction with the U.S. Employment Service of the Department of Labor. These employment services charge no fee and make placements for all types of jobs; some even offer free career guidance and aptitude tests.

3. "Help-wanted" ads in newspapers and professional or trade journals. Virtually every newspaper in the country has ads listing vacancies for various jobs. There are also job vacancies listed in trade and professional journals. Since these usually require that you apply by mail, an impressive resume is imperative.

4. Private employment agencies. You can register with an agency and wait to be called, or apply directly for a job that is advertised in a periodical. Agencies generally require you to sign a contract that obligates you to pay a fee if the agency places you. Read these contracts carefully; the small print may reveal that you owe the agency the fee even if you're fired after one week. Agency fees may run from 5 to 15 percent of your annual starting salary. In the upper-income job brackets, agency fees can sometimes be as much as 30 percent of your first year's salary. Those agencies that receive their commissions from employers are usually free to applicants.

5. Office of Personnel Management. The federal government's Office of Personnel Management publishes information on job opportunities for government civilian jobs, both within the United States and overseas. For information, check with your local post office or write to the Office of Personnel Management, Washington, DC 20415.

6. Periodicals. Some periodicals, such as *Kiplinger's Personal Finance* and *Business Week,* offer job-outlook or jobs-in-demand sections each year in their January or February issues. These can be valuable sources for college graduates who want to know what to expect when job hunting, the kinds of jobs available, and what employers are looking for.

▶ PREPARING A WINNING RESUME

For almost all job applications, you must submit a **resume.** Because personnel officers in corporations read thousands of them every year, your resume should create the best possible impression in order to give you a competitive edge over other job seekers. Remember, your resume is an advertisement for yourself.

▶ Keep It Brief

Since your resume is, in large part, bait for the interview, it need not be an entire dossier, starting out with letters of commendation from your junior-high-school principal. Nor should it list your every accomplishment, information about your outside interests, or the backgrounds of your parents.

▶ Presentation of Your Resume

Your resume should be typed on one or more sheets of high-quality rag bond. A good resume is usually professionally printed, not photocopied. Remember, the appearance of a resume is like the appearance you will make for an interview: First impressions count in both cases.

▶ Format of Your Resume

You needn't write a resume as if it were an application for college. In other words, don't put the word NAME before your name. The fewer headlines, the better, but you can divide your resume into sections for easy readability. A suggested outline follows.

1. *Personal data.* Begin with your name, address, and telephone number at the top of your resume.

2. *Employment objective.* Indicate the kind of job (or jobs, as long as they are within the same general area or industry) that you are seeking.

3. *Education.* List all schools you have attended and all other relevant academic information, as follows:

  a. Name and city/state of high school and the date you graduated (omit high school if you have a higher degree).

  b. Names and cities/states of colleges or universities you have attended, degrees received, and dates.

  c. Major and minor subjects and other courses related to your job goal.

  d. Scholarships, honors, and any extracurricular activities that may indicate social or leadership abilities.

4. *Work Experience.* Any work experience you have could be a valuable asset when applying for a job. Depending on the job you are applying for, you may wish to put the work-experience summary before the summary of your educational background.

5. *Miscellaneous.* Any abilities you have that may be appropriate to the job you are seeking should be listed. Depending on your prospective employer's needs, foreign-language skills, for example, or the ability to operate special equipment may be a strong selling point.

6. *References*. Give the names, positions, and addresses of three persons who have direct knowledge of your work competence. If you are a recent graduate, you can list teachers who are familiar with your capabilities. It is courteous to obtain permission from those whom you wish to use as references.

▶ The Do's and Don'ts of Resume Preparation

Experts in the field of resume preparation offer the following guidelines.

1. Make sure you proofread your resume so there are no typographical or spelling errors.
2. Make sure there are no errors in grammar. When in doubt, ask someone who knows.
3. First impressions are important. Therefore, have your resume professionally printed on good quality paper. Don't use colored or perfumed paper. Don't include a picture of yourself on the front.
4. Describe yourself honestly. Don't exaggerate. If you're young, be candid about your experience—or lack of it.
5. Don't cram your resume with useless information.
6. State very succinctly and clearly a job or career objective.

Exhibit F–1 shows a sample resume based on the preceding suggestions. There are other possibilities, of course, but the main things to keep in mind are clarity, brevity, and the relevance of your resume's content to the kind of job you seek.

▶ LETTER OF APPLICATION

When you send your resume to a prospective employer, you also will want to send a cover letter or a letter of application. This is the customary way to ask for a personal interview for a job. Exhibit F–2 shows a typical letter of application—in this case, for a sales job. Spend some time preparing the letter, making sure it is brief, to the point, yet personal. Whenever possible, address your letter to a specific person.

Once your application letter and resume have earned you an interview, consider these other pointers that can improve your chances of landing the job.

▶ HOW TO BE INTERVIEWED

Remember that the personnel officer of the company interviews many prospective employees. You must somehow convince the interviewer that you are as good as or better than anyone else who is being considered for the job. Basically, your interview should be constructed to convince the prospective employer that you will fulfill his or her needs. To do that, you must be prepared.

One skill that ranks high on the list of employers who are interviewing is the ability of the job candidate to communicate well. If you know something about the company, it will help you to relate your background to the company's needs and to communicate effectively with your interviewer. Information about prospective companies can be found by looking at some of the following sources:

1. *Moody's Manuals*
2. *Fitch Corporation Manuals*
3. *Thomas' Register of American Manufacturers*
4. *MacRae's Blue Book*
5. Company annual reports

Here are some suggestions for a successful interview.

1. Be a few minutes early.
2. Come with a copy of your resume.
3. Always maintain eye contact and listen attentively.
4. Be honest and frank, but don't make derogatory comments about a previous employer.
5. Let your interviewer offer you information on benefits, salary, and agency fees (if any).
6. Dress appropriately; first impressions are important.
7. Remember, personality counts, too. Be well rested for the interview, be alert and forthcoming in your responses, and be courteous to, and thoughtful of, everyone included in the interviewing process.
8. Have answers ready. Try to imagine a variety of questions you may be asked during an interview and prepare a few answers in advance. Then rehearse your answers.

▶ SOME FINAL POINTERS ON JOB HUNTING

Think of job hunting as a full-time (or part-time, depending on your work or school circumstances) job. Manage your time well and be methodical in your search. Consider your job search as work you are doing for yourself, and don't take "time-outs" from the job. After all, you're the employer!

The key to success in job hunting is motivation. If you are motivated, you will follow many of the suggestions in this section. If you feel that you need some more professional advice, consider seeking the services of a professional resume writer, generally someone associated with a private employment-counseling firm. If you need help with interviews,

▶ **Exhibit F–1   A Sample Resume**

Jane D. Jones   (date of resume)
593 Ninth Avenue
Anytown, Ala 35204
(555) 422-2824

EMPLOYMENT OBJECTIVE: Reporter, copy editor

EDUCATION

Standard State University, University City, Ala. B.S.,
   cum laude, 1982
Major: Journalism, *Minor:* Psychology. *Other courses:*
   Beginning and advanced photography
Honors: Phi Kappa Phi
Extracurricular activities: Editor of college newspaper.
   Served earlier as copy editor and reporter.

EXPERIENCE

September 1981–June 1982. Correspondent in University
City for *Anytown Gazette,* Anytown, Ala.

June–August 1981. *Anytown Gazette.* Although working as
a copy runner, I received a number of editorial
assignments. Besides covering meetings and writing
obituaries, I did a feature series with photographs on the
county arts group. (Attached is a photocopy of stories I
wrote.)

Summers, 1979 and 1980. Wilder Dress Shop, 215 Main
Street, Anytown, Ala. Salesclerk.

REFERENCES

Prof. J. W. Wynn, School of Journalism, Standard State
University, University City, Ala. 34205

Mr. William T. Ryan, editor, *Anytown Gazette,* Anytown,
Ala. 35204

Mrs. Dora Cohen, assistant professor of journalism,
Standard State University, University City, Ala. 34205

Source: Adapted from *Merchandising Your Job Talents,* U.S. Department of Labor.

▶ **Exhibit F–2   A Sample Letter of Application**

San Francisco, CA 94102
(415) 778-0000
(date)

Mr. Wilbert R. Wilson
President, XYZ Company
3893 Factory Boulevard
Cleveland, Ohio 44114

Dear Mr. Wilson:

Recently I learned through Dr. Robert R. Roberts of Atlantic
and Pacific University of the expansion of your company's
sales operations and your plans to create a new position of
sales director. If this position is open, I would appreciate
your considering me.

Starting with over-the-counter sales and order service, I
have had progressively more responsible and diverse
experience in merchandising products similar to yours. In
recent years I have carried out a variety of sales promotion
and top management assignments with excellent results.

For your review I am enclosing a resume of my
qualifications. I would appreciate a personal interview with
you to discuss my application further.

Very truly yours,

John W. Doe

Enclosure.

Source: Adapted from *Merchandising Your Job Talents,* U.S. Department of Labor.

practice with a friend or with someone who works in the placement center at your college or university. Without a doubt, job hunting requires a great deal of effort.

▶ SUMMARY

1. Aptitude can determine which career you pursue. It is important to determine early in life whether you have the appropriate aptitude for a specialized career, such as in professional sports or the arts.
2. You can obtain information on occupations from *The Encyclopedia of Careers and Vocational Guidance, The Occupational Outlook for College Graduates, The College Placement Annual,* and other publications.
3. You can obtain further information on jobs from private employment agencies, state employment agencies, your local college placement centers, and "help-wanted" ads in newspapers and professional journals.
4. A resume is bait for an interview. It should be a brief outline of your experience and education, not your entire life history.
5. Successful interviewing requires that you follow a few rules. Among the most important are these: Be a few minutes early, be honest and frank, and obtain information about the company before the interview.

▶ QUESTIONS FOR THOUGHT AND DISCUSSION

1. Can you think of a way to measure your aptitude for a career you are considering?
2. Who can use the services of a college or university employment office?
3. Who should seek the aid of private employment agencies in finding a job?

▶ THINGS TO DO

1. Find out as much as you can about the occupation you think you want to enter.
2. Make up a sample resume. What do you think it lacks that would impress a potential employer?
3. If your college media center has a videotape of a job interview, watch it carefully and make notes of possible things to remember and practice yourself.
4. Talk to three friends or relatives who are (happily) employed. Ask them how they got their jobs and what they think led to the success of their job interviews (if they were interviewed).

▶ SELECTED READINGS

▶ "Best Jobs For the Future." *U.S. News & World Report,* November 11, 1991, pp. 62–64.
▶ Bolles, Richard N. *What Color Is Your Parachute?* Berkeley: Ten Speed Press (published annually).
▶ *Dictionary of Occupational Titles.* 4th ed. supplement. Washington, DC: U.S. Government Printing Office, 1986.
▶ Moreau, Dan, and Bertha Kainen. "Job Interviews: Answers That Get You Hired." *Changing Times,* April 1989, pp. 53–55.
▶ *Federal Civilian Employment.* Washington, DC: Government Printing Office, 1988.
▶ *Jobs for the Future.* Washington, DC: U.S. Government Printing Office, 1987.
▶ Kocher, Eric. *International Jobs: Where They Are, How to Get Them: A Handbook for Over 500 Career Opportunities around the World.* Reading, MA: Addison-Wesley, 1984.
▶ *Matching Personal and Job Characteristics.* Available free from the Consumer Information Center, Pueblo, CO 81009.
▶ Parker, Jana. *The Damn Good Résumé Guide.* Berkeley: Ten Speed Press, 1986.
▶ *Résumés, Application Forms, Cover Letters, and Interviews.* Available from the Consumer Information Center, Pueblo, CO 81009.
▶ U.S. Department of Labor, *Merchandising Your Job Talents,* Washington, DC: U.S. Government Printing Office, 1986.

CHAPTER 8

You Have to Live with What You Have

PREVIEW

▶ What is the value of a budget?
▶ How can a budget be a part of an individual's or family's plan to achieve long-term goals?

▶ What special budget problems may college students have?
▶ What steps can consumers take to construct a useful budget?

▶ Why is record keeping important?
▶ What kinds of budgeting assistance are available to consumers?

> We can't buy everything we'd like to buy.

American consumers are rich. That is, we are rich compared with the Korean consumer, the Indian consumer, the African consumer, the Spanish consumer, or the Venezuelan consumer. The average per capita income in the United States is considerably higher than the per capita income in most other countries in the world.

But per capita income does not tell the story we want to tell. Exhibit 8–1 shows the different percentages of U.S. families that make particular amounts of income, ranging all the way from poverty to extreme opulence. Most of us find ourselves somewhere in the middle range. We're not destitute, because we do have some form of income, but, on the other hand, we're not Bill Gates either.

All of us, whether rich or poor, have this in common: we can't buy everything we'd like to buy. In other words, we all face the universal problem of scarcity. All of us operate with a limited income and amount of wealth we can spend. Because everyone faces this universal problem of scarce resources, personal money management is important for all of us, no matter what our income level.

CONSUMERS NEED A SPENDING PLAN

We've established the fact, then, that even extremely wealthy people need a spending plan. Consider the case of Donald Trump, who in 1990 controlled assets that included an airline, hotels, a railroad yard, and several casinos in Atlantic City. He also was in debt $3.8 billion and not able to make his payments on time. To obtain $60 million in additional credit in June of 1990, Trump was forced to agree to reduce his personal monthly spending from the $583,000 he spent in May of 1990 to $450,000. Although most people would be happy to "scrape by" on $450,000 a month, Trump's situation demonstrates the universal problem of scarcity that forces everyone to make choices no matter who they are or what they own. A spending plan—more commonly called a budget—helps us make these choices.

Planning a budget and attempting to follow it force the issues of scarcity and opportunity cost out into the open. Budgeting also necessitates decision making and the establishment of priorities. If you include a trip to Mexico in your budget, you will realize that somewhere along the line another item or items must be cut out. A budget, then, helps you manage your money in a more or less systematic and rational manner. It is also a control mechanism that causes you to be aware of the decisions you are actually making—deci-

▶ Exhibit 8–1   **Money Income of Families by Income Level, 1990**

Level of Annual Money Income	Number of Families in This Group (thousands)	Number of Families as Percent of All Families
Less than $10,000	6,234	9.4%
$10,000–$14,999	4,974	7.5
$15,000–$24,999	10,877	16.4
$25,000–$34,999	10,744	16.2
$35,000–$49,999	13,331	20.1
$50,000–$74,999	12,071	18.2
$75,000 and over	8,158	12.3

Statistical Abstract of the United States (Washington, DC: U.S. Government Printing Office, 1992), p. 449.

sions that are being made even if you don't wish to acknowledge them. Some of you may be able to determine instantaneously the tradeoffs and opportunity costs involved every time you make a purchase. But most of us would benefit from a budget. With it, we may be able to hold in check undirected spending activities that can lead to unhappiness and, occasionally, to financial disaster.

> Problems related to money are the most frequent cause of family fights.

DEMOCRATIC DECISION MAKING

If, in your situation, more than one person is affected by how each month's income is spent, then you have to choose how decisions will be made. Will decision making be unilateral or democratic? That is, will everybody involved in the family or spending unit participate? If not, some of those whose lives are affected may, at one time or another, feel cheated, left out, or imposed upon.

In most families today the "breadwinner" is no longer automatically allowed all the financial decision-making powers. And, of course, in most American households there is more than one person who is employed. Moreover, the unemployed members of a household who perform chores such as cooking and cleaning are making a contribution to the welfare of their family no less than those who are working for an income outside their home. Hiring a housekeeper or a nanny, for example, is an expensive proposition that can cost as much as $20,000 a year or more. The point to remember in preparing a budget, therefore, is that people should have a voice in it whether their contribution is made in the form of earned income or completing household chores.

It is important to work out money problems within a family unit in a cooperative way. Surveys have shown that problems related to money are the most frequent cause of family fights. Unfortunately, people who fight over money are likely to fight over other matters as well, at least in part because it becomes difficult for them to communicate when they are already angry about their financial problems.

It goes without saying that getting everybody within a spending unit to agree on budget allocations will not always be easy—or even possible. And, even in households that do engage in democratic decision making, usually the votes of the older and more experienced individuals (read: parents) carry the most weight. Nonetheless, the participation of all members of the family or spending group in the budget-making process has a very positive function. It forces each member of the group to consider the wants and needs of the others, and it acquaints each individual with the fact that not all wants and needs can be met. This knowledge can help a great deal in making sacrifice and compromise more acceptable, especially if each person's wishes and views have been treated fairly and reasonably by the others.

THE FAMILY COUNCIL

Money is a sensitive issue in any family, and in the busy world of today, the right moment for discussing the budget sometimes comes around very infrequently. One way to overcome this difficulty is by holding a family meeting, or *family council,* to decide on budgeting issues. You may wish to start with a casual meeting. If this doesn't work, try a more formal setting. It's helpful, too, if everybody in the spending unit knows of the meeting a day or so in advance. This will allow each individual some time for reflection on what he or she really needs or wants, or wants to complain about.

Resolving financial problems through family councils and shared decision making is an important part of creating and adjusting both short- and long-term budgets.

In some situations, communication on paper may be easier than verbal communication. If there is a quarrel about family spending priorities, you might suggest that each family member write down a list of individual priorities in descending order and then compare the lists. If the going gets rough, you might even want to tape-record—and then listen to—the family money fights. Frequently, those who argue don't really hear themselves. In the bargain-making process, contracts—between parents and teenagers, for example—might be created.

COLLEGE AND BUDGETING

The 1990s has seen a steady increase in the cost of obtaining a higher education at the same time that the level of financial aid and scholarships offered at many institutions has declined. Also, a growing number of college students are parents and have family responsibilities to bear. Consequently, making and following budgets is even more important for college students today than in the past.

When college students prepare budgets, they need to plan the use of their time as well as the use of their money. Students can often increase their income by finding a job, or by increasing the number of hours they work at a job they already have. They must remember, however, that their basic purpose in attending college (and in paying the associated costs) is to obtain an education that should increase their future income. Students need to be sure that working more hours while in school does not prevent them from achieving their full academic potential. In cases where students can't be successful in their courses and meet their financial needs at the same time, they may consider taking a semester off to earn more money or attending school part time while they work more hours.

Many college students borrow to pay for all or part of their college expenses. This choice is often unavoidable for students who want to complete their education quickly and who are not able to obtain other types of financial assistance. When students borrow, they should keep in mind the fact that they will be required to repay their loans. It is easy to borrow more money than is necessary to be able to buy a few "extras" while attending school. These extras, however, will increase the amount of payments due after graduation. Often a better choice is to live with less now to avoid having to make do with less in the future. This is particularly true for people who have long-term goals that include borrowing for other purposes later on. For example, a person who has a $25,000 student loan to pay off may find it more difficult to qualify for a mortgage even years after he or she graduates.

When students are parents, they may be tempted to try to give their children all the toys, trips, clothes, and other material possessions other children might have. Students with children, however, need to keep the purpose of their education in mind. Although paying for tuition, books, and other supplies may prevent parents from buying as much for their children now, their education should enable them to give their children a more financially sound future. Bringing older children into the budgeting process is often a good idea so they can understand why they may not have all the toys or clothing they want at the present.

> To be able to clarify your values, you first have to formulate your goals.

BUDGET MAKING, GOALS, AND VALUE CLARIFICATION

In Chapter 3, we discussed value clarification—how you decide what your goals are, what your values are, and what they mean with respect to how you should spend your time. Ultimately, this all relates to what kind of life you want to lead. Now you can put this abstract problem into perspective by applying it to an actual dollars-and-cents decision-making process—budget formulation. When you sit down alone or with the other members of your spending unit, you have to consider the values that you place on the various things you want to do with the income available. To be able to clarify your values, you first have to formulate your goals and those of the spending unit as a whole. Then you must set *priorities* among your goals. These priorities will be related to three general types of goals you probably will set for yourself or your household—short-term, intermediate, and long-term.

Consider an example. Suppose you set a long-term goal to improve your skills and physical condition so you can join and become a leader of your school's basketball team. This long-term goal would probably force you to make certain short-term and intermediate-term goals: making the second-string squad as a first step, buying a pair of expensive athletic shoes, spending at least an hour a day shooting the ball from beyond the 3-point line, and running every day to improve your wind. In general, short- and intermediate-term goals contribute to achieving long-term goals, whether these goals are athletic or financial in nature.

Consider another possible long-term goal—that of acquiring a genuine appreciation of the arts for yourself and your family. Short-term goals, such as going to a museum once a month or purchasing art appreciation books, and an intermediate-term goal of saving enough money for season tickets to the opera, might be involved in meeting this goal.

> A budget should not be a straitjacket but rather an indication of direction that will change.

More basically, you may have the goal of seeing that your family is well nourished and adequately housed or that it has sufficient medical protection or safe, comfortable transportation. Here, your goals may require choices such as stinting on housing to provide adequate food, or on transportation to provide medical protection.

Essentially, everybody's main goal is to be happy. The problem is clarifying your values enough so that you can establish goals that, taken together, will spell happiness for you and for those around you. When you formulate a budget, you can see exactly what these goals cost. You are forced to rethink and to reformulate your values when you realize that they are either unattainable or extremely costly, in the sense that you must forgo other desired or necessary things.

Goal definition and value clarification are integral parts of budget formulation and may be considered the only ways to design a satisfactory budget that works. Remember, though, a budget should not be a straitjacket but rather an indication of direction that will change, depending on changes in individual and family situations.

HOW DOES THE TYPICAL HOUSEHOLD ALLOCATE ITS INCOME?

Averages sometimes can be deceiving. But it may be instructive for you to see how typical households in the United States allocate their disposable (after-tax) incomes to the many competing demands. Exhibit 8–2 shows how an average American family spends its take-home income. A large chunk usually goes for housing services and household operation (including utilities and maintenance). Another large chunk goes for food. Food, housing, and household operation expenses often account for more than 60 percent of the average American family's after-tax expenditures in any one year. Personal care, clothing, and medical care constitute another large part of each family's budget in the United States. Medical care alone represents an increasingly large percentage of total U.S. consumption spending; we discuss the reasons for this increase and the future of medical-care expenditures in Chapter 19.

▶ **Exhibit 8–2** **Typical Distribution of Personal Consumption Expenditures, 1991**

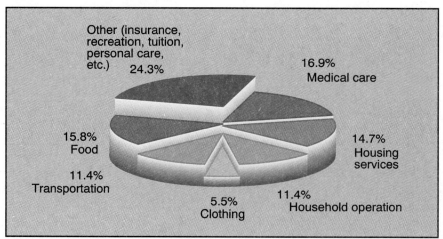

Other (insurance, recreation, tuition, personal care, etc.) 24.3%

16.9% Medical care

15.8% Food

14.7% Housing services

11.4% Transportation

5.5% Clothing

11.4% Household operation

As income goes up, spending for food generally falls and housing expenditures rise as percentages of total income. That means that, as our incomes increase, we buy proportionally more housing and proportionally less food. Housing, then, is often considered after a certain point to be a **luxury good,** for people buy a disproportionate amount of it as they become wealthier. Food, on the other hand, has the opposite characteristic and is, therefore, considered a necessity.

We have to be careful of such labels as *luxury* and *necessity,* however, because they have some subjective connotations. One person's luxury may be another person's necessity, and vice versa. Most of us have a hard time determining our own values and goals, let alone those of other people. But that's exactly what we attempt to do when we consider somebody else's spending to be "wasted" on so-called luxury items.

Luxury good
A good whose purchase increases more than in proportion to increases in income. Jewelry, gourmet foods, and sports cars usually fall into this category.

CREATING A BUDGET PLAN

Very briefly, these are the basic steps in creating a spending plan, a budget, that will be discussed in greater detail in the following paragraphs:

1. Identify and prioritize the goals you would like to achieve through your budget.
2. Analyze your income and spending patterns by keeping records for a month or two.
3. Determine **fixed expenses,** such as rent and any other contractual payments that must be made, even if they come due infrequently (such as insurance and taxes).
4. Determine **flexible expenses,** such as those for food and clothing.
5. Balance your fixed and flexible expenditures with your available income. If a surplus exists, you can save it or apply it toward the cost of achieving more of your goals. If there is a deficit, you need to examine your flexible expenses with an eye to reducing or eliminating some of them. You may also reexamine your fixed expenses to determine if any of them may be reduced in the future.
6. Evaluate your current spending patterns. Ask yourself if they will help you achieve your long-term goals. Do they form the basis for a responsible long-term budget? What changes could increase the satisfaction you receive from the money you spend?

Fixed expenses
Expenses that occur at specific times and cannot be altered. Once a house is purchased or rented, a house payment is considered a fixed expense; so is a car payment.

Flexible expenses
Expenses that can be changed in the short run. The amount of money you spend on food can be considered a flexible expense because you can buy higher- or lower-quality food than you now are buying. These are also known as variable expenses.

Note that so-called fixed expenses are necessarily fixed only in the short run. In the longer run, everything is essentially flexible or variable. You can adjust your fixed expenses by changing your standard of living, if necessary.

The Importance of Keeping Records

A budget is only as good as you make it—through good record keeping. Budget making, whether you are a college student, a single person living alone, or the head of a family, will be useless if you don't keep records. The best record keeping system is one that is both convenient to maintain and efficient. Paying bills by checks is one way to ensure both a record of your payment (in the check register) and a receipt (your cancelled check, when the bank returns it to you). Those expenditures can then be listed easily on a ledger at the end of every month. A special note, or receipt, of all cash expenditures—placed routinely in a specific container in your home—can help you keep track of your cash outflow. Again, at the end of each month, these can be entered into your ledger to create, along with expenses paid by check, a complete listing of monthly expenses.

Constructing a One-Month Budget Worksheet

In preparing a long-term budget, your first task is to construct a *one-month budget worksheet* to help you gain an understanding of your current spending patterns and to help you test your ideas for your budget. First, you should list your sources and amounts of income. If you receive money only from your parents or relatives, or from a scholarship or fellowship, then you know what your income will be. If, on the other hand, you earn all or part of your income, you must estimate what your net income for the month and year will be after withholding is taken from your gross pay for income taxes and Social Security. The easiest way to do this is to base your estimate on a recent paycheck stub.

Your next step is to identify and total the fixed expenses you must pay each month. Keep in mind that your budget worksheet should include a share of expenses that must be paid during the year, but not in each month. If your car insurance is $1,200 a year, for example, then you should be setting aside $100 each month to cover this expense even if you have already paid your bill for this year. The same sort of procedure may be used to set money aside for a future expense you know you will have to pay, like the purchase of schoolbooks or equipment for a required class you know you will take.

You also need to identify and estimate the amounts you believe you will spend on flexible expenses like food, entertainment, and similar goods or services. For most students, these expenses make up roughly one-third of their spending, although special situations may change the share for you.

Finally, compare the amounts of your expected income and spending. If your spending is less than your income, you may be able to save money or allocate more of it to other types of flexible spending. If, on the other hand, you realize that you have been planning to spend more than you will receive, you should review your expenses to see where you can make cuts.

The "Application" activity at the end of this chapter will help you understand how a one-month budget worksheet may be prepared to help you meet your financial goals.

Developing an Annual Budget Worksheet

After completing your one-month budget worksheet, you need to see how it works. Keep careful records of your income and spending and see if they are essentially the same as your budget. If they are, you may consider yourself an exception: most people encounter unexpected expenses that force them to make adjustments in their budgets. If the exhaust system on your car falls off, for example, you will need to have it repaired regardless of your budget. This may force you to cut down on entertainment expense. Or you may experience a particularly cold winter month, forcing your heating bills up higher than expected. These examples demonstrate why people should always try to have some unallocated funds in their budgets to cover emergencies.

Completing a series of three or four one-month budgets may be necessary for you to become confident in your understanding of your financial needs and resources. When you feel you have this understanding, it is time to make a long-term, or annual, budget worksheet. This document should be directed toward achieving long-term goals in addition to covering day-to-day expenses.

In long-term budgets many fixed expenses turn into flexible expenses. If you find that the rent on your apartment is so high that you are unable to save or buy other goods and services you need, you can look for a less expensive place to live, or try to find another person to share your apartment and its costs. If your car loan payments and insurance bills are too large, you might consider trading down to a less expensive car, or using public transportation instead of owning a car at all.

Long-term budgets may also help you evaluate your financial situation. For example, your long-term budget may cause you to see that you really need to earn more money if you want to accomplish your long-term goals. You might consequently choose to work more hours during your spring break or summer vacation than you would have if you had had no long-term plan. Long-term budgets tend to give people a sense of direction or purpose that helps them make more responsible consumer choices. You would be less likely to go out with your friends on weekends if you knew you would be able to take a vacation or buy a new car by saving the money that would have been spent on such outings.

REVIEWING YOUR BUDGET

Every successful budget requires a review of what has happened. You must be aware, however, that the money spent during the first several months in a particular category may be a very different amount from the money budgeted. That is to be expected; the budget will become more realistic as the process continues. Every few months, analyze your budget to see which categories are seriously out of line with reality.

It's also a good idea to rethink the budget process itself every few months. With time, you and/or the *spending unit*—those who decide what to spend—can predict relatively accurately what size each budget category should be. The next step is to determine for each category whether the maximum amount of satisfaction is being obtained from the budgeted income. If it isn't, perhaps one category should be expanded while another one is contracted. Thus, a budget will be continuously updated to reflect the spending unit's understanding of the level of satisfaction it is receiving from each budget category. Additionally, family changes will cause changes in budget categories. For instance, when children grow up, expenditure patterns change for the family unit, and when a homemaker goes to work, income patterns also change.

FITTING IT ALL INTO A LIFETIME PLAN

Today there is much talk about early retirement and the decisions that must be made if it is to be a happy period. There is also much talk about how increased leisure time will be spent and the need to purchase more leisure-related products. These matters should be considered as part of a lifetime plan, one that is revised periodically to take account of changing values, income, and consumption situations.

Lifetime planning actually is based on the establishment and subsequent accomplishment of both mundane and lofty goals. As a consumer, you might begin your planning by drawing up monthly and yearly lists of goals, tasks, and ideas. The monthly list, for example, would tell you when to schedule maintenance on your car, when to have services performed on household appliances, what days sales are coming up at various stores, and so on. The yearly list, of course, can do the same thing but probably will be more general and less specific.

Your long-term goals, those you hope to achieve in five, ten, or even fifteen years, will be much broader and will have to be revised to remain realistic. Your five-year goal may be to obtain a bachelor's degree, to learn how to ski or play tennis better, to become fluent in Spanish, or to become an active participant in a minority-affairs program. To attain those goals, you have to lay your yearly, monthly, weekly, and even daily plans with your future firmly in mind. Every once in a while, you have to take stock of your current position and your progress toward the various goals contained in the different plans. You probably will want to include in your evaluation those members of the spending unit who would be most affected by the different plans.

Periodically, you should confer with all members of the family spending unit to determine where each stands and where the family as a whole wants to be a year from now, five years from now, and so on. If a new house with a view of the ocean is what everyone really wants, you might decide to devise a program to attain that goal. That program might require sacrificing many consumption expenditures over the next few years in order to save enough for the down payment on that house. But if the family is united in its desire to meet that goal, the sacrifices may be made quite willingly.

Long-range planning is quite simple in concept but sometimes difficult to put into operation, mainly because people don't always like to face the reality of what is entailed in attaining certain goals. For example, the only way you can save is to consume fewer goods and services. And if you want to consume more goods and services, you will need to make more income. In most cases, the only way you can make more income is to become more productive in your job or to change jobs. That may involve going to night school, taking additional training, or working on weekends. If you're aware of such requirements, then you may be more willing to accept the cost of attaining a particular goal for yourself and/or your family.

BUDGET-ASSISTANCE PROGRAMS

A number of resources are available to help you with your budgeting or to assist you if you are having difficulties meeting your financial goals.

Budget Software

In recent years, computer software for budgeting has proliferated to the point that there are now hundreds of programs available. If you have a personal computer, a computer budget program might be useful in helping you record and categorize your income and expenses. Some of the software can be used in conjunction with tax-preparation software (see Consumer Issue H). Budget programs with this capacity include Andrew Tobias's *Managing Your Money* and Intuit, Inc.'s *Quicken*. These and other money-management computer programs can be obtained for prices of $50 and up.

Consumer Credit Counselors

If you are having difficulties with budgeting or debt management, there is a nationwide organization you can turn to for advice and counseling. Consumer

Credit Counselors, Inc., is a nonprofit organization that offers financial counseling and budgeting services at no charge. If you need to do more than just trim your budget, this organization also has a debt-management program that can assist you. Although there is a fee for the latter service, it is often nominal and may be waived in some cases. If you wish to contact Consumer Credit Services, which has 400 offices in the United States, look in the White Pages of your local telephone directory, or write

National Foundation for Consumer Credit, Inc.
8701 Georgia Ave., Suite 507
Silver Spring, MD 20910

The National Foundation can direct you to the nearest local office.

▶ SUMMARY

1. Even the richest among us do not have an unlimited budget and must, therefore, make choices.

2. Budgeting, or making a spending plan, forces you to realize that you face the constraint of a limited income and that you must make tradeoffs among those things you desire to purchase.

3. Democratic decision making means involving all members of the spending unit in the budget-making process. Holding a formal or informal family council is one way to allow each member of the family or spending unit to participate in budget formulation. Learning about tradeoffs and budget constraints is a valuable lesson in economics for children, as is the hands-on experience they obtain from managing allowances.

4. A typical household in the United States spends about 60 percent of its after-tax income on food, housing, and household operation expenses. As a family's income goes up, the percentage spent on food decreases and the percentage spent on housing increases.

5. Goals should be set according to your priorities. Short-term, intermediate, and long-term goals must be realistic, and striving to attain them may involve making tradeoffs.

6. The first step toward a realistic budget plan is keeping accurate records and constructing a monthly budget worksheet. Once this is done, longer-term budgeting can be undertaken and an annual budget formed.

7. The overall purpose of budgeting is to ensure that you get the best returns—in terms of health and happiness—from your income. This means your lifetime plan must be the ultimate framework for your daily, monthly, and annual budgeting strategies.

8. A number of good software programs are available to assist you in your budgeting effort. Another source of assistance is Consumer Credit Counselors, Inc., a nonprofit nationwide program to assist consumers in budgeting and debt management.

▶ QUESTIONS FOR THOUGHT AND DISCUSSION

1. Do you know anybody who does not face a budget constraint?

2. Do you think citizens of the United States have different problems working within their budget constraints than do citizens of India or Turkey?

3. It is sometimes argued that budget making and time planning reduce spontaneity. Do you agree or disagree? Is there any way the two can be reconciled?

4. Democratic decision making by way of a family council sounds old-fashioned to many individuals. What might be a more modern alternative?
5. How much voice do you think a teenager should have in family budget making?
6. Why do Americans spend proportionally more on housing than on food as their incomes increase?
7. Why must tradeoffs be made?
8. "If I only had 50 percent more income, I could buy everything I wanted." Evaluate this statement. Have you ever made it? Has it proved to be true?
9. Although very few people do serious lifetime planning, don't most individuals implicitly have a plan?

▶ **THINGS TO DO**

1. With the help of your reference librarian, go back to the earliest publication you can find from the Department of Labor, Bureau of Labor Statistics, and see what the average American family budget looked like then. How has it changed over the years? Are we spending more or less on food? On housing? What about taxes? A useful publication you may use is *Historical Statistics of the United States,* published by the U.S. Government Printing Office.
2. Make a detailed list of your short-term, intermediate, and long-term goals. How do these goals fit in with your overall values?

▶ **APPLICATION**

Prepare a one-month budget worksheet for yourself by completing each of the following steps. Use the left-hand column for estimated amounts. Record the actual amounts at the end of the month in the right-hand column. You will probably want to copy these forms rather than marking in your text.

1. *Estimate your income for the next month.*

	Estimated	Actual
Money provided by relatives, or from scholarships or fellowships	$_____	$_____
Expected net wages (after withholding)	$_____	$_____
Other sources of income	$_____	$_____
Total expected income	$_____	$_____

2. *Estimate your fixed expenses for the next month.*

	Estimated	Actual
Rent or mortgage payments	$_____	$_____
Utilities (heat, electricity, etc.)	$_____	$_____
Loan payments (car, credit card, etc.)	$_____	$_____
Insurance ($\frac{1}{12}$ of annual costs for car, renters, homeowners, life, etc.)	$_____	$_____
College costs ($\frac{1}{12}$ of annual costs for tuition, books, lab fees, etc.)	$_____	$_____
Other fixed expenses	$_____	$_____
Total fixed expenses	$_____	$_____

3. *Estimate your flexible expenses for the next month.*

	Estimated	Actual
Food in your home	$_____	$_____
Eating out	$_____	$_____

Household items	$_____	$_____
Transportation (gas, oil, bus fare, etc.)	$_____	$_____
Clothing	$_____	$_____
Personal items	$_____	$_____
Gifts for others	$_____	$_____
Entertainment (movies, sports, etc.)	$_____	$_____
Other	$_____	$_____
Total flexible expenses	$_____	$_____
Total fixed expenses (from above)	$_____	$_____
Total expenses	$_____	$_____

4. *Compare your total expected income with your total expected expenses to determine if you should anticipate a shortage or surplus of money at the end of the month.* If you do, you may want to adjust the amounts you have allocated for flexible expenses. Keep careful records of your income and spending over the month and record them in the right-hand column. Compare your estimates with what actually happened. You may choose to make adjustments in your budget and try it again for another month.

▶ **SELECTED READINGS**

▶ *The Complete Guide to Managing Your Money.* New York: Consumer Reports Books, 1989.

▶ Kutner, Lawrence. "Parent and Child." *New York Times,* December 15, 1988, p. 22.

▶ Loeb, Marshall, *Marshall Loeb's 1992 Money Guide.* Boston: Little, Brown, 1992.

▶ Money Management Institute. *Children and Money Management.* Available for $1 from Money Management Institute, Household Financial Services, 2700 Sanders Rd., Prospect Heights, IL 60070.

▶ "Pocket Guide to Money." *Consumer Reports,* January 1989, p. 18.

▶ Silver, Mark. "Curing Kids Who Want It All." *U.S. News & World Report,* March 20, 1989, pp. 83–85.

▶ "Strategies for the Stages of Life." *Fortune,* Special Issue, Fall 1991.

▶ Tucker, James F. *Managing Your Own Money: A Financial Guide for the Average Wage Earner.* New York: Norton, 1988.

▶ U.S. Department of Agriculture. *Managing Your Personal Finances.* Vol. 1. *The Principles of Managing Your Finances.* Home and Garden Bulletin #HG-245-1, October 1986.

▶ Weiner, Leonard. "Sizing Up Your Finances." *U.S. News & World Report,* June 8, 1987, pp. 52–64.

Budgeting Time for Recreation and Leisure

GLOSSARY

BED-AND-BREAKFAST a business run by an individual who rents rooms in his or her home and provides breakfasts to travelers.

TIME-SHARING PLAN an agreement through which consumers purchase the right to use a vacation facility for a specified period of time each year.

You may have heard the saying, "All work and no play makes Jack a dull boy." The idea is that people won't have a rewarding life if they work so many hours that they have little time left to enjoy themselves. When consumers construct budgets, they often forget about planning for recreation and leisure time. Yet, a spur-of-the-moment choice to buy a boat or take a vacation is not likely to be the best use of your earnings or time any more than other consumer choices that are not carefully made. Budgets that include plans for recreation and leisure time are more likely to result in personal satisfaction.

▶ THE GROWTH OF RECREATION

When consumers use time for recreation they make a tradeoff with other uses they could have made of their time. In 1890 the average American employee worked almost 55 hours a week. By 1990 average weekly hours at work had fallen to slightly more than 39 for full-time employees. This steady decline may be seen in Exhibit G–1. Millions of other Americans work at part-time jobs that leave them even more time for other activities. Labor-saving devices like washing machines and microwave ovens, and other new products like ready-to-eat and take-out foods, and wash-and-wear clothing, have allowed the average American consumer to enjoy a better standard of living and provided more leisure time for recreational activities.

Americans are also devoting a growing share of their spending to recreational products and activities. In 1933 only 4.7 percent of the average American's spending was used for recreation. Exhibit G–2 shows that by 1993 this share had reached 7.7 percent of consumer spending. American consumers increased their spending for recreation per person by more than 500 percent in the 60 years between 1933 and 1993, even after this spending was adjusted for inflation.

Americans use their increased leisure time in a variety of ways. They travel more and participate in more organized sports. Many people have purchased equipment like swimming pools or boats that allow them to enjoy their recreation without leaving the area of their home or community. Many consumers use their time to visit national and state parks. The list goes on and on.

▶ VACATIONS

Between 1975 and 1990 spending on tourism in the United States grew from almost $95 billion to over $350 billion a year. In the same time, employment in the travel industry almost doubled. Although these figures show how tourism has grown, it is less clear that there has been a corresponding increase in people's enjoyment and satisfaction. Consumers benefit from careful shopping when they spend their recreation dollars. There are many steps you can take to control your costs and make your vacation a success.

▶ Investigate Your Alternatives

If you plan to visit an unfamiliar place, before you leave be sure to investigate what there is to see and do at your destination. The American Automobile Association (AAA) publishes travel guides full of detailed information about points of interest, hotels, restaurants, and directions for how to reach these places. These guides are free to AAA's members.

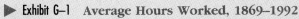

▶ **Exhibit G–1** Average Hours Worked, 1869–1992

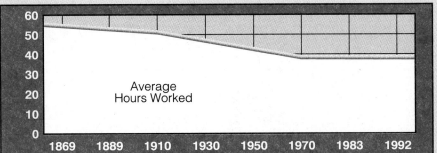

Average Hours Worked

| 60 | 50 | 40 | 30 | 20 | 10 | 0 |

1869　1889　1910　1930　1950　1970　1983　1992

▶ **Exhibit G–2 Percent of Personal Consumption Expenditures Devoted to Recreation**

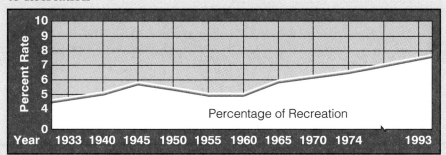

Back in 1933, only 4.7 percent of present consumption expenditures were devoted to recreation. This percent has been rising ever since, today reaching 7.7 percent or more. (The 1993 figure is an estimate.)

Another useful source that may be used for free in most libraries is the various editions of the *Mobil Travel Guide* which contains listings of hotels and restaurants that have paid to have their names included. Although many fine establishments will not appear because they have not paid a fee, consumers can be reasonably sure the ones that are included will meet minimum standards of quality and that their prices will be within the ranges indicated in these booklets. Many listed firms provide discount coupons in the *Mobil Travel Guide* as well as giving discounts directly to AAA members. Other travel guides with specific and useful in formation may be found in most libraries.

Another way to find a place to stay is by using the toll-free numbers provided by many hotel and motel chains. You can find these numbers in the Yellow Pages of most telephone books, listed under "motels/hotels." You will be limited to the ones that maintain an 800 number, but you can be reasonably sure that they will meet minimum standards.

One choice you should not overlook is staying in a **bed-and-breakfast.** These are rooms rented in private homes from individuals who also serve you breakfast. They often provide a separate bath and entry. There are organizations of bed-and-breakfasts that publish lists of their members' establishments with brief descriptions. Most libraries have books that tell about bed-and-breakfasts in different regions of the country. You may also write to the chamber of commerce in towns you intend to visit and ask for a local listing of these businesses. An advantage of staying at a bed-and-breakfast is the opportunity it gives you to gain personal knowledge of the area you are visiting and to plan the best use of your time.

Some consumers prefer to rent condominiums or apartments instead of staying in a hotel, particularly if they expect to stay in one location for several days or more. Condominiums offer more space than most hotels, plus the use of a kitchen, which can save you the cost of some or all restaurant meals. A problem with many condominium rentals is that you may have to make your own beds and wash your own dishes. They do offer lower-cost vacations, however, particularly for larger families. Travel agencies have access to listings of condominiums that may be rented, or you can write to local chambers of commerce.

▶ **Time-Sharing Plans**

One method that may reduce vacation costs is a resort **time-sharing plan.** Under these agreements you buy the use of a resort facility for a specified period of time (most often two weeks) each year. You are then allowed either to use your time in your own resort or trade your time with someone else who owns a similar plan in another vacation spot.

In some time-sharing plans, you buy only the right to use a facility that belongs to someone else. In others, you actually become a part-owner of a condominium. Ownership plans can be quite expensive, requiring initial payments that are typically between $8,000 and $15,000. They will also require the payment of a maintenance fee that may be as much as $150 a year. The advantage of these plans is the opportunity they provide to earn a capital gain if the property increases in value. Of course they may also result in a loss if the property's value falls, and they may be difficult to sell quickly.

Generally, time-sharing plans are most appropriate for consumers who are financially able to commit a substantial amount of money over an extended period of time. Although many time-sharing plans are legitimate and offer consumers quality vacations at reasonable cost, some have involved deceit and fraud. Have a lawyer examine any time-sharing plan agreement before you sign it. For further information, write to the American Land Development Association, Resort Time-Sharing Council, 1000 16th Street, N.W., Washington, DC 20036.

▶ Cutting Vacation Costs

Planning, and a willingness to cut some corners, may save you a significant amount of your travel money. Here are some suggestions for reducing your vacation costs. Travel agents and budget travel books may provide others.

1. Take vacations in off-seasons when possible. Hotel and resort rates may be reduced by as much as 50 percent. Trips to Europe in October, for example, are less costly than similar vacations in July. The historic buildings, museums, and theaters are the same regardless of when you go and are also less likely to be crowded by other tourists. Timing is a crucial factor in saving money on vacations.

2. Take advantage of airfare bargains. Always book your flights well in advance of the dates you intend to travel, and inquire about rates with several travel agents. If you can be flexible in the time you are willing to fly, you often can find lower rates. Also, charter flights may be available through travel agencies at much lower costs than regularly scheduled flights. There are drawbacks to charter flights, however. They often depart at late hours and are well known for not leaving or arriving on time. Some charter organizations have gone out of business, leaving passengers with worthless tickets. Buying travel insurance may be worth the money if you use a charter airline.

3. If you are a student, obtain an international student identity card from the Council on International Educational Exchange, 777 United Nations Plaza, New York, NY 10017. Many hotels, restaurant, theaters, and museums give discounts to people who have such cards.

4. Investigate the benefits and costs of passes that provide unlimited travel on trains or buses. In Europe you can buy the Eurail pass. U.S. bus lines sometimes make available similar passes.

5. Consider staying in youth hostels, inexpensive dormitory-style accommodations that exist throughout the world. Fees in the United States range from $5 to $10 a day. In other countries the fees may be somewhat higher or lower but will always be much less expensive than staying in a hotel. For information on youth hostels, write the American Youth Hostels, AYH National Campus, Delaplane, VA 22025.

6. Choose hotels or motels that do not charge extra for parking. Consider older, downtown hotels that most likely have lower rates than newer suburban motels.

7. Remember, it is not necessary to eat every meal in a restaurant. Having picnics along the road or even in your car can be fun and is always less expensive than restaurant meals.

8. Shop around for your best travel deal. If you know where you want to go, invest the time and money to make calls to several hotels or resorts to find what each has to offer. It is not necessary to stay in a hotel that is on the beach to enjoy the beach, for example. Staying a few blocks away may save you money and allow you to get a better night's sleep because of less noise. And don't pay for more room than you need. Essentially, a hotel is mostly a place to sleep. An impressive lobby with extra-thick carpets will not improve the quality of your rest.

▶ PARTICIPATING IN SPORTS

More and more Americans are using their leisure time to participate in various sports. The number of recreational golfers, for example, increased from about 15 million to 25 million in the 1980s. Adult softball teams grew from 110,000 to 184,000 in the same time. The number of U.S. skiers almost doubled, and bicyclists increased by roughly 50 percent. Participation in many other sports has grown at similar rates.

Taking part in recreational sports requires a commitment of time and money. American consumers spent more than twice as much for sports equipment in 1990—almost $46 billion—than they did in 1980—about $17 billion. This growth in spending is not surprising. Consider the costs of being a golfer as an example. In 1990 a basic set of golf clubs cost at least a few hundred dollars, and a consumer could easily spend a thousand dollars or more on them. Greens fees and club memberships cost the average golfer another $700 each year. Almost 500 million 18-hole rounds were played in 1990, of which roughly half involved the rental of a golf cart. When the cost of food and beverages consumed before or after playing golf are included, an estimated $25 billion was spent on this sport in 1990. Similar data can be found for other sports.

Generally, sports equipment can be rented at a fraction of the cost of buying your own. For example, a set of downhill ski equipment that cost at least $500 could be rented at most ski resorts for $40 to $60 a day in 1992. Many consumers have purchased expensive ski equipment before they were sure that they would continue with the sport, or that the particular type of equipment they chose was the best for their needs. People who want to buy such sports equipment may benefit from investigating publications like *Consumer Reports*.

Buying sports equipment is often the result of social pressure as much as need. Choosing the absolute best equipment may be rational for Olympic Games contenders, but it seems less reasonable for those who ski only a few times a year. In the 1980s sales of skiing equipment grew by 80 percent, reaching an annual average of $613 million. Some of this money could certainly have been saved if consumers had rented equipment until they were sure they needed their own, and learned what type was the best choice for their money.

▶ BUYING RECREATIONAL VEHICLES

Total sales for recreational vehicles—pleasure boats, motor homes, snowmobiles, and all-terrain vehicles and bicycles—increased by almost 200 percent in the 1980s. In 1980 for example, 2.7 million new pleasure boats were sold. In 1990 these sales exceeded 9.2 million. Although owning a boat or a motor home is often an enjoyable experience, it is also an expensive proposition. Consumers need to make the decision to buy such a product only after careful evaluation of their costs and benefits.

Let's consider the choice of buying a motor home as an example. Many consumers picture leisurely drives through the countryside, cooking their own meals, and staying in picturesque campgrounds with all the comforts of home. And they imagine having these benefits at a fraction of the cost of renting a room in a hotel and eating out in restaurants. They probably fail to realize all the costs involved in this dream. Most experts believe that owning and using motor homes for vacations increases the cost of recreation.

A typical new motor home in 1992 cost in the range of $25,000 to $40,000 depending on its size and features. However, motor homes are not only expensive to buy, they are very costly to own and operate. Insurance for a motor home may cost $1,000 or more each year. These vehicles are expensive to register in most states because they are heavier than ordinary cars. They get poor gas mileage and tend to be expensive to repair. When you park them in a commercial campsite, or even in a state or national park, you can expect to pay a fee of $10 to $20 a night. They are not convenient to park or easy to drive, particularly in cities.

The greatest expense of buying a new motor home for most people is the cost of depreciation. Motor homes do not hold their value well. They commonly lose as much as 50 percent of their value in their first two or three years of use. They are also often hard to sell.

The average cost of owning a motor home has been estimated to range from $6,000 to $10,000 a year. You can stay in a hotel and eat out for many days for that amount of money. If you ever decide to own a motor home, consider buying a used one that has already suffered much of the rapid depreciation that takes place in the years after it is first sold. In any case, don't expect to save money unless you have a large family and spend many days on vacation each year.

▶ VISITING NATIONAL AND STATE PARKS

For generations our national and state parks have been a popular destination for recreational trips. In 1989 patronage of national parks exceeded 250 million visitor days; another 688 million visitor days were recorded at state parks. American consumers spent more than $500 million for entry fees to make these visits. Our parks have become so popular that some have become overcrowded and have even begun to limit the number of people who may visit on a given day. Traffic jams on roads in Yellowstone National Park commonly reduced the speed of traffic to little more than ten miles an hour during summer days in the 1980s.

To make the best use of public parks, consumers may choose to travel at times that are not the most popular. You can call the park's information center (the number can be found in most travel guides) about the best times to visit. At the same time, you may make reservations at the many superior hotels and resorts that exist around our parks. It is usually impossible to stay in these facilities without making reservations months in advance. Even making advance reservations for a campsite is usually necessary.

One reason our parks are so popular is their relatively low prices, made possible because the cost of maintaining them has traditionally been shared between those who use them and taxpayers in general. In 1988 only about 8 percent of the cost of running our national parks came from entry fees. The remainder came from government appropriations and fees paid by businesses for the right to operate in the parks. Presidents Reagan, Bush, and Clinton suggested that entry fees be increased to cover a larger share of the cost of operating our parks. In general, most members of Congress, and many consumers, have opposed these suggestions, because higher fees could limit the use of national parks to people who have substantial incomes. As our government experiences continued budget deficits, such fees will likely increase in the future.

▶ MAKING TIME FOR LEISURE

Many people who do not have the time or can't afford vacations spend their leisure time at or near their homes. They take walks in parks or play games with their children. Although staying near your home is often a less expensive use of recreational time, it is often not free. In 1990, for example, over 1 million Americans purchased home swimming pools. The average price for an above-ground pool at that time was $3,600 and for in-ground pools the average was just over $13,000. The chemicals and electricity to run a pump for a pool add more than another $150 to this cost each year.

Some consumers relax by working in their gardens, but even this can be expensive. In 1989 Americans spent more than $7.2 billion on nursery products. Other types of spending in 1989 that could be considered recreational included $2.8 billion on renting videotapes, $5.4 billion on photographic equipment, and more than $5 billion on pets and pet supplies.

Recreation and leisure are necessary to refresh your body and your mind. Most people are more productive if they devote a reasonable share of their time to having a good time. Yet, some people never seem to find time for recreation. When they are not working at a job to earn an income, they are engaged in accomplishing tasks around the house. Such people need to take control of their lives by scheduling in time for rest and recreation. It is desirable to find a balance between work and play that best fits one's needs and personality.

A budget can help in this regard. The planning process can help you put into perspective the kind of life you wish to lead. Devoting time and money to recreation and leisure is a tradeoff. Most people can't earn money or advance their careers while they are having fun. But is working and earning money all you want out of life? How much more is another dollar worth if you don't have time to spend it? The procedure of making a budget, and setting various short-term and long-term goals in the process, can help you sort out these lifestyle issues.

▶ SUMMARY

1. American consumers now have more leisure time than in the past and are devoting a growing part of their earnings to recreation.
2. Spending on tourism has increased by more than 280 percent since 1980. Consumers may make better spending choices for their vacations by availing themselves of the information in various tour guides, including those provided by the AAA and *Mobil Travel Guides*.
3. Consumers might also consider the costs and benefits of staying in bed-and-breakfasts, condominiums, and less expensive hotels and motels, or of joining time-sharing plans.
4. More consumers are using leisure time to participate in sports. Spending on sports equipment and activity almost tripled in the 1980s. Before consumers buy sports equipment, they can investigate their alternatives by studying *Consumer Reports* and other similar publications. A good choice for many people is to rent equipment, at least until they know whether they want to pursue the sport and, if so, what type of equipment suits them best.
5. Sales of recreational vehicles like boats and motor homes grew rapidly in the 1980s. Although these products can be the source of consumer

satisfaction and enjoyment, they rarely save money. Most new recreational vehicles suffer rapid rates of depreciation in the first years after they are purchased.
6. A large number of consumers spend their leisure time at or near their homes. Even this may involve the spending of substantial amounts of money when a swimming pool or video equipment is involved.
7. Consumers can gain the most satisfaction from their lives by choosing the balance between work and leisure that best meets their personalities and financial needs.

▶ QUESTIONS FOR THOUGHT AND DISCUSSION

1. What changes in society have taken place that allow American consumers to devote more of their time and earnings to recreation?
2. What types of tradeoffs do consumers make when they go on vacation?
3. Why might it be more economical to rent recreational equipment rather than buy it?
4. Why do people need to devote at least some time and money to recreation?

▶ THINGS TO DO

1. Investigate forms of recreation that you or your friends participate in that were not available when your parents were your age. How are these activities related to our greater income and technological advancements? What activities do you think your children might participate in when they are your age?
2. Visit a motor home or boat dealership. What sort of sales pitch does the salesperson give you? Are you told about the money you can save or the fun you will have? What do you believe you are not told that you should know about?

Paying for Government

▶ Why are taxes necessary?
▶ How has the federal government's use of tax revenue changed

in recent years?
▶ What principles are different taxes based on?

▶ Why has the manner in which federal income tax liability is determined changed in recent years?

Fiscal Year	Individual Income and Social Security Taxes as Percent of Federal Spending
1960	52.0%
1965	51.2
1970	58.2
1975	59.0
1980	62.5
1985	62.9
1990	62.3

Source: Based on data from *Statistical Abstract of the United States* (Washington, DC: U.S. Government Printing Office, 1991).

Our government provides numerous goods and services, such as a court system, police, firefighters, public schools, public libraries, and myriad other programs that most citizens could not afford to pay for themselves. These goods and services help the people of our nation live better and our economic system operate more efficiently. However, all government services must be paid for in one way or another.

The government raises money to pay its expenses by shifting purchasing power from people and business to its own spending, either through taxes or borrowing. In Exhibit 9–1, you can see that in most recent years an increasing portion of federal tax revenue has been paid by individuals through income taxes and Social Security taxes. In 1960 individuals paid 52 percent of total federal tax revenues. By 1990 this proportion had reached 62.3 percent. This means that, on average, Americans now work more days to earn the money that they pay to the government in taxes than they worked in previous years.

In 1992 the Tax Foundation of Washington, D.C., estimated that the average American worked from the first of the year until May 8, the date the Tax Foundation dubbed "Tax Freedom Day," to earn tax money. Only after that date is the average American working for him- or herself. Exhibit 9–2 shows that in 1930 "Tax Freedom Day" fell on February 13. Of course, the government provided far fewer goods and services at that time. Exhibit 9–3 compares sources of federal revenue and types of spending in 1970 and 1990. What do these graphs show about changes in the role of the federal government in our lives?

THE WHYS AND HOWS OF TAXATION

Governments—federal, state, and local—have various methods of taxation at their disposal. The best known, of course, is the federal personal income tax. At the state and local levels, property taxes make up the bulk of the taxes collected. In addition to these taxes, there are corporate income taxes, sales taxes, excise taxes, inheritance taxes, and gift taxes, not all of which can be investigated in detail here.

First, a Little Theory

Naturally, everybody would prefer a tax that someone else pays. Because we all think that way, no tax could be devised that everyone would favor. Economists and philosophers have come up with alternative justifications for different ways of taxing. The two most prevalent principles of taxation are benefits and ability to pay.

The Benefit Principle   One widely accepted doctrine of taxation is the *benefit principle*. According to this principle, people should be taxed in pro-

► Exhibit 9–2 Tax Freedom Day

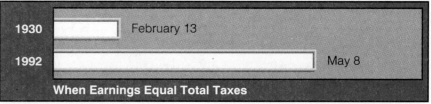

| 1930 | February 13 |
| 1992 | May 8 |

When Earnings Equal Total Taxes

► Exhibit 9–3   The Federal Government Dollar

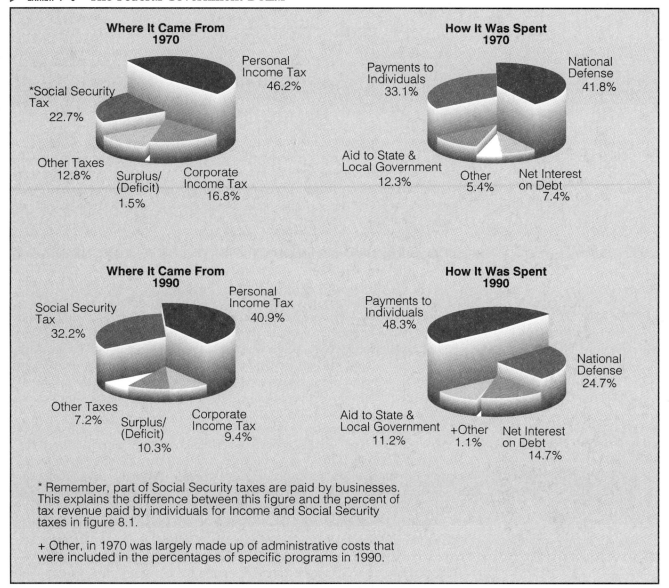

**Where It Came From
1970**

Personal Income Tax
46.2%

*Social Security Tax
22.7%

Other Taxes
12.8%

Surplus/ (Deficit)
1.5%

Corporate Income Tax
16.8%

**How It Was Spent
1970**

Payments to Individuals
33.1%

National Defense
41.8%

Aid to State & Local Government
12.3%

Other
5.4%

Net Interest on Debt
7.4%

**Where It Came From
1990**

Personal Income Tax
40.9%

Social Security Tax
32.2%

Other Taxes
7.2%

Surplus/ (Deficit)
10.3%

Corporate Income Tax
9.4%

**How It Was Spent
1990**

Payments to Individuals
48.3%

National Defense
24.7%

Aid to State & Local Government
11.2%

+Other
1.1%

Net Interest on Debt
14.7%

* Remember, part of Social Security taxes are paid by businesses. This explains the difference between this figure and the percent of tax revenue paid by individuals for Income and Social Security taxes in figure 8.1.

+ Other, in 1970 was largely made up of administrative costs that were included in the percentages of specific programs in 1990.

portion to the benefits they receive from government services. The more they benefit, the more they should pay; if they benefit little, they should pay little. This principle of taxation has problems in application, however. First of all, how do we determine the value people place on the goods and services the government provides? Can we ask them? If people think that others will pay their way, they will claim, on being asked, that they receive no value from government services. For example, they will say they are unwilling to pay for national defense because they do not want it, it is of no value to them. This is the **free-rider problem.** We are free riders if we think we can get away with it. If you think everybody else will pay for what you want, then you will gladly let them do so. The problem is schematized in Exhibit 9–4. How much national defense will you benefit from if everyone pays except you?

Free rider problem
When individuals attempt to receive benefits from a good or service without paying their appropriate share.

▶ Exhibit 9–4 Scoreboard for National Defense

	If you pay	If you do not pay
If everyone else pays	$300,000,000,<u>300</u>	$300,000,000,000
If no one else pays	$300	$0.00

$300,000,000,000. How much will there be if you also pay? $300,000,000,<u>300.</u> If you think everyone else will pay, won't you be tempted to get a free ride?

One way out of this dilemma is to assure that the higher a person's income, the more services he or she receives and, therefore, the more value he or she gets from goods and services provided by the government. If we assume that people receive increases in government services that are *proportional* to their incomes, then we can use this benefit to justify requiring them to pay more taxes.

The Ability-to-Pay Principle The second principle of taxation states that those who are able to pay more taxes *should* pay more taxes. Obviously, people who make more money generally should be able to pay higher taxes. But we do make them pay taxes that go hand-in-hand with income (a proportional system)? Or do we make them pay taxes that increase, but at a rate that is not in proportion to their incomes (a regressive system)? To answer these questions, we must decide whether their ability to pay rises faster than, in proportion to, or slower than their incomes. Whatever assumption we make determines whether we use a progressive, proportional, or regressive tax system. The ability-to-pay principle would lead us to recommend progressiveness only if we assume that ability to pay rises more rapidly than income.

Proportional taxation

A taxing system in which all people pay the same share of their income in tax.

Proportional taxation is a system by which taxpayers pay a fixed percentage of every dollar of income. When their incomes increase, the taxes they pay increase. If the proportional tax rate is 10 percent, you pay 10 cents in taxes out of every dollar you earn. If you earn $1,000, you pay $100 in taxes; if you earn $1 million, you pay $100,000 in taxes. Exhibit 9–5 illustrates the principle of proportional taxation.

There are few if any examples of proportional taxes in the United States. Even Social Security and Medicaid taxes, in which all wage earners pay a set percent of their income up to a maximum amount, are not proportional because these taxes are not charged on some types of income, like interest and dividends, and earned income over the maximum is not taxed.

Progressive taxation

A taxing system in which the greater your income is, the greater the share of that income you will pay in tax.

At this point, we should contrast proportional taxes with **progressive taxation.** If a tax is progressive, the more you earn, the more you pay in taxes, as with the proportional system; but, in addition, the *percentage* taken out of each additional dollar earned rises. We can describe progressiveness as

▶ Exhibit 9–5 **A Proportional Tax System**

INCOME	PROPORTIONAL RATE	TAX
First $100	10%	$10
Second $100	10%	$10
Third $100	10%	$10
Total Income: $300		**Total Tax: $30**

INCOME	MARGINAL RATE	TAX
First $100	10%	$10
Second $100	20%	$20
Third $100	30%	$30
Total Income: $300		**Total Tax: $60**

a system by which the **marginal tax rate** goes up. In the example illustrated in Exhibit 9–6, the first $100 of income is taxed at 10 percent, the next $100 at 20 percent, and the third $100 at 30 percent.

Probably the best example of a progressive tax is the federal (and most state) income tax. Although the use of deductions and exemptions (these will be discussed later in this chapter) allows some people with large incomes to pay little tax, for most people, the percentage of their income that is paid in tax increases with the amount of their income.

Can the benefit principle of taxation be used to justify progressiveness? Yes, it can. The only additional assumptions needed are: (1) the *value* people obtain from increased goods and services provided by the government goes up faster than their income, and/or (2) the *amount* of government goods and services received goes up faster than income. The benefit principle alone, without one of these two assumptions, cannot be used to justify progressive taxation.

As you might suspect, **regressive taxation** is the opposite of progressive taxation. A regressive tax system takes away a smaller and smaller additional percentage as income rises. The marginal rate falls and is usually below the average rate. As an example, imagine that all revenues of the government were

Marginal tax rate
The share of the next dollar earned that must be paid in taxes.

Regressive taxation
A taxing system in which the greater your income is, the smaller the percent of that income you will pay in tax.

Taxes on gasoline, tobacco products, and alcoholic beverages are all regressive. For example, the 36¢ gasoline tax indicated in the photograph would be a larger share of most students' relatively low incomes, but a smaller share of most professors' incomes.

obtained from a 99 percent tax on food. Because we know that the percentage of income spent on food falls as the total income rises, we also know that the percentage of total income that would be paid in taxes under such a system would likewise fall as income rises. It would be a regressive system.

The **excise tax** (a tax collected from the product's producer) on gasoline is a good example of a regressive tax. For people who have large incomes, the tax is a much smaller part of their incomes than it is for those who have small incomes. The exact amount that is charged per gallon varies from state to state, but suppose that the tax is 15 cents per gallon in your state. If you earn $100,000 a year and purchase 1,000 gallons of gasoline, the $150 tax you pay is .15 percent of your income. If the same $150 tax is paid by Joe who earns only $10,000, it would be 1.5 percent of his income. Therefore, the gasoline tax is regressive, because it is a larger portion of Joe's smaller income.

Most taxes imposed by state or local governments tend to be regressive. These include taxes on tobacco products, liquor, sales, and property.

PERSONAL FEDERAL INCOME TAX

As mentioned earlier, the personal income tax system in the United States is progressive. In 1986, for example, prior to the tax-reform legislation, there were 15 income-tax brackets, each with a progressively higher marginal tax rate. The highest tax rate was 50 percent. This did not mean, however, that if you were in the 50-percent bracket you had to pay a 50-percent tax on *all* your income but only on the income that exceeded a certain amount.

The tax-reform legislation of 1986 greatly simplified matters by reducing the number of tax brackets to only three. Regardless of the number of brackets, tax rates that increase with taxable income clearly demonstrate the progressive nature of federal income taxes for most Americans.

THE ETHICAL CONSUMER

Shopping at Smokin' Joe's

Federal law recognizes Native American (Indian) tribal governments as being independent nations. Native Americans do not collect or pay federal, state, or local taxes on money earned on their reservations. In the 1980s many stores were opened on tribal lands where no taxes were collected. One such store is Smokin' Joe's on the Tuscarora Reservation in Niagara County, New York. In 1992 Joe, a Native American, sold gasoline for $.99 a gallon when gas stations only two miles away from the reservation charged $1.21. The difference in price was the federal and state gas tax that Joe didn't collect from his customers. Thus, consumers buying gasoline from Joe benefited from paying a lower price while Joe earned the same profit as the other gas stations. Although the treaties signed by the federal government and Native American leaders probably were not intended to allow non–Native Americans a way to avoid paying taxes, federal and New York State courts have ruled Joe's store is legal under these agreements. When federal, state, and local governments lose tax revenue from people who shop at Joe's, other taxpayers have to pay a larger portion of the tax burden. Although consumers who shopped at Joe's were not breaking any laws, do you believe they were being ethical? What would you do if you lived near Joe's? Would you buy his gasoline or would you pay the tax?

How Our Progressive System Evolved

The Constitution gives Congress the authority "To Lay and collect Taxes, Duties, Imposts and Excises. . . ." No reference was made to an income tax at the time the Constitution was drafted. But in 1894 the Wilson-Gorman Tariff Act provided for individual income taxes of 2 percent on incomes above $4,000. The country knew about income taxes from the period during the Civil War, when $4.4 million of such taxes were collected. Nonetheless, the concept of income taxation set forth by the Wilson-Gorman Tariff Act was violently challenged and had to be settled by a Supreme Court decision in 1895. Finally, in 1913, the Sixteenth Amendment was passed:

> The Congress shall have power to lay and collect taxes on incomes, from whatever source derived, without apportionment among the several States, and without regard to any census or enumeration.

Section 2 of the Underwood-Simmons Tariff Act of 1913 provided for a 1 percent rate on taxable income, with an exemption of $3,000, plus $1,000 more to a married head of household. Notice the concept of exempting the first several thousand dollars of income from taxes. This has continued to the present time in the form of personal exemptions and standard deductions.

The Underwood-Simmons Tariff Act also provided for a surtax that was levied progressively on income over $20,000, with a maximum total tax rate of 7 percent on income over $500,000. These taxes may seem paltry in comparison with today's rates, but they were considered quite large in those times. The concept of progressiveness introduced in 1913 met with considerable debate, which continued for several years thereafter.

Undoubtedly, progressiveness is here to stay, at least in principle, but the apparently progressive nature of our personal income tax system is considerably less obvious than it once was. Before 1961 the maximum federal income tax rate was a whopping 91 percent; by 1980 it had been lowered to 70 percent; between 1981 and 1983 it was reduced to 50 percent; after 1986 it became effectively 33 percent; and in 1990 it was once again lowered, this time to 31 percent. These reductions were no accident, and they were not intended to be just a tax break for the wealthy. The intent of lowering the maximum tax rate, and marginal tax rates in general, was to encourage people to work harder to earn and produce more, and thereby help our economy grow and become more productive.

In 1993 President Bill Clinton and Congress passed legislation that increased the maximum tax rate to 36 percent for married Americans who earned over $140,000 in taxable income a year, and charged an extra 10% for taxpayers with taxable incomes over $250,000, bringing their rate to 39.6 percent. This act reversed the trend of lowering tax rates in the preceding 30 years.

A Complicated Tax System

When the federal personal income tax was first levied, it was a fairly straightforward, simple tax on income. Taxpayers had little difficulty calculating how much tax they had to pay the government. During the following decades, however, federal income tax laws became an increasingly complicated morass of rules and regulations that confused and frustrated most taxpaying citizens. It is estimated that in recent years the cost of filling out federal income tax forms, measured in people's time, has been somewhere between $15 billion

Loopholes
Legal methods of reducing tax liabilities.

Capital gain
An increase in the value of something you own. Generally, you experience a capital gain when you sell something you own, such as a house or a stock. You compute your capital gain by subtracting the price you paid for whatever you are selling from the price you receive when you sell it.

and $20 billion! And this doesn't include the fees many individuals pay to accountants and lawyers each year for tax assistance.

The creation of various tax **loopholes,** or exceptions to regulations, to shelter certain income from taxation is the major reason why our tax system has become, in the words of no less a personage than Albert Einstein, "the hardest thing in the world to understand." These loopholes are shelters that have allowed individuals in high income brackets to take advantage of various business incentives, such as accelerated depreciation, the deduction of intangible oil-drilling expenses, capital-gains preferential rates, and so on. Additionally, Congress created numerous tax loopholes to encourage specific types of activities. For example, consider all the energy tax credits that were available in the last decade for individuals who incorporated energy-conserving technology when constructing or altering their homes and/or business properties. By doing so, these individuals took advantage of tax loopholes while being encouraged—and rewarded—by the government to conserve precious energy.

Until recently, one of the biggest loopholes in personal-income taxation concerned capital-gains rates. A **capital gain** is defined as the positive difference between the buying and selling price of a capital asset, such as a stock, a bond, or a house. If you buy a share of Silver Syndicate Mining stock for $13 and, being a financial wizard, are able to sell it for $67, your capital gain is $54. In the past, only 40 percent of capital gains has been considered taxable income. Over the years, until the Tax Reform Act of 1986, special-interest groups succeeded in getting more and more of their income classified as capital gains in order to reduce the tax due on such income. President Clinton has stated that he would like Congress to reinstate a tax reduction for long-term capital gains in some situations.

Attempts at Tax Reform

Legislation creating tax shelters for special-interest groups obviously complicated our tax system. And the incredible numbers of loopholes and complexities have diluted the progressiveness of our so-called progressive tax system. That is, those with the highest income often have paid the least in taxes because of the numerous tax shelters available to them. In the past two decades, Congress has passed various tax reform acts in an effort to close these loopholes, but those most negatively affected have resisted such legislation. For example, when the 1969 Tax Reform Act finally was put into law, it had been so totally amended that even attorneys and accountants had difficulty figuring out how to use it. Cynics renamed the 1969 legislation the Lawyers' and Accountants' Relief Act because these professionals doubtless would benefit: Mere mortals would seek their help—for a fee—in figuring out how to complete the bewildering new tax forms.

The 1976 Tax Reform Act did reduce, to some extent, the number of loopholes that high-income individuals could exploit. It eliminated the possibility of writing off a larger sum than actually had been invested in a particular project, such as cattle raising or oil drilling. It also increased taxes that had to be paid on any income that previously was sheltered from income taxes. Other tax reform measures were passed in the early 1980s. The most significant tax legislation to be passed in recent years—and, some say, since the personal income tax first was introduced—was the Tax Reform Act of 1986, which eliminated many deductions that had often been used by individuals and business to reduce their tax liabilities.

▶ SUMMARY

1. Taxes are paid to finance the expenses of government. The personal federal income tax, the most important source of government income in this country, accounts for about 46 percent of all federal revenues.

2. The two best-known principles of taxation are the benefits principle and the ability-to-pay principle.

3. Taxes may be classified into three types of structures: *proportional,* in which all taxpayers pay the same percent of their incomes in tax; *progressive,* in which the percent of income that is taken in taxes grows as income increases; and *regressive,* in which the percent of income that is taken in taxes declines as income increases.

4. There are few if any examples of proportional taxes. The federal income tax is progressive for most people, and most state and local taxes tend to be regressive.

5. The personal federal income tax in the United States is a progressive tax. A federal income tax was authorized by the Sixteenth Amendment to the Constitution in 1913, and the progressive nature of our tax system was allowed for in the Underwood-Simmons Tariff Act of the same year.

6. In the decades prior to 1986, Congress created many tax loopholes and shelters, either in response to the needs and lobbying efforts of special-interest groups or to encourage specific types of activities. As many high-income taxpayers thus were able to shelter large amounts of their income from taxation, our taxation system became both less progressive and inordinately complicated.

7. In the years between 1970 and 1990 Congress passed a series of tax laws that reduced tax rates and eventually eliminated many of the tax loopholes that individual taxpayers and businesses had used to reduce their tax liabilities.

▶ QUESTIONS FOR THOUGHT AND DISCUSSION

1. Why do you think the concept of progressive taxation is so popular in the United States?

2. Which aspect of government expenditures do you think is most important for your own well-being?

3. Which principle of taxation do you think best justifies progressive taxation?

4. Would you prefer to have most taxes collected from individuals or from corporations?

5. How do tax loopholes hurt or help you as a consumer?

6. Can you envision a fairer taxation system than the one we have in the United States today?

▶ THINGS TO DO

1. Review recent news magazines or periodicals to find at least one suggestion made by members of each major political party to change federal taxes. Describe and evaluate each of these suggestions. What would their impact probably be on consumers?

2. Call or visit a consultant at the nearest (free) financial planning service. (Your local bank probably can direct you to one.) Find out from the consultant the best ways to "shelter" part of your income from taxation.

▶ APPLICATION

Refer to Consumer Issue H to help you complete the following exercise:

Use the information given about Shelly and Paul's income to recommend whether this couple should use the standard deduction for a married couple filing a joint return ($5,700 in 1991) or itemize their deductions on Schedule A of form 1040. Explain your recommendation.

Their adjusted gross income was $34,561.82.
They paid medical and dental expenses that totaled $3,291.05
They paid $893.25 in property taxes.
They paid $1,894.57 in state income taxes.
When they bought a car they paid $654.27 in sales tax.
They paid $2,120.62 in interest on their mortgage.
They paid $892.43 in interest on their credit card account.
They made contributions of $320 to charities.
Paul's home computer was stolen. It was not insured. It had a value of $1,200.
They did not move.
Shelly spent $290 for uniforms she needed for her job.
Shelly paid $360 for union dues.
Shelly and Paul paid a tax preparer $150 to do their taxes last year.
They had no other miscellaneous deductions to claim.

▶ SELECTED READINGS

▶ Anthony, Joe. "How I Survived a Tax Audit." *Changing Times,* May 1990, pp. 39–44.

▶ Borger, Gloria. "The Short, Unhappy Life of Tax Reform." *U.S. News & World Report,* February 13, 1989, p. 27.

▶ Dorfman, John R. "There'll Be Few Ways to Escape New Tax Bite." *Wall Street Journal,* October 26, 1990, p. B1.

▶ "Finding a Good Tax Preparer." *Consumer Reports,* March 1991, pp. 20–21.

▶ Lamante, D. "Defensive Tax Planning." *Black Enterprise,* October 1991, pp. 84–85.

▶ McCormahy, K. "The Verdict on the New Tax Forms, OUCH!" *Kiplinger's Personal Finance Magazine,* November 1991, p. 96.

▶ "Meet the New Tax Law." *Consumer Reports,* March 1991, pp. 143–145.

▶ "Tax Returns by The Book." *U.S. News & World Report,* March 18, 1991, p. 92.

▶ "Weeding Out Your Home Files." *Kiplinger's Personal Finance Magazine,* January 1991, pp. 41–47.

Preparing Your Income Tax Return

GLOSSARY

DEDUCTION Different types of expenses taxpayers may subtract from their income before figuring their tax liability.

EXEMPTION An amount of income that may be subtracted from income for each person a taxpayer supports.

FILING STATUS The family situation under which taxes are filed: single, married filing jointly, head of household, etc.

STANDARD DEDUCTION An amount all taxpayers are allowed to subtract from their income before figuring their tax liability. The amount varies depending on the taxpayer's filing status.

W-2 FORM The form used by employers to report employee income and withholding to the employee and the government.

It is safe to say that most people don't enjoy paying income taxes. Whether we like it or not, though, income taxes are here to stay, and over 150 million Americans filed personal income tax returns in 1992. As taxpayers and citizens, we are ethically bound to pay our fair share of the cost of government. However, we have no moral or legal obligation to pay more than the law requires. By keeping good financial records, choosing the appropriate tax forms, and completing them correctly, taxpayers can make sure that they pay no more than their legal share.

▶ KEEPING COMPLETE RECORDS

Although taxpayers are furnished with records of many types of income they receive, they are responsible to gather other types of information they need to complete their tax returns. As a general rule, the more you earn and spend, the more important it is to have accurate and complete records.

▶ Information You Receive from Others

At the end of the year employers are required to provide each of their employees, and the federal and state governments, with copies of the **W-2 form,** showing employee gross income and amounts withheld for federal income tax, Social Security and Medicare, and state and local income tax. Employees must include one copy of this form with their tax return.

Banks report interest paid to taxpayers on Form 1099 INT, copies of which are sent to each depositor and to the Internal Revenue Service (IRS). It is important for taxpayers to report all of this interest income. The IRS enters amounts of interest reported by banks into computer files for each taxpayer. If you fail to report the correct amount of interest income you received, chances are very good that you will be audited.

Corporations report dividends paid to stockholders on Form 1099 DIV. Again, this information is provided to both stockholders and the IRS. Failure to report dividends accurately will almost certainly result in an audit of a tax return.

▶ Information You Must Gather for Yourself

Records of many other types of income, such as self-employment earnings, rents, or interest paid by one individual to another, must be kept by taxpayers themselves and reported on their tax returns. Failure to do so is not as likely to result in an audit but still is against the law and can lead to the imposition of interest, penalties, and in some cases jail terms when tax evasion is proved.

It is also important for taxpayers to maintain records of their spending and their contributions to charities so they will be able to determine if they should itemize their **deductions**—expenses that can be subtracted from income before figuring the amount of tax owed. To claim $150 spent on an eye examination and new glasses as a deduction on your income tax, for example, you must be able to prove you spent this money if you are audited. Keeping receipts will also remind you of your deductible spending when you prepare your tax return. The types of spending that are deductible are described in Exhibit H–1.

▶ CHOOSING AND COMPLETING THE PROPER FORM

There are three basic forms taxpayers must choose among when they file their tax returns. Each offers benefits and costs taxpayers must weigh to know if the form is right for their personal situation.

▶ Forms 1040 EZ and 1040 A

The simplest way to file an income tax return is to use Form 1040 EZ. This form was given its name because it is relatively easy (EZ) to

► Exhibit H–1   **Deductible Expenses—1992**

► *Medical and dental expense*—if amounts exceeded 7.5 percent of adjusted gross income.

► *Taxes paid*—state and local taxes paid, but not sales taxes.

► *Interest paid*—interest payments and certain other payments on home mortgages and some other types of interest, but not interest paid on most consumer loans after 1990.

► *Gifts to charity*—charitable contributions of either cash or property (additional forms required for large donations of property).

► *Casualty and theft losses*—uninsured losses resulting from accidents or theft if amounts exceeded 10 percent of adjusted gross income and had values over $100.

► *Moving expenses*—cost of moving that was necessary to accept new employment and was more than 35 miles from the former place of employment (additional forms required for this deduction).

► *Job expenses and most other miscellaneous deductions*—part of many job-related expenses and costs associated with completing tax returns if amounts exceeded 2 percent of adjusted gross income.

► *Other miscellaneous deductions*—for example, part of the loss from a failed pension plan if amount exceeded 2 percent of adjusted gross income.

complete. To use this form in 1992 taxpayers had to be single, under 65, and not blind. They must have provided their own support so they can claim themselves as an **exemption**—taxpayers are allowed to reduce their taxable income for each exemption they claim, that is, for each person they support. Their taxable income had to be less than $50,000, and less than $400 of it could come from interest income. They could have no adjustments to their income, they could owe no special taxes (such as for self-employment), and they could claim no tax credits (for low-income parents). Although this may seem like a long list of qualifications, almost one-third of the returns filed in 1992 used Form 1040 EZ.

Many people who were married, over 65, had additional exemptions they could claim, or who had income from sources that disqualified them from using Form 1040 EZ,

could still file their returns using the relatively simple Form 1040 A. However, the fact that a person is qualified to use Form 1040 EZ or 1040 A does not necessarily mean he or she should choose to do so. A form that allows itemized deductions (discussed shortly) may be more beneficial. If either Form 1040 EZ or 1040 A is used, the taxpayer is required to use the **standard deduction** for his or her **filing status,** or family situation (single, married, etc.). Exhibit H–2 shows the standard deductions that could be claimed on 1992 tax returns.

► Form 1040 for Itemized Deductions

Form 1040 allows taxpayers to list, or "itemize," deductible expenses on Schedule A and subtract them from income before figuring tax liability. If the amount of itemized deductions is greater than the standard deduction, this is the form to use. The list

of expenses that could be claimed as deductions in 1992 appears in Exhibit H–1.

To itemize deductions, taxpayers must keep accurate and complete records of expenses. Records of most of these costs will not be provided by any organization, and the taxpayer's failure to keep these records may cause him or her to pay more tax than would have otherwise been legally required.

After *taxable income*—that is, the amount of income you must pay tax on—is determined, you will find the tax owed in a table at the back of the tax instruction booklet. Exhibit H–3 shows part of this table.

► DO YOU NEED HELP?

Anybody who itemizes deductions faces at least a minimal ordeal in deciphering and applying current tax laws. One way to ease your tax burden is to hire a tax accountant or other tax preparer to help you in this task. But do you really need help? This is a question you need to ask yourself before tax season comes around. When you have only a few weeks left to file, it is too late to take many steps that could reduce your tax liability.

The complexity of your financial situation and the tax returns you will

► Exhibit H–2   **Standard Deduction for 1992 Federal Tax Returns**

Filing Status	Standard Deduction
Single (if you could be claimed as a dependent by someone else, this amount was $600 in 1992)	$3,600
Married, filing joint return, or qualifying widow(er) with dependent child	6,000
Married, filing separate return	3,000
Head of household	5,250

Section 7.

1992 Tax Table

Use if your taxable income is less than $100,000. If $100,000 or more, use the Tax Rate Schedules.

Example. Mr. and Mrs. Brown are filing a joint return. Their taxable income on line 37 of Form 1040 is $25,300. First, they find the $25,300–25,350 income line. Next, they find the column for married filing jointly and read down the column. The amount shown where the income line and filing status column meet is $3,799. This is the tax amount they must enter on line 38 of their Form 1040.

Sample Table

At least	But less than	Single	Married filing jointly *	Married filing separately	Head of a household
			Your tax is—		
25,200	25,250	4,275	3,784	4,736	3,784
25,250	25,300	4,289	3,791	4,750	3,791
25,300	25,350	4,303	(3,799)	4,764	3,799
25,350	25,400	4,317	3,806	4,778	3,806

If line 37 (taxable income) is—		And you are—				If line 37 (taxable income) is—		And you are—				If line 37 (taxable income) is—		And you are—			
At least	But less than	Single	Married filing jointly *	Married filing separately	Head of a house-hold	At least	But less than	Single	Married filing jointly *	Married filing separately	Head of a house-hold	At least	But less than	Single	Married filing jointly *	Married filing separately	Head of a house-hold
		Your tax is—						**Your tax is—**						**Your tax is—**			
0	5	0	0	0	0	1,300	1,325	197	197	197	197	2,700	2,725	407	407	407	407
5	15	2	2	2	2	1,325	1,350	201	201	201	201	2,725	2,750	411	411	411	411
15	25	3	3	3	3	1,350	1,375	204	204	204	204	2,750	2,775	414	414	414	414
25	50	6	6	6	6	1,375	1,400	208	208	208	208	2,775	2,800	418	418	418	418
50	75	9	9	9	9	1,400	1,425	212	212	212	212	2,800	2,825	422	422	422	422
75	100	13	13	13	13	1,425	1,450	216	216	216	216	2,825	2,850	426	426	426	426
100	125	17	17	17	17	1,450	1,475	219	219	219	219	2,850	2,875	429	429	429	429
125	150	21	21	21	21	1,475	1,500	223	223	223	223	2,875	2,900	433	433	433	433
150	175	24	24	24	24	1,500	1,525	227	227	227	227	2,900	2,925	437	437	437	437
175	200	28	28	28	28	1,525	1,550	231	231	231	231	2,925	2,950	441	441	441	441
200	225	32	32	32	32	1,550	1,575	234	234	234	234	2,950	2,975	444	444	444	444
225	250	36	36	36	36	1,575	1,600	238	238	238	238	2,975	3,000	448	448	448	448
250	275	39	39	39	39	1,600	1,625	242	242	242	242						
275	300	43	43	43	43	1,625	1,650	246	246	246	246	**3,000**					
300	325	47	47	47	47	1,650	1,675	249	249	249	249	3,000	3,050	454	454	454	454
325	350	51	51	51	51	1,675	1,700	253	253	253	253	3,050	3,100	461	461	461	461
350	375	54	54	54	54	1,700	1,725	257	257	257	257	3,100	3,150	469	469	469	469
375	400	58	58	58	58	1,725	1,750	261	261	261	261	3,150	3,200	476	476	476	476
400	425	62	62	62	62	1,750	1,775	264	264	264	264	3,200	3,250	484	484	484	484
425	450	66	66	66	66	1,775	1,800	268	268	268	268	3,250	3,300	491	491	491	491
450	475	69	69	69	69	1,800	1,825	272	272	272	272	3,300	3,350	499	499	499	499
475	500	73	73	73	73	1,825	1,850	276	276	276	276	3,350	3,400	506	506	506	506
500	525	77	77	77	77	1,850	1,875	279	279	279	279	3,400	3,450	514	514	514	514
525	550	81	81	81	81	1,875	1,900	283	283	283	283	3,450	3,500	521	521	521	521
550	575	84	84	84	84	1,900	1,925	287	287	287	287	3,500	3,550	529	529	529	529
575	600	88	88	88	88	1,925	1,950	291	291	291	291	3,550	3,600	536	536	536	536
600	625	92	92	92	92	1,950	1,975	294	294	294	294	3,600	3,650	544	544	544	544
625	650	96	96	96	96	1,975	2,000	298	298	298	298	3,650	3,700	551	551	551	551
650	675	99	99	99	99							3,700	3,750	559	559	559	559
675	700	103	103	103	103	**2,000**						3,750	3,800	566	566	566	566
700	725	107	107	107	107	2,000	2,025	302	302	302	302	3,800	3,850	574	574	574	574
725	750	111	111	111	111	2,025	2,050	306	306	306	306	3,850	3,900	581	581	581	581
750	775	114	114	114	114	2,050	2,075	309	309	309	309	3,900	3,950	589	589	589	589
775	800	118	118	118	118	2,075	2,100	313	313	313	313	3,950	4,000	596	596	596	596
800	825	122	122	122	122	2,100	2,125	317	317	317	317	**4,000**					
825	850	126	126	126	126	2,125	2,150	321	321	321	321	4,000	4,050	604	604	604	604
850	875	129	129	129	129	2,150	2,175	324	324	324	324	4,050	4,100	611	611	611	611
875	900	133	133	133	133	2,175	2,200	328	328	328	328	4,100	4,150	619	619	619	619
900	925	137	137	137	137	2,200	2,225	332	332	332	332	4,150	4,200	626	626	626	626
925	950	141	141	141	141	2,225	2,250	336	336	336	336	4,200	4,250	634	634	634	634
950	975	144	144	144	144	2,250	2,275	339	339	339	339	4,250	4,300	641	641	641	641
975	1,000	148	148	148	148	2,275	2,300	343	343	343	343	4,300	4,350	649	649	649	649
1,000						2,300	2,325	347	347	347	347	4,350	4,400	656	656	656	656
1,000	1,025	152	152	152	152	2,325	2,350	351	351	351	351	4,400	4,450	664	664	664	664
1,025	1,050	156	156	156	156	2,350	2,375	354	354	354	354	4,450	4,500	671	671	671	671
1,050	1,075	159	159	159	159	2,375	2,400	358	358	358	358	4,500	4,550	679	679	679	679
1,075	1,100	163	163	163	163	2,400	2,425	362	362	362	362	4,550	4,600	686	686	686	686
1,100	1,125	167	167	167	167	2,425	2,450	366	366	366	366	4,600	4,650	694	694	694	694
1,125	1,150	171	171	171	171	2,450	2,475	369	369	369	369	4,650	4,700	701	701	701	701
1,150	1,175	174	174	174	174	2,475	2,500	373	373	373	373	4,700	4,750	709	709	709	709
1,175	1,200	178	178	178	178	2,500	2,525	377	377	377	377	4,750	4,800	716	716	716	716
1,200	1,225	182	182	182	182	2,525	2,550	381	381	381	381	4,800	4,850	724	724	724	724
1,225	1,250	186	186	186	186	2,550	2,575	384	384	384	384	4,850	4,900	731	731	731	731
1,250	1,275	189	189	189	189	2,575	2,600	388	388	388	388	4,900	4,950	739	739	739	739
1,275	1,300	193	193	193	193	2,600	2,625	392	392	392	392	4,950	5,000	746	746	746	746
						2,625	2,650	396	396	396	396						
						2,650	2,675	399	399	399	399						
						2,675	2,700	403	403	403	403						

Continued on next page

* This column must also be used by a qualifying widow(er).

– 35 –

need to file are the most important factors in determining whether you should seek help in tax preparation. Simply having a large income does not necessarily mean you need assistance. A person might earn $250,000 but have a relatively simple tax return if the income is totally from wages and there are no special deductions. (Such a person, however, would probably benefit from tax planning that would make his or her return more complex but would also reduce the taxes owed.) A self-employed person earning only $25,000 from a business operated out of his or her home might need to complete more complicated forms and might need help in tax planning more than the individual with the larger income.

▶ Do You Need a Tax Preparer or a Tax Planner?

A tax preparer and a tax planner do not offer the same services. A *tax preparer* will complete necessary tax forms based on information supplied by his or her customers. A *tax planner*, however, helps customers arrange their financial situation to reduce the amount of their tax liability. If you hire someone to help you with your taxes, you need to decide which sort of service you need. A person with relatively little income and no special financial problems probably does not need the services of a tax planner.

Thousands of individuals and businesses offer both of these services. The best way to begin selecting one is to ask friends and relatives for their recommendations. Another source of information is the Yellow Pages of your phone directory. They list a selection of nationally franchised operations that are well qualified to complete relatively simple returns. H&R Block, which has roughly 7,000 offices throughout the nation, is an example. Also, many individuals offer tax preparation services, some being former IRS employees or at least having passed tests on tax preparation issued by the U.S. Treasury. These individuals will be advertised as *enrolled agents*.

If you have more complicated needs, you may want to hire a certified public accountant (CPA) who has special training in tax matters. CPAs will charge more for their services than firms like H&R Block, but if they are able to save their customers taxes because of their specialized knowledge, they are worth the extra expense.

The most expensive tax help is offered by tax attorneys. Only people who have special needs or face legal problems related to their taxes should consider this type of help. Paying an attorney $500 to save $100 in taxes makes little sense. Indeed, any type of tax planning should be reserved for people who are wealthy enough, or are in situations complicated enough, to make them worthwhile.

▶ Do's and Don'ts of Hiring Tax Help

Following are some guidelines for selecting help in tax preparation or planning if you determine you need it.

1. Be wary of tax preparers who promise to give you a check for your refund immediately. The preparer is probably offering you a loan on which you will pay interest.

2. Never sign a blank return.

3. Never sign a return prepared in pencil; it can be changed later.

4. Never allow your refund check to be mailed to the preparer.

5. Be wary of tax advisers who "guarantee" refunds, who want a percentage of the refund, or who supposedly "know all the angles."

6. Avoid a tax preparer who advises you to overstate deductions, omit income, or claim fictitious dependents.

7. Make sure the tax preparer signs the return he or she prepares and includes his or her address and tax identification number. (You, however, are legally responsible for virtually all errors on your return, no matter who fills it out, unless there is a blatant case of fraud brought against the tax preparer.

8. Be wary of preparers who claim they will make good any amounts due because of a mistake on your return. Usually, the preparer means that he or she will pay the penalty cost; the tax money due must come from you.

9. Find out the educational background of the preparer. Has that person a degree in accounting?

10. Use only preparers who have permanent addresses so you will have no difficulty finding that person a few months later if problems develop.

▶ TAX GUIDES

Even if you hire somebody else to prepare your tax return, it is a good idea to be somewhat versed in the tax laws affecting your financial situation. Even a minimal knowledge of these laws can help you get the most for your money from a tax preparer and help you take full advantage of the law if you prepare your tax return yourself.

Every year numerous tax guides are published and marketed. Some of the best known are Lasser's *Your Income Tax,* H&R Block's *Income Tax Workbook,* and Arthur Young's *Tax Guide.* Recently, the editors of

Consumer Reports have begun to market an annual guide entitled *Guide to Income Tax Preparation*. You can also get *Your Federal Income Tax* free from the Internal Revenue Service in your area, and the IRS has numerous other free instruction booklets for every imaginable deduction for which you may be eligible.

► TAX SOFTWARE

In recent years the quality of computer tax software has been notably improved, and there are now a number of highly rated programs on the market. One of them is ChipSoft's *Turbo Tax* (for IBM computers). Others include SoftView's *MacInTax* (for Macintosh, Apple II, and IBM computers), and Legal Knowledge Systems' *Ask Dan about Your Taxes* (for IBM computers). These programs sell for $75 and up, depending on whether you want the program for just the federal 1040 return or for state taxes as well.

Remember that software is just that—software. It will help to sort, categorize, and analyze tax information, and perhaps even prepare your return, but it cannot make decisions for you; that is, these programs are not substitutes for qualified, human tax advisers.

► MINIMIZING YOUR TAXES— AND YOUR TAX TIME

Americans in general may be very honest. The IRS estimates that fully 92 percent pay their lawful due to the government. Being honest, though, does not mean you shouldn't take advantage of what is legally your right. That is, you can be very honest and report all income but, at the same time, make sure that you take all legitimate deductions. You owe that to yourself and to your family.

Consult current tax guides, or check with an accountant, to find out what deductions you can take to help reduce your federal income taxes. Whenever you are uncertain about the acceptability of the deduction, you might consider taking a chance. Many deductions are subject to interpretation by the IRS; that is, they are ambiguous, and, if you are audited, you stand as good a chance of winning your case as not winning it. At the most, because this action does not involve fraud or anything illegal, you pay only an interest-rate penalty on the taxes due.

Remember, it's not worthwhile for you to spend weeks filling out tax forms to save a mere $25. You must figure out at what point you should *stop* trying to reduce your tax burden. This, of course, is a function of your tax rate. If you are in the 15 percent bracket, every extra dollar you can find as a legal deduction saves you on average only 15 cents. If it takes you an extra hour to find $10 more of deductions, the benefit to you of those $10 of deductions is on average only $1.50. Is your time worth more than $1.50 an hour?

► WHAT IF YOU CAN'T PAY?

One out of every four people who owe taxes on April 15 cannot pay them at that time. If this should happen to you, file your return anyway. When the Internal Revenue Service later sends you a bill for the taxes due, if you still don't have enough funds to cover the amount, pay what you can and make arrangements with IRS personnel to pay the remainder as soon as possible. You may want to take out a loan to pay the government its due. If you fail to pay, the IRS can attach your paycheck, your bank account, your car, and even your home, if necessary,

to collect the taxes. Rarely, though, does the IRS resort to such drastic measures if an individual makes an earnest effort to pay the debt.

If you fail to file your return, you will face a fine of at least 5 percent (and possibly as much as 25 percent) of the amount you owe, in addition to about ½ percent charged each month for late payment.

Another alternative is to file Form 4868, which provides an automatic extension beyond April 15 for filing your return. This does not eliminate or postpone your tax liability, which must be estimated and paid. It does, however, provide extra time to obtain documents that will allow you to pay the smallest legal amount possible.

► HOW TO AVOID A TAX AUDIT

Being audited by the IRS is time-consuming, often traumatic, and may cost you more tax dollars. Thus, astute taxpayers try to minimize the chances of being audited. Exhibit H–4 shows the percentage of individual returns that are audited. You will note that the higher the income, the greater the chance of a tax audit. Overall, your chances of being audited are one in a hundred. If your income is relatively low and you do not itemize deductions, your

► Exhibit H–4 **Percentage of Individual Returns that are Audited**

NONBUSINESS INCOME	CHANCES OF AN AUDIT
Under $10,000 (1040 A)	.53%
$10,000 to $25,000 (nonitemized)	.64
$10,000 to $25,000 (itemized)	1.30
$25,000 to $50,000	1.40
$50,000 and up	2.24

chances of being audited become much slimmer.

What Prompts an Audit?

The IRS computer system is programmed to select for an audit returns that don't conform to normal patterns of income and deduction levels. What those patterns are is a well-kept secret, however, and the IRS changes the patterns every few years to prevent taxpayers from "beating the computer." Frequent targets for audit by the IRS are tax returns claiming certain types of deductions, such as travel and entertainment expenses, self-employment deductions, charitable contributions, casualty losses (theft, for example), passive losses, and individual retirement accounts. Audits also are made when an individual who is not qualified to do so uses head-of-household tax tables. For example, two formerly married individuals with joint custody of their children can't both claim to be the head of the household.

A tax audit might also be conducted for the following reasons:

1. Savings and loan associations, employers, and Social Security wage reports revealed information that did not agree with the tax return.
2. More than one return was filed under the same Social Security number.
3. There was a discrepancy between the state income tax return reported by state tax agencies and the federal income tax return.
4. The wrong tax table was used.
5. There were computation errors.

Backing Up Your Deductions

Using a computer, of course, does not mean that deductions on your claim will automatically be accepted. Human classifiers at the IRS are trained to spot deductions that are not normal. If, for example, you have extremely high medical expenses one year, make a separate schedule of them and attach copies of all the bills to your return. This will assist the classifier and perhaps save you a trip to the local field office. On the other hand, it's inappropriate to overdo the extra schedules. To reduce your chances of being audited, verify, when you file, anything that might stand out and raise questions.

Human classifiers can quickly spot inconsistencies, so avoid such inconsistencies if possible. Your income after deductions must be enough to buy such essentials as food and clothing, so don't overdo the deductions. And business expenses must be appropriate for your occupation.

HOW TO SURVIVE A TAX AUDIT

Should you receive in the mail a note from the IRS that says, "We are examining your federal income tax return for the above year(s) and we find we need additional information to verify your correct tax," don't despair. Many individuals are audited randomly, even though their returns seem to be in order. And approximately one-fifth of those who are audited leave the IRS office without owing more in taxes.

Prior to your scheduled audit, remember that personal attitude helps in a successful negotiation with the auditor. Therefore, you should:

1. **Be prepared.** You will be given at least six weeks to prepare for your interview with the IRS auditing agent. Use this time to study the facts in your case and, if possible, the law relating to the specific deductions being questioned.
2. **Be businesslike.** Answer the letter from the IRS promptly and help the agent dispose of major issues quickly during the initial interview.
3. **Be cooperative.** Answer all questions, but do not volunteer unsolicited information, unless, of course, the agent has overlooked something that could alter things in your favor.

Using Those Records

When you are audited, you realize how important record keeping is. An IRS auditor has the right to disallow completely unsubstantiated itemized deductions or to reduce them to what he or she might consider "reasonable." When you are asked to verify specific itemized deductions, provide only the information relating to those deductions, and provide it as completely as possible. You don't want to give the impression that you are hiding something.

For most individuals who are audited, negotiations with the IRS agent proceed smoothly. Once an agreement is reached, you will sign a form stating that you will pay the taxes you owe. See Exhibit H–5 for ten do's and don'ts when you get called in for an audit.

If You Disagree with the Agent

If there is still a disagreement after the audit is completed, you will get a copy of the agent's audit report, together with a letter telling you of the various rights you have to appeal the findings.

At this point, you are given 30 days to act. One way you might have your complaint resolved is by taking it to an IRS *problem resolution officer* (PRO). There are currently 73 of these officers, one in each IRS district office and service center. The PRO has five working

Here are some hints from tax adviser Paul N. Strassels on how to act if the IRS calls you in for an audit.

Do dress the way you normally do for business—whether in a finely tailored suit or in jeans. But don't flaunt wealth with expensive jewelry.

Do act natural—but if you can't help being visibly jittery, then tell the auditor you're nervous.

Do take the audit seriously. Don't joke about it with the auditor or be flippant in your answers.

Do bring along a tax adviser, and let him do the talking whenever you can.

Don't antagonize the auditor by being late.

Don't volunteer information, be chatty, or go to lunch with the auditor.

Don't walk in without any records—or try to overload the auditor with material. It can backfire on you.

Don't rush the auditor or allow yourself to be rushed.

Don't try for sympathy, plead that "everyone does it," or lash out at taxes in general. It's a waste of time.

Don't underestimate the auditor or be shocked if "he" is a she.

Source: *U.S. News and World Report*, March 24, 1980, p. 81; and Paul N. Strassels (with Robert Wood), *All You Need to Know about the IRS* (New York: Random House, 1979).

---

days within which he or she must settle your claim or advise you as to its status and direct you to someone who can settle it for you. If the PRO or other IRS personnel cannot create a satisfactory solution, you can request a conference with the IRS Appeals Division. The IRS appeals officer is allowed to weigh your appeal against the costs of possible court litigation. These conferences are usually informal, especially if the amount in question is $2,500 or less.

If the agent's position is upheld, you have two alternatives. You can pay the additional tax or wait for a 90-day letter, which will mean that going to court is the only remaining method of continuing the case.

▶ Going to Tax Court

If you decide to take your case to tax court, you must file your petition within the 90 days. If the disputed sum isn't over $10,000, the tax court will handle your case informally as a small-case claim in its Small Claims Division. If the decision goes against you in this court, you will have to pay the additional taxes.

Think carefully before you go to tax court, however. Statistics show that the chances of winning your case are not very great. Because of this, many taxpayers choose to have their case heard in a district court,

where the chances of success are much higher. Before you use this court, however, you must pay the taxes in dispute.

Obviously, the best thing to do is to try to avoid a dispute in the first place by keeping the best records you can. And, if a dispute does arise, do all you can to settle it with the auditing agent, a PRO, or—if it gets to this point—the IRS appeals officer.

▶ COMPUTERIZING THE TAX SYSTEM

Not only are taxpayers making more use of computers for tax purposes, but so is the IRS. In 1986, for the first time, taxpayers were able to file their returns with the IRS electronically. Approximately 25,000 people opted for this "paperless filing" procedure, which allowed the data on the tax forms to be transmitted directly from the tax preparer's office to an IRS computer over telephone lines. By 1988, nearly 600,000 taxpayers filed their returns electronically, and the IRS anticipates that eventually some 35 million individuals—about a third of the taxpaying population—will eventually file their returns via computers.

The IRS restricts the electronic-filing option to those who do not owe any taxes. Also, only IRS-

designated and IRS-approved accountants and other tax preparers can transmit returns electronically. By 1989, there were more than 4,000 tax preparers and computer operators in 36 states who had been qualified by the IRS to file tax returns directly into government computers. By 1990, electronic filing services were available in all 50 states. To find out whether there is such a service in your area, check with your local IRS office or call the IRS national toll-free number, 1-800-424-1040.

One advantage of filing electronically is that the error rate is reduced—to about 3 percent versus 20 percent for paper returns. Another advantage is that you will likely receive your refund more quickly. Of course, the disadvantage is that you have to pay for the service—currently anywhere from $10 to $30 or more.

▶ SUMMARY

1. Taxpayers need to keep accurate and complete records of their income and expenses to help them complete their tax returns. Some types of income will be reported to taxpayers and to the IRS by employers, banks, and corporations. Records of other types of income and all types of expenses must be main-

tained by individual taxpayers.

2. Taxpayers must choose which of three basic forms to use when they file their tax returns. Although forms 1040 EZ and 1040 A are less difficult to complete, taxpayers must use the standard deduction if they use these forms. People who have more deductible expenses than their standard deduction will benefit by using Form 1040 and Schedule A to file their tax returns.

3. Consumers should remember that tax preparers and tax planners do not provide the same services. Tax preparers may help people complete tax forms, but they will not be able to reduce a person's tax liability below what it otherwise would have been. In general, the need of a taxpayer to hire a professional preparer depends more on the complexity of the tax forms that need to be completed than on the amount of money earned. Tax planners, in contrast to tax preparers, help people who have substantial incomes arrange their finances in a way that will reduce their tax liabilities.

4. Your first decision at tax time is whether or not to hire a tax preparer to assist you. Your answer should depend on the complexity of your return, not on the amount of your income.

5. If you need assistance, there are numerous sellers of tax services available, including certified public accountants, storefront tax-preparation operations such as H&R Block, and tax attorneys. As with your other consumer choices, you need to guard against unethical or fraudulent service providers.

6. Some knowledge of current tax laws will be useful even if you hire tax help, because it will help you discuss your tax situation more intel-

ligently with your tax preparer and take greater advantage of his or her expertise. Annual tax guides published early in the year and free publications from the IRS can equip you to take maximum advantage of tax laws.

7. Computer software is available for tax-preparation assistance. Such programs can help you organize your tax data and make appropriate entries on your return, but they are not substitutes for human decision making.

8. If you itemize your tax return, you will need to document each deduction with appropriate records. Records of all expenses that are being deducted and of all income must be kept to support your tax return.

9. If you are uncertain about the acceptability of a deduction because the law is ambiguous, you have the option of taking or not taking the deduction on your return. If the IRS disagrees with your interpretation, the most that can happen is that you will have to pay an interest-rate penalty on the taxes due—as long as no fraud is involved.

10. In preparing your tax return, remember that your time is valuable, too. Therefore, search for possible tax-saving deductions only as long as the dollars you save outweigh the cost of the time it takes to save them.

11. If you can't pay the taxes you owe, file your return anyway and make arrangements with the IRS to pay the amount due as soon as possible.

12. Your chances of being audited by the IRS can be reduced by taking the standard deduction instead of itemizing your deductions or, if you itemize, by attaching appropriate documentation to your return for

unusual or unusually large deductions. On average, only one out of a hundred taxpayers is audited.

13. If you are audited by the IRS, be prepared, businesslike, and cooperative. Bring records to the interview with the IRS agent so that you can substantiate all claims that you made on your tax return. If you disagree with the IRS agent, you can take your complaint to an IRS problem-resolution officer. If you are still unsatisfied, you can appeal to an IRS appeals officer to hear your case. If IRS personnel can't satisfactorily resolve the problem, you can take your case to tax court or to a district court.

14. The IRS now allows for the electronic submission of tax returns, but only if the taxpayer owes no taxes and only if the return is transmitted by an IRS-approved computer transmission service.

▶ QUESTIONS FOR THOUGHT AND DISCUSSION

1. When would it not pay to keep meticulous records for tax purposes?
2. When is it definitely a waste of time to have an accountant or other tax preparer fill out your tax returns?
3. What is the cost to you of deducting an expense from your income before paying taxes if a tax audit determines that the deduction is not legitimate?

▶ THINGS TO DO

1. Send away for free booklets from the IRS. See if you can find information that will be useful for your own tax planning.
2. Try to find out from the IRS what percentage of taxpayers are audited every year.
3. Buy one of the best-selling tax guides. Read through it to see if you can get a general feeling for how

our tax system works. Do you think we need further simplification of our tax laws?

▶ SELECTED READINGS

▶ Arthur Young & Co. *The Arthur Young Tax Guide*. New York: Ballantine Books. Published annually.

▶ Ashton, Betty. "Sailing Through Tax Season." *Guide to Living on Your Own*. Boston: Little, Brown, 1988, pp. 53–68.

▶ Block, Julian. "Taking the IRS to Court." *American Way*, March 15, 1987, pp. 58–64.

▶ Consumer Reports Books. *Guide to Income Tax Preparation*. New York: Consumer Reports Books. Published annually.

▶ Deutsch, Claudia H. "Audited? No Need to Panic." *New York Times*. March 5, 1989, p. 24.

▶ *Ernst & Young Tax Guide 1992*. New York: John Wiley & Sons, 1991.

▶ Fink, Robert, and Sandor Frankel. *You Can Protect Yourself from the I.R.S.* New York: Fireside House, 1987.

▶ *Guide to Income Tax Preparation*. Fairfield, OH: Consumer Reports, 1991.

▶ *How to Prepare Your Personal Income Tax Return*. Englewood Cliffs, NJ: Prentice-Hall. Published annually.

▶ Janssen, R. F. "Last Minute Hints for Taxpayers." *Business Week*, March 11, 1991, p. 110.

▶ Lasser, J. K. *Your Income Tax*. New York: Simon & Schuster. Published annually.

▶ "Let Your Computer Help You Out." *U.S. News & World Report*, March 14, 1988, p. 74.

▶ Lewis, Peter H. "Electronic Assistance for Those 1040 Forms." *New York Times*, March 7, 1989, p. 26.

▶ McCormally, Kevin, and Bertha Kainen. "Timely Answers to Taxing Questions." *Changing Times*, April 1989, pp. 48–51.

▶ Meadows, Laura L. "Electronic Filing Speeds Refunds." *New York Times*, March 5, 1989, p. 27.

▶ *Money* (January issues containing special tax reports).

▶ "Tax Software." *Money*, January 1989, p. 105.

▶ Weiner, Leonard. "A Plug-in, High-cost Fast Refund." *U.S. News & World Report*, March 6, 1989, p. 65.

▶ Weinman, Sidney. "Oh No! A Letter from the IRS." *Sylvia Porter's Personal Finance*, October 1988, pp. 67–69.

▶ Wool, Robert. "How to Pay $0 Taxes." *Money*, April 1989, pp. 163–70.

▶ Yang, Catherine. "Filing a Tax Return That Doesn't Set Off Alarms." *Business Week*, March 6, 1989, pp. 104–105.

▶ *Your Federal Income Tax*. Available free from the Internal Revenue Service.

Major Consumption Expenditures

C H A P T E R 10

The 600^+ Billion American Diet

PREVIEW

▶ How do Americans choose the food they eat?

▶ How do government labeling and inspection requirements affect consumers?

▶ What types of additives are used in foods we eat, and how might they affect consumers?

▶ What steps can consumers take to assure themselves of eating a balanced diet?

▶ What are the benefits and costs of convenience foods?

▶ Are brand-name foods better than store-brand, or generic products?

In one year, the total amount of money that Americans spend on food products is staggering—over $650 billion in 1992 alone. Americans consume approximately one-fourth of the world's total agricultural output. We are feeding a very large and hungry stomach. We buy our food products at more than 300,000 retail stores that carry an average of 25,000 different products on their shelves at any one time. The number of brands of different types of foods— canned peas, carrots, soups, cereals—is probably many thousands when you include all the regional specialties you can buy.

CHOOSING THE FOOD WE EAT

Even though we spend more than $650 billion a year on food, that represents only 15.8 percent of disposable personal income in the United States. Exhibit 10–1 shows that the percentage of American income spent on food consumption has actually been falling. Is this surprising? Well, it shouldn't be. Ask yourself how much more food you could buy if you doubled your income. You could certainly buy better quality, and perhaps you could eat in restaurants more often. But there is a limit, at least for most of you, and that limit is a physical one. Your stomach can hold only so much at any one sitting, and your body will maintain its weight only if you do not take in more calories than you use. If people's expenditures for food had kept pace with their incomes over the past 150 years in the United States, we would be a nation of balloons, running into each other and having trouble sitting in chairs, driving cars, and getting on buses. (Americans do weigh more, on average, though, than populations in other countries of the world.)

In 1856 a German statistician, Ernst Engel, made some budgetary studies of family expenditures and found that as family incomes increased, the *percentage* spent on food decreased—not the total amount of food, of course, but the percentage. A family making $60,000 a year certainly spends more on food than a family making $30,000 a year. But even though the richer family has

▶ **Exhibit 10–1** **Percentage of Total Income in the United States Spent on Food**

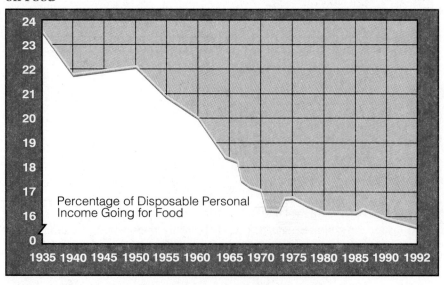

Percentage of Disposable Personal Income Going for Food

1935 1940 1945 1950 1955 1960 1965 1970 1975 1980 1985 1990 1992

UNIT 3   MAJOR CONSUMPTION EXPENDITURES

an income twice as large as the other family's, the richer family does not spend twice the amount that the other family spends on food.

Engel's Law has fairly universal applicability, not only through time but also across nations at any given moment. Recall our discussion of this in Chapter 8 in reference to the budgets of different families. Richer nations spend a smaller fraction of their total national income on food than do poorer nations, and we can predict that, in the United States, if we become richer, our expenditures on food will become a smaller percentage of total expenditures.

Engel's Law
A proposition, first made by Ernst Engel, that states that as a family's income rises, the proportion spent on food falls.

GOVERNMENT LABELING AND INSPECTION REQUIREMENTS

Because food is an essential part of every consumer's budget, the government has, through the years, established a system of inspection and labeling designed to help us make wiser choices about the food products we buy. You may not be aware of it, but the government is constantly inspecting meat-packing houses and various food-processing establishments to ensure that our food is processed in a clean, bacteria-free environment so we won't suffer any harmful effects of improper food processing. In addition, the government requires fair packaging and labeling of food products by means of the Fair Packaging and Labeling Act of 1966 and other federal laws.

Fair Packaging

The Fair Packaging and Labeling Act of 1966 came about as a result of numerous complaints directed at packagers. The quantity of packaged contents was often inadequately or confusingly disclosed; there was no uniform designation of quantity by weight or fluid volume. For example, one producer would measure by ounces, while a competitor would measure by the quart or by quarts and ounces combined. In addition, there was criticism of the use of adjectives such as "giant" or "jumbo," and designations of servings as small, medium, and large, without any standard of reference.

The Fair Packaging and Labeling Act applies to such consumer commodities as foods, drugs, devices, and cosmetics that are subject to the federal Food, Drug and Cosmetic Act, and to any other article customarily purchased for sale through retailers for consumption by individuals or for "use by individuals for purposes of personal care or in the performance of services ordinarily rendered within the household." The act does not apply to tobacco, meat, poultry, and any other products already covered by federal laws.

The act authorized the secretary of commerce to attempt to limit "undue" proliferation of product package sizes, that is, a variety of sizes that causes consumers to suffer an "unreasonably" impaired ability to make product comparisons. The secretary may request manufacturers, packers, and distributors to participate in the development of a voluntary product standard for the packaging of a commodity. If no standard has been adopted within one year after such a request, or if the voluntary standard adopted is not observed, the secretary of commerce is supposed to report such determination to Congress.

Food Labeling

Under the authority of the Fair Packaging and Labeling Act and other federal laws, the Food and Drug Administration (FDA) requires that every package of food, drugs, or cosmetics contain the following information on its label:

When you do your grocery shopping do you bother to read the labels? If you don't, do you really know what you are buying? Why is it important for food labels to be clear and easy to understand?

1. The name of the product.
2. The name and address of the manufacturer, packer, or distributor.
3. The net contents by weight, volume, or count.
4. Details of dietary characteristics, if applicable.
5. Mention of whether the product contains artificial coloring, flavoring, or chemical preservatives.

Standards of identity are provided by law for some food products, such as mayonnaise and bread, for which the contents have been traditionally well known. In foods with a standard of identity, certain ingredients must be present in a specific percentage—otherwise the food may not use the standard name. For foods without a standard of identity, ingredients must be listed on the label.

In 1991 the FDA announced new standards for labeling food products. The new standards were finalized in 1992, to be implemented in 1994. These rules aim to make nutritional information provided on labels much more specific and usable than before. The FDA was authorized to set these new rules by the Nutrition Labeling and Education Act of 1990.

Prior to 1991, only about half of all packaged food products sold in the United States provided nutritional labeling. Under the new rules established by the FDA virtually every packaged food product will carry nutritional information that lists calories per serving and amounts of carbohydrates, fat, fiber, protein, sugar, and salt, in addition to data on vitamins and minerals.

New standard serving sizes for many products will be almost as important as nutritional information per serving. In the past, many manufacturers of food products have been able to mislead consumers by labeling their products with serving sizes that were either unrealistically small—to make them seem low in calories or fat—or unrealistically large—to make them appear to be high in protein or vitamins and minerals. The 1991 FDA rules set standard serving sizes for 176 categories of food products; these standard sizes will enable consumers to compare the nutritional values of similar products.

One purpose of the new rulings was to encourage food producers to reformulate their products to make them more healthful. The reasoning was that businesses producing food products falsely marketed as being healthful and low in fat would probably choose to change their products to match the advertising rather than give up the advertising.

The 1990 labeling law is also important because it is the first time the FDA and the U.S. Department of Agriculture (USDA) have worked together to set standard labeling rules. For example, consumers can now compare the nutritional value of packaged pepperoni pizza (regulated by the USDA) against packaged cheese pizza (regulated by the FDA).

In addition to regulations of what food producers must include on their labels, there is an even longer list of terms they may not use except in special cases (see Exhibit 10–2). No product may be called "fresh" unless it has never been processed, frozen, or preserved. "More" can be used to describe a product's contents only when 10 percent or more of the desired ingredient has been added. "Light" may be used to describe a product only when it has at least one-third fewer calories than comparable products. Producers will not be able to get around this rule by changing the spelling of the word—by calling a product "Lite," for example. The list goes on and on.

Some producers have complained about the new rules and restrictions. One consultant to the food industry is quoted as saying, "It's very hard to describe some products fairly and accurately and still make them saleable. If you are producing "Cocoa Flavored Sugar Bomb Breakfast Cereal," for example, saying that it is bad for your health (which may be true) is not likely to increase your sales.

Estimates are that the relabeling effort will cost the food industry between $2 billion and $3 billion. However, supporters of the new ruling believe that it may save as much as $100 billion in reduced health care costs as people choose to eat better diets.

USDA Grades

In addition to FDA labeling requirements for canned or processed foods and meat inspection, the U.S. Department of Agriculture (USDA) provides for grade marks on various meats and fresh produce. These grades are meant to inform the consumer about the level of quality.

Meat All fresh meats sold by retailers, with the exception of pork, are *voluntarily* labeled as to grade. Currently, the top grade available in supermarkets is "prime," followed by "choice," and then by "select." Grading for quality should not be confused with inspection. All meat sold for human consumption is inspected for wholesomeness. Grading is voluntary and is usually a measure of the taste qualities of the meat, which have to do with the fat content or marbling of the beef. For example, prime cuts of beef have more fat than the choice and select grades, and that is one of the reasons prime beef is more palatable (and more expensive) than the leaner grades. Today, most (92 percent) of the beef available in supermarkets and restaurants is graded choice; only 3.1 percent is graded prime, and 4.6 percent (a small, but rising percentage) is graded select.

Poultry Poultry, which was not under federal inspection standards until the Poultry Products Inspection Act of 1968, is now subject to USDA grading. Poultry is graded solely on physically observable characteristics, such as

Acidulants or acidifiers   Acids that have many food uses—as flavor-enhancing agents, as preservatives to inhibit growth of micro-organisms, as antioxidants to prevent discoloration or rancidity, and to adjust the acidity in some foods.

Anti-caking agents   Substances used to prevent powdered or granular foods from absorbing moisture and becoming lumpy. They help products like table salt and powdered sugar flow freely.

Antioxidants   Preservatives that prevent or delay discoloration in foods, such as cut potatoes and sliced apples. They also help keep oils and fats from turning rancid. Examples: BHA, BHT, propyl gallate.

Cholesterol   Fat-like substances found in foods of animal origin (meat, poultry and dairy products) but not in foods from plants. Cholesterol is essential to body functions. But because the body can make what it needs, the amount in some people's diets is often excessive, increasing the risk of heart disease.

Emulsifiers   Widely used in food processing, these agents stabilize fat and water mixtures so they will not separate. For example, in mayonnaise, egg yolks act as emulsifiers to keep the oil from separating from the acids (vinegar or lemon juice). Lecithin, derived from soybeans, acts as an emulsifier in such foods as chocolate and margarine.

Fats   A major source of energy, they also play a key role as carriers of fat-soluble vitamins (A, D, E, and K). Fat is a constituent of most foods of plant and animal origin.

Fatty acids   The major constituents of fat. Fats in foods are a mixture of saturated and unsaturated fatty acids. Fats with a high proportion of saturated fatty acids are solid or nearly solid at room temperature and are found in larger amounts in foods of animal origin. Fats with mostly unsaturated fatty acids are liquid at room temperature and are found in largest amounts in plant oils, such as safflower, sunflower, corn, soybean, canola, and cottonseed oils.

Fiber   Provides bulk or roughage in the diet. Fiber is derived from such plant-derived foods as cereal grain products, vegetables, fruits, seeds, and nuts.

Flavor enhancers   Help bring out the natural flavor of foods. Examples: Monosodium glutamate (MSG), disodium guanylate, and disodium inosinate.

Grains   Hard seeds of cereal plants, such as wheat, rice, corn, and rye. Whole grains contain the entire seed of the plant.

Humectants   Chemicals such as glycerol, propylene glycol, and sorbitol that are added to foods to help retain moisture, fresh taste, and texture. Often used in candies, shredded coconut, and marshmallows.

Hydrogenated and **partially hydrogenated** Labeling terms that describe the process of adding hydrogen to an unsaturated fat to make it saturated; for example, oils may be hydrogenated to various degrees to make them suitable for use in products such as margarine. The more an oil is hydrogenated, the more saturated fatty acids it contains.

Leavening agents   Substances such as yeasts and baking powders that are used to make foods light in texture by forming carbon dioxide gas in the dough.

Niacin   A water-soluble B vitamin that is important for the health of all body cells. The body needs it to use oxygen to produce energy.

Refined flour   Type of flour produced by milling grains to a fine white consistency. Refining removes bran, fiber, and some other nutrients. Enriched flour has iron and three B vitamins added to levels required by the FDA.

Riboflavin   A water-soluble B vitamin that helps the body obtain energy from foods and aids in the proper functioning of the nervous system, in growth, and digestion.

Sequestrants   Chemicals used to bind trace amounts of metal impurities that can cause food to become discolored or rancid. EDTA is an example.

Sodium   A chemical in some foods. Essential for regulating body fluids and muscle function, excessive amounts have been linked with an increased risk of high blood pressure.

Stabilizers and thickeners   Substances that give foods a smooth, uniform texture. They also protect foods from adverse conditions, such as wide temperature fluctuations and physical shock during distribution. The most common thickening agents are starches (cornstarch and wheat starch) and modified food starches. Other types include carrageenan, locust bean gum, agar, sodium alginate, gelatin, and pectin.

Sugar-free/sugarless   A food can be labeled sugar-free and still contain calories from sugar alcohols (xylitol, sorbitol, and mannitol), provided the basis for the claim is explained. Saccharin is a nonnutritive sweetener—that is, it has no calories. Aspartame has the same calories as sugar, but is so much sweeter that only small amounts are needed to provide the desired sweetness in a product. Hence, its caloric contribution is almost negligible.

Source: U.S. Department of Agriculture.

Free   Contains no more than an amount that is "nutritionally trivial" and unlikely to have a physiological consequence.

Fresh   Can refer only to raw food that hasn't been processed, frozen, or preserved.

Calorie-Free   Has fewer than 5 calories a serving

Sugar-Free   Has less than 0.5 gram of sugar a serving.

Sodium-Free/Salt-Free   Has less than 5 milligrams of sodium a serving.

Low Sodium   Has less than 140 milligrams of sodium per serving or per 100 grams of food.

Very Low Sodium   Has less than 35 milligrams per serving or per 100 grams of food.

Low Calorie   Has fewer than 40 calories per serving or per 100 grams of food.

High   A serving provides 20 percent or more of the recommended daily intake of the stated nutrient.

Source of   A serving has 10 percent to 19 percent of the recommended daily intake of the nutrient.

Reduced Sodium   Has no more than half the sodium of a comparison food.

Reduced Calories   Has one-third fewer calories than comparison food.

Less   Term may be used to describe nutrients if the reduction is at least 25 percent.

Light   Term may be used on foods that have one-third fewer calories than a comparable product. Any other use of "light" [or alternate spellings such as "lite"] must specify whether it refers to the look, taste or smell; for example, "light in color."

More   Term may be used to show that a food contains at least 10 percent more of a desirable nutrient, such as fiber or potassium, than a comparable food.

Fat-Free   Has less than 0.5 gram fat per serving, and no added fat or oil.

Low Fat   Has 3 grams or less fat per serving or per 100 grams of the food.

(Percent) Fat-Free   Term may be used only in describing foods that qualify as low-fat.

Reduced Fat   Has no more than half the fat of an identified comparison. *Example:* "Reduced fat, 50% less fat than our regular brownie. Fat content has been reduced from 8 grams to 4 grams." To avoid trivial claims, reduction must exceed 3 grams of fat per serving.

Low in Saturated Fat   Has 1 gram or less of saturated fat per serving, and not more than 15 percent of the food's calories come from saturated fat.

Cholesterol-Free   Has less than 2 milligrams of cholesterol per serving and has 2 grams or less of saturated fat per serving.

Low in Cholesterol   Has 20 milligrams or less cholesterol per serving or per 100 grams of food, and 2 grams or less of saturated fat per serving.

Source: U.S. Department of Agriculture.

Other Food Products   The USDA also grades other food products, such as eggs and milk and fresh fruits and vegetables, usually those that come prepackaged. In this area particularly, the grading is often misleading. For example, "U.S. No. 1" is the third grade for apples, but the second grade for grapefruit and the first grade (top grade) for pears. Similarly, "U.S. No. 1 Bright" represents the second grade of oranges, not the top grade, as might be assumed.

Food Labels and the Consumer

All federal efforts to ensure that food products are truthfully labeled are aimed at providing consumers with information so that they may make rational choices. Nutrition labels are a special boon to consumers, who can see at a glance the nutritional content of the food and compare it with other products to make healthful choices. It takes little effort, for example, to detect from the nutrition labels which of two cereals contains the most nutrients. New rules have made labels much easier to understand than those used in the past. Exhibit 10–3 demonstrates differences between older and newer food labels.

The Cost of Labeling

It is important to remember that, although food packaging and labeling laws benefit consumers greatly, any increased information, regulations, and other changes in labeling policies mean added costs for food manufacturers. Much of this expense is passed on to the consumer in the form of higher prices for food items.

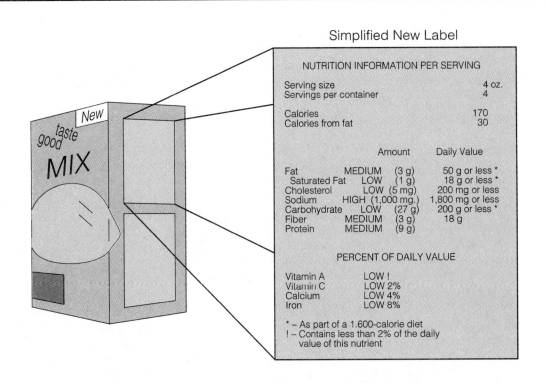

Simplified New Label

NUTRITION INFORMATION PER SERVING

Serving size		4 oz.
Servings per container		4

Calories		170
Calories from fat		30

	Amount		Daily Value
Fat	MEDIUM	(3 g)	50 g or less *
Saturated Fat	LOW	(1 g)	18 g or less *
Cholesterol	LOW	(5 mg)	200 mg or less
Sodium	HIGH	(1,000 mg.)	1,800 mg or less
Carbohydrate	LOW	(27 g)	200 g or less *
Fiber	MEDIUM	(3 g)	18 g
Protein	MEDIUM	(9 g)	

PERCENT OF DAILY VALUE

Vitamin A	LOW !
Vitamin C	LOW 2%
Calcium	LOW 4%
Iron	LOW 8%

* – As part of a 1.600-calorie diet
! – Contains less than 2% of the daily
   value of this nutrient

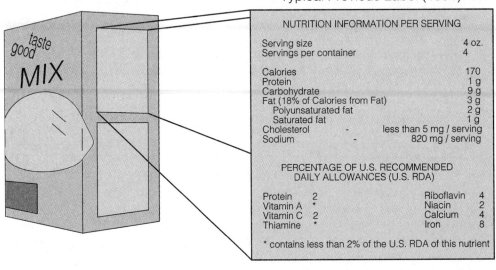

Typical Previous Label (1991)

NUTRITION INFORMATION PER SERVING

Serving size	4 oz.
Servings per container	4

Calories	170
Protein	1 g
Carbohydrate	9 g
Fat (18% of Calories from Fat)	3 g
Polyunsaturated fat	2 g
Saturated fat	1 g
Cholesterol –	less than 5 mg / serving
Sodium –	820 mg / serving

PERCENTAGE OF U.S. RECOMMENDED DAILY ALLOWANCES (U.S. RDA)

Protein	2	Riboflavin	4
Vitamin A	*	Niacin	2
Vitamin C	2	Calcium	4
Thiamine	*	Iron	8

* contains less than 2% of the U.S. RDA of this nutrient

THE GLOBAL CONSUMER

Should There Be Truth in Exporting?

Consumer protection in the United States has resulted in an ever-growing responsibility for manufacturers to provide information on product labels that will help American consumers make informed decisions. Many of these same products, however, ranging from baby formula to frozen raviolis, are sold in other nations without the nutritional and other types of information that their labels must provide in the United States. In many cases this may not pose a serious problem, but in some it clearly does.

In the 1960s and 1970s baby formula produced in the United States and in Europe was heavily promoted in South America, Africa, and the subcontinent of Asia. Unfortunately, many people who bought this product lacked an un-

derstanding of how it should be used. They could not read the directions and were not provided with verbal instruction. Because they were poor, and the product was expensive, they often diluted it with water drawn from wells that were polluted or contained bacteria. Their children became sick. If they had instead continued nursing their babies, they would have avoided these problems. The advertising promoted a product that proved harmful because consumers lacked necessary nutritional information about it.

Consider the sales of exported American tobacco products. Although health warnings must be printed on these products in the United States, this is not required in most nations. U.S. tobacco exports have been most successful in Asia,

where tobacco consumption is growing at a rate of almost 2 percent a year. In Japan, for example, in 1991, 61 percent of all adult men smoked and almost 15 percent of all women. Imported American cigarettes account for close to 20 percent of sales in Japan. Similar trends may be seen in other nations where smoking American cigarettes is often seen as a sign of affluence or status. These tobacco products are surely causing illness among people who use them, but they are given no health warning on the package.

Do you believe American manufacturers have a responsibility to print nutritional information or health warnings on their exported products? Would this put American products at a competitive disadvantage in world markets?

NUTRITION

In the mid-1970s, studies by the Food and Drug Administration and various Senate committees created government concern about a "wave of malnutrition" in the United States. Much of this malnutrition was attributed to an overconsumption by Americans of sugars and fats, especially fat from meat products, since the turn of the century. Since 1977 the Department of Agriculture and the FDA have recommended that Americans generally strive to reduce their "current intake of total fat, saturated fat, and cholesterol." These government efforts have been joined in the private sector by the American Heart Association, the National Cancer Institute, and numerous other health-oriented groups, as well as nutritionists.

Have these appeals been effective? Are Americans changing their dietary habits and consuming less fat? Yes—to some extent. Data from the Department of Agriculture and the American Heart Association indicate that between 1977 and 1986 Americans reduced their fat intake from 41 percent of their daily diet to 37 percent. Still, they haven't reached the dietary goals set by the American Heart Association: a daily diet consisting of 30 percent fat, 15 to 20 percent protein, and 50 to 55 percent carbohydrates (some health experts recommend that fat consumption be reduced even further—to 25 or even 20 percent of

▶ Exhibit 10–4   Recommended Dietary Allowances

SEX-AGE CATEGORY	AGE		WEIGHT		HEIGHT		FOOD ENERGY	PROTEIN
	Years		Kilo-grams (kg)	Pounds (lb)	Centi-meters (cm)	Inches (in)	Calories (cal)	Grams (g)
	From	To						
Infants	0	0.5	6	13	60	24	kg×115 lb×52.3	kg×2.2 lb×1.0
	0.5	1	9	20	71	28	kg×105 lb×47.7	kg×2.0 lb×0.9
Children	1	3	13	29	90	35·	1,300	23
	4	6	20	44	112	44	1,700	30
	7	10	28	62	132	52	2,400	34
Males	11	14	45	99	157	62	2,700	45
	15	18	66	145	176	69	2,800	56
	19	22	70	154	177	70	2,900	56
	23	50	70	154	178	70	2,700	56
	51 +		70	154	178	70	2,400ᵃ	56
Females	11	14	46	101	157	62	2,200	46
	15	18	55	120	163	64	2,100	46
	19	22	55	120	163	64	2,100	44
	23	50	55	120	163	64	2,000	44
	51 +		55	120	163	64	1,800ᵃ	44
Pregnant							+300	+30
Lactating							+500	+20

ᵃAfter age 75 years, energy requirement is 2,050 calories for males and 1,600 calories for females.

Source: U.S. Department of Agriculture.

the daily diet). That Americans continue to consume too much fat, especially saturated fat, was stressed by U.S. Surgeon General Everett C. Koop in his 1988 "Surgeon General's Report on Nutrition and Health." His prescription was a familiar one: Eat less fat-containing foods and more fruits and vegetables.

Recommended Dietary Allowances

To inform their citizens of the nutrients required to maintain health, many countries have developed nutrient standards. In the United States, these standards are the **recommended dietary allowances (RDAs),** which list the recommended daily intakes of nutrients—protein, vitamins, and minerals—that normal, healthy people require. Although the RDAs are published by the government, they are created by a highly qualified group of scientists selected by the National Academy of Sciences. Exhibit 10–4 shows the RDAs that have been established for the following groups of individuals: infants up to age 1, children from age 1 to 10, males from age 11 up, females from age 11 up, and pregnant and lactating women. RDAs have been determined for virtually every important nutrient needed each day by these groups of people.

To simplify RDAs, nutritionists have condensed them to the **U.S. recommended daily allowances (U.S. RDAs).** The U.S. RDAs take the *maximum amount* of each nutrient needed for the following categories: infants, children, children over age 4 and adults, and pregnant and lactating females.

Recommended dietary allowances (RDAs)

A system devised by the National Academy of Sciences in which a specified daily intake of particular vitamins and nutrients is given for infants, children, males, and females, as well as pregnant and lactating women. Not to be confused with U.S. recommended daily allowances.

U.S. recommended daily allowances (U.S. RDAs)

Related to recommended dietary allowances but in a simplified form. The U.S. RDAs are the maximum amount of each nutrient needed for four broad categories of the population.

	MINERALS		VITAMIN A		THIAMIN	RIBO-FLAVIN	NIACIN	ASCORBIC ACID
CALCIUM	PHOS-PHORUS	IRON	Retinol equiv. (RE)	Interna-tional units (IU)				
Milli-grams (mg)	Milli-grams (mg)	Milli-grams (mg)			Milli-grams (mg)	Milli-grams (mg)	Milli-grams (mg)	Milli-grams (mg)
360	240	10	420	1,400	0.3	0.4	6	35
540	360	15	400	2,000	.5	.6	8	35
800	800	15	400	2,000	.7	.8	9	45
800	800	10	500	2,500	.9	1.0	11	45
800	800	10	700	3,300	1.2	1.4	16	45
1,200	1,200	18	1,000	5,000	1.4	1.6	18	50
1,200	1,200	18	1,000	5,000	1.4	1.7	18	60
800	800	10	1,000	5,000	1.5	1.7	19	60
800	800	10	1,000	5,000	1.4	1.6	18	60
800	800	10	1,000	5,000	1.2	1.4	16	60
1,200	1,200	18	800	4,000	1.1	1.3	15	50
1,200	1,200	18	800	4,000	1.1	1.3	14	60
800	800	18	800	4,000	1.1	1.3	14	60
800	800	18	800	4,000	1.0	1.2	13	60
800	800	10	800	4,000	1.0	1.2	13	60
+400	+400	18+[b]	+200	+1,000	+.4	+.3	+2	+20
+400	+400	18	+400	+2,000	+.5	+.5	+5	+40

[b]The increased requirement cannot be met by ordinary diets; therefore the use of supplemental iron is recommended.

Additionally, the U.S. RDAs recommend a larger quantity than the RDAs established by the National Academy of Sciences whenever evidence appears that the population is lacking in a nutrient—for example, riboflavin. Food for infants or children uses only U.S. RDAs for that age group. FDA rules imposed in 1992 no longer require extensive RDA information on food labels because such lists were found to be confusing to many consumers.

Basic Food Groups

To calculate whether your daily diet contains the amount of nutrients prescribed by the U.S. RDAs is a difficult and time-consuming endeavor. To simplify your task, the Department of Agriculture developed, beginning in 1956, dietary guidelines based on basic food groups. Originally, these groups were called the "basic four" and consisted of (1) vegetables and fruits; (2) breads and cereals; (3) milk and cheese; and (4) meat, poultry, fish, and beans. As you can see in Exhibit 10–5, a fifth group (fats, sweets, and alcohol) has been added—to be used only as "extras" in the diet.

By selecting foods from these basic food categories in the recommended amounts per day, you can be fairly sure that you will obtain a nutritionally balanced diet. The nutrients will in most cases take care of themselves, and vitamin and mineral supplements should not be necessary—unless prescribed by a physician. To reduce fat intake, select products within each food group that are low in fat content—skim milk instead of whole milk, for example. To

FOOD GROUP AND NUMBER OF SERVINGS	COUNT AS A SERVING	NUTRITIONAL BENEFIT	USE IN MEALS
FRUIT VEGETABLES **4 or more**	• ½ fruit or typical portion as served— • 1 orange or banana • ½ medium grapefruit or cantaloupe • 1 wedge of lettuce • 1 bowl of salad • 1 medium potato	*Vitamin A*—Dark-green and deep-yellow vegetables. Eat often. *Vitamin C*—Citrus fruits (oranges, grapefruit, tangerines, lemons), melons, berries; have one serving per day. Tomatoes, dark green vegetables; have one serving every day. *Riboflavin, folacin, iron, magnesium*—Dark-green vegetables. *Fiber*—Unpeeled fruits and vegetables, especially those with edible seeds. *Starch*—Potatoes (white and sweet), corn, green peas. Low in fat and calories; no cholesterol.	• Serve raw or cooked. • Use in salads or as side dishes. • Use fruits as juice and occasionally in desserts (cobblers, pies, and shortcakes). • Use vegetables in casseroles, stews, and soups.
BREAD CEREAL **4 or more**	Products made with whole-grain or enriched flour or meal— • 1 slice bread • 1 biscuit or muffin • ¼ to ½ cup cooked cereal, cornmeal, grits, macaroni, noodles, rice, or spaghetti, 1 ounce ready-to-eat cereal	*B vitamins and iron*—Most whole-grain and enriched breads and cereals. *Zinc, magnesium, folacin, and fiber*—Whole-grain products. *Protein*—A major source in vegetarian diets. *Lower in calories*—If prepared and served with little or no fat and sweets.	• Have at all meals and snacks. • Serve at breakfast as toast, muffins, pancakes, or grits, cooked or ready-to-eat cereals. • Use at lunch or dinner as macaroni, spaghetti, noodles, or rice in a casserole or side dish, and breads in sandwiches—hot or cold. • Use crackers or cereals as snacks. • Have occasionally as a baked dessert, such as cake, pastry, or cookies made from whole-grain or enriched flour.
MILK CHEESE Teenager: 4 or more Adult: 2 or moreᵃ	• 8 ounces milk or yogurt • 1 ounce Cheddar or Swiss cheese = ¼ cup milk • 1 ounce processed American cheese = ⅔ cup milk • ½ cup ice cream or ice milk = ¼ cup milk • ½ cup cottage cheese = ¼ cup milk.	*Calcium*—Major source in American diets. *Protein, riboflavin, vitamins B₆, B₁₂, and A.* *Vitamin D*—If product is fortified. *Lower calories and fat*—Lowfat or skim milk products. Items fortified with vitamins A and D contain the same amount of nutrients as whole milk products.	*Milk:* • As a beverage at meals and snacks. • On cereals. • In soups, main dishes, custards, puddings, baked goods. For variety, replace part of milk with: • Yogurt. • Cheese (plain, on crackers, or in sandwiches, salads, and casseroles).

FOOD GROUP AND NUMBER OF SERVINGS	COUNT AS A SERVING	NUTRITIONAL BENEFIT	USE IN MEALS
MEAT, POULTRY FISH & BEANS **2 or more**	2 to 3 ounces of lean cooked meat, poultry, or fish without bone. Equal to 1 ounce of meat: • 1 egg • ¼ to ½ cup cooked dry beans, peas, soybeans, or lentils • 2 tablespoons peanut butter • ¼ to ½ cup nuts or seeds • 2 ounces of bologna	*Protein, iron, zinc, vitamins B_6 and B_{12} and other minerals and vitamins.* *Vitamin B_{12}*—Only foods of animal origin. *Zinc*—Red meats and oysters are the better sources. *Iron*—Red meats are important sources. *Magnesium*—Dry beans and nuts. *Lower calories and fat*—Dry beans and peas, red meat with fat parts trimmed away, poultry with skin removed, and fish. *Relatively low in cholesterol*—Fish and shellfish, except for shrimp. None in dry beans and peas. (Organ meats and egg yolks have the highest amount.)	• Main dish. • Ingredient in a main dish—soup, stew, salad, casserole, or sandwich.
FATS SWEETS ALCOHOL **Little or none required, unless for calories**	No serving size defined, as no number of servings is suggested. Includes— • Butter, margarine, mayonnaise, other salad dressings • Sugar, candy, jams, jellies, syrups • Soft drinks, other highly sugared beverages • Wine, beer, liquor • Unenriched, refined bakery products	*Calories.* *Vitamin E*—Vegetable oils. *Essential fatty acids*—Vegetable oils. *Vitamin A*—Butter and margarine.	• Ingredients (sugar and fats) in recipes • Added to foods at table—sugar on cereals, dressings on salads, and spreads on bread. • Expensive "extras"—candy, soft drinks, and alcoholic beverages.

ªThree servings for women who are pregnant and 4 servings for women who are nursing.

reduce sodium intake, select foods from each group that are low in sodium. The FDA recommends between 1,100 and 3,300 milligrams of sodium per day as a safe amount (for the record, a teaspoon of salt contains nearly 2,000 milligrams of sodium). Remember, too, that eating a variety of the foods within each group will help to ensure a healthy intake of nutrients.

In 1991 an attempt was made to change the way the four food groups were presented to the public. An "Eating Right Pyramid" showed the food groups in a pyramid with fruits and vegetables at the top and meats and dairy products at the bottom. The intent of the pyramid may have been to leave the impression among consumers that eating fruits and vegetables is better for your health than eating meat and dairy products. The food pyramid chart was discarded on April 25, 1991, less than two months after it had been suggested. Part of the reason may have been the pressure applied to the Department of Agriculture by meat and dairy product producers.

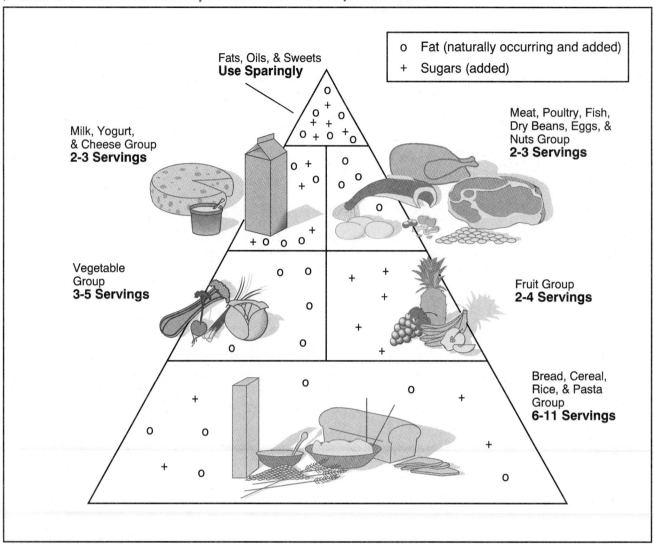

The restructured food group pyramid with four layers shown in Exhibit 10–6 was approved in May 1992. In this new pyramid, complex carbohydrates like bread, rice, and potatoes make up the largest layer on the bottom. The next layer contains fruits and vegetables. The third layer includes meat, fish, and dairy products. The peak is for sugar and fat. The idea is that the higher a food group is on the pyramid, the less of it you should eat each day.

FOOD ADDITIVES

More and more chemicals seem to be getting into the foods we eat, and many consumers, government officials, and nutritionists believe that such additives are causing health problems. Broadly defined, a food additive is any substance that is added to a food product either directly or indirectly. The FDA estimates that at least 2,800 substances are intentionally added to foods, and as many as 10,000 other compounds or combinations of compounds find their way into various foods during the processing, packaging, and storing of food products.

Classification of Additives

Several government agencies have been granted authority to regulate the use of additives in products that cross interstate lines. Meat products are controlled by the U.S. Department of Agriculture, and other food products are regulated by the U.S. Food and Drug Administration. Since 1958 manufacturers of additives have been required to prove that the additives are safe for human consumption. All additives in common use prior to 1958, however, were exempted from this requirement. These additives are placed on one of two lists: Generally Recognized as Safe (GRAS) or Prior Sanction. Presumably, all the items on these lists are assumed to be safe because they have withstood the test of time. Saccharin was on the GRAS list, however, and sodium nitrate was on the Prior Sanction list. Studies show both saccharin and sodium nitrate may cause cancer in laboratory animals when administered in doses larger than any consumer is likely to use.

Any additives tested after 1958 have been either rejected or placed on an Approved list. Whenever an additive on the market is found to be hazardous, it is placed on a Banned list. If there are serious doubts concerning an item on the GRAS, Prior Sanction, or Approved lists, the item is placed on an Interim list.

Direct Additives

Most of the substances added to food are for the purpose of improving its nutritional quality or to preserve its freshness for marketing purposes. Some direct additives are in the form of vitamins and minerals that might otherwise be lacking in a person's diet or that have been destroyed or lost in the processing of the food product. Other substances are added to make food taste better. Approximately 98 percent of all direct additives are in the form of sugar, salt, corn syrup, citric acid, baking soda, vegetable coloring agents, mustard, and pepper. According to the FDA, food flavors constitute the largest single category of food additives. Some consumers have questioned the necessity of using artificial flavors, but there has been less criticism of this form of food additive than of food-coloring agents, preservatives, and artificial sweeteners.

Food Colors The Color Additive Amendments, passed in 1960 (amending the Food, Drug and Cosmetic Act), require certification by the FDA of all colors made from potentially harmful chemicals. Until the food color Red No. 2 was declared unsafe and banned in 1976, it was one of the most common food additives. There are still quite a few artificial colors used in foodstuffs for humans, even though questions about their safety still exist. Two of the most widely used are Red No. 40 and Yellow No. 5, and both are under fire because of reports of possible health risks.

Preservatives Many chemicals are added directly to food substances as preservatives. For example, sodium nitrate is a red coloring agent that inhibits the growth of botulism germs in hot dogs, bacon, and luncheon meats. Alone, sodium nitrate seems to be relatively safe in extremely small quantities. Nonetheless, experiments have shown that when sodium nitrate joins with naturally produced proteins called amines, the result is nitrosamines. It is believed that nitrosamines may cause cancer in humans because they have been shown to cause cancer in animals. There is clearly a tradeoff here: Sodium nitrate preserves food longer, but it may cause cancer.

Artificial Sweeteners Artificial sweeteners, such as saccharin (Sweet 'n Low) and cyclamate, usually used in conjunction, and, more recently, aspartame (NutraSweet, Equal) and acesulfame-K (Sweet One), are also used as direct additives in foods. The health risks posed by some of these artificial sweeteners have caused much controversy. In the cases of both saccharin and cyclamate, animal tests produced evidence that they are carcinogenic. On the other hand, there has been no evidence that *persons* using saccharin or cyclamate have contracted cancer. The so-called Delaney Clause of the 1958 Food and Drug Amendment requires, nonetheless, that any direct additive found to be cancer-causing (carcinogenic) in animals must be banned from human food. In short, "No additive shall be deemed . . . safe if it is found to induce cancer when ingested by men or animals." Cyclamate was banned in 1970 on the basis of the Delaney Clause when that sweetener was found to cause bladder tumors in rats. In 1977, when Canadian tests showed that saccharin was carcinogenic in rats, a proposed ban was withheld because of public furor. Congress voted an 18-month delay on banning saccharin that has since been extended several times, and saccharin is still being used in food products.

With the advent of aspartame on the market in the early 1980s, consumers were given an alternative. Aspartame is considered to be much safer for human consumption than saccharin, although products containing aspartame must bear a warning on their labels cautioning people with the rare genetic disease of phenylketonuria against its use. Sweet One is the only artificial sweetener currently on the market that doesn't require a warning label—as yet.

Indirect Additives

A potentially serious health problem arises with indirect additives, such as chemicals used on produce to control pests, control growth, or preserve freshness and appearance. These indirect additives are not listed on any labels, and consumers usually have no way of knowing—short of extensive research—what produce has been subject to chemical (or radiation) treatment. Consumers must rely on the FDA's judgment as to what kind of chemicals, in what amounts, are safe to ingest. The FDA regulates indirect additives by setting up tolerance levels, expressed in parts per million or billion, of carcinogenic or other harmful chemical substances.

How Safe Is "Safe"?

Some consumers believe that it is difficult—if not impossible—to determine "safe" amounts of any harmful substance and thus seriously question the value of the FDA list. One of the major problems with food additives is their unknown long-term effects. When taken in small quantities, they appear to be safe under most circumstances. When taken over a long period of time, they may be cancer-causing. Cancer may take as long as 40 years to develop, so we don't know very much about such long-term effects, particularly for additives that have just recently been used in or on foodstuffs.

Consumer Confusion

Another problem is that consumers often receive mixed signals about the relative safety of certain additives. Growth hormones added to beef by cattle farmers, for example, pose a significant health risk according to some health-advocacy groups. And the fact that the European Economic Community banned beef imports from the United States in late 1988 because of these potentially dangerous additives created even more widespread concern over this problem. On the other hand, the World Health Organization and the FDA both maintain that the tiny amount of growth hormones in beef poses no health threat. In the midst of this confusion was the concern expressed by the Centers for Disease Control (CDC) that the stir over beef obscured the more genuine threat caused by adding antibiotics to chicken feed to prevent disease. According to the CDC, the antibiotic regimen breeds antibiotic-resistant strains of the bacteria that cause salmonella and other serious illnesses. Certainly, reports of salmonella have been increasing, although thorough cooking will kill the bacteria.

American consumers also received conflicting messages about the chemical daminozide (known by the trade name Alar), which in 1989 was being used on an estimated 5 percent of the red apples marketed in the United States to produce uniform growth and ripening. While the Environmental Protection Agency noted that the chemical seemed to pose a significant risk of cancer in humans, it nonetheless allowed the product to remain on the market for 18 months until studies of the chemical's effects could be completed. In the meantime, an environmental group warned that preschoolers (who eat more apples than adults) could face as much as 910 times the acceptable cancer risk if they ate the daminozide-treated apples. Who or what is the consumer to believe?

Tradeoffs We Make When We Buy Food

Buying food, as with any other consumer choice, forces us to make tradeoffs. The most tasty food products may be bad for our health. Those that are easiest to prepare often cost more and may not be as nutritious as other foods that are less convenient. Finding the best food purchases often forces consumers to take more time shopping. In the end, each consumer must decide what tradeoff offers the most value for his or her food dollars and personal time and effort.

HEALTH, NATURAL AND ORGANIC FOODS

Many consumers worry about possible harmful effects of eating foods that contain additives. As a result, they choose to trade off the cost of higher prices for the benefits of purchasing "health" or "natural" or "organically grown" foods, which are supposedly free of harmful substances. These three types of food are often lumped together, and thus definitions become hazy. The following broad definitions are fairly widely accepted, however.

1. Health foods may include vegetarian and dietetic foods and other products not necessarily free of chemical additives.
2. Natural foods do not contain artificial ingredients, preservatives, or emulsifiers.
3. Organic foods are grown without the use of chemically formulated fertilizers or pesticides.

The problem with these definitions is that the terms are not defined by law. How do we really know what is natural and healthful? Do organic fertilizers produce more nutritious fruits and vegetables, as some people suggest? At one

> Buying food, as with any other consumer choice, forces us to make tradeoffs. The most tasty food products may be bad for our health.

time, the Federal Trade Commission attempted to ban the use of such words as *organic, natural,* and *health* as they pertain to foods because of their vagueness and the possibility of deceiving the consumer. Although many products thus labeled are both healthful and economical, some others may not be, and the consumer is advised to be wary when shopping for them. There is no guarantee, for example, that a food marketed as "organic" really hasn't been exposed to pesticides or pesticide residues in the soil in which it was grown, and there is no way for the FDA to police these products. Likewise, food supplements labeled as "natural" sources for vitamins and minerals may or may not be that. As discussed in Chapter 6, this is an area where fraud can easily be perpetrated on health-conscious consumers.

THE GROWING TREND TOWARD CONVENIENCE FOOD

The food industry is now providing us with buttered peas, frozen corn on the cob, stuffed baked potatoes, cheese in a spray can, complete frozen dinners, frozen tacos, and so on. You name it, and you can buy it already prepared. Just pop it into the oven (conventional or microwave) and wait.

Why Convenience Foods?

Why are Americans buying so many convenience foods? The answer is quite simple: Our high incomes prompt us to place a high value on our time. Americans are no lazier than other people. We simply are willing to pay more in both money and possibly lower food quality to save time. We prefer to use our time in ways other than food preparation.

Convenience foods require almost no preparation. You need none of the pots and pans and cutting utensils of old for something that is already chopped, frozen, buttered, and ready to eat after only heating. Certain convenience foods give you less nutrient value than if you spent the time making the dish yourself. Again, that is just part of the price you pay for convenience, and you should be aware of it. People more concerned about nutritional value and those who dislike consuming large quantities of food additives shy away from convenience food, but they pay a price for that. People who always cook meals from scratch spend more time in the kitchen than those who settle for TV dinners or canned foods. We can make no ultimate judgment about whether convenience foods are good or bad for the American consumer. As long as you know what you are getting, then you can make the choice.

Perhaps it is incorrect to lump all convenience foods together. While some, such as Tang, increase sugar in the diet, and others, such as frozen cream pies, are essentially nonfoods, others provide real convenience. Frozen string beans, for example, give you a reasonably fresh vegetable out of season with the time-consuming preparation job (that is, cutting and cleaning) already done.

The trend toward packaged foods is definitely on the upswing; restaurants, even some of the best ones, now have frozen convenience foods on their menus. It might surprise you to find that some parts of a $45 meal in an expensive French restaurant are frozen foods. Actually, you shouldn't be surprised; the cost of food-preparing labor in restaurants has risen so much that to stay in business, even the best restaurants have to cut corners. And one way to do so is to buy convenience foods.

The cost of convenience is often an important factor in consumer decision making. While convenience foods may cost more than foods prepared at home, consumers using such foods pay a lower "time cost" in preparing them.

Fast Foods Aren't Necessarily Junk Foods

In the first decade of this century, two items were marketed that were to change the course of American life: the hamburger and the Model-T Ford. Since then, eating on the run has been increasingly common for Americans, and fast-food restaurants have met this demand with more and more offerings in more and more cities across the nation. Long criticized as sources of "junk food," these restaurants have changed their image. Starting with Wendy's in 1979, most fast-food chains introduced salad bars along with fish and chicken sandwiches as alternatives to the ubiquitous hamburger. By the late 1980s, in response to pressure from health-advocacy groups, Burger King, McDonald's, Hardee's, Wendy's, and Taco Bell had eliminated some, if not all, of the highly saturated fats they had been using in cooking.

Even nutritionists admit that it is possible to buy nutritious foods on the run, but they caution that consumers should be selective and watch the fat and sodium content of the fast foods they choose. This task has become much easier in recent years as many fast-food restaurants have begun to provide nutritional information about the products they sell. In all, the verdict remains generally the same as it has for years: Although an occasional meal at a fast-food restaurant won't harm anybody, a steady diet of such foods and too little in the way of nutrition-dense foods—those rich in minerals and low in calories—could eventually cause health problems.

> Even nutritionists admit that it is possible to buy nutritious foods on the run.

GETTING THE MOST FOR YOUR FOOD-SHOPPING DOLLAR

We all have different buying habits, and how much time we want to spend shopping for groceries determines to a great extent our shopping tactics. As we noted in discussing convenience foods, our time has value for us, too. If we walk into a supermarket and buy the items we need without regard to price, we will obviously spend less time than the careful shopper who reads labels and compares food quality and costs. We will also very likely spend more money. But how much more?

To answer this question, the editors of *Consumer Reports* conducted an experiment, reported in the March 1988 issue. Two individuals were given an identical shopping list and asked to purchase all of the items on the list from a large, modern A&P store. One shopper was asked to buy impulsively, without regard to price; the other was instructed to choose carefully, comparing nutritional value and prices. The result? The impulsive shopper selected an array of mainly name-brand products, the total cost of which was $110.05. The careful shopper, on the other hand, purchased mainly store brands and paid a total of $59.35. Clearly, there are savings to be had in shopping for groceries, if you want to take the time to comparison-shop.

Are Name-Brand Foods Better?

As a corollary to the preceding experiment, the editors of *Consumer Reports* also conducted a series of studies comparing the quality of name-brand food products with store and generic brands in the same food category. Foods were rated by taste experts as well as nutritionists, and nonfood products (such as aluminum foil or plastic wrap) were judged on the basis of durability, ease of handling, and other factors. The store brands selected for the study were those of Safeway and Pathmark. The results of the tests showed that the store brands were of equal or higher quality than name brands in seven of the ten food categories studied. The generic brand could compete in only one category—canned vegetables—in which it was rated equal in quality to the store brand, and both the generic brand and store brand were rated higher in quality in this category than name brands.

Although this ratio may not hold with other store brands, which vary in quality from store to store, it does underscore what many consumers have suspected for some time—that the most significant difference between name-brand and store-brand foods may be just the price, at least in the majority of cases. Why, then, do food buyers continue to purchase name brands? You probably already know the answer. For example, if you have eaten a certain Kellogg's cereal for years, that cereal is a known quantity to you. You can predict that it will contain certain nutritional values and have a specific taste and texture. This predictability may be important for you—it can save on shopping time and reduce your risk of ending up with a cereal not as good. Of course, exposure to name brands through advertising also induces many consumers to purchase such products, simply because the product names sound familiar. For the price-conscious consumer, however, a little venturesomeness in the supermarket can cut food costs considerably.

The Psychology of Selling Food

The wise consumer will also be on the alert for special marketing tactics employed by food sellers to lure customers to certain displays in their stores and tempt them to purchase their products. Say that you go to the supermarket to purchase a gallon of milk—at least, that's all you had in mind to purchase. But the milk is at the back of the store—and not by accident. To get to it, you must first pass through an aisle filled on both sides with food products, probably a frozen food section (since food marketers rate frozen foods as an "impulse buy"), and perhaps some end-aisle displays of special sale items. You might also need to resist purchasing the product promoted at a strategically placed "sampler station" or the bakery products that smell so good. In short, you will be exposed to numerous temptations to buy more than the milk—or whatever items you have on your grocery list.

Food marketers know that the rate of exposure is directly related to sales and that approximately 65 percent of all food sales result from impulse buying. So be prepared to have your senses of sight, taste, and smell all targeted for this exposure when you enter a supermarket.

Unit Pricing

An important tool consumers may use to compare prices and make better choices is *unit pricing*. Unit prices appear on tags below the product's location on the grocery store shelf. The tags identify the product, its total price, the size of the container, and its price per amount, or unit. These units may be expressed in terms of ounces, quarts, pounds, or many other types of measure depending on the product in question. The advantage of unit pricing to the consumer is that similar products can be compared easily regardless of the size of their containers. For example, one brand of detergent might come in a 48-ounce bottle at a price of $2.99, while another brand is offered in a 64-ounce bottle for $4.19. In this case, would you be able to do the math quickly and easily in your head to know which had the lower price? Most people couldn't. But if unit prices are given, you will know at a glance that the first product's price is 6.23 cents per ounce, while the second costs 6.55 cents per ounce.

Electronic Price Scanning and the Consumer

Electronic price scanning, which has led to time-saving benefits for consumers and sellers alike, has also created a problem for consumers: the increasing lack of item pricing of food products. In some states, by law, each item on display must have a price tag on it. In states without such laws, however, many food sellers have stopped pricing each item. Of course, the price of each food product is shown somewhere nearby—on the shelf below it, usually—but often it is difficult to tell which product corresponds to which price marker.

If this is a problem at the market or markets at which you shop, complain about it to the store owners or managers. The more consumers complain, the more likely it is that the store or stores in question will change their policies—as they have in some areas in response to consumer concerns.

▶ SUMMARY

1. The percentage of total U.S. income spent on food has been declining steadily since this nation was founded. This is characteristic of goods that are necessities as opposed to luxuries. As income rises, the percentage spent on necessities falls. A German statistician named Ernst Engel made this discovery in 1856, and it is now called Engel's Law.

2. Under the Fair Packaging and Labeling Act of 1966 and the Nutritional Labeling and Education Act of 1990, the labels of most consumer products must clearly indicate, among other things, the product's name, the name and address of its manufacturer, and the nutritional value of its contents per standard serving size. The manufacturer must also comply with limitations on the words that may be used to describe the product.

3. Nutrition labeling is required for products containing added nutrients or for which a nutritional claim is made. Nutrition labels must list the amount of nutrients contained in the product, as well as total calories, serving size, amount of calories and certain nutrients per serving, and so on. This kind of labeling has been especially helpful to consumers who want to compare nutritional values, as well as prices, when they shop for food.

4. Special labeling is also required for diet or dietetic foods or any foods designated as low-calorie or reduced-calorie products.

5. The U.S. Department of Agriculture provides grades for meats, fresh produce, poultry, and other items. These grades reflect taste, not nutritional, qualities. Grades for produce can be confusing owing to the use of similar names, such as "U.S. Fancy," to represent different grades for different fruit categories.

6. Labels and grades help consumers make more rational choices. Some consumers want even stricter labeling requirements and fuller disclosure by manufacturers as to product contents.

7. It is important for the consumer to be aware of the fact that increased labeling imposes a cost on food manufacturers—a cost that is usually passed on to the consumer in the form of higher food prices.

8. American government agencies and private health groups have been increasingly concerned over the nutrition of Americans, particularly the overconsumption of fats and the linkage between fat intake and illness. Although Americans appear to be changing their dietary habits and consuming less fat, the unhealthy diet of many Americans continues to be a major health issue.

9. Recommended dietary allowances were developed by the National Academy of Sciences to measure the nutrient value of different foods for comparison purposes. These have been condensed to the U.S. recommended daily allowances, which are used in product labeling.

10. A good way to ensure a nutritious diet is to select foods in the recommended amounts from the following basic food groups: (1) fruits and vegetables, (2) bread and cereals, (3) milk and cheese, and (4) meats, fish, poultry, and beans. Fats and sweets, a fifth group, affect only the taste of food and are to be used sparingly.

11. Food additives are substances added directly or indirectly to food products. Direct additives generally consist of flavoring, coloring, preserving, and sweetening agents. Indirect additives result from the use of chemicals or other substances in the growing or packaging process. Much controversy and uncertainty exists concerning the long-term effects of many of these additives.

12. Health, natural, and organic foods are often lumped together and hazily defined. These foods are difficult for the FDA to control, and the consumer is advised to be cautious when purchasing them.

13. There is a growing trend toward frozen convenience foods or fast foods because, as Americans become richer, they are willing to pay more to save time. That is, their higher incomes lead them to place a higher value on their time, and they therefore rate the ease of using convenience or fast foods higher than the improved quality or lower cost of foods they prepare themselves.

14. By comparing the nutritional value and prices of food products, consumers can cut their food costs considerably and still achieve a healthy diet. Because comparison-shopping requires additional time, some consumers prefer to purchase only familiar products (such as name brands), often paying a higher price for them.

▶ QUESTIONS FOR THOUGHT AND DISCUSSION

1. What is the most important aspect of your diet—taste, nutrition, variety, cost, or convenience?

2. How do you think Americans will shop for and prepare their meals ten years from now? Do you foresee much change?

3. What are the benefits of food additives?

4. What differences do you believe the Nutritional Labeling and Education Act of 1990 has made in the way typical Americans shop for food?

5. Why do Americans continue to consume higher amounts of fats than those recommended by the leading health institutes and organizations?

6. Do you comparison-shop for food? Why or why not?

▶ THINGS TO DO

1. Write down what you eat for the next seven days then answer these questions. How closely did you stick to the recommended minimum servings of the basic food groups? How many foods did you eat that could be considered convenience foods?

2. Select a certain food category, such as TV dinners or cereals, and compare the information on the labels of each brand available. Is there a wide variance? Do the prices of the brands have much to do with nutritional value?

3. At your local meat market, try to determine the differences among the various grades of meat. Ask the butcher if there is a distinct difference between the top two grades of meat and if the top grade is worth the extra price. Also ask him or her which grade of meat is healthiest, in terms of fat content.

▶ APPLICATION

Visit a grocery store where you or another member of your family shops for food. Choose five food products that your family commonly uses and compare their unit prices with those of competing products. Does your family tend to consume food products that are more or less expensive than most other similar goods? What reasons can you give that explain your family's shopping habits?

▶ SELECTED READINGS

▶ Begley, Sharon, and Mary Hager. "Guide to the Grocery." *Newsweek,* March 27, 1989, pp. 20–25.

▶ Brody, Jane E. "Healthy Words to Live By." *Modern Maturity,* October–November 1988, pp. 48–53.

▶ Hamilton, Eva, et al. *Nutrition: Concepts and Controversies.* St. Paul: West, 1988.

▶ Hayton, B. "When Less Is More." *FDA Consumer,* November 1991, pp. 8–11.

▶ "Healthy Labels, Healthy Food," *New York Times* (editorial), March 13, 1989, p. 24.

▶ Hunter, B. T. "Cholera and the Food Supply." *Consumers' Research,* December 1991, pp. 8–9.

▶ Hunter, B. T. "Food for Thought." See issues of *Consumers' Research.*

▶ Lehman, Phyllis. "More Than You Ever Thought You Would Know about Food Additives." *FDA Consumer,* February 1988. Available from the Food and Drug Administration, 5600 Fishers Lane, Rockville, MD 20857.

▶ Money Management Institute. *Your Food Dollar.* Rev. 1988. Available for $1 from the Money Management Institute, 2700 Sanders Rd., Prospect Heights, IL 60070.

▶ National Cancer Institute. *Diet, Nutrition, and Cancer Prevention: The Good News.* Washington, DC: U.S. Government Printing Office, 1986.

▶ *Nutrition and Your Health: Dietary Guidelines for Americans.* Available free from the Consumer Information Center, Pueblo, CO 81009.

▶ Rosewicz, Barbara. "Pesticide Risk from Apples: Who's Right?" *The Wall Street Journal,* March 10, 1989, pp. B1, B13.

▶ Shapiro, Laura, et al. "Warning! Your Food, Nutritious and Delicious, May Be Hazardous to Your Health." *Newsweek,* March 27, 1989, pp. 16–20.

▶ Silberner, Joanne. "A Call to Get the Fat Out." *U.S. News & World Report,* August 8, 1988, pp. 59–61.

▶ U.S. Department of Agriculture. *Making Food Dollars Count: Nutritious Meals at Low Cost.* Home and Garden Bulletin No. 240. Washington, DC: U.S. Government Printing Office, 1987.

▶ U.S. Department of Agriculture. *Nutritive Value of Foods.* Home and Garden Bulletin No. 72. Washington, DC: U.S. Government Printing Office, 1988.

▶ Whitney, Eleanor N., and Eva Hamilton. *Understanding Nutrition.* St. Paul: West, 1987.

Shopping for the Lo-Cal Diet

GLOSSARY

COUNTING CALORIES Keeping track of the calories you consume in your food versus the calories you expend by various activities. If you eat more calories than you expend, you will gain weight; if you expend more calories than you eat, you will lose weight.

DIET OR DIETETIC FOODS Low-calorie or reduced-calorie food, or food intended for a special dietary purpose—for example, low-sodium diets.

LIGHT, LITE, OR REDUCED CALORIE Foods that contain one-third fewer calories per serving than comparable unmodified food products. If the word "light" is used to describe a food's appearance the label must state that the word is being used in this way.

LOW CALORIE Foods that contain no more than 40 calories per 100 gram (3.5 ounce) serving.

LOW IN SATURATED FAT Foods that have 1 gram or less of saturated fat per serving and in which no more than 15 percent of the calories come from saturated fat.

REDUCED SODIUM Foods that contain no more than half the sodium of an identified comparison food.

Americans are trimming down (or trying to) with a vengeance. And for good reason: An increasing number of health problems are being linked to excess weight: heart disease, high blood pressure, kidney problems, diabetes, malnutrition, and complications of pregnancy—as well as psychological and social problems. More recently, cancer has been added to the list. Overall, it is now estimated that the mortality rate for people who are even 10 percent overweight is increased by 20 percent over a 25-year period.

Whether for health or appearance reasons, we are in the midst of a diet craze. One recent study revealed that 90 percent of those Americans surveyed wanted to lose weight, and 35 percent wanted to lose at least 15 pounds. In 1989 weight-conscious Americans spent over $12 billion for diet-related foods, drugs, and other products, up from $5 billion spent in 1986, only three years earlier. Weight-reducing purchases ranged from the sublime (low-calorie but nutritious foods) to the near-ridiculous ("appetite-suppressant" sunglasses). According to the Food and Drug Administration (FDA), millions of consumer dollars were spent on gimmicks, potions, and other diet products that are largely worthless for effective and healthy long-term weight control. The FDA urges consumers to avoid products that promise the impossible and, instead, to follow a sensible diet plan. Most nutritionists agree that, although there may one day be a magic cure for the problem of being overweight, in the meantime the safest and surest way to lose weight is simply to count your calories.

With the advent of an astonishing array of low-calorie and reduced-calorie foods to choose from, counting calories is no longer the ordeal it once was. It is now possible to reduce your caloric intake substantially without changing your eating habits very dramatically. In this Consumer Issue, we look at the growing diet-food marketplace and suggest some ways the diet-conscious consumer can get the most nutrition (and least weight) for his or her diet dollar.

▶ THE DIET-FOOD MARKETPLACE

Diet foods and beverages, while not new, have in the past several years increased in sales to the point where they now represent one of the fastest-growing segments of the American food industry. There is now a much greater choice of calorie-saving food available to consumers. You can buy low- or reduced-calorie versions of bread, cheese, mayonnaise, margarine, cake and pancake mixes, jams and jellies, syrups, salad dressings, ice cream, gelatin desserts, frozen foods and dinners, as well as beer and wine; the list is seemingly endless. Recently, meat and poultry processors and marketers have also entered the fitness-food arena with lean beef and poultry.

These products and many more are available at most supermarkets around the country. Some of them you will find in diet-food sections in supermarkets or, in many cases, shelved with other similar, nondiet foods. Reduced-calorie versions of a regular food product are now usually placed near the unmodified food, which makes comparison of price and nutritional and caloric content easy.

► DIET FOOD LABELING

Prior to their regulation by the FDA, so-called **diet (dietetic) foods** often contained as many calories as their regular counterparts. But current FDA rules, which became effective in 1992, ended this confusion. Exhibit I–1 shows a typical diet-food label today. Moreover, it is now possible for a consumer to know the nutritional and caloric contents of almost any food product, regardless of whether it is labeled "diet" or not. The Nutritional Labeling and Education Act of 1990 led to the establishment of specific definitions for terms used to describe dietary foods. These were listed in Exhibit 10–2 in Chapter 10. The imposition of these rules on food manufacturers has made the jobs of consumers less demanding but has not eliminated their need to use judgment when making food purchases. This fact is made clear by the examples that follow.

In the past, the words "light" or "lite" on a food label had little meaning. Many food producers plastered the words on their labels without regard to actual fat or caloric content. Sometimes "light" referred to the color of the product. Light olive oil, for example, meant the product wasn't as dark in color as some other oils. Many consumers did not realize how the word was being used and bought the product thinking it was more healthful than other oils, when in fact all were 100 percent fat.

Since the implementation of the Nutritional Labeling and Education Act, **"light"** (or **"lite"**) must mean the product has at least one-third fewer calories than other similar products. (This labeling, unfortunately, applies only to products regulated by either the FDA or the U.S. Department of Agriculture.) However, a problem still exists with such labeling.

Just because a product is labeled "light" does not mean it is healthful, but consumers tend to think so. Take potato chips, for example. People who need to reduce their consumption of fat may avoid ordinary potato chips but feel safe buying the light version. Yet, light potato chips still provide more than 50 percent of their calories from oil.

Much the same can be said about many products that are advertised as being **low in saturated fat** or having **reduced sodium.** Foods low in saturated fat may nevertheless have too much unsaturated fat for healthy eating. Low-sodium foods must have half the amount of sodium (salt) of other products. But for a person on a salt-restricted diet, half the salt of an ordinary potato chip is still far too much.

The labeling of light wines and beers does not fall under the jurisdiction of the FDA—except in the case of wines that contain less than 7 percent alcohol by volume. Labeling guidelines for these beverages have been established by the Bureau of Alcohol, Tobacco, and Firearms, and, to date, their caloric labeling has been voluntary. Generally, light beer and wines contain 25 to 35 percent fewer calories than the regular products.

Low-calorie, reduced-calorie, and

► Exhibit I–1 **A Reduced-Calorie Food Product Label**

This Product is Low Fat, Low Sodium

	Heart-safe Helpings Spring Vegetable Noodles	Daily Dietary Recommendations*
Sodium	450mg	2,400
Cholesterol	12mg	300mg
Fat	6g	50g**

**50 g fat based on a 1,500 calorie per day diet.
*The National Research Council. *Diet and Health; Implications for Reducing Chronic Disease Risk.* Washington D.C.: National Academy Press, 1989- Recommended maximum sodium intake of 2,400 mg per day; Less than 300 mg cholesterol per day; Daily fat intake not to exceed 30% calories from fat. Individual calorie needs vary, please note that it is important to consider your diet over time

Nutrition Information		Servings Per Container: 1	
Calories 240		Fat 6g	
Protein 16g		Polyunsaturated 2g	
Carbohydrate 30g		Monounsaturated 3g	
		Saturated 1g	
		Cholesterol 12mg	
		Sodium 450mg	

Ingredients
Tomato Puree, Cooked Enriched Macaroni Product, Part Skim Ricotta Cheese (Whey, Pasteurized Part Skim Milk, Vinegar, Carrageenan), Tomatoes, Spinach, Zucchini, Mushrooms, Carrots, Onions, Romano Cheese (Made From Cow's Milk), Sugar, Dehydrated Onion, Modified Food Starch, Spices, Granulated Garlic, Salt, Hydrolyzed Plant Protein, Olive Oil, Xanthan Gum, Autolyzed Yeast Extract, Calcium Chloride, Citric Acid.

light food products often achieve their reduced caloric content by cutting down on the fat content of the ingredients used—using skim or low-fat milk instead of whole milk, for example. Light beer and wines achieve fewer calories by cutting down on carbohydrates or alcohol, or both. Many of the diet products available are low in calories because artificial sweeteners have been substituted for sugar. This is particularly the case with diet beverages that use saccharin, aspartame, or a relatively new sweetener, acesulfame-K.

▶ PRICES

Increased competition by manufacturers vying for a share of the growing diet-food market has lowered the prices of these foods considerably in the last several years. Some low-calorie food items are now even less expensive than similar "regular" food products, as can be seen in Exhibit I–2. Here we compare caloric content and prices for seven types of food products; in only three cases

were the diet versions more expensive than the regular product. If the present trend in diet-food production continues, consumers can look forward to even lower prices in the future.

By comparison-shopping and planning your dietary needs carefully, you can now get a great deal for your diet-food dollar. Forming a rational weight-control program can help you maximize the benefits to be obtained from available diet products and prices.

▶ DON'T BE MISLED

When shopping for a healthy diet, watch for claims that might be misleading. "No cholesterol" on the label of a jar of peanut butter, for example, may tempt you to believe that that particular brand is healthier for you than the others on the shelf. What the label doesn't say is that no other brand of peanut butter has cholesterol, either. A box of cookies may be labeled "baked in pure vegetable oil"—which may lead you to

assume that the product is low in saturated fat. In fact, it could easily contain one of the tropical oils, which are high in saturated fat and may be more damaging to cardiovascular health than any other type of oil.

Careful reading of labels can help you avoid being misled to a certain extent. Until recently manufacturers were not required to disclose on food labels whether the fats contained in their products were saturated or unsaturated. Concerned about the link between nutrition and health, the National Research Council recommended fuller disclosure on food labels to encourage manufacturers to make low-fat and low-sodium foods more available. In the meantime, some consumer advocates who were not content to wait for congressional action embarrassed manufacturers—through page-size ads in leading newspapers and other tactics—into switching from the cheaper, highly saturated tropical oils to partially unsaturated vegetable oils.

▶ A SENSIBLE DIET PLAN

The following suggestions may help you devise a healthful and effective diet plan.

1. Determine your caloric needs. To benefit from **counting calories,** you need first to know how many pounds you want to lose—or what weight you wish to maintain. Weight control is—theoretically, at least—a simple matter of addition and subtraction. A certain amount of caloric intake is necessary to maintain each pound of your body weight. How many calories are required depends on how active you are and how much energy (read: calories) you expend in daily exercise and activity. Exhibit I–3 lists the approximate

▶ Exhibit I–2   **Price and Calorie Comparisons of Seven Low/Reduced-Calorie and Light Foods with Regular Food Products**

	CALORIES/SERVING	PRICE/QUANTITY[a]
Smuckers Strawberry Preserves	35/tsp.	13.1¢/oz.
Estee Imitation Strawberry Preserves	2/tsp.	14.6¢/oz.
Zesty Italian Dressing (Kraft)	80/tsp.	13.9¢/oz.
Zesty Italian Reduced-Calorie Dressing (Kraft)	16/tsp.	13.9¢/oz.
Hellman's Mayonnaise	100/tbsp.	6.5¢/oz.
Weight Watchers Reduced-Calorie Mayonnaise	40/tbsp.	5.3¢/oz.
Log Cabin Syrup	156/oz.	$2.89/24 oz.
Log Cabin Lite Syrup	80/oz.	$2.89/24 oz.
Breyers Yogurt (Low Fat)	230/8 oz.	69¢/8 oz.
Breyers Yogurt (No Fat)	160/8 oz.	69¢/8 oz.
Kraft American Pasteurized Cheese Slices	90/oz.	18.4¢/oz.
Kraft Light and Lively American Pasteurized Cheese Slices	70/oz.	19.6¢/oz.
Lemon Jell-O (Regular)	80/½ cup	36¢/pack
Sugar-free Lemon Jell-O	8/½ cup	46¢/pack

[a]Prices charged in Buffalo, New York, in 1992.

Exhibit I–3 Daily Calorie Requirements for Levels of Activity

METABOLIC RATE	MEN	WOMEN
Sedentary[a]	16 cal/lb of body weight	14 cal/lb of body weight
Moderate[b]	21 cal/lb of body weight	18 cal/lb of body weight
Active[c]	26 cal/lb of body weight	22 cal/lb of body weight

[a]Includes activities that involve sitting most of the day, such as secretarial work and studying.
[b]May include activities such as walking, gardening, and housework.
[c]May include dancing, skating, and manual labor—for example, farm work or construction work.

Source: Nutrition Search, Inc., *Nutrition Almanac,* 2d ed. (New York: McGraw-Hill, 1984), p. 283.

number of calories required to maintain one pound of body weight for men and women and for three different metabolic rates—sedentary, moderate, and active. If, for example, you are a moderately active woman and your weight is 120 pounds, you will need to consume about 2,160 calories per day (120 × 18) to maintain that weight. If you want to lose ten pounds, you will need to eat fewer calories or exercise more—or both. Generally, whenever you consume 3,500 fewer calories than you expend through exercise, you will lose one pound. Thus, if you reduce your caloric intake by 1,000 calories per day (or by 500 calories per day and use up the equivalent of the other 500 calories in increased exercise), you will lose two pounds per week. In five weeks, you will have attained your desired weight. Since there are additional health benefits to be obtained by exercising, increased activity usually is recommended as a component of a healthful diet plan. Exhibit I–4, which lists the approximate calories "burned" per hour for a variety of activities, will help you relate exercise to energy expenditure expressed in calories.

2. Plan for a moderate weight loss. If you plan to lose weight, aim for a moderate weight loss of one to two pounds per week. This represents the maximum weight loss recommended by physicians for healthful and effective dieting. Beware of fad diets and diet products that promise a weight loss of "ten pounds in three days" or "five pounds overnight"; these usually result only in a temporary weight loss—if any—and often the weight loss is achieved through dehydration.

3. Obtain a calorie counter. In order to plan for your shopping and dietary goals, you will need to buy or borrow a nutrition manual or calorie guide that lists the caloric (and, optimally, the nutritional) contents for various foods. Nearly every major bookstore has a variety of such offerings to choose from, and many of these books now include a long list of fast foods, by brand name, as well.

Exhibit I–4 Expenditure of Caloric Energy per Hour for Various Activities

ACTIVITY	CALORIES EXPENDED PER HOUR	ACTIVITY	CALORIES EXPENDED PER HOUR
Ballroom dancing	330	Preparing a meal	198
Bed making	234	Roller skating	350
Bicycling 5½ mph	210	Running 10 mph	900
Bowling	264	Scrubbing floors	216
Bricklaying	240	Sitting and eating	84
Carpentry	408	Sitting and knitting	90
Desk work	132	Sitting in a chair reading	72
Driving a car	168	Skiing	594
Farm work in field	438	Sleeping (basal metabolism)	60
Gardening	220	Standing up	138
Golf	300	Sweeping	102
Handball and squash	612	Swimming (leisurely)	300
Horseback riding (trot)	480	Tennis	420
Ironing (standing up)	252	Volleyball	350
Lawn mowing (hand mower)	462	Walking (2.5 miles per hour)	216
Painting at an easel	120	Walking downstairs	312
Piano playing	150		

Source: Nutrition Search, Inc., *Nutrition Almanac,* 2d ed. (New York: McGraw-Hill, 1984), p. 4.

4. Know your eating habits. The aim of a good diet plan is to change what you eat, in terms of calories, rather than when or how you eat. The key is to change your food-shopping habits so you have the right foods available when you need them. If you like to spend time cooking and preparing meals at home, shop accordingly. If you are a snacker, shop for low-calorie snack foods. If you eat on the run and prefer frozen dinners occasionally, substitute the low-calorie brands for the regular frozen dinners.

5. Look for low-calorie alternatives when eating out. Shop around for restaurants in your area that may offer **low-calorie** cuisine in addition to their traditional selections. Such restaurants are now increasing in number, and, if you live in a large metropolitan area, it won't be too hard to find one.

6. Remember the basic food groups. Malnutrition is, unfortunately, a not uncommon consequence of dieting for many consumers—particularly for those who opt to emphasize one food group over another. Most nutritionists agree that if you select your calories—sparingly—from the recommended basic food groups discussed in Chapter 10, you can maintain a reasonably balanced nutritional input.

7. Keep a record. Because each individual's metabolic rate—the rate at which calories are expended through activity—varies considerably, you can get a clear idea of your own particular caloric needs only through trial and error. A journal helps. After a few weeks of recording the calories you consume per day and the amount of exercise you undertake, you will be able to approximate fairly closely how many calories and how much exercise you need to attain, or maintain, your desired weight level.

▶ WHEN YOU CAN'T
DO IT YOURSELF

Many dieters find it difficult—if not impossible—to lose weight without some kind of external support. If you are among them, you may choose from among several diet programs that, for a price, offer support and in some cases special diet food and medical supervision.

The lowest-cost programs are TOPS and Overeaters Anonymous. These are informal, nonprofit groups that stress motivation and positive reinforcement. Overeaters Anonymous focuses less on weight than on learning how to stop eating compulsively. It is patterned after Alcoholics Anonymous and offers similar emotional and psychological support.

Weight Watchers costs a little more and is a more structured program. Nutrition specialists consider Weight Watchers to be among the best programs because it helps you develop eating habits that can keep your weight off once you have lost it.

The most structured and most expensive programs are Diet Center, Nutri/System, and the liquid-diet plans, such as Optifast. These programs are supervised by medical and psychological specialists and require special food supplements or food products. The liquid-diet plans, which are the most expensive and fastest-growing diet programs, are supposedly safe—unlike those of the 1970s that nearly vanished from the marketplace after 60 people died of protein starvation. The strictest of the liquid-diet programs is Optifast, which requires a totally liquid diet for the first 12 weeks and then a gradual reintroduction of food by the dieter. Optifast is available only for those who are at least 40 to 50 pounds overweight.

▶ SUMMARY

1. An increasing number of health problems are being linked to overweight and obesity: heart disease, hypertension, diabetes, malnutrition, complications of pregnancy, and cancer. It is estimated that the mortality rate for people even 10 percent overweight is increased by 20 percent over a 25-year period.

2. Americans are in the midst of a dieting craze and in 1989 spent over $12 billion for diet products. Nutritionists recommend that consumers avoid fad diets and quick-weight-loss programs and instead aim for a moderate, rationally planned weight loss.

3. Reducing caloric intake is not difficult with the many low-calorie and reduced-calorie foods now available in supermarkets.

4. In 1990 Congress passed the Nutritional Labeling and Education Act that required the FDA to establish standards for nutritional information that must be included on food labels. These rules were suggested by the FDA in 1991 and implemented on May 1, 1993. The result has been much more uniform and understandable labels that consumers can use easily. An extensive list of words that can be used only to describe products that meet specific standards was created. The FDA also established standard serving sizes for most food products.

5. Prices for diet food products have decreased substantially over the past several years as more and more manufacturers have entered this market. In some cases, low- and reduced-calorie foods are less expensive than regular food products.

6. Seven steps to successful, and healthful, dieting are suggested for the weight-conscious consumer: (1) Determine your caloric needs by calculating what weight loss, if any, you wish to achieve; (2) plan for a moderate weight loss of one to two pounds a week; (3) obtain a calorie counter—a book or manual listing calories for different foods; (4) know your eating habits and shop accordingly; (5) look for low-calorie alternatives when eating out; (6) remember to include foods from the recommended basic food groups daily to ensure adequate nutrition; and (7) keep a record of your caloric intake and expenditure to determine your own personal caloric needs.

7. Numerous diet programs are available for those who find it difficult to diet without external emotional or psychological support or a structured diet program.

▶ QUESTIONS FOR THOUGHT AND DISCUSSION

1. It is estimated that 90 percent of those who lose weight fail to keep it off for a period of several years. To what extent do you think these dismal results are due to psychological and emotional factors? Do you think that the increasing availability of diet foods will change these statistics in the future?

2. Do you think that the danger of being overweight should, in any circumstances, outweigh the possible risks posed by some of the food additives—particularly sweeteners—in diet food products?

3. The American population is considered to be the most overweight population in the world. Why is this?

4. What do you think is the primary motive for the millions of Americans who are dieting—health or appearance?

5. Americans tend to regard slimness as an ideal—an ideal that's implicitly promoted by the fashion industry. Is this because a trim body is healthier, or is there some other reason?

▶ THINGS TO DO

1. Assume you are on a reducing diet of 1,500 calories per day. Create a weekly menu within this calorie range—making sure to include foods from the recommended basic food groups for each day.

2. Call or write the nearest FDA Consumer Affairs Office. Ask what the FDA does to regulate the manufacture and marketing of diet products that are ineffective and possibly dangerous to consumers' health.

3. Call or write the President's Council on Physical Fitness, 450 5th St., N.W., Suite 7103, Washington, DC 20001, (202) 272-3421. Ask for information relating food and exercise programs to physical fitness.

▶ SELECTED READINGS

▶ *About Body Wraps, Pills, and Other Magic Wands* (564N). Available free from the Consumer Information Center, Pueblo, CO 81009.

▶ *Diet Books Sell Well But. . . .* Available free from Consumer Information Center, Pueblo, CO 81009.

▶ *Everybody's Walking.* Available from the President's Council on Fitness and Sports, 450 5th St., N.W., Suite 7103, Washington, DC 20001.

▶ *Exercise and Weight Control.* Available for $1.25 from the Consumer Information Center, Pueblo, CO 81009.

▶ Freedman, Alix M. "New Sweeteners Head for the Sugar Bowl." *The Wall Street Journal,* February 6, 1989, p. B1.

▶ Hellmich, Nanci. "Weighing Fat and Sodium in Diet Dinners." *USA Today,* February 16, 1989, p. 4D.

▶ Henderson, Nancy, and Adrienne Blum, "Crying the Weight-Loss Blues." *Changing Times,* April 1989, pp. 75–78.

▶ Papazian, R. "Product Bans and Controversies." *FDA Consumer,* October 1991, p. 10.

▶ *Planning a Diet for a Healthy Heart.* Available free from the Consumer Information Center, Pueblo, CO 81009.

▶ *Saccharin, Cyclamate and Aspartame.* Available free from the Consumer Information Center, Pueblo, CO 81009.

▶ Stockton, William. "Balancing the Equation of Fat and Exercise." *New York Times,* December 12, 1988, p. 21.

▶ *Weight Loss.* Available free from the Food and Drug Administration, 5600 Fishers Lane, Rockville, MD 20857.

▶ Willis, Judith. "How to Take Weight Off (and Keep It Off) without Getting Ripped Off." Available free from the Food and Drug Administration, 5600 Fishers Lane, Rockville, MD 20857.

CHAPTER 11

More Than Just Keeping Warm

PREVIEW

▶ What determines our clothing choices?

▶ How do clothes fit into family budgets?

▶ What tradeoffs do consumers make regarding the price, quality, and style of clothing they buy?

▶ How can consumers judge the quality of different clothing items?

▶ Who determines what styles of clothing are fashionable?

▶ What federal laws govern the labeling of clothing products?

▶ What can consumers do to be more successful clothing shoppers?

> Just as variety in diet contributes to more than physical well-being, so, too, can clothing be one of the material aspects of life that contributes to self-esteem and thus happiness.

It is estimated that American families spent over $215 billion on clothing in 1991. Together, all of us purchased $215 billion worth of shoes, pants, hats, jockey shorts, brassieres, panties, hose, suits, ties, shirts, skirts, and socks. Clothing expenditures account for more than 7 percent of the typical American's total budget. Clothing is a major industry, now employing more than a million workers in any one year. The fashion business, of course, occupies large amounts of advertising and media space and probably, for many people, a significant amount of mental space.

CLOTHES, FAMILY HAPPINESS, AND BUDGET FORMATION

How a family dresses can sometimes enhance family satisfaction. Some may find this idea reprehensible because it puts too much emphasis on a material, instead of a spiritual, aspect of life. But just as variety in diet contributes to more than physical well-being, so, too, can clothing be one of the material aspects of life that contributes to self-esteem and thus happiness. The fact remains, for example, that parents who approve of how their children dress are often more satisfied and proud to be the heads of the family. Similarly, children as well as their parents may take great pleasure in being part of the family unit that "dresses up" to go to religious services or to visit friends. But each member of the family has his or her own idea about what fashions are appropriate for himself or herself and for the others in the family. This may cause conflicts within the family or spending unit for two reasons. For one, the family's budget will, by necessity, curtail some of the clothing expenditures desired by each member. And, for another, members of the family whose clothing habits are significantly different from those of other members may feel pressure to conform.

To avoid the problem of family conflicts about individual dressing styles, it is important that as children mature their individuality be recognized and respected. This is something that can be discussed during family councils or between individual members of the spending unit. Because clothing habits reflect each person's values and aesthetics, no set rules about dressing can be absolute for any person at any time. If one member of the spending unit wishes to rebel and buy clothes that are indeed different from everyone else's, this attempt at individuality must not only be understood but also accepted (at least in part). As with everything else, compromises will have to be made about dressing habits within a spending unit, as well as about the amount of each member's clothing expenditures. There are many factors that can affect the tradeoffs people make between the kinds and amounts of clothing they buy.

WHY SO MANY CLOTHES?

The typical American has more clothes than are actually needed to provide physical protection from the cold, sun, wind, and rain. Obviously, most clothing is no longer so much a necessity as it is a consumer good that gives pleasure to the wearer.

Customs

The types of clothes we buy are often determined by customs in the community, although in the United States this is less true today than in the past.

It is certainly only by custom that men wear trousers and women wear skirts. After all, in Scotland, some men also wear skirts; and in the United States, more and more women are wearing pants whenever and wherever they wish without being exposed to ridicule or discrimination. Why do men wear ties and collars while women usually do not? Again, the only explanation is custom.

Customs are not created in a vacuum; most are created to appease or satisfy a large segment of the population. Once customs are well established, they change very slowly. They are hard to alter, simply because the majority of the society accepts them or even enjoys them. Only when a significant and aggressive minority finds certain customs disturbing are they changed.

Aesthetic Considerations

Clothing that pleases us as wearers and that we think pleases those who see us can positively affect our attitude and increase our confidence. One of the strongest motivations of dress is preservation of the self-image of the wearer through the enhancement of the body. This is an aesthetic consideration—that is, one having to do solely with beauty. Even among primitive tribes, self-adornment is a stronger motivation than protection from the elements or thrift or durability. And this motivation in clothing selection has nothing to do with snobbery. It merely indicates a positive self-concept that is healthy and beneficial.

Values

People generally express their values, attitudes, and interests by the choices they make. To a great extent, values help determine our choice of behavior and influence much of our decision making during the course of our lives. In this sense, clothing choices make a statement about those ideas we consider important in our day-to-day living and, whether consciously or unconsciously, about the beliefs about ourselves that we would like others to share.

Our individual values, however, are closely linked to a much broader value system, one that we learn from our culture, family, friends, and our own experiences. Taken together, these values are known as a *value pattern*. This pattern includes all those things we consider important, and it helps organize them into some kind of functioning order. Clothing, then, can be said to reflect not only those values instilled in us by society but also our own individual attitudes and values.

Studies on the emphasis that we, as groups and individuals, give to clothing have found that clothing choices reveal attitudes most often related to conformity, self-expression, aesthetic satisfaction, esteem, comfort, and economy. For example, if you place a great deal of importance on conformity, you will make choices that reflect the clothing fashion of your peers. If you are more concerned with aesthetic satisfaction, you might choose clothing for its stylishness, fabric quality, or for the pleasure derived from being considered well-dressed. If you are more concerned with economy, your clothing choices will express the practicality, durability, and price of the item.

Even though our values are often expressed by our clothing choices, many times values conflict, and compromises must be made. For example, a person may value conformity in dress, but his or her budget might place constraints on that desire. That latest style that everyone is wearing may be too expensive. Clearly, a compromise must be made.

Group Identification

Another aspect of clothing involves group identification. Clothing styles tell the outside world something about an individual's personality and lifestyle. Clothing will convey a message to others about what you do, what you believe, and what you are. In particular, clothing appearance and style may identify an individual with a particular group. Advertisers are well aware of this function of clothing and, as discussed in Chapter 5, have successfully promoted name brands and designer labels by linking them to certain age groups or to certain social characteristics.

The wearing of a particular style of clothing can also help create an identity for an individual. Teenagers, for example, often dress in a manner contrary to what is normal for the family in which they have been raised. This seeming rebellion is often no more than an external expression of the teenager's search for his or her unique identity as a young adult. From infancy on, children learn their own identity by distinguishing themselves as separate individuals from their parents and others closest to them. By the time children reach their teens and exercise some control over clothing choices, they are also becoming aware of the relationship between clothing and personality or self-image. Often, teenagers need to try on a number of identities—expressed in clothing styles—before they find one that fits comfortably. This is a normal part of the maturation process.

DURABILITY VERSUS PRICE

Parents should help their children realize that styles come and go. As a matter of fact many people accuse the clothing industry of creating obsolescence. The ultimate in planned obsolescence was a phenomenon that appeared in the 1970s: paper underwear, paper dresses, and other items made out of paper products that were thrown away after being used several times. But, at least in this case, the obsolescence was planned by the consumer, because those who bought such articles did so knowing that they would soon be thrown away. Nobody was being fooled, for the manufacturers told consumers explicitly how many times they could plan on wearing such a piece of clothing. Information wasn't a problem.

Normally, *durability* in clothing is directly related to its price. You usually have to pay more for materials that last longer, and that price may be more than you wish to pay. Depending on your tastes and your budget, you may be better off buying less durable clothes and replacing them more often—especially if the cost of cleaning rises relative to other costs. Whenever the maintenance costs of an item go up relative to other costs (such as the purchase price), you have more incentive to replace the item rather than to maintain and repair it.

Once you know that durability is *itself* a good, you can make more rational choices when buying clothing. You are purchasing a suit or a dress, for example, because of the *service flow* it yields per unit time period. Thus, if you buy a jacket that you think will last five years, you should figure out what the cost per year is; if it costs $100 but another jacket that will last only one year costs $75, the first jacket is obviously not more expensive in cost per service flow per year.

In your own shopping forays, remember that you should figure out the cost per year of owning a piece of clothing. It's also important to understand the maintenance costs of particular materials. A clothing label that says "dry clean only" may indicate that the item will cost you more to maintain than another item in the same line labeled "may be machine washed." This kind of information is important in determining the relative costs of different pieces of clothing (and is also a good reason for labeling requirements).

INDICATIONS OF QUALITY

To get the most quality for your dollars, it is important to be able to recognize which garments will perform better and longer than others. How can you distinguish quality in clothing? Generally, there are two broad indications—fabric content and the skill with which the garment was put together.

Fabric Content

You can tell the fabric content of any garment you wish to purchase by reading its label—which is required by law to be attached to every clothing item marketed in the United States. Higher-quality fabrics will consist either of all natural fibers (such as wool, cotton, or silk) or a good blend of these with manufactured fibers (such as nylon, polyester, or acrylic). Manufactured fibers are often used to lend durability and ease of care to fabrics. Cotton-polyester blends, for example, are popular today because they combine the comfort of pure cotton with the durability and ease of care ("wash and wear") of polyester.

Fiber content won't tell you everything about fabric quality, however. The durability and overall performance of a particular fabric also has to do with yarn size, tightness of weave, fabric finishes, and other treatments. In nylon products, for example, yarn size can create either one of the strongest fabrics (such as "rip-stop" nylon used in tents and sleeping bags) or one of the most fragile, such as in hosiery, with many variations in between. A loosely woven fabric will not perform as well as one with a tight, smooth weave. To check for tightness of weave, you can hold a garment up to the light. If the light shows through, this means the weave is loose—and of lesser quality than a tightly woven fabric. Finishes can also alter the performance qualities of fabrics. Cotton, for example, is one of the most absorbent fibers, but it can be made water-resistant, as in the case of polished cotton.

In sum, content labels, although very helpful to consumers, do not indicate entirely how a given fabric will perform for you. Because of this, it is a good idea to save your clothing receipts until you've worn a garment a time or two and washed it (or had it dry cleaned) at least once. It is also useful to know something about manufactured fibers (such as synthetics and acrylics), since they are being used increasingly in the garment industry. Exhibit 11–1 contains a list of the most commonly used manufactured fibers and their performance characteristics. For more information on the history and current production of manufactured fibers, you can obtain (for $5.00) *The Manufactured Fiber Fact Book* (and a free fiber chart) from:

American Fiber Manufacturers Association, Inc.
1150 17th St., N.W., Suite 310
Washington, D.C. 20036
(202) 296-6508

MAJOR GENERIC FIBERS AND TRADE NAMES		CHARACTERISTICS	MAJOR DOMESTIC AND INDUSTRIAL USES
ACETATE Ariloft Celebrate Chromspun	Estron Loftura	Luxurious feel and appearance; wide range of colors and lusters; excellent drapability and softness; relatively fast-drying; shrink-, moth-, and mildew-resistant.	*Apparel:* Blouses, dresses, foundation garments, lingerie, linings, shirts, slacks, sportswear. *Fabrics:* Brocade, crepe, double knits, faille, knitted jerseys, lace, satin, taffeta, tricot. *Home Furnishings:* Draperies, upholstery. *Other:* Cigarette filters, fiberfill for pillows, quilted products.
ACRYLIC Acrilan Bi-Loft Creslan Fi-lana Orlon	Pa-Qel Remember So-Lara Zefkrome Zefran	Soft and warm, wool-like, light-weight; retains shape; resilient; quick-drying; resistant to moths, sunlight, oil, and chemicals.	*Apparel:* Dresses, infant wear, knitted garments, skirts, ski wear, socks, sportswear, sweaters, work clothes. *Fabrics:* Fleece and pile fabrics, face fabrics in bonded fabrics, simulated furs, jerseys. *Home Furnishings:* Blankets, carpets, draperies, upholstery. *Other:* Hand-knitting and craft yarns.
ARAMID Kevlar	Nomex	No melting point; highly flame-resistant; high strength; high resistance to stretch; maintains its shape and form at high temperatures.	Hot-gas filtration fabrics, protective clothing, military helmets, protective vests, structural composites for aircraft and boats, sailcloth, tires, ropes and cables, mechanical rubber goods, marine and sporting goods.
MODACRYLIC SEF		Soft, resilient, abrasion- and flame-resistant; quick-drying; resists acids and alkalies; retains shape.	*Apparel:* Deep pile coats, trims, linings, simulated fur, wigs and hairpieces. *Fabrics:* Fleece fabrics, industrial fabrics, knit-pile fabric backings, non-woven fabrics. *Home Furnishings:* Awnings, blankets, carpets, flame-resistant draperies and curtains, scatter rugs. *Other:* Filters, paint rollers, stuffed toys.
NYLON A.C.E. Anso Blue "C" Cadon Cantrece Capima Caplana Caprolan Captiva Compet Cordura Courtaulds Crepeset	Cumuloft Hydrofil No Shock Patina Shareen Shimmereen Tolaram Ultron Vivana Zafran Zefsport Zefstat Zeftron	Exceptionally strong, supple, abrasion-resistant; lustrous; easy to wash. Resists damage from oil and many chemicals. Resilient; low in moisture absorbency.	*Apparel:* Blouses, dresses, foundation garments, hosiery, lingerie and underwear, raincoats, ski and snow apparel, suits, windbreakers. *Home Furnishings:* Bedspreads, carpets, draperies, curtains, upholstery. *Other:* Air hoses, conveyor and seat belts, parachutes, racket strings, ropes and nets, sleeping bags, tarpaulins, tents, thread, tire cord, geotextiles.
OLEFIN Avtex Elustra ES Fiber Hercuson Nouvelle	Marquesa Lana Marvess Patlon Spectra Tolaram	Unique wicking properties that make it very comfortable. Abrasion-resistant; quick-drying; resistant to deterioration from chemicals, mildew, perspiration, rot, and weather; sensitive to heat; soil resistant; strong, very lightweight. Excellent colorfastness. (Spectra is a high performance fiber with unequaled strength-to-weight ratio, excellent chemical, stretch, cut, and abrasion resistance, plus optimum flex fatigue and superior dielectric constant.)	*Apparel:* Pantyhose, underwear, knitted sports shirts, men's half hose, men's knitted sportswear, sweaters. *Home Furnishings:* Carpet and carpet backing, slipcovers, upholstery. *Other:* Dye nets, filter fabrics, laundry and sandbags, geotextiles, automotive interiors, cordage, doll hair, industrial sewing thread.

MAJOR GENERIC FIBERS AND TRADE NAMES		CHARACTERISTICS	MAJOR DOMESTIC AND INDUSTRIAL USES
POLYESTER A.C.E. Avlin Ceylon Comfort Fiber Compet Dacron E.S.P. Fortrel Golden Glow Golden Touch	Hollofil Kodaire Kodel KodOfill KodOsoff Silky Touch Strialine Tolaram Trevira Ultra Touch	Strong; resistant to stretching and shrinking; resistant to most chemicals; quick-drying; crisp and resilient when wet or dry; wrinkle- and abrasion-resistant; retains heat-set pleats and creases; easy to wash.	*Apparel:* Blouses, shirts, career apparel, children's wear, dresses, half hose, insulated garments, ties, lingerie and underwear, permanent press garments, slacks, suits. *Home Furnishings:* Carpets, curtains, draperies, sheets and pillow cases. *Other:* Fiberfill for various products, fire hose, power belting, ropes and nets, thread, tire cord, sails, V-belts.
PBI PBI	Arozole	Highly flame resistant. Outstanding comfort factor combined with thermal and chemical stability properties. Will not burn or melt. Low shrinkage when exposed to flame.	Suitable for high-performance protective apparel such as firemen's turnout coats, astronaut space suits and applications where fire resistance is important.
RAYON Avril Avtex Beau-Grip Coloray Courtaulds Courcel Durvil	Fiber 40 Fiber 240 Fibro Zanaire Zankare Zankrome Zantrel	Highly absorbent; soft and comfortable; easy to dye; versatile; good drapability.	*Apparel:* Blouses, coats, dresses, jackets, lingerie, linings, millinery, rainwear, slacks, sports shirts, sportswear, suits, ties, work clothes. *Home Furnishings:* Bedspreads, blankets, carpets, curtains, draperies, sheets, slipcovers, tablecloths, upholstery. *Other:* Industrial products, medical/surgical products, non-woven products, tire cord.
SPANDEX Lycra		Can be stretched 500 percent without breaking; can be stretched repeatedly and recover original length; lightweight; stronger, more durable than rubber; resistant to body oils.	*Articles (where stretch is desired):* Athletic apparel, bathing suits, delicate laces, foundation garments, golf jackets, ski pants, slacks, support and surgical hose.
SULFAR Ryton		High-performance fibers with excellent resistance to harsh chemicals and high temperatures. Excellent strength retention in adverse environments; flame-retardant; non-conductive.	Filter fabric for coal-fired boiler bag houses, papermakers' felts, electrical insulation, electrolysis membranes, filter fabrics for liquid and gas filtration, high-performance composites, gaskets and packings.
Hoechst Celanese		Softens at low temperature; high resistance to chemicals; nontoxic.	Used in industrial applications as a bonding agent for non-woven fabrics and products such as tea bags and automotive headliners.

Source: Manufactured Fiber Producers Association, Inc.

Tailoring

There is more to quality clothing than just fabric content and characteristics. For example, if you compare shirts selling for $15 to $20 at Sears with shirts in an exclusive men's store selling for five times those prices, you might find that the fabric content is very similar, if not virtually identical. What makes the shirts in the exclusive men's store more expensive? Generally (at least to a great extent), the higher price indicates the higher quality of craftsmanship that went into making the more expensive shirt.

Labels won't tell you how well a garment is tailored—cut and sewn together. This is something you will have to judge for yourself, and it's not always easy unless you've taken a course in tailoring or done a little research. Some indications of quality craftsmanship are quite visible, however, and can be quickly checked:

1. In plaid or striped fabrics, do the plaids or stripes match at the seams and armholes?
2. Are the stitches neat and even along the seams, edges of the pockets, and behind the collar?
3. Are the inside seams well finished? A finished seam will be either stitched at the edge or cut with pinking shears to prevent raveling of the material.
4. Is there a generous back seam? This is typical of well-made men's clothing to allow for adjustments in the fit of the garments.
5. In heavy-duty clothing, such as work clothes or jeans, are the seams flat-felled (doubled over and stitched twice on the outside)? This gives added durability under stress.
6. Is there double stitching at stress points in the garment—such as around the armholes and on the pockets?
7. Do the buttonholes fit the button tightly?
8. In men's jackets or women's blazers: Is there a felt backing on the collar? This helps retain the collar's shape.
9. In men's shirts: Are the front corners reinforced?

Perhaps the best way to familiarize yourself with quality in clothing is to go to the most expensive stores and try on some of their clothes. How do they feel? How do they fit? Look closely for some of the qualities just mentioned. If you have never done so, it might even be worth investing in one or two clothing items of superior quality to learn their performance characteristics. Then, in the words of clothing designer Egon von Furstenburg, "having tried the best, you will be better able to achieve the best look at any price."

THE POWERFUL FASHION INDUSTRY

Planned obsolescence in clothing is created not only by the mass production of lower-quality wearing apparel but also by changing clothing styles. You might have purchased a coat two years ago for $300, but, for all its durability, you aren't happy about wearing it today because it's out of fashion.

Who Dictates Fashion?

The immense size of the fashion industry and its apparent influence on our buying habits lead us back to the eternal question of consumer versus producer sovereignty. Are fashions dictated by you, the consumer, or are they dictated by the whims of designers and producers? Nobody will ever know who truly decides what will or won't be fashionable, but obviously consumers have some say in the matter. Since the 1970s, for example, when American women rejected the heavily promoted "midiskirt," women in this country have shown an increasing reluctance to have the length of their hemlines determined by designers in Parisian or other dress salons. Generally, Americans have voted with their dollars for more flexibility in fashion, and the fashion world has responded by offering not just one "look" per season but numerous style options.

In the marketing of style, as with other consumer products, these options increasingly are related to different age, social, or professional groups. The promotion of fashion as an external expression of a particular lifestyle or self-image is even more finely tuned in the marketing of designer labels.

The Designer Craze

The creators of fashion have at no time been more visible than during the past decade. Once distant and aloof from all but the most elite social groups, dress designers are now heavily involved in mainstream American markets—at least their names are. The designer craze began in the late 1970s, when designer labels were placed on the back pockets of jeans. Such labels now appear on almost every product imaginable. You can even buy designer chocolates (Bill Blass) or designer cigarettes (Yves St. Laurent).

What's in a Name?

If you buy a pair of Oleg Cassini slacks, will their quality be better than another pair of slacks without a designer label? Possibly, but not necessarily. This is because, although designers usually control carefully their top-of-the-line production, they often have little to do with the production of garments or other items manufactured for mainstream consumption. Most of the millions of designer products filling our shops and stores today are produced and marketed not by the designers themselves but by manufacturers who purchase from a designer the right to use the designer's name in the marketing of a particular product or product line. As a result, quality control is usually about the same as it is in the garment industry as a whole—where an estimated 10 percent of all garments produced contain flaws.

Not only might you find a garment of equal (or even superior) quality for a lower price than that marked on a garment carrying a designer label, you might even find the identical garment (under a different label) at a lower cost.

Designer clothing can be attractive and popular, and might—or might not—be better constructed than similar garments. What is certain is that it will be more expensive. Do you believe buying designer clothing is a wise consumer choice? When you look in your closet how many examples of designer clothing do you see?

Betsy Ashton, former consumer affairs correspondent for the "CBS Morning News," has interviewed dozens of clothing designers, manufacturers, and retailers on the subject of labels. She tellingly reports how, on one occasion, she

> watched as one manufacturer produced a line of suits. Into one batch, his seamstresses sewed a designer label. He said those suits would have a retail price of $350 at a fashionable department store. Into another batch of exactly the same suits were sewn the private label of a moderately priced store. Their retail price would be $189. Same suit, different label.[1]

It is estimated that this so-called label-switching occurs on at least 30 percent of all garments produced.

What You Pay For

When you buy designer clothing, you are truly paying for the label in the sense that you absorb part of the royalty costs the manufacturer must pay to the designer for the use of the name. In addition, the marketing of designer products requires extensive (and expensive) advertising. These costs are also factored into the price you must pay.

Does this mean you shouldn't buy designer clothing? Of course not. But you should be aware of what you are paying for. If quality alone is your concern, it can be found under other labels as well, labels that aren't as heavily advertised as name brands and designer labels are. And if you do wish to buy designer clothing, off-price stores offer a lower-cost alternative. Stores such as Loehmanns, T. J. Maxx, Marshall's, and others, by purchasing production overruns or end-of-season styles, can offer name brands and designer labels for up to a 50-percent discount and still make a profit.

MAIL-ORDER SHOPPING

Recent years have witnessed explosive growth in the number of firms that offer mail-order clothing to American consumers. Hardly a day goes by without one or more catalogs appearing in your mailbox. Although these firms may offer quality and convenience, consumers should be aware of the trade-offs they make when they patronize mail-order businesses.

The most obvious advantage of mail-order shopping is its convenience, allowing people to avoid traveling to crowded stores that may not have products in stock they want to buy. Other possible advantages include choosing from a wider selection, avoiding sales tax, and using 24-hour toll-free numbers that allow consumers to shop at any time of day.

Disadvantages are equally obvious. First, mail-order prices may be higher than those charged in local stores. Without shopping around, you won't know. Also, mail-order clothing may not fit. Garments that look wonderful on professional models in catalogs may not look so good on our less-than-perfect bodies at home. It is impossible to judge the quality of a garment's construction or the feel of its fabric from a picture. And if you need to return a mail-order item, you almost always have to pay shipping charges.

Before you decide to purchase mail-order clothing, be sure you understand the firm's return policy. Can you return a purchase if you simply don't like it?

---

1. Betsy Ashton, *Guide to Living On Your Own* (Boston: Little, Brown, 1988), p. 168.

Is there a time limit on when you can return a garment for a full refund? Who pays for return shipping? Will your account with the firm be credited, or will you receive a refund?

FACTORY OUTLET SHOPPING

Many clothing manufacturers have established their own retail outlets in recent years that often offer name-brand products at much lower prices than typical department stores. There are a number of reasons from a business's point of view to open such stores. Probably the most important reason is to expand the size of the market they may sell to. Many people who would never consider buying name-brand products at full price are happy to buy these goods when their prices have been reduced. The manufacturers are able to keep a larger share of the retail price of the goods because there are no independent retailers to take a cut. These stores also provide a way to move garments with outdated styles, those that have not sold well, and "seconds," or products that have minor defects that prevent them from being sold at full prices.

Factory outlet stores offer consumers the opportunity to buy quality clothing at substantially reduced prices if they are careful shoppers. However, although many "seconds" are perfectly usable, some are not. There is little advantage in buying a garment at a low price if it falls apart the first time it is worn. Also, not all prices at factory outlet stores are the lowest available. Ordinary department stores frequently run sales of the same products at even lower prices. Another potential problem to look out for are these stores' return policies. Most of them do not give cash refunds, and some will not take products back even in exchange after a few days post purchase.

CLOTHING SALES AND SPECIALS

Most consumers take special delight in getting more quality for less money, and this can often be achieved by purchasing goods on sale. Often, however, consumers will buy clothing they don't need—and maybe don't even like that much—simply because it is available at a reduced price.

Don't assume that just because an item is on sale it is *necessarily* a good buy. Sellers are well aware of the fact that such words as "on sale" or "slashed prices" can cloud a consumer's judgment as to the quality or desirability of goods. The continual sales offered in clothing stores would not exist if they weren't profitable for merchants.

Sales can be profitable to sellers because the regular prices of most of their merchandise contain a large retail markup in price (on average, 50 percent). This means that for items with a high retail price markup, sellers can "slash" the price by more than a third and still make a profit. It also means that the sale price offered at one store may be the same as (or even more than) the regular price of goods of the same quality at another store. A good way to avoid being conned by a sale price into buying something you don't really want or need is to ask yourself the question: Would I like this garment if it weren't on sale? If your answer is no, it's not a bargain at any price.

This does not mean you shouldn't take advantage of genuine sales. Most clothing stores routinely have sales at certain times during the year to clear their inventories of the previous season's stock and make room for new purchases. Other clearance sales are held to unload overpurchased quantities of goods. "Loss leaders"—items sold at sometimes below-wholesale cost to promote a new product or entice buyers into a store—are also offered occasionally by stores. If you watch for these kinds of sales, you can usually get good-quality merchandise at a low cost. A little comparison-shopping will help you to learn when a reduced price is—or is not—a bargain.

LABELING LAWS

As mentioned earlier, the government requires that all clothing manufacturers affix labels to their products disclosing fabric content and other information, such as care required. Labeling laws help not only consumers but also manufacturers, by protecting them against the possibility that less-than-ethical competitors might profit from misleading consumers about the contents of their products.

Labeling requirements were established by three legislative acts: the Wool Products Labeling Act, Fur Products Labeling Act, and Textile Fiber Products Identification Act. All are enforced by the Federal Trade Commission (FTC). In addition, since 1972 the FTC has required that all clothing must carry a label indicating the type of care required for proper maintenance.

Wool Products Labeling Act

The Wool Products Labeling Act of 1939 protects producers, manufacturers, distributors, and consumers by requiring that manufacturers' labels clearly state

---

THE GLOBAL CONSUMER

If the Price Is Right, Should You Care How the Product Was Made?

We all know that clothing imported from less-developed nations is often inexpensive because of the low wages their workers are paid. Clearly, American consumers have benefited from being able to buy inexpensive clothing. Probably many Americans feel they are helping workers in other countries by providing them with jobs. This is not always the case.

In 1992 a situation that appears to have involved a condition close to slavery was uncovered on Saipan (part of a semi-independent island nation in the Pacific that has close

political ties with the United States). An American citizen of Chinese heritage recruited citizens of China to work in his factory on Saipan. The facility looked much like a prison. It had barbed wire fences, guards who carried guns and patrolled with dogs, and apparently forced labor. Once workers arrived at the factory, they were not allowed to leave but were forced to work seven days a week for roughly $2 an hour. They were housed in metal buildings that were hot and poorly ventilated. Their food was often substandard. The garments these workers produced were sold

to large American firms with the label "Made in the USA" printed on them. American consumers then purchased them under labels that included Levi Dockers. The American firms that bought the clothing stated they were unaware of how the garments were produced and stopped purchasing them once the conditions on Saipan came to light.

Do you believe American consumers bear any responsibility for working conditions that exist in other countries or even in the United States? Is there anything they could realistically do about situations like this?

---

the type of wool and all other fibers making up 5 percent or more of the fabric content. The FTC has established the following definitions for the use of wool.

1. *Reprocessed wool.* Fibers that have been previously woven or felted into a wool product that was never used by consumers.
2. *Reused wool.* Fibers taken from a used wool product and reused in another garment.
3. *Virgin wool.* Wool that has never been used to make another product.

Fur Products Labeling Act

Passed in 1951, the Fur Products Labeling Act requires that labels indicate the type of fur, the country of origin of an imported fur product, whether the fur has been dyed or tinted, and whether the garment is made from scraps of fur. The act is designed to protect consumers and competitors by making it unlawful to misbrand, falsely advertise, and falsely invoice fur products. It was originally passed in part because of the widespread use of exotic-sounding euphemisms such as "Baltic Lion" and "Isabella Fox" for such unexotic furs as rabbit, dogskin, skunk, or alley cat. The Fur Act goes one step beyond the Wool Act in that it requires informative advertising as well as labeling of fur products.

Textile Fiber Products Identification Act

Under the United States Textile Fiber Products Identification Act of 1958, *all* textile products must contain the following information on the label:

1. The generic (nontrademark) name of the fibers (such as cotton or polyester) listed in order of predominance by weight.
2. The percentage of each fiber making up 5 percent or more of the product's weight.
3. The name of the manufacturer.[2]
4. The country of origin of an imported fiber.

Care Labeling

Care-instruction labels are a great aid in purchasing clothing. Care instructions are required by an FTC trade rule effective since 1972 and revised in 1983 to ensure more complete and consistent care instructions. The rule specifies that all fabrics be labeled as to the laundering or dry cleaning that will be required to maintain the garment's original character. In other words, you can now gauge how much time or money may be expended to maintain the garment you purchase. Labels vary from "dry clean only" to "leather clean only" to "machine wash, warm, tumble dry," and so on. Some manufacturers have added even further care categories than those specified by the FTC. And the regulation does not apply solely to prefabricated garments; people who choose to sew for their families are also being given care labels with each piece of fabric to sew into the finished garment.

In specifying washing and drying methods and temperatures, use and type of bleach, and temperatures for ironing, if needed, manufacturers are encouraged to use common terms from a glossary that is part of the revised FTC rule.

---

2. Information concerning the manufacturer (name, address, and so on) may be either placed on the label itself or represented on the label by a number, which is assigned by the government. Directories containing these numbers (called R.N. or W.P.L. numbers) and the manufacturers they represent are available in most large libraries.

The glossary is intended to standardize words and directions on labels. "Machine wash, warm," for example, would uniformly mean machine wash at a temperature between 90 and 110 degrees Fahrenheit.

Dry-cleaning instructions have to specify the type of solvent to be used if not all commercially available solvents are appropriate. If an item can fare well with either dry cleaning *or* washing, the label must say so. However, the manufacturer is not required to warn you about any *unsafe* care procedures for the garment.

Permanent-care labels are required for the first time on suede and leather items, upholstered furniture, draperies, sheets, bedspreads, and so on. The rule further requires that labels be available to fabric and carpet retailers to pass on to consumers.

Consumers need to remember that there is usually a tradeoff between price and ease of care. Garments treated with materials that make them easy to take care of have higher costs of manufacturing. These costs are passed on to consumers in higher prices. Consumers must decide what the best tradeoff is for them.

FLAMMABILITY STANDARDS

In 1953 Congress passed the Flammable Fabrics Act in response to public indignation over the deaths and injuries caused by highly flammable wearing apparel. This act prohibited "the introduction or movement in interstate commerce of articles of wearing apparel and fabrics which are so highly flammable as to be dangerous when worn by individuals." A 1967 amendment to the act specifically prohibited the manufacture and sale of any product, fabric, or related material that fails to conform to an applicable standard or regulation.

Since the passage of the act, the government has created numerous regulations for its implementation. Flammability standards have been established not only for wearing apparel but also for such items as mattresses, mattress pads, and carpets (over a certain size). To further protect against flammability in children's sleepwear, in 1971 the government mandated that fabrics used for such garments be treated by a flame retardant. Various chemicals have been used for this purpose. One of them, Tris, was very effective, but it was banned in 1977 because it was thought to be carcinogenic.

TIPS FOR SUCCESSFUL CLOTHES SHOPPING

Because clothing has a psychological as well as a practical dimension, no one can tell you what kind of clothes to buy or even how much money you should spend on your wardrobe. Those questions will obviously depend on your tastes and on your budget. To get the most for your shopping dollar, however, you might find it useful to ask yourself the following questions the next time you contemplate investing in a new item of clothing.

1. Does the garment fit properly? A poorly fitting garment will be neither becoming nor comfortable. Although in many cases clothing can be adjusted to fit, in some stores you may need to pay extra for the service.

2. Does the garment fit your wardrobe? If you purchase a pair of slacks or a new skirt, you will get far more use out of the item if you have other clothes in your wardrobe to coordinate with it.

3. Does the garment suit your personality? Or, to rephrase the question, can you envision at least three events or occasions at which you would feel comfortable wearing the garment? If you can't, you might want to rethink your decision to purchase it.

4. How long will it be in fashion? If it's a trendy item, don't plan on more than a year's worth of wear. Classic clothes—basic suits, blazers, simple designs, and so forth—tend to be stylish year after year. Judge the investment you make accordingly.

5. If the item is on sale, will it continue to be fashionable in the coming season or seasons? Again, this will depend on how classic the design is.

6. What maintenance costs—in both time and money—are involved? Because of such costs, you may wear a garment that requires dry cleaning less often than one that doesn't. Garments that need to be ironed also have a time cost.

7. Does the color suit you? Some colors look splendid on some people, while they make others look bleached out or even ill. If you're unsure of whether a given color becomes you, it probably means you won't be happy with the garment.

8. Is the quality of the item worth the price? This question can be answered only by learning what's available at other stores at the same price.

9. Can you afford it? This is probably the most important question of all. Whenever you're unsure of whether you should make the investment, sleep on it. If others, such as family members, will be affected by your decision, talk it over with them. Don't buy on impulse.

10. Finally, when in doubt, don't buy it.

▶ SUMMARY

1. Perceived clothing needs can easily lead to conflicts in the family budgeting process. It is important to try to reach a compromise between individual tastes and family dressing habits.

2. Our clothing choices are determined by more than the simple need to protect ourselves from the environment. Custom, aesthetic considerations, and psychological factors also influence how we dress.

3. Generally, we pay more for more durable clothing. When you're deciding what clothes to buy, take into account how long they will last. Then you can compare clothes on the basis of price per year rather than total purchase price.

4. Clothing of good quality depends both on fabric content and on how well the garment is tailored. Fabrics containing a good blend of natural and manufactured fibers are popular today because they promote durability and ease of care.

5. In the past decade, the fashion industry has created more flexibility in style options. To a great extent, this reflects the industry's response to the needs and wishes of consumers.

6. Designer labels do not necessarily indicate that the garments are of quality superior to similar or identical garments marketed under private labels. This is because part of the price you pay for designer clothing goes toward the manufacturers' added advertising (and sometimes royalty) costs.

7. Clothing merchants have frequent sales because they know that consumers will be more likely to buy goods if the price is reduced. Often, however, because of a retailer's high price markup, the reduced price at one store may be as high as (or higher than) the regular price at another for

goods of the same quality. Consumers should look for genuine clearance sales for price bargains.

8. Three federal statutes—the Wool Products Labeling Act, the Fur Products Labeling Act, and the Textile Fiber Products Identification Act—require that manufacturers affix labels to their products disclosing fiber content and other information. Under a Federal Trade Commission regulation of 1972, as revised in 1983, care labeling is also required.

9. The Flammable Fabrics Act, as amended, requires that the manufacture and sale of fabric or fabric products conform to an applicable standard or regulation. Numerous standards have since been established to implement the act.

▶ QUESTIONS FOR THOUGHT AND DISCUSSION

1. To what extent—if any—are your clothing choices dictated by what your family wears? By what your friends wear?

2. How large a role does fashion play in your choice of wearing apparel?

3. Do you agree that clothing imparts information to the onlooker? Or do you think "you can't judge a book by its cover"?

4. Do you think that members of a family unit should be concerned with the clothing tastes of the other members?

5. How do you explain the popularity of designer labels?

▶ THINGS TO DO

1. Go to an expensive clothing store and examine closely two or three items in a particular category of clothing, such as shirts, dresses, jackets, or slacks. Look at the labels, feel the fabrics, and check for tailoring qualities. Then do the same thing for clothes in the same category at an inexpensive clothing store. Make a list of the similarities and differences that you observed.

2. Go to a nearby fabric store and ask the salesperson to identify for you the most important characteristics of the following natural fibers: wool, cotton, and silk. Ask to see the most expensive and least expensive fabrics in each category and note what the price differences reflect.

3. Make a list of all the clothes in your closet that you no longer wear. Write beside each item the reason you no longer wear it. Now ask yourself the following questions: How important is stylishness in your choice of clothing? How important is variety? How important is durability? And, finally, how much have you spent for clothing in excess of what was really necessary?

▶ APPLICATION

Interview five people who hold different types of jobs—for example, a laborer, executive, lawyer, salesperson, teacher, secretary, etc. Ask these people to explain how important they feel the manner of their dress is to the success they can achieve in their careers. Use this information to help you write an essay in which you evaluate the often quoted phrase, "dress for success." Does it hold true for all workers? Why do the people you interviewed make different tradeoffs when they buy clothing?

▶ SELECTED READINGS

▶ Ashton, Betsy, "Behind the Labels: Fashion on a Shoestring." *Guide to Living on Your Own,* Boston: Little, Brown, 1988, pp. 168–70.

▶ Borrus, A. and P. Engardio. "Customs Tears Into the Rag Trade." *Business Week,* December 30, 1991, pp. 51–52.

▶ *Care Labels.* Available for 50 cents from the Apparel Trade Commission, 6th St. and Pennsylvania Ave., N.W., Washington, DC 20580.

▶ Hollen, Normal, et al. *Textiles.* 6th ed. New York: Macmillan, 1988.

▶ Konrad, W. "The Textile Industry Is Looking Threadbare." *Business Week,* September 16, 1991, p. 114.

▶ Loeb, Marshall. "Discount Stores." *Marshall Loeb's 1992 Money Guide.* Boston: Little, Brown, 1992, pp. 306–308.

▶ Money Management Institute. *Your Shopping Dollar.* Available for $1 from Money Management Institute, 2700 Sanders Rd., Prospect Heights, IL 60070.

▶ Prud'homme, A. "What's It All About, Calvin?" *Time,* September 16, 1991, p. 114.

▶ "What Shapes the Style?" *Working Woman,* November 1991, pp. 106–107.

Putting a Roof
Over Your Head

▶ What factors enter into our housing decisions?

▶ What are the benefits and costs of renting or buying a home?

▶ What kinds of services do real estate agents provide?

▶ How may you negotiate a housing transaction?

▶ What are common sources and types of mortgage loans?

▶ What are closing costs?

If you happen to be an Eskimo living in the Yukon Territory, putting a roof over your head is complicated but not impossible: You make an igloo. If you happen to live in the bush country of Tanzania, putting a roof over your head takes some time, but eventually your thatch hut will be just what you need. If you were a pioneer settling on some cleared land in the Old West, putting a roof over your head would have meant building a log cabin or a sod house.

Today, by way of contrast, if you are Mr. and Mrs. Average American, to purchase a new, three-bedroom, two-bathroom home and the land under it, you will have to pay about $125,000. In all, Americans today pay more than $280 billion a year to purchase new homes.

WHY ARE WE WILLING TO PAY SO MUCH?

Early Americans must have had just as many fanciful ideas about how they would like to live as we have. But today, some of us—in fact, most of us—live like kings compared to earlier Americans. Why is this so? Is it simply because we earn more money? No, the reason we live better than our ancestors is because our economic system has become more productive over the years. On average, in each of the last 150 years the quantity of goods produced in the United States per person has increased by about 1.5 percent. A great deal of this extra production has been allocated to consumer goods in general and to housing in particular. Most Americans live well because we really do like to cater to our fancies. We like the good life, and that includes a spacious home, often with unique features.

It is also important to remember that when we buy or rent houses or apartments, we are also buying the services they yield—just as we do when we purchase clothing or cars or anything else that lasts. When we buy a house, we buy not simply the house but also the pleasure we derive from living in it month in and month out. And that pleasure is a function of the house's size, the convenience it offers, how pretty the view is, what the neighborhood is like, and everything else that can contribute to our happiness when we are home. Generally, the reason that there is "no place like home" is that all of us try to make our homes as special as possible so that we get maximum utility, or service from them. It is important, then, to realize that when a consumer buys a $200,000 house, it is because this dwelling offers a perceived larger flow of services per month than could be obtained by purchasing a $100,000 house.

The actual price American consumers pay for housing at any time and in any location depends on (1) the amount of money they have and are willing to spend on housing and (2) the quantity of housing units that exist. In Chapter 1 you learned that these are the forces of demand and supply. If, for example, you want to buy a house near the ocean in a nice neighborhood of San Diego, California, you should expect to pay more than for a similar house located in the frozen woodlands of northern Minnesota, far from any major city. The number of people who have money to spend and want to live in San Diego far exceeds the number of houses available there. On the other hand, houses in cold climates, located away from job centers are deemed less desirable and thus cost less.

RENTING VERSUS BUYING

At some point, you may be faced with the question of whether you should rent or buy a home. In this section we look at some of the factors that you will want to consider in making your decision. We then devote the rest of the chapter to a discussion of home purchasing. That does not mean that everybody should—or can—buy instead of rent. More space is given to the home-buying process simply because it is a more complicated procedure. Renting a home, however, also involves specific procedures and legalities with which you should be familiar, and these are discussed in Consumer Issue J.

Advantages of Renting

In many cases, your budget will determine whether you can afford to rent or to buy. But the budget is not the only factor in your decision. Consider, for example, the following advantages of renting, instead of buying, a place to live:

1. Even given constraints, renters are more mobile than homeowners.
2. No down payment is involved; nor is a credit check normally necessary prior to renting a house or an apartment (although there may be a breakage or cleaning deposit).
3. Renters don't face the maintenance tasks and expenses that accompany homeownership.
4. The exact cost of housing services can be calculated easily for the period of the lease.
5. Future housing needs in terms of family size do not have to be estimated carefully.
6. Renters often have the use of common facilities—such as a swimming pool, a tennis court, or a sauna—that would be expensive to purchase when buying a home.
7. Renting offers new members of a community an opportunity to become familiar with an area before investing in a house.
8. There is no loss of interest on investment of savings.
9. There is no liability of ownership.
10. Renting may be the only affordable alternative for many consumers.

Advantages of Buying

There are also, of course, undeniable advantages to buying a housing unit.

1. You can remodel your home or make it into anything you want.
2. A home offers an investment option that historically has been a good hedge against inflation.
3. Home ownership causes you to save, because part of your monthly payments creates equity interest in the housing unit.
4. Owning a home gives you the tax benefits of being able to deduct interest payments and property taxes from your income before paying taxes—although how much of a saving this will represent depends on your tax rate.
5. Owning a home provides people with an asset that may be borrowed against, making it easier for them to obtain credit for other purposes.

The tax benefits of home ownership are often the most compelling factor in the decision of whether to rent or buy. This is because, if you buy a house and borrow the money to pay for it, all the interest you pay to the bank or mortgage company can be deducted from your income before you pay taxes. For most consumers, this represents a sizable savings.

For example, suppose you bought a $100,000 house and were somehow able to borrow the entire $100,000. Let's say that the interest you paid every year on that $100,000 came to $12,000. You would be able to deduct that $12,000 from your income before you paid taxes on it. If you were in the 28-percent tax bracket, you would get a tax savings of $3,360; the interest on your loan would, in effect, be costing you only $8,640. Now you know why, as people get into the higher income-tax bracket, it generally is more advantageous to buy a house instead of renting.

Taxes and housing are related in another way. If you buy or build a house for $60,000 and sell it ten years later for $120,000, you have made $60,000. You will be taxed on that sum, for it is a *capital gain*. But if you buy another house of equal or higher value within two years, you pay no taxes on that profit at all until much later. Additionally, you are allowed one exclusion from the payment of capital gains on the sale of your own residence after you reach the age of 55. Currently, you can exclude up to $125,000 of capital gains (profits) on the sale of your personal residence once you reach that age.

An additional tax benefit might be obtained if you qualify for a *home equity loan,* which is like a second mortgage. In a home equity loan, your equity interest in your home (what you have paid toward its purchase, aside from interest, plus any appreciation in its market value since you purchased it) is given as security for the loan. Under the Tax Reform Act of 1986, the interest you pay on a home equity loan is fully tax-deductible—in contrast with the interest paid on other types of consumer loans.

How Much Can You Afford?

Before you go house-hunting, you should determine how much you can afford to pay. There is no point in looking at homes that cost more than you can afford. Remember, it's easy to get carried away when buying housing services. A nice house is something in which you and your family can take pride. Owning a home also—albeit often unfairly—makes you appear in the eyes of others to be a more responsible and committed member of the community. The tax and other advantages of homeownership discussed earlier can also be persuasive. But, as mentioned earlier, although your budget shouldn't be the sole determining factor in deciding whether to purchase a home, it is nonetheless a very important one.

Mortgage
A loan obtained for the purpose of purchasing land or buildings, in which the property is pledged as security.

Initial Costs   Unless you are among the fortunate few, you will probably need to finance your home purchase by obtaining a **mortgage**—which is a loan for purchasing property in which the property is pledged as security. Only rarely, however, will the mortgage cover 100 percent of the purchase price. From 10 to 20 percent of the purchase price will usually be required as a down payment, and you will be expected to pay this at the time of purchase. In addition to your down payment, you will also need to pay *closing costs*. These costs, which we discuss later in the chapter, usually range between 3 and 6 percent of the home's purchase price. In sum, if you want to buy a $100,000 house and finance it with a mortgage loan, you will not only need a good credit rating and dependable source of income—and an income high enough to qualify for the loan—you will also need to have as much as $25,000 available to cover the initial purchasing costs.

Checklist for Calculating Total Housing Expenses

HOUSING EXPENSES PER MONTH	CURRENT	FUTURE
Mortgage payments	_____	_____
Property taxes	_____	_____
Insurance	_____	_____
Heating oil, gas, or wood	_____	_____
Gas, electricity, water, telephone, sewage	_____	_____
Yard care, trash pickup, etc.	_____	_____
Savings fund for repairs, remodeling, and maintenance	_____	_____
Other	_____	_____
Total	_____	_____

Monthly Costs   The checklist in Exhibit 12–1 can be used to help estimate the monthly expenses you will pay as a homeowner. Your largest monthly expense is, of course, your mortgage payment. The size of your monthly mortgage payment will depend both on the amount of the loan and on the interest rate charged by the lender. Exhibit 12–2 shows what your monthly payment would be for different amounts at different interest rates. For amounts above $100,000, add to the payment the amount of the payment corresponding to the additional amount. For example, for a $120,000 loan at 8 percent interest your monthly payment would be $733.77 plus $146.75, or $880.52.

Some lenders agree to pay taxes and insurance for the buyer. These costs are then factored into the monthly payment. The payments given in Exhibit 12–2 do not include taxes and insurance, so you will need to include them separately on your list of estimated monthly expenses. Taxes vary considerably, depending on the location of your home and other factors. The best way to anticipate what your taxes will be is to check either with the previous homeowner or with the local county assessor's office. To help determine what your insurance costs might be, refer to the discussion of homeowners' insurance in Chapter 20.

Several rules of thumb may be used when buying a home. One is that you spend no more than one-third of your household income each month on

▶ Exhibit 12–2 **Monthly Mortgage Costs**

MORTGAGE LOAN	MONTHLY PAYMENT OF PRINCIPAL AND INTEREST AT:				
(For 30 Years)	8%	10%	12%	14%	16%
$ 10,000	$ 73.38	$ 87.76	$ 102.86	$ 118.41	$ 134.48
20,000	146.75	175.51	205.72	236.97	268.95
30,000	220.13	263.28	308.59	355.47	403.43
40,000	293.51	351.03	411.45	473.95	537.91
50,000	366.89	438.79	514.31	592.44	672.38
60,000	440.26	526.55	617.17	710.93	806.86
70,000	513.64	614.31	720.03	829.42	941.33
80,000	587.02	702.06	822.90	947.90	1,075.81
90,000	660.39	789.82	925.76	1,066.39	1,210.29
100,000	733.77	877.58	1,028.62	1,184.88	1,344.76

housing costs. Another is that the maximum amount you should pay for a house is two and one-half times your annual household income. Housing prices vary dramatically from region to region, though, so you will need to decide on the basis of your income and the housing market in your area what amount you can and should pay.

When estimating what it will cost to own a home, be sure to allow a wide margin (at least 2 percent of the purchase price per year) for repairs and maintenance. Houses have a tendency to fall apart just like anything else, and homeowners commonly face many unanticipated, and expensive, repairs. The wage inflation of people who come to fix your sprinkler system, your clogged drain, your leaking roof, or your broken furnace is among the highest in the nation. In addition to repairs, you will incur routine maintenance costs—for law and garden upkeep, for example, or for repainting either the exterior of your house or its interior or both.

Software to Help

Calculating whether to rent or to buy can become somewhat complicated when you try to account for such factors as inflation in your analysis. A software program developed by the Real Estate Center at Texas A&M University can help you compare more accurately the costs of renting versus buying a home. The program, called *Real Estate Applications Software Directory,* is available for IBM PCs or compatible computers and costs $45 plus $1 P&H. To order it, or to obtain more information, write or call the Real Estate Center at:

Real Estate Center
Texas A&M University
College Station, TX 77843-2115
(409) 845-2031

IF YOU DECIDE TO BUY

Part of the American dream is home ownership. Let us assume that you share that dream and are planning to buy a house. Let us further assume that you have determined how much you can afford to spend for a home, know the city or area in which you wish to locate, and have an idea of the approximate size and style of home you wish to buy. The next step, then, is to locate the specific house that suits you and your housing needs. How do you do this?

Looking through the classified ads in the newspaper is one way. These ads offer a free information search and can give you some general ideas of what you can obtain at what price. And, should you decide to buy a house offered for sale directly by a current owner, you could save money because the seller does not have to pay a 6-percent to 7-percent commission to a real estate broker for selling services—a cost that is passed on to you in the form of a higher purchase price. Frequently, however, the ads you see in the paper are placed by real estate agencies, so it may or may not pay you to spend hours and hours searching for information through the classified ads.

What Does a Real Estate Agent Do?

Essentially, real estate agents are information brokers. They provide buyers and sellers of houses with information. Information, remember, is a costly resource. This is particularly true with such a nonstandard product as a house.

If You Can Afford It, Should You Be Able to Do It?

There are more than 2.5 million Americans who have a net worth of $1 million or more. Indeed more than 500,000 people in this country are worth over $10 million. Many of these people could afford to buy or build almost any type of home they would like. But should they be allowed to just because they can afford to?

Consider the case of Donald Leroy Bren. In 1990 he owned more land than any individual in the country. His properties include a 64,000-acre tract of land on the Pacific coast of California and one-sixth of the land in Orange County.

Estimates of Bren's total wealth reach into the $4 billion range. He uses much of his time and money building housing developments in Orange County that some people say are dull and monotonous, because the houses are mostly Spanish-style stucco with orange tile roofs. There are areas where they go on for mile after mile. An anti-growth movement began to pressure the Irvine City Council to restrict the growth of Bren's developments in the 1980s, claiming they contributed to air pollution and to general overcrowding in the area. This group has met with some success. In one case, the city council

voted four to one against allowing Bren to develop a 400-acre subdivision in a rural canyon.

Bren's biggest objective is to build a posh residential resort in the last undeveloped stretch of southern California coastline. Many people have lined up against his plan. But who is right? Bren paid for the land. He owns it. Should others be able to tell him what to do with his property? What of the people who would like to live in his development? Should they be allowed to buy Bren's houses simply because they can afford to? What do you believe the ethical choices are?

Every house is different from every other one, and it is difficult to get buyers and sellers together for such nonstandard products. Generally, for standard products, or even for nonstandard products that do not cost very much, there are no agents. But a house is generally the largest purchase any family will make. For that reason, a consumer about to purchase a house is usually willing to spend more time and money gathering information. The real estate agent can save information costs by helping to match the wants of buyers with the products offered by sellers.

A real estate agent can help in other ways. The agent generally knows the area well and can furnish information on schools, sources of financing, repair services, and closing costs that you wouldn't be able to find in the classified ads. Since some agents are better informed than others, it is usually worthwhile to shop around for the right one. After an agent has shown you a few houses, you will sense how serious the broker is about servicing you and also whether he or she understands your tastes and preferences in housing.

Real estate agents, because they normally receive a commission (a percentage of the selling price) from the seller, are more likely to have the seller's interest at heart than the buyer's. This means that you should be careful not to let the realtor know things you don't want the seller to know—such as how high you are willing to go in price. Some home buyers, for this reason, hire a real estate broker to act solely as a "buyer's agent"—who, in return for perhaps a flat fee from the buyer, will promote the buyer's interests in negotiations with the seller.

When prospective home buyers work with a real estate agent, can they be sure this person will put their best interests first? Real estate agents earn their commission when a sale is made. The larger the price, the more they receive. Although real estate agents can help locate appropriate housing, consumers should use their own judgment when they make an offer on a home that is for sale.

How to Bargain

Most Americans are unaccustomed to bargaining because goods and services are sold at set prices. But buying a house is a different situation. The asking price generally is not the final sale price. If you are unaccustomed to bargaining for a house or you feel uncomfortable doing it, you can let a real estate agent do it for you.

You might get a general idea of how much profit the seller is trying to make by finding out what was paid for the house before. You can look at the deed to the house, which is a public document, at the office of the county clerk or county registrar of deeds. You can find out what the house cost by looking at the federal tax stamps affixed to the deed when the ownership was transferred. For example, if the stamps cost $1.10 for every $1,000 and a deed has $33 worth of stamps, the owner paid $30,000. (Don't forget the impact of inflation on the pricing during the years since the person purchased the house.)

Many times, sellers do not expect to get the prices they are asking on their houses. They set a price that they think may be, say, 5 or 10 percent more than the price they will finally receive. It is up to you to find out how far they will go in discounting that list price. You can start by asking the real estate agent whether he or she thinks the price is "firm." because the broker's commission is a percentage of the sale price, the higher the price, the more the agent benefits, but not if it means waiting months or years for a sale. The broker's desire to get that commission as soon as possible is an incentive to arrange a mutually agreeable price so that a deal will be made. On an $85,000 list price, for example, you may want to offer $79,000 on condition that you receive the refrigerator, freezer, washer, and dryer that are already in the house. This sort of bargaining happens all the time. You should not accept the list price just because you think you want the house. Before you make an offer, though, certain basic, common-sense precautions must be taken.

Before You Sign Anything

Before you sign anything, make sure you are getting a house that is structurally sound. The list of questions in Exhibit 12–3 indicates specifically what you want to know. You can pay an expert to go over everything in the house that

▶ Exhibit 12–3   **Checklist for Inspecting a House**

Basement
Has the basement leaked within the past two years? _____
What basement waterproofing repairs have been made within the past two years? _____

Roof
What type of roof is it? _____
How old is it? _____
Has the roof leaked within the past two years? _____
What roof repairs have been made within the past two years? _____

Plumbing
Has the plumbing system backed up within the past two years? _____
What repairs or servicing has been done within the past two years? _____

Heating
How old is the heating system? _____
Is heat provided to all finished rooms? _____
Is it: ☐ Gas   ☐ Electric   ☐ Oil   ☐ Other?   When was it last repaired or serviced? _____

Air Conditioning
Is there a central air-conditioning system? _____
If yes, is it provided to all finished rooms? _____
Comments: _____
How old is it? _____ Is it: ☐ Gas   ☐ Electric?
When was the last time it was repaired or serviced? _____

Utilities
How much is the average monthly bill for: Electricity $_____, Gas $_____, Oil $_____?
Other than the central heating and air-conditioning systems, are any appliances, fans, motors, pumps, light fixtures or electrical outlets in need of repair? _____

Fireplace
Is the fireplace in working condition? _____
When was it last repaired, serviced or cleaned? _____
Comments: _____

Windows
Are there any storm windows or screens on the premises that are not installed? _____
Specifics: _____

Floors
What type of floor is under areas covered by wall-to-wall carpeting? _____
☐ Finished hardwood   ☐ Plywood   ☐ Other
Is flooring material the same for all covered areas? _____
Specifics: _____

Gutters
Do gutters and downspouts need any repairs other than routine maintenance? _____
Specifics: _____

Hot Water Heater
How old is the hot-water heater? _____ What is its capacity in gallons? _____
When was it last serviced or repaired? _____

Rainwater
Does the property ever have standing water in front, rear or side yards more than 48 hours after a heavy rain? _____
Location: _____

Electrical
Do fuses blow or circuit breakers trip when two or more appliances are used at the same time? _____
Specifics: _____

Locks
Are all outer door locks in working condition? _____
Will keys be provided for each lock? _____

Insulation
Is there insulation in the ceiling or attic? _____
The walls? _____
Other places? _____

Notes:
_____
_____
_____
_____

Source: Montgomery County (Md.) Office of Consumer Affairs.

could cause problems—wiring, frame, plumbing, sewage, and so on. The typical cost for an inspection runs between $175 and $500. It is money well invested unless you are an expert at figuring out what can go wrong with the house just by looking at it. Ask your real estate agent about whom to contact, or look at the listings under "Building Inspection Service" or "Home Inspection Service" in the Yellow Pages. Again, these companies are selling the same thing a broker is selling—information. Such information can save you hundreds, if not thousands, of dollars in repairs you would later discover had to be made. Often, if a building inspector discovers structural faults in a house, you can have the seller agree to pay for the repairs even after you take over the house. Or this can be a bargaining point: The price you agreed on can be reduced by the amount of repair costs. Make sure the purchase contract specifies that the contract is contingent on the results of any inspections you want to have made and that any arrangements you make with the seller concerning necessary repairs are also written into the contract.

MAKING THE OFFER

Generally, when you have decided to buy a house, you make an offer and put it in writing. You also must put up **earnest money,** or deposit binder money. The earnest agreement or binder states in some detail your exact offering price for the house and lists any other things that normally are not

Earnest money
Sometimes called a deposit on a contract or an offer to purchase a house. It is the amount of money you put up to show that you are serious about the offer you are making to buy a house. Generally you sign an earnest agreement, or a contract that specifies the purchase price you are willing to pay for the house in question. If the owner selling the house signs, then you are committed to purchase the house; if you back down, you could lose the entire earnest money.

included with a house but are to be included in this deal, such as a washer or dryer. Within a specified time period, the seller of the house either accepts or rejects the earnest agreement or binder. If the seller accepts and you try to back down, the earnest money you put up, which may be several thousand dollars, is legally no longer yours. But sometimes you can get it back even when you decide against the house after signing the agreement. In any earnest agreement, it is often wise to add an escape clause if you are unsure about getting financing. Put in a statement such as, "This earnest agreement is contingent on the buyer's obtaining financing from a bank for [X thousand] dollars." Remember, the earnest agreement offer is *your* proposal. Put in what *you* want. Let the seller change it; then you review it.

If the earnest or binder agreement has been accepted, then a contract of sale is drawn up. This is sometimes called the *sales contract*. Usually, the signing of a contract of sale is accompanied by a deposit, which may be 10 percent of the purchase price paid to the seller. Often the buyer merely adds to the existing earnest money to bring it up to the desired amount.

The deposit may be put into an escrow account or a trusteed savings account that earns interest from the time it is paid to the seller to the time the buyer takes possession of the house. When any substantial sum is involved, it is, of course, advantageous to the buyer to have the deposit put into a trusteed savings account with the interest accruing to the buyer rather than the seller. This is particularly advantageous if there is a large time difference between the signing of the conditional sales contract and the actual date of possession of the house.

TITLE EXAMINATION

After the sales contract has been negotiated, the buyer or buyer's attorney (or the broker, escrow agent, or title insurance company) will begin the **title** examination (or "search"), which entails examining the history of all past transfers and sales of the piece of property in question. Every county has a filing system where deeds, plats, and other instruments are recorded.

The title examiner will generally obtain an **abstract** from a private abstract company. This document lists all the records relating to a particular parcel of land. After reading the abstract, the examiner will give an opinion as to the validity of the title.

On the basis of this examination, a **title insurance** policy can be drawn up guaranteeing that if any defects arise in the title, the title company itself will defend for the owner and pay all legal expenses involved. Note that this may sound better than it actually is. Title insurance generally does not cover government actions that could restrict use of ownership of the property you just bought. Often, title insurance excludes mechanics' liens not recorded with the proper official agency when the policy was issued. In other words, if work was done on the house and not paid for by the former owner, it is possible, even with the title insurance, that you could end up paying for that work. You should always ask the seller for a copy of paid bills for any obviously recent repairs or additions to the home.

Title search and insurance are important parts of the home-buying process. When you purchase something as expensive as a house, you must be sure that you really own it and that no one with a prior claim can dispute your title to the land and structure.

Title
The physical representation of your legal ownership of a house. The title is sometimes called the deed.

Abstract
A short history of title to land; a document listing all records relating to a given parcel of land.

Title insurance
Insurance that you pay for when you buy a house so you can be assured that the title, or legal ownership, to the house is free and clear.

DIFFERENT TYPES OF ROOFS

By far the most popular type of residence in the United States (and also the most expensive in terms of energy and maintenance requirements) is the single-family, detached dwelling. But numerous multifamily dwellings are also available to us, to rent or to buy. For home buyers, the three most significant alternatives to the single-family, detached dwelling are cooperatives, condominiums, and townhouses.

Cooperatives

Cooperative
An apartment building or complex in which each owner owns a proportionate share of a nonprofit corporation that holds title or a legal right to use the building.

In a building of **cooperative** apartments, each dweller owns a **pro rata** (proportionate) share of a nonprofit corporation that holds a legal right to that building. In addition, a member of a cooperative

Pro rata
Proportionately; that is, according to some exactly calculable factor.

1. Leases the individual unit he or she occupies.
2. Accepts financial responsibility for his or her own payments and, in addition, accepts responsibility for increases in assessments if one or more members fail to make their payments.
3. Pays a monthly assessment to cover maintenance, service, taxes, and mortgage for the entire building.
4. Votes to elect a board of directors.
5. Must obtain approval from the corporation before remodeling, renting, or changing his or her unit, or selling his or her share in the corporation.

Cooperative housing grew slowly until 1950, when Congress passed legislation that allowed the Federal Housing Administration (FHA) to insure the mortgages of cooperative housing units. Although much cooperative housing has been produced for middle-income families, today co-ops are more popular among higher-income families in large eastern cities, particularly New York, Boston, and Washington, D.C.

Co-ops themselves are nonprofit organizations and are, therefore, owned and operated solely for the benefit of the members. The FHA estimates that the cost of living in a cooperative apartment is about 20 percent less than renting a comparable apartment from a private landlord. In addition, co-op owners reap the various tax advantages of owning a home. Basically, all local taxes and interest on the mortgage for the prorated share in the cooperative are deductible from income before taxes are paid. Because this benefit is not directly available to renters, it is one reason a number of people prefer to join a cooperative instead of renting an apartment, even though an apartment in a cooperative building looks the same and gives the same types of housing services. These tax advantages are also gained by owners of condominiums.

Condominiums

Condominium
An apartment house or complex in which each living unit is individually owned. Each owner receives a deed allowing him or her to sell, mortgage, or exchange the unit independently of the owners of the other units in the building. Title to a condominium also gives the purchaser shared ownership rights in common areas.

In **condominiums,** which represent a newer type of ownership than the cooperative,[1] the apartment dweller has the legal title to the apartment that he or she owns. A condominium owner, however,

1. Has a joint ownership interest in the common areas and facilities in the building, such as swimming pools and tennis courts.

---

1. Although the condo concept is very old (such arrangements existed in ancient Rome and medieval Europe), in this country legal obstacles impeded its growth until 1961, when the Federal Housing Administration was authorized to insure condominium mortgages.

2. Must arrange for his or her own mortgage and pay taxes individually on the unit.

3. Must make separate payments for building maintenance and services.

4. Does not accept financial responsibility for other people's units or their share of the overall operating expenses.

5. Votes to elect a board of managers that supervises the property.

6. Has the right to refinance, sell, or remodel his or her own unit.

In many situations, owners who want to sell their condominium apartments are under fewer restrictions than are owners of co-op units. With a condominium, if the owner of a unit defaults on a payment, it affects only the owner's own mortgage. In the case of a cooperative unit, any owner who defaults causes the other co-op members to chip in to cover what has been defaulted. Also, condominium owners usually are free to rent or lease their units to anyone.

Townhouses

A **townhouse** is a regular house with a yard or garden area but with common sidewalls. The obvious advantage of a townhouse is economy, for its construction permits savings on the cost of land, insulation, windows, foundation, roof, and walls. Some townhouses are sold as condominiums. One disadvantage of such housing units may be lack of adequate soundproofing as a result of shared walls and the proximity of neighbors.

Townhouse
A house that shares common sidewalls with other, similar houses.

PAYING FOR YOUR HOME

More than 90 percent of all people who buy homes do so with a mortgage loan, which, as mentioned earlier, is a loan that a bank or trust company makes on a house. In some states, you hold the title to the house; in others, the mortgagee does. In several states, a special arrangement is made whereby the borrower (mortgagor) deeds the property to a trustee—a third party—on behalf of the lender (mortgagee). The trustee then deeds the property back to the borrower when the loan is repaid. If the payments are not made, the trustee can deed the property to the lender or dispose of it by auction, depending on state law. As the mortgagor, you make payments on the mortgage until it is paid off.

Sources of Mortgages

Most mortgage loans are made by savings and loan associations, but there are many other sources for mortgages as well. These include mortgage companies, commercial banks, and mutual savings banks, as well as special institutions that, in certain circumstances, may give you a mortgage loan—such as pension funds, mortgage pools, insurance companies, mortgage investment trusts, and state and local credit agencies.

Comparison-Shopping

Given the variety of sources available for mortgage loans, the wise consumer will want to shop around for the best deal available. One way to do this is to check with a mortgage-reporting service. If one is available near you, the local mortgage officer at your bank or at other lending institutions in your community will know of it. The local real estate board, or perhaps your broker if you are using the services of one, may also be able to refer you to this kind of service.

There are also computerized mortgage-search services that you might want to use. For example, HSH Associates of Butler, 1200 Route 23, Butler, NJ 07405 (201-838-3330), is a mortgage-search service that you can contact directly. For $20, you can obtain from HSH a homebuyer's kit that includes the latest weekly report on mortgage loan terms in 36 states and 50 major metropolitan areas.

Mortgage Talk

When you shop for a mortgage, you should know the language of the mortgage trade. Some terms that you will want to understand are *discount points, prepayment privilege, prepayment penalty,* and *amortization schedule.*

Discount points

Additional charges added to a mortgage that effectively raise the rate of interest you pay.

Discount Points Sometimes obtaining a mortgage involves paying **discount points.** This is merely a device to raise the effective interest rate you pay on a mortgage. It is often used when there are restrictions on the legal interest rate you can be charged for your mortgage loan. You may think this unfair, but if you are faced with the possibility of either paying the discount points or not getting the loan at all, you may decide to pay the implicitly higher interest rate. A point is a charge of 1 percent of the amount of a loan. Typically, two points are charged for each one-fourth of 1 percent difference between the rate available on conventional mortgages and the ceiling rate on Federal Housing Administration and Veterans Administration mortgages. Points also are charged on conventional mortgages in several states, such as Florida and California. Basically, this amounts to prepaid interest. This charge may be assessed against the buyer, or the seller, or both. To see how a discount-point system works, say you have to pay four discount points on a $25,000 loan; that means that you get a loan of $25,000 minus 4 percent of $25,000, making the loan only $24,000. You pay interest on the full $25,000, however. Some states have laws against discount points, and the FHA and VA have restrictions on buyers paying points, so they are charged to the seller. But ultimately they tend to be passed on to the borrower in the form of a higher price.

Prepayment privileges

In a mortgage loan with prepayment privileges, you can prepay your loan before the maturity date and not have to pay a penalty.

Prepayment Privilege If the mortgage terms allow for **prepayment privileges,** then you can prepay your mortgage before the maturity date without penalty. You might want to do this later on if interest rates in the economy fall below what you actually are paying. You could pay the mortgage off by refinancing it at a lower interest charge. Charging prepayment penalties is against the law in many states.

Amortization schedule

A table showing the amount of monthly payments due on a long-term loan, such as a mortgage; it indicates the exact amounts going toward interest and principal.

Amortization In calculating the cost of credit for a large loan, such as a mortgage, you will need an **amortization schedule,** which will show you what portions of each monthly payment go to the interest and to the principal on your loan. Lenders usually provide mortgagors with such schedules; if they don't, ask for one. For the first several years of your mortgage loan, you will be paying primarily interest on your mortgage, so the amount owing on the principal of the loan declines very slowly. But it does decline, and, as it does, the monthly interest is accordingly reduced. By the end of your payment schedule, your payment will mostly be on the principal.

THE KINDS OF MORTGAGES

Numerous types of mortgages are now available. Although you may not be eligible for two of them, the rest are available from the same sources: commercial banks, savings banks, mortgage banks, savings and loan associations, and insurance companies.

> Conventional loans can be arranged on just about any terms satisfactory to both parties.

Conventional (Fixed-Rate) Mortgage

With a conventional mortgage loan, the money the lender risks is secured only by the value of the mortgaged property and the financial integrity of the borrower. To protect the investment from the start, the conventional lender, such as a savings and loan association, ordinarily requires a down payment of anywhere from 5 to 25 percent of the value of the property, depending on market conditions. Some private insurers will protect lenders against loss on at least a certain portion of the loan. When such extra security is provided, the lender may go to a higher loan figure. The borrower, of course, pays the cost of the insurance.

Most conventional mortgages are given at a fixed rate of interest—which is determined by conditions in the credit market—and repaid over a period of 15, 20, 25, or 30 years. If you expect the interest rate to rise in the future, a fixed-rate mortgage would be advantageous to you, because the amount of interest you pay would not change over the period of the loan. If, however, interest rates are high when you are looking for a mortgage, other options may be more favorable to your pocketbook. If you make a very large down payment thus lowering the risk of lending for the lender, you may get a slightly lower interest rate, perhaps a fraction of a percent below the prevailing local rate.

Conventional loans can be arranged on just about any terms satisfactory to both parties. Different lenders favor different arrangements, so it pays to shop around. And because most borrowers pay off their mortgages well before maturity, it is wise to look around for liberal conditions on prepayment; you don't want to pay a penalty if you wish to prepay your loan.

Adjustable-Rate Mortgage

An adjustable-rate mortgage (ARM) loan carries an interest rate that may change over time, instead of a fixed interest rate. The rate is pegged to interest-rate changes in the financial market, as determined by the movement of any public index of interest rates that can be checked by borrowers and that are not under the control of lenders. ARMs allow lenders to keep their flow of funds in step with changing conditions, and this, in turn, could make home loans easier to come by when money is tight. You may get a fractionally lower interest rate at first or be offered other inducements by lenders to make future uncertainties more palatable. If you consider obtaining an ARM you should be sure to ask about its *yearly cap* (how much the interest rate can be increased in a year), *lifetime cap* (the maximum the interest rate can ever be raised to), and how often the interest rate may be adjusted in each year.

Although ARMs accounted for less than 40 percent of new mortgages in 1992, they made up 60 percent of them in the late 1980s, probably because of the high interest rates that were charged on conventional mortgages at that time.

Graduated-Payment Mortgage

A flexible type of mortgage called a graduated-payment mortgage allows borrowers to tailor their mortgage to their income over time. Monthly payments are arranged to start out low and to increase later on, perhaps in a series of steps at specified intervals. The term of the loan and the interest rate remains unchanged.

This type of mortgage benefits mainly first-time home buyers who look forward to higher earnings in the future and the ability to afford higher payments at a later time. One disadvantage of the graduated-payment mortgage is the possible "negative amortization" in the early years, which means that, for a time, your debt grows instead of diminishing.

Rollover Mortgage

In a rollover mortgage, the rate of interest and the size of the monthly payment are fixed, but the whole loan—including principal, rate of interest, and term—is renegotiated, or "rolled over," at stated intervals—usually every three to five years. If interest rates go up, you can expect to be charged more when you renegotiate, but you'll also have the opportunity to adjust other aspects of the loan—such as term and principal. Or you can pay off the outstanding balance without penalty. Renegotiation is guaranteed.

Obviously, lenders benefit from rollover mortgages, as they do from ARMs. Benefits to the borrower are the same as those obtained from ARMs, with this plus: Periodic renegotiation gives you a chance to rearrange the loan to suit your changing needs without all the expense of refinancing.

Exhibit 12–4 compares monthly payments on a $30,000, 30-year, 9-percent loan for a standard mortgage, an adjustable-rate mortgage, a rollover mortgage, and a graduated-payment mortgage.

Shared-Appreciation Mortgage

Another approach to house-purchase financing in the 1980s is the shared-appreciation mortgage. This is a form of equity sharing whereby one or more other investors (which could be a savings and loan institution, an individual, or other investors) agree to pay part of the loan, the down payment, or closing costs in exchange for part of the equity in your home.

Consider an example. A house buyer wishes to obtain a $75,000 mortgage on a $100,000 house. A savings and loan association may agree to lend the $75,000 at five percentage points lower than the going mortgage rate of interest. In exchange, the lender has a claim on a one-third share of the appreciated value of the house. If the house is sold ten years later for $200,000, the increased value is $100,000. The lender would receive one-third of that, or $33,333.33. The attraction of a low rate of interest on the mortgage is obvious, but there are drawbacks. Subject to Internal Revenue Service rulings, the overall tax savings for the borrower may be less than if he or she had chosen a conventional mortgage with a higher rate of interest. There is also a problem with valuation of home improvements; if, indeed, the lender has a claim on one-third of the increased value, even if some of that appreciation is due to the homeowner's own improvements, there is less incentive to make those improvements.

VA Mortgages

Veterans Administration (VA) mortgages (GI loans) can be obtained only by qualified veterans or their widows. The interest rate charged is administered

The loan is for $30,000 over a 30-year term, assuming an increase in interest rates from 9% to 12% after the first five years of the mortgage where applicable.

MONTHLY PAYMENTS	CONVENTIONAL MORTGAGE FIXED AT 9%	ARM INITIAL INTEREST RATE 9%, ADJUSTED TO 12% OVER 5 YEARS	FIVE-YEAR ROLLOVER INITIAL INTEREST RATE 9%, ADJUSTED TO 12% AFTER 5 YEARS	GRADUATED PAYMENTS	
				5-YEAR 7½% INCREASE	3% INCREASE
Year 1	$ 241	$ 241	$ 241	$ 182	$ 200
2	241	252	241	196	206
3	241	263	241	211	212
4	241	273	241	226	219
5	241	284	241	244	226
6	241	294	292	262	233
11	241	294	292	262	270
OUTSTANDING BALANCE					
Year 1	$29,795	$29,795	$29,795	$30,533	$30,304
2	29,570	29,592	29,570	30,945	30,562
3	29,326	29,389	29,326	31,212	30,765
4	29,057	29,184	29,057	31,306	30,908
5	28,764	28,976	28,764	31,197	30,983
10	26,828	27,618	27,416	29,098	29,975
TOTAL PAID					
Year 1	$ 2,896	$ 2,896	$ 2,896	$ 2,188	$ 2,408
2	5,793	5,922	5,793	4,540	4,888
3	8,690	9,075	8,690	7,070	7,443
4	11,586	12,356	11,586	9,788	10,075
5	14,483	15,764	14,483	12,710	12,785
10	28,969	33,435	32,026	28,419	27,607
30	86,900	104,122	102,197	91,254	92,335

rather than determined strictly by the forces of supply and demand in the money market. The VA loan is guaranteed rather than insured. That is, the government simply promises that, on an approved loan, it will guarantee repayment of 60 percent of the loan. The borrower has no insurance premium to pay.

Loans with nothing down are possible under the VA program, often for amounts up to $125,000 and for up to 30 years. You cannot get a loan on a VA-financed house for more than the VA appraisal of its current market value, however. Nor can you mortgage it for longer than the VA estimate of its remaining economic life. All VA loans can be prepaid without penalty. VA loans are also available for second mortgages and for mobile homes.

Although the Veterans Administration makes some mortgage loans directly to veterans in some circumstances, usually they are handled by savings and loan associations and other sources of mortgage loans.

FHA Mortgages

The Federal Housing Administration (FHA) issues insurance covering the entire amount of an FHA loan. This added security enables qualified borrowers to obtain a much more generous loan in relation to the value of the property than they could obtain with an uninsured loan. FHA loans are attractive to many home buyers because they often finance 95 percent of the purchase price of a home, and there are no penalties for prepayment. On the other hand, as with VA loans, it may take several weeks to have your application processed because of government red tape.

You can apply for an FHA-insured mortgage loan just as you would apply for any other loan. The lender—be it a savings and loan association, mortgage company, or commercial bank—will supply you with the necessary forms and help you complete them. If willing to make the loan, the lender will notify the FHA of your loan application. The FHA, in turn, will assign an approved private appraiser to whom the loan application is sent. When the appraisal has been completed, the application will be forwarded to the FHA for review, approval, and commitment.

Although the FHA has no arbitrary rules on age or income, these factors are considered for their possible effect on your ability to repay the loan over the period of the mortgage.

The FHA also sponsors a subsidy program for low- and moderate-income families. In this program, down payments can be as low as several hundred dollars and interest as low as two to five percentage points.

The big difference between FHA loans and so-called conventional loans is that the FHA interest is not determined strictly by market conditions but is set at an arbitrary rate by the secretary of the U.S. Department of Housing and Urban Development. Usually, the secretary tries to fix a rate below the lowest prevailing market rate.

CREATIVE FINANCING

The term *creative financing* is commonly used to describe loans either provided by a source other than the traditional lenders or with contract features that make them more attractive to mortgagors. Exhibit 12–5 describes some alternative methods of financing a home.

Because interest rates on existing mortgages are sometimes lower than current interest rates, *mortgage assumptions* can at times be attractive to potential buyers. Note, however, that there are usually two problems associated with assuming an existing mortgage.

1. FHA and VA loans can be assumed at the same rate by a new borrower, but conventional loans might contain a *due-on-sale clause,* which states that the balance of the loan must be paid when the home is sold.
2. Even if the existing loan can be assumed, it might represent such a small part of the purchase price that the borrower will have to arrange a second mortgage or come up with a larger down payment.

Perhaps the easiest and least expensive way to finance the purchase of an existing home is by the use of a mortgage assumption with the seller holding a *second mortgage* (called a *purchase money mortgage*) for the balance of the purchase price. The terms and conditions of the arrangement can be tailored to fit the financial requirements of both the buyer and seller. The main obstacle to this type of arrangement is finding a seller who doesn't immediately need to take his or her *equity* in cash from the sale of the residence. Your real estate agent should be able to help you in your search for this type of financing.

Land sales contract. The buyer and seller form a land sales contract (also called *contract for deed* or *installment sales contract*) under which the buyer promises to make monthly payments to the seller until the property is paid for. The buyer does not receive title to the property until the loan is completely paid.

Lease-purchase option. The buyer rents the property until he either moves out or exercises his option to buy it. This can be a profitable arrangement if the option price turns out to be less than the market value of the house when the option is exercised. A disadvantage is that lease payments are not tax-deductible. And a lease option is not a way to circumvent a due-on-sale clause because most such clauses say the loan must be paid off if the owner gives anyone a lease that contains an option to purchase the property.

Ground lease. The buyer buys the house but leases the ground under it. This arrangement requires a lower down payment for a mortgage because the value of the land is not financed. Usually, the lease contains an option to buy within a few years. A ground lease can help make a mortgage affordable, but lease payments aren't deductible, and not owning the land may make the house harder to sell.

Wraparound mortgage. Suppose the seller has an assumable mortgage with a below-market interest rate: a five-year-old, $33,000, 9-percent loan now paid down to $31,631 with 25 years left to go. He sells you the house for $70,000, and you make a 20-percent down payment of $14,000. A lender (who could be the seller) gives you a wraparound mortgage in the amount of $56,000 at 11 percent for 25 years.

You make a monthly payment of $548.86 on the $56,000 loan. The lender in turn makes the $265.53 payment for you on the original loan, which you have assumed. The lender pockets the $283.53 difference. Because, in effect, he lent you only $24,369 ($56,000 minus $31,631), his return is about 14 percent ($283.33 × 12 ÷ $24,369), not the 11 percent for the wraparound.

In many cases, real estate agents have suggested that home sellers offer to be the wraparound lenders for potential buyers. The purported advantages of such an arrangement could be misleading, however. The seller could get exactly the same return by letting the buyer assume or buy the property subject to the first mortgage and by taking back a second mortgage with an interest rate equal to the return he'd get using a wraparound. The seller's return and the buyer's total payments would be exactly the same either way.

Balloon payment. In a balloon-payment loan contract, a borrower agrees to make a lump-sum payment of the loan balance at the end of a certain period, typically two to ten years. In the meantime, periodic payments are set up as if the loan were going to run for much longer. This arrangement keeps current payments down and gives the borrower an opportunity to sell the property or refinance the loan before the balloon comes due.

MORTGAGE REPAYMENT TERMS

Traditionally, a 30-year payment schedule has been the favored term for repaying a mortgage. In recent years, however, many homebuyers have been opting for repayment over a shorter period of time to reduce the amount of interest they must pay for the loan.

THE 15-YEAR MORTGAGE

If you pay off your mortgage in 15 years, the amount you pay each month will be, of course, substantially higher. But you can also reduce the interest paid on the loan. For example, assume that you want to borrow $100,000 toward the purchase of a new home. As indicated in Exhibit 12–6, if you select a 30-year repayment schedule, your interest rate will be 10 percent, your monthly payments will be $877.58, and the total interest will be $215,926. If, however, you repay the loan over a 15-year period instead, your interest rate will be 9.75 percent, your monthly payment will be $1,059.33, and you will pay only $90,685 in interest. In sum, you will reduce the loan interest by $125,241!

Extra Payments

Another way to save on interest is to take out a conventional, 30-year fixed-rate mortgage but—in addition to making the required monthly payments—

Repayment Possibilities on a $100,000 Mortgage with a 10 Percent Interest Rate*

TYPE OF REPAYMENT	TERM TO MATURITY	TOTAL INTEREST	REGULAR PAYMENT	TOTAL ANNUAL PAYMENTS	TOTAL INTEREST SAVED
30-year mortgage					
Conventional	30 yr.	$215,926	$ 877.58	$10,531	None
Additional $25 per month toward principal	25 yr. 10 mo.	$179,261	$ 902.58	$10,831	$ 36,665
Additional $100 per month toward principal	19 yr. 3 mo.	$125,417	$ 977.58	$11,731	$ 90,509
Extra monthly payment each year toward principal	21 yr. 4 mo.	$142,498	$ 877.58	$11,408	$ 73,428
Biweekly mortgage	20 yr. 9 mo.	$139,109	$ 438.81	$11,409˙	$ 76,817
15-year mortgage	15 yr.	$ 90,685	$1,059.33	$12,712	$125,241

*The 15-year rate is 9.75 percent, reflecting the reduction lenders usually offer in return for a shorter repayment period.

Source: *U.S. News & World Report*, February 22, 1988, p. 91.

make extra payments periodically toward the principal. As Exhibit 12–6 shows, even $25 extra per month will result in an interest reduction of $36,665—and you will pay off the loan four years and two months sooner.

If you are interested in using a computer to help choose the best mortgage for you, you could purchase a copy of Kiplinger's *CA-Simply Money*. This software provides payment schedules and calculates monthly and total interest costs of various mortgage plans you could choose. In 1993 the first million people to request this program received the software free. You may order a copy for yourself by calling 1-800-373-3666.

Biweekly Payments

Some lending institutions offer yet another alternative—biweekly, instead of monthly, payments. With a biweekly repayment schedule, you pay half of your regular monthly payment every other week. As you can see in Exhibit 12–6, by making biweekly payments you can reduce the interest you pay by $76,817 and pay off the loan in 20 years and 9 months instead of 30 years. In essence, what happens is this: Because there are 52 weeks in a year, the 26 payments you make add up to more than 12 monthly payments. In effect, you make the equivalent of an extra monthly payment each year. In addition, the more frequent payments have the effect of reducing the principal on which interest is calculated just enough each month to net you further savings.

CLOSING COSTS

Closing—also called *settlement* or *closing escrow*—is the final step in buying your home. An escrow agent is a neutral third party who keeps your deposit and any pertinent documents until the sale is finalized—which happens at the time of closing. At the close of escrow, the escrow agent will give your deposit and loan funds to the seller and have the deed recorded. You will receive a copy of the deed by mail within about 30 days after it has been recorded.

Several costs must be paid, in cash, at the time of closing; these are fees for services, including those performed by the lender, escrow agent, and title company. These costs can range from several hundred to several thousand dollars, depending on your mortgage and other conditions of purchase, and often home buyers are not aware of them until the time of closing. To be prepared for these out-of-pocket expenses, you should try to obtain in advance an estimate of what they will be. In the initial stages of house hunting, ask your realtor to give you a broad idea of what the closing costs might be.

Once you've applied for a mortgage, federal law requires the lender to send you an estimate of the closing costs within three days. You may be able to negotiate with the seller to pay for some of the closing fees, with the results of your negotiation being included in your purchase agreement. Under the 1976 Real Estate Settlement Procedures Act, the lender must do the following when you borrow money to pay for a house.

1. The lender must send you, within three business days after you apply for a mortgage loan, a booklet prepared by the U.S. Department of Housing and Urban Development outlining your rights and explaining settlement procedures and costs.

2. The lender must give you, the applicant, within that three-day period an estimate of most of the settlement costs.

3. The lender must clearly identify individuals or firms that he or she may require you to use for legal or other services, including title insurance and search.

4. If your loan is approved, the lender must provide you with a truth-in-lending statement showing the annual interest rate on the mortgage loan.

5. Lenders, title insurers, and others involved in the real estate transaction cannot pay kickbacks for referrals.

For further details about RESPA regulations, write the Assistant Secretary for Consumer Affairs and Regulatory Functions, Real Estate Practices Division, Department of Housing and Urban Development, Room 4100, Washington, DC 20410.

▶ **SUMMARY**

1. Individuals purchase or rent a house or apartment in order to obtain the flow of services from that particular asset.

2. Renting is an attractive alternative to buying because there is greater freedom of mobility, no down payment, no maintenance tasks, and the exact cost can be determined easily.

3. A decision to rent or buy often rests on whether the added costs of purchasing a house are offset by equity and tax savings.

4. The costs of owning a home include not only initial costs (down payment, closing costs, and so on) but also the costs of repairing and maintaining the home over time.

5. If you are buying a house, you will probably find the services of a real estate agent helpful. Remember, however, that the cost for those services—paid for by the seller—will ultimately be passed on to you in the form of a higher purchase price.

6. A real estate agent essentially brings together the buyers and sellers of homes. He or she is, therefore, a provider of information. Since different agents may be more or less helpful, depending on your preferences in housing and how seriously you are looking, it pays to shop around for the right broker. You might also consider hiring one as a "buyer's agent" to act specifically on your behalf.

7. Buyers and sellers commonly bargain over the price of a house.

8. It is usually advisable to have a building-inspection service inspect the home you wish to buy before you make any offer. The price for such an inspection is small compared with the costs you may incur without one.

9. Cooperatives and condominiums are popular types of ownership arrangements. The co-op is a nonprofit organization that is owned and operated solely for the benefit of its members (the individuals who own residences in the building).

10. The owner of a condominium has title to the unit he or she occupies and has fewer restrictions than a co-op owner.

11. Numerous types of lending institutions offer numerous types of mortgages. Shop around for a mortgage just as you shop for anything else. Seek out the best deal in terms of the down payment required, the annual percentage interest rate charged, and whether or not there is a penalty for early prepayment in case you decide to sell the house for a few years.

12. Before shopping for a mortgage, buyers should understand the terminology commonly used in the mortgage trade, including such phrases as discount points, prepayment privilege, and amortization schedule.

13. Various types of mortgages are available from lending institutions, including conventional (fixed-rate) mortgages, adjustable-rate mortgages (ARMs), graduated-payment mortgages, rollover mortgages, and shared-appreciation mortgages. In addition, government-guaranteed mortgages, such as a VA mortgage or an FHA mortgage, can be obtained.

14. Creative financing of mortgages is frequently done through special agreements made between the seller and the buyer.

15. The amount of interest paid for a mortgage loan can be reduced substantially by paying the loan over a shorter period of time and/or by making extra payments toward the principal.

16. Closing costs are out-of-pocket expenses that must be paid at the time of closing. These costs are for services performed by the lender, escrow agent, title company, and other services.

17. The Real Estate Settlement Procedures Act of 1976 requires that all closing costs and procedures be specifically outlined to you by the lender before you buy a home. The lender must comply with the various requirements of the act within designated time periods.

▶ QUESTIONS FOR THOUGHT AND DISCUSSION

1. Why do you think housing is such a special commodity?

2. If you had to live in either a co-op or a condominium, which would you choose? Why?

3. Would you prefer to buy a new or a used house? Why?

4. Do you think real estate brokers charge too much for their services?

5. In bargaining over the price of a house you are thinking of buying, how would you determine what price to offer the seller?

6. Why might you want to pay on a mortgage for 30 years instead of 15 years?

▶ THINGS TO DO

1. Visit a local real estate agency and ask a realtor about housing prices in your area. What is the average price of a new home versus a used home? How do these prices compare with the national average for both types of homes?

2. Talk with some homeowners you know and ask them about maintenance and repair expenses. How much did they pay in the last year for maintenance and repair work? How many of these expenses were anticipated?

3. Find out how property taxes are determined in your area and how the money is spent.

▶ APPLICATION

Complete a checklist similar to the list in Exhibit 12–3 for inspecting the building you live in. Would you be able to sell this property if you owned it? What features would you emphasize to prospective buyers? What subjects would you try to avoid? How does this exercise demonstrate the importance of asking many questions when you consider buying a house?

▶ SELECTED READINGS

▶ Fried, Carla A. "How to Buy Your First House." *Money,* April 1989, pp. 137–143.

▶ Giese, W. "Bargains, Houses." *Kiplinger's Personal Finance Magazine,* July 1991, pp. 48–49.

▶ "The High Cost of American Homes." *Consumers' Research Magazine,* September 1991, pp. 10–14.

▶ *Home Buyer's Checklist.* Available from National Homebuyers and Homeowners Association, 1225 19th St., N.W., Washington, DC 20036.

▶ Loeb, Marshall. "Your Home." *Marshall Loeb's 1992 Money Guide.* Boston: Little, Brown, 1992, pp. 177–212.

▶ McDonald, E. M. "Mortgages That Look Best at Today's Rates." *Money,* December 1991, pp. 35–36.

▶ Miller, Peter. *The Common Sense Mortgage.* New York: Harper & Row, 1987.

▶ Money Management Institute. *Your Housing Dollar.* Available for $1 from Money Management Institute, 2700 Sanders Rd., Prospect Heights, IL 60070.

▶ *The Mortgage Money Guide: Creative Financing for Home Buyers.* Available free from the Federal Trade Commission, 6th St. and Pennsylvania Ave., N.W., Washington DC 20580.

▶ Pollan, Stephen. *The Field Guide to Home Buying in America.* New York: Fireside, 1988.

▶ Rowland, Mary. "When Renting Makes More Sense." *New York Times,* March 4, 1990, p. 29.

▶ *Second Mortgage Financing.* Available free from the Federal Trade Commission, 6th St. and Pennsylvania Ave., N.W., Washington, DC 20580.

▶ Sims, J. "When It Pays to Swap Your Mortgage." *Money,* December 1991, pp. 124–126.

▶ Thomsett, M. *How to Buy a House, Condo, or Co-op.* New York: Consumer Reports, 1990.

▶ U.S. Department of Housing and Urban Development. *Settlement Costs.* Washington, DC: U.S. Government Printing Office (latest edition).

▶ *Using Ads to Shop for Home Financing.* Available free from the Federal Trade Commission, 6th St. and Pennsylvania Ave., N.W., Washington, DC 20580.

▶ "Your Home." *Changing Times,* March 1990, pp. 26–28.

GLOSSARY

LEASE A contract by which one conveys real estate for a specified period of time and usually for a specified rent; and the act of such conveyance or the term for which it is made.

WARRANTY OF HABITABILITY An implied warranty made by a landlord to a tenant that leased or rented residential premises are in a condition that is safe and suitable for human habitation.

Many houses, condominiums, apartments, mobile homes, and other dwelling units are rented by their owners to tenants. Some of these are rented on a month-to-month basis with the rent paid in advance; the renter or tenant automatically has the right to live in the apartment for the next month. In this type of tenant/landlord relationship, the contract may be terminated on a month's written notice. Given the proper month's notice, the rent can be raised at any time, or the tenant can be asked to leave. There are advantages and disadvantages to this short-term contract. On the one hand, renters can move when they wish without giving a long advance notice. But, on the other hand, there is the possibility of being asked to leave on short notice or of finding the rent raised sooner than had been anticipated.

Alternatively, renters may obtain a **lease.** This is simply a long-term contract that binds both landlord and tenant to specified terms. It is usually for one year and generally requires two months' rent in advance and perhaps one month's rent as a cleaning, breakage, or security deposit.

If you have decided you wish to rent, you face at least four concerns:

1. Obtaining information on rental units available.
2. Making sure you get the rental unit that's right for you.
3. Making sure the contract or lease is appropriate.
4. Knowing what to do when you have valid complaints after you have rented the housing unit.

▶ INFORMATION ABOUT RENTAL UNITS

There are basically four sources from which you can obtain information about potential rental units.

1. Ads in the local newspapers.
2. Property management firms and real estate agencies.
3. "For Rent" signs in front of apartment buildings and houses.
4. Friends and acquaintances.

Any or all of these options for finding a rental unit may be helpful, depending on what you are looking for and in what area. If you wish to rent housing near a campus, for example, you can often simplify your task by looking at the rental ads in the campus paper, by checking the campus bulletin boards, and by driving around nearby residential areas, where there are bound to be some "for rent" signs posted. If you are looking for an apartment in a specific area of a city, visit the offices of some of the larger apartment complexes in that area to see if there may be an expected vacancy.

Most people, at one point or another in their search, look at the classified ads in the local newspaper. Even if you don't find your rental through the ads, you will have gained some valuable information on approximately what is available and for what price.

If you want some assistance in finding a place to rent, or in narrowing the options, you might consult a property management firm, which will try to match your needs with the housing available in a given area. Many realty offices also offer this type of service to potential renters. These intermediaries are paid by homeowners—in the form of a commission of 10 percent or so of the monthly rent—to secure renters for their housing units; if you do pay for these services, it will be in the form of higher rent. Generally, though, such units will be priced according to the going market rate for housing. This type of service is particularly helpful to families moving into a new area, because the property agents can advise the newcomers about the locations of good schools, the virtues of particular neighborhoods, and so on. To contact a property management group, look in the Yellow Pages under "Real Estate—Management" or "Real Estate—Rental Services."

You need to be careful when enlisting the help of a rental service. While some of them may be respectable realty firms, others may be less than ethical in their practices. Some of these agencies, for example, practice a form of bait-and-switch. They put an ad in the local newspaper for an extremely advantageous rental unit, but when you call the agency, you are told that you must pay an advance fee for an "exclusive" list of available houses and apartments. When you ask for the address of the "too-good-to-be-true" rental unit listed in the newspaper, you are told that that particular unit has been rented, "but we have lots of other listings." Because of such practices, it is a good idea to check with the local Better Business Bureau before doing business with a rental agency to learn if there have ever been any complaints about it.

In your search for a rental unit, you may find it useful to contact the Department of Housing and Urban Development (HUD) and ask for their current list of fair market rates for rental housing. They list these rates for various types of dwellings in every county and metropolitan area of the country and update their information annually. To obtain this information, write the Office of Economic Affairs, Department of Housing and Urban Development, 451 7th St., S.W., Washington, DC 20410, or call (202) 707-1422.

▶ MAKING THE RIGHT CHOICE

When looking for a rental unit, it is often helpful to carry a checklist with you to make comparisons. That way, you won't sign a lease on an apartment or house only to discover that you had forgotten to inquire about an essential feature of the rental unit that you now find doesn't exist. Exhibit J-1 is a partial checklist; you can draw up your own and add questions that you consider important.

▶ THE THORNY PROBLEM OF SECURITY DEPOSITS

It is virtually impossible to rent any type of housing unit without first paying a security and/or cleaning deposit. Typically, you can expect to pay the equivalent of a month's rent

as security and, possibly, an additional fee (often a half-month's rent) as a cleaning deposit. The amounts of such deposits are, theoretically at least, to be returned to you when you leave the rental unit, if it is clean and in good condition.

Landlords argue that such deposits are needed because they protect landlords against damages to their property by renters. Renters, however, have found that it is sometimes very difficult to get their deposits back when they leave. You can look at deposits in either of two ways. You can abandon from the outset the prospect of getting your deposit back and consider it additional rent; in this case, divide the number of months you plan to live in the rental unit into the amount of the security deposit, and you will come up with your monthly surcharge. Or you can attempt from the beginning to have a strong case in favor of getting the money back. To do that, consider the following suggestions:

1. Go through the apartment with the manager or owner the day you move in, marking down every single indication of wear and tear or damage that already exists. Make sure you have a copy of that set of notations; sign it yourself, and have the landlord who is with you sign it. Better yet, have it notarized. In some cases, it might be better to live in the apartment a few days to find out in more detail what doesn't work. This is particularly true if you have rented a furnished apartment or house.
2. Retain copies of all bills for improvements, repairs, or cleaning that you had done as evidence that you carefully maintained the unit.
3. Take fairly detailed snapshots showing the condition of the apartment when you moved in and when

you leave. Have them developed by a company that puts the date on the picture.
4. If the building you live in is sold, obtain a letter from the former owner explaining who is holding the security deposit money.
5. Find out what local regulations require you to clean before you move out of an apartment. You may need only to sweep the floor in some locations, while in others you may be required to clean more thoroughly.

If you follow these five suggestions, you will be ready to go to court if your deposit is not refunded. When you are clearly prepared, most landlords will return your security deposit.

▶ MAKING SURE THE LEASE IS OKAY

Most standard-form leases seem to put everything in favor of the landlord (who usually provides it!). Before signing a lease, read it over carefully, including the fine print, to make sure you are not signing away any of your rights as a tenant.

▶ Clauses to Avoid

There are a number of clauses that you may want to attempt to delete from the lease.

Confession of Judgment If your lease has this provision, your landlord's lawyer has the legal right to go to court and plead guilty for you in the event that the landlord thinks his or her rights have been violated—that is, that the property has been damaged or the terms of the lease have not been met. If you sign a lease that has a confession-of-judgment provision, you are admitting guilt before committing any act. Such a clause is, in fact, illegal in some states.

▶ Exhibit J–1 **Shopping for an Apartment**

	APARTMENT A	APARTMENT B	APARTMENT C	APARTMENT D
Monthly rent (including all expenses that you have to pay directly, such as utilities, recreational fees, parking fees, etc.)				
Size of security or cleaning deposit				
Are pets allowed?				
Is there a manager or superintendent on the premises at all times?				
Garbage-disposal facilities?				
Laundry equipment available on the premises?				
Is the laundry room safe?				
When can the laundry room be used?				
Is there a lobby?				
Is there a security officer?				
Will you have direct access to your unit?				
If there is an elevator, what is its condition?				
Is the apartment close to public-transportation if you need it?				
Is it close to food stores?				
Entertainment?				
Other shopping?				
Are there sufficient electrical outlets?				
Are carpets and drapes included?				
Is there enough closet space?				
Are there safe and clearly marked fire exits?				
Are the tenants around you the ones you want to live near (children, singles, retired, etc.)?				

Waiver of Tort Liability   If this provision is in your lease, you have given up in advance the right to sue the landlord if, in fact, you suffer injury or damage because of your landlord's negligence. (If such a clause is illegal in your state, however, it will not hold up in court even if you have signed it.)

Arbitrary Clauses   These are any clauses that give the landlord the ability to cancel the lease because he or she is dissatisfied with your behavior. Some leases include clauses that

1. Forbid immoral behavior.
2. Forbid hanging pictures on the wall.
3. Forbid you to have overnight guests. (This is usually done by requiring that the apartment be occupied only by the tenant and members of the tenant's immediate family.)
4. Forbid you to sublease your rental unit to another person.

5. Allow the landlord to cancel the lease and hold you liable for rent for the balance of the lease if you are one day late in your rent payment.
6. Allow the landlord to enter your apartment when you are not there.
7. Make you liable for all repairs.
8. Make you obey rules that have not yet been written.

▶ Clauses to Add to Your Lease

There are also a number of clauses that you may wish to have added to your lease. The following are some examples.

1. If the person renting the unit to you says that it comes with dishwasher, disposal unit, and air conditioner, make the lease specifically list these items.
2. If you have been promised the use of a recreation room, a gymnasium, a parking lot, or a swimming pool, make sure that the lease says so specifically. Also, have it indicate whether or not you must pay extra for the use of those facilities.
3. If the landlord has promised to have the apartment painted, have this indicated in the lease. If you wish to choose the color, also have that in the lease.
4. In certain cases, you may be able to negotiate a right to premature cancellation if you are transferred to another job. Usually, however, you must negotiate the amount you pay the landlord for exercising this privilege. Ideally, it will be less than the security deposit.
5. If you wish to have any fixtures, shelves, furnishings, and so on that you install become your property when you leave the premises, specify this in the lease.

▶ WHEN YOU HAVE TROUBLE WITH YOUR LANDLORD

Under the laws of most states, landlords are held to a **warranty of habitability.** This means that the landlord implicitly warrants to the tenant that the leased or rented residential premises are in habitable condition—that is, in a condition that is safe and suitable for human living. This warranty is violated whenever a landlord fails to provide essential services that affect a tenant's health and safety.

If you believe that your landlord has violated the warranty of habitability or has in some other way treated you unfairly, there are several steps you can take.

1. Explicitly indicate what your grievance is, such as uncomfortably low (or high) temperatures, a stopped-up sewage system, a continuously leaking toilet, a refrigerator whose freezing compartment doesn't work, and so on.
2. Make several copies of the complaint list. Mail one to the manager (and one to the owner, if two individuals are involved), and keep one for yourself. If there is an organized tenants' group in your area, send a copy to it also.
3. If you receive no response from the manager or owner of your rental unit, contact the agency that administers the housing code in your area and request a visit from a housing inspector, in hopes that he or she will certify the validity of your complaint.
4. If difficulties persist, your best recourse is to contact your state consumer protection bureau (see Consumer Issue B). Since landlord-tenant laws vary from state to state, the state consumer protection bureau will be able to advise you on state laws, as well as direct you to

personnel who may be able to assist you.

▶ Withholding Rent

If your complaints are serious enough, you may, in some states, have the legal right to withhold part or all of your rent until the complaint or complaints are satisfied. Approximately half the states allow the tenant to deduct repairs that are the landlord's responsibility from the rent; they also provide for not paying any rent when the dwelling is uninhabitable. There may be a dollar limit on the amount you can deduct for repairs, however, depending on the state you live in. Again, your state's consumer protection bureau can advise you on this.

▶ A Final Alternative

If your rental situation is truly disagreeable, you might consider looking for another apartment where you won't have similar problems. When one manufacturer's product does not satisfy you, you often turn to a competitor. The same principle could be applied to rental units.

▶ SUMMARY

1. Some tenants rent an apartment, house, or other dwelling unit from month to month. This short-term rental agreement can be terminated by either the landlord or the tenant with one month's notice.
2. A long-term rental contract is called a lease. In a lease agreement the landlord and tenant are bound by certain specified terms, such as the length of time the tenant will lease the premises, the monthly or yearly lease amount, a description of the property and equipment covered by the lease.
3. Information about rental units can be obtained from newspaper ads, property management groups

and real estate agencies, "for rent" signs on apartment buildings and houses, and friends and acquaintances.

4. When comparing apartments, a fairly sophisticated checklist can be used to make a more objective survey.

5. If you desire to have your security (cleaning or breakage) deposit returned to you when you vacate a rented unit, you must take certain precautions, such as going through the unit with a manager or landlord the day you move in and checking off all damage that has already occurred. You also may want to retain copies of bills for improvements, repairs, and cleaning and take snapshots of the condition of the apartment when you moved into it.

6. When signing a standard-form lease, avoid confession-of-judgment, waiver-of-tort-liability, and arbitrary clauses.

7. Grievances with managers or owners can be handled through a housing agency in your city or an organized tenants' association. You may wish to check with your state's consumer protection bureau for assistance.

▶ QUESTIONS FOR THOUGHT AND DISCUSSION

1. Assume you are contemplating renting a well-maintained apartment for $625 a month. What kind of security deposit, if any, would you require of your renter?

2. Why do you think certain apartment owners consistently are able to keep all or part of the security deposits they collect from renters?

3. Do you think confession-of-judgment clauses should always be illegal?

4. What are the advantages and disadvantages of renting an apartment in a large complex and a small duplex, respectively?

▶ THINGS TO DO

1. Assume you are contemplating renting a well-maintained apartment for $625 a month. Write down the essential provisions you would want to include in a lease agreement.

2. Obtain a standard-form lease contract. What kind of arbitrary clauses, if any, are included in the form? Make a list of any changes you would like to make on the form if you were the renter. Assume you are the landlord and do the same.

3. Check to see if there is a tenants' organization in your area. Your county consumer affairs office or local legal-aid society may be able to help you. Find out if the tenants' organization is attacking some of the problems mentioned in this Consumer Issue.

▶ SELECTED READINGS

▶ Ashton, Betsy. "Finding a Place to Live." *Guide to Living on Your Own.* Boston: Little, Brown, 1988, pp. 70–93.

▶ Clarkson, Kenneth W., et al. "Landlord-Tenant Relationships." *West's Business Law.* 4th ed. St. Paul, MN: West, 1988, Ch. 55.

▶ Hayden, Delores. *Redesigning the American Dream.* New York: W. W. Norton & Co., 1984.

▶ "Home Prices." *Changing Times,* January 1989, pp. 50–59.

▶ King, R., Jr. "From Bombay to L.A." *Forbes,* November 12, 1990, p. 124.

▶ *Landlords and Tenants: Your Guide to the Law.* Available for $2 from the American Bar Association, 750 North Lake Shore Dr., Chicago, IL 60611.

▶ "Look Before You Lease." *Changing Times,* February 1985, pp. 59–62.

▶ Money Management Institute. *Your Housing Dollar.* Available for $1 from Money Management Institute, 2700 Sanders Rd., Prospect Heights, IL 60070.

▶ Saltzman, Amy. "To Buy or to Rent Is a Question for the '90s." *U.S. News & World Report,* April 17, 1989, pp. 68–70.

▶ Strozier, Robert M. "How to Evict Your Landlord." *The Atlantic Monthly,* February 1984, pp. 89–90.

The Appliance Society

▶ What are consumer durable goods?

▶ How should I decide when to buy a consumer durable?

▶ What steps can I take to get the best deal on a consumer durable?

▶ Should I buy consumer durables on credit?

▶ What should I look for when I purchase a personal computer?

Consumer durable goods
Consumer goods with a lifetime that exceeds one year—for example, washers, dryers, refrigerators, and stereos.

Service flow
The flow of benefits received from an item that has been purchased or made. Consumer durables generally give a service flow that lasts over a period of time. For example, the service flow from a VCR may be a certain amount of satisfaction received from it every year for five years.

Once we've bought or rented a place to live, our next concern is to equip that dwelling with an array of appliances and furniture that makes our lives easier, cleaner, more comfortable, more entertaining, more economical, and often more complicated. Both types of products, furniture and appliances, are examples of **consumer durable goods**—"durable" meaning that they should have a useful lifetime of several years or more. Consumer durables commonly found in our homes include washing machines, refrigerators, stoves, microwave ovens, living room and bedroom furniture, tables and desks, and so on. (The next chapter examines another consumer durable—the automobile.) To get an idea of just how durable some of these consumer durable products really are, study Exhibit 13–1, which shows the percent of new appliances that required repairs in their first year of ownership. Although you should investigate information about specific brands, this type of information can help you decide how important warranties for these products are.

All consumer durable goods have the following characteristics.

1. They yield a **service flow** over their useful lifetimes—that is, a flow of benefits or satisfaction.
2. The purchase price is greater than the value of one year's service flow because consumer durables last for more than one year.
3. Their purchase is often financed on credit.
4. They wear out or depreciate.
5. They must be cared for and repaired.
6. They often are replaced when no longer usable.
7. They may be covered by some form of property insurance.
8. They represent status symbols.
9. There has been growing difficulty in disposing of worn-out consumer durables.

▶ Exhibit 13–1   **Percent of New Appliances Requiring Repairs in First Year of Ownership, 1990**

TYPE OF APPLIANCE	PERCENT REPAIRED IN FIRST YEAR
Top-loading washing machine	21.3%
Electric clothes dryer	14.9
Side-by-side refrigerators	
without ice-maker or water dispenser	14.3
with ice-maker and water dispenser	25.3
Top-freezer refrigerators	
without ice-maker	9.9
with ice-maker	19.1
Microwave ovens (full size)	10.7
Electric ranges	11.2
Dishwashers	16.7
Television sets	
13-inch	4.6
19- and 20-inch	7.7
25- and 27-inch	9.3
Compact-disc players	6.6
VCRs	17.9
Air conditioners	4.6

THE DURABLE GOODS SOCIETY

The ownership of appliances, particularly small appliances, has grown dramatically in the last decade. Just look at Exhibit 13–2, which shows the growth in consumer appliances from 1970 to 1989. In 1970 virtually no one had VCRs, calculators, or hand-held dryers. Nineteen years later, over 31 percent of U.S. homes had VCRs, 59 percent had hand-held hair dryers, and over 99 percent had calculators.

CONSUMER DURABLES AS AN INVESTMENT

Buying durable consumer goods may be regarded as a type of investment. When you spend your money to buy a durable good, you expect to receive a flow of usefulness over time that will have greater value than other uses for your money. Consumers should not think of such purchases as a cost that is paid in only one year.

Consider the decision to buy a washing machine as an example. Although the initial price of a washing machine may be $600, it probably will last ten years or more. The cost of doing your laundry each year, then, is $60 for the machine plus the cost of water and electricity to run it—say, another $60 per year. However, that isn't the end of it. If doing your washing at a coin laundry for $5 each week is your alternative, buying the machine will save $140 each year ($5 × 52 weeks = $260 − $120 = $140 saved a year). When you also consider the cost of transportation to a coin laundry, and the value of time you would spend there while your clothes are being washed, your savings are even greater. Similar savings may be realized when we purchase freezers, sewing machines, microwave ovens, or dishwashers. A method of evaluating the costs and value of appliances over their useful lives is presented in the next section of this chapter.

Even furniture that does not provide a service of measurable value may still be evaluated in terms of time. For example, a new bed probably will not save you money or increase your income, but if it helps you sleep and feel better for the next ten years, its $400 price may be worthwhile. After all, $400 divided by the next 3,652 days (10 years) is only 11 cents a day. Would you be willing to pay 11 cents each day to feel better? A way to buy the use of consumer durables without making an investment is described in the Consumer Close-Up.

EVALUATING THE PURCHASE OF A CONSUMER DURABLE

In many respects, a consumer durable good is just like a machine that a business buys. Businesses are able to reach decisions on the profitability of investing in different types of business equipment, and we can use a similar analysis to determine whether or not a new consumer durable should be purchased. That is, when and how much should you invest in new furniture, a new washing machine, a new refrigerator, or a new dryer?

We do this by looking at the costs and then the benefits of the purchase of a consumer durable item. Let's think in terms of all costs and all benefits being expressed in dollars per year. Consider a hypothetical example in which you are debating the advisability of purchasing a freezer to store food purchased on sale in larger quantities for a longer period of time.

▶ Exhibit 13–2 **Growth in Consumer Appliance Ownership**

APPLIANCE	1970	1989
Calculators	—	99.4%
Clothes dryers	44.6%	67.0%
Clothes washers	62.1%	81.2%
Dishwashers	26.5%	61.0%
Drip coffee makers (on a stand)	—	47.0%
Hair dryers (hand-held)	—	59.0%
Home freezers	31.2%	49.2%
Room air conditioners	40.6%	67.4%
Television (color)	42.5%	94.1%
VCRs	—	31.4%
Telephone answering machines	—	31.8%
Home computers	—	13.0%

Source: Adapted from *Merchandising Magazine*.

Beware of Rent-to-Own Agreements

Consumers who are short of cash or who have been denied credit are sometimes tempted by offers of rent-to-own plans promoted by some appliance stores. Under these plans, a buyer "rents" an appliance by paying a weekly or monthly charge. At the end of a specified time, he or she is given ownership of the product by the store. Does this sound fair to you? Research on these agreements clearly shows that consumers should avoid them if they possibly can.

The Journal of Consumer Affairs completed a survey that compared the cost of buying a 19-inch color television by paying cash or by using a rent-to-own plan. It discovered that the cash price ranged from $325 to $399 for the TV depending on the store where it was purchased. However, under rent-to-own plans the consumers paid anywhere from $720 to $1,213 for the same television. These agreements allow stores to avoid legal limits on interest rates they charge because

they "rent" the appliances instead of selling them. Interest rates in many cases would have to be in the 100-percent to 150-percent range per year to result in similar costs to the consumer.

If you really need a product you can't afford to buy new, it is usually better to purchase a used model rather than agree to a rent-to-own contract. The best choice may be to put off the purchase until you have saved enough money to pay cash.

The Cost Side of the Picture

The cost side of any durable good will, at a minimum, include depreciation, operating costs, repairs, and interest, not to mention the *time* costs spent on repairs.

Depreciation

A reduction or loss in value that occurs as a result of wear and age.

1. *Depreciation.* Let's take a simple example in which a freezer has a ten-year life period, at the end of which it has a zero value and must be scrapped. Its full purchase price is $600; the average annual **depreciation** will be $60 a year. Actually, this is an understatement of depreciation in the first year and an overstatement of what it is in the later years of the useful life of the freezer. It would be virtually impossible to sell it at the end of one year for $540. Just as with automobiles (discussed in Chapter 14), equipment in the home depreciates more the first year than in subsequent years. We'll ignore that fact for the moment.

2. *Operating costs.* Most durable goods, and particularly a freezer, use some form of energy. In this case, it is electricity. As discussed in Consumer Issue L, energy guides are now available for freezers, refrigerators, room air conditioners, and so on. Therefore, it is easy for you to estimate what it will cost per year to operate a particular appliance. To help estimate operating costs, you can also refer to Exhibit 13–3, which gives an estimate of the typical wattage of a number of household appliances and the average kilowatt hours (KWH) used per month by a family of four. To compute your own average usage per month, multiply the number of KWH in the second column by the charge per KWH of your local utility company. For simplicity's sake, let's assume that your operating cost for the freezer will be $70 per year.

3. *Repairs.* A freezer probably will have to be serviced occasionally over the ten-year period. You might even buy a service contract that would explicitly require a payment of so much per year in exchange for complete coverage

Exhibit 13–3 Cost of Operating Selected Major and Minor Appliances per Month*

APPLIANCES	TYPICAL WATTAGE	AVERAGE MONTHLY KWH USE	CUSTOMER USES
Water heater	4,474	500**	
Refrigerator/freezer—standard	326	125	
Refrigerator/freezer—frost-free	615	188	
Freezer—standard 16 cu. ft.	341	100	
Freezer—frost-free 16 cu. ft.	440	150	
Range—with oven	12,200	100	
Lighting	Misc.	100	
Water pump	400	100	
Furnace fan	420	90	
Clothes dryer	4,856	5 × No. of loads	
Clothes washer (water not incl.)	512	10	
Dishwasher (water not incl., one load per day)	1,200	30	
Television—B&W (solid-state)	45	20	
Television—color (solid-state)	145	45	
Stereo	109	9	
Radio	71	7	
Electric blanket	177	22	
Water bed heater (with thermostat)	Misc.		
Coffeemaker	1,200	12	
Fry pan	1,196	10	
Microwave oven	1,500	8	
Toaster	1,146	5	
Garbage disposal	445	5	
Misc. small appliances	Misc.		
Electric heaters	Misc.		
Air conditioners	Misc.		
Hot tub (103°F/1.5 KW/1 HP)			
Fiberglass/insul. 300 gal.	2,250	560	
Dry wood/insul. 442 gal.	2,250	920	
Wet wood/insul. 442 gal.	2,250	1,560	
Other			
Total			

*For a 1,500 sq. ft. home of a family of four.
**Add 100 KWH for each additional person.

of all replacement parts and labor. Let's say that would cost, on average, $65 per year (either for directly paid repairs or for a service contract).

4. *Interest.* If the $600 for the freezer has to be borrowed, then an explicit interest payment must be made. On the other hand, if you have $600 in your savings account and withdraw it, you are paying an *implicit* interest rate equal to the interest forgone on that $600. Let's say that the $600 is in an account yielding 7 percent per year. Interest of 7 percent times $600 equals $42 a year in lost interest (ignoring compounding).

5. *Total costs.* We find, then, that the total annual cost, on average, of service from the freezer is

Depreciation	$ 60
Operating costs	70
Repairs	65
Forgone interest	42
TOTAL	$237

Now we'll turn to the benefit side.

Benefits

The benefits of having a freezer include, but are not limited to, reduction in food bills, convenience, reduced food spoilage, and less time and gas spent on shopping trips.

1. *Reduction in food bills.* Depending on the size of the freezer, the owner can take advantage of sales on meat, frozen fruit juices, frozen vegetables, ice cream, fish, poultry, and a few other items that can be frozen and stored. Also, the freezer allows the owner to grow vegetables in a home garden and store them for the winter. Finally, some foods can be bought in bulk at reduced per-unit prices—for example, a side of beef. Let's assume that, over a one-year period, this saves the owner $150.

2. *Convenience.* It is certainly more convenient to pop into the laundry room or the garage and remove a few steaks for dinner than to go to the market. It is difficult to put a dollar figure on this arrangement, but if you value such convenience very highly, this will be an important benefit factor.

3. *Less time and gas spent on shopping trips.* If you can spend less time going shopping by doing it less often because of the freezer, then we can place a value on your saved time in terms of opportunity cost. Again, it is difficult to talk in terms of what this opportunity cost is without knowing specifically your alternatives and the value you place on them. We can get a monetary handle on the reduction in gas costs and automobile expenses in general, however, by looking at the price of an average trip to the grocery store. Let's assume that the total saved in opportunity costs and reduced automobile expenses is $75 a year.

4. *Other benefits.* These include less spoilage of food, the ability to store more leftovers, and the ability to prepare large quantities of food in advance.

5. *Total benefits.* We can add up the total benefits as follows.

Reduced food bill	$150
Convenience	?
Reduced time and automobile expenses	75
Other	?
TOTAL	$225 + ? = ?

If those items for which we entered a question mark had a combined value of more than $12.00, we would have to say that the benefits outweigh the costs for this particular durable good.

The Special Case of Buying Furniture

A decision to buy furniture is more difficult for many consumers to make than deciding when to buy an appliance like a freezer or a new stove. The reason is that the value of the enjoyment we receive from furniture is hard to quantify, or put a value on. Although we all could get by using furniture that cost only a few hundred dollars at a secondhand store, most of us would rather have better furniture in our homes. But why is this so? A chair is still a chair whether it is made of plastic and steel tubes, or of solid oak and is hand-carved. What value do we receive from owning a piece of fine furniture, and how can we measure this value?

One of the best ways to measure the value of furniture we buy is to think of its value in terms of other items we have to give up to be able to afford it. Does owning a new living room set mean we can't afford decent clothing or are unable to buy the new tires we need for our car? The furniture's cost may be looked at in terms of the value we would place on having these other products.

Like other durable goods, the value of furniture should be considered over time. A fine dining room table may last the rest of our lives, while a less expensive model may fall apart after a few years. In the long run, a table that costs $1,500 could be less expensive than one that costs only $350 but must soon be replaced.

Judging the quality of furniture is often something we need guidance in. *Consumer Reports* has published a number of articles over the years that make recommendations on how to choose furniture as well as appliances. It is worth the investment of time to look up this information when you are considering spending a significant amount of money for any durable consumer good.

PLANNING IS IMPORTANT

Different consumer durables last for different periods of time. They must, therefore, be replaced at different periods of time. For example, the average replacement age of a washing machine is 13 years; a refrigerator, 17 years; an electric dryer, 14 years; a freezer, 16 years; and an electric range, 17 years. These figures will change, depending, to some extent, on how well the item is taken care of, its initial quality, and the frequency of its use. For example, a washing machine will last longer in a family where there are no children because it will not be used as often.

Given that major appliances have a limited life, you must plan for potential future use, not just for what may be needed for the next year or so. For example, a couple setting up a household and planning to have children may consider purchasing a larger-capacity refrigerator and range in anticipation of having more mouths to feed in a few years. The same would be true for a washing machine. It may be more expensive to buy a small clothes washer now and have to replace it with a larger-capacity one three years later when there is another person in the family.

Putting Together a Spending Plan

Exhibit 13–4 presents a sample spending plan for you to fill out. Some people like to plan one year ahead; others, two; and others, three. The planning period really is a function of how rapidly you believe your economic situation is going to change. The faster you think it will change, the shorter your planning period should be.

If the total cost of the household equipment that you plan to buy or replace during the planning period exceeds the amount of money you anticipate you will have available, then obviously you must change your plans. You can postpone or eliminate purchases; you also can look for substitutes. If, initially,

PURCHASES OF CONSUMER DURABLES	ESTIMATED COSTS	DATE OF ANTICIPATED PURCHASES	AMOUNT OF MONEY TO ACCUMULATE EACH PLANNING PERIOD
Washer			
Dryer			
Refrigerator			
Freezer			
Range			
Oven			
Microwave Oven			
Dishwasher			
Trash compactor			
Vacuum cleaner			
Carpets (list each room separately)			
Furniture (list each room separately			
Blender			
Toaster			
TV			
Stereo			
VCR			
Home computer			
Water bed			
Other consumer durables			

COST OF OPERATION AND SERVICING	ESTIMATED COST	ESTIMATED FREQUENCY	AMOUNT OF MONEY TO ACCUMULATE EACH PLANNING PERIOD
Washer			
Dryer			
Other			

Total amount of money available to spend for purchase and servicing of consumer durables during planning period: _____

you cannot afford a new washing machine, then you can use laundromats. If you desire a larger-capacity refrigerator but cannot afford one, you will substitute your time, effort, and the use of your car in going to the store more often.

Shopping for Safety

Because safety may be one of the most important aspects of any product you buy, it is important to consider the safety features of the consumer durables on your shopping list. In Exhibit 13–5, you can check off the safety features that are available for the items you wish to buy.

THE QUESTION OF BUYING ON CREDIT

We noted earlier that one of the characteristics of a consumer durable good is that it is often purchased on time through the credit market. What should the wise consumer do when deciding how to finance the purchase of a new washer or dryer or freezer? That is a question we answer in Chapter 16 and in Consumer Issue N. Basically, the *reason* you are borrowing money has little to do with whether or not you *should* borrow it. What is important is that you maintain a safe debt load. Just because you are able to obtain relatively easy financing for a new washer or dryer does not automatically mean that you should buy it on credit. If doing so will put you over your estimated safe debt load, then you definitely should not buy on credit. If you cannot afford a new washer or dryer at that particular time, then you will have to make do with what you have. That may mean going to a laundromat, but it will also mean staying out of financial difficulties and having greater peace of mind.

It really isn't correct to say that paying cash is the least expensive method of payment just because you pay no finance charges. When you purchase a consumer durable good on credit, you are buying two separate items. One is the durable good, such as the washer or dryer; the other is the use of someone else's money for a specified period of time. In both cases, a cost is involved: In the latter, it is interest; in the former, it is the purchase price or annual average price per year of useful life of the equipment. As in all cases when purchasing credit, you must use the same shopping techniques you would use to buy anything.

Even if you plan to pay for a new appliance or other home furnishing immediately, you might consider the benefits of charging the purchase on a credit card—and then paying the bill before interest is charged on the balance. This is because, under the Fair Credit Billing Act (see Chapter 16), if a dispute arises between you and the merchant over the product, you can refuse to pay the credit company for that charge until the dispute is resolved. Furthermore, the credit company must intervene to help settle the dispute. Another advantage offered by some credit card companies, such as MasterCard and American Express, is that they may extend the manufacturer's warranty on any product you purchase with their cards or offer a warranty if none exists.

BARGAINS IN SHOPPING

If you are about to purchase a household appliance or other item, check the local newspaper for current sales being held by department stores and other retailers. If the item you want to buy isn't on sale, you might call some of the major stores in your area and ask when they are planning sales of the type of appliance or equipment you are looking for.

Many major retailers—J.C. Penney, Sears Roebuck, Macy's, and several others—have warehouse outlets for their surplus goods. If one of these is located in your area, you may be able to find new merchandise for significantly lower prices. There are also a growing number of discount houses and off-price stores where brand-name merchandise can be obtained for much less than you would have to pay in a department store or other retail outlet.

There are also a number of options if you are shopping for used appliances or equipment. Scanning the classified ads in a newspaper is sometimes a good way to find essentially new items at drastically reduced prices. When you're in the market for a major appliance, browse through the classified section of your newspaper. You may be amazed to find just what you want—at bargain prices.

You also may want to check out many other places where you can purchase secondhand items, including flea markets, garage sales, secondhand stores, and auctions. A growing number of consumers are attending government auctions to find used merchandise. Several government departments and agen-

▶ **Exhibit 13–5** **A Safety Checklist for New and Used Appliances**

☐ **1.** When door or cover is open, washer, dryer, dishwasher, or microwave oven automatically stops.

☐ **2.** The "off" controls are clearly indicated.

☐ **3.** Both stationary and portable appliances have three-pronged grounding electric plugs, particularly those to be used outdoors or in damp places (not necessary, however, on toasters and open-coil heating units).

☐ **4.** Trash compactors and self-cleaning ovens have safety locks so they cannot be opened during operation.

☐ **5.** Refrigerators, dryers, and freezers have doors that can be pushed open from inside so that children cannot be trapped.

☐ **6.** Control knobs are beyond the reach of small children.

cies—including the General Services Administration, the Department of Defense, the Internal Revenue Service, the Customs Service, and the Postal Service—have periodic auctions where they sell surplus government and civilian property. For household items, the best auctions are those conducted by the Customs Service, the IRS, and the Postal Service—where confiscated or abandoned personal possessions are sold. Thousands of these government auctions are held each year. If you want to obtain more information about them, call your regional Federal Information Center (see Consumer Issue B). They will direct you to the appropriate regional office of the department or agency you wish to reach.

Finding a good price is always satisfying for consumers; however, we should be suspicious of offers that seem too good to be true. The Consumer Close-Up demonstrates the need to carefully investigate offers of goods or services at prices that are unrealistically low.

CONSUMER CLOSE-UP

The Sofa Swindle

Olivia Taylor-Young was not unfamiliar with how swindles work; in fact, as she states, she "writes about the law for a living." Nonetheless, she fell victim to the tactics of a wily upholsterer. Her tale of woe began when she saw an ad in the paper that read. "Reupholstery. Sofa, $89. Chair, $59. Includes labor. Free estimates, pick-up and delivery." It was a dream come true for our consumer, who had been considering having her sofa reupholstered but had given up the idea after two months of comparison-shopping had informed her it was simply too costly.

She called the number in the ad and met with the upholsterer the next day. He showed her many beautiful fabric samples, and, after Taylor-Young had selected one, informed her that the price wouldn't be $89 but $395. Although surprised and uncomfortable at the deception, she agreed to go ahead with the deal and gave the uphol-

sterer a $50 deposit. The quality of the fabric was worth the $395. She was told that it would take about two weeks for the fabric to arrive and that her sofa would be picked up at that time.

Having heard nothing from the upholstering service for a month, Taylor-Young called them to learn that her fabric had "just arrived." A few days later, the service picked up her sofa, and all appeared well—until, not long thereafter, she received a call from the firm informing her that the fabric she had chosen had arrived "flawed" and was now out of stock. She would have to select another. The next day a young woman came to Taylor-Young's door with a much smaller selection of fabric swatches. The swatches were vastly inferior in quality to the swatches of the original selection—but the price was the same. Only then did the pieces of the puzzle fit together into a picture of fraud: The ad was the bait; the quality fabric was the hook; and

the substitution of an inferior fabric for the quality fabric was the sinker.

Eventually, after a series of unpleasant encounters and threats of legal action, Taylor-Young got her couch back—recovered in the fabric of her choice for the agreed price of $395. Too late, she learned from the Better Business Bureau that they had a file on the upholstering service, and, had she called them earlier, they would have warned her not to do business with the upholstery firm. Taylor-Young also learned that the district attorney's office had a case pending against the upholsterer and assumed that the seedy upholstery service would soon be out of business. But she underestimated the resources of this particular con artist. Six months later, on opening her morning paper, she noticed to her surprise and dismay a very familiar ad: "Reupholstery. Sofa, $95. Chair, $59. . . ."

The decision to buy a personal computer is more complex than most choices consumers make. Unlike refrigerators, televisions, or furniture, the value of a computer depends on the software that is loaded into its memory. To make the best choice possible, consumers need to consider the programs they will use as well as the capacity of the machine they purchase.

BUYING A PERSONAL COMPUTER

This section is about purchasing a personal computer—for fun, for home use, or for business purposes. The most versatile personal computers with a variety of add-ons will allow you to play games; create works of art; track the stock market; schedule your airline flight; write letters, term papers and theses; compose electronic music; and do your accounting.

Shopping for a personal computer is much more complicated and time-consuming than shopping for a TV or VCR. With these products there is a limited range of criteria to consider when making a purchase. You can easily judge a TV's picture and sound quality by turning it on. If you play a videotape on a VCR, you can tell if it produces a quality picture, has a fast-forward feature, and so on. These products perform a limited number of functions that may be quickly and easily evaluated. A problem in choosing personal computers is that with different software they are able to do a seemingly unlimited number of tasks. It would be surprising if any consumer understood every possible use of any computer he or she was considering buying. When consumers buy personal computers they most often have a number of tasks in mind they would like the machine to carry out. They should realize, however, that the reasons they might need a personal computer for today could be quite different from their needs a year from now. The bottom line on all this is that most consumers need help in choosing the best personal computer for their needs.

Where to Look for Help

Salespeople always offer information about computers they offer for sale, both orally and with printed materials. The problem is that people who really don't understand computers are not likely to understand much of what they hear or read. Words like *megabytes, hertz, random access memory,* or references to 286, 386, or 486 chips are meaningless to many people. It is therefore easy for unscrupulous salespeople to take advantage of such consumers and convince them to buy more sophisticated (and more costly) equipment than they need. If all you are ever going to do with a computer is keep household expenses on file and write a few letters, you don't need a machine that could keep all the records for a business, including inventory, sales data, and tax information.

Consumers who are not comfortable choosing a computer should seek the assistance of someone who understands computers and who has no vested interest in which model is purchased. There are many people who have this sort of information. One source is to inquire with user groups. These are people who own computers and meet to share information and give advice. Many businesses employ people who have knowledge of computers and are often happy to provide individuals with advice. You should also investigate *Consumer Reports* and other consumer publications for information. Always be sure that the capabilities of the computer you buy may be added to in the future if your needs change. When you buy a computer you are making an important choice, not only in terms of how you spend your money now, but also in terms of the quality of service you will receive from the computer over the next five to ten years that you use it. Saving $300 on a computer that fails to meet your needs is not a real saving.

Evaluating Computer Hardware

Hardware
Computer equipment, including the computer itself and all input and output peripherals.

Computer **hardware** consists of the computer itself and the input devices (such as a keyboard) and output devices (such as a printer) that attach to it. When you shop for a computer, make comparisons based on the following attributes of both the hardware and the store that's going to sell it to you.

1. Ease of use.
2. Availability and quality of software that is compatible with the hardware.
3. Expandability in terms of more memory and more peripherals.
4. Support, consisting of an 800 number to call for assistance and perhaps magazines and local user groups that specialize in this particular computer.
5. Repair, in terms of speed and location. (For example, does the store offering you the computer have factory-authorized repair on the premises?)

Computer Exchanges

Before purchasing a new personal computer, you might want to check what are called *computer exchanges.* These are computer-brokerage services that match up potential sellers of used computers with potential buyers. While some of the computers offered through these exchanges are manufacturers' closeouts—brand new computers in their original boxes, unopened—most are used computers for sale by regular computer users who have upgraded to a more powerful system.

There are more than one hundred of these computer exchanges across the country; we list a few of them and their telephone numbers below.

▶ Boston Computer Exchange (Boston, MA), (617) 542-4414.
▶ Computer Brokerage Services, Inc. (New York, NY), (212) 947-7848.
▶ Mathewson Associates, Inc. (Norfolk, VA), (804) 624-9639.
▶ Computer Exchange Northwest (Seattle, WA), (206) 820-1181.

Finding the Right Software

Software consists of the programs that make your computer do the things you want it to do. You can evaluate software by looking at the following three areas.

1. *Ease of use.* Is the software "user friendly"—that is, is it easy to understand and operate? Does it have self-explanatory "help" screens with instructions built into the program? How much of what you need to know is provided in the form of a helpful "menu" that simply lists things from which to choose?

2. *Support.* Is there written support from the software publisher that explains everything? Is there an 800 number to call to get an explanation of something you don't understand? If not, can your dealer tell you about the software and its problems?

3. *Warranty.* What if it doesn't work? Can you send it back? Do you get a backup copy of the program so, if the first one fails, the second one will work for you?

Software can be purchased from mail-order discount houses. Any computer magazine will show how you can save up to 40 percent on many packages. You can also rent software to try it out before you buy it. Or you can use a "demo," or "demonstration disk," that allows you to try out a limited version of the software. Again, any current issue of a computer magazine will carry advertisements of companies that rent software programs.

Software
Programs that direct the computer in problem solving and other tasks. Software programs are packaged in the form of cassette tapes, cartridges, or diskettes.

BUYING TIPS

It is impossible to present in this brief space all the different principles that relate specifically to buying each available major and minor appliance—as well as to give characteristics of different types of rugs, furniture, and bedding. We can, however, present a few general principles that might help you make decisions on consumer durables.

1. *Be prepared.* Check consumer information publications to learn about price and quality variations for the product you want to purchase. For example, if you are buying a carpet for the first time, you probably—if you are like most consumers—know very little about carpet fibers, construction, and performance. A little consumer research can help you avoid some costly mistakes.

2. *Comparison-shop.* Always check with at least two or three dealers before you buy—but don't "overspend" your time in comparison-shopping.

3. *Don't forget convenience.* Keep the convenience factor in mind when comparison-shopping. For example, if you truly dislike cleaning ovens, then a self-cleaning oven is important, even though its operating costs may be quite high.

THE ETHICAL CONSUMER
"I'll Make a Copy for You"

A problem of the computer age arises because computer software does not fit the traditional definition of property. The crime of theft, for example, traditionally has involved the unauthorized taking and carrying away of another's property. But if you make a copy of a program that you own and give it to someone else, what have you "stolen"? Wasn't it your program and your disk it was copied onto? What has been taken without permission is the right of the firm that spent money and time to develop the program to earn a just profit for its effort and investment.

Giving others free copies of software you own reduces the income of the firm that produced the program. This may increase the price for people who buy the program and reduce the incentive the firm has to produce new, and even better programs in the future. The owners might say, "Why bother, when we can't earn a decent return?"

Giving away or selling copies of programs is against the law, but it involves an ethical dilemma as well. If you don't sell your program, or give it to many people, the chance of ever being caught is quite small. It often comes down to your willingness in effect to give something away that doesn't belong to you. This kind of decision is made by individuals based on their own moral values. Would you give away a computer program? Would you use one that was given to you? What is the ethical choice for you?

4. *Don't let the seller decide what you want.* Remember that sellers promote their highest-quality (and most expensive) wares and may try to convince you that you need a higher-quality product. But you know your needs better than the seller. For example, you may want to carpet a back room that is rarely used. For that you do not need the most durable carpet on the market—although the seller may think you do.

5. *Ask about seller services and warranties.* One of the easiest things to overlook in the excitement of purchasing a new piece of furniture or a desired appliance is the fact that it may turn out to be imperfect—it may be broken when you unpack it at home, it may malfunction, and so on. It is important to anticipate such future problems at the time of purchase and to ask the seller exactly what will happen if something goes wrong. Will you have to return the product yourself to the manufacturer, or will the seller repair the item in-house? What kind of warranty exists, and what exactly is warranted and for how long? Don't be embarrassed to repeat your questions until you thoroughly understand, and agree to, what is being promised and warranted.

6. *Read the contract.* This is probably the most important thing you can do to protect yourself as a buyer. Read your purchase contract carefully and make sure that whatever the sales agent has told you is in the contract itself. The law is usually very reluctant to help those who don't read what they sign before they sign it.

7. *Remember—if a deal sounds too good to be true, it probably is.*

▶ SUMMARY

1. Consumers purchase consumer durables that often yield a service flow over a lifetime, are often financed on credit, wear out, and must be cared for and replaced.

2. The purchase of a consumer durable involves part consumption and part saving because the durable, by definition, does not wear out immediately. To make rational decisions when buying equipment, consumers must undertake a cost-benefit analysis.

3. Costs of a durable good include, at a minimum, depreciation, operating costs, repairs, and forgone interest. When making a purchasing decision, these costs should be weighed against the potential benefits of owning the durable good.

4. Because major appliances have a limited life, it is useful to set up a household plan to determine needed purchases and replacements.

5. It is important to consider safety features of consumer durables, as safety may be one of the most important aspects of any product you buy.

6. Whether or not credit is used to purchase a durable good should depend on the consumer's already existing debt load.

7. Consumers can make considerable savings by looking for sales and shopping at warehouse outlets, secondhand stores, auctions, and so on.

8. Consumers who have limited knowledge of computers and their capabilities should seek assistance when considering such a purchase. Assistance provided by manufacturers and salespeople, although often useful, is likely to be biased. Consumers should also read various computer publications and ask advice of people who possess computer knowledge but have no vested interest in a particular type of computer.

9. Things to consider when buying a personal computer are ease of use, the availability and quality of compatible software, future potential for expandability, support (phone numbers to call for information, for example), and the convenience of repair services.

10. You can evaluate software by answering three questions: (1) Is it user friendly? (2) Is it well supported—in terms of written explanations and sources for additional information? (3) Does it have a good warranty?

11. Some tips on how to purchase consumer durables include being prepared by checking some consumer publications before you go shopping; comparison-shopping at two or three dealers; shopping for convenience as well as price; checking seller services and warranties; and reading the contract before signing it.

▶ **QUESTIONS FOR THOUGHT AND DISCUSSION**

1. Why is the purchase of a VCR a form of saving?
2. Is there any special reason individuals associate buying consumer durable goods with buying on credit?
3. Why must we consider interest if we purchase a consumer durable with cash?
4. Assume you are shopping for a new printer for your computer. Your local dealer charges $300 more than a distant mail-order house does for the same printer. From which store would you make your purchase? What factors would influence your decision? What if the price difference were only $100?

▶ **THINGS TO DO**

1. Calculate the amount that you saved in the purchase of a durable good that you now own. (Hint: Figure out how many years it will last.)
2. Go to one or more computer stores in your area and look at the types of home computers available. Compare at least two computers in terms of

price, performance, and warranties.

3. Take the safety checklist, Exhibit 13–5, with you to an appliance store. Are there any particular brands of appliances that do not conform to these safety standards? If so, ask the salesperson if he or she knows why.

▶ **APPLICATION**

Identify a new type of appliance or piece of electronic equipment intended for home use that you do not understand well. Investigate the benefits and costs of buying one of these products, and list them in two columns on a sheet of paper. Use these lists to explain why you would or would not choose to purchase the product at the present time.

▶ **SELECTED READINGS**

▶ Ashton, Betsy. "The Shopping Game." *Guide to Living on Your Own.* Boston: Little, Brown, 1988, pp. 151–191.

▶ Berkman, Sue. "Used Computers: The New Bargain." *Good Housekeeping,* April 1989, p. 238.

▶ *Byte.* Various issues.

▶ *Computer Buyer's Guide and Handbook.* Various issues.

▶ Flint, J. "Consumer Durables." *Forbes,* January 8, 1990, pp. 142–144.

▶ Goldstein, Sue. *Secrets from the Underground Shopper.* Dallas: Taylor Publishing Co., 1986.

▶ Loeb, Marshall. "Your Spending." *Marshall Loeb's 1992 Money Guide.* Boston: Little, Brown, 1992, pp. 305–314.

▶ "Major Appliance Buying Guide." *Consumers Digest,* March–April 1989, pp. 33–52.

▶ "Major Kitchen Appliances." *Consumer Reports,* December 1991, pp. 57–58.

▶ Money Management Institute. *Home Furnishings and Equipment.* Available for $1 from Money Management Institute, 2700 Sanders Rd., Prospect Heights, IL 60070.

▶ Sellers, P. "A 1990s Consumer Goes Shopping." *Fortune,* July 29, 1991, p. 122.

▶ Zemke, Ron. *The Service Edge.* New York: Plume, 1989.

Servicing Your Consumer Durables

GLOSSARY

SERVICE CONTRACT For an annual fee, the appliance owner receives a contract allowing for all repairs to be made without further payments.

Virtually all consumer durable goods require some type of servicing and care throughout their useful life. In fact, homeowners can attest that the more appliances there are in the household, the more time and money they must spend having them repaired.

▶ PROS AND CONS OF A SERVICE CONTRACT

Whenever a new appliance is purchased—particularly a washer, dryer, freezer, refrigerator, and, to a lesser extent, stereo equipment—it is possible to purchase a **service contract** that covers all parts and labor for a specified period after the full or limited warranty runs out. For example, if you purchase a refrigerator from J. C. Penney or from Sears, the store will offer you a full service contract for a specified amount of time. In a sense, a service contract is really a form of insurance. You pay a predetermined amount of money each year to avoid the possibility of having to pay a larger amount on costly repairs. You are betting that you would have paid a larger amount in repairs than the service contract actually costs. The seller of the service contract is betting that, on average, for all the individuals who purchase such contracts, the repairs will cost less than the total amount collected. Clearly, on the average, the sellers of service contracts must be right, because they profit from these arrangements. Does that mean that you always lose out by purchasing such a contract? No, you don't. That would be equivalent to saying that you lose out on a life insurance policy unless you die prematurely. If a service contract is regarded as insurance, then buying it makes sense for individuals who do not want to face the prospect of unusually large repair bills at any time during the year.

There is another positive aspect to purchasing a service contract. You may decide to have smaller, less important repairs performed more frequently under a service contract than you would if you had to pay each time you called the serviceperson. In so doing, you may extend the useful life of the appliance, thereby delaying the need to replace it. If, for example, you buy a VCR, for maximum performance and durability you should have it cleaned once a year. If you purchase a service contract that costs $22 per year and an annual cleaning of your VCR is included for that price, then (if it costs approximately $22 to have your VCR cleaned) you don't lose by purchasing the service contract. In fact, you gain, because, having paid for the contract, you will be more motivated to have your equipment cleaned annually.

Except in a few situations, however, if you do buy a service contract, you should do so after the warranty period is up, if the seller allows this. That will give you time to base your decision on the performance of the appliance during the warranty period. Refrigerators, freezers, and clothes dryers have very low repair frequency rates during the second through fifth years. Unless you bought a lemon, which should be obvious during the first year, the money spent on a service contract for any of these appliances is probably unwarranted. The same holds for a central-heating furnace until it is several years old.

▶ Cost of a Service Contract

Exhibit K–1 gives the annual cost by year of service contracts for a TV and a washer. In addition, there is a total cost over the six-year period. As the exhibit shows, the annual cost rises as the unit becomes older. When looked at over a six-year period, the total service contract costs seem quite out of proportion to the cost of the appliances. Thus, one might conclude that a service contract is best suited for individuals who do not take care of their appliances.

▶ The ''90'' Rule

Industry sources frequently cite what they call the "90" rule: If an appliance goes 90 days without breaking, it probably will not break for quite a while. Since most appliances are covered by warranty during this initial period, you might question the wisdom of paying more money for a service contract. According to John Gooley, retired service manager for the National Association of Retail Dealers of America, the odds are that if a product performs well during the warranty period, it will continue to do so, and what repairs

▶ Exhibit K–1   Cost per Year of Service Contract over Six-Year Period

| Appliance | ANNUAL COST BY YEAR OF OWNERSHIP | | | | | |
	1 and 2*	3	4	5	6	Total Cost for Six Years
Clothes washer	$45	$45	$49	$50	$ 58	$247
Color TV	58	71	81	89	102	401

*Cost of coverage for years 1 and 2 were added together because many service contracts handle them this way. This simply means that part or all of the first year's coverage is reflected in the warranty.

might be necessary will be less than the cost of a service contract. *Consumer Reports* and many other consumer protection organizations generally recommend against the purchase of service contracts.

▶ **BEFORE YOU CALL A SERVICEPERSON**

Because service calls are costly, you should first go through the following checklist to see if you can solve the problem yourself.

1. Make sure that you have read carefully and followed all the manufacturer's instructions. In many instruction booklets for durable goods, there is a troubleshooter's checklist that may help you solve your problem simply. Many dollars are wasted on unnecessary service calls. Paying a serviceperson to unplug the drain in a self-defrosting refrigerator, something the owner could have done easily with the help of the instruction booklet, is a case in point.
2. Check fuses or circuit breakers.
3. Make sure gas, water, or electric connections have been turned on correctly.

If all else fails call the serviceperson and give the model number of your appliance (taken from the nameplate). This way you won't pay for two service calls: one to see what was wrong and the second to bring a part that could have been in the serviceperson's truck to begin with.

▶ **WHAT TO DO WHEN YOU HAVE A COMPLAINT**

If you have a complaint about a consumer durable that has not been satisfied by the seller of that good, you may wish to contact the company that manufactured or distributed the product. A polite letter telling what has happened and what you want the company to do about it usually will bring some action. Address your letter to the customer relations department; be sure you make a copy of your letter and that you enclose *copies* of sales slips, guarantees, agreements, cancelled checks, receipts, or contracts. Never mail the originals! Send your complaint either by certified or registered mail, return receipt requested.

If you still do not receive satisfaction, you may wish to contact one of the following private organizations.

1. Appliances: Major Appliance Consumer Action Panel (MACAP); see Exhibit K–2. You can call Westinghouse at (800) 245-0600 and Whirlpool at (800) 253-1301. For other manufacturers, write the consumer relations department at the address given on the model and serial number plate or in the instruction manual. If you have lost your appliance instruction manual, write American Home Appliance Manufacturers at the same address as MACAP or call (800) 621-0477.
2. Carpets and rugs: Carpet and

Rug Institute, 1100 17th St., N.W., Washington, DC 20036.
3. Electronic equipment: Electronic Industries Association, 2001 "I" St., N.W., Washington, DC 20006, (202) 457-4977.

If you still do not receive satisfaction, you may wish to contact the National Council of Better Business Bureaus or your state's consumer

▶ Exhibit K–2   **The Right Way to Complain**

If you have a problem that you haven't been able to solve locally, write or call the manufacturer, giving all details. If that doesn't resolve the difficulty, write MACAP, 20 N. Wacker Dr., Chicago, IL 60606, or telephone toll free (800) 621-0477.

Include the following information:

☐ Your name, address, and telephone number.

☐ Type of appliance, brand, model, serial number.

☐ Date of purchase.

☐ Dealer's name and address and service agent's name and address if different from dealer's.

☐ Clear, concise description of the problem and service performed to date.

MACAP cautions that it is important to keep receipts of repairs even when a service call is under warranty. The receipts may be required to prove an appliance needed excessive repairs and should be replaced.

protection agency, both of which are listed in Consumer Issue B.

▶ SUMMARY

Service contracts are available on most appliances. As a general rule, you should wait and see how the appliance performs during the warranty period before purchasing a service contract, if the seller will allow you to purchase one later. Experts suggest that if there are no problems within the first ninety days of ownership of a new appliance, it is unlikely that future repairs will be substantial enough to warrant the expense of a service contract.

2. Before you call a serviceperson in for repairs, make sure that you have read carefully and followed all the manufacturer's instructions; check fuses or circuit breakers; and make sure that gas, water, or electric connections have been turned on correctly.

3. If you have a complaint about a consumer durable that the seller will not satisfy, you can write directly to the manufacturer. If still unsatisfied, you can turn to industry consumer action panels, such as MACAP, for assistance.

▶ QUESTIONS FOR THOUGHT AND DISCUSSION

1. When would it be advisable to purchase a service contract on a major or minor appliance?

2. Do you think you get more for your dollar by buying used, rather than new, appliances or equipment?

3. How much consideration do you give to maintenance and repair costs when you buy new equipment for your home?

▶ THINGS TO DO

1. Write to MACAP to obtain information on how successful that organization has been in handling consumer complaints.

2. Go to two or three appliance dealers and ask what service contracts, if any, they offer for specific types of appliances. How do these contracts compare in terms of price per year and coverage?

3. Write to the Federal Trade Commission, 6th St. and Pennsylvania Ave., N.W., Washington, DC 20580, and ask for a copy of the *Facts for Consumers* pamphlet on service contacts. Summarize the FDA's recommendations.

▶ SELECTED READINGS

▶ Ashton, Betsy. "Questioning Service Contracts and Extended Warranties." *Guide to Living on Your Own.* Boston: Little, Brown, 1988, pp. 186–187.

▶ Clark, Brooks. "Extended Service Contracts: Just Say No." *Sylvia Porter's Personal Finance,* October 1988, p. 44.

▶ Loeb, Marshall. "Beware of Service Contracts." *Marshall Loeb's 1989 Money Guide.* Boston: Little, Brown, 1988, pp. 313–314.

▶ Moreau, Dan, and Adrienne Blum. "Appliance Service Contracts: Why the Dealer Wins." *Changing Times,* January 1989, pp. 83–86.

▶ *Service Contracts.* Available free from the Federal Trade Commission, 6th St. and Pennsylvania Ave., N.W., Washington, DC 20580.

▶ "What to Do If Your Appliance Breaks Down." *Consumers' Research,* January 1990, p. 35.

Reducing Energy Costs

GLOSSARY

ENERGY BUDGET   A record of a family's energy-consumption expenses, which is formulated to make family members more conscious of the kilowatt hours used during a given time period and to limit those hours to reduce energy costs.

ENERGY LABELS   Labels attached to new appliances that inform purchasers of the amount of energy each labeled appliance will require. Energy labeling of major appliances is mandated by the Energy Policy and Conservation Act of 1975.

HOME ENERGY AUDIT   A thorough check of your home to evaluate how much energy is being wasted. A home-energy auditor will recommend energy-saving steps you can take to reduce fuel and electric bills. Most public utilities offer this service free.

Once you have purchased or rented a home, your main housing concerns will be monthly mortgage or rent payments and utility and maintenance costs. Although the oil shortages of the 1970s are no longer with us, the energy-conservation awareness that they created in Americans has lasted into the 1990s. Consumers have learned that it is not only possible but surprisingly profitable to cut back on energy consumption.

This Consumer Issue examines various ways to conserve energy. In each instance, however, remember the primary rule for rational consumer decision making: *Engage in an activity only up to the point where the last few dollars in cost are matched by an equal amount of benefits.* Otherwise, you'll be spending more of your resources than you'll be receiving in benefits.

▶ SET UP AN ENERGY BUDGET

A good way to begin the process of cutting energy corners is to set up an **energy budget.** Just as you do when you draw up a regular household budget, you should start by monitoring and recording existing expenses—in this case, utility expenses. Study your electric bill, for example, and note how many kilowatt hours (KWH) you use per day. Check your electric meter when certain appliances are running to determine which are the most expensive to use. If you've never read an electric meter, it can be a little confusing; Exhibit L–1 shows you how to read it correctly.

It also helps to have an idea of which appliances are the most expensive in terms of wattage used. Exhibit L–2 gives you an idea of the relative costs of different electrical appliances in a typical home.

An effective energy budget must involve all members in a household unit. As you would when formulating a household budget, discuss together plans for reducing energy consumption and the things that each member can do to achieve the overall goal of reducing energy expenditures. One advantage of such family discussions is that they can promote an awareness of energy costs among household members—and this is the first step toward reducing those costs.

▶ REDUCING ENERGY USE OF APPLIANCES

There are many ways you can save on the energy costs of using home appliances without sacrificing much comfort. Saving energy is like any other activity: It can quickly become a habit, a routine part of your life. Although the following list is by no means complete, you can save many dollars a year if you apply these energy-saving tips carefully to your daily activities.

▶ Hot Water Is Expensive

As you can see in Exhibit L–2, the amount of energy consumed by hot-water heaters is second only to that of electric heating equipment. Here are some pointers to help you save on hot-water costs.

1. *Fix a leaky faucet.* Leaky faucets are not only annoying but costly—especially if they are hot-water faucets. Drops add up quickly to gallons, as you can see in the following chart.

30 drops per minute
= 90 gallons per month
= 22 KWHs per month

60 drops per minute
= 192 gallons per month
= 48.38 KWHs per month

90 drops per minute
= 310 gallons per month
= 77.64 KWHs per month

120 drops per minute
= 429 gallons per month
= 106.83 KWHs per month

2. *Lower the thermostat.* A setting of 120 degrees is a good temperature for normal home use. If you have a dishwasher, use water heated to 140

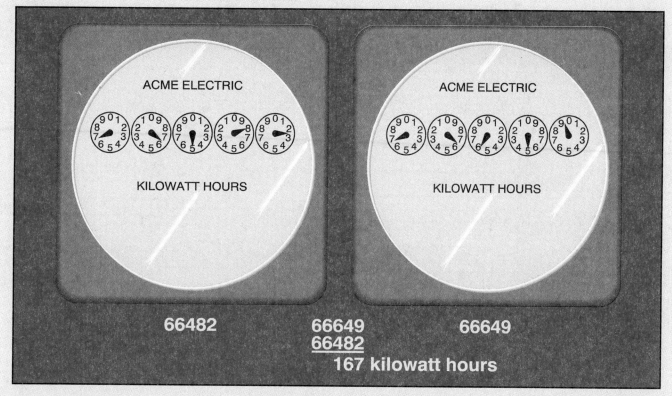

ACME ELECTRIC

KILOWATT HOURS

ACME ELECTRIC

KILOWATT HOURS

66482   66649   66649

66482

167 kilowatt hours

degrees—depending on the manufacturer's specifications. You may want to try living with even lower settings.

3. *Showers or baths?* A shower requires approximately six to eight gallons of water per minute; it takes between 30 and 35 gallons to fill an average-sized bathtub. Enough said.

4. *Water restrictors.* Installing water restrictors in your showerheads can reduce the water flow to two to three gallons per minute. The best ones reduce the flow without sacrificing the hard spray many people like.

5. *Is your water heater the right size?* Oversized water heaters waste money and energy. If you're building or remodeling, consider buying one to suit your family's needs.

6. *Insulate hot-water pipes.* If your hot-water pipes are located in an

unheated area, wrapping the pipes with pipe insulation will cut heat loss.

7. *Insulate your hot-water heater.* Likewise, if your water heater is in an unheated area, wrapping it in insulation will save heat. Many public-utility firms will install this insulation free for you.

8. *A timer for your hot-water heater?* Some households spend $45 to $50 to install a timer on their hot-water heater. If you use hot water at certain times of the day on a routine basis, this can save you a few dollars. Otherwise, the small savings wouldn't be—for most people—enough to offset the inconvenience.

9. *Become hot-water conscious.* Simply by becoming hot-water conscious, you can find ways to lower your use and your water-heating costs.

▶ **Your Refrigerator-Freezer**
Next to heat and hot water, your refrigerator-freezer is probably your greatest energy-using appliance. Here are some suggestions to consider for reducing its cost.

1. *Frost-free freezers cost more.* Frost-free freezers, on average, use approximately 150 KWHs per month, compared with 100 KWHs for a standard freezer. Although the tradeoff in terms of convenience is obvious, you should be aware of this extra usage in drawing up your energy budget. For maximum efficiency, a standard freezer should be defrosted whenever the frost is one-quarter of an inch thick.

2. *Check the seals on your refrigerator-freezer.* If a dollar bill placed in the door can be pulled out easily, it's time for a new seal.

▶ Exhibit L–2   Where the Watts Go

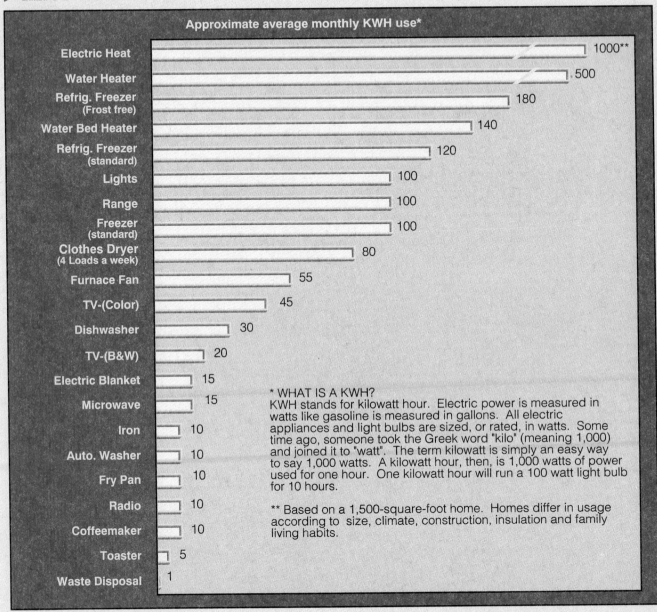

Approximate average monthly KWH use*

Appliance	KWH
Electric Heat	1000**
Water Heater	500
Refrig. Freezer (Frost free)	180
Water Bed Heater	140
Refrig. Freezer (standard)	120
Lights	100
Range	100
Freezer (standard)	100
Clothes Dryer (4 Loads a week)	80
Furnace Fan	55
TV-(Color)	45
Dishwasher	30
TV-(B&W)	20
Electric Blanket	15
Microwave	15
Iron	10
Auto. Washer	10
Fry Pan	10
Radio	10
Coffeemaker	10
Toaster	5
Waste Disposal	1

* WHAT IS A KWH?
KWH stands for kilowatt hour. Electric power is measured in watts like gasoline is measured in gallons. All electric appliances and light bulbs are sized, or rated, in watts. Some time ago, someone took the Greek word "kilo" (meaning 1,000) and joined it to "watt". The term kilowatt is simply an easy way to say 1,000 watts. A kilowatt hour, then, is 1,000 watts of power used for one hour. One kilowatt hour will run a 100 watt light bulb for 10 hours.

** Based on a 1,500-square-foot home. Homes differ in usage according to size, climate, construction, insulation and family living habits.

Otherwise, a lot of energy can be wasted.

3. *Increase the temperature setting.* Thirty-nine degrees is usually adequate in the food compartment, and 5 degrees in the freezer will keep food in good condition for about four months.

4. *Keep the door shut.* If you have teenagers in your household, your refrigerator door is probably open as often as it is closed. Although this is a hard habit to break, keeping the doors to your refrigerator and freezing unit shut will represent a savings.

5. *Cool foods before refrigerating or freezing them.* It takes less energy to chill or freeze your foods if they are cool when you put them into the refrigerator or freezer.

▶ Other Household Appliances and Energy Users

1. *Electric ranges.* Oven cooking can be less expensive than cooking on the top of the range. Entire meals, including frozen vegetables, can be cooked at the same time in the oven. If possible, bake several items at once to conserve energy costs.

Most ovens will preheat in ten minutes, but preheating is necessary for only some foods. Meats and casseroles generally do not require a preheated oven; but if you are baking breads, cakes, or souffles, you will need to preheat the oven.

Thaw frozen foods before cooking when possible. A frozen roast, for example, may take an extra hour to cook. Be sure to turn the oven off as soon as you are through using it; accidentally leaving it on is costly.

Generally, electric fry pans, broilers, slow cookers, and other countertop appliances use less energy than stove tops or ovens.

2. *Dishwashers.* Wait until you have a full load before running your dishwasher. Some dishwashers now have "power saver" cycles—an option that can save you the heating expense of the normal "dry" setting. If your dishwasher doesn't have this feature, open the door after the last rinse and allow the dishes to air dry.

3. *Washers and dryers.* You can save further on hot-water usage by doing full loads instead of partial ones, or by making sure the machine is set properly if you do have a small load. Use cold water for washing and rinsing whenever possible.

4. *Home-entertainment equipment and small appliances.* Color and instant-on television sets draw considerable current—as much as five 100-watt bulbs, so turning them off when nobody's watching represents a noticeable savings over time. Instant-on TVs draw some current continuously even when the set is not in use. If you are planning to be away from your home for a day or

two, it makes sense to disconnect the cord of this type of set from the electrical outlet. Transistor radios use little energy, but stereo systems have a heavier draw; turn them off if nobody's listening.

If you're a coffee drinker, using a thermos instead of your automatic coffee maker to keep your coffee hot will save a few dollars per month. Other small appliances— mixers, toasters, electric toothbrushes, and so on—really don't use much energy.

5. *Turn the lights off when possible.* Turning lights off when they're not in use is one of the most visible energy-saving techniques you can employ. Even if the cost saving is minimal—and it may be—turning off lights can increase your energy-saving consciousness.

You can probably think of other ways to save on energy used by home appliances. Remember, though, that when reducing energy expenses means sacrificing some convenience you now enjoy, you may or may not find it economical to make the tradeoff. Remember the opportunity cost of your time!

▶ USING ENERGY LABELS WHEN YOU MAKE A CONSUMER APPLIANCE DECISION

Information on relative energy costs for various brands and models of major appliances is now available to consumers in the form of **energy labels** attached to new products. Information on these labels is based on tests of appliance energy use under controlled laboratory conditions designed to simulate home use. Energy-cost labeling of major appliances is mandated by the Energy Policy and Conservation Act of 1975, Title III, Part B, for these appliances:

air conditioners, dishwashers, clothes washers and dryers, televisions, refrigerators, freezers, water heaters, humidifiers and dehumidifiers, ovens and ranges, furnaces, and heating equipment other than furnaces. Exhibit L–3 shows a typical energy-cost label. Notice that the *estimated* yearly energy cost is $80 for this particular refrigerator. But to find out your *actual* energy cost, you need to know the cost per kilowatt hour of electricity in your area. For example, if electricity costs you 10 cents per kilowatt hour, your annual cost for operating that refrigerator would be $119 a year.

▶ REDUCING HOME HEATING AND COOLING COSTS

There are numerous ways to reduce home heating and cooling costs. One way to start is to arrange for a **home energy audit,** which is an attic-to-basement inspection of your house by an energy expert. Most public utility companies will do this free of charge. The audit will show you where effective improvements can be made and how much money they can save you, as well as how long it will take you to recover your investment. For more information on getting a home energy audit, contact your local utility company or your state energy office.

In the meantime, the following suggestions can save you money on heating and cooling costs.

1. *Stop air leaks.* Air leaks can account for as much as one-third of winter heating and summer cooling bills. Caulking and weatherstripping windows and doors can save up to 10 percent on your fuel bills. Also, closing the drapes at night will cut down on drafts. To save even more, consider installing storm windows and insulated draperies.

▶ Exhibit L–3 **Sample Energy Label**

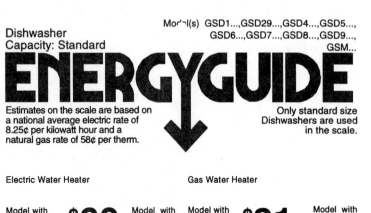

Dishwasher
Capacity: Standard

Model(s) GSD1...,GSD29...,GSD4...,GSD5...,
GSD6...,GSD7...,GSD8...,GSD9...,
GSM...

ENERGYGUIDE

Estimates on the scale are based on a national average electric rate of 8.25¢ per kilowatt hour and a natural gas rate of 58¢ per therm.

Only standard size Dishwashers are used in the scale.

Electric Water Heater

Model with lowest energy cost
$46

$60

▼ THIS MODEL

Model with highest energy cost
$82

▼ Estimated yearly energy cost

Gas Water Heater

Model with lowest energy cost
$25

$31

▼ THIS MODEL

Model with highest energy cost
$46

▼ Estimated yearly energy cost

Your cost will vary depending on your local energy rate and how you use the product. This energy cost is based on U.S. Government standard tests.

How much will this model cost you to run yearly?

with an electric water heater

Loads of dishes per week		2	4	6	8	12
Estimated yearly $ cost shown below						
Cost per kilowatt hour	4¢	$ 9	$19	$ 28	$ 38	$ 57
	6¢	$14	$28	$ 42	$ 57	$ 85
	8¢	$19	$38	$ 57	$ 76	$113
	10¢	$24	$47	$ 71	$ 94	$142
	12¢	$28	$57	$ 85	$113	$170
	14¢	$33	$66	$ 99	$132	$198

with a gas water heater

Loads of dishes per week		2	4	6	8	12
Estimated yearly $ cost shown below						
Cost per therm (100 cubic feet)	40¢	$ 9	$17	$26	$34	$51
	50¢	$ 9	$19	$28	$37	$56
	60¢	$10	$20	$30	$40	$61
	70¢	$11	$22	$33	$44	$65
	80¢	$12	$23	$35	$47	$70
	90¢	$12	$25	$37	$50	$75

Ask your salesperson or local utility for the energy rate (cost per kilowatt hour) in your area, and for estimated costs if you have a propane or oil water heater.

Important Removal of this label before consumer purchase is a violation of federal law (42 U.S.C. 6302)

Dwg. No. 165D4334P018

3. *Control the thermostat.* The Department of Energy suggests that consumers set their thermostats to 65 degrees in winter and 78 degrees in summer to conserve energy. This can be done manually or with an automatic setback device that currently costs as little as $40. Ceiling fans can circulate the air to make higher temperatures in summer seem cooler and to distribute the warm air from your furnace (which rises to the ceiling) in winter.

4. *Insulate furnace ducts.* This is one of the most cost-effective steps you can take in most colder areas. You simply wrap the heating ducts that pass through unheated areas with insulation (similar to the way a hot-water heater is wrapped). If this measure is a do-it-yourself project, it becomes particularly cost-effective.

▶ **Should You Heat Your Home with Wood?**

In 1972 only 160,000 wood-burning stoves were sold. Today wood-burning stoves are being sold at a rate of more than 1 million per year. Obviously, this is becoming a popular form of heating homes. But is home heating by wood less costly than heating by electricity, propane, natural gas, coal, or fuel oil? There's no easy answer, because how much you save depends on how costly your wood is. Depending on the area in which you live and the efficiency of your stove, you will require between five to ten cords of wood to heat your house during the winter. If you can obtain wood at little or no cost, then wood-burning represents a substantial savings. If, however, you have to pay $150 a cord for wood, you may not be so eager to trade in your gas heater for a wood-burning stove. If you decide to change to wood, however, there

2. *Check your insulation.* After air leaks have been stopped, you may be able to reduce your heating and cooling bills by as much as 20 to 30 percent by properly insulating your home. If you already have insula-tion, check the R-value of the insulating material to see if it is appropriate to your climate. R-values are insulation-efficiency ratings; the higher the R-value, the more effective the insulating capacity.

are certain dangers of which you should be aware.

► Dangers in Heating with Wood

1. *Be aware of the fire hazard.* In an effort to obtain a quick heat buildup, many wood-burning stove users start an excessively hot, fast-burning fire. The stove and its vent pipe become so hot that they can ignite adjacent combustible floors or walls. Additionally, the disposal of ashes may cause a fire if they are incompletely extinguished. Special care must be taken to insulate flue pipes that connect the stove to the chimney. If a flue pipe passes through a wall, it must be insulated, or a thimble must be put around it that keeps the hot pipe away from any combustible wall materials.

2. *To prevent your own or your neighbor's roof from catching fire, you must keep the stovepipe and chimney clean.* Constant use of a wood-burning stove will cause an accumulation of creosote that can start a chimney fire. You may have to hire professional chimney cleaners to remove these deposits.

3. *You must be especially aware of the danger of carbon-monoxide poisoning.* This problem is unknown to many users of wood-burning stoves and often underestimated by others. For example, an unvented room heater for a mobile home must never be installed in a sleeping room. Proper ventilation is extremely important for preventing carbon-monoxide poisoning.

4. *Wood-stove pollution.* Wood-burning stoves account for nearly half the emissions of substances known as polycyclic organic matter, a group that contains several cancer-causing compounds. They have also been responsible for extensive air pollution in certain areas of the country, such as Reno, Nevada; Juneau, Alaska; parts of Idaho and Oregon; and the ski-resort areas of Colorado. Some of the recently manufactured stoves contain features that help to reduce toxic emissions. If you already own a wood-burning stove, you may wish to write to the Environmental Protection Agency to find out what you can do to modify it to produce fewer toxic emissions. An EPA booklet has been published for consumers and can be obtained free from the Environmental Protection Agency, Office of Public Affairs, Washington, DC 20460.

► CONCLUSIONS

This Consumer Issue has presented some of the ways you can conserve energy in your home. As technology changes, numerous new energy-saving devices will become available. Additionally, as the relative prices of different energy sources change, you will be forced to make decisions about conserving different types of energy in different ways. Today, the print and broadcast media frequently present us with ideas about how to conserve energy. Listen, read, think, and then make your own energy-conserving decisions.

► SUMMARY

1. The first way to start saving on energy expenses is to become energy-conscious and to monitor your utility costs. Involving each family or household member in an energy budget plan can increase awareness of energy use.

2. There are a number of ways to reduce the energy costs of using home appliances. Next to home-heating equipment, the hot-water heater is the most expensive home appliance, in terms of energy use. Cutting back on hot-water usage can represent a substantial cost saving.

3. There are also a number of ways to reduce the costs of operating your refrigerator-freezer, kitchen range, and other household appliances.

4. Heating and cooling a home represents the single largest utility expenditure. Stopping air leaks, properly insulating your house and furnace ducts, and controlling the thermostat effectively can significantly reduce heating and cooling costs.

5. Burning wood to heat a dwelling may or may not be cost-effective, depending on where you live and the availability of wood. Every wood-burning-stove owner should be aware of certain risks posed by these stoves, as well as the toxic pollution they create.

► QUESTIONS FOR THOUGHT AND DISCUSSION

1. In what ways would you not want to cut energy costs in your home? What tradeoffs would you be unwilling to make between convenience and savings?

2. If you practiced all the energy-saving techniques mentioned in this Consumer Issue, by what percentage do you think your electric bill would be reduced per month?

3. Does saving on energy costs necessarily involve sacrifice?

4. Do you think low-income people who cut energy costs still spend a higher or lower percentage of their income on electric bills than do high-income people who don't monitor their energy usage?

► THINGS TO DO

1. List the ways you would be willing to reduce energy consumption in your home; note which ones would involve trading convenience for lower costs.

2. Check with your local utility company or companies to find out what free energy-saving services they provide to consumers and what other energy-saving programs they may know about.

3. Draw up an energy-saving checklist based on the tips given in this Consumer Issue. Interview three or four friends or relatives to see how their energy-saving practices (or lack of them) compare.

▶ SELECTED READINGS

▶ *The Do's and Don'ts of Home Insulation.* Available for 50¢ from the Consumer Information Center, Pueblo, CO 81009.

▶ *A Guide to Superior Energy Efficiency in Homes.* Available from Mineral Insulation Manufacturers Association, 1420 King St., Alexandria, VA 22314.

▶ *Heating with Wood.* Available free from the Consumer Information Center, Pueblo, CO 81009.

▶ Horowitz, S., and J. Parmelee. "How to Save Energy and a Bundle on Your Utility Bill." *Kiplinger's Personal Finance Magazine.* November 1991, p. 90.

▶ *How to Keep Warm and Cut Your Fuel Bill.* Available free from the Department of Energy, Technical Information Center, P.O. Box 62, Oak Ridge, TN 37830.

▶ *Money Saving Tips for Home Appliances.* Available for 50¢ from the Consumer Information Center, Pueblo, CO 81009.

▶ Nulty, P. "Finding a Payoff in Environmentalism," *Fortune,* October 21, 1991, pp. 79–80.

▶ *Tips for Energy Savers.* Available free from the Department of Energy, Technical Information Center, P.O. Box 62, Oak Ridge, TN 37830.

▶ *Wood Burning.* Available for 50¢ from HouseMaster of America, 421 W. Union Ave., Bound Brook, NJ 08805.

Getting There Is Half the Worry

PREVIEW

▶ How much do we spend on transportation?

▶ What benefits do consumers receive and what costs do they pay as the result of owning a car?

▶ How might consumers decide whether to buy a new or a used car?

▶ How can you be a smart car shopper?

▶ What choices are available to consumers who want to finance the purchase of a car?

▶ How can lemon laws help consumers?

▶ How can consumers benefit from using public transportation?

> One out of every six jobs in the United States is concerned with automobiles in some way.

The twentieth century in America has been called the Age of the Automobile. From a modest beginning at the turn of the century, when a few courageous souls drove around in Stutz Bearcats and Hupmobiles until Henry Ford developed low-cost mass-production techniques to put out an $870 "Tin Lizzie," right into the 1990s, when fully 90 percent of all American families own cars, the automobile has become a pervasive part of American life.

WE DEPEND ON CARS IN MANY WAYS

In the United States almost 150 million cars flood our roads and highways. In recent years, our annual car sales have amounted to about 12 million vehicles. The value of these sales totaled roughly $160 billion in 1991. Although the American automobile industry is shrinking, it is still huge. One out of every six jobs in the United States is concerned with automobiles in some way. Whether people are factory workers in Detroit or Tennessee, repair people in dealerships, advertising executives in New York City, or employed unloading ships from Japan, their jobs depend on our "love affair" with the automobile.

THE TREND TOWARD SAFER AUTOMOBILES

For decades, many have depicted the automobile as a four-wheeled rolling coffin, because so many Americans—currently about 50,000 per year—lose their lives in vehicle accidents. For younger Americans—those between 5 and 34 years of age—traffic accidents are the leading cause of death. In addition, over 2 million individuals are injured annually as a result of car accidents.

Many highway deaths could have been avoided had the drivers been more careful. But, according to some observers, many others could have been avoided if additional safety features were required on automobiles. In 1958 the Ford Motor Company tried to sell additional safety features to the American car-buying public, but sales declined and Ford lost money. Finally, after the exposé by Ralph Nader in his book *Unsafe at Any Speed,* Congress passed the National Traffic and Motor Vehicle Safety Act of 1966, the basis of most of the current safety requirements on automobiles.

Safety Requirements

Some of the requirements imposed on car manufacturers by the National Highway Traffic Safety Administration have been

1. Dual braking systems.
2. Nonprotruding interior appliances.
3. Over-the-shoulder safety belts in the front seat.
4. Head restraints on all front seats.
5. Seat-belt warning systems and ignition interlocks.
6. Collapsible, impact-absorbing arm rests.
7. Impact-absorbing instrument panels.

In 1984 the National Highway Traffic Safety Administration took another major step toward increasing auto safety. Under its regulation of that year, all car manufacturers were required to include passive-restraint safety features—such as air bags or automatic safety belts—in their new cars, beginning with the 1987 models. This rule has been implemented gradually, applying only to

10 percent of the 1987 models, 25 percent of 1988 models, 40 percent of 1989 models, and 100 percent of 1990 models.

Costs and Benefits of Safety Devices

Automobile safety devices raise the cost of automobiles, and you, the consumer pay for the safety directly out of your pocket. Air bags are particularly costly, adding $600 or more to the price of your new car.

On the benefits side, however, safety features such as seat belts are responsible for reduced injuries and fatalities from auto accidents. A recent University of Chicago study indicates, for example, that the use of seat belts reduces the severity of injuries by 60.1 percent—even more significantly than previously thought. Because air bags are judged to be an even safer precaution against injury, many consumers are willing to pay the higher price for this safety. This consumer demand is being met by manufacturers, who are increasingly offering air bags as an alternative to automatic safety belts in passenger vehicles.

Safety and Sobriety

Drunk drivers are responsible for slightly more than half of all traffic fatalities each year, according to the National Highway Traffic Safety Administration. And for every death, 20 more people are injured in alcohol-related car accidents. Shocking as these figures are, they are lower than they have been in the past. In 1982, for example, 57 percent of traffic accidents resulting in deaths were alcohol related; by 1989 this figure had dropped to 51 percent.

Several factors have been responsible for this decline in drunk-driving fatalities. Among them are the stiffer penalties now being imposed on drunk drivers in nearly all states, as well as the fact that more of the population— either by law or by choice—now wear seat belts or have some kind of passive-restraint system protecting them during accidents. There has also been a growing perception on the part of the American public of the risks involved in driving while intoxicated—thanks largely to the efforts of a single organization, Mothers Against Drunk Drivers (MADD), which has been campaigning for more stringent laws since 1980. Students Against Drunk Drivers (SADD) has joined this campaign in recent years.

Another reason for the decline in deaths related to intoxication is that almost all states have passed laws mandating 21 as the minimum age for purchasing alcoholic beverages. Studies have shown a direct relationship between the minimum drinking age and the number of traffic fatalities in the 18-to-21-year-old age group. Nationwide, fatal traffic accidents have been reduced by an estimated 15 percent in this age group as a result of the higher drinking age required under state laws.

THE SOCIAL COSTS OF DRIVING

When you get into your car and fire it up, you incur, in addition to the private costs discussed below, the **social costs** of driving. You are all aware of them, particularly if you live in Los Angeles, New York, or Washington, D.C. One of the biggest social costs of driving has been air pollution. That engine does not just pull your car around. It also emits by-products that, when added together, do little good for your lungs or mine. This is, of course, why the federal government as well as individual states regulate the pollution output of automobile engines. And this is also why cars with pollution-abatement

> One of the biggest social costs of driving has been air pollution.

Social costs
The costs that society bears for an action. For example, the social costs of driving a car include any pollution or congestion caused by that automobile.

equipment do not run as efficiently as cars did 15 years ago. It has not been easy to eliminate the harmful by-products of internal combustion.

Thus, you, the individual driver, are forced to take account of the social cost you impose on the rest of society in the form of pollution. When you have no alternative but to purchase automobile engines that have pollution-abatement equipment, you pay directly in the form of a higher purchase price and indirectly in the form of reduced power and higher gas consumption.

Private automobile transportation has other social costs. One of them is congestion. Congestion on bridges, highways, and in inner cities is a problem of social concern, even though private individuals, at least until now, have not been forced to pay the full price of driving their cars. That price includes making other people late for work or making them spend more time in their own cars. In other words, simply by driving onto a crowded bridge, you slow down everybody else somewhat. When you add up the value of everybody else's time, you see that you impose a pretty high cost. And the same is true of every other person on that bridge.

THE PRIVATE COSTS OF DRIVING

Private costs
The costs that are incurred by an individual and no one else. The private costs of driving a car, for example, include depreciation, gas, insurance, and so on.

The cost of driving a car involves more than making a monthly payment, although that is part of it. The **private costs** of driving include such things as wear and tear, repairs, gas and oil, insurance, and taxes, in addition to the price of the car and interest payments, if the car is financed. Exhibit 14–1 shows the brands of automobiles that had the lowest estimated costs in 1991. It is difficult to say exactly what the per-mile cost of owning and operating a car would be for any individual because there is such a wide range of insurance costs and driving styles. Your driving costs probably fall somewhere between 25 cents and 40 cents per mile.

The Repair Industry

Some consumer economists believe that preventive maintenance avoids large repair bills. This is true, but you must take account of the maintenance costs themselves. In the long run, it may be cheaper not to keep your car in perfect condition but, rather, to let some things (other than brakes, tires, and safety-related parts) wear out and replace them only when they do or to trade in your car every few years. Some state governments buy fleets of cars that they do not service at all for a year and then trade in. This seems to be cheaper than trying to maintain the cars; as the prices of repair services rise, this prac-

▶ Exhibit 14–1 **Lowest-Cost Automobiles for 5 Years and 70,000 Miles**

Money magazine reported the following car models as being the least expensive to own and operate in 1991. Their figures include estimates for depreciation, insurance, maintenance, financing, gasoline, and oil.

PRICE RANGE	LEAST EXPENSIVE CAR
Under $10,000	Honda Civic two-door hatchback
$10,000 to $15,000	Honda Civic DX four-door sedan
$15,000 to $20,000	Geo Prizm LSI four-door sedan
$20,000 to $30,000	Volvo 240 four-door sedan
Over $30,000	Mercedes-Benz 190 E 2.6 four-door sedan

Source: Jerry Edgerton, *Money*, November 1991, p. 174.

tice will become still cheaper by comparison. Thus, you have two choices: You can buy a car that you expect to keep for only a short period of time, or you can buy a car that has a reputation for very low service requirements. Each year, the April issue of *Consumer Reports* recounts its readers' experiences with the repair needs of different makes and years of cars. This is an important aid when you try to assess the annual cost of operating an automobile.

Individuals who purchase automobiles often are unaware of the necessity of regular servicing. Furthermore, many automobile drivers could, if they wanted to, save considerable dollars by learning a few elementary maintenance techniques. Numerous adult education classes in auto mechanics are available in high schools, community colleges, and elsewhere throughout the country. Anybody seriously concerned with reducing repair costs would be advised to take one of these classes.

The Cost of Depreciation

With the possible exception of paying for insurance, which will be discussed in Chapter 20, depreciation is the greatest cost of owning an automobile. Cars lose value as they grow older even if they are driven only a few miles each year and have not worn out. They depreciate because dealers and people are willing to pay less money for an older car than for a newer model. Remember, the market value of any product is measured in terms of what someone else is willing to pay for it. Although different models of cars depreciate at different rates (see Exhibit 14–2), a good rule of thumb is that a car will lose about one-fifth of its value each year you own it. Suppose you spend $20,000 on a new car. When it is one year old it will probably be worth about $16,000, or one-fifth less than its purchase price. Its value will fall by roughly another fifth, or $3,200, to $12,800 in the second year you own the car. By the end of the third year its value will be about $2,560 less, or $10,240. The longer you own a car the less it will depreciate in each year. However, there is another factor to consider. As automobiles become older they also require more maintenance. A five-year-old car may not depreciate much in a year, but it will probably need more repairs than a new automobile.

Getting Good Repairs

Every car owner faces the problem of having his or her car repaired. Finding a good repair shop or an honest mechanic may be a difficult job. Car repairs can also be very expensive—as is evidenced by the fact that Americans pay

▶ Exhibit 14–2   **Resale Values of Different Models of Automobiles**

MODEL	1988 PRICE	1990 VALUE	PERCENT OF PURCHASE PRICE RETAINED
Honda Accord DX Sedan	$10,535	$ 8,925	84.7%
Toyota Corolla Deluxe	8,989	7,275	81.8
Oldsmobile Cutlass Ciera	10,656	8,275	77.7
Mercedes-Benz 300E	42,680	30,250	70.9
Chevrolet Blazer	16,500	11,550	70.0
Cadillac Sedan DeVille	23,049	15,975	69.3
Plymouth Voyager LE	18,500	11,950	64.6
Hyundai Excel GLS	7,750	4,600	59.4

approximately $50 million a year for these services. For tips on how to find reliable mechanics and car-repair services, see Consumer Issue E.

DECIDING WHEN TO BUY

At what point does it make sense to stop spending money on repairs for your old car and purchase a new, or different, one? An older model, if it has been well serviced and maintained over the years, can sometimes go 100,000 miles before requiring a new transmission or other major repairs. If you have an older car and if your mechanic thinks it is in relatively good condition, don't panic at just one repair bill. Remember, it costs less to own and operate an older vehicle than it does a new one *if* that vehicle has been well maintained.

The decision to repair or replace ultimately depends on what your repairs are costing in terms of both money and inconvenience and on what your mechanic predicts about future repairs. Leil Lowland, in *Shopping the Insider's Way,* has devised a formula you may wish to use in making repair-or-replace decisions. Lowland suggests you divide the book value (BV) of the car into the repair estimates (RE) to obtain the replacement percentage (RP). For example, a $500 repair estimate on an $2500 car works out to 20 percent. If the RP is 25 percent or less, Lowland says go ahead with the repairs; if the RP is 40 percent or more, replace the automobile.

SHOULD YOU BUY A NEW OR USED CAR?

When most of us go out to purchase transportation, we are tempted to buy something new. There are certainly good reasons for buying a new car instead of a used one. A new car has never been owned by someone else; therefore, you have to worry only about how you will treat it during its first few years, not about how it was treated beforehand. A new car may be safer, it may run more smoothly, it may be more stylish—although today these various aspects are not as subject to annual changes as they were in the past.

You may choose a new car simply because you like to have new things. The depreciation you learned about in the previous section, however, will lower a new car's value $1,000 or more the moment you drive it out of the dealer's parking lot. Buying a used car allows you to avoid the rapid depreciation in the car's value that takes place in its first years of ownership.

On the other hand, in some cases, when you buy a new car, you get the benefit of an extremely desirable warranty. Some car manufacturers offer warranties on almost everything for a specified amount of mileage or period of time: 12,000 miles or twelve months to 70,000 miles, or seven years. Some warranties have certain exclusions to watch for, and there may be some limitations based on dealer participation in the manufacturer's program. You can find out what the specific warranty coverage is by discussing it with your dealer.

LEASING VERSUS BUYING

Many individuals no longer buy new cars. Rather, they lease one from a new-car dealer for usually a four-year period. Leasing automobiles became popular during the 1980s because of the convenience it offers to consumers. No down

> ▶ Exhibit 14–3   **Leasing versus Buying: A Cost Comparison**

The car used in this example is a 1992 Cadillac Sedan DeVille with a suggested retail price—excluding dealer preparation to make the car ready for delivery, destination charge, taxes, and registration fees—of $28,950.

BUY THE CAR	LEASE THE CAR
Terms: 20% down; balance financed at 8.9% for five years.	*Terms:* 5-year (60-month lease).
Down payment: $5,790.	*Up-front payment:* $760; includes the first month's payment and a refundable deposit of $380.
Monthly payment: $480.	*Monthly payment:* $380.
Total cost: $34,590.	*Total payments:* $22,800.
After 5 years: You own the car.	*After 5 years:* You have an option to buy the car at the end of the lease for $13,896. If you do, you will have spent
Bottom line: Your total cost, $34,590, is less than the $35,612 total for leasing and then buying. But monthly payments would be higher, and the down payment might be hard to come up with. You should also consider the number of miles you are likely to drive. The lease will cost you more if you drive more than a total of 75,000 miles in the five years.	$36,696 in total. But you could have invested the $5,030 difference between the down payment to buy and the $760 up-front payment to lease. In a 5-year deposit at 5% compounded annually, that $5,030 would have earned $1,084 in interest. Subtracting that from the $36,696 total, your leasing cost is $35,612 (although tax considerations will raise that amount).

payment is required (although a refundable security deposit—normally the equivalent of one month's payment—is generally requested), and lease payments are usually smaller than loan payments would be on a financed car. Additionally, you don't have to bargain with a dealer over price, and you don't have to worry about reselling the car eventually.

Offsetting these benefits of leasing is one major disadvantage: At the end of the lease period, you don't have a car. Many leases will allow you to purchase the car at the end of the lease term for its "residual value," a price usually preset at the time the lease is initiated, but this price may be more than you feel a four-year-old car is worth. Some studies indicate, however, that even if you pay this higher price to purchase the car after the lease has expired, you may come out about the same financially as you would had you financed a car over the same period. Exhibit 14–3 shows the results of one such study.

Whether you should lease or buy will depend largely on your individual situation and anticipated use of the car. Most leases, for example, limit the mileage included in the lease price to between 12,000 and 15,000 miles a year. If you plan to drive more than 15,000 miles per year, the cost of your lease will increase—because at the end of the lease term you will be required to pay for that excess mileage (currently between 6 and 12 cents per mile). If you think you will want to upgrade to a new car before the lease term expires, this will cost more also—a penalty will be charged for breaking the current lease and re-leasing another car. Another factor to consider is that, at the end of the lease term, you will be charged for any "excess" wear and tear on the leased car. Finally, you should bear in mind that credit requirements for leasing a car are as strict as, and in some cases stricter than, they may be for buying.

THE GLOBAL CONSUMER

It Isn't Easy to Buy American

Although many people would like to buy American-made cars it is very difficult to determine what an American car is. In recent years foreign-owned firms like Toyota, Honda, Mazda, and Nissan have built factories to assemble automobiles in the United States. Some of these cars now include as much as 60 percent American-manufactured parts. At the same time, many cars that have American nameplates are entirely or partially produced in other countries. In 1991, for example, the Ford Crown Victoria was produced in Canada, the Pontiac LeMans was made in Korea, and the Dodge Stealth was imported from Japan. On a showroom floor these cars may have looked American, but they weren't.

Inroads by foreign manufacturers can be seen in sales figures. In March of 1991, 730,000 cars were sold in the United States. Of this number, 543,000 (74 percent) were assembled in the United States and 187,000 were imported. Foreign-owned firms, however, accounted for 15 percent of the domestic production in 1991. The market share of U.S.–owned firms fell to just 63 percent of total sales. Even cars that were assembled in the United States by American firms often contained 40 percent or more of foreign-made parts. Do you feel buying an American car is a wise choice for our economy? How could you make sure you were buying an American car if you wanted to?

IF YOU DECIDE TO BUY A NEW CAR

If you opt to buy a new car, you will have to decide what kind of car you want, what options to include, and what price you want to pay. Since the purchase of a new car often represents a substantial expenditure, you will want to gather sufficient information before you actually buy.

The First Step—Getting Information

You can start your market research by asking relatives and friends about their experiences with different cars. Additionally, you can glance through such auto-enthusiast periodicals as *Car and Driver* and *Road and Track*. Finally, you'd do well to check the April issues of *Consumer Reports* that contain test results on various new cars.

You will be better prepared to bargain if you have some idea what the dealer has paid for a certain car and for various options. You can learn this information from auto guides sold at bookstores and newsstands, such as the December issue of *Kiplinger's Personal Finance*, *Edmund's New Car Prices*, and Car/Puter's *Autofacts*. Alternatively, you could write Consumer Reports Auto Price Services or write or call Car/Puter or Nationwide Auto Brokers and request a computer printout of list prices and options for hundreds of models and makes of cars. Each service charges a $10-to-$20 fee for its services.

> Nationwide Auto Brokers, Inc.
> 17517 West Ten Mile Rd.
> Southfield, MI 48075
> (800) 521-7257 (toll free)
> (313) 559-6661 (Michigan only)

Car/Puter International, Inc.
1500 Cordova Rd., Suite 309
Ft. Lauderdale, FL 33316
(800) 221-4001 (toll free)
(305) 462-8905 (Florida only)

Consumer Reports Auto Price Services
P.O. Box 570
Lathrup Village, MI 48076
(written inquiries only)

Once you have adequate information about the list price of a new car you are interested in purchasing, you will be able to evaluate the dealer's markup—the difference between what the dealer pays for a car and what is shown on the sticker pasted to the car window—and determine the bargaining margin. Dealer markups vary widely, depending on the size of the car and whether it is domestic or imported. Exhibit 14–4 lists the average markup for various categories of vehicles.

Shopping by Phone

Although many dealers refuse to give out prices over the telephone and others will give you only the sticker price, there are some, especially foreign-car dealers, who will tell you exactly what your final cost will be. In fact, if you are assertive enough over the telephone, sometimes you can negotiate a deal without ever visiting the showroom. Consider the following tactic. Call the dealer and ask to speak to a salesperson. Immediately indicate that you were just disappointed by a competing dealer who had "low-balled" you. That is, you had been quoted one price, and then the salesperson upped that figure when you were just about to close the deal. Telling the salesperson this over the phone reveals that you have shopped around, are serious, and won't accept a higher-than-stated price. When the salesperson on the phone suggests a particular figure for the car you want with the options you want, ask him or her if that is the best possible offer. In many cases, the salesperson will be forced to be honest with you and probably will offer you a lower price just to get you into the showroom.

What Type of Car to Buy?

Deciding what new car to buy depends at least in part on how much money you want to spend. You should figure out the exact yearly out-of-pocket costs you will incur for different price ranges and then decide what you are willing to pay. Remember, many times when you go up the ladder of car prices, you are not buying any more safety or speed but only styling, prestige, and so on. Be aware of the price you are paying for these qualities.

You also should be aware of the various operating costs of the new cars you are considering. Compacts are cheaper to run than full-sized cars, but they hold fewer people comfortably and less baggage, and generally they give you less protection in a big crash.

Options

The options you choose also should depend on your tastes relative to your income. Some options are wise to take, even if you don't want them. It would be ridiculous to try to get a stick shift on a Cadillac because, when you want to sell the car, few people would want to buy it. You also should consider

▶ **Exhibit 14–4** Dealer's Markup for Various Categories of Vehicles

You can estimate the dealer's cost on a given vehicle by multiplying the sticker price by one of the percentages below. The result will be the dealer's likely profit margin—and your margin for bargaining. For example, the dealer's profit on a domestic compact with a sticker price of $10,000 would be approximately 13 percent, or $1,300.

Mini-compacts	6 to 9 percent
Subcompacts	10 percent
Subcompacts, imported	9 percent
Compacts	13 percent
Compacts, imported	10 percent
Intermediates	17 percent
Full-size	21 percent
Luxury full-size	21 percent
Luxury imports	16 percent
Pickups and vans	20 percent
Pickups, imported	13 percent

Source: *Sylvia Porter's Personal Finance*, October 1988, p. 33; adapted from James Ross, *How to Buy a Car* (New York: St. Martin's Press, 1988).

things like power steering and power brakes on larger cars because without these features large cars are very hard to sell (and very hard to drive and park while you own them).

Tires are an important feature on any car and something on which you won't want to compromise. Radial tires seem to offer the most protection, the safest handling, and sometimes the longest life. Today, many new cars come with radials; if the car of your choice comes without them, you should consider immediately trading in the standard tires for radials.

Another accessory you definitely should consider is a rear-window defogger. Most cars now have them as standard equipment, but some do not. If you live in a cold climate, the extra $30 to $60 is well spent; on cold mornings, a defogger improves rear-window visibility. Of course, the assumption is that you are willing to pay for safety; only you can decide whether you are.

Air conditioning may seem like a luxury to many people, but it is very difficult to resell a car in Sun Belt states without it. Therefore, in those states where it is hot much of the year, air conditioning should be considered a necessity.

Exhibit 14–5 is a chart you can complete to compare the actual cost of four different types of cars you may want to buy with different options.

▶ Exhibit 14–5   **Price Comparison Chart**

LIST PRICE	CAR #1	CAR #2	CAR #3	CAR #4
OPTIONS				
Power steering and brakes	_____	_____	_____	_____
Automatic transmission	_____	_____	_____	_____
Nonstandard engine	_____	_____	_____	_____
Air conditioning	_____	_____	_____	_____
Rear-window defogger	_____	_____	_____	_____
Special radio/tape deck	_____	_____	_____	_____
Limited slip differential	_____	_____	_____	_____
White-wall tires	_____	_____	_____	_____
Tinted glass	_____	_____	_____	_____
Vinyl roof	_____	_____	_____	_____
Tires—radial, oversized, or snow	_____	_____	_____	_____
Speed control	_____	_____	_____	_____
Power door locks	_____	_____	_____	_____
Power windows	_____	_____	_____	_____
Remote side-view mirrors	_____	_____	_____	_____
Compact disc player	_____	_____	_____	_____
Other	_____	_____	_____	_____
TOTAL COST	_____	_____	_____	_____
Subtract trade-in or down payment	_____	_____	_____	_____
TOTAL AMOUNT TO BE PAID TO DEALER	_____	_____	_____	_____

Dealer Add-ons

In addition to factory options, dealers often try to sell consumers special add-ons that most often increase the dealer's profit rather than the value of the car. Almost all new cars sold in the United States, for example, have been built and treated to resist rust. Many new cars have "rust-through" warranties that last for as many as 100,000 miles. Still, some dealers try to convince consumers to spend an extra $300 to $500 to have their cars "rust-proofed." Dealers are also likely to offer special waxes or leather treatments. They often encourage consumers to buy extended protection plans. In general, dealers benefit much more from these add-ons than consumers.

GETTING THE BEST DEAL ON A NEW CAR

Once you have obtained enough information to know what kind of car you are looking for and in what price range, your next step is to locate that car at the best price. Depending both on the dealer you buy from and on your bargaining skills, you can pay more or less for the same car with the same accessories.

Using a Buying Service

If you want to avoid all the haggling and frustrations associated with bargaining for a new car, you may wish to use a *buying service,* which is simply an intermediary that offers the car at a price of $50 to a few hundred dollars above factory cost, depending on the basic price and the size of the car. You buy the car from a regular dealer but at a guaranteed price. Nationwide Auto Brokers and Car/Puter offer buying services in addition to their computerized price lists. Another buying service is Amway Auto Network, of Ada, Michigan, which you can call toll free at (800) 992-6929. Expect to pay a fee ranging from $34 to $119 to use these services. Many American Automobile Association (AAA) affiliates offer buying services also, and you can find information regarding these by calling your local AAA. Other brokers may be listed in the Yellow Pages of your telephone directory under "Auto Brokers" or "Automotive Services." Warranties, rebates, and service are the same through these brokers as through your local dealer.

Those who do not favor car-buying services contend that, since the buyer does not usually select the dealer, the service after the sale may be less dependable, more inconvenient, and more costly than had the car buyer chosen the dealer. Since service is a major concern of a new-car owner, the reputation and location of the dealer are important factors in making a buying decision.

The Dealer

In shopping around for a dealer, you will want to keep in mind the following things.

1. Location. Where to buy depends on a number of factors, the most important being how far the dealer is from your job or home. After all, you must take the car in for servicing, and a new car, no matter how good it is, is going to have at least a few problems in the beginning. If you value time and convenience highly and if you can conveniently leave your car at the dealer's facility and walk to work or walk back home, you will be ahead of the game.

2. Dealer service facilities and personnel. To find out about the dealer's service facilities and personnel, ask specific questions about them, such as: What does the dealer do to make service easier for customers? What are the size and reputation of the service department? How long is service work guaranteed—no days, 30 days, or 90 days? How much electronic diagnostic equipment does the shop have? Are there provisions for replacement transportation while your car is in for service? When is the service department open? All these questions are important and should not be treated lightly because, as we all know, cars, whether they be new or used, require servicing.

3. Dealer reputation. Talk to customers who have bought from the dealer and have used the dealer's service department to find out how satisfied they are. Or better yet, take your present car in for servicing and see how satisfied you are with the service department. (This is important for both new and used-car purchases).

4. The deal offered. Obviously, the deal offered is the most important consideration. You may be willing to pay a *slightly* higher price at a specific dealer you like very much and who has a good reputation for service. Shopping around is, of course, a necessary step for most people when they buy a car.

TRADING IN YOUR OLD CAR

When you trade in your old car, you can be fairly certain you will get no more than the standard trade-in price listed by the National Automobile Dealers Association in its *Official Used Car Guide,* or "blue book." It might be a good idea for you to look up this information yourself. Most banks and many libraries have a copy you may use.

Here is an area where private sellers are just as guilty of irresponsibility as dealers. We've all heard about people trying to trade in lots of problems. Usually, they assure the dealer that the old clunker is running perfectly.

It is generally a good idea to bargain on your trade-in *after* you have completed the new-car sale with the dealer. Then you won't have to deal with the "high-ball" gimmick. The salesperson will quote you a price for your used car as a trade-in that exceeds by $200, $300, or even $500 its blue-book value. Presumably, you might be deluded into thinking that you are getting a bargain; however, the additional price you receive for your trade-in will merely be included somewhere else in the price of the new car. You can assume that you will get the wholesale price of the car as a trade-in if it is in good condition. You can also attempt to sell the used car yourself, but remember that you must incur the time and hassle costs of doing so (for example, changing the title, taking care of sales taxes, and so on).

IF YOU BUY A USED CAR

If you decide to buy a used car, you must think about several other things. Because you do not know how any given car was treated by its previous owner, you must be especially careful about its condition. One way to make certain that nothing major will go wrong is to have an independent mechanic check out the car before you commit yourself to buying it. You may be charged for this, just as you will be charged by a building inspector who checks out a house you want to buy. You are buying information from the mechanic, information that may save you hundreds of dollars in the future. The mechanic may point out that the transmission is about to go, that the gaskets leak, and so on. You may wish to take the car to an electronic diagnostic center that will charge from $15 to $50 to analyze electronically all major aspects of the car you intend to buy. Generally, these centers do not do repair work. Their technicians usually can indicate, however, what it will cost to have the used car repaired if anything shows up in their diagnosis.

Another way of insuring yourself against major repair expenses is by working with used-car dealers who have written warranties on their products. Sometimes you have to pay for such a warranty, and sometimes its price is merely included in the price of the used car. You are buying a type of insurance that costs you a little in the beginning but reduces the probability that you will pay out a lot in the future. Very rarely, a used car may still be covered by the manufacturer's one-year, 12,000-mile or two-year, 24,000-mile warranty. Because such a used car is worth more to you than those without warranties, you will be willing to pay more.

One thing you can check out yourself is whether a used car has been in a major accident. Look for mismatched colors in the paint and for ripples, bumps, and grainy surfaces on the body work. These will indicate extensive repainting and, therefore, extensive repairs. Such discoveries may not dissuade you from wanting to buy the car, but they should persuade you to have some shop testing done by an independent mechanic.

There are numerous ways to examine a prospective used-car purchase. The section on buying a used car in any annual *Consumer Reports Buying Guide* gives you more than a dozen on-the-lot tests and eight to ten driving tests you can do yourself. It also tells you approximately what each repair job will cost if you notice something wrong. Because nothing can duplicate a shop test by a good mechanic, however, this step is highly recommended unless you have an extremely good warranty with the deal. You also might be able to get a helpful brochure from your local consumer-affairs office. If you are purchasing a used car from a dealer, ask the dealer if he or she will give you the name and address of the car's previous owner. Then query this person on possible problems, defects, or advantages of the car.

> Do not automatically accept the credit that the dealer offers you when you decide to buy a car. Shop around for credit just as you shop around for anything else.

FINANCING THAT PURCHASE

A new or used car is usually such a major purchase that at least part of it has to be financed by credit. Do not automatically accept the credit that the dealer offers you when you decide to buy a car. Shop around for credit just as you shop around for anything else. Fortunately for you, the Truth-in-Lending Act of 1968 requires every lender to disclose the total finance charge and actual annual interest rate to be paid. Thus, the credit offered you by the dealer can be compared with the credit offered you by competing sources, such as banking institutions and finance companies. Remember, if you default on your car payment, your car may be repossessed. This is a real possibility: In some states, finance companies can take your car away from you without a judicial hearing. Do not buy a car that is more expensive than you know you can afford.

Where to Borrow for a Car

There are numerous sources for automobile loans: life insurance policies, savings and loan or commercial banks, credit unions, auto insurance companies, and auto dealers themselves.

Life insurance loans are possible if you have a whole life policy (see Chapter 21) that has been in effect for at least a few years. It will have accumulated cash value, and you can borrow up to that amount from the company. The maximum annual percentage rate for a life insurance loan is often limited to 8 percent by law. The only problem with taking out such a loan is that it reduces the amount of life insurance you have in effect.

A passbook loan is available if you have a savings account. The bank or savings and loan association may lend as much as 90 percent of the amount on deposit. The bank will freeze enough to cover the unpaid balance on a loan, but the entire account will continue to earn interest.

Generally, credit unions offer the most beneficial rates on automobile loans; so if you are a member of one or can become a member without too much trouble, find out what you will be charged there.

Banks are the second most commonly used source of automobile financing, after the auto dealers themselves. What your local banker will charge you depends on your credit rating, the amount of down payment or trade-in value on the car you are buying, and the general state of the economy.

Auto insurance companies sometimes issue car loans through a bank or through their own subsidiaries. To find out if your auto insurance company does this, call your agent.

You will find that if you go to a small-loan company, you will pay the highest annual percentage fee for an auto loan.

What Length of Loan to Take Out

Most consumer experts recommend that automobile loans be taken out for the shortest period possible. They point out that you end up paying a relatively high interest charge when you take out a three- or four-year car loan. Additionally, you end up having a hefty balance to pay if you are ready to trade in your car before the end of four years.

Does that mean that you should not take out a four-year auto loan? No, not necessarily. You really are asking a question about how much you should be in debt; the fact that it concerns an automobile is irrelevant. If you think you would be uncomfortable having a debt outstanding for four years, then that may be a reason to opt for a shorter time period. If you do so, however, you must use more of your discretionary funds to pay off the automobile loan's monthly payment, and you will, therefore, have less to spend on other items during that period. The fact that it costs you in additional charges to keep an auto loan outstanding longer should not be surprising. You are asking to use someone else's money for a longer period. As with all borrowing decisions, you must balance the benefits of having more cash available for other purchases against the increased cost for borrowing more or for borrowing for a longer period of time. Exhibit 14–6 shows what it costs in finance charges per $1,000 of a car loan.

KNOW YOUR LEMON LAWS

All states have now passed lemon laws that pertain to new-car sales and service. In effect, if your new car has a serious problem that can't be fixed in a

Annual Percentage Interest	ONE YEAR		TWO YEARS		THREE YEARS		FOUR YEARS	
	Monthly Payment	Total Finance Charge	Monthly Payment	Total Finance Charge	Monthly Payment	Total Finance Charge	Monthly Payment	Total Finance Charge
5	$86	$27	$44	$ 53	$30	$ 79	$23	$105
6	86	33	44	64	30	95	23	128
7	87	38	45	75	31	112	24	150
8	87	44	45	85	31	128	24	172
9	87	49	46	96	32	144	25	194
10	88	55	46	107	32	161	25	217
11	88	61	47	118	33	178	26	240
12	89	66	47	130	33	196	26	264
13	89	72	48	141	34	213	27	288
14	90	78	48	152	34	231	27	312

Note: Figures have been rounded to nearest dollar.

reasonable time, either you get your money back or you get a new car. Most states say you've purchased a lemon if, within its first year or 12,000 miles, your car has a serious defect that an authorized facility hasn't been able to repair in four attempts or if the car has been out of service for 30 days. Generally, defects must be covered by the manufacturer's warranty and must substantially reduce the use, safety, or value of your vehicle.

If you are a new-car owner, you may want to contact the Center for Auto Safety (2001 S St., N.W., Suite 410, Washington, DC 20009) for a free information sheet that summarizes all lemon laws, which vary from state to state; send a self-addressed, stamped envelope along with your request for the lemon-law chart. You can also call your state's attorney general's office for information on your state's lemon law and how to use it if you have purchased a lemon. The Consumer Close-Up describes actions taken by one consumer to receive fair treatment when he bought a car that was a lemon.

When consumers negotiate to buy new automobiles they know that if the car they buy is defective, state lemon laws will force dealers to repair or replace the car, or refund their money. Some dealers argue that lemon laws make cars more expensive and prevent some people with lower incomes from purchasing a vehicle of their own. Do you think this is a valid argument?

Lemon Laws and "Emotional Distress"

In October of 1989, Anthony Kwan of San Francisco purchased his "dream car," a brand-new Mercedes-Benz 300E for more than $45,000. The car came with a 48-month or 50,000-mile warranty. Contrary to Kwan's expectation of years of trouble-free driving, the car started to malfunction within several weeks of its delivery. In the first year Kwan reported problems that included engine oil and water leaks, rough running, malfunctions in the engine warning lights, and defects in the car's cooling and heating systems.

He took the car to the dealer ten times, where it was left for a total of 30 days for repairs.

Kwan finally wrote to Mercedes-Benz of North America demanding that his money be refunded. The firm refused. Kwan then filed suit against Mercedes-Benz under California's lemon law, charging the firm with violating both the written warranty and implied warranties of merchantability and fitness. He sought damages based on the cost of the car, loss of its use, wages he lost when he was unable to drive to work, and the cost of the attor-

ney he hired to sue the firm. Kwan also sued for the cost of the rental car he used while the case was in trial.

Kwan's case was settled in August of 1992 when a jury awarded him $186,278 in damages. Included in that amount was $10,000 that was designated to compensate Kwan for his "emotional distress, aggravation, and inconvenience."

Source: "Mercedes Ordered to Pay $186,278 for Lemon," *Automotive News,* August 10, 1992, p. 17.

Arbitration Programs

Most states' lemon laws require an aggrieved new-car owner to notify the dealer or manufacturer of the problem and provide the opportunity to solve it. If the problem remains, the owner must then submit complaints to the program specified in the manufacturer's warranty before taking the case to court. Your owner's manual will tell you which arbitration program applies to your car.

Most major car companies use their own arbitration panels. Ford and Chrysler, for example, have the Ford Consumer Appeals Board and the Chrysler Customer Arbitration Board, respectively, to which lemon-law disputes are submitted. Some companies, however, such as General Motors, subscribe to independent arbitration services, such as those provided by the Better Business Bureau. These arbitration services are free to consumers, and lawyers are not involved. You simply explain your problem to the arbitration panel or board, in person or in writing, and submit any evidence you feel is necessary to back up your claim—such as an independent mechanic's evaluation of your car's problem. The board will rule within 60 days on whether your car is a lemon and whether it will be replaced, the price refunded, or otherwise. Often, disputes are settled before they get to the arbitration stage. General Motors, for example, settles approximately 90 percent of disputes prior to arbitration.

Although decisions reached by these groups are usually binding on manufacturers, they usually are not on car owners, who are free to sue in court if they are not satisfied with the results of arbitration. Even if arbitration does not result in a consumer receiving a new car or a refund of the purchase price it often results in complaints being resolved. Automobile manufacturers tend to repair defects that have led to arbitration.

Criticism of Industry Arbitration Panels

Although arbitration boards must meet state and/or federal standards of impartiality, some consumers have voiced doubts that industry-sponsored arbitration boards are truly impartial in their decisions. In response to consumer pressure, to date six states (Connecticut, Massachusetts, Montana, New York, Texas, and Vermont) and the District of Columbia have established mandatory, government-sponsored arbitration programs for lemon-law disputes. The rulings by these government boards would seem to justify consumer complaints of industry partiality in arbitration: According to the Center for Auto Safety, the government-sponsored programs gave refunds in 58 percent of their first 2,598 cases—which is six times the number of refunds given by industry arbitration boards.

THE ALTERNATIVE OF USING PUBLIC TRANSPORTATION

> Many Americans could save hundreds or even thousands of dollars every year if they would use public transportation instead of owning a car.

Many Americans could save hundreds or even thousands of dollars every year if they would use public transportation instead of owning a car. The alternative of public transportation is most often available to consumers who live in urban areas.

Think of the costs of owning a car that could be saved. In 1992 depreciation, insurance, gas and oil, parking fees, and other costs paid by Americans for the typical car totaled roughly $6,000. This figure was much larger in cities where parking alone could cost $100 or more a month.

Public transportation is often more convenient than using a car. If you take a bus to work you do not need to worry about finding and paying for a place to park that may be blocks from your job. When you need to use a car, van, or truck for special purposes, you can rent one for $50 or $100 per day. Although this may seem expensive, it is much less than the cost of owning a car. It is fair to say that for many consumers owning a car is more a luxury than a necessity.

Public Transportation Over Greater Distances

When consumers need to travel between cities there are often several alternative forms of public transportation they might choose. Interstate bus lines, such as Greyhound or Trailways, offer low-cost transportation between most major cities and many rural areas. Trains are another alternative that is relatively quick and inexpensive. Since the deregulation of airline travel in the 1970s the cost of flying has fallen significantly.

Finding Low-Cost Travel by Air

The cost of air travel varies widely depending on where and when you choose to travel. Airlines continually adjust prices to try to fill flights and maximize their revenue. If you call today for a 9:00 A.M. flight tomorrow and you want to return the following day, you should expect to pay a high price. However, if you are willing to fly on a Thursday afternoon and return Tuesday evening sometime next month, and you make your reservations at least two weeks before you travel, you will receive a much lower price.

Consumers should realize that many less expensive tickets are not refundable. If you want to be sure you can fly on a particular day and at a specific time, you might purchase a full-price, refundable ticket for the flight you want. Then you might call different travel agents at different times to see if you can find a better price for the same flights. If you can, you can book the new reservation and cancel the first one. If you never find a better price, at least you have the flight you need. This does cause more work for the airline, but it also improves your chance of paying the lowest possible price for your travel.

Airline prices and billing procedures change frequently. By the time you read this text, new developments probably will have changed the way to get the best price. You should always check with several travel agents and consult recent travel publications in your library to find the method that currently offers the best alternative for your needs.

Advantages of Special Vacation Plans

A number of organizations offer special vacation plans for people who are able to leave on short notice. When a tour is planned for 40 people but only 38 tickets are sold, the agent who organized the tour may be happy to sell the remaining two tickets at half-price or even less instead of taking a total loss on the cost. Organizations that specialize in this sort of discount travel often advertise in travel sections of the Sunday issues of major newspapers. Two that are well known are Unitravel, 1177 N. Warson Rd., P.O. Box 12485, St. Louis, MO 63132 (800-325-2222); and Moment's Notice, 425 Madison Ave., New York, NY 10017 (212-486-0503). If you buy a travel package from this sort of organization, it is often a better choice to charge it so you may be able to dispute payment if the trip does not live up to what was promised.

▶ **SUMMARY**

1. The automobile industry in the United States is huge. Currently, Americans spend more than $160 billion for passenger vehicles and purchase more than 12 million cars per year.

2. There are approximately 50,000 traffic fatalities per year in the United States, and traffic accidents are the leading cause of death for those between 5 and 34 years of age.

3. Beginning with the passage of the National Traffic and Motor Vehicle Safety Act of 1966, the federal government has been active in regulating the auto industry to promote safer vehicles by requiring that autos be equipped with certain safety devices. Safety features raise the prices of automobiles, and consumers thus pay for the additional protection they receive.

4. Stiffer penalties for drunk driving, laws mandating a higher drinking age in many states, and greater awareness by Americans of the risks of drunk driving have all contributed to the reduction in alcohol-related traffic fatalities and injuries.

5. Some of the social costs of driving are pollution and traffic congestion.

6. The private costs of driving a car will vary according to the age of the car, its size, insurance costs, and driving styles. For most American consumers this cost will fall in a range between 25 cents and 40 cents per mile.

7. When making a decision about replacing an existing car, you should consider the costs of owning and operating a new car versus your existing older car and the costs of repairs in terms of time and inconvenience compared with the book value of the older car.

8. Before you buy a new car, you should consider the benefits that you might obtain by leasing one instead. Leasing a car offers several advantages and is often no more expensive in the long run than financing a new car.

9. Since a new car represents a substantial expense for most people, you should conduct some market research before you buy one. Knowing the list price that dealers pay for new cars and new-car accessories can help you shop comparatively among dealers.

10. Auto brokers can provide factory-cost information on new cars and actually buy a car for you for a few hundred dollars above cost.

11. Because new cars generally have problems that you will want the dealer to take care of, the proximity of the dealer and the dealer's willingness to handle such warranty problems are important considerations when deciding where to buy a new car.

12. The purchase of a used car requires as much shopping as for a new car, or more, for the mechanical condition of the car is now in question. If you wish to have a warranty, you can purchase a used car from a dealer offering a one-month or 300-mile warranty for a somewhat higher price.

13. Shop for automobile financing just as you shop for any other product. Shop on the basis of the down payment required, set-up charges, actual finance charge, and actual annual interest, as well as the number of months required to pay. Remember, the sooner you pay off the loan, the less interest you pay. On the other hand, if your payments are high relative to your income, you will have less money for other purchases.

14. All 50 States plus the District of Columbia have some form of lemon law governing new-car performance. If you feel you have purchased a lemon, check with the Center for Auto Safety or with your state's attorney general's office for information on lemon laws.

15. Consumers can often save time and money by using public transportation, especially if they live in urban areas.

16. Various forms of public transportation are available for travel over greater distances. Although bus lines and trains offer the lowest prices, the cost of air transportation is also less than it was before deregulation. Consumers should be aware that low-price airline tickets often are not refundable.

▶ QUESTIONS FOR THOUGHT AND DISCUSSION

1. What is the most important safety feature a car can have?

2. If you were shopping for a new car, what would be the primary factor in your decision making—safety, economy, comfort, or appearance?

3. Do you think more Americans should use mass-transit systems—such as buses, subways, trains, and so on—instead of private automobiles for routine commuting to and from work?

4. Can the government do more, in your opinion, to promote safer driving habits in America? To create safer automobiles?

5. If the long-run cost were about the same, would you prefer to lease or buy a car?

▶ THINGS TO DO

1. Check with the Department of Motor Vehicles in your area to find out what penalties are imposed on drunk drivers and what the state law is regarding the use of seat belts.

2. Write or call the consumer protection division or attorney general's office in your state (see Consumer Issue B) and ask to have sent to you any information available on your state's lemon law and how it is enforced.

3. Even if you are not in the market for a new car, try shopping for one over the phone. Pick a particular make, body style, and set of accessories.

Call five different new-car dealers in your area. See if you can get an actual quote on the phone. Are there any significant differences among the quotes?
4. Go to the library and get the latest December issue of *Annual Buying Guide* of *Consumer Reports*. Look at the section on buying a used car. Could you perform the eight to ten on-the-lot tests given in that section? Have you ever tried the driving tests given in that section when you were looking for a used car?

▶ APPLICATION

Comparison-shop for a three-year, $10,000, new-car loan. How much difference is there in the interest rates you would have to pay to borrow from different lending institutions, in your monthly payments, and in your total cost of borrowing the money? What factors do you believe cause different lending institutions to charge different rates? Are there any factors you should consider in taking out a loan other than the interest rate? If so, what are they and why are they important?

▶ SELECTED READINGS

▶ "Bumper to Bumper Auto Care." *Nation's Business*, October 1991, pp. 70–71.
▶ *Buying a Used Car*. Available free from the Federal Trade Commission, 6th St. and Pennsylvania Ave., N.W., Washington, DC 20580.
▶ *A Consumer Guide to Vehicle Leasing*. Available free from the Federal Trade Commission, 6th St. and Pennsylvania Ave., N.W., Washington, DC 20580.
▶ "Dealing With the Dealer." *Consumer Reports*. December 1991, pp. 125–127.
▶ Joseph, Anthony. "How to Make Your Car Last 150,000 Miles." *Consumers Digest*, May–June 1989, pp. 16–25.
▶ Keller, M. "The Educated Consumer." *Motor Trend*, December 1991, p. 134.
▶ National Highway Safety Traffic Administration. *Consumer Information Series*. Available free from the National Highway Safety Commission, NEF-10, 400 Seventh St., S.W., Washington, DC 20590.
▶ *New Car Buying Guide*. Available free from the Federal Trade Commission, 6th St. and Pennsylvania Ave., N.W., Washington, DC 20580.
▶ *Your Driving Costs*. Available free from the American Automobile Association, 8111 Gatehouse Rd., Falls Church, VA 22047.
▶ Washington, F. "The Knock in the Engine." *Newsweek*, November 11, 1991, p. 52.
▶ "When You Should Lease, Not Buy." *Money*, November 1991, pp. 50–51.

Financial Management

CHAPTER 15

Banks and the Banking System

PREVIEW

▶ What is the Federal Reserve System, and how does it operate?

▶ What types of checkable accounts are available from different depository institutions?

▶ How do you decide which bank and which types of bank accounts are best for you?

▶ What are the rights and responsibilities of consumers who use banks?

▶ What are electronic fund transfer systems, and how do they operate?

We live in a money economy. We use currency consisting of various denominations of bills and coins, and we also use checks and their equivalent, which are processed through our banking system. Understanding how that system works and what services banks can offer you is an important aspect of consumer economics. This chapter looks at the banking system as a whole, the types of checkable accounts and other services that various banks offer, and the possibility of someday having a cashless society.

DEPOSITORY INSTITUTIONS

In earlier editions of this book, this chapter was concerned only with commercial banks. The definition of a commercial bank was a financial institution that could accept checkable-account deposits, otherwise known as *demand deposits*. For many years, commercial banks dominated the checkable-account market. That is to say, they were the only financial institutions legally allowed to let people write checks on checkable-account balances. All this changed, however, in 1980 when Congress passed the historic Depository Institutions Deregulation and Monetary Control Act. The term *depository institution* was put in the title of that act for a very good reason. Commercial banks are not the only depository institutions in our nation. Rather, a host of financial institutions permit consumers to make deposits. The term **depository institution,** then, includes commercial banks, savings and loan associations, credit unions, mutual savings banks, and brokerage firms. In any event, the 1980 act lifted the restrictions on all those depository institutions that had been unable to offer checkable accounts to banking customers. Eventually, virtually all differences among depository institutions will disappear. Therefore, even though this chapter is titled "Banks and the Banking System," the information contained in it does not apply only to those financial institutions that call themselves banks; rather, it applies to all depository institutions. Instead of using the cumbersome words *depository institutions,* we simply refer to them as banks throughout this chapter and Consumer Issue M.

To understand our banking system, we have to understand the regulating agency that controls it.

Depository institution
Any institution that can accept deposits; commercial banks, savings and loan associations, mutual savings banks, brokerage houses, and credit unions are depository institutions.

FEDERAL RESERVE SYSTEM

In the U.S. banking system, the monetary authority, or Federal Reserve System, determines the quantity of money in circulation. The Federal Reserve System, often called *the Fed,* was established in 1913 with the passage of the Federal Reserve Act under President Woodrow Wilson. According to its preamble, it was "an act to provide for the establishment of Federal Reserve banks, to furnish an elastic currency, to afford means of rediscounting commercial paper, to establish a more effective supervision of banking in the United States, and for other purposes."

Structure and Powers of the Federal Reserve System

Currently, the Federal Reserve System consists of 12 Federal Reserve banks that have 25 branches, a Board of Governors consisting of 7 members nominated by the president for 14-year terms, a Federal Open Market Committee, and other less important committees (see Exhibit 15–1).

At the top of the system is the Board of Governors. Then there are the 12 Federal Reserve banks, which have 25 branches throughout the country. About 5,000 member banks are part of the Federal Reserve System. The Federal Reserve also sets reserve requirements for all other depository institutions.

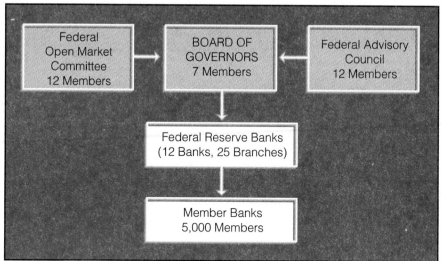

The Federal Reserve System is charged with carrying out monetary policy that is intended to stabilize the economy and help it run more efficiently. All depository institutions in the United States must follow at least some of the rules established by the Fed. These may lead to higher or lower interest rates, to more or less money being available for banks to loan. For example, in the spring of 1992, the amount of money banks were required to hold on reserve for checking deposits was reduced from 12 percent of these deposits to only 10 percent. This allowed banks to increase the amount of money they loaned.

A Clearinghouse for Checks

The Federal Reserve System has greatly simplified the clearing of checks—the method by which checks deposited in one bank are transferred to the banks on which they were written. Let's say that Mr. Ortiz of Chicago writes a check to the Fabian family in San Francisco. When the Fabians receive the check in the mail, they deposit it in their bank. Their bank then deposits the check in the Federal Reserve Bank of San Francisco. That bank, in turn, sends it to the Federal Reserve Bank of Chicago. That Federal Reserve Bank then sends the check to Mr. Ortiz's bank, where the amount of the check is deducted from Mr. Ortiz's account. We show how this is done in Exhibit 15–2.

DIFFERENT TYPES OF CHECKABLE ACCOUNTS

There are numerous types of checkable accounts available through banks and other financial institutions. We discuss the major types here.

Minimum Balance

Minimum-balance accounts give you unlimited checking at no charge per check or deposit so long as you maintain a specified balance, such as $200,

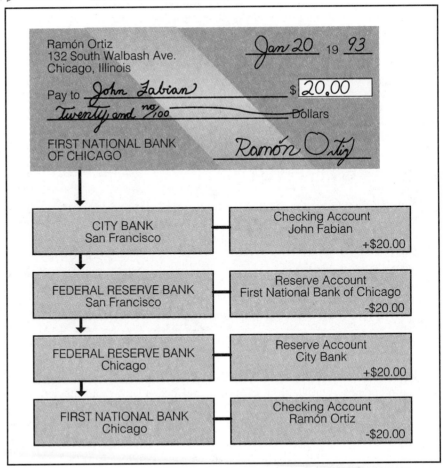

Ramón Ortiz
132 South Walbash Ave.
Chicago, Illinois

Jan 20 19 93

Pay to John Fabian $ 20.00

Twenty and no/100 ——————— Dollars

FIRST NATIONAL BANK
OF CHICAGO   Ramón Ortiz

CITY BANK
San Francisco

Checking Account
John Fabian
+$20.00

FEDERAL RESERVE BANK
San Francisco

Reserve Account
First National Bank of Chicago
−$20.00

FEDERAL RESERVE BANK
Chicago

Reserve Account
City Bank
+$20.00

FIRST NATIONAL BANK
Chicago

Checking Account
Ramón Ortiz
−$20.00

$300, or $500. Whenever the account balance falls below the specified balance in any month, a service charge is added.

There are two basic ways banks determine the minimum balance in an account. It may be measured by taking an average of the balance from each day in the month, or by using the smallest balance on any day of the month. In general, the first method is more beneficial to consumers. Suppose a consumer had an account with a $500 minimum balance. He or she might need to pay bills early in the month, reducing the balance in the account to, say, $200. By depositing enough money later to bring the balance up to $800 in the second half of the month, the consumer can maintain the average minimum balance and thus avoid fees. If the account balance is determined by the smallest amount, it won't matter how much is deposited later in the month—the consumer will still have to pay a fee.

Although minimum-balance checkable accounts are advertised as "free," they clearly are not. If you have to keep $500 as a minimum balance in your checkable account for a one-year period, then you have lost the *potential* interest you could have earned in a savings account during that time. If the interest rate you could have earned in a savings account for that one-year period is 6 percent, you would have been charged implicitly 6 percent times

$500, or $30 per year, for the so-called free minimum-balance checkable account.

Free Checking

Accounts termed *free checking* give you unlimited checking at no charge with no strings attached—no required minimum balance, no monthly maintenance fee, and so on. Generally, such accounts are rare and are usually offered only to a limited number of customers—for example, to elderly persons and students. Often, however, smaller banks will offer free checkable-account services in order to lure business away from the larger, more established banks.

Analysis, or Transaction, Plan

With the *analysis plan,* or *transaction plan,* you are charged for every transaction you make, including deposits. At the end of the month, the total amount of transactions fees charged to you is reduced by a credit that is based on your average balance during that month. The higher the average balance you maintain, the lower the final service charge is. As an example, one plan might charge you 12 cents for each check and 6 cents for each deposit. On the other hand, it will give you a 20-cent credit for each $100 average balance maintained. If you average twenty checks a month plus two and one-half deposits a month and maintain an average balance of $100, this analysis-plan account would cost you $28.20 a year.

Activity, or ''Per Check,'' Plan

With the *activity plan,* or *per-check plan*—often called a *special checkable account*—your monthly fee is based on the amount of your banking activity. There are two separate charges: a flat monthly "maintenance" fee and a charge for every check written. Usually, the monthly fee is 50 cents to $1, and the check fee is 10 to 20 cents. This particular account is most suited to customers who write relatively few checks (five to ten) a month. For an individual who averages twenty checks a month, the annual cost for this account would be $45—if the per-month fee is 75 cents and the per-check fee is 15 cents.

Package Plan

Many banks offer a combination all-in-one *package plan.* Generally, you're charged a single monthly fee—probably $7 to $10—that entitles you to something called a *Blue Chip,* a *Gold,* or an *Executive Account.* Included may be the following services:

1. Unlimited check writing.
2. Personalized checks, sometimes with your picture embossed on them or with a reproduction of a famous painting or a landscape in your area.
3. Overdraft protection. (If you write checks for more money than you have in your account, funds will be transferred automatically from either a credit card account or a personalized line of credit.)
4. A safe-deposit box.
5. Free traveler's checks, cashier's checks, and money orders.
6. Sometimes, preferred interest rates on personal loans.
7. Free term life insurance.
8. Possibly a credit card—such as MasterCard or VISA.

Package accounts apparently benefit only those customers who make heavy use of virtually every type of bank service. Usually, most of the services offered by package accounts are used by very few individuals who have such accounts. Moreover, a number of services attached to package accounts are often offered to other customers free of charge anyway, such as free-rein lines of credit.

Overdraft Accounts

Customers who can supply satisfactory credit ratings may be able to obtain an *overdraft account,* where the bank automatically lends the customer money when his or her checkable-account balance falls below zero. Thus, instead of refusing payment on checks written on a negative balance, the bank lends the customer a specified amount and automatically deposits that amount into the account. Most plans lend a minimum of $100 and add to the account in multiples of $100. Although few banks actually will lend you the exact amount of your overdraft or negative balance, you would be better off if they did because you would pay interest only on the smaller sum.

Most overdraft accounts require that you make a special deposit at regular intervals and indicate that it is to pay off the loan. Some banks automatically deduct a part of the loan from your regular checkable account after you have made deposits in it later in the month. Many overdraft accounts charge a service fee in addition to interest every time they add to your account. Thus, the total cost of an overdraft account loan may be quite high.

NOW and Super NOW Accounts

Negotiable order of withdrawal (NOW)
The equivalent of a check covered by a special type of interest-earning account.

Super NOW account
A checking-type account available in most commercial banks in which market rates of interest are paid, provided that a minimum balance (originally $2,500) is maintained in the account.

Virtually all banks offer a **negotiable order of withdrawal (NOW)** account, which, in essence, is a combined checkable and savings account. With a NOW account, you receive interest on your checkable-account balances provided you keep a certain minimum balance, such as $500.

Starting in 1983, banks were allowed to offer **Super NOW accounts** yielding rates of interest that are governed by market conditions. For example, when Super NOW accounts started, most of them offered 8½ to 9 percent per annum interest on account balances, compared with 5¼ percent interest earned on regular NOW accounts. The only catch was that the customer had to keep a minimum balance in the Super NOW account of $2,500. In any month when the balance fell below $2,500, the interest earned for the entire month would only be equivalent to that paid on a regular NOW account. With the deregulation of banking institutions, however, the minimum-balance requirement has changed. It now varies from bank to bank. Some banks have also combined their NOW and Super NOW accounts into one account and pay a higher interest rate for balances above a certain amount.

Money Market Deposit Accounts

Money market deposit account (MMDA)
A checkable account on which a depository institution can pay a market-determined interest rate.

The Garn–Fernand St. Germain Depository Institutions Act of 1982 allowed banking institutions to offer **money market deposit accounts (MMDAs)**— that is, checkable accounts that draw a rate of interest comparable to what would be earned by depositing funds in a money market mutual fund (see Chapter 18). This type of account limits the customer to a specified number of transactions on the account per month, only some of which may be in check form. Some banking customers who have large deposits keep only a small working balance in either a NOW or Super NOW account and the rest in an insured money market deposit account.

Asset Management Accounts

In the late 1970s, a new type of financial service appeared in the form of *asset management accounts.* Such accounts are offered by brokerage firms (such as Merrill Lynch), by banks (such as Citibank), retail stores (such as Sears), or other corporations and include a variety of financial services in one account.

The first such account was offered by Merrill Lynch. Its brokerage account, called Cash Management Account, or CMA, has the three characteristics of a regular stock brokerage account, through which stocks and bonds may be bought and sold. Such an account also allows investors to buy stocks and bonds with borrowed money. If at any time there are idle cash balances in the CMA, they are invested in a money market fund, earning market rates of interest. This is similar to having money in a money market deposit account at a regular depository institution.

Additionally, customers with a CMA receive books of checks and a credit card from a cooperating bank. When you write a check, it is presented to the bank for payment. The bank informs Merrill Lynch, which then transfers money from your cash balance or money market fund to the bank. You also may use your credit card to charge your purchases. These, too, are presented for payment to the bank, which again collects the funds from your Merrill Lynch account. At the end of each month, you receive a comprehensive statement detailing the transactions and the status of the account.

With the advent of asset management accounts, we have moved one step closer to both nationwide banking and one-stop financial service. Clearly, the differences among financial institutions are rapidly diminishing. It is interesting to note that savings and loan associations now also offer brokerage services to their customers.

> With the advent of asset management accounts, we have moved one step closer to both nationwide banking and one-stop financial service.

SELECTING THE RIGHT ACCOUNT

To decide which type of bank account is most appropriate for you, you will want to do the following:

1. Determine how many checks you write per month. If you write fewer than fifteen, you are a light check writer; you are average if you write fifteen to twenty-four; and you are a frequent check writer if you average more than twenty-five.

2. Determine the average amount of money you keep in a checking account over and above what you actually use. Many individuals play it close, depositing just enough to cover the checks they are going to write. Others maintain a cushion of several hundred dollars for unforeseen expenses.

Now you can decide which plan you should consider. If you write fewer than five or six checks per month, you should either put your funds into a money market mutual fund (explained in detail in Chapter 18), or, if you can meet the minimum-deposit requirement, you should put them into a Super NOW account or a money market deposit account at a depository institution.

If you are a heavy check writer and if you keep a very low average balance in your account, you should shop for a bank that charges a small service fee or nothing at all for an unlimited number of transactions, provided you keep a small balance in the account. The key point to remember in finding the right bank and banking services is to shop around and to ask questions. Banking personnel won't always tell you right away the best deal they have to offer.

It is important that you come in with the exact information about your average banking activities and then be aware of the various accounts that are available.

CERTIFIED CASHIER'S AND TRAVELER'S CHECKS

Certified check
A check the bank has certified, indicating that sufficient funds are available to cover it when it is cashed.

When a person writes a check, it is assumed that he or she has enough money on deposit to cover that check when it is presented for payment. In some situations, however, particularly when the buyer and seller of goods or services are strangers to each other, it is important to be certain that the bank will honor a check. There are three special kinds of checks that can be used to ensure this. A **certified check** is one for which the bank guarantees payment and sets aside funds from the depositor's account to cover the check. If you need to have a check certified, you simply write out a check as you usually would and take it to your bank, requesting certification. The usual method of certification is for the cashier or teller to write across the face of the check, over the signature, a statement that it is good when properly endorsed. The bank will then deduct the amount of the check from your account and transfer the funds to its own certified-check account. In effect, the bank agrees in advance to accept your check when it is presented for payment and to make the payment from the reserved funds. Certification can be requested by yourself or by the payee or other holder of your check.

Cashier's check
A check drawn on the bank by its own order to a designated person or institution. A cashier's check is paid for before it is obtained.

A **cashier's check** is one drawn on a bank by itself to the order of a designated person. For example, if you want a cashier's check, you purchase the check from the bank—that is, you pay the bank in advance for whatever amount the check is drawn for—and then the bank writes a check on its own funds to whomever you specify.

Traveler's check
A check purchased from a financial institution and signed by the purchaser at the time it is purchased. The check can be used as cash upon a second signature by the purchaser. It has the characteristics of a cashier's check.

A **traveler's check** is a form of guaranteed check similar to a cashier's check and is often used in lieu of cash when traveling. Traveler's checks, like cashier's checks, are written by a financial institution—such as American Express—on itself. You can purchase traveler's checks in banks. You must sign each check at the time it is purchased and again when it is cashed. When you choose a brand of traveler's check to purchase, it is important to find out how much trouble you will have to go to in order to replace them if they are lost or stolen.

SELECTING THE RIGHT BANK—BEWARE BEFORE YOU DEPOSIT

Are all depository institutions created alike? Certainly not. Some actually are safer than others. Deposits in virtually all depository institutions are insured, usually up to a limit of $100,000, by the Federal Deposit Insurance Corporation (FDIC) or by the Savings Association Insurance Fund (SAIF). But just because an agency of the federal government insures your deposit doesn't mean you want to take a chance on putting your money into a financial institution that may fail. Although you'll get your deposits back, up to $100,000, it may take time. To check the financial condition of the depository institution in which you place your money, contact your local Federal Reserve bank to find out if the financial institution in which you are interested has been placed on a list of "problem banks." Exhibit 15–3 shows you why it pays to select your bank with some care. Although the number of bank failures peaked in 1989 and fell to an estimated 137 in 1991, a total of more than 800 banks failed in the years between 1985 and 1991.

The Thrift Industry Disaster

Most Americans are aware of the many failures of savings and loan associations (S&Ls) in the late 1980s and early 1990s. You may have heard that American taxpayers will eventually pay over half a trillion dollars to "bail out" the S&L industry. That is roughly $2,000 for every man, woman, and child who lived in the United States in 1992.

The roots of the S&L disaster can be found in the banking regulation of the 1950s and 1960s. At that time S&L associations were limited in the kinds of deposits they could accept and the loans they could make. They could not take commercial deposits or offer checking accounts. They were allowed to make loans only for mortgages and some home improvements. They were intended to serve the needs of small savers and borrowers, those whom larger commercial banks were less interested in serving.

The S&Ls were assured a low-cost source of deposits because of a rule made by the government called *Regulation Q*. This regulation set a maximum interest rate that could be paid on savings deposits of less than $100,000. Small savers earned the same low interest rate no matter where they deposited their money. S&L representatives acted friendly and interested in consumers, so small savers often chose to deposit their money in S&L accounts. The S&Ls used the money to make long-term loans for mortgages at a fixed interest rate. This seemed to be a safe way to do business. Depositors earned 5 percent, borrowers paid 7 percent, and the S&Ls kept the other 2 percent to pay their costs.

In the 1970s the government changed the rules. New types of deposits were created that allowed small savers to earn much higher rates of interest on their deposits. To keep small savers from withdrawing their money, the S&Ls had to pay interest rates that were as high as those offered by other institutions. By the early 1980s these interest rates were as high as 12 percent to 14 percent. The S&Ls still earned their income from long-term, fixed-interest-rate mortgages that paid 7 percent to 8 percent a year. Many S&Ls lost large amounts of money as the result of this situation.

Congress and the president tried to help S&Ls in 1982 when the Garn–Fernand St. Germain Act was passed. This law allowed savings and loans to make some commercial loans; for the first time they could finance shopping centers and oil exploration, and make many other types of investments. This ability to make new types of loans did not change the fact that S&Ls still had billions of dollars tied up in fixed-interest-rate mortgages. They continued to lose money every year on these loans. If the S&Ls were to stay in business, they had to earn large profits from the new types of loans to make up for the money they were losing on mortgages. This encouraged S&Ls to make investments that promised large returns but also had large risks. Many of these investments failed, and the S&Ls took huge losses.

There have been a substantial number of people involved in the S&L crisis who were dishonest, who committed fraud, or who showed poor judgment. The problem, however, had its roots in the regulations established by our government. It would be difficult to find any one person who is most responsible for what happened. Clearly, the bulk of the cost will be paid by American taxpayers. In addition, many individuals lost the money they deposited in excess of the $100,000 limit that was insured by the Federal Savings and Loan

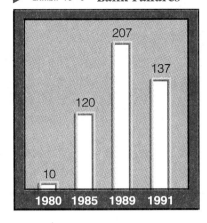

▶ Exhibit 15–3 **Bank Failures**

> Writing out a check is, on the surface, very easy. There are, however, certain errors you can make that can cause problems later.

Insurance Corporation. The S&L disaster demonstrates the need of American consumers to be careful where they deposit their money.

HOW TO AVOID BANKING PROBLEMS

Once you open a checkable account and start writing checks, a number of problems can arise. This section looks at some of the precautions you can take to protect yourself against potential pitfalls in banking.

Writing Checks

Writing out a check is, on the surface, very easy. There are, however, certain errors you can make that can cause problems later.

1. *Postdating a check.* In postdating a check, or writing a future date on it, you take a chance that the bank might slip up and cash the check before its postdated date. Thus, if you postdate a check in hopes of having sufficient funds to cover it on that future date, you might end up with an overdraft.
2. *Making checks out to "cash."* Making a check out to "cash," except when you are right in front of a bank teller's window, is not advisable. Anyone can cash checks made out that way. If you lose such a check, it is the same as losing currency.
3. *Improperly filling out the amount.* It is often easy to be careless and leave spaces before and after the words and numbers indicating the amount of the check. If you do this, you risk an alteration that will increase the apparent amount of the check.

Endorsing a Check

Whenever you cash a check that has been made payable to you or attempt to deposit it to your bank account, you will have to *endorse* it first. This means you will sign your name on the back of the check so it can be cleared and the money it represents transferred to you or your bank account. To endorse a check properly, you should sign your name exactly as it is written on the face of the check. If your name has been misspelled or incorrectly written, endorse it with the incorrect version and then write your correct name below it.

You should make your endorsement on the back of the left-hand side of the check. Recently, the Federal Reserve System has requested that bank customers place their endorsements *only* within the top one and one-half inches on the back of the left-hand side of the check. The rest of the space can then be used for bank endorsements as the check is processed through the banking system.

There are three types of endorsements. A *blank endorsement* is simply your name written on the back of the check. A blank endorsement allows anybody in possession of the check thereafter to cash or deposit it, after further endorsing the check with his or her own name, or to transfer it to another.

A *special endorsement* is when you specify a particular individual as the recipient of the funds. "Pay to the order of Annabel Maitland [signed] Sharon Cross" is an example of a special endorsement.

A *restrictive endorsement* indicates, above your signature, "for deposit only." With this type of endorsement, nobody else can cash the check or deposit it into an account other than your own.

Consumers should never endorse a check until they are actually at a teller's window in a bank. Remember, when a check has been endorsed it is just like cash. If a consumer loses an endorsed check, anyone can cash it.

Stale Checks

A check that is more than six months old is considered a *stale check.* Banks have the option of paying or not paying stale checks. Although the bank might, as a courtesy, consult its customer to ask whether the check should be paid, the bank is not required to do so. This means that if you receive a six-month-old check from someone, you may not be able to cash it; similarly, if you receive a check and hold it for six months or more before depositing or cashing it, you may not be able to receive the money that the check represents. In your own accounting, you need to remember not to "forget" about checks you have written, even if they're now a year old; they still *could* be cashed. To ensure that your bank won't accept a check you wrote that has since become stale, you can submit a *stop-payment order* to your bank, as discussed next.

Stop-Payment Orders

If you wish to stop a check from being collected after you have given it to someone, you can issue a **stop-payment order.** The bank will then refuse to honor the check. When you think a check has been lost or stolen, or when you realize you have purchased defective merchandise with a check, a stop-payment order is worth the $10 to $20 a bank will charge.

Generally, a phone call will stop payment on a check for only 14 days; written notice will stop payment for six months, after which time it can be renewed. Once the stop-payment order has been issued, the tellers in the bank are requested not to pay that particular check. The stop-payment information is also put in the computer in order to reject the check if another bank presents it in the bank-clearing process. A stop-payment order can be made only on a regular check from a checkable account; cashier's and certified checks cannot be stopped. A typical stop-payment order is shown in Exhibit 15–4.

Stop-payment order
An order to one's bank not to honor a particular check when it is presented for payment.

TO THE (BANK NAME)
STREET ADDRESS
CITY, STATE
DATE OF ORDER   ACCOUNT NUMBER

Please STOP PAYMENT on my (or our) check drawn on your bank, described as follows.

NO: DATED   PAYABLE TO   AMOUNT: $

REASON: DUPLICATE ISSUED?

THIS REQUEST IS MADE WITH THE UNDERSTANDING THAT THE BANK WILL USE REASONABLE PRECAUTION IN FOLLOWING YOUR INSTRUCTION BUT IN CONSIDERATION OF THE ACCEPTANCE OF THIS REQUEST. IT IS EXPRESSLY AGREED THAT THE BANK WILL IN NO WAY BE LIABLE IN THE EVENT THE CHECK IS PAID. IF PAID THE SAME DAY YOUR ORDER IS RECEIVED OR IF PAID BY OVERSIGHT OR INADVERTENCE OR IF BY REASON OF SUCH PAYMENT OTHER CHECKS DRAWN BY THE UNDERSIGNED ARE RETURNED FOR INSUFFICIENT FUNDS AND THE UNDERSIGNED FURTHER AGREES TO INDEMNIFY THE BANK AGAINST ALL EXPENSES AND COSTS THAT IT MIGHT INCUR BY REASON OF REFUSING PAYMENT ON SAID CHECK.

EXPIRATION DATE

IT IS HEREBY AGREED AND UNDERSTOOD THAT THIS ORDER WILL REMAIN IN EFFECT FOR A SIX MONTH PERIOD UNLESS OTHERWISE DIRECTED AND THE BANK WILL CHARGE $5.00 FOR EACH SIX-MONTH PERIOD OR PORTION THEREOF THAT THIS ORDER IS IN EFFECT THE BANK MAY CHARGE MY ACCOUNT WITH THIS AMOUNT

ORDER RECEIVED BY   IN PERSON   BY LETTER   SIGNATURE OF MAKER

BANK NOT LIABLE IF CHECK HAS BEEN CASHED IN THE SAME DAY THIS ORDER WAS ACCEPTED.

Deposit Holds

When you deposit checks into your account, don't assume that you will be able to withdraw—either in cash or by check—the funds immediately. Banks are allowed to hold deposited checks for a certain period of time so that they can ascertain whether checks are good before paying them. Hold periods vary from bank to bank, and all banks are now required to disclose their hold policies to customers.

Until recently, some banks would hold deposits for as long as two weeks. Lengthy hold policies benefited banks because, if checks cleared before the end of the holding period, the banks could invest and earn interest on the funds until the hold period elapsed and the funds had to be made available to the customer. Consumer complaints and public concern over the unfairness of such lengthy holds led Congress in 1987 to pass the Expedited Funds Availability Act, which required that new availability schedules be effected as of September 1, 1988. Under this act, certain kinds of deposits—government checks, checks on an account in the same bank, cash deposits, and electronic transfers—must be available for withdrawal by the depositor by the next business day following the deposit. Other local checks (checks on banks within the same Federal Reserve region) can be held no longer than three business days and nonlocal checks for no longer than six business days. On September 1, 1990, these time periods were reduced even further—to one business day for local checks and four business days for nonlocal checks. The act also provided that all bank customers must be allowed to withdraw up to $100 from the total of any checks deposited on the previous business day. Any state laws that require shorter hold periods are unaffected by the federal act.

Avoiding Bounced Checks

If you write a check and don't have sufficient funds in your account to cover it, the check will "bounce." Your bank will immediately notify you by mail of the problem and charge your account with a fee—which might range anywhere from $6 to $30 or even more. The payee—the person to whom you gave the check—might also charge a fee for the bad check.

If you are a long-time customer of the bank and have made deposits at regular intervals, the bank might go ahead and pay the check for you and charge your account with an overdraft for the amount of the check. Essentially, if the bank does this, it is temporarily loaning you the amount of the check, and you must reimburse the bank immediately. Frequently, however, the bank will simply return the check to the payee or other person who presented it for payment. When this happens, the payee or other holder can come directly to you and demand payment or redeposit the check in the hope that on the second collection attempt you will have enough money in your account to cover the check.

Bouncing checks can be more than embarrassing; it can also create legal problems for you. If you write a check and are unable to cover it, you could become involved in a civil lawsuit; and, if intent to defraud is involved, you could be criminally prosecuted for writing bad checks.

One way to ensure that you don't ever bounce a check is to arrange with your bank to have an *overdraft account,* a type of account that was discussed earlier in this chapter. Another way to avoid bounced checks is to keep good records so that you know at all times how much money you have in your checkable account. By entering the amount of each check you write in your check register and comparing your record with the monthly bank statement, you can avoid the problem of bounced checks.

RECONCILING YOUR BANK BALANCE

Every month, you will receive a bank statement and a set of canceled checks. (You should have your deposit slips already.) It is important that you reconcile your bank balance with your checkbook or set of check stubs so you know exactly how much you have in the bank, can catch any mistakes the bank might have made, and can find out if someone has not cashed a check you wrote.

Since you may have written checks immediately before the closing date on your bank statement which have not been paid by the bank yet, the balance in your checkbook rarely will be exactly the same as the balance on your bank statement. Thus, you must reconcile the two by taking account of deposits you made that did not show up on your bank statement and checks you wrote that have not yet been processed. A simple procedure for reconciling your bank statement is as follows.

1. Sort your canceled checks, either numerically or by date issued.
2. Deduct from your checkbook balance any service charges—for new checks, overdraft charges, and so on—not previously recorded.
3. Enter your bank statement balance (T). $ _____
4. After adding up all the checks outstanding that are not reflected on your bank statement, subtract the total of these unpaid checks (U) from the bank balance entered above and obtain a new balance here. $ _____ (= T − U)
5. Add up any deposits you made that did not show on your bank statement and put them here (D). $ _____
6. Now obtain your final balance by adding the unreflected deposit total (D) to the new balance you found in Step 4 (T − U). Your final balance is T − U + D.

▶ Exhibit 15–5 **Reconciling Your Bank Statement**

1. Adjust the balance in your checkbook for service charge and other bank charges and credits shown on the bank statement but not recorded in your checkbook.
2. See that all deposits made by you are properly credited.
3. See that all checks enclosed in your statement are checks issued by you.
4. Check each paid check against your checkbook stubs. List all checks outstanding in the space provided here.

Checks outstanding not charged to account				
No.	$		Bank balance shown on this statement	$_____
			ADD+	
			Deposits not credited in this statement	$_____
				$_____
				$_____
			TOTAL	$_____
			SUBTRACT– Checks outstanding	$_____
Total	$		BALANCE	$_____
			(Should agree with your checkbook balance)	

This final balance should be the same as your checkbook balance after the service charge and any other bank charges have been deducted.

Exhibit 15–5 shows the steps to follow in reconciling your bank balance.

Don't destroy your checks and the bank statement after you reconcile your bank balance. For income tax purposes, it's a good idea to keep bank statements and canceled checks for at least three years. Some people keep them longer in case there is a dispute with the Internal Revenue Service.

HOW TO SETTLE A COMPLAINT WITH A BANK

Because so many of our personal financial transactions filter through the banking system, it is possible that at some point an error will be made and a dispute may arise between you and the bank. Because the error could have a long-lasting effect on your financial status and an impact on others involved in the transaction, it is important to try to settle it quickly.

As a first step, you should contact the bank directly and explain the problem, of which the bank may not even be aware. Many banks have designated employees to deal with these problems. For example, you may have deposited money that was credited to the wrong account; this deposit will fail to appear on your monthly checkable-account statement. In most cases, errors and misunderstandings can be corrected at this level. If, however, you cannot resolve the dispute to your satisfaction by dealing directly with the bank, you may

TYPE OF BANK	IDENTIFICATION MARKS	WHERE TO COMPLAIN
National bank	The word "national" appears in the bank's name, or the initials N.A. appear after the bank's name.	Consumer Activities Division Comptroller of the Currency 250 "E" Street, S.W. Washington, DC 20219 (202) 622-2000
State bank, member Federal Reserve, FDIC insured	Look for two signs at the bank: "Member, Federal Reserve System" and "Deposits Insured by Federal Deposit Insurance Corporation."	Consumer Affairs Board of Governors Federal Reserve System 20th St. and "C" Street, N.W. Washington, DC 20551 (202) 452-3946
State nonmember bank or state-chartered mutual savings bank	FDIC sign will be displayed; Federal Reserve sign will not.	Office of Consumer Affairs Federal Deposit Insurance Corporation 1776 "F" Street, N.W. Washington, DC 20429 (800) 934-3342 or (202) 898-3536
Federal savings and loan association	A sign on the door or in the lobby featuring an eagle surrounded by the words, "Backed by the full faith and credit of the United States Government."	Office of Thrift Supervision Office of Community and Consumer Division 17th and G Sts., N.W. Washington, DC 20552 (202) 906-6000
Federal credit union	Sign will be displayed reading "Member, National Credit Union Administration."	National Credit Union Administration Office of Public and Congressional Affairs 1776 G St., N.W. Washington, DC 20456 (202) 682-9600

take your complaint to one of the agencies that regulates your bank. These are indicated in Exhibit 15–6.

ELECTRONIC FUND TRANSFER SYSTEMS

The application of computer technology to banking, in the form of **electronic fund transfer systems (EFTS),** promises to relieve banking institutions of the burden of having to move mountains of paperwork in order to process fund transfers. An **electronic fund transfer** is a transfer of money made with the use of an electronic terminal, a telephone, a computer, or magnetic tape. Automatic payments, direct deposits, and other fund transfers are now made electronically; no physical transfers of cash, checks, or other negotiable instruments are involved. Through the use of EFTS, transactions that would otherwise take days can now be completed in minutes.

Electronic fund transfer systems (EFTS)
Systems used to transfer funds electronically.

Electronic fund transfer
A transfer of funds with the use of an electronic terminal, a telephone, a computer, or magnetic tape.

Types of Electronic Transfers

There are principally four types of EFTS in use: (1) automated teller machines, (2) point-of-sale systems, (3) systems handling direct deposits and withdrawals of funds, and (4) pay-by-telephone systems.

Debit card

A plastic card similar to a credit card that allows a consumer to use a computerized banking system.

Automated Teller Machines   A major EFTS development has been the automated teller machine (ATM), also called a customer-bank communication terminal or remote service unit. ATMs are located either on a bank's premises or at convenient locations such as supermarkets, drugstores, and shopping centers. The card that you use to activate an ATM is called an *access card* or **debit card** and is accompanied by a personal identification number (PIN) that is given only to the account holder—a number that is meant to be kept secret so as to inhibit others' use of the card. A sample debit card is shown in Exhibit 15–7.

Once the debit card activates an ATM, the ATM can receive deposits, dispense funds from checking or savings accounts, transfer funds between accounts, make credit-card advances, and receive payments on loan accounts. ATMs are usually connected on-line to the bank's computers. To avoid the unauthorized withdrawal of money from your account through an ATM you should never allow anyone else to use your card or provide someone with your PIN number. The possible result of doing this is demonstrated by the Consumer Close-Up.

Point-of-Sale Systems   It is now possible for consumers to transfer funds directly to merchants to pay for purchases. On-line terminals are located at checkout counters in, for example, supermarkets. Instead of receiving cash or

a check from the customer, the checkout person inserts the customer's debit card into a terminal, which reads the data encoded on the card. The computer at the customer's bank verifies that the card and identification code are valid and that there are enough funds in the customer's account to cover the purchase. After the payment is made, the customer's account is debited for the amount of the purchase.

For the grocer, direct payment from customers by means of **point-of-sale systems** carries, under current law, less risk of nonpayment or bounced checks. For the customer, the electronic transfer makes bills and check writing unnecessary.

Point-of-sale system

An electronic customer-merchant-bank communication terminal that, when activated by a debit card and a personal identification number (PIN), can debit the customer's account to cover a purchase from the merchant.

Preauthorized Direct Deposits and Withdrawals   Automated clearinghouses are similar to the ordinary clearinghouses in which checks are cleared between banks. The main difference is that entries are made in the form of electronic signals; no checks are used. Thus, these systems do not further automate the handling of checks; they replace checks. This type of EFTS allows a bank to complete a transaction for less than the cost of clearing a check.

A direct deposit may be made to a customer's account through an electronic terminal when the customer has authorized the deposit in advance. The federal government often uses this EFTS to deposit Social Security payments directly into beneficiaries' accounts. Similarly, an employer may agree to make payroll and pension payments directly into an employee's account at specified intervals.

A customer may also authorize the bank (or other financial institution at which the customer's funds are on deposit) to make automatic payments at regular, recurrent intervals to a third party. For example, insurance premiums, utility bills, and home mortgage and automobile installment loan payments may sometimes be made automatically.

Pay-by-Telephone Systems   When it is undesirable to arrange in advance for an automatic payment—as, for example, when the amount of a regular payment varies—some financial institutions permit their customers to pay bills through a pay-by-telephone system. This allows the customer to access the institution's computer system by telephone and direct a transfer of funds. Utility bills frequently are paid directly by customers using pay-by-telephone systems. Customers may also be permitted to transfer funds between accounts—for example, to withdraw funds from a savings account and make a deposit in a checking account—in this way.

Protection with Electronic Banking

Electronic banking obviously poses certain problems. When you write a check, it has your signature on it and it leaves a paper trail of evidence. And if someone forges your name on a check, you have the evidence before you. With electronic transactions, however, there is no such evidence, and consequently disputes can easily arise. For example, what if another person, without your permission, uses your debit card and your PIN to initiate a banking transaction? What is your liability? Or what if you suspect the bank's computer made a mistake? What can you do?

In 1978 Congress addressed these and other problems involved in electronic banking by passing the Electronic Fund Transfer Act (EFTA). In addition to providing a basic framework "establishing the rights, liabilities, and responsibilities of participants in electronic fund transfers," the EFTA gave the Federal Reserve Board the authority to issue rules and regulations to help implement the act. The Federal Reserve Board's implemental regulation is called **Regulation E.** This regulation spells out the respective responsibilities of banks and consumers when disputes arise over electronic fund transfers. Generally, whenever you open a bank account that uses electronic banking, the bank must inform you of your rights under the EFTA and Regulation E. Consumer Issue M looks more closely at some of the potential problems you may encounter with EFTS and at your rights, as a consumer, in electronic banking transactions.

Regulation E
The set of rules issued by the Federal Reserve Board to protect users of electronic banking services.

THE TREND TOWARD A CASHLESS SOCIETY

The efficiency and convenience of electronic transfers have led many observers to assume that America is in the process of becoming a cashless, checkless society. This could well be true—certainly, an increasing number of banking and sales transactions are being conducted by means of computers rather than with cash or checks. But the pace of our advancement toward a cashless society is considerably slower than visionaries of a decade or two ago imagined it would be. Americans continue to pay most of their bills with checks and write, on average, 20 checks each month. And an increasing number of checks—currently, close to 60 billion—are written and processed by the banking system each year in this country. To the surprise of many, Americans have also failed to jump at the ultimate electronic banking opportunity: home banking via one's personal computer. When this convenient method of banking was introduced in the early 1980s, the banking industry believed that it would become widely adopted; but, so far, it has not been. Only a tiny fraction (approximately 100,000) of the 28 million households that have personal computers subscribe to this service, and, because of the lack of consumer demand, the number of banks offering such programs has dwindled from 70 several years ago to 36 at the present time.

Undoubtedly, some of this resistance to cashless transactions is due to force of habit, as well as concerns about computer reliability and computer breakdowns. But it very likely also reflects some genuine consumer concerns over computerized transactions. A major disadvantage of payment of bills via computer is that you do not have the **float time** that checks provide. If you purchase a product from a department store through a point-of-sale electronic system, for example, the amount of the purchase is immediately deducted from your account balance at your bank. When you write a check to pay for goods or services, you can stop payment on the check if a problem with the seller arises. Check float also allows you time to add funds to your account, if necessary, to cover the check before it arrives at your bank for payment.

Another consumer concern that will be discussed in Chapter 23 is the loss of privacy that results from computerized transactions. Once your name and personal data are entered into a computer file, you cannot be certain about who might have access—legally or illegally—to that information.

In addition, as we all know, computers can make mistakes and they can break down. They also leave fewer records of our transactions, which can present problems when disputes arise.

Despite these disadvantages, it is evident that electronic fund transfer systems are here to stay, as they obviously offer many advantages to consumers as well. Because it is important to know your rights when using EFTS, we discuss that topic in Consumer Issue M.

Float time
The time between the issuance of a check and the deduction of the amount of the check from the drawer's account.

▶ SUMMARY

1. The Depository Institutions Deregulation and Monetary Control Act of 1980 allowed savings and loan associations and savings banks to compete more directly with commercial banks for deposits and loans. This has fundamentally changed the American banking system.

2. The Federal Reserve System was established in 1913 and consists of 12 member federal banks with 25 branches. One of the major functions of the Federal Reserve System is to serve as a clearinghouse for checks.

3. There are several types of checkable accounts available in commercial banks: minimum-balance, free, analysis or transaction, activity or per-check, package, overdraft, NOW, Super NOW, and money market deposit accounts. Some banks, brokerage houses, and other firms offer asset management accounts, which combine investment activities and checkable accounts.

4. Pursuant to legislation passed at the end of March 1980, all banks that are federally insured, including credit unions, can offer negotiable orders of withdrawal or interest-bearing checkable accounts.

5. When shopping for a bank account, you should have a fairly clear idea of how many checks you will write a month and how much money you plan to keep in your account. This will help you determine which of the various types of checkable accounts available will best suit your particular needs. When selecting a bank, check with the Federal Reserve System to make sure the bank of your choice has not been placed on the list of problem banks.

6. A certified check is one for which the bank guarantees payment and for which funds from the depositor's account have been specially set aside by the bank for payment of that particular check. A cashier's check is one drawn by the bank on its own funds and payable to a person designated by the purchaser. A traveler's check is a check that is purchased from a financial institution and signed by the purchaser at the time of purchase and that can be used as cash upon a second signature by the purchaser; it is similar to a cashier's check.

7. To avoid potential problems, it is important to write and endorse checks properly, to be aware that stale checks may or may not be honored by the bank, to know how to issue a stop-payment order on a check if this should be necessary, and to realize that banks may hold your deposits for a day or more before you can withdraw the funds by check or in cash.

8. To avoid the embarrassment and potential legal problems that could result from bouncing checks, you can arrange with your bank to have an overdraft account. Good record keeping will also help to ensure that you don't write checks when you have insufficient funds in your account to cover them.

9. Monthly reconciliation of your bank statement with your check register allows you to keep informed of the status of your account and your current balance.

10. When you have a complaint with your bank, contact the bank directly and explain the problem. If you cannot settle the dispute directly with the bank to the your satisfaction, contact the appropriate agency listed in Exhibit 15–6.

11. Electronic fund transfer systems allow vast sums of money to be transferred from account to account without mountains of paperwork and in a shorter time period than is the case with checks. The four principal types of electronic transfer systems in use are automated teller machines, point-of-sale systems, preauthorized direct deposits and withdrawals, and pay-by-telephone systems.

12. The rights and obligations of banks and consumers in EFTS are spelled out by the Electronic Fund Transfer Act of 1978 and the Federal Reserve Board's implemental regulation, Regulation E.

13. The pace of America's advancement toward a cashless, checkless society is slower than visionaries of previous decades imagined it would be. Force of habit, concerns about computer reliability and computer breakdowns, and concerns over the lack of float time and privacy resulting from EFTS are some possible reasons for the resistance displayed by Americans to cashless transactions through EFTS.

▶ QUESTIONS FOR THOUGHT AND DISCUSSION

1. In what circumstances would you prefer to receive a certified or a cashier's check instead of a regular, personal check?

2. Is it true that traveler's checks are as good as cash, as is often claimed?

3. What is an overdraft account, and what advantages (and disadvantages) are associated with such an account?

4. What are some ways in which the deregulation of the banking industry has affected consumers?

5. Why do you think some people choose to use a debit card to make purchases instead of a check when it means that money will be taken from their accounts immediately?

▶ THINGS TO DO

1. Visit several types of financial institutions (commercial banks, savings and loan associations, and so on) in your community and ask each of them what kind of services it offers to consumers. Write down their answers and

then compare your lists. Are there more similarities than differences, or vice versa?

2. Go to three commercial banks in your area and ask them to explain to you what kinds of checkable accounts they offer and the differences among them. Find out the specific names each bank gives to the various types of accounts discussed in this chapter.

▶ APPLICATION

Assume that you deposited $649.70 in your checking account on the 23rd of last month. You have recently received notification that several of the checks you wrote to pay bills have bounced, although you believe there was enough money in your account to cover them. You have been told you will be charged a fee of $15 for each of these checks. Today you received your monthly statement from the bank and discovered that your account was credited with only $64.97 for your deposit on the 23rd. You have kept your deposit slip, which clearly shows the $649.70 amount.

Write a letter to the bank explaining the problem and demanding a specific solution. There is no need to be rude or insulting. The person who reads your letter did not make the mistake. However, it is necessary that you make your expectations clear.

▶ SELECTED READINGS

▶ Ashton Betsy. "Banking Smart." *Guide to Living on Your Own*. Boston: Little, Brown, 1988, pp. 3–14.

▶ Bohlman, Herbert M., et al. "Checks and the Banking System." *The Legal Environment of Business*. St. Paul: West, 1989, pp. 240–251.

▶ Clarkson, Kenneth W., et al. "Checks and the Banking System." *West's Business Law*. 4th ed. St. Paul: West, 1989, ch. 27.

▶ Elias, S. and L. Goldoftas. "Stopping Payment on a Check." *Consumers' Research Magazine,* May 5, 1990, pp. 25–27.

▶ Loeb, Marshall. "Your Best Deals in Banking." *Marshall Loeb's 1992 Money Guide,* Boston: Little, Brown, 1992, pp. 344–345.

▶ *Making Deposits: When Will Your Money Be Available?* Available free from the Board of Governors of the Federal Reserve System, Room M-P-503, Stop 138, 20th and C Sts., N.W., Washington, DC 20551.

▶ Miller, Roger LeRoy, and Robert W. Pulsinelli. *Modern Money and Banking,* 2d ed. New York: McGraw-Hill, 1989.

▶ Vogel, T. "Have a PC? Now You Can Chuck Your Checkbook." *Business Week,* September 3, 1990, p. 113.

Coping with Computerized Banking Services

When you use electronic fund transfer systems (EFTS), any number of problems might arise. Your debit card could be lost or stolen, and somebody else—if the person knows your PIN—could withdraw funds electronically from your account. The computer could make a mistake—or you might make a mistake but assume it's the bank's fault. You might want to stop the bank from making a preauthorized fund transfer, but how—and when—must you go about it? In such situations, you need to know your rights as established by the Electronic Fund Transfer Act (EFTA) of 1978. This Consumer Issue looks at some of the common problems experienced by EFTS users and at the rights of consumers under the EFTA.

► IF YOU LOSE YOUR DEBIT CARD

If you lose your debit card, or if it is stolen, you should notify your bank right away. Under the EFTA, if you notify your bank of the loss or theft within two business days, you will be liable for only $50 of any unauthorized transfers from your account. If you don't notify the bank until af-ter the second business day, your liability climbs to $500. Your liability may be unlimited if you fail to notify the bank within sixty days of your receipt of a periodic statement that reflects an unauthorized transfer.

► WHEN MISTAKES OCCUR

If you find an error on your bank statement, you need to notify your bank of the error within 60 days af-ter receiving the statement, or you will lose your right to have the mis-take corrected. The notification can be oral or written, but it must con-tain the following information:

1. Your name and account number.
2. A statement that an error has been made and the amount of the error.
3. The reasons why you think the error occurred.

The bank is required to investigate the problem and report the results of its investigation to you within 10 business days. If a full investigation requires more than 10 days, the bank can take up to 45 days—but it must recredit your account with the disputed amount until the problem is resolved. After the bank has con-cluded its investigation, it must give you a full, written report of the bank's conclusions—even if no mis-take was made. Banks are held to strict compliance with the EFTA, and if your bank fails to adhere to the letter of the law of the EFTA, it will be held liable for treble damages (three times the amount of provable damages) to you, the consumer.

► HOW TO STOP A PREAUTHORIZED TRANSFER

As the name implies, a preauthor-ized transfer is one that is authorized by you in advance through a special arrangement you make with your bank. The authorization must be in writing, and the bank must give you a copy of the authorization when the arrangement is made. But what if you want to stop a preauthorized payment from being made? Perhaps you want to make a payment in per-son or for some other reason don't want the bank to go ahead with the transfer.

Under the EFTA, you can request the bank to stop the transfer at any time up to 3 business days before the transfer is scheduled to be made. You can notify the bank orally or in writing of your wishes, although, if the notification is oral, the bank may require written confirmation of the notification within 14 days.

► DISCLOSURE OF TERMS AND CONDITIONS

The EFTA requires that the terms and conditions of electronic fund transfers involving a customer's ac-count be disclosed in readily under-standable language at the time the customer contracts for the services. Included among the required disclo-sures are the following, some of which have already been discussed:

1. The customer's liability for unau-thorized transfers resulting from the loss or theft of a debit card, code, or other access device.
2. Whom and what phone number to call to report a theft or loss.
3. The charges for using EFTS.
4. What systems are available and the limits on frequency and dollar amounts.
5. The customer's right to see evi-dence of transactions in writing.
6. How errors can be corrected.
7. The customer's right to stop pay-ments.
8. The bank's liability to the cus-tomer.

9. Rules concerning the disclosure of account information to third parties.

▶ RULES TO REMEMBER WHEN USING EFTS

Rule 1. Always wait for ATM's record of your transaction, and check it before you leave. Such records tell you the amount, date, and location, as well as the type of transaction. This information, on paper, allows you to verify the bank's monthly statement when you receive it. Also, if you have a dispute, it helps to have the actual receipt from the machine.

Rule 2. When you make a mistake that cannot be corrected at an ATM, pick up the customer-service phone immediately. This same advice holds true if the machine ever short-changes you.

Rule 3. Keep all records. Put them in your wallet or purse and then collect them for reconciliation at the end of the month.

Rule 4. Transfer your EFTS records to a checkbook, and keep a running balance.

Rule 5. Reconcile your monthly statement, canceled checks, and ATM records at the end of every month, just as you would with a regular checking account. You'll have to keep a detailed record of your ATM transactions to do so.

Rule 6. Don't share your PIN, or secret code, or your debit card with anyone. If you have a choice, don't choose a PIN that uses your name, initials, birthdate, or parts of your phone number, Social Security number, or account number.

Rule 7. If you are using an ATM, have anyone with you step aside so the transaction can't be observed. Do it politely or with humor, but don't take no for an answer. If someone is waiting behind you or beside you, shield your actions on the numbered keys with your free hand.

▶ SUMMARY

1. To cope properly with electronic fund transfer systems (EFTS), you need to know your rights as a consumer under the Electronic Fund Transfer Act of 1978.

2. If your debit card is lost or stolen, notify your bank of the loss or theft within two business days; your liability will be only $50 for any unauthorized transfer from your account. Notification after the second business day increases your liability to $500, and if no notification is given after 60 days from the receipt of a bank statement that shows an unauthorized transfer, your liability may be unlimited.

3. If you notice an error on your bank statement and notify your bank within 60 days of receiving the statement, the bank is required to investigate the problem and report its conclusions to you within ten business days. If a longer time is necessary, the bank can take up to 45 days, but it must recredit your account for the disputed amount until the problem is resolved.

4. You can stop your bank from making a preauthorized transfer from your account, provided you make your request at least 3 business days before the transfer is scheduled to be made.

5. The EFTA requires that all of the terms and conditions pertaining to electronic fund transfers, including the bank's and the customer's respective obligations in EFTS, be disclosed to any customer who contracts for EFTS services.

6. To guard against problems in EFTS, be sure you keep transaction receipts, keep a running balance of your account, reconcile your monthly statement, don't share your PIN or debit card with anyone, and don't let anybody observe you punch in your PIN at an automated teller machine.

▶ QUESTIONS FOR THOUGHT AND DISCUSSION

1. Do you think EFTS will eventually replace all cash and checks in our society?

2. In your opinion, do you think point-of-sale systems make it harder or easier to engage in impulse buying?

3. If you lose your debit card, should you notify the bank even if nobody else knows your PIN?

4. Can you envision any circumstances in which you would ever let another person use your debit card and PIN to withdraw funds from your account?

▶ THINGS TO DO

1. On a sheet of paper, create three columns under the headings of cash, checks, and EFTS. Under each heading, list the advantages and disadvantages you feel are associated with each method of payment.

2. Go to a major bank in your community and ask what types of EFTS are available to consumers through that bank. Find out if any point-of-sale systems exist in your community and, if so, how they operate.

▶ SELECTED READINGS

▶ Ashton, Betsy. "Dealing with Machine Mania." *Guide to Living on Your Own*. Boston: Little, Brown, 1988, pp. 8–10.

▶ Clarkson, Kenneth W., et al. "Electronic Fund Transfers." *West's Business Law*. 4th ed. St. Paul: West, 1989, ch. 28.

▶ Davis, K. "The Supercharged ATM

Card." *Kiplinger's Personal Finance Magazine,* August 1991, p. 244.

▶ Loeb, Marshall. "Automatic Teller Machines." *Marshall Loeb's 1989*

Money Guide. Boston: Little, Brown, 1992, pp. 348–350.

▶ Wilson, Virginia. "The Era of Debit Cards." *Newsweek,* January 2,

1989, p. 51.

▶ Zinn, Laura. "Electronic Banking May Have to Log Off." *Business Week,* April 10, 1989, p. 75.

The Overextended American

In 1786, in the city of Concord, Massachusetts, the scene of one of the first battles of the Revolution, there were three times as many people in debtors' prison as there were in prison for all other crimes combined. In Worcester County, the ratio was even higher—twenty to one. Most of the prisoners were small farmers who could not pay their debts. In August 1786, mobs of musket-bearing farmers seized county courthouses to halt the trials of debtors. Led by Daniel Shays, a captain from the Continental Army, the rebels launched an attack on the Federal Arsenal at Springfield; although they were repulsed, their rebellion continued to grow into the winter. Finally, George Washington wrote to a friend:

> For God's sake, tell me what is the cause of these commotions. Do they proceed from licentiousness, British influence disseminated by the Tories, or real grievances which admit to redress? If the latter, why were they delayed until the public mind had become so agitated? If the former, why are not the powers of government tried at once?

THE INDEBTED SOCIETY

Interest
The cost of using someone else's money.

The majority of Americans have outstanding *installment debt* at any given time. In other words, they have received money from a lender and contracted to pay back what is owed plus **interest** over a certain period of time—say, monthly for four years. At the start of 1992, the total amount of consumer credit (not including mortgages) was $730 billion—equal to more than one-fifth of personal disposable income. Clearly, we are an indebted society, and buying on credit is part of the American way of life. A number of sources are available to supply that credit for us.

SOURCES OF CREDIT

The numerous sources for today's consumer can be divided into two general categories:

1. Sources of credit for consumer loans.
2. Sources of credit for consumer sales.

The first category relates to direct loans that a consumer can obtain. The second category relates to the extension of credit along with the purchase of some item, such as a stereo.

Sources of Consumer Loans

There are a number of sources to which consumers can turn for direct loans.

Commercial Banks The most obvious place to obtain credit is a commercial bank. The personal-loan departments of commercial banks extend about 50 percent of the loans for automobile purchases, as well as about 20 percent of all loans for other consumer goods. In general, these banks are full-service commercial banks that have personal-loan departments.

Consumer Finance Companies Consumer finance companies make small loans to consumers at relatively high rates of interest. Interest rates are typically very high because consumer finance companies cater to a higher-risk clientele. That is to say, they incur a higher risk of nonpayment on their outstanding loans than do commercial banks. They must be compensated for this higher risk by receiving a higher interest rate. Approximately 20 percent of installment credit is financed by these small-loan companies.

Credit Unions Credit unions are a special type of consumer cooperative agency; only members may borrow from a credit union. Teachers and workers belonging to large unions or companies often have the opportunity to join their own credit unions. Credit unions account for about 15 percent of all personal consumer credit.

Loans on Your Life Insurance If you have a life insurance policy with a cash value (see Chapter 21), then you may be able to obtain a relatively low-cost loan on that policy. You usually pay something less than 10 percent for a loan on the value of your policy. You cannot be turned down for a loan from your insurance company, and no questions are asked about how you plan to use the money, because it is *your* money. Your credit rating has nothing to do with whether you get the loan. You can take as long as you wish to repay. In fact, whenever the policy becomes payable—either because it matures or the owner of it dies—any outstanding loan is deducted from the amount of the insurance claim that the company must pay. Hence, any loan you take out reduces your insurance protection.

Other Approximately 10 percent of consumer loans are extended by other types of lenders. Pursuant to the 1980 Depository Institutions Deregulation and Monetary Control Act, savings and loan associations and savings banks are now allowed to make some personal loans to consumers. Student loans, which are guaranteed by the government but administered through banks, also (when they become due) become installment debt. Brokerage houses are a relatively new source of consumer credit for their customers. They have traditionally made loans to customers for purposes of purchasing stocks and bonds on credit. Recent changes, however, have allowed customers to borrow—by writing checks on their asset management accounts (see Chapter 15)—up to a certain percentage of the value of their investments held by the brokerage firm.

Cash advances on major credit cards, such as MasterCard, VISA, Sears's Discover card, or American Express's new Optima card, are another source of installment credit if the loan is repaid over time and draws interest.

Sources of Consumer Sales Credit

In addition to direct loans, consumers also obtain credit by purchasing products on the installment plan or by using their credit cards.

Automobile Dealers and Financial Services Installment loans to pay for the purchase of an automobile are available from car dealers or affiliated financial agencies, such as General Motors Acceptance Corporation. Automobile loans account for approximately 40 percent of all installment debt in the United States.

Credit Cards Today, there are more than 1 billion credit cards in use in America. Two of the most widely known bank credit cards, MasterCard and

VISA, account for nearly 300 million of these—that's more than one bank card for every adult in the United States. Other credit cards are American Express, Diners Club, and Sears's Discover card. In addition to these major credit cards, most retail outlets offer some form of credit to their customers. Virtually all of the major department stores, such as Sears, J. C. Penney, Marshal Fields, Montgomery Ward, and others, provide individual credit cards to their customers for use in making purchases at their stores. Oil companies such as Shell, Amoco, and Conoco also make it possible for their customers to purchase their products on credit with the use of a credit card.

Credit cards have become an important source for consumer sales credit, as well as for direct loans in the form of cash advances, as already mentioned. Approximately 25 percent of all installment debt is created by credit cards. The average monthly credit card balance per person in the United States is now approximately $1,500, and millions of Americans have balances exceeding $2,500.

WHY BORROW?

Why should you ever borrow money? Some of you may answer, "There's no reason you should. Pay cash for everything and never have debt hanging over your head." This is still the attitude throughout much of Europe, where many people are reluctant to borrow to purchase goods and services.

The reason most of us borrow might be explained this way. Suppose you have decided that you want to buy an automobile. Now, you're not buying an automobile *per se;* you're really buying the *services* from that automobile for each day, week, month, and year that you will have it. In fact, what is really important to you is the cost per *service flow* per period. In other words, what does it cost you per month to operate that Buick Skylark or Ford Mustang? What will it cost you per month or per year to buy a new car instead of

Although buying on credit can be a wise consumer choice, in many situations consumers should resist this temptation to avoid going too far into debt. Retailers encourage consumers to buy on credit to increase their sales and profits. While the extra spending this causes may be good for business, it can spell disaster for consumers who fail to control their credit buying.

keeping your old one? Cars are *consumer durables,* as are houses, TVs, VCRs, computers, water beds, and other things that last a relatively long time. You do not consume such durable items immediately; rather, you consume the services from them over a period of time.

When you go to the movies, on the other hand, you consume that movie during the hour and a half or two you are there, and you also pay for that movie when you consume it. When you go out to dinner, you eat the meal and then you usually pay for it on the spot. What are you doing when you consume things and pay for them at the same time? You are timing the payment for the good or service with the rate at which you are consuming it. Why not think of this as the reason for borrowing? You want to synchronize the payments for the services you are consuming from a consumer durable, such as an automobile, with the services themselves. Therefore, you do not feel obliged to pay for the car with cash because you are going to be using it for a certain number of years. *When you borrow, then, you are merely synchronizing your cash outlay to correspond more or less with the service flow from the good you purchased.* That is a valid reason for borrowing.

There are, of course, other reasons why you may wish to borrow money. They include:

1. Taking advantage of advertised specials when you are short of cash.
2. Consolidating bills.
3. Having a safeguard in emergency situations.
4. Being able to shop or travel without having to carry large amounts of cash.
5. Increasing future earning power, such as obtaining a loan to expand or to introduce a new line of merchandise.
6. Attending school.

Of course, most people don't explicitly think of credit in these terms. Rather, they reason that, because they don't have enough cash to purchase an item they want, such as a car, they must borrow.

SAVING VERSUS CREDIT BUYING

A very astute savings and loan association once ran an ad in some national magazines pointing out that if you were to save for 36 months to buy a car for $10,000, you would have to put into the bank only $9,200, the other $800 being made up by the interest you receive over the three years. On the other hand, if you bought the car immediately and paid for it over 36 months, not only would you not receive interest on your savings, but you would have to pay a finance charge on the installment debt. The total price of the car might be $11,600. There is obviously a big difference between $9,200 and $11,600. The conclusion, according to the savings and loan association: It is better to save now and buy later than to buy now and go into debt.

Is anything wrong with the reasoning in that ad? First of all, the interest on your savings account is taxable by the federal government and some state governments. Additionally, the price of the car will rise with inflation during the three-year period. If the interest rate on your savings account does not reflect the inflation rate, the arithmetic will clearly be off. Also, a crucial point was left out: During the three years in which you saved, you would not be enjoying the services of the car or of the other things you could buy. You would be putting off your purchase for three years. Most people do not want to wait that long; they would prefer to have the services of the car immediately and pay the finance charge to do that. After all, the finance charge is merely a payment for using somebody else's money so that you can consume and that other person—the saver who decided not to consume—cannot.

You may therefore decide that the implicit utility you get per service flow of whatever you buy is greater than the interest payments you have to pay your creditor to get the total amount of money to buy the goods right away. No moral judgment need be passed here: It is simply a question of comparing costs and benefits. The benefit of borrowing is having purchasing power today; the cost is whatever you have to pay in finance charges. Obviously, if the cost were zero, you would borrow as much as you could because you could buy everything you wanted today and pay back whatever you owed at some later date without any penalty. In fact, the ultimate consumer probably would like to die with an infinite debt. That way, the person could consume all he or she wanted at everybody else's expense. Of course, when you buy something on credit with no intention of paying back that loan, there is little difference between that action and stealing.

The benefits of borrowing are something that only you can decide. But we should all be aware of the costs of borrowing. There is a very definite relationship between rising prices and high interest rates. But the relationship is not the simple one of causation that you may have been taught to expect. Contrary to popular belief, high interest rates do not and cannot, in the long run, *cause* inflation. When prices are rising, interest rates will have an inflationary premium tacked on to them. A simple example will show you why.

Suppose you are a banker who has been loaning out money at 5 percent a year for the last 20 years. Suppose also that, for the last 20 years, there has been no inflation. That 5 percent interest you have been charging is the *real* rate of interest you are receiving. It covers your costs and gives you a normal profit for your lending activities.

Now prices start rising at 5 percent a year, and you expect that they will rise at that rate forever. If someone comes in to borrow money, how much do you think you would want to lend at the 5 percent rate of interest that you have always charged? Think about it. Say a person comes in to borrow $1,000 for a year. At the end of the year, with an inflation rate of 5 percent, the actual purchasing power of that $1,000 paid back to you will be only $950. If you ask for 5 percent, or $50 dollars in interest payments, you will be compensated *only* for the erosive effect of inflation on the value of the money you lend out.

Obviously, you will want to tack on an inflationary premium to the real interest rate that you had been charging when there was no inflation and none was anticipated. Hence, in periods of inflation, we find the inflationary premium tacked on everywhere. It is not surprising, then, that, during an inflationary period when prices are rising at 10 percent a year, interest rates may be 15 percent. (See Exhibit 16–1.)

You, the demander of credit, or the potential debtor, should not be put off by a higher interest rate. After all, you are going to be repaying the loan in cheapened dollars—that is, dollars that have lost part of their purchasing power through inflation. In fact, some interest rates did not react very rapidly to rising inflation in the early 1970s. Credit unions, for example, were giving out automobile loans at an effective interest rate of 8 percent per annum. Since the rate of inflation was 6 percent, those loans cost people only a 2 percent real rate of interest. For example, the author took out a National Defense

▶ **Exhibit 16–1   The "Real" Rate of Interest**

The rate of interest you are paying on a $1,000 loan for one year.	15%
The (expected) rate of inflation (loss in value of money) this year.	10%
The difference between the rate of interest you are paying and the loss in the value of dollars you will pay back.	5%

So 5 percent is the real rate of interest you pay when you are charged 15 percent on a loan and the rate of inflation is 10 percent.

(This example ignores tax deductions, which may reduce real interest rates even more on certain loans, such as home mortgages.)

Education Act student loan while he was in college in the 1960s. The rate of interest on those loans was then 3 percent. When he paid them back, however, the inflation rate was nearly 9 percent. Therefore, he made a profit of 6 percent by holding off repaying those loans; that is, he actually *made* money on the loans. This is not the kind of deal most people get, however, because potential creditors generally tack on inflationary premiums whenever they think inflation is gong to occur.

WHAT IT COSTS TO BORROW

Why do you have to pay to borrow? Because somebody else is giving up something. What are they giving up? Purchasing power, or command over goods and services today. For other people to give up command over goods and services today, they have to be compensated, and they usually are compensated with what we call interest. Ask yourself if you would be willing to loan $100 to your friend with the loan to be paid back in ten years, with no interest—just the $100. To do this, you would have to sacrifice what the $100 would have bought, while your friend enjoyed it. Most people will not make this sacrifice with no reward except as a strictly charitable act (and they also want to be compensated for any risk of not being repaid).

Interest Rate Determination

Think of the interest rate you pay on a loan as the price you pay the lender for the use of his or her money. What determines that price is no different from what determines the price of anything else in our economy. The various demands and supplies for credit ultimately result in some sort of interest rate being charged for the different forms of credit.

But we cannot really talk about a single interest rate or a single charge for credit. Interest rates vary according to the length of a loan, the risk involved, whether the debtor has put up something as **collateral** for the loan (that is, secured it), and so on. One rule is fairly certain: The greater the perceived risk, the more the creditor will demand in interest payments from the debtor. Don't be surprised, then, that interest rates in the economy range all the way from relatively low to relatively high. Much of that difference in interest rates has to do with the riskiness of the loan.

Finance Charges

The cost of credit varies, not only among individuals for the reasons just given, but also among different lending institutions, some of which will charge more than others. The **finance charge** is the total amount you will pay to use credit. This charge includes interest costs, any required credit-insurance premiums or appraisal fees, and other related service charges.

By far the largest part of finance charges is the interest you will pay for your loan. If, for example, you wish to buy a car for $7,500 but have only $1,500 in cash, you will have to borrow the other $6,000. The cost of borrowing that $6,000 will depend on two factors: the **annual percentage rate (APR)** and the length of the loan.

The annual percentage rate is the cost of credit calculated on a yearly basis. The total amount of interest you pay for your loan will be determined by the length of the loan. A $6,000 loan for four years, for example, at an APR of 14 percent would cost $487.56 more in interest than would a three-year loan for

Collateral
The backing that people often must put up to obtain a loan. Whatever is placed as collateral for a loan can be sold to repay that loan if the debtor cannot pay it off as specified in the loan agreement. For example, the collateral for a new-car loan is generally the new car itself. If the finance company does not get paid for its car loan, it can then repossess the car and sell it to recover the amount of the loan.

Finance charge
The total costs you pay for credit, including interest charges, possible credit-insurance premium costs and appraisal fees, and other service charges.

Annual percentage rate (APR)
The annual interest cost of consumer credit.

	APR	LENGTH OF LOAN	MONTHLY PAYMENT	TOTAL FINANCE CHARGE	TOTAL COST
Creditor A	14%	3 years	$205.07	$1,382.52	$7,382.52
Creditor B	14%	4 years	$163.96	$1,870.08	$7,870.08
Creditor C	15%	4 years	$166.98	$2,015.04	$8,015.04

the same amount, as can be seen in Exhibit 16–2. Does that mean you shouldn't get a four-year loan? Not necessarily. You will also note in Exhibit 16–2 that the monthly payment for those four years will be substantially less than it would be for a three-year loan; to pay off the loan in three years, you would pay $41.11 more a month. Depending on your personal situation, you might prefer to make lower monthly payments for a longer period of time.

Consumer Credit Legislation

With hundreds of billions of dollars in consumer credit outstanding, the opportunity for abuse is great. A series of laws has been passed that are intended to protect consumer rights and prevent the exploitation of borrowers by unscrupulous lenders.

TRUTH IN LENDING

The Truth-in-Lending Act, which is Title I of the Consumer Credit Protection Act of 1968, is essentially a disclosure law. Most kinds of installment debts now have to be properly labeled so that the consumer knows exactly what he or she is paying.

The congressional purpose of the act was "to insure a meaningful disclosure of credit terms so that the consumer will be able to compare more readily the various credit terms available to him and avoid the uninformed use of credit." The act, based on the consumer's right to be informed, requires that the various terms used to describe the dollar cost of credit, such as interest, points, and so on, be described and disclosed under one common label, *finance charge*. Likewise, it abolishes all the various terms used to describe the cost of credit in percentage terms, such as discount rates, add-ons, and the like, and prescribes a uniform method of computation of a single rate known as the *annual percentage rate*.

The Truth-in-Lending Act also grants the consumer-borrower a **right of rescission** (cancellation) for certain credit contracts. (This is also called a *cooling-off period*.) Section 125 of the act gives the consumer three business days to rescind a credit transaction signed with a door-to-door salesperson that results or may result in a lien on the consumer's home, or on any real property that is used or expected to be used as his or her principal residence. The right of rescission is designed to allow the person additional time to reconsider using the residence as security for credit. This right of rescission does not, however, apply to first mortgages on homes.

The Truth-in-Lending Act also regulates the advertising of consumer credit. One of the primary purposes of the act's advertising requirements is to eliminate "come-on" credit ads. For example, if any one important credit term is mentioned in an advertisement—down payment or monthly payment—all other important terms also must be defined.

Right of rescission
The right to cancel a contract or an agreement that has been signed. For example, if you sign an agreement to buy a set of encyclopedias from a door-to-door salesperson, you have the right to cancel the agreement within a three-day period in some states.

A Tale of Woe

Under the Truth-in-Lending Act, a consumer's liability for the unauthorized use of his or her credit card is limited to $50. But what, exactly, constitutes "unauthorized" use? One consumer, Robert Martin, learned the hard way. Martin loaned his American Express credit card to an associate, E. L. McBride, and told McBride that he could charge up to $500 on the card. As a precaution, Martin also wrote to American Express and requested that the charges on his account be limited to $1,000. Two months later, however, Martin re-

ceived a bill from American Express showing a balance of $5,300 on his account.

Martin refused to pay the unauthorized portion of the charges, claiming that he was protected under the Truth-in-Lending Act from all but $50 in liability. When American Express sued Martin for the money, however, Martin learned that his interpretation of the term *authorized* was not that intended by the Truth-in-Lending Act as interpreted by the court. In the eyes of the court, Martin had voluntarily permitted McBride to use his credit

card and thereby *authorized* its use. McBride had neither stolen the card nor obtained it from Martin under conditions of fraud or duress. Since McBride's use of the card was authorized, the $50 liability limit provided for under the Truth-in-Lending Act did not apply. Although Martin could sue McBride for unauthorized use, he couldn't avoid payment to American Express on the basis of the Truth-in-Lending Act. A costly lesson in the letter of the law.

A 1970 amendment to the act provides federal regulations on the use of credit cards. This amendment prohibits the unsolicited distribution of new credit cards and also establishes a maximum limit of $50 on liability for the unauthorized use of each of such cards; that is, the owner of a lost or stolen card that has been used illegally by another person cannot be made liable for more than $50 of illegal purchases. The Consumer Close-Up shows how important it is to avoid allowing others to use your credit card. A 1982 amendment to the act required that all installment credit contracts be written in easily readable and understandable English so that consumers clearly understand any credit terms and conditions of the contract.

The Truth-in-Lending Act does not actually assure protection, only information. But information can be valuable, because it allows you, the consumer who is looking for credit, to shop around, to see exactly what you are paying, and to know exactly what you are getting into. The Truth-in-Lending Act requires that an accurate assessment of the annual percentage rate be given, and that's what you should look at when you compare the price of credit from various dealers and companies. In addition, you may want to look at the finance charge, which is the total number of dollars you pay to borrow the money, whether directly or in the form of deferred payments on a purchase. These total finance charges include all the so-called carrying charges that sometimes are tacked onto a retail installment contract plus such things as "setup" charges and mandatory credit life insurance.[1] These all contribute to your costs of having purchasing power today instead of waiting, of having command over goods and services right now, and of taking that command away from somebody else. Expressed as a percentage of the total price, it

---

1. Credit life insurance, which is discussed in Chapter 21, usually isn't a good deal.

gives your annual percentage interest rate. In some cases, it may be very high indeed.

REGULATION OF REVOLVING CREDIT

Many credit card companies currently impose an annual membership fee. This fee is at least $15 dollars, but it could be as much as $250. So even if you pay your account within the billing period, you still won't receive free credit if you are required to pay a membership fee. In addition, for those people who do not pay off their accounts during the billing period, the creditor will impose a monthly finance charge of generally 1 to 1½ percent. The creditor computes the finance charge by multiplying the monthly rate times the outstanding balance. Creditors will use one of the following different techniques to compute the outstanding balance and finance charges on revolving credit accounts.

1. *Previous-balance method*—Here the creditor computes a finance charge on the previous month's balance, even if it has been paid.
2. *Average-daily-balance method*—The finance charge is applied to the sum of the actual amounts outstanding each day during the billing period divided by the number of days in that period. Payments are credited on the exact date of payment.
3. *Adjusted-balance method*—Finance charges are assessed on the balance after deducting payments and credits.

It's important to know which method is used in assessing the finance charge you pay, because the different methods can result in quite different finance charges. For example, assume your opening balance or previous monthly balance was $300. You paid $100 on the account, which was credited on the fifteenth day of the month. The monthly interest rate is quoted at 1½ percent (18 percent annual rate). Exhibit 16–3 shows that the same monthly finance percentage rate can result in a sizable difference in finance charges based on

▶ Exhibit 16–3 **Computing Finance Charges Using Three Different Methods**

METHOD	OPENING BALANCE	OUTSTANDING BALANCE (1)	MONTHLY INTEREST RATE (2)	FINANCE CHARGE (1) × (2) = (3)
A. Previous balance	$300	$300	1.5%	$4.50
B. Adjusted balance	300	200	1.5%	3.00
C. Average daily balance	300	250	1.5%	3.75

A. Previous balance—The interest rate of .015 is multiplied times $300 to obtain the finance charge of $4.50. It is important to note that the lender gives no credit for the $100 payment received on the fifteenth when computing the outstanding balance.
B. Adjusted balance—The interest rate of .015 is multiplied times $200 to obtain the finance charge of $3.00. The creditor uses only the ending balance for the period as the outstanding balance.
C. Average daily balance—The interest rate of .015 is multiplied times $250 to obtain the finance charge of $3.75. The $250 average daily balance was calculated as follows:

Number of days	X	Balance	= Total balance
15	X	$300	$4500
15	X	200	$3000
			$7500

Total balance, divided by number of days in month (billing period) ($7,500/30) = Average daily balance ($250)
With this method, the creditor considers the average daily balance as the outstanding balance.

what the creditor considers the outstanding balance. The same monthly finance charge of 1½ percent results in three different annual rates of interest, depending on which computational method the creditor uses.

The Truth-in-Lending Act requires that all revolving credit contracts and monthly bills state the "nominal annual percentage rate," which equals 12 times the monthly rate. As Exhibit 16–3 illustrates, however, sometimes the annual percentage rate can be misleading when comparing revolving credit accounts. In 1988, Congress addressed this problem by passing the Fair Credit and Charge Card Disclosure Act. Under this act, lenders must reveal to any consumers applying for credit accounts the following information:

1. The annual percentage rate of interest, including the way the rate is calculated if the rate is variable.
2. All fees, including annual fees, minimum finance charges, transaction charges, cash-advance fees, late fees, and over-the-limit fees.
3. The length of the grace period, if any. (A *grace period* is that period of time during which no interest is charged on your account balance.)
4. The method used to calculate the monthly account balances against which the lender applies interest or finance charges.

EQUAL CREDIT OPPORTUNITY

Since October 1975, when the Equal Credit Opportunity Act went into effect, it has been illegal to discriminate on the basis of sex and marital status when granting credit. Regulations pursuant to the act issued by the Federal Reserve Board prohibit:

1. Demanding information on the credit applicant's childbearing intentions or birth-control practices.
2. Requiring co-signatures on loans when such requirements do not apply to all qualified applicants.
3. Discouraging the applicant from applying for credit because of sex or marital status.
4. Terminating or changing the conditions of credit solely on the basis of a change in marital status.
5. Ignoring alimony and child-support payments as regular income in assessing the creditworthiness of the applicant.

Basically, the Equal Credit Opportunity Act reaffirms a woman's right to get and keep credit in her own name rather than that of her husband (or of her former husband, if she is divorced). Women who wish to establish their own lines of credit are advised by bankers to do the following:

1. Open checking and savings accounts in your own name.
2. Create a separate credit record, assuming you can afford it.
3. Open a charge account at a retail store. When applying, list only your own salary, not that of your spouse.
4. Apply for a bank credit card.
5. Finally, take out a small loan and repay it on time. Even if you don't need it, this would speed up the establishment of your credit reliability.

Today, a woman has the legal right to credit for her husband's credit cards. In other words, all new accounts automatically give credit references to all those on the application, including the wife.

FAIR CREDIT BILLING ACT

Basically, under the rules set up pursuant to this act, you can withhold payment until the dispute over a faulty product that you purchased with your credit card is resolved. The purchase must be for more than $50 and must have taken place within your state or 100 miles of your home. It is up to the credit card issuer to intervene and attempt a settlement between you and the seller. You do not have unlimited rights to stop payment. You must exercise a good-faith effort to get satisfaction from the seller before you do so. The rules seem to be in the consumer's favor, however. You don't even have to notify the credit card company that you are cutting off payment (on that item). You just wait for the company to act. It is probably a good idea, however, to let the company know what you are doing. Ultimately, you can be sued by the credit card company if no agreement is reached.

Other rules were also set up in the Fair Credit Billing Act. If you think there is an error in your bill, the credit card company must investigate and you can suspend payments until it does so. You simply write to the credit card company within 60 days of getting the bill, briefly explaining the circumstances and why you think there is an error. It is a good idea to include copies (not the originals) of the sales slips at issue. Under the law, the company must acknowledge your letter within 30 days and resolve the dispute within 90 days. During that period, you don't have to pay the amount in dispute or any minimum payments on the amount in dispute. And, further, your creditor cannot charge you finance charges during that period for unpaid balances in dispute. It cannot even close your account; however, if it turns out that there was no error, the creditor can attempt to collect finance charges for the entire period for which payments were not made.

FAIR CREDIT REPORTING ACT

The Fair Credit Reporting Act (Title VI of the 1968 Consumer Credit Protection Act) was passed in 1970 and went into effect in 1971. Under this law, you have recourse when a credit-investigating agency gives you a bad rating. Now, when you are turned down for credit because of a bad credit rating, the company that turned you down must give you the name and address of the credit-investigating agency that was used. The same holds true for an insurance company.

The 1971 act was meant to regulate the consumer credit-reporting industry to ensure that credit-reporting agencies supply information that is equitable and fair to the consumer. The problems that led to passage of the act seem to have been the reporting of incorrect, misleading, or incomplete information, as well as one-sided versions of disputed claims. A 1991 Consumers Union survey of credit bureau reports showed that 50 percent of the files investigated contained at least one error. In addition, many people were concerned about the invasion of privacy in the distribution of such reports to those who did not really have a legitimate business need for them. These reports often contained material about a person's general reputation, personal characteristics or mode of living, and character. The act applies not only to the usual credit bureaus and investigating concerns but also to finance companies and banks that routinely give out credit information other than that which is developed from their own transactions.

Under the rules of this law, a credit bureau must disclose to you the "nature and substance of all information" that is included under your name in its files. You also have the right to be told the sources of just about all of that information. If you discover that the credit bureau has incomplete, misleading, or false information, the Fair Credit Reporting Act requires that the bureau investigate any disputed information "within a reasonable period of time." Of course, the credit bureau is not necessarily going to do it, but you do have the law on your side, and you can go to court over the issue. In addition, at your request, the credit bureau must send to those companies that received a credit report in the last six months a notice of the elimination of any false information from your credit record. Finally, if the credit bureau does not correct your information, you can file a personal version concerning any disputes that is limited to 100 words in length. In 1991, TRW, one of the three largest credit-reporting businesses, announced it would provide free copies of credit reports once a year to people who request them.

Even if you have not been rejected for credit, you still have the right to go to a credit bureau and find out what your file contains. You also have the right to ask the credit bureau to delete, correct, or investigate items you believe to be fallacious or inaccurate. The credit bureau then has the legal right to charge you for the time it spends correcting any mistakes.[2] Also, the Fair Credit Reporting Act specifically forbids credit bureaus from sending out any adverse information that is more than seven years old. But there are important exceptions. Bankruptcy information can be sent out to your prospective creditors for a full ten years. And there is no time limit on any information for loans or life insurance policies of $50,000 or more or for a job application with an annual salary of $20,000 or more. That means that adverse information may be kept in your file and used indefinitely for these purposes.

> Even if you have not been rejected for credit, you have the right to go to a credit bureau and find out what your file contains.

FAIR DEBT COLLECTION PRACTICES ACT

In 1977 Congress passed the Fair Debt Collection Practices Act. The purpose of the act is to regulate the debt-collection practices of persons who collect from consumers whose debts arise from purchases that are primarily for personal, family, or household purposes. The act prohibits the following debt-collection practices:

1. Contacting the consumer at his or her place of employment if the employer objects.
2. Contacting the consumer at inconvenient or unusual times, such as three o'clock in the morning, or contacting the consumer at all if he or she is represented by an attorney.
3. Contacting third parties other than parents, spouses, or financial advisers about the payment of a debt unless the court authorizes it.
4. Using harassment and intimidation, such as abusive language, or using false or misleading information, such as posing as a police officer.
5. Communicating with the consumer after receipt of notice that the consumer is refusing to pay the debt, except to advise the consumer of further action to be taken by the collection agency.

---

2. In some states, such as California, legislatures have mandated a maximum fee that can be charged by credit bureaus for such information.

Personal bankruptcy offers people who have gotten in over their heads a chance to "wipe their slates clean" and start over. Many people have been forced into bankruptcy by conditions that were beyond their control. Sharon and Billy Grona, for example, had successfully operated children's clothing stores for years in Texas when a faltering economy and rising interest rates wiped them out. Their bankruptcy relieved them of their debt, but what of their creditors who never collected the more than $100,000 they were owed? Bankruptcy does not eliminate the cost of debt; it simply moves it from the debtor to the creditor.

Some people believe it has become too easy and too acceptable to file personal bankruptcy. Many law firms and individual attorneys advertise that consumers may quickly and easily eliminate their debt burdens for as little as $500 in legal fees. A Nashville attorney shows videotapes that explain the bankruptcy process to prospective clients. The idea is to increase the number of bankruptcy cases he is able to take on. There are also many do-it-yourself bankruptcy publications. Nolo Press in Berkeley, California, sells a bankruptcy manual for $25.95 (1-800-992-6656). You can even purchase bankruptcy forms from stationary stores, and obtain assistance in preparing them

from Legal Alternatives, Inc., of Portland, Oregon (1-800-626-2642).

Although under current law, filing for personal bankruptcy is clearly legal under any circumstances, some people do not believe it is an ethical choice for non-emergency cases. They suggest that it has become too easy for consumers to borrow and not pay their debts. What is your opinion in this issue? Would you consider filing for bankruptcy? Under what circumstances?

The enforcement of this act is the responsibility of the Federal Trade Commission. The act provides for damages and penalties that can be recovered for violation, including attorneys' fees.

▶ SUMMARY

1. The majority of Americans have outstanding installment debt at any given time.

2. The sources of credit are many, including commercial banks, consumer finance companies, credit unions, credit card companies, and retail stores.

3. Individuals borrow in order to obtain the services of large consumer items without paying for them at one time. The installment payments can be thought of as matching the service flow from whatever was purchased, such as a house or a car.

4. Interest is the payment for using somebody else's money. As such, it is like any other price. Interest rates must take account of the rate of inflation. Hence, interest rates are relatively high when the rate of inflation is high.

5. The real rate of interest you pay on a loan is the stated rate of interest minus the rate of inflation.

6. The Truth-in-Lending Act requires that both the total finance charge and the annual percentage rate be clearly stated on a loan agreement (except on first mortgages on homes).

7. Lenders use three methods to compute the actual percentage rate you pay on an open-ended credit account: previous balance, average daily bal-

ance, or adjusted balance. The resultant finance charge can vary considerably, depending on the method employed. Under the Fair Credit and Charge Card Disclosure Act of 1988, lenders have to disclose to consumers which method of computation is used.

8. Since October 1975, when the Equal Credit Opportunity Act went into effect, it has been illegal to discriminate on the basis of sex and marital status when granting credit.

9. The Fair Credit Billing Act and the Fair Credit Reporting Act offer protection to the consumer in the areas of disputed charges on credit card bills and in credit-reporting practices.

10. In 1977, the Fair Debt Collection Practices Act was passed to protect consumers from unfair debt-collection practices.

▶ QUESTIONS FOR THOUGHT AND DISCUSSION

1. Does easy access to credit and charge cards make it easier or harder to stick to a budget?

2. What is the difference between credit and debt?

3. The interest rate charged by different lenders varies tremendously. How can you account for the differences?

4. Does it seem fair that those who pay cash usually pay the same price as those who use a credit card?

5. Can you think of some very specific reasons why you would ever want to borrow money? Or ever have?

6. Is it better to save and buy? Or to buy and go into debt?

7. Do you think it is appropriate that interest rates be regulated?

8. During the early 1970s the rate of inflation exceeded the rate of interest that some borrowers had to pay on their loans. What does that mean about the real rate of interest those borrowers were paying?

9. If you are charged a setup fee in addition to some annual percentage rate to borrow money from a credit card company, should that setup charge be included as part of the total finance charge? Would this raise or lower the annual percentage rate of interest?

▶ THINGS TO DO

1. See if you can find a self-supporting adult who has never gone into debt. (If you find one, ask how and/or why this is so.)

2. Select a consumer durable good, such as an automobile or an expensive stereo. Call around to find out where you could get the best loan to purchase it. If there are substantial differences in annual interest rates charged for the loan, try to determine why.

3. Ask your neighborhood retailers who accept credit cards whether they give a discount for cash. If they don't, find out why or why not.

▶ APPLICATION

Write a letter to a local credit-reporting service asking how you can obtain a copy of your credit history. (You can select a service from the Yellow Pages in your telephone book or ask at your bank.) When you receive the report, review it to see if it contains any mistakes. If it does, write to have the mistakes corrected.

▶ SELECTED READINGS

▶ Bamford, Janet, et al. *Complete Guide to Managing Your Money.* New York: Consumer Report Books, 1989.

▶ *Buying and Borrowing: Cash In on the Facts.* Available free from the Federal Trade Commission, 6th St. and Pennsylvania Ave., N.W., Washington, DC 20580.

▶ *Buying on Time.* Available from the New York State Banking Department, 2 World Trade Center, New York, NY 10047 (latest edition).

▶ "The Cheapest Credit Cards." *Consumers' Research Magazine,* September 1991, pp. 29–35.

▶ *Consumer Handbook to Credit Protection Laws.* Available free from the Federal Trade Commission, 6th St. and Pennsylvania Ave., N.W., Washington, DC 20580.

▶ *Credit and Charge Card Fraud.* Available free from the Federal Trade Commission, 6th St. and Pennsylvania Ave., N.W., Washington, DC 20580.

▶ Loeb, Marshall. "Your Borrowing." *Marshall Loeb's 1992 Money Guide,* Boston: Little, Brown, 1992, pp. 362–379.

▶ McDonald, E. M. "Slash Your Finance Charges with a Low-Rate Credit Card." *Money,* December 1991, pp. 21–22.

▶ Money Management Institute. *Managing Your Credit.* Available for $1 from Money Management Institute, 2200 Sanders Rd., Prospect Heights, IL 60070.

▶ Power, C. "Card Wars: My Value Is Bigger Than Your Value." *Business Week,* November 11, 1991, p. 138.

▶ Quinn, Jane Bryant. "Let Them Eat Credit." *Newsweek,* November 18, 1991, p. 56.

▶ Seligman, D. "Credit Card Follies." *Fortune,* December 16, 1991, pp. 147–148.

▶ Wiener, Leonard. "Cards That Try Harder." *U.S. News & World Report,* January 21, 1991, pp. 77–81.

Coping with the Credit Maze

Some consumer economics books give you cut-and-dried formulas to tell you when you should borrow. It is not unusual to find a financial adviser telling consumers that they should borrow only for major purchases, such as automobiles or houses. Just about everyone who buys a house automatically assumes that it is respectable to borrow; very few of us are in a position to pay out $80,000 or more for the full cost of a house. Because we know that the housing services we consume per month represent a very small part of the total price (because houses last so long), there seems to be no advantage in spending all that cash; instead, we take out a mortgage. The same holds for cars, especially new ones. A car is such a large expense that very few of us pay for it in cash. After houses and automobiles, though, the reasoning gets pretty fuzzy. Is it all right to buy a stereo on credit? Some financial advisers say yes, and some say no. Is it all right to buy furniture on credit? Some advisers say yes, some say no. Of course, for clothes and food most financial advisers are adamant about the desirability of paying cash.

When you think about it, the reasoning behind such cut-and-dried rules is pretty shaky. Gertrude Stein once wrote that a rose is a rose is a rose; and so, too, a dollar is a dollar is a dollar. Does it matter what you say your dollar is going to buy? You can't earmark it. If you make $100 a week and you spend $10 for clothes, $50 for food and lodging, and the rest on entertainment, how do you know which dollar you used for "essentials"—food and lodging and clothes—and which dollar you used for "nonessentials"—entertainment? You don't know because you can't tell one dollar from another. What does it matter if you say you are going to use credit to buy your clothes and pay for your entertainment with cash? It doesn't matter.

What is important is for you to decide what percentage of your anticipated income you are willing to set aside for fixed payments to repay loans. You should care about the total commitment you have made to creditors. You want to make sure you have not over committed yourself. Exhibits N–1 and N–2 may help you determine how much you should borrow.

▶ SHOPPING FOR CREDIT

Once you have decided that you want to buy some credit—that is, you want to get some goods now and pay for them later—then you should shop around.

The Truth-in-Lending Act, which requires full disclosure of the annual interest rate charged, makes shopping much easier than it used to be. You can now contact lending institutions and learn within a relatively short period of time which offer the lowest interest rates. To find the lowest interest rates on credit cards, you can contact Bankcard Holders of America and obtain a list of U.S. banks that offer the lowest rates. To obtain a list, send $1.50 to Bankcard Holders of America, 560 Herndon Parkway, Suite 120, Herndon, VA 22070.

▶ Exhibit N–1 **Rules for Borrowing**

There are two rules to consider for borrowing:

1. *Never overcommit yourself.*
2. *Limit the times you borrow money but maximize the amounts borrowed,* because this way you will pay the lowest interest charges. In other words, don't borrow several small amounts at one-week intervals; wait and borrow the total amount all at once.

▶ **Exhibit N–2   Determining a Safe Debt Load**

First, you must determine your spendable income per month.
Enter it here. $_____

Next, determine your monthly debt payments.
1. Automobile $_____
2. Appliances   _____
3. Cash loan   _____
4. Others   _____
                                    Total $_____

Now, determine your monthly payments as a percentage of spendable income. Then, look at the following guidelines.

DEBT GUIDELINES: PAYMENTS AS A PERCENTAGE OF
SPENDABLE MONTHLY INCOME.

PERCENTAGE	CURRENT MONTHLY DEBT LOAD	CAN I ASSUME ADDITIONAL DEBT?
Less than 15%	Within safety limits	Yes.
15–20%	Right at limit	Yes, but be careful.
21–30%	Overextended	No, no, no.
Above 30%	On the verge of going under	Perish the thought!

▶ WHAT IS THE MAXIMUM YOU CAN BORROW?

If you go to a bank or a credit company and ask for a loan, the loan officer probably will require you to fill out a form. On this form, you list your **liabilities** and your **assets** so that the credit officer can estimate your **net worth.** Essentially, you have to list all your assets—whatever you own—and all your liabilities—whatever you owe. The difference is your net worth. (See Exhibit N–3.) Obviously, if your net worth is negative, you will have a hard time getting a loan from anybody unless you can show that your expected income in the immediate future will be substantial.

You still do not know what your maximum credit limit is. That, of course, depends on the loan officer's assessment of your financial position. This will be a function of your net worth, your income, your relative indebtedness, and how "regu-lar" your situation is. Regularity means different things to different people, but it generally means the following:

1. You have been working regularly for a long period and, therefore, have been receiving regular income.
2. Your family situation is stable.
3. You have regularly paid your debts on time.

Or your creditworthiness can be measured by the three "Cs" that loan officers use as a guide to lending:

1. Capacity to pay back.
2. Character.
3. Capital or collateral that you own.

Loan officers may sometimes appear to discriminate against people with unstable living situations—that is, those who have unstable jobs, unstable family situations, and the like. That may or may not be true, depending on your definition of discrimination. But a loan officer is supposed to make decisions that maximize the profits for his or her company. At the going interest rate, the loan officer may decide to eliminate people who are high risks: Loans will be refused to people whose records indicate they will not pay their debts as easily or as regularly as those people who seem more stable. If you are a credit buyer with an unstable living situation, one way you can persuade loan officers not to refuse you is to discuss your problems candidly with them and produce a past record of loan repayments that shows stability in spite of your unstable situation. Or, alternatively, you could offer to pay a higher interest rate.

▶ WHERE SHOULD YOU GO FOR A LOAN?

For some asset purchases, you immediately know where to go for a loan. If you are buying a house, you obviously don't go to your local small-loan company; you go to a savings and loan association, a commercial bank, or a mortgage trust company, or you sign a contract with the seller of the house. The real-estate agent usually helps the buyer of a house secure a loan. If you want to shop around, the easiest thing to do is to call various savings and loan associations and banks to see what interest rates they are charging or visit those that won't reveal that information over the telephone. Chapter 12 discusses in more detail what you should look out for when borrowing money on a house.

To borrow for a car, again you probably won't go to the small-loan company around the corner. Rather, you should go to a credit union or a commercial bank, where the loan for a car will cost less. Note that the interest rate for a new car is usually

Estimated amounts, end of this year.

ASSETS

House (including furniture)—market
value _____

Car(s)—resale value _____

Life insurance—cash value _____

Bonds, securities—market value _____

Cash on hand _____

Other (for example, stereo, cameras,
savings accounts, land) _____

TOTAL ASSETS _____

LIABILITIES _____

Mortgage _____

Loans _____

Other _____

TOTAL LIABILITIES _____

NET WORTH
December 31, 19_____ _____

An annual net-worth statement may help you and/or your family keep track of financial progress from year to year. Essentially, your net worth is an indication of how much wealth you actually own. We generally find that young people have low net worths—or even negative net worths: that is, they owe more than they own—because they are anticipating having higher income in the future. As individuals and families get farther down the road, their net worth increases steadily, only to start falling again, usually when retirement age approaches and the income flow slows down or stops completely, thereby forcing the retired person or couple to draw on past accumulated savings. This very simplified statement of family net worth can be filled out easily. Just make sure you include all your assets and all your liabilities. Assets are anything you own, and liabilities are anything you owe.

---

lower than for a used car. Why? Because the car is used as collateral, and a new car is generally easier to sell than a used car. You should note also that, if you buy a car that is technically brand new—that is, you would be the first owner—but you purchase it after next year's models have entered the showroom, the lending agency may consider that to be a used car and charge you the higher rate of interest.

If you want to borrow money for purchases of smaller items, a credit union might be the cheapest source of credit. The next best deal would probably be offered by a bank. If you use a credit card to make your purchase, you should be sure to pay off the balance before the end of your billing period, even if this means you must borrow from another source to do it. This will allow you to avoid paying the high interest rates usually charged on credit card debt.

The key to purchasing the best credit deal is to treat credit as a

good or service and to use the same shopping techniques for purchasing credit that you would use to purchase anything else. Your shopping should stop after you've found the best car deal, for example. You may not be getting the best deal possible if you buy the credit for the car from the dealership or its affiliate. You may do better by going to your local commercial bank. But you can't predict: You have to compare.

If you wish to figure out what it would cost to borrow $1,000 for any specified period of time, look at Exhibit N–4. It shows different specified annual percentage rates for different time periods.

▶ **THE RULE OF 78**

Suppose you took out a loan for 12 months and wanted to pay it back after five months. The bank or finance company normally uses what is called *the rule of 78* to calculate what you owe in terms of the percentage of the total year's interest that would have been earned had

you carried out the full contractual agreement.

If you pay off the loan after one month, then, based on the rule of 78, you will have to pay your creditor $^{12}/_{78}$ths of the year's total interest. This is equivalent to 15.38 percent of one year's interest owed. On the other hand, the exact proportional amount of interest that you would have paid on such an installment contract for one month would equal $^{1}/_{12}$th of the year's total interest, or 8.33 percent. Notice the penalty for such an early repayment: You pay almost double the interest for that one-month loan than is stated in the installment contract.

If you keep the loan for two months and then repay it, you end up having to pay (12 + 11)/78ths, or $^{23}/_{78}$ths of the total year's interest. Again, comparison shows that the $^{23}/_{78}$ths equals 29.49 percent, and $^{2}/_{12}$ths equals 16.67 percent. You almost double the effective amount of interest that you pay over what you would have paid had you kept the

▶ Exhibit N–4   Cost of Financing $1,000 on the Installment Plan

PERCENTAGE RATE (ANNUAL)	LENGTH OF LOAN (MONTHS)	MONTHLY PAYMENTS	FINANCE CHARGE	TOTAL COST OF LOAN
9.25%	6	$171.19	$ 27.14	$1,027.14
	12	87.57	50.84	1,050.84
	24	45.80	99.20	1,099.20
	36	31.92	149.12	1,149.12
10.5%	6	171.81	30.86	1,030.86
	12	88.15	57.80	1,057.80
	24	46.38	113.12	1,113.12
	36	32.50	170.00	1,170.00
12%	6	172.55	35.30	1,035.30
	12	88.85	66.20	1,066.20
	24	47.07	129.68	1,129.68
	36	33.21	195.56	1,195.56
13%	6	173.04	38.24	1,038.24
	12	89.32	71.84	1,071.84
	24	47.54	140.96	1,140.96
	36	33.69	212.84	1,212.84
15%	6	174.03	44.18	1,044.18
	12	90.26	83.12	1,083.12
	24	48.49	163.76	1,163.76
	36	34.67	248.12	1,248.12
18%	6	175.53	53.18	1,053.18
	12	91.68	100.16	1,100.16
	24	49.92	198.08	1,198.08
	36	36.15	301.40	1,301.40

loan outstanding. In sum, then, using the rule of 78 to calculate early repayment results in the lender obtaining more than a strictly prorated distribution of interest.

Consider another example. If you are making an early repayment on a two-year loan with 24 equal installments, you would use the rule of 300.[1] If you repaid the loan after one month, you would owe $^{23}/_{300}$ths of the total amount of interest that would have been paid over a two-year period (since there are 24

monthly installments). That means you would pay 8 percent of the total as opposed to the prorated distribution of interest that would equal $^1/_{24}$th, or 4.17 percent.

Lenders do not have to calculate what you owe in this step-by-step manner because they use prepared tables. The method used to prepare the tables, however, is similar to the process just described.

▶ THINGS TO WATCH FOR

You must be careful when you look at loan agreements because all have various contingency clauses written into them that may or may not affect you.

---

1. Because $(1 + 2 + 3 + 4 + 5 \ldots + 24)$ = 300.

▶ Acceleration Clauses

If you sign a credit agreement with an **acceleration clause**—meaning that the entire debt becomes due immediately if you, the borrower, fail to meet any single payment on the debt—you probably could not pay such a large sum. Obviously, if you could not meet a payment on the debt because you lacked the money, you certainly would be unable to pay off the whole loan at once. The addition of an acceleration clause in a credit agreement increases the probability that whatever you bought on credit will be repossessed.[2]

▶ Add-on Clauses

You also should be aware of what is called an **add-on clause** in installment contracts, particularly when you go shopping for furniture and appliances. An add-on clause essentially makes earlier purchases security for the more recent purchase. Let's say that you buy furniture for your living room from a particular store on an installment contract. Six months later, you decide that you want new furniture for a bedroom. You return to the same store and also buy the bedroom furniture on an installment contract. If there is an add-on clause and you default on the installment contract for the bedroom furniture, you not only can lose that furniture but all the items you purchased for the living room, even if you have paid for that furniture after making the second purchase.

---

2. Since loans with acceleration clauses usually can be obtained at relatively lower interest rates, they still may be a good deal for people who rarely or never default on loan payments.

▶ Balloon Clauses

Balloon clauses are defined as terms of installment loan contracts that require, after a period of time, specific payments more than twice the normal installment payments. For example, a contract may indicate that $100 a month is due for eleven months; then a single payment of $600 is due in the twelfth month. If you cannot pay the $600, you either have to refinance or, possibly, lose the item purchased on credit. ("Interest only" loans are balloon loans.)

▶ Garnishment (Wage Attachment)

It is also possible for a court order to allow a creditor to attach, or seize, part of your property. Your bank account may be attached and used to discharge any debts, or your wages may be **garnished.** That is, if a judgment is made against you, your employer is required to withhold your wages to pay a creditor.

The Federal Garnishment Law, effective July 1, 1970, is part of the Consumer Credit Protection Act. It limits the portion of an employee's wages that can be garnished. Garnishment can be no more than the lesser of the following:

1. Twenty-five percent of take-home pay.
2. The amount by which take-home pay is in excess of 30 times the federal minimum hourly wage.

The act also prohibits firms from firing an employee because of a single wage garnishment proceeding.

▶ GIVING YOURSELF THE BEST CHANCE

How do you give yourself the best chance to get the loan you want? Make sure you plan ahead. Credit experts suggest you do the following:

1. Verify with credit-reporting agencies the information about you contained in their files. You can do this by calling the local credit bureaus or reporting agencies listed in your Yellow Pages to see if they have a file on you and if any national reporting agency has a file. Then, either visit or write to the relevant agency or agencies and request a copy of your file. You will probably have to pay a fee, but it will be worth it. If you find that any information is missing or incorrect, rectify the situation immediately.
2. If you do not have any credit history, start now by opening a checkable and a savings account in your own name. Take out a small loan and repay it on time, and also attempt to get a bank credit card or a store charge account.
3. When filling out a loan application, answer *all* questions.
4. Make a copy of your loan application so that every time you apply for a new loan you can repeat all the information that you have used before. Lenders usually open a new file for every new type of loan.
5. Comparison-shopping is useful, but don't try to obtain the same type of loan from several lenders at the same time. Your credit record may then show a streak of applications, which will raise questions among potential lenders.
6. If a lender turns you down, find out why. The rejection may be the result of inaccurate information that was supplied by a credit-reporting organization. The Fair Credit Reporting Act of 1971 gives you the right to a copy of this information, and you should take steps to correct it if it is wrong. See Exhibit N–5.
7. Remember, a refusal is not permanent. You may want to try again, even with the same lender.

▶ Reasons for Refusing Credit

Lending institutions that turn down your request for credit are required to explain the reasons for their decision. They typically offer the following reasons for refusing credit to individuals:

1. Insufficient length of local residence.
2. Insufficient income.
3. Inability to verify employment.
4. Excessive obligations.
5. Insufficient credit history.
6. Negative credit history.

▶ How to Improve a Bad Credit Rating

Once you've gotten into credit difficulties and have a bad credit rating, it may be very difficult to clear the slate and start anew. But it can be done. For one thing, credit-reporting agencies are prohibited from giving out negative information that is more than seven years old—except in the special circumstances discussed in Chapter 16. In the meantime, you should try to rebuild your credit record slowly, starting with applications for department store charge accounts, for which the requirements are usually not as stringent as for major bank cards. Another possibility is to apply for a guaranteed bank credit card. Certain banks will issue you a MasterCard or other bank credit card, for example, if you deposit a specified amount of cash as collateral for the card. Your credit limit on the card will be equal to (or probably somewhat lower) than the cash on deposit. If you fail to pay your credit card debt, the bank can draw on the cash deposit to cover the charges made on the card. For a list of banks that offer

▶ **Exhibit N–5   What You Can Do to Protect Yourself against Unfair Credit Reports**

If you are trying to get insurance, credit, or a job, you may be subjected to a personal investigation. Under the Fair Credit Reporting Act of 1971:

☐ The company asking for the investigation is supposed to let you know you are being investigated.

☐ You can demand the name and address of the firm hired to do the investigating.

☐ You can demand that the investigating company tell you what its report contains—except for medical information used to determine your eligibility for life insurance.

☐ You cannot require the investigators to reveal the names of neighbors or friends who supplied information.

If the investigation turns up derogatory or inaccurate material, you can:

☐ Demand a recheck.

☐ Require the investigators to take out of your file anything that is inaccurate, and send a new report to anyone who has received an incorrect report about your credit history in the past six months.

☐ Require them to insert your version of the facts, if the facts remain in dispute.

☐ Sue the investigating firm for damages if negligence on its part resulted in violation of the law and caused you some loss—failure to get a job, loss of credit or insurance, or even great personal embarrassment.

☐ Require the company to cease reporting adverse information after it is seven years old—with the exception of a bankruptcy, which can remain in the file for ten years.

---

guaranteed credit cards, contact Bankcard Holders of America at 560 Herndon Parkway, Suite 120, Herndon, VA 22070, (800) 638-6407.

Another way to repair a damaged credit rating, if you can afford it, is to open a savings account with a moderate deposit of perhaps $1,000. Leave this money on deposit but borrow against it. The bank will be willing to make such a loan because it has your $1,000 if you fail to make your payments. Make regular payments over the term of the loan to demonstrate your ability to handle money in a responsible way. This will cost you some money in extra interest (the difference between what the bank pays you for your deposit and what you pay the bank for the loan) but it is probably money well spent.

▶ Fraud and Your
   Credit Rating

Many millions of consumers have black marks on their credit records because of the fraudulent use of lost or stolen credit cards or other types of credit fraud. Credit fraud and how

to protect yourself against it is discussed in Chapter 6.

▶ DEBT'S DANGER SIGNALS

If you observe any of the following, you are in danger of overextending yourself financially.

1. You consistently postpone or avoid paying your bills because you lack sufficient income to pay them.
2. You begin to hear from your creditors.
3. You have no savings, or not enough to tide you over a financial upset.
4. You have little or no idea what your living expenses are.
5. You use a lot of credit, have charge accounts at a number of stores, carry several credit cards in your wallet, and you pay only the monthly minimum on each account.
6. You don't know how much your debts total.

▶ HOW TO KEEP FROM
   GOING UNDER

To prevent yourself and your family from getting into deeper financial

trouble, consider some of the following commonsense actions.

1. Itemize your debts in detail, making sure you note current balances, monthly payments, and dates when payments are due.
2. List the family's total *net* income that can be counted on every month.
3. Subtract your monthly living expenses from your net income. Don't include the payments on debts you already have. The result will be the income you would be able to spend if you had no debts. Now subtract the monthly payments you are committed to making on all your debts. If you come out with a minus figure, you are obviously living beyond your means. If you come out with a very small positive figure, you still may be living beyond your means.
4. If you think that your spending unit is, in fact, living beyond its means, you must inform your family that the money situation is tight. Tell them that you and every other spender in the family unit will have to cut expenses, such as those for recreation, food, and transportation.

CREDIT COUNSELING SERVICES

If you still have difficulties making ends meet after you've tried the foregoing suggestions, you might check with a credit counseling service. The best way to locate such a service in your area is to contact the National Foundation for Consumer Credit (NFCC) and ask for a list of nonprofit counseling services that have offices near you. You can contact the NFCC at 8611 2nd Avenue, Suite 100, Silver Spring, MD 20910, (301) 589-5600. There are some 350 nonprofit credit counseling organizations in the United States, and they are usually better than the for-profit organizations, which charge more for their services. Although the nonprofit organizations charge no fee, they will ask for a contribution, on average about $10, and perhaps small fees for certain debt-repayment services, depending on the assistance they render to you.

According to the NFCC, of those consumers who turned to its credit counselors for help in 1988, 33 percent settled their own financial problems satisfactorily after credit counselors advised them on how to manage their money so that all bills could be paid. With 39 percent of the clients counseled, the clients arranged to make monthly payments to their counselors, who then distributed the funds among creditors under a specially arranged payment schedule. The remainder of those counseled could not be helped because their situations were too critical, often because of marital problems or drug abuse.

PROS AND CONS OF DEBT CONSOLIDATION

Although most credit-counseling organizations are bona fide consumer groups that will act in your interest, be wary of commercial enterprises that advertise help in debt consolidation. They might claim they can consolidate all your debts into one fixed monthly payment that will be lower than the total of what you are paying now to all your creditors. Rarely, though, is this claim true; in most instances you won't actually pay a smaller interest rate by consolidating your debts instead of paying them separately. Remember, you have already incurred setup charges in taking out the various lines of credit that you want consolidated. Credit companies won't render a service unless they make profit on it. So if you let a credit company pay off all your existing debts and then lend you the total amount that they paid, you will have to incur the setup charge for that.

Sometimes, however, debt consolidation actually *may* save you some money. If, for example, you consolidate all your revolving credit accounts that charge you 18 percent into one 12-percent credit-union loan, you will be better off (assuming there are no early-payment penalty charges on the revolving credit accounts).

Furthermore, it may be more *convenient* for you to have all your loans consolidated into one big one. Then you have to write only one check a month instead of many. But this service comes with a charge. You may, in fact, have a smaller monthly charge, but it will be for many more months, and you ultimately will pay higher finance charges for the whole consolidation package and, thus, a higher total payment. If you detest keeping records and writing out lots of checks, you may want to incur this additional cost (and additional debt) by taking a loan consolidation. However, you should be very careful to keep the result of such a loan in perspective. Many consumers react to a lower total monthly payment by going out and taking on more debt that makes their credit problem even greater. As long as you realize that nobody gives you anything for free, you can make a rational choice, knowing that there are always costs for any benefits you receive. Loan consolidation certainly isn't going to pull you out of dire financial trouble; the only way out is either to make a higher income or cut back on your current consumption so you can pay off your debts more easily. (You could, of course, sell some of your assets to pay off your debts.)

SUMMARY

1. There is no definite way to decide which purchases should be bought on time and which should be bought with cash. Rather, your total outstanding debt should not exceed what you can handle.

2. You can determine your safe debt load by adding up all your outstanding debt, which includes loan payments, department store payments, credit card payments, overdue telephone and electricity accounts, and so on. If your monthly payments on outstanding debt (excluding mortgage or rent payments for your home) equal 20 percent or less of your after-tax income, you have a relatively safe debt load. If they equal more than 20 percent of your after-tax income, however, you've probably overextended yourself and may need to reduce your credit purchases.

3. To determine your net worth, add up all your assets, which include the market value of your house, your car(s) your bonds,

stocks, and other possessions. After you subtract what you owe, such as your house mortgage and other loans, you have your net worth.

4. When applying for a loan, you must realize that the loan officer will look at your capacity to pay back, your character, and what collateral you can produce to back up the loan.

5. When you shop for credit, shop as if you were buying any other good or service. Look for the best deal by calling around to get various offers of interest rates and monthly payments. Be sure to contact appropriate sources for the type of loan you are seeking.

6. The rule of 78 is used by banks and finance companies to calculate what you owe if you prepay a loan.

7. Things to watch for in credit contracts are acceleration, add-on, and balloon clauses. Also, remember that a certain amount of your wages can be garnished if you fail to meet your loan payments.

8. Before applying for credit, know where you stand by checking with local credit bureaus to learn your credit rating and to correct any errors that might exist. If you have no credit history, it is a good idea to create one by opening checkable and savings accounts, applying for loans against your savings, and so on. And, when applying for a loan, make sure you complete the application correctly and thoroughly and keep a copy of your application.

9. If you are refused credit, the Fair Credit Reporting Act allows you to demand that the firm hired to do the credit check tell you what its report contains, that it do a recheck, and that it insert in its report your version of any facts in dispute.

10. Some of debt's danger signals are consistently postponing payment of bills because of insufficient in-

come, being contacted by creditors, having no savings or insufficient savings to tide you over in a financial crisis, not knowing what your expenses are, using a lot of credit but paying only the monthly minimum on each account, and not knowing what your debts total.

11. To keep from going under, you can itemize your debts and payment amounts and due dates and subtract the total monthly payments you must pay from the income you have left over each month after living expenses have been met. Then, if you are spending beyond your means, it will be evident, and you will need to take steps to reduce spending.

12. Credit counseling services aid many consumers in managing their debt problems. A leading source of credit counseling services is the National Foundation for Consumer Credit.

13. Be wary of debt-consolidation schemes. Although some are genuinely beneficial, generally they are overpriced.

▶ QUESTIONS FOR THOUGHT AND DISCUSSION

1. Is it important for you to determine why you are borrowing money before you borrow? Would you feel safer borrowing money to buy a durable consumer good, such as a refrigerator, TV, or stereo, than for a vacation?

2. Do you think it is unfair for loan officers to delve into your character before they decide whether you are a good credit risk? Why or why not?

▶ THINGS TO DO

1. Using Exhibit N–2, determine your safe debt load or the debt load of your parents. How much are you or they overextended or underex-

tended? (Is it possible to be under-extended in debt?)

2. Call several banks or the credit departments of various stores in your area and ask them to send you a loan application. Fill out the personal net-worth statement. Familiarize yourself with the various terms. If you do not know what they mean, ask your instructor or go to a dictionary. If it is appropriate, attempt to determine your net worth for the past five years. Has it gone up or down?

3. Call or write your regional office of the Federal Trade Commission. Ask how the FTC enforces the Truth-in-Lending Act. See if their methods of enforcement have changed over the last few years.

▶ SELECTED READINGS

▶ *Building a Better Credit Record: What to Do, What to Avoid.* Available free from the Federal Trade Commission, 6th St. and Pennsylvania Ave., N.W., Washington, DC 20580.

▶ *Buying and Borrowing: Cash In on the Facts.* Available free from the Federal Trade Commission, 6th St. and Pennsylvania Ave., N.W., Washington, DC 20580.

▶ Davis, D. "Bank Cards: How to Get What Is Rightfully Yours." *Kiplinger's Personal Finance Magazine,* July 1991, p. 26.

▶ Feinberg, A. "Pitfalls of Borrowing." *Working Woman,* November 1991, p. 62.

▶ Keller, John. "A T & T Launches Its Credit Card For Consumers." *The Wall Street Journal,* March 27, 1990, p. B7.

▶ Loeb, Marshall. "Your Borrowing." *Marshall Loeb's 1992 Money Guide,* Boston: Little, Brown, 1992, pp. 362–379.

▶ Meehan, John. "Picking a Path

through the Plastic Jungle." *Business Week,* August 6, 1990, pp. 84–86.

▶ Money Management Institute. *Managing Your Credit.* Available for $1 from Money Management Institute, 2200 Sanders Rd., Prospect Heights, IL 60070.

▶ Protect Yourself Against Advance-Fee Loan Scams." *Consumers' Research Magazine,* December 1991, pp. 16–19.

▶ Quinn, Jane Bryant. "Protecting Your Good Name." *Newsweek,* August 12, 1991, p. 64.

▶ Smart, Tim. "Mad as Hell About Late Fees." *Business Week,* January 24, 1992, p. 32.

Going Into Personal Bankruptcy

GLOSSARY

BANKRUPTCY The state of having come under the provisions of the law that entitles a person's creditors to have that person's estate administered for their benefit.

In 1978 Congress passed a new **bankruptcy** law that represented the first complete revision of U.S. bankruptcy laws since 1898. The new act was amended by the Bankruptcy Amendments and Federal Judgeship Act of 1984 to streamline even further the mechanics of bankruptcy and to make them as fair as possible for both creditors and debtors. The act was further amended in 1986 to allow bankruptcy relief to family farmers. The basic intent of bankruptcy law remains the same, however: to provide a fresh start for individuals and businesses that suffer financial failure.

WHY SO MANY BANKRUPTCIES?

In 1976 the number of Americans who filed for bankruptcy was 193,000. By 1980 this figure had climbed to 409,000. By 1991 the 1980 number had almost doubled— to over 872,000. According to the International Credit Association, 26 million consumers were in financial trouble at that time, and more than 3 million of that group were on the verge of bankruptcy.

Why are so many consumers going into bankruptcy? There seems to be no one answer to that question. After a study of the problem, the Federal Reserve Board concluded that the increase in bankruptcies was related to a parallel increase in consumer debt. On the other hand, the National Association of Credit Unions reports that the number of consumers who default on their debts has actually remained about the same over the past ten years. The association suggests that the increase in the number of bankruptcies is due to the fact that more people now use bankruptcy as a form of default than previously.

While bankruptcy may carry less of a stigma today than it has in the past, and obviously more consumers are opting for bankruptcy than used to be the case, it nonetheless can be very costly to an individual. Once you have gone into bankruptcy, it is very difficult to reestablish credit as long as the bankruptcy proceeding remains on your credit record (under current laws, for ten years). Because of this black mark on one's credit record, some consumers who have resolved their financial problems through bankruptcy have referred to their decision as a "ten-year mistake." The point of this discussion is to emphasize that before you choose bankruptcy as an option, you should explore very thoroughly all other alternatives. Bankruptcy should be considered only as a last resort.

If you do decide to file for bankruptcy protection, however, you have, basically, two choices: Chapter 7 and Chapter 13 of the federal Bankruptcy Code both provide personal relief for debtors. Chapter 7 is often called *straight bankruptcy,* or *ordinary bankruptcy,* whereas Chapter 13 is basically a *debt-repayment plan* worked out by the bankruptcy court between a debtor and his or her creditors.

FILING FOR CHAPTER 7 BANKRUPTCY

A Chapter 7 filing, the more drastic bankruptcy plan, in effect clears the slate of all obligations except "nondischargeable" debts such as alimony, child support, taxes, and government-insured loans. The law permits one Chapter 7 filing every six years. If you file for straight bankruptcy, you will usually need the services of a lawyer. You must list all your debts and assets and turn control of your assets over to the court. A trustee is named to check on those assets available for distribution to creditors.

Exemptions

An individual debtor is entitled to exempt certain property from the property of the estate. Before the enactment of the new bankruptcy law, state law exclusively governed the extent of the exemptions. Federal bankruptcy law, however, now establishes an exemption scheme for debtors. An individual debtor (or husband and wife who file jointly) now has the option of choosing between the exemptions provided under the applicable state law or the federal exemptions. Federal bankruptcy law exempts the following property:

1. Up to $7,500 in equity (the difference between the resale value and the amount owed) in the debtor's residence and burial plot.

2. Interest in a motor vehicle up to $1,200.

3. Interest, up to $200 for any particular item, in household goods and furnishings, wearing apparel, appliances, books, animals, crops, or musical instruments. (The 1984 amendments, however, limit the total of all items to $4,000.)

4. Interest in jewelry up to $500.

5. Any other property worth up to $400, plus any unused part of the $7,500 homestead exemption up to an amount of $3,750.

6. Interest, up to $750, in any tools of the debtor's trade.

7. Any unmatured life insurance contract owned by the debtor.

8. Certain interests in accrued dividends or interest under life-insurance contracts owned by the debtor.

9. Professionally prescribed health aids.

10. Social Security and certain welfare benefits, alimony and support payments, and certain pension benefits.

11. Certain personal injury and other awards.

▶ Advantages and Disadvantages of Straight Bankruptcy

The benefit of declaring straight bankruptcy is that most debts are "erased" except for taxes, alimony, and support payments, and the debts that others have cosigned for you (which now become their debts), plus any secured debts.

The disadvantages have already been mentioned: You no longer have control over all your property, and bankruptcy puts a black mark on your credit record. Furthermore, you will incur further debt. After all, you have court and lawyers' costs, which together might run between $500 to $1,000. And, remember, you can't file for bankruptcy again for another six years.

▶ CHAPTER 13 PLANS

Under bankruptcy law, you may choose a Chapter 13 repayment plan. This is basically a debt-consolidation program with legal safeguards that permits you to stretch out your payment of bills. You can develop a plan for full or even partial repayment of debts over an extended period of time. It is a meaningful alternative to full bankruptcy litigation. Any individual with regular income who owes unsecured debts of less than $100,000 or secured debts of less than $350,000 can be a Chapter 13 debtor. Under the old law, only a wage earner was eligible for such relief; the person with a small business was excluded. Now the sole proprietor of a small business can also use this plan, as can individuals living on welfare, Social Security, fixed pensions, or investment income.

Chapter 13 continues the old law insofar as the debtor is given the exclusive right to propose a repayment plan. No creditor can force a debtor into a plan that he or she does not wish to accept. The plan may provide for repayment over a period of up to five years. It may also provide for payment of claims only out of future income or out of a combination of future income and the liquidation of some of the debtor's currently owned property. Once a Chapter 13 plan has been approved, all creditors must stop collection efforts and suspend interest and late charges on most kinds of debts. Each month, the debtor turns over a specified amount of money to a court trustee, who then dispenses it to the creditors. As long as the plan is working, the debtor may keep all of his or her assets.

One of the major benefits of a Chapter 13 plan is that you may end up paying off your debts at less than 100 cents on the dollar. If you repay at least 70 percent of your debts, you do not have to wait the usual six years until you file for bankruptcy again.

▶ SUMMARY

1. Current bankruptcy law in this country is based on legislation first passed in 1898, as revised and amended in 1978, 1984, and 1986. The purpose of bankruptcy law is to provide a fresh start for individuals and businesses that suffer financial failure.

2. The number of personal bankruptcies continues to climb and is now double what it was in 1980.

3. Personal bankruptcy relief is obtained under Chapter 7 and Chapter 13 of federal bankruptcy law.

4. Chapter 7 (ordinary or straight) bankruptcy allows a debtor to have all debts erased, except for certain nondischargeable debts such as alimony, child support, taxes, and government-insured loans. A debtor can file for Chapter 7 relief once every six years.

5. Federal bankruptcy law exempts certain property from a debtor's assets to be distributed in bankruptcy. Up to $7,500 of the value of one's home, for example, is excluded from bankruptcy proceedings and can remain the debtor's property following bankruptcy.

6. The major advantage of Chapter 7 bankruptcy is that a debtor can have all debts (except those that are not dischargeable in bankruptcy) erased. The major disadvantage is a black mark on the debtor's credit record.

7. Chapter 13 bankruptcy offers debtors who qualify an alternative to ordinary bankruptcy. Under Chapter 13 of the federal bankruptcy law, the debtor can arrange for full or partial payment of debts over a period of time.

▶ QUESTIONS FOR THOUGHT AND DISCUSSION

1. Are bankruptcy laws fair to creditors? To other consumers?

2. Who pays for the debts that are "erased" in bankruptcy?

3. Do you think that our bankruptcy laws make it too easy for consumers to shed their debt?

4. Certain debts, including child support, taxes, and government-insured loans, such as student loans, are not dischargeable in bankruptcy. Do you think they should be?

▶ THINGS TO DO

1. Call or write the National Foundation for Consumer Credit at 8611 2nd Avenue, Suite 100, Silver Spring, MD 20910, (301) 589-5600, and ask its representative what percentage of those who seek credit-counseling services eventually petition for bankruptcy. Also ask if this percentage has grown in the past decade.

2. Visit several financial institutions in your community and ask what percentage of loans are uncollectible or only partially collectible owing to bankruptcy proceedings of the debtors.

3. Call or write your state's consumer protection bureau (see Consumer Issue B) and ask for information on bankruptcy proceedings. Are your state's bankruptcy exemptions more favorable than the federal exemptions listed in this Consumer Issue?

▶ SELECTED READINGS

▶ Caplovitz, David. *Consumers in Trouble: A Study of Debtors in Default.* New York: Free Press, 1987.

▶ Clarkson, Kenneth W., et al. *West's Business Law,* 4th ed. St. Paul: West, 1989, ch. 31.

▶ Davis K. "Bankruptcy: The 10-Year Mistake." *Kiplinger's Personal Finance Magazine,* October 1991, pp. 89–92.

▶ Kosel, Janice. *Bankruptcy: Do It Yourself.* Berkeley, CA: Nolo Press, 1983.

▶ Lindsay D. "Where the Money Goes." *Washingtonian,* October 1991, p. 21.

Saving

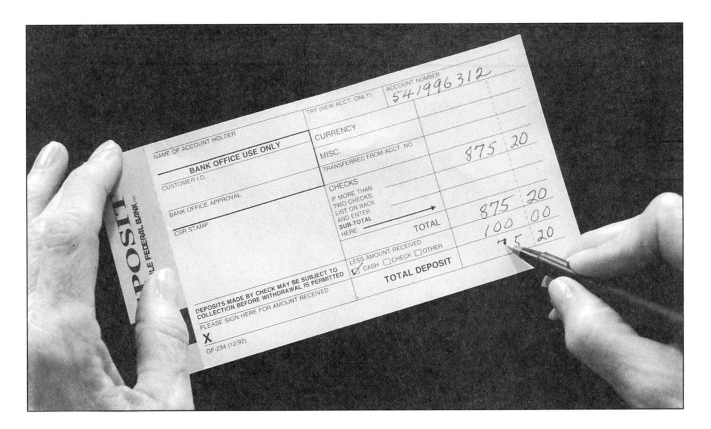

▶ What are the advantages of regular saving?

▶ What factors determine how much you can save?

▶ What is the nature of compound interest?

▶ What are the costs and benefits of different depository institutions and methods of saving available to consumers?

▶ How can consumers save through buying government securities?

Saving

The act of not consuming or not spending your money income to obtain current satisfaction.

Over the past several years, Americans have **saved,** on average, between 4 and 6 percent of their after-tax income. This may not sound too impressive if we compare it to the saving rate in Japan (17 percent) or West Germany (13 percent) but it does represent a total saving in the United States of nearly $220 billion per year. The tendency to save has existed ever since this country was founded, and the proportion of income not consumed—that is, saved—has remained relatively constant over time, although it has been relatively lower in recent years. Exhibit 17–1 shows the amount of money saved in various years in the United States. The growth is largely the result of our increased income, not because of an increase in our rate of saving per dollar earned.

WHY SAVE AT ALL?

When most people think of saving, they immediately think of saving *for* some special item, such as a down payment on a new house, a vacation next summer, a new car, or a microcomputer. But another way to look at saving is to take a long-term view.

The reason you want to save may be either to leave a large estate to your heirs or to provide for yourself and your family during periods when your income is abnormally low, such as when you might be disabled or after you retire. You can look at saving, then, as a way to spread your consumption over your lifetime so that it remains smooth even when your income fluctuates or sometimes falls to zero, especially after you retire.

Even if you are just barely making a living, you know that you will need to make important purchases in the future. The chances are better than 4 in 5 that you either are or will become a parent. Children are very expensive. Most Americans have bought or would like to own a home of their own. Cars, furniture, vacations, education for you or your children, all add to the list of reasons why you should try to save. Finally, consumers need to plan for financial security in their retirement years.

▶ Exhibit 17–1   **Personal Savings in the United States**

Personal saving in the United States has been going on at a fairly steady rate of 4 percent to 6 percent of disposable personal income (after-tax income) over the past four decades. The increase in the amount saved is largely the result of increased disposable income.

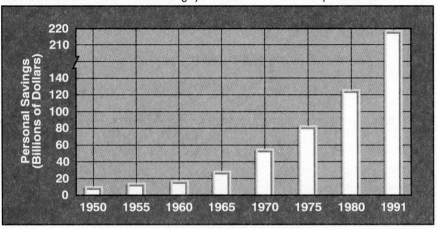

Saving is more than a tradeoff between the value you could receive from spending money now and the value you would receive from spending the money you save in the future. The value of saving includes the sense of security that having money set aside gives people. It is hard to quantify this value, but it is real. Knowing you have money you can use if you need to is an important value for most people.

Even people who have very little income can usually find some part of their spending they could reduce or eliminate to start to save. If you can't save much, setting aside just a few dollars a week at least gets you into the habit of saving. Later, when you finish school, your income should grow, and the habit of saving will help you put away that nest egg for the future.

WHAT DETERMINES HOW MUCH YOU SAVE?

If you want to save something for that proverbial rainy day, what determines the amount you save? We can offer a few ideas here. Obviously, the return you can earn on your savings is one factor that helps you determine how much of your current income you are willing to set aside for the future. If banks are paying 10 percent interest on deposits, you know the $100 you save this month will grow to be $110 a year from now. The extra $10 you will earn may encourage you to save more of your income. However, if the bank is paying only 3 percent interest, the extra $3 you would have a year from now would provide less of an incentive to save. The level of interest rates, then, is one factor that influences how much we save.

Saving and Expected Rates of Inflation

Another consideration in how much we save is the expected rate of inflation. When people believe the purchasing power of the dollars they save will fall, they are less inclined to save. Suppose you are convinced that the prices of most products you want to buy will increase by an average of 10 percent in the next year and the banks are paying only 5 percent interest for deposits. In one year you would need $110 for products you could purchase with $100 today. However, if you save your money, you will earn only $5 in interest on your savings (and you will pay tax on your interest income). You will therefore lose more than $5 worth of purchasing power (in terms of next year's prices). This could encourage you to buy goods you want now instead of saving up for them.

On the other hand, if interest rates are greater than the expected rate of inflation, people will be more inclined to save, because the purchasing power of their savings will grow. Exhibit 17–2 shows the amount of money that would have the same purchasing power in the future as $1,000 would have now if there were 4 percent or 7 percent rates of inflation. The relationship between expected rates of inflation and the interest you receive from your savings, then, is an important factor to consider when you decide how much to save.

Taxes and Saving

Most often, the interest consumers earn from saving is taxed by both the federal and state governments as ordinary income. There are some exceptions to this rule, which will be discussed in Consumer Issue P. You know that different people pay taxes in different brackets (percentage rates of their taxable

▶ Exhibit 17–2 **The Impact of Inflation on Savings**

YEARS TO SAVE	ANTICIPATED RATE OF INFLATION	INFLATION EQUIVALENTS OF $1,000
30 Years	7%	$8,117
	4%	$3,114
25 Years	7%	$5,725
	4%	$2,714
20 Years	7%	$4,039
	4%	$2,223
15 Years	7%	$2,849
	4%	$1,821
10 Years	7%	$2,010
	4%	$1,491

income). In 1993 the highest federal bracket was 39.6 percent. People with large incomes who lived in New York City, for example, also had to pay nearly 8 percent of their income in state income tax and another 2 percent in city income tax. Their effective total tax rate was almost 50 percent (although the state and local taxes might have been deductible from their income for federal tax purposes). Such a high tax rate would almost certainly have discouraged these people from saving as much as they otherwise would. On the other hand, people with lower incomes might have been able to keep all or most of the interest income they earned from saving. They had a better incentive to save, though probably much less ability.

Your Saving Goals

One of the most important reasons to save has little to do with inflation, interest rates, or taxes. It has a lot to do with individual purpose. People usually find a way to save when they have an important reason to save. If you want to save for the down payment on a house, for a dependable car, or to pay your tuition next semester, you will probably save even if you are forced to do without a few goods you would like to have now. Having a clear understanding of why you are saving is probably the most important factor (other than income) in a successful savings plan. If you don't know what you are saving for, you probably won't save very much.

Other Determinants of the Rate of Saving

Of course, to decide whether to save, or how much to save, you consider more than the interest rate on your savings; you also consider the value you place on consumption today as opposed to consumption tomorrow. Obviously, when you put off spending $100, you do not get the pleasure from whatever you might have spent it on. If you are impatient, even a high interest rate on savings may not induce you to save much. Those of you who are not so impatient about consuming may save more.

Another major determinant of how much of your current income you think you should save is the variability of your income. For example, people who have stable incomes from secure employment positions generally save a smaller percentage of their income than do people who are in business for themselves. Obviously, the more variable your income, the more likely you are to have years when your income is lower than usual. Hence, during years when it is higher than usual, you generally will save more.

Moreover, how much you will save depends on how much future retirement income you decide you should have and on how much you earn. To help determine how much you will have in the future, you must understand compound interest. Obviously, if you earned no interest at all, your total savings at the end of a specified period—say, 30 years—would be exactly what you put in. But that is not what usually happens; usually you earn interest on whatever you save.

THE NATURE OF COMPOUND INTEREST

If you decide to save by not consuming all your income, you can invest what you save. You can put it in the stock market, or you can buy bonds—that is, lend money to businesses or government. You also could put it in your own business. In any event, you might expect to make a profit or interest every

This table shows the value of a dollar at the end of a specified period after it has been compounded at a specified interest rate, compounded once a year at the end of every year. There are other ways of compounding interest, such as semiannually (once every six months), daily, and continuously. The actual compound factor in this exhibit would have to be altered for each compounding scheme. Clearly, the more frequently a given interest percentage is compounded, the larger the return after a given period of time.

YEAR	3%	4%	5%	6%	8%	10%	20%	YEAR
1	1.03	1.04	1.05	1.06	1.08	1.10	1.20	1
2	1.06	1.08	1.10	1.10	1.17	1.21	1.44	2
3	1.09	1.12	1.16	1.19	1.26	1.33	1.73	3
4	1.13	1.17	1.22	1.26	1.36	1.46	2.07	4
5	1.16	1.22	1.28	1.34	1.47	1.61	2.49	5
6	1.19	1.27	1.34	1.41	1.59	1.77	2.99	6
7	1.23	1.32	1.41	1.50	1.71	1.94	3.58	7
8	1.27	1.37	1.48	1.59	1.85	2.14	4.30	8
9	1.30	1.42	1.55	1.68	2.00	2.35	5.16	9
10	1.34	1.48	1.63	1.79	2.16	2.59	6.19	10
11	1.38	1.54	1.71	1.89	2.33	2.85	7.43	11
12	1.43	1.60	1.80	2.01	2.52	3.13	8.92	12
13	1.47	1.67	1.89	2.13	2.72	3.45	10.70	13
14	1.51	1.73	1.98	2.26	2.94	3.79	12.80	14
15	1.56	1.80	2.08	2.39	3.17	4.17	15.40	15
16	1.60	1.87	2.18	2.54	3.43	4.59	18.50	16
17	1.65	1.95	2.29	2.69	3.70	5.05	22.50	17
18	1.70	2.03	2.41	2.85	4.00	5.55	26.60	18
19	1.75	2.11	2.53	3.02	4.32	6.11	31.90	19
20	1.81	2.19	2.65	3.20	4.66	6.72	38.30	20
25	2.09	2.67	3.39	4.29	6.85	10.80	95.40	25
30	2.43	3.24	4.32	5.74	10.00	17.40	237.00	30
40	3.26	4.80	7.04	10.30	21.70	45.30	1,470.00	40
50	4.38	7.11	11.50	18.40	46.90	117.00	9,100.00	50

year in the future for a certain period of time. To figure out how much you will have at the end of any specified time period, you have to compound your savings, using a specified interest rate. Say you put $100 in a savings and loan association account that yields 5 percent per year. At the end of one year, you have $105. At the end of two years, you have $105 plus 5 percent of $105, or $5.25, which gives you a total of $110.25. This same compounding occurs the third year, the fourth year, and so on.

The power of **compound interest** is truly amazing. Exhibit 17–3 shows $1.00 compounded every year for 50 years at different interest rates. At an interest rate of 8 percent, $1.00 will return $46.90 at the end of 50 years. Thus, if you inherited a modest $20,000 when you were 20 years old and put it in an investment that paid 8 percent compounded annually, at 70 years of age you would have $938,000. It's not so hard to understand how some people become millionaires! It usually does not take much business acumen to get an 8 percent rate of return in the long run. Somebody who had invested in the stock market 50 years ago could have received much more than 8 percent.

Exhibit 17–4 shows an example of the difference between compound and simple interest. In Exhibit 17–5, you can see what $1,000 will compound to in ten years at different interest rates and also what would happen if you deposited $1,000 each year for ten years.

Compound interest

When interest is paid on interest that has already been earned on a deposit or a loan.

► Exhibit 17–4   **Compound versus Simple Interest**

At 5 percent simple interest, 1¢ would become in 1992 approximately $1 had it been invested at the birth of Christ.

On the other hand, 1,990 years later, the 1¢ invested at 5 percent compounded annual interest grows to about $12,728 followed by 36 zeros!

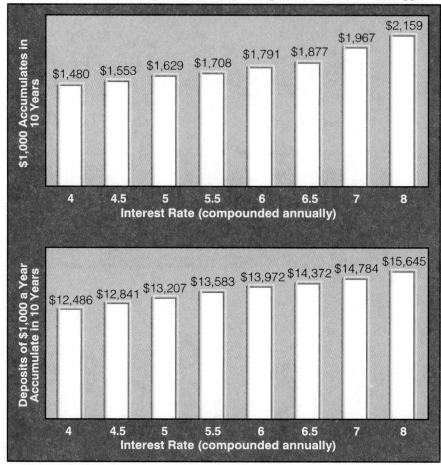

Exhibit 17–5 How Compound Interest Helps You Build a Nest Egg

ALTERNATIVE VEHICLES FOR SAVING

After deciding to save, you must choose where to save. Where will your money provide the tradeoff between interest, safety, and accessibility that is best for you? A wide selection of savings vehicles is available to consumers.

Passbook Savings Accounts

With passbook accounts, banks and thrifts give depositors a book in which a record of deposits, interest, and withdrawals are recorded. Actually, some banks no longer provide passbooks because all transactions are computerized. There are two basic types of passbook savings accounts that may be opened. Individual accounts are owned by only one person while joint accounts are owned by two people, most often a husband and wife.

Time Deposits

A major savings choice in the United States is the **time deposit,** a savings instrument that, in principle, cannot be turned into cash until a specified amount of time has passed after the request for cash is made. Additionally, the money usually must remain on deposit for a specified period of time for

Time deposit
Deposits that in principle cannot be withdrawn until the end of a specific period of time. This right of a bank, however, is not generally exercised.

it to earn interest. The most common types of time deposits are savings accounts in commercial banks, savings and loan associations, and credit unions.

A major virtue of time deposits is their liquidity. A **liquid asset** is one that readily can be turned into buying power. Even though, in principle, you must wait a specified period of time before a time deposit can be turned into buying power, in practice, institutions offering time deposits rarely, if ever, require such a waiting period. Hence, the owners of time deposits can turn them into buying power rapidly.

Why Use Time Deposits

Time deposits are a popular form of savings for personal investment for the following reasons.

1. Time deposits in federally insured accounts are insured up to $100,000, and the owner is virtually guaranteed that the **principal** will never be lost. Moreover, the value of the time deposit does not fluctuate as does, for example, the value of stocks purchased. The interest paid on time deposits is certain, and there is rarely, if ever, a default (nonpayment).

2. Because it is easy to "get in and out" of time deposits, many individuals use them to accumulate funds to transfer to another investment or to purchase a consumer durable good.

3. Since time deposits are highly liquid, the individual owner can liquidate them for immediate buying power to cover unexpected doctor bills, casualty losses, or other emergencies.

Disadvantages of Time Deposits

A major disadvantage of time deposits is their relatively low rate of return. Note, though, that one reason the rate of return on time deposits is so low is that the risk of losing your money is also low. It is usually difficult, if not impossible, to obtain a higher rate of return without incurring greater risk. And it is usually difficult to obtain a higher rate of return without purchasing investment assets, which certainly are less liquid than time deposits.

Types of Time Deposits

During the 1980s a plethora of savings instruments became available to the average saver. These instruments are being offered by commercial banks and the so-called thrifts—savings and loan associations, mutual savings banks, and credit unions—as well as certain brokerage houses and even retail stores, such as Sears. By the time you read this text, even more savings instruments may be offered by the various financial institutions in the United States.

You have to be careful in determining exactly what the options are because banks and thrifts call their time deposits by different names. Here are some of the best-known types of time deposits.

Club Accounts and Bonus Savings Accounts   There are several special types of savings accounts that enable customers to save for a special goal. Chanukah, Christmas, and vacation *club accounts* encourage you to accumulate savings, usually by depositing a fixed amount for 50 weeks. Often, little or no interest is paid on these accounts, but they give you an incentive to save. If the bank does offer interest, you don't receive it unless you keep your money on deposit for a requisite number of months. Consumers usually could accomplish the same results as those offered by these accounts if they

Liquid asset
An asset that can be easily turned into cash.

Principal
A capital sum that is distinguished from interest; it is the original amount deposited or loaned.

saved regularly in an ordinary passbook account. And the passbook account would place no withdrawal restrictions on them.

Bonus savings accounts are passbook-type accounts that pay a slightly higher interest rate if a minimum required balance is maintained and/or a minimum holding period is used. The bonus-type account reverts to a regular account if any of the stipulations are violated.

Certificate of deposit

A federally insured deposit that cannot be cashed in before a specified time without paying an interest-reduction penalty.

Certificates of Deposit   You can obtain **certificates of deposit (CDs)** for varying periods—from seven days to five or more years—that will yield substantially higher interest rates than passbook savings accounts. A minimum investment of at least $500 is normally required to open a CD. If you must obtain cash before the maturity date of the CD, however, you will have to pay a penalty. For accounts of 7 to 31 days, and the 91-day account, you lose all interest for early withdrawal. For the six-month CD, you lose three months' interest for early withdrawal. Obviously, these savings certificates are not appropriate if you think you will need cash before the CD matures.

The yield on a savings certificate will depend on its *term*—that is, the time period between opening the CD and its maturity date—and prevailing interest rates at the time it is opened. In mid-1988, for example, the average annualized yield on a six-month CD was 7.1 percent, and 8.5 percent for the CDs with a five-year term. By 1992 all interest rates had fallen significantly, leaving the annualized yield on a six-month CD at 3.83 percent while five-year CD yields were as high as 5.02 percent. At any point in time there is a tradeoff between accepting a yield that is tied in for a long term or a short term. When you have a long-term CD, you will not be hurt by falling interest rates, but you also will not be able to take advantage of any higher rates that might occur. You also need to consider when you will need the money. There is no point in putting your money in a five-year CD if you know you will need it in two years. You will be forced to pay an interest penalty if you withdraw your money before the CD matures.

When you open a CD, be sure to find out whether the bank will pay you simple interest or compound interest, because the yield will be substantially lower if simple interest is paid. For example, if you buy a $1,000 five-year CD paying a simple interest rate of 10 percent, your return will be $100 in interest every year for a total of $500. If the interest is compounded annually, however, you will end up with $610 when the CD matures.

Judging which banks pay the best interest on their CDs is easier since the passage of the Truth in Savings Act, which took effect on June 21, 1993. This law requires banks to advertise a standard interest rate called the **annual percentage yield (APY)** that must be figured in the same way by all banks.

Annual percentage yield (APY)

The standard annualized return on a savings deposit that all savings institutions must provide to depositors under the Truth in Savings Act of 1993.

FLOATING-RATE DEPOSIT ACCOUNTS

Banks, thrifts, and other financial institutions now offer a variety of floating-rate deposit accounts. These differ from time deposits in that there is no fixed date of maturity. Often, however, you are not guaranteed a particular interest rate for more than a very short period of time. We already talked about these accounts in the chapter on banking, but will review them here.

NOW and Super NOW Accounts

It is possible to obtain a relatively low but guaranteed rate of interest on your checkable-account balance by opening a NOW checking account. If you can meet the minimum-deposit requirement, you can open a Super NOW account and obtain an interest rate that is considerably higher than NOW account interest rates. One major benefit of NOW and Super NOW accounts is that they are insured by an agency of the federal government—the Federal Deposit Insurance Corporation (FDIC) for banks, the Savings Association Insurance Fund (SAIF) for savings and loans, and the National Credit Union Administration (NCUA) for credit unions—up to a maximum of $100,000.

Money Market Deposit Accounts

Virtually all banks and thrifts offer some form of money market deposit accounts. These offer higher interest rates than many alternative types of deposits at a thrift or bank and still grant some flexibility. That is to say, you can, without penalty, make a certain number of deposit or withdrawal transactions on the account each month. The minimum deposit in such an account will be determined by the institution offering the account. You will earn an interest rate approximately equal to the interest rate available on money market deposit accounts offered by brokerage houses. The big difference is that your money market deposit account in a bank or thrift is insured by one of the previously mentioned agencies of the federal government. Flexibility, high interest yields, and insurance make these accounts attractive to many savers.

U.S. SAVINGS BONDS

You can also buy savings instruments from the U.S. government. Savings bonds are probably the safest of all savings outlets because they are backed by the federal government. Savings bonds can be redeemed six months after purchase or kept for as long as 40 years—at which time they cease to draw interest. They can be purchased from banks, thrifts, and credit unions, or through a payroll-deduction plan offered by your employer. The most popular of the government savings bonds among small savers are the Series EE bonds.

Series EE Bonds

EE bonds can be purchased in denominations ranging from a minimum of $50 up to $10,000. When you buy an EE bond, you pay half of the bond's face value. The bond then increases in value every six months until its full value is reached—which usually occurs within ten to twelve years. EE bonds held for five years earn interest at a guaranteed rate of 4.0 percent, compounded semiannually. Any EE bond purchased and held for longer than five years pays you a variable interest rate equal to 85 percent of whatever the yield on five-year U.S. Treasury securities averages over your holding. For example, if the rate on the Treasury's five-year securities averages 10 percent, your bond would earn 8.5 percent. If there is a steep drop in interest rates, however, you are protected: you are guaranteed the minimum yield of 4.0 percent.

Many savers purchase EE bonds because of the tax advantages they offer. Interest on these bonds is not taxed by the federal government until the bond is redeemed, and EE bonds are exempt from state and local taxes. The Technical and Miscellaneous Revenue Act of 1988 made these bonds especially attractive to people who are saving for their or their children's education. Under this act, the interest earned on EE bonds is not taxable by the federal government even on redemption if the interest is applied toward educational expenses for the bondholder or his or her dependent. This exemption from

Buying savings bonds is a safe and easy way for consumers to put money away for their future. Savings bonds pay a guaranteed rate of interest when held for five or more years and may be redeemed at any commercial bank after they have been held for six or more months.

federal taxation is phased out, however, for those with incomes of $60,000 and higher.

Series HH Bonds

HH bonds can be obtained in exchange only for EE bonds that have matured. They are issued in denominations ranging from $500 to $10,000 and, unlike EE bonds, are purchased at their face value—that is, you would pay $500 for a $500 HH bond. You obtain the interest on the bond via a Treasury check twice a year, and, at the bond's maturity, you also get exactly what you paid for them. Currently, HH bonds have a ten-year maturity, and an interest penalty is levied if they are redeemed before they mature.

As with EE bonds, interest earned on HH bonds is exempt from state and local taxation. In addition, federal tax on the interest earned on the EE bonds which were traded for the HH bonds is not paid until the HH bonds mature. You will, however, pay federal tax on interest paid to you on the HH bonds as you receive it.

If you wish to obtain current bond rates or more information about U.S. savings bonds, check with your local bank or savings institution—or with any Federal Reserve bank or branch. You can also call toll free (800) US-BONDS for bond information.

TREASURY SECURITIES

Treasury bills, notes, and bonds are yet other alternative and safe outlets for your savings dollars. Treasury bills, or T-bills, are sold in minimum denominations of $10,000 and can be purchased with varying maturities—of three, six, and twelve months. Notes are usually sold in minimum denominations of $5,000 if their maturities are less than four years and in minimums of $1,000 if they mature in four years or more. You can purchase bonds in minimum denominations of $1,000, but only with maturities of ten years or more.

One of the main benefits offered by Treasury securities is that interest you earn is exempt from state and local taxes. Another advantage is the attractive interest rates—which are generally competitive with money market fund rates—that you can obtain without the degree of risk associated with investments in mutual funds or corporate bonds.

You can buy Treasury issues through any Federal Reserve bank or branch, or, for a fee, from commercial banks or brokerage houses. You can also order them by mail, using forms obtained from a Federal Reserve bank. Recently, the Treasury has a new service for investors, called the Treasury Direct Book-entry Securities System. With Treasury Direct, the Treasury securities you purchase can be maintained by you in book-entry form. This means that engraved certificates will not be issued; instead, you will receive a statement of account that will provide you with a record of your portfolio of Treasury securities. Book-entry systems have been available for T-bill holders for years, but Treasury Direct expands the system to include notes and bonds as well. For more information concerning Treasury Direct Securities, you can write to the Department of the Treasury, Bureau of the Public Debt, Securities Transaction Branch, 13th and C Sts., S.W., Washington, DC 20239.

HOW MUCH TO SAVE?

This chapter has explained why people save and described some popular saving outlets. In the following chapter, we discuss other areas where savings dollars can go, such as stocks, bonds, artwork, real estate, and the like. Remember, any money that is saved or invested is income that is not spent in the current year. Thus, every individual and family faces the decision of how much current income should be set aside for future consumption. The average rate of saving in the United States has remained around 4 to 6 percent in the past several years. Therefore, you might want to save the average or, say, 5 percent.

No fixed rules can be made for everyone, however. When you're young, your rate of saving may be negative; that is, you may borrow in addition to spending all your year's income. When you're older, your rate of saving may hit the national average or even be greater. Then, of course, when you retire, your rate of saving may become negative again as you consume the fruits of your past saving.

▶ SUMMARY

1. Individuals save in order to provide for income during periods when their earning capacity falls, such as during sickness or after retirement. In addition to the rate of return or interest you obtain from your savings, the variability of your income also will determine how much you save. The higher the interest paid and the higher the variability of your income, the more you will save.

2. In our competitive society, very few things come free of charge. Hence, no investment can guarantee you a higher-than-normal rate of return unless you undertake substantial risk—that is, a high chance of losing everything.

3. When trying to figure out how much total savings you will have accumulated after a certain length of time and number of deposits, you should consult a compound-interest table such as the one presented in Exhibit 17–3. If, for example, your savings were invested at an average of 8 percent, at the end of 20 years every dollar invested will have grown to $4.66.

4. A wide variety of savings instruments is now available to the average saver. Among these are passbook savings accounts, club accounts, bonus savings accounts, various small-scale certificates of deposits, and large-scale certificates of deposit. These accounts usually require specified minimum balances and/or have fixed maturity dates and interest rates.

5. Banks and thrifts also offer floating-rate deposit accounts, which have no fixed maturity dates. Often, however, these accounts do not guarantee the saver fixed interest rates for long periods. NOW, Super NOW, and money market accounts are examples of floating-rate accounts that require minimum balances and are insured by agencies of the federal government.

6. The federal government also offers savings instruments. The most popular are the Series EE bond and the Series HH bond. The minimum denomination for a Series EE bond is $50, with a maturity date of ten to twelve years and a maximum annual investment of $10,000. Series HH bonds are issued in denominations ranging from $500 to $10,000 and are available only in exchange for matured EE bonds. The tax advantages of savings bonds, as well as their government backing, make them attractive saving vehicles for consumers.

7. Treasury bills, notes, and bonds are also available as vehicles for your savings. These securities offer good rates of return without the risk of mutual fund or corporate securities investments.

8. No fixed rules can be made for how much individuals should save. Typically, saving rates vary with age, starting out at possibly a negative rate, then a positive rate during one's middle years, and again a negative rate during retirement when savings are drawn on for current expenses.

▶ QUESTIONS FOR THOUGHT AND DISCUSSION

1. When do you think an individual should start planning for financial security later in life?

2. Do you think Americans save too little of their income?

3. Why do you need to consider the rate of inflation when you invest your savings?

4. What are the costs and benefits of buying a five-year CD that yields 5 percent interest instead of a one-year CD that pays 3.5 percent interest?

5. "Poor people barely have enough to survive on and, therefore, cannot save anything for a rainy day." Do you agree with this statement?

▶ THINGS TO DO

1. Try to figure out what percentage of your income you save. Remember that the purchase of a so-called consumer durable, such as a television set, a VCR, a house, or a car, is a form of saving because you receive implicit income from that consumer durable for a long period of time. The income you receive is the satisfaction you obtain from the durable.

2. Assume that, by the time you retire at age 65, you want to have saved $100,000. Also assume that you can earn 8 percent per year on your savings. Determine from Exhibit 17–3 how much you have to put in the bank today to have $100,000 at age 65 at an 8 percent rate of return.

▶ APPLICATION

Assume that you have inherited $10,000 that you want to save for the next two years. Investigate alternative vehicles for saving that are currently available to you in your community. List five alternatives with their respective terms and interest yields. Choose the one you would be most likely to use. Write an essay that explains why you made your choice by describing the advantages and disadvantages of each of the alternatives you identified.

▶ SELECTED READINGS

▶ *Credit Union Statistics.* Available free from the National Credit Union Administration, 2025 M St., N.W., Washington, DC 20456 (latest edition).

▶ "Deposit Insurance Reform is Key to Banking System's Overhaul." *Nation's Business,* July 1991, p. 63.

▶ Egan, J. "Saving," *U.S. News & World Report,* July 15, 1991, p. 60.

▶ *Financial Tools Used in Money Management.* Available for $1.75 from the Consumer Information Center, Pueblo, CO 81002.

▶ *Getting Started.* Available free from American Express Co., World Financial Center, New York, NY 10085.

▶ Gould, Carole. "Planning for the Inevitable Rainy Day." *New York Times,* January 8, 1989, p. 15.

▶ "How to Make Sure Your Money Lasts a Lifetime." *Money,* June 1991, pp. 84–88.

▶ Loeb, Marshall. "Your Savings." *Marshall Loeb's 1992 Money Guide,* Boston: Little, Brown, 1992, pp. 340–360.

▶ Luciano, Lani. "Starting Out: First Steps to a New Goal." *Money,* April 1989, pp. 177–178.

▶ Miller, A. "How to Live Better on Less." *Working Woman,* July 1991, p. 28.

▶ "Pocket Money Guide." *Consumer Reports,*" February 1989, p. 78.

▶ Quinn, Jane Bryant. *Making the Most of Your Money,* New York: Simon & Schuster, 1991.

▶ *The Savings Bonds Question and Answer Book.* Available free from the U.S. Department of the Treasury, Savings Bonds Division, Washington, DC 20226.

▶ Sloane, Leonard, *Book of Personal Finance,* New York: Random House, 1992.

▶ Tucker, James F. *Managing Your Own Money: A Financial Guide for the Average Wage Earner.* New York: Norton, 1988.

▶ Whittingham-Bernes, D. "Smart Money Moves You Can Make Today." *Black Enterprise,* July 1991, pp. 44–48.

How to Save

Americans, on average, save relatively little of their disposable income. Many don't save at all. The need to save, however, remains the same for everyone. If you think of saving as a necessity, rather than an option, your chances of success at saving will be greater.

▶ HOW TO START SAVING

▶ Get into the Habit

If you have had difficulty saving successfully in the past and want to develop the habit of saving, the amount that you save is not important. What is important is that you begin to save something from each paycheck or other source of income *before* spending any of it on anything else. Many financial planners recommend that you save 10 percent of your income, because this figure is easy to remember and to calculate. But you need to be realistic in your planning, especially when you first undertake the discipline of saving. If 10 percent is too much, save less—5 percent or perhaps even as little as 3 percent. You will find that, as you form a habit of saving, it becomes less and less painful to "pay yourself" higher amounts.

Some individuals find it helpful to enlist outside help in saving. One way to do this is to arrange with your employer to have a certain percentage of your paycheck automatically deducted and placed in a savings vehicle—such as a credit union account or U.S. savings bonds.

▶ Setting Up an Emergency Fund

If you don't already have money set aside for an emergency, here's where you'll want to begin to build up your savings. It is generally advisable to keep the equivalent of either three months' salary or enough to cover your necessary expenses for three months in a special, readily accessible fund for emergencies. Once you have this cushion to fall back on in case of unforeseen financial need, you can begin to plan your savings around goals that you wish to achieve in the future.

▶ Establishing Your Goals

Perhaps the most important thing you can do for yourself, if you wish to save successfully, is to clarify your future spending goals. This is because saving requires a sacrifice; that is, you sacrifice the pleasure of spending your money now in favor of spending it in the future. And it will be hard to motivate yourself to make that sacrifice unless you have some specific short-term and long-term goals in mind for your savings. Knowing your goals will not only make it easier to save but also will help you determine how much to save and, to some extent, where to place your savings.

▶ WHERE TO PLACE YOUR SAVINGS

In shopping around for the right account in the right institution for your savings, one of your primary concerns will be with the amount of interest you can earn. If you want to keep your savings in an account where it is readily accessible to you, you will probably opt for a regular savings account or—if you can meet the minimum-deposit requirement—an interest-earning NOW, Super NOW, or money market deposit

(MMDA) account. On the other hand, if you can part with your money for a longer period of time, higher interest rates can be obtained by investing in certificates of deposit (CDs) or Treasury securities. Clearly, you will face a tradeoff between liquidity (the ability to have immediate access to your fund) and obtainable interest rates.

▶ Don't Be Afraid to Commit Funds to CDs

You may be reluctant to take out a long-term CD in times of relatively low interest rates; this could, you might reason, tie up your funds at a low rate, and, if interest rates were to rise, you would lose out. Such is not necessarily the case, according to financial planner Steven Enright of Hillsdale, New Jersey. Enright suggests that your best CD strategy should be to get the highest yield by signing up for long-term CDs but with the idea of pulling your money out and putting it in a new CD if interest rates increase—notwithstanding the fact that you will pay an early-withdrawal penalty on the first CD. For example, suppose you have deposited $10,000 in a five-year CD that pays 8 percent interest and has an early-withdrawal penalty of three months' simple interest. After five years, your deposit plus interest would come to $14,690. If, however, after one year you switched to a four-year CD paying 8.51 percent or higher, you would end up with $14,700 or more, even after paying an early-withdrawal penalty on your first CD. Clearly, though, the closer you get to the CD's maturity, the higher the new rate must be to make the switch worthwhile.

▶ Local versus Out-of-State Accounts

Most people prefer to have their savings in a local institution, both for the sake of convenience and because it may make it easier to obtain a loan when necessary. If obtaining a high yield on your savings is your sole concern, however, you may want to do some comparison-shopping, not only within your city but also among various banking institutions around the country. Just about every bank or savings and loan institution will accept out-of-state deposits, and you might be able to earn 2 to 3 percentage points more on your savings by undertaking a market search of available interest rates outside your local area.

Two weekly banking newsletters can help you in this search: *100 Highest Yields,* P.O. Box 088888, North Palm Beach, FL 33408 ($98 for one year), and *Tiered Rate Watch,* P.O. Drawer 145510, Coral Gables, FL 33114 ($99 a year). Both newsletters list federally insured depository institutions and can tell you which institutions are offering the best rates.

Most savings institutions will arrange to give you an account number over the telephone, after which you can endorse a check for deposit to that account and send it by mail to the institution.

▶ THE SAFETY FACTOR—IS YOUR DEPOSIT INSURED?

The failure of numerous savings and loan institutions in recent years has brought home to many the importance of federal insurance for savings deposits. Although you might be able to obtain a higher interest rate at one of nearly a thousand savings banks in the United States that are privately insured, the risk you take will also be greater.

When shopping among various time-deposit institutions, you should find out if your deposit will be insured. In most savings banks and commercial banks, your deposit will be insured by the Federal Deposit Insurance Corporation (FDIC). Deposits in savings and loan associations are most often insured by the Savings Association Insurance Fund (SAIF). Credit union deposits are usually insured by the National Credit Union Administration (NCUA), which supervises the National Credit Union Shareholders Insurance Fund.

Currently, each depositor is protected to an upper limit of $100,000 should the covered savings institution fail. It is important to understand just how this $100,000 protection limits your potential loss.

▶ Applies to a Single Depositor

The $100,000 protection applies to the total number of accounts a single depositor has under his or her name within a single bank. Thus, if you were to have a $56,000 savings account in one bank and also $50,000 in a checkable account, you would be insured up to $100,000, not $106,000. If you have accounts in the same name in a main office and in one or more branches of the insured bank, the accounts are added together to determine your insurance.

▶ Splitting Your Funds among Banks and Accounts

If you have so much of your savings in time deposits that you reach the maximum limitation on insurability, you can either split your funds among a number of banks or split your funds among a number of accounts. For example, if you are married, you can have an account, your spouse can have an account, and you both can have a joint account. Thus, your maximum insurability as a unit is increased to $300,000. If you have children, you can set up guardian or trustee accounts that are insured separately.

You should investigate the current status of deposit insurance if you have more than $100,000 to deposit. In 1991 and 1992 bills were discussed in Congress that would have limited the total insurance per individual to $100,000 regardless of where or how it was deposited.

▶ SUMMARY

1. The best way to start saving is to think of saving as a necessity, rather than an option.

2. An excellent way to save is to pay yourself first out of your paycheck by setting aside 5 to 10 percent of your income before making any purchases.

3. The first step in building up your savings is to create a special emergency fund as a cushion against unforeseen financial needs.

4. Setting specific future goals is a vital step in a savings program. Generally, the clearer the goals, the easier it is to motivate yourself to save for them.

5. A primary concern in shopping for the right account in which to place your savings will be the interest your savings can earn. Both the amount of your deposit and the amount of liquidity you desire will affect the rate of interest you can obtain.

6. Depositing funds in long-term CDs at low rates of interest need not tie up your funds and prevent you from obtaining higher interest rates later. Depending on a CD's maturity date, it might be worthwhile to break the CD, pay the early-withdrawal penalty, and open a new, shorter-term CD at a higher rate of interest.

7. Deposits in most savings and commercial banks are insured by the Federal Deposit Insurance Corporation. The Federal Savings and Loan Insurance Corporation insures accounts in most savings and loan institutions, and credit union deposits are usually insured by the National Credit Union Administration. If you want to be assured that your savings are safe, you must choose an account that is covered by one of these federal insurance programs.

8. Most insured deposit accounts have a limit of $100,000 in protection.

9. In 1992 it was possible to split up your funds among different banks and accounts in order to insure all your deposits. New banking laws may have outlawed this practice by the time you read this text.

► ## QUESTIONS FOR THOUGHT AND DISCUSSION

1. In your opinion, what is the relative importance of short-term goals and long-term goals in a savings plan? In your personal situation, which would take priority?

2. How is saving important to your financial security?

3. Do you think it is possible for even the poorest individual or family to save?

► ## THINGS TO DO

1. Assume you want to deposit $1,000 in a banking institution as savings. Go to two or three local banks and find out what types of accounts at what rates of interest they offer. Choose the account that best suits your needs, and list the reasons why.

2. Determine one future goal you would like to achieve or a purchase you wish to make. Taking both inflation and taxes into consideration, determine how much you would have to save per month to reach this goal in six months and one year, respectively.

► ## SELECTED READINGS

► Brown, C. M. "A Lifetime of Financial Planning." *Black Enterprise*,

October 1991, pp. 42–44.

► *Getting Started.* Available free from American Express Company, World Financial Center, New York, NY 10085.

► Loeb, Marshall. "Out of State Deposits." *Marshall Loeb's 1992 Money Guide,* Boston: Little, Brown, 1992, p. 355.

► Maners, J. "The Right Way to Save on Your Own." *Money,* November 1991, pp. 104–106.

► *Personal Money Management.* American Bankers' Association, 1120 Connecticut Ave., N.W., Washington, DC 20036. Latest edition.

► Quinn, Jane Bryant. "How to Save for College." *Newsweek,* October 21, 1991, pp. 52–54.

► "Saving for College." *Consumer Reports,* October 1991, p. 661.

► Wasik, John F. "How to Get the Highest Return on Your Savings." *Consumers Digest,* May–June 1989, pp. 51–55.

Investing

PREVIEW

▶ What is the relationship between the risk and the rate of return on an investment?

▶ What are the differences between common stocks, preferred stocks, and corporate bonds?

▶ What are capital gains and losses?

▶ How do mutual funds work?

▶ Why is financial planning for retirement important for young people?

THE SIMPLE FACTS ABOUT INVESTING

There are many things you can do with your accumulated savings. You can keep all or part of them in cash, which earns no interest at all and, in fact, loses value at the rate of inflation. You can put them into a savings account that gives a relatively low rate of interest but is extremely secure. You can invest your money in shares of stock of various corporations. You can invest it in U.S. savings bonds. You can purchase land. You can purchase consumer durable goods, such as cars, houses, and stereos, that yield a stream of services over their lifetime. In other words, you can do an infinite number of things with your savings. What you *should* do depends on your goals; what your goals are will tell you how much risk you want to take.

There is an unfortunate fact to which we have alluded time and again: You cannot get anything free. If you go into an investment deal with the idea that you'll make a killing, you may be sure that the risk you are undertaking is relatively high.

RISK AND RATE OF RETURN

The higher the prospective rate of return you expect to get on any investment, the greater the risk you take. That is why, if you are offered a "deal" that you are told will earn you a 50-percent profit a year, you may be certain that the risk of losing everything you invested is pretty high. The reason you cannot get a high rate of return without taking a high risk is that no particular investment is necessarily better than any other, at least unless you have some pretty specialized information. Let us explain this by a specific example—making money on the stock market. But, first, we need a few facts.

SOME FACTS ABOUT THE STOCK MARKET

Stock market
An organized market where shares of ownership in businesses are traded. These shares generally are called stocks. The largest stock market in the United States is the New York Stock Exchange.

The **stock market** is the general term used for all transactions that involve the buying and selling of shares of stocks issued by companies. These stocks are pieces of paper giving the owner the right to a certain portion of the assets of the company issuing the security. Say a company wishes to expand its operation. It can obtain the money for expansion by putting up part of the ownership of the company for sale. It does this by offering stock for sale. If a company worth $1 million wants $200,000, it may sell stock. Suppose you alone own the company, and you arbitrarily state that there are 100,000 shares of stock that you own completely; you would then have to put out on the market about 20,000 shares of your stock, which you would sell at $10 a share. You would get the $200,000 for expansion, and the people who paid the money would receive 20,000 shares of your stock. They would have claim to one-sixth of whatever profits the company earned because their stock represents one-sixth of the firm's new total value of $1.2 million (your original $1 million plus their $200,000).

There are many different submarkets within the stock market. At the top of the ladder are the big ones: the New York Stock Exchange and the American Stock Exchange. Measured by dollar value, about 65 percent of all stock transactions are carried out at the New York and the American Stock Exchanges. There are also regional stock exchanges throughout the country, as well as the national and regional over-the-counter (OTC) markets. The OTC markets are somewhat less organized than the New York, American, and regional exchanges. Stocks on OTC markets usually trade stocks in companies that are small and less well known than the companies on the major stock exchanges. More than 50,000 different stocks are bought and sold on the OTC market.

Common Stock

Most stock that is owned and traded in the United States is **common stock.** Common stock has **equity** because it represents a share of ownership in a corporation. Owners of common stock may receive a share of the firm's profit in *dividends,* an amount that often varies with the firm's success. If the firm does well, the dividend could be large; if it does poorly, no dividend may be paid at all. For this reason, there is more risk associated with owning common stock than with many other types of business investments.

Preferred Stock

Preferred stock also represents ownership, or equity, in a corporation. It is different from common stock in at least two important ways. Owners of preferred stock have no vote in choosing the firm's board of directors. They must rely on the owners of common stock to choose the directors who will run the firm. However, they have a right to the profits and assets of the firm before the owners of common stock.

Another important difference is that, unlike common stock, preferred stock pays a fixed dividend that does not change over time regardless of the amount of a firm's profit. Although it is possible for a corporation's board of directors to choose not to pay preferred stock dividends if the firm is losing money (as Chrysler Corporation did in 1979), these dividends generally must be made up before any common dividends can be paid in successful years. Also, if the firm fails, assets that remain after its other debts are satisfied will be paid to preferred stockholders before common stockholders receive anything. For these reasons the risk of buying and holding preferred stock is less than that of owning common stock.

Corporate Bonds

A *corporate bond* is basically an IOU, or a promissory note of a corporation, usually issued in multiples of $1,000. A **bond** is evidence of a debt in which the issuing company promises to pay the bondholder a specific amount of interest for a specified length of time and then to repay the loan on the expiration date. In every case, a bond represents debt of the issuing corporation. Its holder is a creditor of the corporation and not a part-owner.

Interest on a bond and its principal must be paid on time, or the firm is in default and may be forced into bankruptcy by the bondholder. In such cases, bondholders have a right to the firm's assets before either the common or preferred stockholders. See Exhibit 18–1 for a summary comparison of common stocks and bonds.

Some types of preferred stock and corporate bonds are *convertible.* This means the owners of these investments may choose to trade them for common stock at a specific rate, often within a specific period of time. The advantage of owning convertible preferred stock or bonds is the opportunity they offer investors to take advantage of a firm's success, which could push the value of its common stock up, while assuring them the security of the preferred stock or bond if the firm is less profitable.

Common stock
A unit of ownership that has a legal claim to the profits of a company. For each share owned, the common-stock owner generally has the right to one vote on such questions as merging with another company or electing a new board of directors.

Equity
A legal claim to the profits of a company. This is another name for stock, generally called common stock.

Preferred stock
A unit of ownership in a corporation; each share entitles the owner to a fixed dividend that the corporation must pay before it pays any dividends to common stockholders; owners have call on the firm's assets before common stockholders if the firm fails, but have no vote in choosing the firm's board of directors.

Bond
A type of debt that a business or a government issues to investors. A bond represents a promise to pay a certain amount of money (called interest) each year. At the end of a specified amount of time, the principal on the bond is repaid to the bondholder.

COMMON STOCKS	BONDS
1. Represent ownership.	1. Represent owed debt.
2. Have no fixed dividend rate.	2. Require interest be paid, whether or not any profit is earned.
3. Allow holders to elect a board of directors, which, in turn, controls the corporation.	3. Usually entail no voice in or control over management.
4. Have no maturity date; the corporation does not usually repay the stockholder.	4. Have a maturity date when the holder is to be repaid the face value.
5. Are issued by all business corporations (and are purchased by stockholders).	5. Need not be issued by corporations.
6. Allow holders to have a claim against the property and income of the corporation after all creditors' claims have been met.	6. Give to bondholders a prior claim against the property and income of the corporation that must be met before the claims of stockholders.

Capital Gains and Losses

Stock can go up and down in price. If you buy a stock at $10 and sell it at $15, you make a *capital gain* equal to $5 for every share you bought and then sold at the higher price. That is called an *appreciation* in the price of your stock, which you realized as a capital gain when you sold it. If the value of your stock falls and you sell it at a loss, you have suffered a **capital loss** because of the depreciation in the market value of your stock. Normally, when you buy a stock that has never paid a dividend, you expect to make money on your investment by an increase in the value of the stock. That is, if the company is making profits but not giving out dividends, it must be reinvesting those profits. A reinvestment in itself could pay off in the future by higher profits. The value of the stock would then be bid up in the market. Your profit would be in the form of a capital gain rather than dividend payments.

Capital loss
The difference between the buying and the selling price of something you own when the selling price is lower than the buying price.

WHAT AFFECTS THE PRICE OF A STOCK?

Some observers believe that individual psychological or subjective feelings are all that affect the price of a stock. If people think a stock will be worth more in the future, they will bid the price up. If they think it will be worth less in the future, the price will fall. That is not a very satisfactory theory, however. Usually, psychological feelings are based on the expected stream of profits that the company will make in the future. Past profits may be important in formulating a prediction of future profits. Past profits are bygones, however, and bygones are forever bygones. A company could lose money for ten years and then make profits for the next fifteen.

If a company hires a new management team that has a reputation for turning losing companies into winning ones, people in the stock market might expect profits to turn around and rise. If a company has a record number of sales orders for future months, one also might expect profits to go up. Whenever profits are expected to rise, we typically find a rise in the value of the stock. That is, people bid up the price of stock. Any information about future profits, therefore, should be valuable in assessing how a stock's price will react.

MAKING MONEY IN THE STOCK MARKET

You probably have heard of the famous investor J. P. Morgan, who supposedly made his fortune by manipulating the stock market. You may have heard of other people who made billions of dollars in recent stock market frauds. Probably the best-known example was Michael Milken, who earned several billion dollars by fraudulently selling *junk bonds*—high yield bonds that are also very high-risk bonds. He was eventually sent to jail and paid more than $1 billion to settle his debts. The point to remember is that most people who have made large amounts of money quickly have done it at the expense of other people. Although it is possible to invest wisely in the stock and bond markets, it is also possible to be "taken" by unscrupulous people. Consumers should never invest their money until they understand what they are investing in. And they should be suspicious of any investment offering an unusually high return.

Getting Advice on the Market

Look in your Yellow Pages under "Stock and Bond Brokers," pick a phone number at random, and call it. Ask to speak with a registered representative or an account executive (in the old days, called "customers' men") and talk to this broker as if you had, say, $10,000 to invest. Ask him or her for advice. You probably will be asked what your goals are. Do you want income from your investment? Do you want growth in your investment? Do you want to take a chance? Do you want to be safe? After you tell the broker the strategy you wish to pursue, you will be told the best stocks to buy. If you ask the broker what he or she thinks the market in general will be doing over the next few months, you are bound to hear an opinion—and an authoritative one at that. After all, if you want to know what to do with your garden, you ask the person who runs the local nursery. If you want to know about your car, you ask your local mechanic. That is, you generally seek out specialists

Consumers can make the best use of stockbrokers to acquire general information about the stock market or about individual firms. History indicates that using the advice of stockbrokers about which stocks to purchase is no more likely to result in a good return than is guessing or using a dart board. For this reason many financial analysts suggest that investors buy into mutual funds that often charge smaller fees and achieve better results than do individual stocks.

in your field of interest. Why not seek out a specialist, then, when you are interested in making money?

A broker is a specialist, one from whom you can get much useful information. A broker can tell you all about the stock market and can give you quotes on all the different stocks—that is, what their prices are and how many of them were sold in the last few days and what the history of the prices has been. You can be told about the various types of securities you can buy—stocks listed on the big exchanges like the New York and the American, over-the-counter stocks that are sold only in very restricted sections of the country, preferred stocks, bonds, convertible debentures, puts, calls, warrants, and so on. A stockbroker is the person you should ask concerning all these different avenues of investment.

But the broker is *not* the one you should ask about which particular stock to buy. *The broker is no more likely to be right than you are.* You might even do well in selecting the stocks to purchase by throwing a dart at a list of stocks on the New York Stock Exchange. If you are shocked by this statement, you should remember that the stock market is very competitive, and obtaining information about it is easy and inexpensive. All stocks and bonds react quickly to changes in economic conditions. They may well react before your broker is able to reach you with recommendations. It is not clear, therefore, that a stockbroker will be able to help you make better investment decisions than if you simply relied on chance.

Public Information

Information flows rapidly in the stock market. If you read in *The Wall Street Journal* that International Chemical and Nuclear (ICN) has just discovered a cure for cancer, do you think you should rush out and buy ICN stock? You might, but you will be no better off than if you had bought any other stock. By the time you read about ICN's discovery (which will mean increased profits in the future for the company), thousands and thousands of other people already will have read it, so the price of its stock will have climbed sky-high. A rule that you should apply, and one that will be explained several times in this chapter, is that *public information does not yield an above-normal profit or rate of return.* Once information about a company's profitability is generally known, that information has a zero value for predicting the future price of the stock. So if you read about a new discovery by Kodak that is going to make immense profits in the future, by the time you go to buy Kodak stock, its price will have already been bid up by people who found out that information before you did. It's a harsh but solid fact that you just can't make a killing by learning about things that a lot of other people already know.

Hot Tips

What about the hot tips your broker might have? First of all, it's highly unlikely that the tips will be true **inside information.** After all, if it were really inside information, why would it be given to you? Why wouldn't the broker take advantage of it, get rich quick, and quit being a stockholder? The broker's information might have come from the brokerage's research department. Almost all stockbrokerage companies have large research staffs that investigate different industries, different companies, and the future of the general economy. These research departments issue statements on different companies and industries in the economy, noting which stocks are underpriced and, therefore, should be bought. *The value of this research information to you as an investor*

Inside information

Information about a company's financial situation that is obtained before the public obtains it. True inside information is usually known only by corporate officials or other insiders.

is zero. You will do no better by following the advice of research branches of your stockbrokerage company than you will by randomly selecting stocks—particularly stocks listed on the New York and American Stock Exchanges. Nevertheless, the amount of research on those companies that is completed by firms, individuals, organizations, governments, and so on is indeed staggering. Because information flows so freely, by the time you receive the results of research on a particular company, you can be sure that thousands and thousands of other people already have found out. And because so many brokerage firms employ research analysts, you can be sure that there are numerous analysts investigating every single company that has shares for sale in the open stock market.

Years of academic research on the stock market have left little doubt that the stock market is, indeed a random walk. What has happened to stock in the past does not matter.

The Random Walk

If you took a high-school physics course, you may recall studying Brownian motion of molecules. The molecules jumped around randomly, and there was simply no way to predict where one would jump next. This is exactly what happens when something follows a *random walk:* It goes in directions that are totally unrelated to past directions. If something follows a random walk, no amount of past information is useful for predicting what will happen in the future. The stock market would be expected to exhibit a random walk merely because it is so highly competitive and because information flows so freely. Examining past prices on the market as a whole or on individual stocks would not be expected to yield any useful information as to prices in the future. Years and years of academic research on the stock market have left little doubt that the stock market is, indeed, a random walk. (If you find out otherwise, you may be able to get rich very quickly.)

A stock is not like a dog—which is to say, it will not eventually come home to its former price. Indeed, because a stock does not know where its home is and does not have a mind or a purpose, what has happened to that stock in the past does not matter. You can find no usable information by examining past stock prices. Or, according to Nobel Prize-winning economist Paul Samuelson,

> Even the best investors seem to find it hard to do better than comprehensive common-stock averages, or better on the average than random selection among stocks of comparable variability.[1]

What about Investment Advisers?

If you wish to have help in making your investment decisions, you can hire an investment counselor or adviser. Generally, when you hire an investment adviser, you sign a contract that gives the adviser discretion over your investment funds. The adviser will then buy and sell securities for you without further authorization. In the past, investment counselors generally were not interested in handling investment accounts of less than $100,000, but owing to competition many of them now offer investment counseling services for much smaller accounts, even accounts for $10,000. Investment counselors are numerous, and many investors—particularly, active investors—turn to them for investment assistance.

---

1. Paul Samuelson, *The Bell Journal of Economics and Management Science* 4 (Autumn 1973), pp. 369–374.

In deciding whether you should hire an investment adviser, you need to keep in mind that whatever profits you may realize on your portfolio because of the counselor's advice does not include the fees for managing your account (typically, ½ to 2 percent of the assets managed, depending on the size of the account) or brokers' commissions that must be paid whenever stock is traded. For example, a typical advertisement for an investment counselor might show you that his or her stock portfolio makes 15 percent a year, rather than the average 8 percent rate of return for all stocks listed on the New York Stock Exchange. But the 15 percent rate does not take into account either the counseling fees or the trading costs. Trading costs (brokers' commissions) can be expensive because investment services usually do a lot of trading: They go in and out of the market—buying today, selling tomorrow. Each time someone buys a stock or sells a stock, that person pays a commission to the broker. Thus, the more trading your investment counselor does for your account, the more trading costs you incur. In fact, investments made through counselors generally do no better than the general market averages because any special profits they make are eaten up by brokerage fees and their own counseling fees.

MUTUAL FUNDS

Mutual fund
A fund that purchases the stocks of other companies. If you buy a share in a mutual fund, you are, in essence, buying shares in all the companies in which the mutual fund invests. The only business of a mutual fund is buying other companies' stocks.

Mutual funds take the money of many investors and buy and sell large blocks of stock; the investors get dividends or appreciation on their shares of the mutual fund. The mutual fund, then, is a company that invests in other companies but does not sell any physical product of its own. You can buy shares in mutual funds just as you can buy shares in General Motors. A study of mutual funds concluded that mutuals that did the least amount of trading made the highest profits, an expected result if you understand the competitive nature of the stock market. Buying into mutual funds provides investors with two important advantages. It diversifies their investments so that they are not too dependent on any one type of stock or bond. Also, mutual funds employ people who will constantly keep track of the fund's investments and, it is hoped, buy and sell investments at the most advantageous times. This is something that most individual investors lack the time to do.

The Two Types of Mutual Funds

A mutual fund or investment trust is principally either of two types: the closed end or the open end. Shares in *closed-end* investment trusts (mutual funds), some of which are listed on the New York Stock Exchange, are readily transferable in the open market and are bought and sold like other shares. *Open-end* funds sell their own new shares to investors, stand ready to buy back their old shares, and are not listed on the stock exchange. Open-end funds are so called because they issue more shares as people want them.

The only commission you pay to buy closed-end mutual funds is the standard commission you would pay on the purchase of any stock. There are two types of open-end mutual funds, no-load and load. The *no-load* mutual fund charges no setup or loading charge for you to get into the fund, whereas the *load* mutual fund charges you about 8 percent to get into the fund. Both may charge a yearly management fee. The salesperson or stockbroker who sells you an open-end mutual fund with a loading charge usually keeps most of that charge as commission. Mutual-fund experts divide open-end and closed-end funds into the following categories.

1. *Income funds.* These funds attempt to achieve high yields by concentrating on high-dividend common stocks or bonds or a combination.
2. *Balance funds.* To minimize risk, these funds hold common stocks and a certain proportion of bonds and preferred stocks.
3. *Maximum capital gains funds—dividend income incidental.* These are often aggressively managed and take higher-than-average risks by buying into little-known companies.
4. *Long-term growth funds—income secondary.* Fund managers go after larger, more seasoned, higher-quality growth stocks that do not generate dividends.
5. *Specialized funds.* Funds that restrict themselves to certain types of securities, such as gold-mining stocks.
6. *Global funds.* Funds that purchase stock issued by firms that are located in other countries or whose business is primarily involved in international trade.
7. *Environmental funds.* Funds that purchase stock issued by firms whose corporate policies are theoretically beneficial to the world's environment.

In addition, there are the following types of closed-end funds.

1. *Real-estate funds.* Otherwise known as REITs, or *real-estate investment trusts,* these are of two types—a *mortgage trust,* which borrows money from banks and relends it at a higher rate to builders and developers, and an *equity trust,* which owns income-producing property.
2. *Dual-purpose funds.* These types of closed-end funds sell two classes of stock—*income shares* and *capital shares.* The first group of purchasers receive all the fund's net income; the second group participates only in capital gains.

Money Market Mutual Funds

Perhaps the most well-known mutual fund today is a *money market mutual fund.* We have already made reference to such funds when we talked about checkable accounts and saving instruments. Banks and thrifts offer money market accounts insured up to $100,000. Alternatively, there are literally hundreds of uninsured but very safe money market mutual funds available to the same investor. The term *money market* refers to the fact that all proceeds are invested in relatively short-term money market instruments, such as Treasury bills, commercial paper sold by reputable corporations, and other short-term debt instruments. There are actually three types of money market funds.

1. *Government funds.* These invest only in U.S. Treasury obligations and those of other federal agencies.
2. *General-purpose funds.* These invest in banks and corporations, as well as in government obligations.
3. *Tax-exempt funds.* These invest in obligations of state and municipal governments whose interest payments are not taxable by the federal government. Typically, investors earn smaller dividends, but the tax-free advantage of these funds is appealing to those investors in the higher tax bracket.

Most money market mutual funds offer check-writing privileges and telephone transfers. There are restrictions, however. For example, checks may have to be for $500 or more in certain funds. The advantage of money market mutual funds is that they often offer higher interest rates than those offered by commercial banks and thrift institutions. As with all investments, those money market mutual funds that offer higher interest rates than others do carry a slightly higher risk. For certain mutual funds to make relatively higher rates of interest, they must invest the proceeds in slightly riskier assets, such as debt obligations of longer maturity and debt obligations issued by corporations that do not have the highest possible security ratings.

A disadvantage to the small saver of money market mutual funds is that they are not insured by an agency of the federal government. Although the uninsured money market funds have a high safety rating, some care should be used in selecting them. To check the rating of a money market fund, you can look it up in a newsletter called *Income and Safety*. This newsletter ranks the largest 135 funds in terms of the maturity, diversification, and quality of each fund's investments. The newsletter can be obtained by writing to *Income and Safety,* 3471 North Federal Highway, Fort Lauderdale, FL 33306, or calling toll-free (800) 327-6720.

IS THERE NO WAY TO GET RICH QUICK?

The general conclusion to be reached from our analysis of the stock market is that all the investing schemes everybody talks about are really quite useless for getting rich quickly. That does not mean, of course, that some people will not get rich by using them. Luck has much to do with making money in the stock market—just as it does with winning at poker or craps. If you do make money with your particular scheme, it does not mean you are extra smart, a better investor, or a prophet. You may be lucky. Or you may make more than a normal rate of return on your invested capital if you spend a tremendous amount of time searching out areas of unknown profit potential. But then you are spending resources—your own time, for example. Your above-average profits can be considered as payment for the time you spent—the value of your opportunity cost—analyzing the stock market and different companies.

The question still remains: How can you make money? Experience suggests that by selecting a variety of stocks from the New York Stock Exchange to invest in, people will earn a return of 8 percent to 12 percent over a number of years. Attempts to earn higher rates of return almost always require investors to accept a higher risk of losing their original investment.

The key to making money in the stock market is to think in long-run terms. As Exhibit 18–2 shows, although in some years your stock investment return may be lower than 10 percent, this lower rate of return will be compensated for by a higher-than-10-percent return in other years. Although you may not be able to "get rich quick" in the stock market, a long-run rate of return of 10 percent can help you create a substantial nest egg to help you achieve your long-term financial goals.

WATCH FOR THOSE SUREFIRE SCHEMES

By now, you ought to be quite suspicious of any special investment deals you hear about. Because so much competition exists in the investment markets and because you, as a single consumer, are not likely to be smarter than any

▶ Exhibit 18–2 Changes in Values of Investments in Stocks and Bonds

The figures in this table represent, not an annual return, but a change in the value of these investments over a period of time.

	1980–82	1983–85	1986–88	1989–90
	Unadjusted for Inflation			
S&P 500*	35.1%	16.5%	42.3%	25.8%
NASDAQ	43.8	5.8	28.8	14.7
Corporate Long-Term Bonds	46.2	27.3	23.0	40.8
U.S. Government Long-Term Bonds	36.8	24.0	17.5	27.1
U.S. Government Short-Term Bonds	41.1	23.6	25.9	27.2
Municipal Long-Term Bonds	32.1	32.4	26.3	23.5
Consumer Price Inflation	20.9	8.0	9.9	10.5
	Adjusted for Inflation			
S&P 500*	11.2%	7.8%	29.5%	13.8%
NASDAQ	18.9	−2.0	17.2	10.4
Corporate Long-Term Bonds	20.9	17.9	11.2	27.5
U.S. Government Long-Term Bonds	13.2	14.8	6.9	15.0
U.S. Government Short-Term Bonds	16.7	11.4	14.6	15.1
Municipal Long-Term Bonds	9.3	22.6	14.9	11.8

*Standard and Poor's (an index of 500 stocks that measure stock-market performance)

Source: based on Statistical Abstracts of the United States, 1991, pp. 475, 513.

THE GLOBAL CONSUMER

Investing in the Global Economy

Many developing nations that experienced difficult economic times in the 1980s have begun to recover and grow at increasing rates in the 1990s. Industrializing countries such as Thailand, South Korea, Argentina, and Indonesia are predicted to experience real growth rates of 7 percent per year during this decade. This growth has been assisted by a combination of factors that include relatively low wage rates, skilled workers, low taxes, and declining transportation costs between countries.

Although the expanding economies in developing countries provide opportunities for American investors who were willing to accept a greater degree of risk, most

Americans lack the skills necessary to invest directly in foreign markets. A number of special mutual funds, however, have been organized that allow Americans to invest in these countries' stocks indirectly. The most successful of these funds is the Templeton Emerging Markets Fund, which increased 216 percent in value between 1987 and 1992. In the same period of time the Standard & Poor's 500 stock index (a gauge of the value of many American stocks) went up 65 percent. Although other emerging nations' funds did not do as well, most did much better than funds that invested in the U.S. economy.

Investors who consider these funds should be willing to take a significant risk for several reasons.

First, if there is political or economic turmoil in these countries, the value of these funds could fall rapidly. This could cause many fund owners to redeem their shares. As a result, the funds' managers would be forced to sell stock at whatever price they could receive. Such a "liquidation" of assets would further depress the funds' value. Events like this took place with a number of funds that had invested in Mexican stocks in the late 1970s. When the Mexican economy experienced difficulties in the early 1980s, some of these funds lost 90 percent of their value. What sort of person do you feel should consider investing in emerging nations' funds? Is this a type of investment you would consider making?

of the experts around, you should consider every single investment as a trade-off between risk and rate of return (and also liquidity). The higher the potential rate of return, the higher the risk. There is no reason why you should expect to do better than average unless you have some special information.

An example is real estate. Will Rogers once said, "It's easy to make money: just figure out where people are going and then buy the land before they get there." Obviously, if Will Rogers was aware of this truism, all the experts knew it, too. What do you think happens when it is known where people will be going? That information will be used by others, who will thereby bid up the price of land in the places where people are going. Only if you think you have such information ahead of everyone else can you expect to make a higher-than-normal rate of return in any type of land investment.

So don't be taken in by a statement such as, "Land is always a safe investment." The value of land can fall like the value of anything else. Even when the overall price of land has been going up for a long time, that does not mean that you will make more than you could make investing money in something else. Although, on average, you might make more in land, on average, you also take a greater risk because land deals frequently fall through completely. Also, recent tax laws make real estate investment less attractive than it once was.

You can think of a thousand and one other investment opportunities to which the same logic applies. Just remember that you do not get something for nothing; any time you do something with your savings, you are going to take a risk, however small. Exhibit 18–2 provides some statistics on returns on stock and bond investments.

PENSIONS AND RETIREMENT FUNDS

For many people, one of the smartest ways to save is to set up a personal pension plan. Depending on your income level and whether you have an employer-provided pension plan, it can be beneficial to save via an individual retirement plan that protects your savings from taxes until you take them out of the plan. There are basically two plans available to individuals whose employers do not provide pension plans or who are self-employed.

Individual Retirement Accounts

Individual Retirement Account (IRA)
An investment account on which the earnings are not taxed until funds are withdrawn from the account, usually at retirement. IRA contributions may also be tax-deductible, depending on one's income level.

Prior to the Tax Reform Act of 1986, the **individual retirement account (IRA)** was a popular legal tax shelter for millions of Americans. If you had an IRA, you could contribute $2,000 per year toward retirement savings and deduct that $2,000 from your taxable income. Married couples could contribute up to $4,000 a year if both spouses worked, or $2,250 if only one spouse earned income. Between 1981, when IRAs first became available to qualified participants, and 1986 IRAs were very attractive, not only because the investments were tax-deductible but also because the earnings on the IRA were untaxed until withdrawn on retirement—when, normally, taxpayers are in a lower tax bracket.

The 1986 act, however, severely restricted these tax benefits of IRAs for single taxpayers who earn $25,000 or more annually and for married couples or self-employed persons whose annual income exceeds $40,000. For every $1,000 of income above these threshold amounts, the allowable $2,000 deduction is reduced by $200, until, as the income level rises, the amount of the

IF YOU ARE COVERED BY A RETIREMENT PLAN AT WORK AND YOUR FILING STATUS IS

And Your Adjusted Gross Income Is		■ Single, or ■ Head of Household	■ Married Filing Jointly (even if your spouse is not covered by a plan at work) ■ Qualifying Widow(er)	■ Married Filing Separately
At Least	**But Less Than**	**You Can Take**	**You Can Take**	**You Can Take**
$—0—	$10,000	Full deduction	Full deduction	Partial deduction
$10,000	$25,001	Full deduction	Full deduction	No deduction
$25,001	$35,000	Partial deduction	Full deduction	No deduction
$35,000	$40,001	No deduction	Full deduction	No deduction
$40,001	$50,000	No deduction	Partial deduction	No deduction
$50,000 or over		No deduction	No deduction	No deduction

IF YOU ARE NOT COVERED BY A RETIREMENT PLAN AT WORK AND YOUR FILING STATUS IS

■ Married Filing Jointly (and your spouse is covered by a plan at work)	■ Single, or ■ Head of Household	■ Married Filing Jointly or Separately (and your spouse is not covered by a plan at work) ■ Qualifying Widow(er)	■ Married Filing Separately (even if your spouse is covered by a plan at work)
You Can Take	**You Can Take**	**You Can Take**	**You Can Take**
Full deduction			
Full deduction			
Full deduction	Full deduction	Full deduction	Full deduction
Full deduction			
Partial deduction			
No deduction			

contribution that is deductible reaches zero. Zero deductibility is reached at incomes of $35,000 for singles and $50,000 for couples who are covered by pension plans through their place of employment. Depending on whether you—or your spouse, if married—is covered by an employer-provided pension plan, you may or may not be able to deduct your IRA contributions. A guide to current tax laws on IRA deductions is presented in Exhibit 18–3.

Even if you are not eligible for an IRA deduction, you may still want to consider making a nondeductible contribution to an IRA because you do not have to pay tax on income earned from your IRA until you begin making withdrawals at age 59½. (You can make withdrawals before reaching that age, but you will have to pay a 10-percent penalty in addition to the tax due unless you are disabled or otherwise qualify for an exemption to the penalty. You must begin making withdrawals by April 1 of the year following the year that you reach 70½.) Since presumably you will be in a lower tax bracket when you reach retirement age, you will thus pay less taxes on your IRA earnings as you withdraw them. In addition, for all nondeductible contributions, you do not have to pay taxes on the principal upon withdrawal.

Keogh Plans

Keogh plans are named after Eugene J. Keogh, the congressional representative from New York who sponsored the Keogh Act of 1962. The Keogh Act was passed to allow self-employed individuals to set up their own pension plans. Keoghs are similar to IRAs in that they allow you to defer tax payments on interest earned in the plan until the time of withdrawal at the age of 59½ or later. As with IRAs, if you withdraw money from your Keogh plan before that age, you face a 10-percent penalty on the amount withdrawn, and you must begin to withdraw from the account by the age of 70½. Unlike IRAs, you can continue contributing to a Keogh plan after retirement for as long as you earn self-employment income.

Even if you are covered by a pension plan at work or have an IRA, you can have a Keogh plan as well—as long as it covers only the income you earn from self-employment. With just a small sideline business, you can set up a Keogh account and save tax dollars while contributing to your retirement fund.

There are a variety of specific Keogh plans to choose from, each with different rules and limitations. If you believe you could benefit from having a Keogh plan, it probably would be wise to find a reputable retirement advisor who can provide you with more specific information.

▶ SUMMARY

1. In the stock market, shares of American businesses are bought and sold just about every weekday throughout the year. When you buy and sell stocks, you may either sell them for more than you paid and experience a capital gain or sell them for less than you paid and experience a capital loss.

2. When you buy a share of stock in a corporation, there is no guarantee that you will receive dividends or that you will make any particular rate of interest on your investment. If you loan money to the company—that is, buy one of its bonds—you are guaranteed, as long as the company does not go bankrupt, a specified dollar interest payment every year and a specified principal payment when the bond matures or when the bond's life runs out.

3. It is generally a waste of time to consult stock market analysts in deciding which stocks to buy for your investment portfolio. The stock market is one of the most highly competitive markets in the world, and any useful information is immediately used by all who receive it.

4. Stockbrokers can explain how the stock market works, the different types of securities you can buy, and so on.

5. Do not be taken in by investment counselors who guarantee you a higher-than-normal rate of return in the stock market. Generally, investment counselors consume any above-normal rates of return in the fees they charge you or the commissions you must pay to buy and sell stocks often.

6. Mutual funds may be an easy answer to your investing problems, for they purchase a wide variety of stocks. It is generally advisable to buy into a no-load mutual fund that has no sales charges. Money market mutual funds provide a relatively safe investment vehicle, although they are not insured by the federal government the way money market deposit accounts are.

7. All schemes to make you richer should be investigated thoroughly, for, on average, they rarely guarantee you a higher-than-normal rate of return unless you accept a higher amount of risk. For example, even though the amount of land is fixed and the population is growing, real estate is not always a good investment. It is an example of public information having zero value as a guide to where to invest your accumulated savings. The same is true for antiques, oil and gas wells, oil paintings, cans of food, and so on.

8. For many people, a good way to save is to set up a pension fund. Two plans available to individuals whose employers do not provide pension plans or who are self-employed are the individual retirement account (IRA) and the Keogh plan.

▶ QUESTIONS FOR THOUGHT AND DISCUSSION

1. "Risk and rate of return are positively related." Do you agree with that statement? Why?

2. Which do you think is a better investment—stocks or bonds?

3. Do you think stockbrokers have more information about which stocks to buy than you have?

4. What is the value of public information?

5. Do you think the small investor should be given special treatment by the stock exchanges and brokerage houses?

6. "The stock market is the backbone of American capitalism." Comment.

7. Do you believe in the so-called random-walk theory of stock prices?

8. Why do you think there were no mutual funds in existence years ago?

9. The value of land has almost always gone up over time. If this is true, why don't investors simply put all their money in land?

▶ THINGS TO DO

1. Call an antique dealer and ask about the investment opportunities in antiques. What's the rate of return on investing in antiques? Is this rate of return higher or lower than what you could expect if you put your money in a savings and loan association?

2. If you live in one of the large cities that has a stock exchange, visit it. You will be able to see a competitive market in action. Also, you can usually pick up information on stock markets and how they work. Call a brokerage firm in your area to ask if there is a national or regional exchange nearby.

3. Look at the financial page of any newspaper. Find out what all the various financial quotations actually mean, either from your instructor or from a stockbroker.

4. List the steps you would follow in purchasing a stock on the New York Stock Exchange.

▶ APPLICATION

Use the *Reader's Guide to Periodical Literature* or a computerized reference guide such as *Infotrac* to identify a recent article that describes how an unscrupulous person or business took advantage of investors. Look under the heading "Fraud" for listings. Write an essay that describes what happened. Explain what the victims should have done to protect themselves.

▶ SELECTED READINGS

▶ "1992 Investor's Guide." *Fortune,* Fall 1991, special issue.

▶ "Black Enterprise Annual Money Management Issue." *Black Enterprise,* October 21, 1991, special issue.

▶ Bodman, J. "Big Ideas." *Kiplinger's Personal Finance Magazine,* August 1991, pp. 28–32.

▶ Cappiello, Frank, and Karel McClellan. *From Main Street to Wall Street: Making Money in Real Estate.* New York: Wiley, 1988.

▶ Givens, Charles J. *Wealth Without Risk*. New York: Simon & Schuster, 1989.

▶ *Investors' Bill of Rights*. Available free from the National Futures Association, 200 W. Madison St., Suite 1600, Chicago, IL 60606.

▶ *Journey through a Stock Exchange*. Available for 75 cents from American Stock Exchange, Publications Dept., 86 Trinity Place, New York, NY 10006.

▶ Lynch, Peter. *One Up on Wall Street,* New York: Simon & Schuster, 1989.

▶ New York Times. *Financial Planning Guide*. Published annually in November.

▶ Quinn, Jane Bryant, "Jane Bryant Quinn's Recession/Inflation/Anything-Proof Guide to Investing." *Working Woman,* October 1991, pp. 48–50.

▶ Rukeyser, Louis. *Louis Rukeyser's Business Almanac*. New York: Simon & Schuster, 1988.

▶ Serwer, A. E., et al. "Your Best Investment Strategy for an Economic Recovery." *Fortune,* July 29, 1991, pp. 29–30.

▶ VanAespel, Venita. *Money Dynamics for the 1990s,* New York: 1988.

▶ *What Is a Mutual Fund?* Available for 50 cents from the Consumer Information Center, Pueblo, CO 81002.

▶ "Where to Invest in 1992." *Business Week,* December 30, 1991–January 6, 1992, pp. 59–64+.

How to Be a Rational Investor

As we have noted, the various schemes you could follow to get rich quickly in the stock market are useless because the stock market is so highly competitive. That is true for just about every investment opportunity into which you could put your savings.

Nonetheless, you need to invest your savings someplace if you wish to have them earn a reasonable rate of return.

▶ HOW TO START INVESTING

There are various ways to start investing, and your choice will depend largely on (1) how much time you want to devote to the process and (2) the extent to which you want—or feel you need—the assistance of professionals.

▶ Investment Clubs

Investment clubs are becoming a popular resource for many who want to learn about the stock market and earn money on their savings at the same time. There are an estimated 30,000 investment clubs across the country. Typically, they have a membership of 15 investors and holdings of around $50,000 or so—meaning that, on average, each member contributes less than $4,000. Some clubs consist of no more than two friends who subscribe to investment newsletters; others are large-scale partnerships of experienced investors who do their own research. Since it often costs quite a bit to join an established club—in order to match the other members' contributions—you might want to consider forming your own club with a friend or group of friends.

The National Association of Investment Clubs (NAIC) (1515 East Eleven Mile Road, Royal Oak, MI 48067) helps new investment clubs get started. On request, they will send you a pamphlet on how to organize an investment club and (for $18) an investor's manual. The annual dues for membership in the NAIC are $30 per club and $10 for each member.

In addition to advising you on how to launch your club, the NAIC will send you a model portfolio, as well as worksheets to help you analyze stocks on your own. Generally, the NAIC advises that you aim for a 15 percent annual growth.

▶ Asset Management Accounts

Asset management accounts, discussed previously in Chapter 15, are offered by a number of major stock-brokerage firms, banks, and other financial organizations. For many who wish to invest in the stock market, as well as have a checkable account and a credit card, these one-stop financial services are certainly something to consider. Combination money market and brokerage accounts let you earn high interest on your cash, buy and sell securities, and borrow on your investment, in addition to offering check-writing services and credit cards.

If you want to open an asset management account (and have the $10,000 or so that may be required to do so), you need to decide which type of institution best suits your needs. If you want investment advice, your best bet is to open an account with a brokerage firm. Discount brokerage service, with commissions that can be 90 percent less than the fees charged by full-time brokers, is available at banks and with mutual funds.

One of the great benefits of an asset management account is the "sweep" feature. Any extra cash in your account above a certain minimum, including dividends and bond income, is automatically reinvested, typically in a money market fund, so your money is constantly earning interest.

▶ Financial Planners

A growing number of consumers are turning to financial planners for help in investment planning and asset management. Most financial planners work independently and charge anywhere between $500 and $5,000 for their services, depending on their client's net worth, the planner's reputation, and whether the planner's fee is based on a commission. Nationwide financial services—such as Merrill Lynch, Prudential-Bache and others—also have financial planners on their staffs. Financial plans from nationwide services are much less expensive and are often offered to customers free of charge.

Unlike investment counselors, who are experts in the stock market and recommend specific stocks and bonds to purchase, financial planners help consumers make overall budgeting, saving, and investing decisions and recommend allocation of funds among different *types* of investments—in order to get the most favorable return for the investors' money.

How Helpful Are Financial Planners? Many consumers have slept better at night and improved their financial situations considerably with the help of financial-planning assistance. But the quality of plans (and planners) varies widely. In 1986 Consumers Union (CU) did some investigating of such services by sending a reporter and her husband to ten different financial planners. The three independent planners the couple visited offered estimates of $1,500, $600, and over $500, respectively, for their financial-planning services. Because of the expense, CU—as most consumers probably would—turned from these planners to the less expensive major

financial-services companies, including Aetna Life & Casualty, Merrill Lynch, the Sears Financial Network, and four others. In each case, the couple submitted fairly specific data concerning their assets, liabilities, income, and future needs. The results? Largely disappointing, according to CU. In the case of the free plans, CU felt they got pretty much what they paid for. And the recommendations in almost all cases reflected the primary business of the company designing the plan. CU was also surprised at the wide variations in what the planners considered suitable for the couple's fairly well-defined needs. The only common recommendation was that the couple prepare wills.

Finding a Good Financial Planner The conclusion reached by Consumers Union doesn't necessarily mean that you should avoid financial-planning assistance; just be cautious. Not only is it very easy to pay for what may be essentially a worthless plan for you, but fraud in the financial-planning industry is on the rise. According to the North American Securities Administrators Association, 22,000 investors lost more than $400 million through financial-planning fraud between

1986 and 1988. To avoid losing your money to a con artist, quiz your potential planning assistant carefully: What are his or her credentials? How can they be checked? What about past performance and track records? References? Is he or she registered with the SEC? And so on. For further details on how to evaluate a financial planner, write to the Federal Trade Commission, 6th St. and Pennsylvania Ave., N.W., Washington, DC 20580, and ask for a copy of its publication, *Money Matters*. This brochure contains a lengthy list of questions to ask financial planners to ensure that you won't be taken in by a bogus planner.

Elements of a Good Financial Plan A good financial plan will include the nine elements listed in Exhibit Q–1. It will also reflect a planning process that usually involves the following steps:

1. *Gathering data.* A good planner will request that you bring all relevant financial information—including bank certificates, insurance policies, tax returns, wills, and other documents—to your first meeting with the planner.
2. *Identifying goals and objectives.* Your goals and objectives will be

▶ Exhibit Q–1   **Elements of a Good Financial Plan**

1. It is clearly written, in language the intended user can understand.
2. Recommendations are clear and unambiguous.
3. It contains a *cash-flow analysis,* a sort of glorified budget, that shows your income from all sources, minus all your expenses.
4. It includes a *net-worth statement* (a snapshot of your assets and liabilities) and examines your current debts to see if any should be consolidated, paid off from other available funds, or refinanced.
5. It includes an examination of your current insurance and recommends ways to bolster your coverage, if necessary, and to save on premiums, if possible.
6. It examines your current investment portfolio and makes recommendations for restructuring your investments if appropriate.
7. It includes a tax analysis and tax-saving suggestions.
8. It touches on retirement planning and estate planning.
9. It includes a statement of your goals, objectives, and tolerance for investment risk.

Source: *Consumer Reports,* January 1986, p. 38.

the foremost concern of your planner. Essentially, this step involves learning why you want financial assistance.

3. *Identifying financial trouble spots.* A good financial planner will be able to identify any trouble spots—if you are underinsured or overinsured, for example, or paying more taxes than necessary.

4. *Following the plan.* A good planner will follow through on recommendations and coordinate the implementation of the plans with others—such as a lawyer—if necessary.

5. *Reviewing the plan periodically.* Usually, a good planner will review your plan with you annually to make sure that the plan is still appropriate to your planning goals.

▶ PICKING A BROKER

If you decide to buy stocks, you usually can do so only through a broker. But, if you use the random-walk theory discussed in Chapter 18, you will need the broker only to execute your orders—that is, to buy and sell stocks. You won't want him or her to advise you about which stocks to buy and which to sell or when to leave and enter the market. You may, therefore, wish to use the services of a discount brokerage firm. Exhibit Q–2 shows an ad for a cut-rate brokerage firm. To do business with a discount broker, you telephone your order in to a trader who buys or sells the stocks you want and later confirms the trade, usually by mail. Most discount brokers have a toll-free number. Within five business days after the transaction, you must either send a check for the securities you bought or deliver the stock certificates of the securities you sold. New customers to discount brokerage firms usually are

▶ **Exhibit Q–2** **Cut-Rate Brokerage Fees**

required to put down part or all of the cash to make their first buy order or to furnish stock certificates before their first sell order. Most discounters base their charges on the size of the transaction. Generally, unless your order is $1,000 or more, you will be better off going to a full-commission broker.

Discounters generally have a two-tiered pricing plan. There is a higher commission rate for trades on major stock exchanges, a lower one for trades on the **third market.** The third market is a network of traders who bypass the major stock exchanges.

In any event, you should pick a broker who meets your needs. If, as many people do, you like having a broker call you often with hot tips, then you want to get an outgoing one who will keep in close touch. But if you value your time and aren't particularly interested in the stockmarket per se, then just call any broker in the book, and let it be known that you never want to be called and that you simply want your orders executed. Because there is a penalty in the form of a higher service charge for smaller orders, wait until you have enough saved to order your shares of stocks in blocks of 100 or more.

If you want to know more about the ins and outs of the stock market, there are hundreds of books to consult. Some of the more recent publications have been included in the "Selected Readings" sections of this Consumer Issue and the preceding chapter. Stock market and investment information can also be found in such publications as *Fortune, Forbes, The Wall Street Journal,* and consumer-oriented magazines such as *Kiplinger's Personal Finance Magazine* and *Money.*

▶ **READING QUOTATIONS ON THE NEW YORK STOCK EXCHANGE**

By far the most well-known public market is the New York Stock Exchange. As with all other stock exchanges, at the beginning of each trading day shares of stock open at the same price at which they closed the day before. At the end of each day, each stock has a closing price. This is the information that newspapers report. The example in Exhibit Q–3 of some of the stocks traded on the New York Stock Exchange is from a typical newspaper financial page. American Stock Exchange quotations are often given in most newspapers, too. Major newspapers throughout the country will also carry regional or local stock exchange listings.

In a listing, each company's name is printed in an abbreviated form. For example, in the listing shown in Exhibit Q–3, *IntPaper* means International Paper. Often, other letters will appear next to the name of the company. For example, the letters *Pf* mean that preferred stock is being quoted in that row. Prices are listed in dollars and fractions of a dollar; for example, the figure 41½ means $41.50.

▶ **READING QUOTATIONS OF OVER-THE-COUNTER MARKET TRANSACTIONS**

Only the most prestigious companies have their stock listed on the New York and American Stock Exchanges. Most securities are traded on what is known as the *over-the-counter (OTC) market.* Dealers in the OTC market are not necessarily affiliated with a securities exchange; rather, they stand ready to buy and sell specified stocks at a specified

bid and ask price. Some OTC securities are listed on the National Association of Securities Dealers Automatic Quotation (NASDAQ) System. The information about OTC securities varies slightly from that given for shares in companies traded on the New York and American Stock Exchanges. Over-the-counter quotations normally list the highest bid and the lowest ask price among dealers at the end of each trading day.

▶ **WHAT ABOUT BONDS?**

Bonds are an alternative to stocks that many people invest in for savings. Unanticipated inflation can make bonds a bad deal, however. This is particularly true, of course, for low-interest U.S. savings bonds, but it may also be true for any other type of bond—federal, state, and municipal government, plus corporate—that is *long term* and has an interest rate that fails to reflect fully the decreasing purchasing power of the dollars you loaned the people who gave you the bond.

In effect, bonds are fixed income-bearing types of investments. You buy a bond, and it yields you a specific annual return in dollars that can be translated into an interest yield. In other words, if you buy a bond that yields you $100 a year and it cost you $1,000, you receive a 10 percent rate of return; if it cost you only $500, you get a 20 percent rate of return. Generally, as with all investments, the higher the rate of return, the higher the risk that the issuer of the bond will not be able to pay interest—or will not be able to pay at all.

If you decide to buy any bonds, make sure you go through a broker who knows what he or she is doing in the bond market. Tell the broker how much risk you are willing to take and when you want the bonds to mature. You can buy bonds that mature in six months or thirty years, if you want. Bonds are issued by the U.S. government and by corporations.

Zero-Coupon Bonds

Corporate and government zero-coupon bonds pay no interest until the bond matures, yet you must pay taxes annually on the *implicit* interest earned. The attraction of these bonds lies in the profits you can accumulate by investing in them, as they are often sold at deep discounts. Zero-coupon bonds may make a good long-term investment for, say, your child's education fund or for your IRA, on which you pay no taxes until later anyway. If you had put $5,000 into a U.S. Treasury zero-coupon bond in mid-1985, for example, by the year 2005 you would receive back $41,000.

Reading Bond Market Quotations

Bonds normally have a face value of $1,000, but they can sell for more or less than that amount. In other words, they sell at a premium or a discount from their face value. Prices for bonds are listed as a percentage of their face value. A figure of 79⅝, for example, means that a $1,000 bond is selling for $79.625.

Exhibit Q–4 is a listing of sample bond quotes from the New York Bond Exchange. Actually, the majority of bonds, including all tax-exempt bonds, are traded in the OTC market. Listings of OTC bond transactions are similar to those for OTC stocks in that the listing will include a bid and ask price. Often, there will be more than one listing of bonds for a particular company; this simply means that the company has different bond issues, each maturing at a different date or having different characteristics.

Tax-Exempt Bonds

Municipal bonds generally are **tax exempt;** that is, the interest you earn on those bonds is not taxed by

Exhibit Q–3   Partial List of New York Stock Exchange Composite Transactions

A	B	C		D	E	F	G	H	I	J	K
					YLD.	P-E	SALES				NET
HIGH	LOW	STOCK		DIV.	%	RATIO:	IN 100S	HIGH	LOW	CLOSE	CHANGE
47¼	39	IntMinl pf		4.00	9.6	...	13	41½	41½	41½	...
62	49½	IntMinl pfA		3.75	6.8	...	328	55	54½	55	+1½
33⅞	26	IntMultfood	IMC	1.18	4.0	12	262	29⅜	28⅞	29¼	+ ⅛
51⅞	39⅝	IntPaper	IP	1.48	3.0	7	2730	49⅝	49	49½	+ ⅜
9½	3⅜	IntRect	IRF		...	...	343	4½	4	4½	+ ½
7⅜	2⅜	IntTech	ITX		...	88	965	5⅜	5¼	5½	− ¼
45	30	IntpubGp	IPG	.80	1.8	16	1805	45	44	44½	+ ¼

These stocks and prices are excerpted from a page in *The Wall Street Journal*. Definitions of the abbreviations used and explanations of the columns are as follows.

A	High:	This is the highest price paid for the stock during the last fifty-two weeks. Stock prices are usually quoted in ⅛ of a point (12½¢) per share or multiple thereof.
B	Low:	This is the lowest price paid for the stock during the last fifty-two weeks.
C	Stock:	This is the name of the company, usually abbreviated.
D	Div.:	This is the annual dividend based on the most recent quarterly or semiannual distribution.
E	Yld. %:	This is the annual dividend amount divided by the closing of the stock.
F	P-E Ratio:	This is the ratio found by dividing the closing price by the most recent twelve months' earnings per share.
G	Sales in 100s:	This is the number of round lots (100 shares each) sold that day. The odd lots, which are less than 100 shares each, are not listed.
H	High:	This is the highest price for the stock on this trading day.
I	Low:	This is the lowest price paid for the stock on this trading day.
J	Close:	This is the price of the stock at the end of the trading day.
K	Net Change:	This is the difference between the closing price of the stock on this trading day and the closing price of the stock on the previous trading day.

▶ Exhibit Q–4   **Reading Bond Quotes**

A	B	C	D	E	F
BONDS		**CUR. YLD.**	**VOL.**	**CLOSE**	**NET CHG.**
AbbtL	11s93	10.8	17	102	…
AlaP	8½s01	9.4	5	90⅛	…
AlaP	10⅞05	10.7	12	101⅜	− ⅜
AlaP	10½05	10.4	25	100⅞	+ ⅜
AlaP	8¾07	9.9	8	88	− ⅛
AlaP	9½08	10.1	10	93¾	− ⅛
AlaP	10s18	10.1	40	99½	+ ½
AlskH	17¾91	16.1	5	110	…
viAlgl	10¾99f	…	26	81	+1½
viAlgl	10.4s02f	…	22	59	+2¾
AlldC	zr92	…	10	72	+ ⅞
AlldC	zr2000	…	34	34⅝	+1⅛
AldC	dc6s90	6.4	8	93¾	+1
AlldC	zr99	…	80	37¾	− ¼
AlldC	zr07	…	10	18½	+ ¾
Alcoa	9s95	9.2	10	97½	+ ½
AMAX	14¼90	13.8	5	103½	+ ½
Amdur	5½93	cv	40	90	…
AAirl	4¼92	5.1	35	83½	+ ⅜
ACeM	6¾91	cv	25	24	

A   Name of the company.
B   Coupon or nominal interest rate of the bond and its due or maturity date.
C   Current yield, or the coupon rate divided by the current selling price (where "cv" appears, the bond is convertible into the company's stock. The price of the conversion is not given, however. Rather, a *Standard and Poor's* or a *Moody's Bond Book* or the financial statement of the corporation will give such information.)
D   Number of bonds sold.
E   Closing price.
F   Net change from the previous trading day's closing price.

the federal government, and, in some cases, it is not taxed by state governments either. Nevertheless, these bonds are not always a special deal. To decide whether a tax-exempt bond is worth buying, you first determine how the yield compares with the rate you can earn on another investment that is not tax exempt—and this will depend, in large part, on your tax rate. Generally, you must determine whether the *after-tax* income you can receive from an alternative investment is greater or less than the (nontaxable) yield on a municipal bond.

Tax-exempt bonds are usually available in both $1,000 and $5,000 denominations. Unfortunately, most of the newer bonds are being issued in $5,000 denominations, so small investors cannot purchase them directly. You can, however, buy shares in tax-exempt bond mutual funds instead of buying the bonds themselves. Exhibit Q–5 gives you a sample of tax-free mutual funds that also allow you to write checks for $500 (or a higher minimum amount) against their accounts. In its September 1991 issue, *Forbes* magazine identified the Vanguard Group as its

"Best Buy" for municipal bond funds. It also identified the "Best Buys" for one-state municipal bond funds that were exempt from both state and federal income taxes. Exhibit Q–5 shows the average annual return from these funds from June 1986 through June 1991. Interest rates fell significantly during these years. As a result, the return on all municipal bond funds are likely to be lower now than these averages. If you would like to receive more information about Vanguard Funds, you may call (800) 662-7447.

Tax-exempt bonds are classified

not only according to the organizations that issue them—states, territories, cities, towns, villages, counties, local public housing authorities, port authorities, water districts, school districts—but also according to the sources of funds that the issuing organizations can utilize to pay interest and principal. As an example, *general obligation* tax-exempt bonds are backed by the full credit, and ordinarily by the full taxing power, of the state or municipality. On the other hand, *revenue* tax-exempt bonds are backed only by revenues from a specific activity, such as a water-supply system or a toll road. In addition, bonds are rated according to their riskiness, ranging from very risky to not risky at all. Owners of bonds issued by New York City found out all too painfully that tax-exempt municipals may not be such a good deal. You have to be wary

about them, as you do about all investments.

You can check several sources to find out about the financial stability of the issuing organization for any bonds you wish to buy. Specifically, you can go to a library to look at *Moody's Bond Record,* where bonds are rated from the highest grade Aaa to the lowest grade C (speculative to a high degree).

▶ REAL ESTATE DEALS

By now you should be suspicious of any investment that promises unusually high yields. There are many real estate deals that do exactly this and should be avoided because they involve large risks. You should be particularly suspicious of telephone solicitations or those that come to you in the mail. Most of the investments offered in this way involve

high commissions for the salesperson, but the property is usually *illiquid* (hard to sell). The fact that many real estate deals border on fraud does not mean that investing in real estate is a bad choice—only that you should be selective about it.

Throughout history, real estate has increased in value at a rate greater than the rate of inflation most of the time. Owning buildings that can be rented generates current income as well. Of course, this type of investment often requires a personal commitment to maintaining property and to dealing with tenants, but it can be financially rewarding. Generally, real estate investments should be looked at as long-term investments. Few people become wealthy in real estate quickly.

▶ ALL THAT IS GOLD DOES NOT GLITTER

What about investing in precious metals? Isn't it a sure thing? The answer is unequivocally no. People who bought gold in 1980 when it reached over $1000 an ounce probably weren't too happy when it fell to $500 an ounce a few months later. To be sure, the price of gold has gone up over time. But that does not mean that you are guaranteed a high rate of return forever. The price of silver also went up. In fact, in 1977 it was selling for $4.41 an ounce, and, during the first couple of months of 1980, it went up to $40 an ounce, but then the price dropped back down to $10 an ounce. Some people made a killing; some people lost a fortune. The price of platinum was $155 an ounce in 1977 and reached $850 an ounce in 1980; by 1985 it was down to $388.

You should not construe these examples to mean that investment in

▶ Exhibit Q–5   Tax-Free Mutual Funds with Check-Writing Privileges

FUNDS	AVERAGE FIVE-YEAR RETURN Jan. 1, 1986—Dec. 31, 1991
Municipal Bond Funds	
Vanguard Muni Bond—Intermediate	8.4%
Vanguard Muni Bond—High-Yield	8.7
Vanguard Muni Bond—Insured Long-Term	8.5
Vanguard Muni Bond—Long-Term	8.6
One-State Funds	
Vanguard California tax-free insured	8.9
Spartan Connecticut Muni High-Yield	8.5
Fidelity Massachusetts Tax-Free High-Yield	9.1
Fidelity Michigan Tax-Free High-Yield	8.6
Franklin Minnesota Insured Tax-Free Incorporated	8.7
Vanguard New Jersey Tax-Free, Insured Long-Term	9.2
Fidelity New York Tax-Free High-Yield	8.5
Vanguard Pennsylvania Tax-Free, Insured Long-Term	9.1

precious metals is not advised. Sometimes it is. A well-diversified investor is the best investor around.

If you wish to diversify your investments, you could indeed have a certain percentage of your investments in precious metals, such as Canadian gold maple-leaf coins, pre-1965 U.S. silver coins, and a variety of other precious metals. But do not assume that you are guaranteed a high rate of return. Nothing is intrinsically a sound investment at all times for all people.

▶ VARIETY IS THE SPICE OF INVESTMENT

It is generally advisable to seek variety in your savings plans for several reasons. First, not all your savings should be in liquid assets. If you unexpectedly require money quickly, you would like to have some cash or savings account reserve that you can take out immediately without losing anything. Remember, however, that you pay a cost for keeping cash—the cost of the rate of inflation that shrinks the purchasing power of those dollars.

The second reason to vary your savings is that you can reduce your overall risk by having a large variety of different investment assets. There are no fixed rules to follow, although many investment counselors have their own. They might suggest

you keep a certain fraction of your assets in cash, a certain fraction in a savings account, and so on. But there is no scientific rule or reason behind such advice. You must decide yourself how much *liquidity* you want, how much risk you want to take, how many long-term investments you want, and how many short-term investments you want.

Remember, as you increase the variety of risks you have in your investment portfolio, you lower the overall risk in that whole portfolio, but you also lower the overall rate of return you will receive. You may want to gamble as part of your investment program. You may want to buy, for example, penny stocks that sometimes jump tremendously in value. You may want to buy stocks on local OTC markets that have a high variability and sometimes really hit. But you certainly should not put all your eggs in this basket, because if you lose, you will have nothing. At the other end of the spectrum, you could be absolutely safe by keeping everything in a savings account; but because you would be unable to make a higher rate of return, you probably don't want to do that, either. Remember successful investment does not mean making a killing. It means avoiding losses that deprive you of retirement savings and, at the same time providing a

normal rate of return on those savings. Any other goals you choose may be costly.

Now take a look at Exhibit Q–6 for various investment vehicles. And then "let the buyer beware."

▶ SUMMARY

1. Ways to start investing include joining an investment club, opening an asset management account, hiring a financial planner to help guide you, or deciding on specific stock purchases and using a brokerage service.
2. Investment clubs are a popular means of learning about the stock market while getting a good return on your savings.
3. Asset management accounts offer both check-writing and credit opportunities and brokerage services. Such accounts are available through banks, mutual funds, brokerage houses, and other firms.
4. Financial planners can be very useful, but care must be taken in selecting one because of the amount of fraud perpetrated by bogus financial planners and planning services.
5. Your choice of a broker will depend on whether you want or feel you need investment advice or just a broker to follow your instructions. Full-service brokers charge higher commissions but will offer you their

▶ Exhibit Q–6 **Average Annual Rates of Return on Various Investments, as of January 1991**

TYPE OF ASSET	1 YEAR	5 YEARS	10 YEARS	20 YEARS
Old masters' paintings	6.5%	23.4%	15.8%	12.3%
Gold	− 0.7	1.0	− 2.9	11.5
Diamonds	0.0	10.2	6.4	10.5
Stamps	− 7.7	− 2.4	− 0.7	10.0
Stocks	11.8	13.3	16.0	11.6
Corporate bonds	14.3	17.6	11.2	9.1
Consumer price index	2.8	4.0	3.7	6.6

Source: *Fortune*, Fall 1991, p. 118; and *Economic Indicators*, various editions.

expertise in making investment decisions. Discount brokers charge less and, if you believe in the random-walk theory, will probably best serve your needs.

6. The New York and American Stock Exchanges list the securities of the most prestigious U.S. companies. The majority of securities are traded in over-the-counter markets. Some of the OTC securities are listed on the National Association of Securities Dealers Automatic Quotation (NASDAQ) System.

7. Bonds, an alternative investment to stocks, are a bad investment in times of unanticipated inflation because bonds are fixed income-bearing types of investments. Zero-coupon bonds are often sold at deep discounts and can be very profitable long-term investments. To determine whether tax-exempt bonds are a good investment for you, you need to compare the yield with other investments that are not tax exempt. Your tax rate will be an important factor in your calculations.

8. In investing your savings dollars, always be aware that high returns also involve a high risk factor. Real estate and precious metals can be good investments, but not for all people.

9. A diversified investment portfolio can help to decrease overall risk. Successful investment means avoiding losses but at the same time providing a normal rate of return on your savings.

▶ QUESTIONS FOR THOUGHT AND DISCUSSION

1. The rate of return on the stock market is basically the rate of return to American business. Do you agree or disagree?
2. Why do you think you can obtain so much free research from various brokerage houses?
3. What do you think determines the price of a stock?
4. What is the difference between a corporate bond and a government bond?
5. Why do you think the interest earned on municipal bonds is not taxed by the federal government?
6. Why is there such diversity of opinion about what constitutes appropriate investments?

▶ THINGS TO DO

1. Ask a stockbroker to send you information on mutual funds in the United States. Find out the characteristics of growth funds versus income funds versus high-risk funds versus low-risk funds. How would you decide which mutual fund to buy? Find out the difference between load and no-load mutual funds. Why would anybody want to pay the sales commission to buy a load fund as opposed to a no-load fund?
2. Look at the "Money & Investing" section in *The Wall Street Journal*, which shows the Dow Jones Industrial Average. Can you see any pattern in what has happened to the average price of stocks?
3. Find out the latest rates for purchasing less than $2,000 worth of stock. Try to determine why some investment brokerage houses charge less than others.

Read two books on the stock market from the list given in the "Selected Readings" section of Chapter 18. Compare the information and/or investment philosophies given in the two books.

▶ SELECTED READINGS

▶ Kuhn, S. E. "America's Best Mutual Funds." *Forbes,* December 30, 1991, pp. 90–92.
▶ Quinn, Jane Bryant. "Muni Bonds: Play It Safe." *Newsweek,* July 15, 1991, p. 41.
▶ Simon, R. "The Unnoticed Risk in Municipal Bond Funds Today." *Money,* October 1991, pp. 53–54.
▶ Rosewicz, Barbara. "Choosing a Financial Planner." *The Wall Street Journal,* November 13, 1987, p. 39D.
▶ Updegrave, Walter L. "How to Launch an Investment Club." *Money,* May 1989, pp. 117–125.
▶ Weaver, P. "Decoding the Prospectus from a Mutual Fund." *Nation's Business,* December 1991, p. 49–50.
▶ Weiss, Gary. " A Down-Home Approach to Savvy Investing." *Business Week,* February 27, 1989, p. 20.

Risk Management

The Health-Care Dilemma

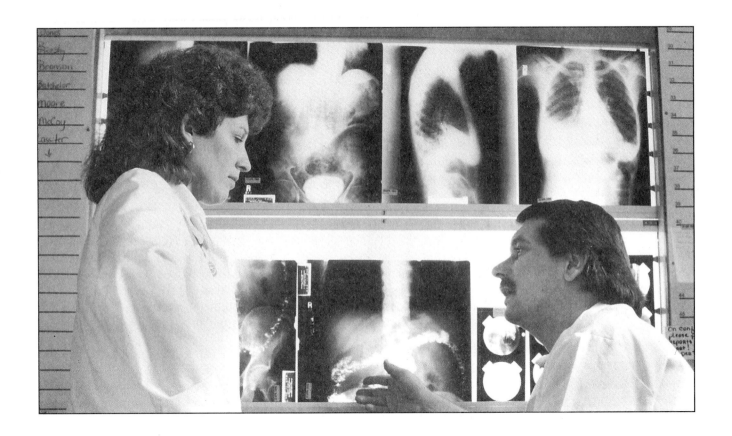

PREVIEW

▶ How does insurance allow consumers to control financial risks?

▶ Why are medical costs so high?

▶ What role does the government play in seeing that health care is provided for Americans?

▶ What types of health insurance are available to consumers?

▶ What steps have been taken to control health-insurance costs?

▶ What benefits and costs might result from a national program of health insurance paid for by the government?

We are all exposed to unknown risks each time we get out of bed. Some risks are small, and even if we do suffer a loss, like breaking a breakfast plate, it makes little difference to our style of life. We should, however, take steps to avoid losses that are greater than we can afford to suffer. To do this most American consumers purchase insurance policies of various types.

THE FOUNDATION OF INSURANCE—RISK POOLING

All types of insurance are based on the principle of shared risk, or *risk pooling*. No matter how careful we are, it is impossible to eliminate every chance we have of suffering a loss to our property or our health, or of causing injuries to others. If risk is spread among many people, however, by having each individual pay money to an insurance company that will compensate those who suffer losses, no individual need suffer a loss that is beyond his or her ability to bear. In effect, each insured party is trading the cost of the insurance for an assurance that he or she will be paid for any covered losses.

To be able to provide this service, insurance companies must be able to predict the probability and value of losses that may be suffered by insured parties. This is accomplished by studying past events and projecting them into the future. Two terms that describe these concepts are *insurable interests* and *insurable risks*.

Insurable interest
Something of value that is to be insured.

Insurable risk
An insurer's understanding of the risk of insuring a particular object or condition.

An **insurable interest** is the property or condition that is insured against loss. There must be some way to determine the value of this interest. An **insurable risk** is the insurance company's understanding of the probability that the insurable interest will suffer a loss, and the estimated value of any loss that may take place. Given enough time to collect and evaluate data concerning past losses, insurance companies can predict with great accuracy the probability of future losses being suffered by different groups of people. They use this information to set premiums that will allow them to pay claims by insured parties and earn a fair return on their investments. Insurance companies are not really in the business of gambling. They are able to calculate the amount of risk they take when they issue insurance policies. This allows them to set prices that almost always yield a profit. The only real danger they take is that of an enormous natural disaster that would cause many of their customers to suffer large losses, or of issuing so few policies that the law of probability will not protect them from the chance of a too-large proportion of their customers suffering losses.

OUR NEED FOR MEDICAL INSURANCE

It probably comes as little surprise to you to learn that American spending on medical care has been growing in money values and as a share of the value of our total production. Medical expenditures increased dramatically in the last 60 years—from $4 billion in 1929 (roughly 4 percent of the value of production in that year) to well over $750 billion in 1993 (about 12 percent of the value of production). As Exhibit 19–1 shows, by the year 2000 medical costs are expected to account for nearly 15 percent of national expenditures. Medical costs have consistently outpaced the rate of inflation in the past decade. In other words, the relative price of health care is higher than it once was. Still, the growth in demand for medical care has resulted in an increase in the

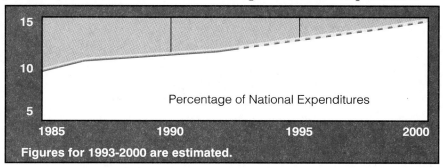

Figures for 1993-2000 are estimated.

amount of care that is delivered to the American people regardless of higher prices.

Although few people expect medical care to be free, many wonder why the cost for health-care services has gone up so much faster than all other costs. There are several reasons for this, and the first has to do with increases in demand brought about by government programs.

THE GOVERNMENT STEPS IN

Before the introduction of *Medicare*—government-subsidized medical care for the aged—congressional estimates of what that program would cost were only a fraction of what the actual cost turned out to be. In the mid-1960s when Medicare was instituted, the actual cost of health-care services to the elderly and others covered under Medicare was drastically lowered, because the government paid the greatest portion of their medical bills. The quantity demanded of health-care services therefore rose so much that the available supply of medical-care services was taxed beyond capacity. The only thing that could give was the price, and it gave. Since then, the Medicare budget has continued to grow to meet ever-increasing prices for medical care. Currently, the Medicare budget is growing at a rate of 14 percent per year. From 1980 to 1990, Medicare spending more than doubled, and it is now growing at twice the rate of medical costs, more than twice the rate of general inflation, and six times faster than the number of beneficiaries in the Medicare program.

The aging of our population indicates that Medicare costs will rise at an even more alarming rate in the near future. According to predictions made by the Office of Management and Budget (see Exhibit 19–2), shortly after the year 2000 we will be paying more for Medicare than for either Social Security or the national defense.

THE INSURANCE FRAMEWORK

Another reason for the increased demand for (and consequent higher price of) medical services has to do with the insurance framework. More than 180 million Americans are covered by some kind of private health insurance— either through a group insurance plan at their place of employment or through individual health policies. Herein lies the problem. Insurance rarely covers as many of the costs incurred for **outpatient services** as it does for **inpatient**

Outpatient services
The services of doctors and/or hospitals that do not require the individual to remain as a registered patient in the hospital.

Inpatient services
Services rendered to an individual by doctors and/or a hospital while the patient remains in the hospital for at least one night.

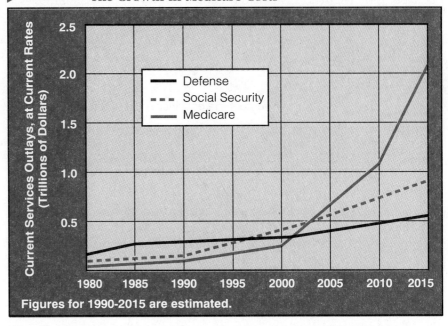

Source: Office of Management and Budget (Washington, DC: U.S. Government Printing Office, 1990).

services.[1] Individuals covered by insurance, therefore, have an incentive to go to the hospital to be taken care of by their private doctors.

Hospitals also have an incentive to use exotic tests when the fees for those tests help pay for the hospitals' investments in the sophisticated technology used to perform them. Until recently insurance plans generally exercised little control over the number of tests and examinations that were performed on patients. In the late 1980s, however, many insurers instituted cost-management systems that have somewhat reduced the number of tests administered.

The lure of private insurance dollars and government assistance with capital costs for Medicare providers probably has encouraged the tendency to build too many hospitals. The result has been that for several years hospitals have been operating at only 60–65 percent capacity. To recoup their overhead costs, these hospitals have had to charge higher prices than they would if they were fully utilized. In addition, to attract doctors—and thus patients—to their services, hospitals feel it necessary to acquire the latest scanners, lasers, magnetic-resonance-imaging equipment, and other high-tech items, even though the same equipment may be available in a hospital only a few blocks distant. Such investments are very costly, and they ultimately result in higher charges to patients who use hospital services. Every year, the daily cost of hospitalization rises significantly. By 1992 the cost of spending one day in the hospital averaged $900.

The problem is that patients covered by health insurance do not pay the *direct* costs of the medical care that they receive. Because of this, they demand more medical services than they otherwise would. This increase in quantity demanded causes medical expenses to rise, if all other things are held constant.

---

1. A few insurance companies are now reversing this situation by requiring outpatient treatment for certain procedures.

Consider an example. When Anna Brown, a courtroom interpreter in Los Angeles, was charged $400 for blood tests while hospitalized for surgery, her husband, Jack, was not at all concerned with the bill until he learned that the insurance company would not pay it because the tests were deemed by the insurer to be unnecessary. At that point, Jack became concerned. So concerned, in fact, that he demanded that the doctor either justify the charges or drop them from the bill. The result? The charges were dropped.

Many consumers have had similar, if less dramatic, experiences. Often, if your doctor learns that your insurance won't cover certain expenses, he or she won't bill you for them. This courtesy to you and your pocketbook is rarely extended to insurance companies, however; on the contrary, insurers must almost universally pay at least the going rate for tests and procedures covered under their policies and—depending on the ethics of the physicians involved—sometimes far more than that.

> The dramatic increase in medical costs in recent years has not been caused primarily by increases in physicians' incomes.

THE SUPPLY OF MEDICAL CARE

Medical care includes but is not limited to the services of physicians, nurses, and hospital staff; hospital facilities; maintenance of the facilities; and medications and drugs. What determines the supply of the most important item—physicians' services—in the total medical care package?

Restricted Entry

Generally, only a small percentage of those who take the Medical College Admissions Test (MCAT) are accepted into medical schools. At the more prestigious schools, such as Harvard Medical School, the percentage of applicants accepted may be as low as 5 percent. Some students apply to as many as ten different medical schools and, when turned down, reapply two or three times. Moreover, probably two or three times as many students do not bother to apply because they know that the odds are against them. Why is there such a large discrepancy between those who want to go to medical school and those who are accepted? If you compare the number of students who wish to attend law school with the number of students who actually go, the discrepancy is much smaller than that for medical school. Obviously, the number of medical schools in the United States is severely restricted, as is the number of entrants into those schools.

Because of the difficulties of getting into the medical profession, doctors have been in short supply relative to the increasing demand for medical care, particularly between 1965 and 1985. As a result, doctors rarely have lacked work or the ability to dictate the terms of their practices and their fee schedules. Their incomes have risen accordingly, as can be seen in Exhibit 19–3; by 1991, the median income for physicians was $145,000.

If a quick glance at Exhibit 19–3 caused you to think that the growth in physicians' incomes has been most dramatic in recent years, you would be wrong. Between 1950 and 1970 there was relatively little inflation in this country. When the growth in physicians' incomes of 172 percent in those years is compared with the total inflation rate of 68 percent, we can see that their real income increased significantly. Between 1970 and 1990, however, physicians' incomes increased by 241 percent while inflation rose 236 percent. Their income in these years increased at about the same rate as inflation, so the dramatic increase in medical costs in recent years has not been caused primarily by increases in physicians' incomes.

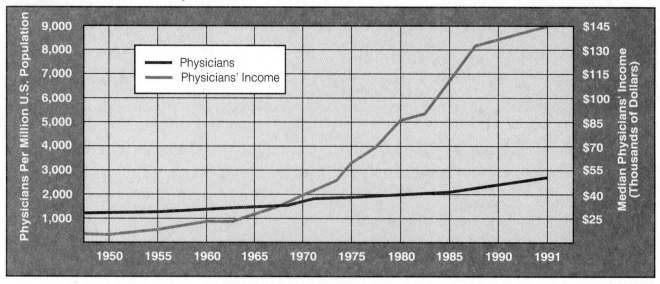

A Surplus Supply?

Ironically, after decades of experiencing a shortage of doctors, our nation soon may find that the reverse is the case. If current estimates are correct, by the year 2000 there will be a "surplus" of doctors.

What has caused this turnaround in the supply of doctors? For one thing, the shortage of doctors in the past two decades and the relative high incomes in that profession drew the maximum number to the medical field. Notwithstanding the limited number of medical schools and the high costs of attending existing medical schools, there has been a gradual increase in the number of graduates in the past several years. In addition, foreign-trained doctors have immigrated to the United States to obtain high-paying jobs. As is indicated by Exhibit 19–4, the supply of physicians relative to the population has increased significantly in the past two decades.

Although the increasing supply of physicians may eventually lower the amount of spending that pays their fees, this may change in the future. A matter of greater concern to many people is the projection that the Medicare program will run out of money sometime soon after the year 2000. This prediction is based on the increasing number of people who will need Medicare and on the increasing cost per patient. This is a conservative estimate, too, because it is based on the assumption that the cost of doctors' fees will grow no more rapidly than other living costs.

If current projections are correct, the number of people who will qualify to receive Medicare benefits will grow by roughly 17 million between 1990 and 2005. At the same time, the number of people who are of working age and will help pay for these benefits will grow by about 30 million. This means that instead of having 7.5 people to help support each person on Medicare, which was the case in 1990, there will be only about 5 people to support one in 2005. People who have studied the financial condition of the Medicare system believe that it will run out of money in that year (see Exhibit 19–5). Either people will be required to pay a larger share of their income to support the system, or the level of benefits will need to be reduced.

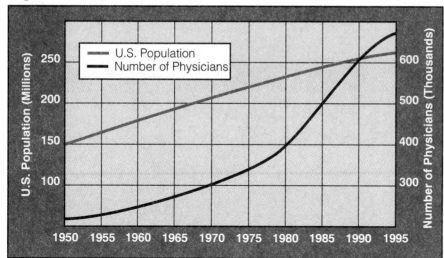

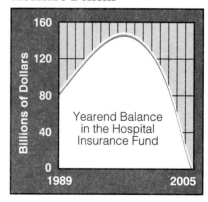

Source: *Business Week*.

DRUG REGULATION AND ITS COSTS

Consumers spend billions of dollars each year for drugs, about half of which are sold by prescription only. Since the Kefauver-Harris Amendment to the 1938 Food, Drug and Cosmetic Act was passed in 1962, the Food and Drug Administration (FDA) has required drug companies to follow quite detailed, extremely lengthy procedures before the FDA will approve a new drug for the market. To test and evaluate a new drug currently takes between 10 and 12 years.

The benefits of this legislation are obvious—Americans can be fairly sure that the drugs they purchase are safe and effective. On the cost side is the suffering of those who are deprived of the benefits of new drugs during the lengthy testing process (except for some drugs for terminally ill patients, for which the FDA requires less testing). Some drugs never reach the market because of FDA uncertainty about their effectiveness and side effects. If aspirin had to meet present requirements for FDA certification, it would probably fail to pass muster because it is not known why it works, and it can have potentially dangerous side effects when taken by children or in large quantities.

The costs that pharmaceutical companies pay for lengthy testing procedures for new drugs are factored into the price that consumers pay for prescriptions for brand-name drugs. The increasing availability of generic drugs, however, is helping to reduce this part of our medical bill. Once the 17-year patent on a brand-name drug expires, the drug can be approved by the FDA for marketing under its generic name, and this is frequently done. Fewer regulatory costs are associated with generic drugs because they require less time for FDA approval—since brand-name equivalents have already been tested. We discuss the cost-saving aspects of generic drugs in Consumer Issue R.

When consumers have prescriptions filled they should ask their pharmacist whether generic versions of the drug they need are available. Even when insurance pays the direct cost of a prescription the higher price of brand-name drugs adds to the cost of the insurance company and contributes to higher premiums that are paid by consumers or their employers.

HIGH-TECH MEDICINE

The application of technology to the field of medicine has resulted in an astonishing array of sophisticated medical equipment and testing procedures. Life-saving artificial organs, organ transplants, wonder biotech drugs, new cancer treatments, in vitro fertilization techniques—these are but a few of the options available today in the medical marketplace. With the aid of technology, diagnostic tests are now available for almost every disorder. It is now possible, for example to run 900 different types of tests on blood alone.

But as those who benefit—or wish to benefit—by these services are learning, high-tech medical care is very costly. The $50 X-ray has now been joined by the $400 CAT (computed tomography) scan and the $1,000 magnetic-imaging-resonance test. Costs for a kidney transplant range from $30,000 to $40,000, and for a liver transplant you can pay anywhere from $135,00 to $500,000. If you have to wait in a hospital intensive-care unit until a donor organ becomes available, your costs could mount to twenty times that of the procedure itself. Increasingly, the lives of premature infants are being saved, but, again, at a cost that may range from $200,000 to $1 million, depending on the medical attention required.

Ironically, researchers and health-care officials initially felt that technological innovations would reduce medical costs as a result of more efficient diagnostic and treatment procedures. It is now becoming clear, however, that these developments have contributed enormously to the high cost of health care in this country. According to some experts, more than 50 percent of the annual inflation in medical costs is due to high-tech medical care.

THE MALPRACTICE SYSTEM

Another contributing factor to the high cost of health care is the need for doctors and hospitals to defend themselves against potential malpractice lawsuits. The increase in malpractice claims has jumped, and so have the size of the awards that juries assign to claimants—today frequently in excess of $1 million. This has meant that doctors and all health-care providers have had to pay higher premiums for malpractice insurance to insure against the possibility of a malpractice claim. Doctors practicing high-risk specialties, such as obstetrics or neurology, face the highest premiums. For example, an obstetrician practicing in Dade County, Florida, currently must pay up to $200,000 for malpractice insurance coverage. This translates into an average insurance cost of $2,000 for every baby delivered! Many obstetricians who cannot recoup these expenses through their fees have simply given up their specialty and concentrated on gynecology—a less risky area—instead.

The fear of malpractice suits has had a strong impact on physicians generally toward their practices and their patients. Increasingly, physicians have been engaging in "defensive medicine"—excessive testing and evaluation procedures and consultations with other physicians—in order to verify their diagnoses and recommendations. All such procedures and consultations entail more costs for insurance providers as well as for the physicians, who must spend more time in record keeping in case their recommended actions need to be justified in a court of law. According to some analysts, defensive medicine is the most expensive aspect of the medical malpractice system, accounting for nearly $50 billion a year in health-care costs.

> The fear of malpractice suits has had a strong impact on physicians generally toward their practices and their patients.

WHO CAN AFFORD THE MEDICAL BILL?

Those who foot the medical bill are the government, insurance companies, employers, and private individuals, and all participants are gradually realizing that they can no longer afford to do so. If present cost trends continue, the government (and taxpayers) cannot continue to pay for Medicare without making totally unsatisfactory tradeoffs—such as national defense or Social Security spending. Insurance companies, which pay the direct costs of medical care for another substantial percentage of Americans, cannot absorb increasing costs without seeing their profit margins shrink. Therefore, insurers pass on these costs to employers and individuals in the form of higher premiums. In the last few years, health insurance premiums have risen dramatically—on average by about 25 percent per year, but in some cases up to 60 percent.

For employers who offer group health insurance coverage to their employees, the cost per employee of this coverage is mounting daily; it now averages almost $4,000 per year. Some corporations pay even more, depending on their benefits package. Chrysler Corporation, well known for its cost-cutting talents, nonetheless paid over $5,000 per employee in 1989. For large firms, health insurance has become the highest cost outlay next to wages.

Because of increased insurance costs, many employers have had to reduce insurance coverage or require employees to share some (or more) of the costs through larger contributions to the plan or higher **deductibles,** or both. Many small businesses have been forced to drop group insurance for their employees entirely, simply as a survival measure. The result of these developments is that employees are now paying higher prices for fewer insurance benefits, and some workers cannot afford health insurance coverage at all.

HEALTH-CARE DILEMMA—OR CRISIS?

Recent surveys conducted in Canada, England, and the United States indicated that the American health-care system is the most expensive, least liked, least fair, and in some ways the least efficient medical system of the three countries. The extent of consumer dissatisfaction came as a surprise to many: Not just a majority, but a full 89 percent of those Americans surveyed believed that a fundamental change in our health-care system was necessary.

Although we pay more for medical care than any other nation on earth, it would appear that Americans do not feel they are getting their money's worth. Despite our technological capabilities, we live, on average, no longer than individuals in other Western countries. Our infant mortality rate remains higher than that of other developed countries—and even that of many Third World countries. Our Medicare program does not cover the single greatest expense of our elderly population: long-term nursing care. Millions of our poor are not receiving adequate health care, and an increasing number of not-so-poor Americans cannot afford the costly high-tech procedures now available. What seems to be occurring more and more frequently is that medical care is allocated to those who can afford it; those who can't, do without. Media exposure of horror stories, such as patients being "dumped" from for-profit emergency rooms because they can't afford to pay for medical services, underscores the plight of the poor under our current system of health care. The disturbing ethical implications of these consequences of high medical costs have led many to conclude that what was perceived as a health-care dilemma in the 1980s has become, in the 1990s, a health-care crisis.

Physicians, employers, insurance providers, and government officials are all seeking solutions to the high cost of health care and its troubling results. The following sections examine both the measures that are currently being undertaken to bring medical costs under control and those that have been proposed for possible future implementation.

TACKLING WASTE AND INEFFICIENCY

In 1989 we spent $155 billion for tests and treatments that had little or no impact on the patients involved. In other words, nearly one-fourth of what we spent for health care in that year was unnecessary. Of the 250,000 expensive coronary bypass surgeries performed each year, 14 percent have been deemed inappropriate. Although more than 200,000 disk surgeries for back pain are performed annually, between 30 and 40 percent of them are inappropriate. According to Edward Pinckney, former editor of the *Journal of the American Medical Association,* well over half of the 40 million medical tests performed each day do not really contribute to a patient's diagnosis or therapy. Fear of malpractice suits, the insurance framework—including both Medicare and private insurance—and the fact that more tests and procedures are available now than in the past have all contributed to the overdose of medical tests and procedures that Americans must pay for.

Discussed next are some of the methods that have been, and are being, used to curb unnecessary and wasteful medical costs. We begin by looking at a type of insurance organization that was developed years ago to provide lower-cost medical services without sacrificing quality medical care—the health maintenance organization.

Health Maintenance Organizations

Health maintenance organizations (HMOs) have for decades offered an attractive alternative to individuals and employers facing high health insurance premiums. One of the oldest and largest of the HMOs, Kaiser Permanente, began in 1933. It was followed by other, similar programs around the country. Today more than 30 million Americans are members of HMOs.

Unlike the fee-for-service standard that has been traditional in private medical practices, HMOs operate on a prepaid plan. Members of an HMO pay a certain, preestablished premium for all medical-care services, which are provided by physicians and hospitals participating in the HMO. Doctors are usually paid a certain fee per patient that is not variable and not related to the patient's income. In other words, it is not possible to price-discriminate in HMOs as it is in fee-for-service practices.

HMO Legislation   In 1973 employees were given the opportunity to switch from standard group-health plans to HMOs by a provision in the Health Maintenance Organization Act of that year. This law required all companies that had 25 or more workers and some kind of group health plan to offer its workers the alternative of participating in an HMO—provided a qualified HMO was in the area and if the employer was first contacted by the HMO organizer. The legislation also required HMOs to accept individual members as well as groups of employees.

Recent amendments to the 1973 law, however, abolished the requirement that employers must offer HMO services if available. As of 1995, that choice will be left up to the employer. Another change created by the amendments is that employers are now free to negotiate rates based on their claims histories rather than paying the same premiums as everyone else. These changes are causing employers to look at HMOs with renewed interest as business firms try to cope with rising insurance premiums.

The Pros and Cons of HMOs   From a patient's point of view, the major criticism of HMOs is that their members cannot choose just any doctor but only one from the list of qualified HMO physicians.[2] There is also concern that, given the profit incentive, doctors operating for a flat fee will not deliver high-quality medical services but skimp on time spent with, and tests run for, each patient. Advocates of HMOs say that, because the worry of paying for each visit to the doctor is removed, people tend to seek treatment earlier, reducing the chances of a serious health crisis. Whatever the reason, studies

Health maintenance organization (HMO)
A type of insurance plan in which members pay a flat fee in return for all medical services, provided they are administered by participating doctors and hospitals.

---

2. Under the new amendments to the HMO Act, HMOs will be allowed, but not required, to permit their members to use non-HMO physicians in some circumstances and be entitled to reimbursement of the cost.

have indicated that HMO members are sent to hospitals 40 percent less often than nonmembers.

Another concern consumers should have in relation to HMOs is their financial stability. The premiums HMOs are allowed to charge in many areas are set by agencies of state governments. In a number of cases medical costs have grown more rapidly than the revenue HMOs have received from the people and organizations they insure. Blue Shield of Western New York, for example, had a negative net worth in the spring of 1992. Although some weak insurers were merged with larger organizations in the early 1990s, and others took steps to strengthen their financial condition by cutting costs, consumers need to be aware of the strength of their insurance provider. If an insurer appears to be having financial difficulties consumers may need to look for other insurance.

Preferred Provider Organizations

Preferred provider organization (PPO)

A type of insurance plan similar to an HMO but more flexible. In a PPO members are allowed to choose the services of non-PPO medical providers in return for a higher copayment or deductible.

Another cost-cutting insurance plan, which is somewhat similar to an HMO, is the **preferred provider organization (PPO).** Here an employer contracts for low-cost insurance coverage in return for having the employees use the services of specific physicians and hospitals that agree to a specific, set schedule of fees. PPOs offer insured employees more flexibility than HMOs in terms of choice because, for a higher deductible and copayment, the employee can see a non-PPO physician. The ability of employers to negotiate insurance bargains through PPOs—which has not been possible with HMOs—has been one of the major reasons for the rapid growth in PPOs in the last few years.

Because of the cost savings available through HMOs and PPOs, more than three-fourths of employees are now covered by these or similar insurance plans. By contrast, in 1984, 85 percent of employees were covered by traditional group policies, under which employees could see any doctor they wished or receive the services of any hospital they chose. As Joseph Califano, Jr., former secretary of the U.S. Department of Health, Education, and Welfare, observed, the era of free choice in medical care is largely over. Such choice has simply become too expensive.

Cost-Management Systems

For some time, a number of insurance companies have required individuals to obtain their preauthorization before hospitalization. If your doctor recommended that you undergo coronary angiography, for example, you (or perhaps the doctor) would first have to call the insurer for approval. Coronary angiography, a diagnostic test used to visualize arteries to the heart, is a very expensive procedure, and the insurance company might request that you get a second opinion to see if it is really indicated.

In the past, preauthorization for physician-recommended procedures was frequently given as a matter of course. As insurance companies fight increasing losses, however, they are devoting more resources to preauthorization and precertification procedures as a way to curb the costs of unnecessary surgeries and expensive diagnostic tests. Increasingly, insurers are consulting computer databases to evaluate whether a patient's symptoms warrant the recommended treatment. Medical Review System, for example, a software program developed by Value Health Sciences of Santa Monica, California, contains detailed indications for 36 of the most common medical procedures. The way this system works is as follows: Before hospitalization, you call your insurance carrier and describe your symptoms and the recommended treatment. A nurse receiving your call asks you a number of questions, which are determined by the computer program, and feeds your answers into the computer. Your answers are then analyzed by the computer to see if the procedure is medically justified. If not, a doctor under contract to the insurance company will check with your physician to make sure that your circumstances warrant the procedure.

Such computer-screening programs have not been greeted with enthusiasm by doctors, who resent being second-guessed by computers. But few doubt that managed health care using precertification on the basis of computer software will spread rapidly. Recognizing the likely inevitability—and the potential benefits—of such programs, some physicians' organizations are beginning to work up their own precertification databases. Even the AMA is now interested, and it is working closely with Blue Cross/Blue Shield and the Health Insurance Association of America to devise comprehensive guidelines for precertification.

Obviously, computer technology is affecting the medical world just as it is all other aspects of life. The role of computers in medical diagnoses and treatment will likely expand in the future. At least one medical visionary, Dr. Paul Ellwood, who pioneered the HMO concept, foresees a national computer network linking all doctors' offices in the country. The computer system would analyze patient data and treatment outcomes fed into it by doctors and provide constant feedback on the results. Such a system would reduce the number of misdiagnosed illnesses and inappropriate treatment procedures—and therefore costs.

Controlling Medicare Costs

For the past decade, the government has been concerned with reducing the high cost of the Medicare program. A major step in this direction was taken in 1983 by the institution of a far-reaching change in the way Medicare costs were reimbursed. Instead of reimbursing hospitals for actual costs, the government established a set fee according to 467 *diagnostic related groups,* or DRGs. By testing and using other diagnostic procedures, physicians determine which DRG applies to a particular patient before hospital admission. The government pays the hospital the specific fee relating to the DRG, regardless of how long the patient is in the hospital or how expensive the care may be.

This "prospective-payment" plan was designed to curb Medicare costs by reducing the length of hospital stays and the number of unnecessary procedures and services. In this, it has succeeded. In the two years following the institution of the prospective-payment system, the average hospital stay for Medicare patients decreased from ten to eight days. Overall, it is estimated that, since its introduction in 1983, the prospective-payment plan has saved the government almost $30 billion in Medicare costs.

The government has found it difficult, however, to deal with the twin needs of cutting medical costs for the Medicare program while also providing necessary care for the increasing number of older Americans. In 1988 an attempt was made to provide "catastrophic-care" coverage for long-term, serious ("catastrophic") illnesses in Medicare patients. This plan was generally opposed because it would have been supported largely by increasing Medicare supplement payments by people enrolled in the system. It also failed to cover the costs of nursing-home care—essential for many older people who suffer catastrophic illness. The law was repealed in 1989, roughly three months after it was put into effect.

THE ETHICAL CONSUMER

Medicare Fraud

Although estimates of Medicare fraud vary widely, figures in the range of $10 billion to $20 billion per year are often mentioned. Despite government attempts to install safety checks in the system, unscrupulous health-care providers are able to charge Medicare for services that were either unnecessary or never performed.

One company, for example, sent a van to old-age homes and told residents they would be given a "free" hearing test if they simply signed a form. The firm billed Medicare $250,000 a year for these tests, which in most cases were totally unnecessary. In another case an anesthesiologist submitted bills for more than 24 hours of service in a single day. In Florida an elderly couple were given "scratch tests" (so named because the skin is broken, or scratched, to admit an allergan) for allergies when they went for a physical. A month later they received notification that Medicare had been billed $900 each for "60 office services." The doctor had apparently charged Medicare separately for each "scratch" that was made, and Medicare was willing to pay. The doctor involved in this incident makes a practice of waiving any bills that patients would normally be required to pay as their part of the cost of treatment. He therefore had many patients who were not likely to complain about him. When the couple involved in this event did complain to Medicare, the amount the doctor received was reduced to $15 for each "scratch."

If you, or a relative or yours, received treatment from a doctor you suspected of submitting inflated bills to Medicare, what would you do? If you complained, you might stop this person from stealing from the system, but his or her patients almost certainly would have to pay more of the costs of any treatment. What do you believe is the ethical thing to do?

Cases of suspected Medicare fraud may be reported by calling a toll-free number at the Office of the Inspector General of the Department of Health and Human Services: (800) 368-5779.

MANDATORY HEALTH INSURANCE COVERAGE

One way to tackle the problem of the growing number of uninsured individuals and the consequent hospital losses due to unpaid hospital bills is by forcing employers to insure their employees. At least 12 states are considering laws to mandate employer-provided insurance coverage, and two states, Hawaii and Massachusetts, already have passed such legislation.

At the federal level, the idea of mandated health benefits was first proposed in 1971, during the Nixon administration, but it was shelved at that time because it was considered to be an inadequate measure by some members of Congress. The idea resurfaced in 1988 but failed to be passed into law. It remained as a part of the Bush administration's suggested health-care plan throughout the presidential campaign of 1992. If this plan had been accepted, it would have required employers either to provide medical insurance for their employees or to contribute to a government program that would help uninsured workers obtain private health coverage.

Mandated insurance benefits (like those supported by former President Bush) have been criticized by some economists as merely payroll taxes in disguise. Employers, they maintain, will end up shifting much of the extra cost back to employees in the form of lower wages—if not unemployment. In short, these critics suggest that mandatory insurance laws could end up hurting the very people they were intended to help.

Other critics of the proposed federal legislation point out that at most it is a stopgap measure. It will not result in health insurance coverage for part-time workers, the unemployed, the poor who live in states that offer little medical assistance to the poor, and the aged—many of whom become impoverished by long-term care expenses.

An alternative plan advocated by President Clinton called for the government to provide basic medical insurance for all Americans. At the beginning of his administration in 1993, it was not clear that Congress would support the plan, spearheaded by his wife, Hillary Rodham Clinton.

SHOULD WE ADOPT A NATIONAL HEALTH PLAN?

How would you like to get all the medical care you need, including preventive checkups and tests, and never see a medical bill or an insurance form? How would you feel if you knew that every other American could do likewise? If the United States were to adopt a national health program similar to that of Canada, that would be the result. Private health insurance and corporate insurance plans would be abolished, and our current mix of public and private health-care systems would be replaced by one comprehensive national program.

The idea of such a program is obviously appealing to many Americans. In a recent survey, 61 percent of those polled indicated that they would prefer Canada's system to our own. And, significantly, a small but growing number of physicians are supporting the idea of a national health program. In early 1989 Physicians for a National Health Program, a group of approximately 1,200 doctors from around the country, proposed that the United States adopt a national program modeled after that of Canada. The proposal, which was published in the *New England Journal of Medicine,* suggested that the implementation of a national health-care program was the only feasible solution for achieving what everybody seems to want: cost containment, preservation of quality, and universal access to medical care. For no more than we are currently paying for health care, we could have a comprehensive program under which all Americans—rich or poor, young or old—would have access to medical care.

Although the American Medical Association (AMA) has not endorsed the proposal, a few other physicians' groups have. Shortly after the first group published its proposal, another article was featured in the same journal. It was entitled, "Universal Health Care: Its Time Has Come." The article emphasized that mandatory insurance laws and cost-cutting modifications to our present system are not enough; too many Americans lack access to adequate health care. John Roberts, a Minneapolis physician, sees a national program as the only means of ensuring more equitable health care. Disease doesn't discriminate on the basis of wealth, and neither should its treatment. In his words, "As a physician, I see daily that disease strikes the rich and the poor, the young and the old, the good and the bad. Shouldn't our treatments be as fair as our illnesses?"

Criticisms of a National Health Plan

Many question whether further government involvement in our health-care system can solve our current problems. Critics of national health care argue that government intervention in the medical arena is one of the primary rea-

Is health care just another
consumer product, or is it a
constitutional right of Americans?

sons for our present difficulties. Government administration of the Medicare program has led to bureaucratic, costly, inefficient, and largely uncaring delivery of health-care services. To look to the government for a solution to a problem it created will only begin the cycle anew and perpetuate—if not worsen—the situation. They suggest that if consumers pay no direct cost for medical care the demand at this "zero" price will far exceed the supply, making it difficult for those who really need medical care to obtain it.

The AMA opposes the adoption of a national health plan for similar reasons. A major concern for physicians is that government-mandated fees would remove the profit motive from the medical enterprise, thus destroying one of the major incentives that lead to quality in patient care and excellence in medical research. For years, American physicians have criticized the British nationalized health system as fostering mediocrity in health care. If the United States were to adopt a national health plan, they believe, similar mediocrity would result. Without freedom of choice on the part of both physicians and patients, the doctor-patient relationships would become impersonal and bureaucratic. Without the economic rewards available through the free-market system, the pace of technological innovation would slow, and fewer and fewer state-of-the-art procedures would be available.

Proponents of a national health plan respond to these arguments by stressing that, given the present circumstances, tradeoffs of some kind will have to be made to ensure that all members of our population receive needed health care. Many supporters argue that the problem with the British plan is lack of funding, not the program itself. Canada's health plan, which is much better funded, has met with greater success. Others who push for a national health program see no reason why quality care and research necessarily should go hand in hand with the profit motive. As an example, they cite the pioneering research on heart attacks that is currently being done in the Scandinavian countries, all of which have strong national health programs.

Health Care as a Consumer Product

At the heart of the debate over the role of the government in providing health-care services is a fundamental question concerning the nature of medical care: Is health care just another consumer product, or is it a constitutional right of Americans? Traditionally, opposition to government involvement in health care has been based, implicitly or explicitly, on the assumption that health care is a consumer product and, as such, should be subject to the laws of the marketplace just as other goods and services are. Government intervention in the medical marketplace leads to inefficiency because it interferes with the working of supply and demand. If the government would stay out of the medical-care market, supply and demand would regulate a price that the market could bear. Cost-conscious consumers would demand less medical care, thus lowering prices. Physicians and medical-service providers who performed badly would see their revenues decline, and those who performed well would reap rewards in the form of profits.

To be sure, not everyone would be able to afford the same degree of medical care under such a system, but more people would receive more, and higher quality, health care than they would under a government-regulated system. There would be no way around the problem that expensive medical treatments would be rationed to those who could afford them, just as there is no way around the problem that not everybody can own a Rolls Royce or a country mansion or that vacation home on the lake.

Those who view medical care as a consumer product are not the heartless, or uncompassionate human beings that they may seem to be. On the contrary, most of them would agree that, ideally, everyone *should* have access to adequate health care. Their position is simply that, from a realistic point of view, this ideal may not be attainable within the framework of our present economic system—which, for all its faults, has succeeded in creating a higher quality of life than any other yet devised. Rather than tossing out our present system, they feel that we should build on its strengths by further cost-cutting measures and by placing more emphasis on the role of charity.

Health Care as a Constitutional Right

At the other end of the debate spectrum are those who maintain that medical care is a right and not a privilege. The first sentence of the U.S. Constitution states that one of the aims of our government is "to promote the general welfare" of its citizens. Since health care is essential to our general welfare, shouldn't the government bear the ultimate responsibility for seeing to it that our health needs are met? A majority of Americans would seem to think so. According to a 1987 survey, nine out of ten Americans polled responded that they felt every American had a right to medical care "as good as a millionaire gets." Only recently, however, have a significant number of Americans wished for more direct involvement of government in health care as a means of securing that right. Although at no time has the average American received medical services comparable to those obtained by millionaires, until recently most Americans at least could be fairly assured of receiving medical treatment during emergencies—and possibly as good as that of a millionaire. If they couldn't pay the bill, the hospitals absorbed the costs and, normally, passed them on to insurance companies through higher billings. That is increasingly no longer the case in some of our cities.

That even a minority of our nation's physicians—who in the past opposed government intervention in the medical-care field—would promote a government-sponsored health program signals the change that is taking place in this country. Old arguments seem to be giving way in the face of new and urgent needs.

Whatever the outcome of the current debate over national health care may be, at the present time you, as a consumer, face the problem of dealing with high medical costs. How you can trim those costs and protect yourself against catastrophic medical bills is the subject of Consumer Issue R.

> Old arguments seem to be giving way in the face of new and urgent needs.

▶ SUMMARY

1. Insurance is based on the concept of shared risk. Insurers are able to provide protection from various types of loss by studying past data to determine the probability of a loss occurring to an insurable interest. This information is used to determine how much an insured party should pay for protection to cover the losses that are claimed and allow the insurance company to earn a profit.

2. In 1990 the cost of medical care in this country was an estimated $700 billion and accounted for approximately 12 percent of our national expenditures. Not only are medical costs rising dramatically, but also the relative price of health care has gone up consistently in recent years.

3. The institution of the Medicare program during the 1960s caused medical costs to rise because of the subsequent increased demand for medical services. The costs of Medicare continue to rise and are expected to be as

high as those for Social Security and national defense programs shortly after the year 2000.

4. The private insurance framework has increased the cost of medical care because medical expenses covered by insurance, particularly hospital expenses, are not paid directly by the individuals receiving the services. This creates a lack of incentive on the part of doctors and patients to control care costs.

5. One of the reasons medical costs have risen is attributed to the limited supply of doctors due to restricted entry into the profession. Although the supply of doctors is increasing, and we may have a surplus of doctors by the year 2000, doctors' charges for medical services still make up a major portion of our overall costs of health care.

6. Government regulation of the drug industry and drug-certification requirements have increased the price that consumers must pay for prescription drugs. The marketing of generic drugs, which require far less testing than new brand-name drugs, has helped to reduce prices for prescription drugs, however.

7. High-tech medical equipment and procedures have brought many (sometimes life-saving) benefits to consumers, but they have also contributed enormously to our health-care costs.

8. The increased number of medical malpractice lawsuits and higher jury awards have meant, in turn, higher malpractice insurance premiums for doctors, especially those in high-risk areas such as obstetrics or neurology. To guard against malpractice suits, doctors engage in the practice of defensive medicine—extensive testing, consulting, and record-keeping procedures—that adds nearly $50 billion a year to our national medical bill.

9. Rising insurance premiums are one of the consequences of rising medical costs. Individuals and employers have faced dramatic premium increases in recent years, and some smaller business firms have been forced to drop insurance coverage for their employees as a result. The growing number of uninsured individuals has become a source of national concern.

10. The growing crisis in health care is being addressed in three ways: by cost-cutting modifications to the present system, by the introduction of mandatory insurance laws requiring employers to provide insurance for their employees, and by proposals for a national, government-sponsored health plan.

11. To curb costs due to waste and inefficiency, employers are turning increasingly from traditional group insurance plans to lower-cost health maintenance organizations and preferred provider organizations. Today, 70 percent of employees are covered under such plans.

12. Some insurers are instituting cost-management programs that use computer databases to determine whether certain medical treatments are medically justifiable. Insurance carriers using cost-management programs require that individuals seeking medical treatment obtain precertification from the insurance company before treatment.

13. To control Medicare costs, the government instituted a prospective-payment plan in 1983. Under this plan, the government pays a pre-established fee, determined by the nature of the patient's illness, to hospitals for treatment given to Medicare patients.

14. Two states have passed mandatory employer insurance coverage for employees, and several other states are considering similar legislation. At the federal level, Congress is also considering a bill that would require employ-

ers to provide health insurance for all full-time workers or face tax penalties.
15. A growing number of Americans, including, significantly, some physicians, support the idea of a national health plan. Issues currently being debated include whether the government has a responsibility to ensure adequate health care for all its citizens and whether further government involvement in health care would improve or only worsen the situation.

▶ QUESTIONS FOR THOUGHT AND DISCUSSION

1. What is the difference between health-care services and other services performed in our economy?
2. Do you think Americans have a right to adequate health care?
3. Should the government pay for long-term nursing care, such as in nursing homes, for the elderly? Or is it the responsibility of individuals to prepare for such costs?
4. Do you believe our growing health-care problems can be solved without resorting to some form of government-sponsored national health-insurance program?

▶ THINGS TO DO

1. Conduct a survey of your friends, relatives, and acquaintances. Ask them how they cope with medical costs, what kind of insurance coverage they have (if any), and whether they are satisfied with the current health-care system. Tally your results.
2. Ask a physician you know about the advantages and disadvantages of a national health plan. Try to determine, on the basis of the answers given, whether the physician regards health care as a right or a privilege.
3. Discuss the arguments concerning medical costs with someone in the medical profession. Are the reasons given in this text and by the person you spoke to the same? If not, how do they differ?

▶ APPLICATION

An idea called the Medical Insurance IRA was suggested as a way to decrease the cost of medical care in the early 1990s. Under this plan employers would set aside an amount of money, say $2,000 for each worker, in accounts that each employee could draw on to pay medical expenses. If the money in each account was not used up in a year, the amount that was left over would be placed in an individual retirement account (IRA) for the employee. If the employee's medical costs were more than $2,000, they would be paid by a normal insurance policy that would be much less expensive to buy because the insurance company would not need to pay the first $2,000 of any employee's medical costs.

Think about this plan. Explain why many people believe it would reduce medical costs. What problems might such a plan cause? To what sort of people would it offer no benefit? Would you support such a plan?

▶ SELECTED READINGS

▶ *AARP Prescription Drug Handbook.* New York: Harper Collins, 1992.
▶ Barrett, S. *Health Schemes, Scams and Frauds.* New York: Consumer Reports Books, 1991.
▶ Buckley, William F. "The Medical Crisis." *National Review,* July 8, 1991, pp. 54–55.

► Califano, Joseph A., Jr. "Billions Blown on Health." *New York Times,* April 12, 1989, p. 19.

► Castro, J. "Condition Critical." *Time,* November 25, 1991, pp. 34–40.

► *The Complete Drug Reference.* New York: Consumer Reports Books, 1991.

► Enthoven, Alain C. "How Employers Boost Health Costs." *The Wall Street Journal,* January 24, 1992, p. B1.

► Fein, Rashi. *Medical Care, Medical Costs: The Search for a Health Insurance Policy.* Cambridge: Harvard University Press, 1986.

► Findlay, Stephen. "Looking over the Doctor's Shoulder." *U.S. News & World Report,* January 30, 1989, pp. 70–73.

► Henderson, H. "How Healthy Is Your Health Insurer?" *Kiplinger's Personal Finance Magazine,* July 1991, pp. 78–80.

► Ingersoll, Bruce. "Amid Lax Regulation, Medical Devices Flood a Vulnerable Market." *The Wall Street Journal.* March 24, 1992, p. A1.

► Loeb, Marshall. "Your Insurance." *Marshall Loeb's 1992 Money Guide.* Boston: Little, Brown, 1992, pp. 547–550.

► Main, J. "The Battle Over Benefits." *Fortune,* December 16, 1991, pp. 91–92.

► Pedolsky, D. M. "Affordable Preventive Care." *U.S. News & World Report,* December 1991–January 1992, p. 63+.

► Quinn, Jane Bryant. "A Buyer's Guide to Cheaper Rates." *Newsweek,* April 23, 1990, p. 50–54.

► Reibstein, L. "Physician, Cut Thy Costs." *Newsweek,* December 23, 1991, p. 41.

► Saddler, Jeanne. "States Test Bare-Bones Health Insurance." *The Wall Street Journal,* July 10, 1990, p. B1.

► Shapiro, J. P. "Real Health-Care Fixes." *U.S. News & World Report,* August–September 1991, pp. 35–36+.

► "Your Solutions to the Health Care Crisis." *Money,* July 1991, pp. 74–77.

► Winslow, Ron. "Managed-Care Networks Show Promise." *The Wall Street Journal,* March 24, 1992, p. B1.

Purchasing Medical Care

GLOSSARY

ANESTHESIOLOGIST A doctor who specializes in administering anesthesia to patients before surgery.

GENERAL PRACTITIONER A doctor who has a family practice rather than a specialized practice.

GENERIC DRUGS Non-name-brand medicines that are often sold at much lower prices than the same name-brand products.

HOSPICE An organization that helps the families of terminally ill patients.

INTERACTIONS Reactions between drugs that sometimes can be life threatening.

PREVENTIVE MEDICINE Medical procedures carried out with the intention of preventing people from becoming ill.

Have you ever gone to work or to school only to have someone say to you, "You look terrible! Why don't you go see a doctor?" Although you may hope to visit a doctor's office only for routine physical examinations, the probability is that sooner or later you will need the services of a doctor, or even a hospital, for illness or injury. In 1990 Americans made almost 1.4 billion visits to doctors' offices. These physicians were paid more than $125 billion for their services. Another $240 billion was spent on hospital care and almost $50 billion for medi-

cine and drugs. Other expenses brought the total spent on medical care to more than $600 billion. The cost of medical care is the most rapidly growing part of the typical American consumer's annual spending.

▶ CHOOSING A DOCTOR

Relatively few doctors are **general practitioners** (GPs) or *family practice physicians*. Of the more than 600,000 physicians in the United States in 1990, only 55,000, or about 9 percent, have this sort of practice. The others all specialize in something. Although GPs earn relatively less than most specialists, they are your first line of defense in protecting your health. Most of the medical care you will need in your life can be provided by one. If you do require the services of a specialist, your family-practice physician can refer you to one.

▶ Choose Your Doctor When You're Healthy

It is vital that you have a working relationship with your doctor that is based on mutual respect and trust. If you do not already have an established relationship with a doctor, the sooner you develop one, the better. To make accurate diagnoses of ailments, a doctor needs to be familiar with you and your medical history. You do not want to find yourself in the position of having to find a doctor quickly and just calling numbers at random from the phone book until you find one who is willing to see you, or of going to an emergency room when you have a medical problem that is not a true emergency and therefore waiting hours for treatment as others are tended to ahead of you. You should choose a doctor when you are

healthy and can take the time to investigate your alternatives.

▶ Pay Attention to Recommendations

One of the best ways to find a good doctor is to ask your friends and acquaintances for recommendations. There is, of course, no guarantee that you will relate well to a doctor just because someone else you know does. However, you may at least eliminate those who are unable to get along with any of their patients. If you have moved from another community where you had a doctor, you might ask him or her for a recommendation or referral. You might also call a local hospital. They sometimes recommend physicians who are popular with other patients. You could also call the local office of the American Medical Association. Do not expect the AMA to evaluate doctors; they will be very hesitant to say anything bad about any doctor. But, they may at least be able to identify doctors who are accepting new patients. Deciding among physicians that are identified is then up to you.

▶ Consider a Doctor's Age and Sex

When you look for a personal physician you should try to choose one you believe you will be able to have a relationship with over an extended period of time. There is a value in choosing someone who is experienced, but there is such a thing as going too far. If you are in your twenties, choosing a doctor in his or her fifties guarantees you the need to find another physician in the future.

Some people are not comfortable discussing personal health problems with a doctor of the opposite sex. If you think you might not be as forthright in discussing your health problems with a doctor of the opposite sex, you should respect your own feelings and select a physician of the same sex.

▶ Consider a Physician's Associations

In most communities some hospitals have better reputations than others. Some may also be more conveniently located to where you live. When selecting a doctor, you should inquire which hospitals he or she is affiliated with. Remember, a doctor who does not work out of hospitals with the best reputations in your community may not be a good doctor.

Consider whether the doctor has an individual practice or is part of a group. If you choose one who is in practice alone, ask who would provide treatment for you if your doctor is out of town when you become ill. When a doctor is part of a group, you should be sure you understand how the group works. Will you always see the same doctor, or will you see whoever happens to be working when you make an appointment? If there is a particular doctor in the group whom you would prefer to avoid, can you request that someone else treat you? If you want to be treated always by a male or female physician, can you request that? Patients need to be sure they understand what they are agreeing to when they choose a doctor who is part of a group.

▶ WHAT IS THE DOCTOR'S ATTITUDE TOWARD YOU?

Although doctors have special knowledge and skills, they are still just people. If your doctor talks down to you, or refuses to answer your questions, or seems uninterested in what you have to say, then you probably need to look for someone else. The attitude of the staff in a doctor's office is often a good gauge of the doctor's character. If they are rude and demanding, then you may be sure, if nothing else, that the doctor is willing to tolerate employees who are rude to patients. This implies a degree of insensitivity that should concern you.

Keep one fact in mind, however: The mere fact that a doctor, or anyone else who provides a service, is friendly and personable does not prove that he or she is competent. Always look beyond the doctor's personality to the quality of the treatment being provided.

▶ LOOK FOR AN INTEREST IN PREVENTIVE MEDICINE

Good doctors are just as interested in **preventive medicine** as in curing a disease you already have. If you are seeing a doctor for the first time, and he or she expresses concern with your weight, your smoking, your high cholesterol, or other similar conditions, it may be one sign that the doctor is truly concerned about your health. You should also expect a doctor to have basic diagnostic procedures carried out after your first visit to establish a "baseline" for your physical condition—data to measure future changes against.

▶ DO YOU REALLY NEED AN OPERATION?

One of the most feared statements any doctor can make is, "You need an operation." The immediate reaction of many consumers is to panic. What they need to do is calmly consider their alternatives, and remember that they are in charge of their own fates.

No reputable doctor will suggest surgery without having a good reason. You should ask for, and expect to receive, an explanation you can understand for why your doctor feels an operation is necessary. Don't be intimidated. It is your body and your life. You have a right to know. If your doctor refuses to provide you with an acceptable explanation, you should look for a new doctor.

Most general practitioners do not perform surgery other than some minor outpatient procedures. If you need an operation, you will probably be referred to a specialist. Again, you should request an explanation from that specialist of what procedures will be used and why they are necessary. There is no value in being rude, but there is value in asking questions that are to the point. If you want to know how much risk is involved you should say so. Asking a question like, "Is this really the best solution?" is not as likely to elicit helpful answers as asking, "What are the risks of this operation?" or "What is likely to happen if I choose not to have it done?"

Although many insurance companies will require a second opinion before they will pay for surgery, you should seek another doctor's opinion whether it is required or not. Estimates made by people who have studied medical care in the United States suggest that between 20 percent and 25 percent of all surgery performed in this country is not necessary. It is usually a good idea not to ask for this second opinion from another doctor who is closely associated with your original doctor. Doctors who work together are not likely to dispute each other's professional opinions. Second Opinion Surgery, which may be reached at 1-800-638-6833, is an organization that identifies physicians in different areas of the country who are qualified to give second opinions for given medical problems.

▶ A Surgeon Is Only Part of a Team

Many consumers mistakenly believe that surgery is sort of a one-person show. The fact is, surgeons operate with the assistance of other medical professionals who are part of a team. Patients should investigate all members of their surgical team. For example, it is very important to know the qualifications of your **anesthesiologist.** You should find out if a certified anesthesiologist will personally administer the anesthesia, or if this person will direct a nurse or a resident doctor to complete the procedure. If someone else will administer the anesthesia, you should find out what this person's qualifications are. In addition, someone on the team should ask you about any allergies you have, your medical problems, if you are taking medication, how you have reacted to anesthesia in the past, or if you have a history of abnormal bleeding. If no one asks for this type of information, you should find out why. The anesthesiologist and other members of the team need to know these facts to provide you with proper care and protect your life.

▶ WHAT MEDICATION IS RIGHT FOR YOU?

Most drugs prescribed by doctors represent no risk, or very little, to most patients. Broad-spectrum antibiotics, antihistamines, and other common drugs are routinely prescribed to help cure many common sicknesses. If you are not familiar with a drug that is prescribed to you, ask your doctor what it is and what it does. If you feel that you

need a more extensive explanation, there are many drug source books you may use in almost every public library. A common one is *The Physicians' and Pharmacists' Guide to Your Medicines,* published periodically by Ballantine Books. This book lists most common drugs by their scientific and trade names. It describes their purpose and possible side effects, and identifies other drugs that should not be taken at the same time.

▶ Beware of Drug Interactions

Many drugs can cause severe and even life-threatening **drug interactions** when taken together. This is less of a danger when all medications you are taking are prescribed by one doctor. It is much more likely to become a danger when you are seeing two or more doctors who do not communicate with each other about your treatment. If you have different drugs prescribed by more than one doctor, you should identify them to your doctors and ask if the drugs are likely to react adversely with each other. In recent years many pharmacies have purchased computers that will flag drugs prescribed to a customer that are likely to interact in a dangerous way. This is one reason to fill all of your prescriptions in the same location.

▶ Taking Too Much of a Good Thing

Consumers should realize that the fact that one tablet makes them feel better does not mean that two tablets will make them feel wonderful. Patients should never take it upon themselves to change the dosage prescribed by their doctors. It is also important to take medication for the full length of time prescribed. Suppose an antibiotic is prescribed for

seven days to fight an infection. If after three days, the symptoms abate, a person might be tempted to stop taking the medication. This would be a mistake. The infection might not be completely gone. It could redevelop and could even become resistant to the antibiotic, making it more difficult to cure in the future.

As a general rule, you should be careful of taking too many antidepressant drugs, painkillers, sleeping pills, or other drugs that affect the level of activity in your body. Never take more of these drugs than have been prescribed by your doctor, and question your doctor about the need for a drug that is prescribed over an extended period of time. Taking any medication that can alter the rate at which your body functions has the potential for harming, or even killing you.

▶ What About Generic Drugs?

It is often possible to purchase non-brand-name **generic drugs** that are much less expensive than their brand-name counterparts. You should ask your doctor or pharmacist if there is a generic alternative for any prescribed drug, even if your insurance pays for the drug. The extra cost of name-brand drugs may force an increase in insurance premiums for your prescription plan and reduce other forms of compensation your employer can afford to provide to you.

▶ A VISIT TO THE EMERGENCY ROOM

At this moment approximately 12,000 people are in the process of being admitted to emergency rooms (ERs) in the United States. Most of them are not seriously injured—only roughly 15 percent are. Whether or not your visit to an emergency room involves a life-threatening situation, there are a number of facts you should know about your rights and responsibilities in an emergency room.

When an Emergency Is an Emergency

Most people who visit emergency rooms are not truly in an emergency situation. Examples of situations that doctors identify as true emergencies include severe bleeding, choking, poisoning, severe chest pain, gunshots or other wounds that have penetrated internal organs, severe burns, and the like. If you visit an emergency room with a true emergency condition, you will probably receive emergency treatment. If your condition does not demand immediate treatment, you will not be served quickly in most cases. Other people will probably receive treatment before you, even if you arrived earlier.

When Your Need Is Urgent but Not Immediate

If you have a fever of 103 degrees, have sprained your ankle, have a cut that you have stopped from bleeding, or have been unable to keep food down for 12 hours and have cramps, you may need care soon, but there is time to consider alternatives. Your first step may be to call your doctor. Many group practices have "emergency" numbers. Others provide their home numbers for emergencies. Of the situations just described, the only one that would have warranted an immediate call is the last, which could indicate a serious internal problem.

If you do call your doctor, he or she will tell you whether or not you need emergency care, and if so, where you should go for it. If you do not succeed in reaching your doctor, you are left with the respon-

sibility of making the decision yourself. In such cases, consumers should realize that not all emergency rooms are equally equipped or able to provide treatment. If you visit an emergency room in a large urban hospital, it may or may not have the most up-to-date equipment and qualified doctors, but it certainly will have many people with true emergencies. You may wait a very long time to be treated.

Smaller or rural hospitals may have no emergency room at all and may have to send you on to a larger facility.

The best choice, if it is available, is likely to be a medium-sized hospital in a relatively affluent area. It is likely to have a well-equipped emergency room and qualified doctors present, or at least on call. An important step you can take now is to identify the best emergency room facility near your home. This is, of course, no use to you if you become ill when you are not near your home. If you need an emergency room when you are on a trip or visiting another city, try to seek recommendations from people who live in the area. Wherever you go, be sure to have the necessary insurance and other medical information with you if you possibly can. No one who has medical insurance should leave home without such information, because people never know when a medical emergency will happen. Not having such information can slow or even prevent necessary treatment.

When You Arrive at the Emergency Room

If the patient who is in pain has not come to the emergency room in an ambulance, it is often better for him or her to stay in the car until contact has been made with the emergency room's officials. When you enter the

emergency room, you will first talk to a trained receptionist or a nurse, whose job is to determine how serious the problem is and how quickly the patient needs treatment. At this point your answers should be brief and to the point. Don't try to tell the person what you think he or she needs to know. You will probably save time by just answering questions and saving any lengthy explanations for doctors later on.

If the problem is a major one, you may wish to have your own doctor or a specialist called in. Many teaching hospitals have interns and residents who are looking for patients with certain conditions that they are interested in learning more about. Although this is reasonable from their point of view, you might prefer an established doctor with more experience.

DEALING WITH A HOSPITAL

No one likes to be in a hospital, but if it is necessary, there are a number of steps you can take to make the best of it. First of all, though, make sure you really need to be hospitalized. Hospitals are intended for people who need medical care that cannot be provided in other settings. Unfortunately, today many people are in hospitals who really shouldn't be there. They may have been admitted because they demanded it, because their doctor found it easier (and possibly more lucrative) to treat them there, because the hospital had empty beds it wanted to fill, because the hospital and/or the doctor wanted to avoid the possibility of being sued for lack of appropriate treatment, or for any number of other reasons.

One of the best reasons for avoiding the hospital when you can is that hospitals are full of sick people. No matter how hard the staff tries to prevent the spread of disease or infections among patients, the potential is always there. A hospital is often a good place to get sick.

Furthermore, hospitals, particularly large ones, often run much like a factory. They are administered by bureaucracies that are separated from those people who provide and receive care. In such situations people may be treated more like numbers than as individual patients. Regrettably, mistakes do take place. Patients are sometimes given inappropriate treatments and harm is done.

▶ When Hospitals are Necessary

If you do have to enter a hospital, probably the most important thing to remember is to ask questions. Yes, the hospital staff is probably overworked and has a thousand other things to do. But that is exactly why you should ask questions. It may be an old saying, but the squeaky wheel does usually get the grease. If you are admitted to a hospital, you should politely ask about anything you don't understand, or that you feel is not being done properly. You might be able to prevent a mistake in your treatment this way.

Whenever you stay in a hospital you may be poked and prodded at regular intervals. This may seem to happen most often late at night. If you find this sort of event happening for no apparent reason, you should ask your doctor what tests are being done and what their purposes are. It is possible for unnecessary tests to inflate your hospital bill in addition to disturbing your sleep. Even if your insurance company pays the bill, you and other consumers pay indirectly through higher premiums.

To find information about a specific hospital or nursing home you may write to the following:

American Hospital Association
840 North Lake Shore Drive
Chicago, Illinois 60611

▶ When Hospitals May Be Avoided

Many medical procedures that were once done in a hospital are now administered on an outpatient basis. This saves money and time. If your doctor has scheduled you for relatively minor surgery, you should inquire whether it could be done on an outpatient basis. Remember, however, that many insurance policies will not cover or will limit their payments for outpatient services.

Another case where it may be better to refuse hospital treatment is when a patient is clearly dying. There are **hospice** organizations throughout the country that can give assistance to the families of people who are terminally ill. Many people who realize they will soon die prefer to spend their final days in the warmth of their homes and with the people they love, rather than in the often cold and sterile environment of a hospital. If you ever find yourself in such a situation, consider contacting your local hospice organization for help and guidance.

▶ CHOOSING A NURSING HOME

Although you may not need the services of a nursing home now, medical records indicate that every American has a better than 50-percent chance of spending at least some time in an intermediate-care facility, or nursing home, before he or she dies. Even if you never enter a nursing home yourself, you almost certainly have a close relative who will.

Nursing homes are particularly worrisome for most families because of their reputation of being little more than holding centers for the elderly and infirm, and because most medical insurance policies will not pay for the costs of the services they provide. In 1992 the average daily cost of nursing-home care was between $70 and $90 a day depending on the state of residency. This is a yearly cost of $25,550 to $32,850 before any special treatments or necessary medications are paid for. It is not uncommon for the cost of keeping a person in a nursing home to exceed $50,000 a year. This kind of expense can quickly eat up savings and leave other family members in poverty.

▶ Is a Nursing Home Necessary?

There are several alternatives to placing a person in a nursing home. One of the most promising is an arrangement that has been called a "nursing home without walls." The "On Lok" program, for example, sends its staff to the homes of the clients, helps them get up in the morning and prepare for a trip to the program's day-care center, where they receive both treatment and stimulation. At the end of the day, clients are returned home with a meal and are helped into bed if necessary. Because there are no sleeping facilities to maintain, the cost of this program is somewhat lower than a typical nursing home, and it allows clients to stay in their homes.

Home health care is another alternative for people who need some help but not 24-hour-a-day assistance. Many businesses and some not-for-profit organizations will send people to help the elderly in their homes. The cost of this service averaged $15 an hour in 1991. There-fore, if assistance is necessary for only an hour or two per day, it can save money. However, if more time is required, this alternative will be more expensive than a nursing home.

Many communities have adult day-care services run either by businesses or not-for-profit organizations. When these programs are appropriate to the needs of clients, they often provide quality care at the lowest possible cost. These programs, however, do not relieve family members of the responsibility of providing care for patients in the morning, at night, or on weekends and holidays. They do offer people an escape from the need to provide full-time care, but they do not take these responsibilities for more than a few hours at a time.

There are a growing number of what might be called halfway houses in the nursing home industry. These are rental apartments that offer a range of services at different costs for elderly people who are able to care for themselves at least partially. Residents are able to opt for various levels of care as their needs change. They may choose to have their meals prepared for them, cleaning and laundry done, and arrangements can be made to have a staff member help them up in the morning or to bed at night. When they need full-time care, they can be transferred from their apartment to a nursing facility that is in the same building complex. This is often the best choice for those people who can afford it.

▶ What to Look for in a Nursing Home

If you believe a member of your family may need nursing-home care, the time to investigate services in

your community is before the need is immediate. The best nursing homes are most often full. You should try to avoid being forced to accept something substandard just because it is the only thing available. Put your relative's name on the waiting lists of your first and second choices and wait for an opening.

Visit nursing-home facilities you are considering and talk to many different people, both staff members and residents who seem to be mentally alert. You do not need to cross-examine residents. Simply ask how they feel about the facility or how they spend their time there, and you will often be able to tell what kind of care they are receiving. Observe whether the facility is clean, whether staff members are friendly and appropriately dressed, whether the residents are clean and well-groomed, the food well prepared, activities for residents provided, therapy equipment available, and so on.

Always ask about arrangements that need to be made for medical care. You should find out if the nursing home has its own pharmacy, or if you will be expected to have drugs delivered with instructions from the patient's doctor. Other questions you should ask are

1. How many registered nurses are available at different times of day?
2. Does the nursing home have its own doctor, or is the patient's doctor expected to provide necessary care?
3. What procedures will be followed if a patient becomes ill and requires hospitalization?
4. What is the ratio of staff to patients?
5. Can physical therapy be carried out at the nursing home, or must patients be transported to other locations?

Try to get a feel for the organization's ability to help patients recover their health rather than simply house them.

▶ Paying for a Nursing Home

If your family has the financial resources to choose any nursing facility regardless of its cost, you are indeed fortunate. For most people who need nursing care, cost is a primary consideration. The rules of when state or federal programs will help pay for nursing-home care, and what specific services are covered, change so often that it is almost pointless to try to explain them here. As a general rule, Medicare will pay for nursing-home care only when a patient has been discharged from a hospital and is not yet able to return home. Medicare in 1992 did not pay for long-term nursing-home care. Many state-administered Medicaid programs will pay for this type of care when an individual's wealth has been exhausted. Some states try to require the patient's children to pay for all or part of the expense. When states pay for nursing-home care, the patient and relatives often have little choice in what facility is used.

Most private medical insurance plans will not pay for nursing-home care except for brief periods of time after a patient has been discharged from a hospital. It is possible to buy nursing-home insurance but it is very expensive. Premiums for older people can be as great as $5,000 a year or more. Even these policies have limitations. They most often will not pay for nursing-home stays made necessary by preexisting conditions (illnesses the patient already had when the policy was taken out). Many financial advisors suggest depositing money that would have been used to pay for such insurance in a special account. Putting $5,000 aside each year for ten years will result in a balance of over $60,000, which would cover the cost of most stays in a nursing home. The fact is that more than half the people who are in nursing homes pay the costs from their own wealth, or are supported by their relatives.

Selecting a nursing home that delivers quality care for a reasonable cost can be very difficult. However, the Health Care Financing Administration has released a state-by-state guide to the nation's 15,000 nursing homes that is of great benefit to comparison-shoppers. The guide, entitled *Medicare/Medicaid Nursing Home Information,* comprises 75 volumes. The volume or volumes containing information on your state's nursing homes can be purchased from the Government Printing Office (GPO), Washington, DC 20402. You first need to write or call the GPO to obtain the document number and the price. To inquire by phone, call (202) 783-3238. You may also check in local Medicare and Medicaid offices, welfare agencies, or in public libraries that may have copies of this publication.

▶ ALWAYS BE WILLING TO ASK FOR HELP

It is impossible to keep up with all the changes in medical care, and most of us lack the expertise to make medical choices without help. We should never be reluctant to ask for such help. There are organizations in virtually every community that provide it. A good place to begin is the closest office of your state health department. People there are trained either to help you with your problem, or to direct you to those who can. For general information,

one of the best sources of information and help about specific diseases is

Center for Disease Control
Health Education Information
1600 Clifton Road, MS-K13
Atlanta, GA 30333

Public Inquiry
(404) 639-3536

AIDS Clearinghouse
(800) 458-5231

Whenever you need to make a choice about medical care, however, you should remember that the final decision is yours. You can and should ask for information and advice, but it is your responsibility to evaluate what others say. Your life is your own, and you should make the important decisions concerning it.

▶ SUMMARY

1. Most of the medical care consumers need is provided by general practitioners who will inform patients when a specialist is needed.
2. Consumers should carefully choose a doctor before one is desperately needed. Friends, relatives, and/or other doctors can make recommendations. A doctor's age, sex, associations, and attitude are all factors consumers should consider.
3. When a doctor recommends surgery, consumers should ask for an explanation of the need and the risk of the operation. A second opinion should be obtained for any serious surgery. Consumers should be sure to talk with the surgeon who will operate and other members of the surgical team. It is particularly important to investigate the anesthesiologist's qualifications.
4. Although most prescription drugs

are safe for most patients, consumers should ask what their purpose and risks are. They should be particularly careful of possible interactions between drugs prescribed by more than one doctor. Patients should always follow their doctor's instructions when they take medications. It is often possible to save money by using generic instead of brand-name drugs.
5. When consumers visit emergency rooms, they should expect the speed of the service they receive to be directly related to the severity of their medical problem. Many people go to emergency rooms for treatments that are not truly emergencies. If your medical needs are not urgent, you may be better off contacting a doctor. When you go to an emergency room, it is important to bring your insurance identification and to be brief and to the point in answering questions about the illness or injury.
6. Consumers should avoid being admitted to a hospital unless they have a clear need for the services only a hospital can provide. In the hospital, patients and their relatives should be sure to ask for explanations for any care they do not understand. If a patient's illness is clearly terminal, it may be better for that patient to be cared for at home or a hospice organization.
7. About half of all Americans will stay in a nursing home before they die. Before having a person admitted to a nursing home, people may want to investigate alternative methods of care. It is better to begin the investigation before such care is absolutely needed. Nursing homes are very expensive, and most medical insurance does not pay for them. More than half of the people in nursing homes today are being supported by private funds.

▶ QUESTIONS FOR THOUGHT AND DISCUSSION

1. How did you choose the doctor you currently use? Are you satisfied with this doctor? Have you ever considered changing to another? If so why?

2. If you were told you needed an operation, what steps would you take before you agreed to the surgery? Explain why you would take each of these steps.

3. Do you ever question the purpose or need of any of the drugs that have been prescribed for you or for other members of your family? Why have you chosen to, or not to, question your doctor about the purpose and need for drugs?

4. Identify the three hospitals that are closest to where you live. If you were injured or became seriously ill, which of these hospitals would you want to be taken to? Give the reasons for your preference.

5. What would you do if you became ill and could not reach your doctor? How would you try to make sure that you received appropriate and timely care?

6. What is your general impression of the care provided by nursing homes in your community? What factors helped form this impression?

▶ THINGS TO DO

1. Interview someone you know who has had a serious injury or illness in recent years. Discuss the quality of the care he or she received. Ask what this person learned from the experience that would cause him or her to act differently if similar circumstances arose in the future.

2. Ask your local pharmacist to explain what laws govern his or her ability to substitute generic drugs for name brands on prescriptions.

3. Visit several local nursing homes. Evaluate the apparent quality of care that is being provided. Which facility would you want a relative of yours to stay in?

4. Call your local social services office and find out the requirements for an elderly person to receive financial aid for nursing-home care in your state.

5. Contact your local hospice organization and ask what sorts of services are provided to terminally ill patients.

▶ SELECTED READINGS

▶ Berman, Henry, and Burhenne, Diane. *The Complete Health Care Advisor*. New York: St. Martin's Press, 1983.

▶ Goldsmith, Seth B. *Choosing a Nursing Home*. New York: Prentice-Hall, 1990.

▶ Horowitz, Lawrence C. *Taking Charge of Your Medical Fate*. New York: Ballantine Books, 1988.

▶ LaMaitre, George D. *How to Choose a Good Doctor*. Andover, MA: Andover Publishing Group, 1979.

▶ *The Medicine Show*. Mount Vernon, NY: Consumer Reports Books, 1983.

Insuring Your Home and Your Automobile

PREVIEW

▶ What types of insurance does a homeowners' policy provide?

▶ Why do renters need insurance protection for their homes?

▶ How can you determine what types and how much insurance is right for you?

▶ What is no-fault insurance?

▶ What determines the cost of automobile insurance?

▶ What steps can you take to control the cost of insurance?

▶ What are your rights if you are refused insurance coverage?

Consumers purchase homeowners' and automobile insurance for two reasons. One reason is, of course, to protect their investments in case of loss. For example, if your house burns down, you're in serious trouble unless you have insurance coverage. You lose not only your personal possessions but also your investment (if your house is paid for). If you have a mortgage on your home, you will end up paying for a house that no longer exists.

The second reason is that consumers need to protect themselves against possible liability claims if their property is the cause of another's harm. If, for example, you are at fault in an auto accident that results in injury or death to another, you may face a lawsuit for damages—possibly in excess of $1 million. Similarly, if someone is injured on your property, you could be sued for damages, even though your only "fault" might be owning the property on which the injury occurred.

People protect themselves against both of these types of potential hazards— loss of property and liability claims—by purchasing homeowners' and automobile insurance.

INSURING YOUR HOME

Part of the process of buying a home is taking out a homeowners' insurance policy. Depending on where you live, the value of your home, and the type of coverage you buy, you can expect to pay anywhere from $200 to $1,000 (or more) a year for homeowners' insurance coverage. You will probably need to arrange for insurance coverage for any house that you pay for through a mortgage before you close on the property. This is because most mortgage holders require the *mortgagor*—that is, the homeowner—to prepay taxes and insurance as part of the monthly house payments. Part of each mortgage payment is placed in a special reserve account (called an *escrow account*) that is usually set up within the lending institution in which money for property taxes and insurance accumulates. The lending institution then makes these payments directly from the account. In this way, the *mortgagee*—the lending institution—does not have to worry about foreclosure on the house because of unpaid taxes or problems if the house is destroyed in a storm or a fire. Escrow accounts, however, pay mortgagees very low rates of interest. If the lending institution will allow borrowers to be responsible for their own taxes and insurance, they will do better financially to take care of these costs themselves by keeping their money in an account that pays a better return.

Types of Homeowners' Coverage

There are two basic types of insurance coverage you can purchase—property coverage and liability coverage. *Property coverage* includes the garage, house, and other private buildings on your lot; personal possessions and property whether at home or while you are traveling or at work; and additional living expenses paid to you if you could not live in your home because of a fire or flood.

There are three types of *liability coverage:* (1) personal liability in case someone is injured on your property or you damage someone else's property and are at fault; (2) medical payments for injury to others who are on your property; and (3) coverage for the property of others that you or a member of your family damages.

There are two types of insurance policies you might buy for your home; one provides just property insurance while the other provides both property and liability insurance.

A standard *fire insurance policy* protects the homeowner against fire and lightning, plus damage from smoke and water caused by the fire and the fire department. If you pay a little bit more, the coverage can be extended to protect you against damage caused by hail, windstorms, explosions, ice, snow, and so on. It is important to include hazards that might be likely in your area, even if the coverage may cost a little more.

A *homeowners' policy* provides protection against a number of risks under a single policy, allowing you to save over what you would pay if you bought each policy separately. It covers both the house and its contents.

There are a number of forms of homeowners' policies, each covering more risks than the other. Exhibit 20–1 shows what each is like. As you can see, the **basic form policy** covers 11 risks, the **broad form policy** covers 18 risks, and the **comprehensive form policy** covers those risks and all other perils, except those listed at the bottom of the chart.

Adding a Personal-Articles Floater Policy   Under the basic homeowners' policy, the contents of your home are insured up to 50 percent of the value of your house, but only for losses resulting from stated perils. You may wish to pay a slightly higher premium to insure specific personal articles such as cameras, musical instruments, works of art, jewelry, or your personal home computer. Under the basic homeowners' policy, for example, there is usually a jewelry cap of a specified sum, such as $1,000. If you apply for a personal-articles floater addition to your homeowners' policy, you will be asked to submit a list of the specific items you want to have covered under it and an affidavit from an appraiser giving their current market value. When you insure under a floater, you have provided all-risk insurance and can omit the covered property from your fire and theft policies.

Personal-Effects Floater Policy   You also can take out a personal-effects floater policy to cover personal items when you are traveling. In most cases, a personal-effects floater isn't necessary because your regular homeowners' insurance covers you. Because a personal-effects floater covers only the articles taken off your property, you still need insurance for them when they are on your property. The policy does not cover theft from an unattended automobile unless there is evidence of a forced entry.

Excess-Liability Policy   The growing number of million-dollar personal-liability lawsuits is causing many Americans to pay between $100 and $200 a year for personal-liability policies that protect them for $1 million above what they carry in their homeowners' (or automobile) policies. Because this kind of policy covers such a broad range of potential liability claims, whether from injuries on your property or from a car accident, it is called an **umbrella policy.** Typically, umbrella policies cover slander and libel defenses, too.

Flood Insurance   You will notice that even a comprehensive homeowners' insurance policy does not cover floods. If you live in an area that may experience flooding, it is advisable to purchase federally subsidized (that is, by all federal taxpayers) flood insurance. You must live in an area designated eligible by the Federal Insurance Administrator of the U.S. Department of Housing and

Basic form policy
A homeowners' insurance policy that covers 11 risks.

Broad form policy
A homeowners' policy that covers 18 risks.

Comprehensive form policy
A homeowners' policy that covers all risks except, usually, flood, war, and nuclear attack.

Umbrella policy
A type of supplemental insurance policy that can extend normal liability limits to $1 million or more for a relatively small premium.

BASIC	BROAD	COMPREHENSIVE	PERILS AGAINST WHICH PROPERTIES ARE INSURED
■	■	■	1. Fire or lightning.
■	■	■	2. Loss of property removed from premises, endangered by fire or other perils.
■	■	■	3. Windstorm or hail.
■	■	■	4. Explosion.
■	■	■	5. Riot or civil commotion.
■	■	■	6. Aircraft.
■	■	■	7. Vehicles.
■	■	■	8. Smoke.
■	■	■	9. Vandalism and malicious mischief.
■	■	■	10. Theft.
■	■	■	11. Breakage of glass constituting a part of the building.
	■	■	12. Falling objects.
	■	■	13. Weight of ice, snow, sleet.
	■	■	14. Collapse of building(s) or any part thereof.
	■	■	15. Sudden and accidental tearing asunder, cracking, burning, or bulging of a steam or hot water heating system or of appliances for heating water.
	■	■	16. Accidental discharge, leakage or overflow of water or steam from within a plumbing, heating or air conditioning system or domestic appliance.
	■	■	17. Freezing of plumbing, heating and air conditioning systems and domestic appliances.
	■	■	18. Sudden and accidental injury from artificially generated currents to electrical appliances, devices, fixtures and wiring (TV and radio tubes not included).
		■	All perils except flood, earthquake, war, nuclear accident and others specified in your policy. Check your policy for a complete listing of perils excluded.

Source: Insurance Information Institute.

Urban Development. Your insurance agent will be able to tell you if you are eligible.

How Much Insurance Should You Have?

You should have 80 percent of the total value of your property insured—that is, 80 percent of its replacement value. You may wish, or be required by the lender, to use the services of a professional appraiser in order to get an accurate idea of the replacement value of your house. You can find appraisers in your Yellow Pages, or your insurance agent, a local home builder, or your banker may be able to help you.

You need not insure your house for more than 80 percent of the replacement value for two reasons. First, the land has a value that would not be destroyed in a fire or flood, and even if the house were totally burned down, the foundation, sidewalks, driveway, and so on would remain. Second, if you have coverage for 80 percent of the replacement value, you can collect the full replacement cost, not the depreciated value, of any damaged property (up to the limits of the policy). For example, say your ten-year-old roof is damaged in a fire, and it costs $3,500 to replace it. If you have at least 80 percent coverage on your house, your insurance company must pay you the full amount of the roof damage, whereas if your house is covered for less than 80 percent of replacement, you will get less. Specifically, you will be paid only that portion of the loss equal to the amount of insurance in force divided by 80 percent of replacement cost of the entire house times the loss on the roof. If your house would cost $60,000 to replace and you have only $30,000 of insurance, then on your roof damage of $3,500, you will be paid:

$$\frac{\$30,000}{\$48,000} \times \$3,500 = \$2,188$$

A little explanation of this formula is in order. The fraction consists of the actual amount of insurance that you had on your structure ($30,000) divided by the amount of insurance you would have to have had to cover 80 percent of the replacement value, or .8 × $60,000 = $48,000.

Homeowners' insurance policies generally insure the contents of a home at their current market value. This means that a dining room table and chairs that cost $3,000 four years ago might be insured for only $1,500 if that is their value as used furniture. Yet it might cost $4,000—that is, even more than the original purchase price—to replace them today because of inflation. It is possible to buy replacement-value insurance for the contents of your home for only a few dollars more each year than an ordinary policy costs.

Periodic Review of Coverage   Although Americans spend billions a year to insure their homes, many still have inadequate insurance coverage. If you already have a homeowners' policy, you should periodically review its provisions to make sure that the policy reflects changes in values brought about by inflation, improvements to your home, or property appreciation. If you live in a house that you bought many years ago, for example, the cost of replacement may be much more than you think. Take that into account when you renew a homeowners' policy. You may want to have an arrangement with your insurance company whereby the value of your insurance is increased by a certain percentage every year or two to keep pace with current price levels.

How to Save on Insurance

There are a number of ways you may be able to reduce the insurance premium you pay without sacrificing coverage. By increasing the deductible, for instance, you can get a much lower premium. In most states, the premium is around 30 percent less for a $500 deductible than it is for a $100 deductible and about 10 percent less for a $250 deductible than a $100 deductible. If you install a burglar alarm, smoke detectors, deadbolt locks, and fire extinguishers, you can also save between 2 to 15 percent on your insurance bill. You may

> Although Americans spend billions a year to insure their homes, many still have inadequate insurance coverage.

also consider moving to a low-crime area where theft insurance will cost less. Sometimes, paying your premiums on a three-year basis rather than a one-year basis can save you money, as can purchasing a package policy rather than separate policies for different perils.

New Home Warranties

In 1974, the National Association of Home Builders (NAHB) established a consumer protection feature called Homeowner's Warranty, or HOW. HOW covers major structural defects on a home for a ten-year period so that subsequent buyers are automatically protected. HOW policies cannot be purchased on the open market; only an active HOW member-builder can sell one along with the house that he or she has built. The builder pays a one-time fee and passes it along to the buyer. Premium costs depend on the location of the house. HOW covers the home in a three-step plan, as follows:

1. During the first year, HOW builders guarantee their new homes to be free from defects in workmanship and materials, major structural defects, and flaws in the electrical, plumbing heating, cooling, ventilating, and mechanical systems.
2. During the second year, the HOW builder guarantees the same items, with the exception of workmanship and materials.
3. For the remaining eight years, the owner is insured against all major structural defects.

Whenever a builder refuses to abide by the terms of the warranty within the first two years (or if the builder goes out of business), the insurance takes over and covers the cost of all authorized repairs after the owner pays the first $250. Historically, over half the claims paid out by HOW have occurred during the initial two-year period.

The Homeowner's Warranty Corporation also makes available a five-year warranty program for remodelers. This plan, introduced in January 1983, guarantees remodeling work done by registered HOW contractors. The coverage is similar to that found in the HOW package for new homes, except that the homeowner pays a deductible.

Buying Repair Insurance

An increasing number of used-home buyers purchase warranties or insurance against defects in the home. These contracts protect new owners against such things as defective plumbing and wiring and sometimes appliance, roofing, and structural defects. Such warranties have been available to buyers of new homes for several years; they are issued through builders affiliated with the National Association of Home Builders. Some plans give protection against major structural defects for up to ten years.

What about Renters' Insurance?

According to the Insurance Information Institute, fewer than one-third of all renters in the United States carry renters' insurance. This is partly because many renters assume their landlords' homeowners' policy will cover any damages to their possessions caused by fire or theft. Unfortunately for many renters, this isn't the case. While it is true that the landlord or owner of your building is liable for damage to the building and for injuries occurring in common areas, such as the lobby or hallway, you are responsible for protecting the inside of your dwelling, and you are liable for accidents that occur there.

Renters' insurance, called a **residence contents broad form policy,** is a policy that covers personal possessions. It includes additional living expenses and liability coverage.

Before you look for a rental policy, make a detailed inventory of your possessions. Decide on the coverage you want and then do some comparison-shopping.

Note that household possessions are sometimes insured for half their value. Everything, including linens and plants, should be listed in your inventory. The inventory list must be kept in a safe place away from the dwelling, and a copy should be given to your insurance agent.

Typically, a renters' policy can be obtained from most property-insurance companies for between $150 and $200 a year. If you have especially valuable equipment or possessions for which you want extra protection, a personal-articles floater can be added—just as in a homeowners' policy—for an additional premium.

Residence contents broad form policy

A renters' insurance policy that covers possessions against 18 risks. It includes additional living expenses and liability coverage in case someone is injured in the apartment or house you are renting.

AUTOMOBILE INSURANCE

When you buy a car, one of the first things you must think about is insuring yourself against theft, fire, liability, medical expenses, and damage related to the automobile. It is foolish to risk driving without automobile insurance. Of the many kinds of coverage you can purchase, the most important is liability insurance.

Liability Insurance

Liability insurance pays when the policyholder is at fault to another person. It covers bodily injury liability and property damage. Liability limits are usually described by a series of three numbers, such as 100/300/50, which means that the policy will pay a maximum of $100,000 for bodily injury to one person, a maximum of $300,000 for bodily injury to more than one person, and a maximum of $50,000 for property damage in one occurrence. Liability insurance also pays for the cost of defending a policyholder should a covered loss result in litigation.

Exhibit 20–2 shows the minimum bodily-injury limits and property-damage liability coverage required by law in the United States and Canada.

Because the cost of additional liability coverage is relatively small, it is wise to consider taking out a much larger limit than you would ordinarily expect to need because awards in personal injury suits against automobile drivers who are proved negligent are sometimes astronomical. Some dependents of automobile accident victims have been successful in suing for $1 million or more.

People who aren't satisfied with the maximum liability limits offered by regular automobile insurance coverage can purchase a separate amount of coverage under an *umbrella policy,* which sometimes goes as high as $5 million in coverage.

Medical Payments Insurance

Medical payments on an auto insurance policy will cover hospital and medical bills and, sometimes, funeral expenses (for those in your car). Medical payment insurance pays regardless of who is at fault in an accident. Some policies allow you to buy medical payment insurance for your passengers. However, you may not want to buy medical payment insurance for your personal cov-

There may have been changes in some states since these data were published. For the latest information, check your own state department of motor vehicles or your auto-insurance agent.

State	Liability Limits*	State	Liability Limits*
Alabama	20/40/10	Montana	25/50/5
Alaska	50/100/25	Nebraska	25/50/25
Arizona	15/30/10	Nevada	15/30/10
Arkansas	25/50/15	New Hampshire	25/50/25
California	15/30/5	New Jersey	15/30/5
Colorado	25/50/15	New Mexico	25/50/10
Connecticut	20/40/10	New York	10/20/5[1]
Delaware	15/30/10	North Carolina	25/50/10
District of Columbia	25/50/10	North Dakota	25/50/25
Florida	10/20/10	Ohio	12.5/25/7.5
Georgia	15/30/10	Oklahoma	10/20/10
Hawaii	15/35/10	Oregon	25/50/15
Idaho	25/50/15	Pennsylvania	15/30/5
Illinois	20/40/15	Rhode Island	25/50/25
Indiana	25/50/10	South Carolina	15/30/5
Iowa	20/40/15	South Dakota	25/50/25
Kansas	25/50/10	Tennessee	20/50/10
Kentucky	25/50/10	Texas	20/40/15
Louisiana	10/20/10	Utah	20/40/10
Maine	20/40/10	Vermont	20/40/10
Maryland	20/40/10	Virginia	25/50/20
Massachusetts	10/20/5	Washington	25/50/10
Michigan	20/40/10	West Virginia	20/40/10
Minnesota	30/60/10	Wisconsin	25/50/10
Mississippi	10/20/5	Wyoming	25/50/20
Missouri	25/50/10		

*The first two figures refer to bodily injury liability limits and the third figure to property damage liability. For example, 10/20/5 means coverage up to $20,000 for all persons injured in an accident, subject to a limit of $10,000 for one individual, and $5,000 coverage for property damage.
[1]50/100 if injury results in death.

CANADA**

Province	Liability Limit	Province	Liability Limit
Alberta	$200,000	Nova Scotia	$200,000
British Columbia	200,000	Ontario	200,000
Manitoba	200,000	Prince Edward Island	200,000
New Brunswick	200,000	Quebec	50,000
Newfoundland	200,000	Saskatchewan	200,000
Northwest Territories	200,000	Yukon	200,000

**In all Canadian provinces except Quebec, the amount of liability insurance shown is available to settle either bodily injury or property damage claims—or both. When a claim involving both bodily injury and property damage reaches this "inclusive" limit, payment for property damage is limited to $20,000 in British Columbia, Manitoba, New Brunswick and Newfoundland, and to $10,000 in the other provinces and territories having "inclusive" limits. Quebec laws provide that people injured in accidents in Quebec be compensated by a government fund. Benefits paid to non-residents are scaled down in proportion to their degree of fault. The $50,000 limit relates to liability for damage to property in Quebec and to liability for bodily injury and property damage outside Quebec.
Sources: American Insurance Association; Insurance Bureau of Canada.

erage through your auto insurance policy if you have sufficient medical coverage through an individual medical insurance policy or through a group policy at your place of employment.

Collision Insurance

Collision insurance covers damage to your car in any type of collision not covered by another insured driver at fault. It is usually not advisable to purchase full coverage (otherwise known as **zero deductible**) on collision. The price per year is quite high because it is likely that, in any one year, small repair jobs will be required and will be costly. Most people take out $100 or $200 deductible coverage, which costs about one-quarter the price of zero deductible.

Comprehensive Insurance

Comprehensive auto insurance covers for loss, damage, or anything on your car destroyed by fire, hurricane, hail, or just about all other causes, including vandalism. It is separate from collision insurance. Full comprehensive insurance is quite expensive. Again, a $100 or $200 deductible is usually preferable.

Uninsured Motorist Insurance

Uninsured motorist coverage insures the driver and passengers against injury by any driver who has no insurance at all or by a hit-and-run driver. Many states require that this coverage be in all insurance policies sold to the drivers. The risk is small, so the premium is relatively small.

Accidental Death Benefits

Sometimes called *double indemnity,* accidental death coverage provides a lump sum to named beneficiaries if you happen to die in an automobile accident. Although it generally costs very little, you may not want it if you feel you have already purchased a sufficient amount of life insurance.

What Determines the Price of Auto Insurance?

It is not uncommon for different prices to be charged for identical insurance coverage, and it therefore pays to shop around before purchasing a policy. But prices can be misleading because different insurance companies offer different qualities of service. One company may be less willing to pay off claims than another; one may have an insurance adjuster at your house immediately if you have a small accident; another may never send one out, leaving you to do the adjusting yourself. Although insurance costs are not consistently related to quality of service, they are consistently differentiated among different classes of drivers.

Why? Simply because the probability that an accident will occur is different for these different classes. Competition among the various insurance companies has forced each one of them to find out which classes of drivers are safer than others and to offer those classes lower rates. For example, statistically, single males from the ages of 16 to 25 have the highest accident record of all drivers. According to the National Safety Council, one-third of the drivers within this group have auto accidents. Some states have a history of higher rates of insurance claim settlements, both in and out of court, which increase the cost of providing auto insurance. For this reason, drivers in such states pay a much higher price for auto insurance—as can be seen in Exhibit 20–3. Statistics also indicate that female drivers have fewer accidents overall than male drivers; therefore, women often pay lower insurance rates for cars that

Zero deductible

In the collision part of an automobile insurance policy, the provision that the insured pays nothing for any repair to damage on the car due to an accident that is the fault of the insured. Zero deductible is, of course, more expensive than a $100 or $200 deductible policy.

New Jersey	$1,444	Arizona	$928	Minnesota	$709
Connecticut	1,281	Colorado	889	West Virginia	708
Rhode Island	1,263	Washington	872	Utah	698
California	1,241	Oregon	835	Tennessee	690
New York	1,108	Virginia	807	Arkansas	672
New Hampshire	1,099	Illinois	801	Indiana	662
Delaware	1,088	Oklahoma	771	Wyoming	633
Pennsylvania	1,074	South Carolina	763	Wisconsin	616
Massachusetts	1,073	Ohio	758	Montana	616
Maryland	1,048	Maine	753	Idaho	608
Georgia	995	New Mexico	749	Nebraska	604
Michigan	975	Alabama	738	Kansas	603
Texas	953	Missouri	736	Kentucky	596
Louisiana	942	North Carolina	725	South Dakota	555
Nevada	940	Mississippi	723	North Dakota	543
Florida	936	Vermont	713	Iowa	466

Source: *Consumers' Research Magazine*, May 1991, page 33.

they use exclusively. Gender-based insurance rates have been under attack in recent years because such a method of rate determination places more emphasis on sex than on safe-driving records, health habits, social habits, and so on. Currently, Hawaii, Massachusetts, Montana, and North Carolina don't allow gender-based auto insurance rates to be applied to their states.

Insurance rates also depend on the following variables:

1. The car you drive.
2. Where you drive (see Exhibit 20-3).
3. What the car is used for.
4. Marital status.
5. Occupation.
6. Safety record.

No-Fault Insurance, Pros and Cons

No-fault auto insurance

A system of auto insurance whereby, no matter who is at fault, the individual is paid by his or her insurance company for a certain amount of medical costs and for the damage to the car.

Original proponents of **no-fault auto insurance** in the 1960s believed that all states in the union soon would adopt the system. To date, however, only 14 of the states and the District of Columbia have "pure" no-fault insurance. Ten other states have a modified form of no-fault, in which no-fault benefits have been simply superimposed on an unchanged liability-based system.

What Is No-Fault?   No-fault auto insurance is basically an extension of the principle of workers' compensation insurance to auto accidents. Under workers' compensation, for example, if a worker is injured, he or she is compensated for sustained injuries regardless of whether the employer or the worker was at fault. Likewise, under a no-fault auto insurance program, your insurance company does not have to decide whose fault the accident was before paying you for medical expenses arising from injuries sustained in that accident. In a traditional, liability-based fault system, a determination must first be made as to who caused an accident. The insurer of the party deemed to be "at fault" then pays the bills—medical bills, auto-repair bills, lost earnings, and, in some cases, pain and suffering—of the other party.

In many no-fault states, a certain dollar threshold—varying between $500 and $4,000—must be met before you are allowed to sue for pain and suffering compensation. In these states, however, a "descriptive" threshold is required.

Six Feet Deep

In 1989 a woman was convicted of having her car buried by a friend and then claiming it had been stolen to collect the insurance. After admitting her crime, she explained that the car had never run properly and that she had not been able to have it repaired satisfactorily. Getting the insurance company to pay for her car seemed like a reasonable choice to her. Although this case is more extreme than many, it demonstrates the willingness of many Americans to file fraudulent claims with insurance companies. They seem to believe that the insurance companies bear the cost of their claims, but in fact these firms only pass the added cost on to all policyholders in the form of higher premiums. Estimates suggest that some degree of fraud is involved in 25 percent of all car repair claims. Most fraudulent claims involve policyholders having preexisting problems repaired at the same time as a legitimate claim is made and charging the insurance company for the entire bill.

Suppose the left front fender of your car was damaged while left in a parking lot. Because you carry a $500 deductible on your policy—more than the repair would cost—you choose not to file a claim. Two weeks later you slide on ice into a ditch, denting the left rear side of the car. No additional damage is done to the already dented front fender. This time the total damage amounts to $2,342 worth of repairs. When you file your claim, would you include the damage to the front fender? If you do, who actually ends up paying the cost of your fraudulent claim? What is the ethical thing to do?

When consumers are involved in accidents in states that have no-fault insurance, they quickly receive payment for their medical expenses from their own insurance company. However, they may be limited in the types of legal action they are able to take against a responsible party. If you were injured in an accident that was caused by another driver would you prefer to have no-fault insurance?

In Michigan, New York, and Florida, accident victims must meet a serious-injury requirement instead of a dollar requirement before they can sue for compensation.

No-Fault versus Liability—Which Is Better? In those states that combine high-benefits programs with a restriction on lawsuits to those with serious injuries only, no-fault works well. This is the case in New York, Michigan, and Florida, where the descriptive threshold limits insurance payments to those who are seriously injured and who need compensation.

A 1984 study by the Department of Transportation revealed that twice as many victims in states with no-fault coverage are being compensated than is the case in states with a traditional liability system. And payments are made more quickly. Most no-fault laws require that payment be made within 30 to 60 days after the submission of the proof of claim. By contrast, in liability states, victims sometimes have to wait months—even years—to be compensated. Furthermore, less money is involved in litigation costs under no-fault, and more of the insurance dollar goes toward benefits; overall, 10 to 15 cents more of each premium dollar goes toward compensation instead of litigation costs.

Many early proponents had expected no-fault insurance programs to result in lower insurance premiums, but this has not been the case. Premiums in no-fault states run about as high as in liability states. This is because more victims are being compensated for medical care, and medical care costs have risen dramatically in the past two decades.

Since the mid-1970s, no additional states (other than the District of Columbia in 1983) have converted to no-fault plans. What happened to no-fault's earlier momentum? A recent *Consumer Reports* study attributes much of the slowdown to the lobbying and pressure tactics of lawyers who have opposed no-fault. Trial lawyers and other critics of no-fault, including consumer advocate Ralph Nader, argue that the liability system is fairer to consumers because it makes those responsible for harms caused by automobiles more accountable. They also argue that no-fault insurance deprives individuals of the right to have their cases heard in court. More generally, however, those no-fault states that offer only skimpy benefits or have only partial no-fault coverage (a mixture of liability and no-fault systems) do not create as favorable an alternative to the liability system as do the high-benefits states previously mentioned—New York, Florida, and Michigan.

In an attempt to please both the supporters and the critics of no-fault and to lower insurance premium costs, some consumer advocates and the insurance industry are proposing a dual-system of insurance within each state. In such a system, drivers would be allowed to chose between no-fault or liability coverage. Those who opt for fault-based insurance would pay higher premiums; those who choose no-fault would pay lower premiums and forfeit the right to sue except in cases of serious injuries or death—in effect, this option would be for true no-fault insurance along the lines of those programs in New York, Florida, and Michigan.

How to Shop for Insurance

Shopping for automobile insurance is usually easier than shopping for a car. You may want to look first to your local credit union or to some special insurance source available to you if you are a member of certain organizations. Sometimes companies get special rates for their employees. If you are a government employee, you can often get special types of automobile insurance from a government employees' insurance company. When comparing insurance companies, remember to look at the service they give. You can shop for insurance by figuring out the exact policy you want, including liability, uninsured motorist, medical, collision, comprehensive, and perhaps towing, with the specific limits you want; then get a written statement from several insurance companies' agents. Insurance premiums can vary by 50 to 100 percent, depending on what company you select.

The insurance agent you work with is also important. If one in your area has a reputation for being fair and knowledgeable, you may want to take suggestions from that person. Again, you are being sold information as part of the package. (You also may be buying "clout" if you are dealing with a company agent rather than a broker for many different companies.)

Exhibit 20–4 will help you compare insurance policies. When calling around to get insurance, you can fill in the chart and compare policies.

The Insurance Information Institute has a hotline you can call for further information on auto insurance. If you have questions about insurance, call its toll-free number, (800) 331-9146.

How to Lower Your Insurance Rates

Following are some tips on lowering your automobile insurance rates.

1. Don't buy coverage that you don't need, such as collision and comprehensive insurance on an older car. For example, if you have a five-year-old car whose blue-book value is relatively low, you may not want to bother with collision insurance because you never collect more than blue-book value (and damage may be more than the car is worth).

2. Avoid high-performance or expensive cars for which auto insurance is much higher.

3. Take a higher deductible on collision and comprehensive insurance. Remember, the higher the deductible, the lower of the premium.

4. See if you qualify for a discount for not smoking, not drinking, belonging to a car pool, having an accident-free record for the past three years or more, or keeping your mileage low each year. If you are a student, ask about discounts for good grades and for driver's education courses.

▶ Exhibit 20–4 **Comparing Auto Insurance Companies**

KIND OF COVERAGE	LIMITS DESIRED	A	COMPANY B	C
1. Liability:				
Bodily injury	$ ____/person, $ ____/accident	_____	_____	_____
Property damage	$ ____/accident	_____	_____	_____
2. Physical damage:				
Compensation for total loss	Only wholesale price available	_____	_____	_____
Collision	$ ____/deductible	_____	_____	_____
3. Medical payments	$ ____/person	_____	_____	_____
4. Uninsured motorist	$ ____/person, $ ____/accident	_____	_____	_____
5. Accidental death benefits	$ ____	_____	_____	_____
6. Towing	$ ____	_____	_____	_____
7. Comprehensive	$ ____/deductible	_____	_____	_____
8. Other	$ ____	_____	_____	_____
ANNUAL TOTAL		_____	_____	_____

5. Don't use your car for work if you can obtain other transportation.

6. Don't duplicate insurance. If you have a comprehensive health and accident insurance policy, then you don't need medical coverage in your automobile insurance plan.

7. Any time your situation changes, notify your company. Do this when your estimated yearly mileage drops, when you join a car pool, when a driver of your car moves away from home, and so on.

The Special Problem of Insurance for Rental Cars

For many years some car-rental firms have pressured customers to purchase *insurance waivers* (special policies that cover damage to rented cars) that cost anywhere from a few dollars to as much as $15 a day. These waivers can almost double the cost of renting a car if they are accepted. Many states (New York, for example) now require insurance companies that do business in these states to automatically provide insurance for rental cars. Before you agree to pay for such a wavier, be sure to check whether you are already covered. The Consumer Close-Up in this chapter addresses this issue.

When You Are Refused Insurance

Sometimes, because of a bad driving record, you will be refused liability coverage by an automobile insurance company. When this happens, you become an **assigned risk.** To get insurance as an assigned risk, you must first certify

Assigned risk
A person seeking automobile insurance who has been refused coverage. That person is assigned to an insurance company that is a member of the assigned-risk pool in the person's state.

CONSUMER CLOSE-UP

A Case of Too Much Insurance

A number of credit card companies, including American Express, now automatically cover the cost of repairing or replacing damaged or stolen rental cars for cardholders *if* the renters use their charge cards to pay for the rental fees. This automatic insurance coverage presents a convenience to consumers, because it relieves them of the necessity of purchasing (at very high rates) rental-car insurance from car-rental firms or the time and trouble of verifying such coverage under their own auto insurance policies.

While on a business trip in 1988, Joe Manusco, president of the Center for Entrepreneurial Management in New York, rented a car from

General Rent-a-Car, Inc., and charged the price of the rental to his American Express card. He knew that, by using his American Express card, the rented car would be automatically covered by insurance. Just to be on the safe side, however, he also purchased insurance from General Rent-a-Car. Mr. Manusco later recalled how self-congratulatory he had been on his "double" coverage: "I figured I'd give myself a gold star for being so safe."

A few days later, when his rented car was stolen, General Rent-a-Car asked him to come up with $7,000 for a new car (because the insurance wouldn't cover the loss until the car was recovered, he was

told). Concerned but not too daunted at this news, Mr. Manusco turned to his alternate insurer, American Express Company. To his dismay, he was told that American Express had voided his insurance coverage. Why? Because he had opted to purchase insurance through General Rent-a-Car. As Mr. Manusco learned later, that is standard policy among credit card companies that offer rental-car insurance to card users.

If there is a lesson to be learned from Mr. Manusco's frustrating experience, it is this: Never assume too much when it comes to insurance—check your coverage carefully before you drive (or rent) a car.

---

that you have attempted within the past 60 days to obtain insurance in the state where you live. A pool of insurance companies (or sometimes the state) will then assign you to a specific company in the pool for a period of three years. At the end of three years, you can apply for reassignment, provided you are still unable to purchase insurance outside the pool.

If you are an assigned risk, you can purchase only the legal minimum amount of insurance in your state. In most cases, you will pay a much higher premium for the same amount of coverage than someone who is not an assigned risk.

▶ SUMMARY

1. Consumers purchase homeowners' and automobile insurance for two reasons—to protect their investments in case of loss and to protect themselves against possible liability claims if their property is the cause of another's harm.

2. There are basically two types of home insurance policies—fire insurance policies and homeowners' policies. Property coverage and liability coverage are both available under homeowners' policies.

3. You should make sure that you obtain sufficient insurance on your house so that at least 80 percent of its replacement value is covered.

4. Special types of insurance can also be added to your basic homeowners' coverage to protect particularly valuable items in your home or to provide extra liability limits.

5. A Homeowner's Warranty (HOW) is a consumer protection feature established by the National Association of Home Builders in 1974. HOW protects against structural defects on a newly built home for a ten-year period. It also makes available a five-year warranty program for remodelers.

6. Renters can obtain insurance coverage for their personal possessions through a renters' insurance policy.

7. Various forms of coverage are available under automobile insurance policies, including liability coverage, medical payments, collision and comprehensive insurance, and uninsured motorist coverage. Accidental death benefits are also obtainable.

8. Auto insurance rates are determined by many factors, including age, gender, the kind of car you drive, where you drive, what your car is used for, marital status, occupation, and safety record.

9. In states that have adopted no-fault auto insurance, the liability-based system is eliminated. Essentially, if you have no-fault insurance, your insurance company pays you in case of an accident, no matter who was at fault.

10. To get the best deal in auto insurance, you need to comparison-shop because rates and claims-handling services can vary considerably for the same kind of insurance coverage. You can lower your insurance premium considerably by taking a higher deductible, searching for discounts for which you might be eligible owing to safe-driving habits and other precautions, reducing the miles driven on your car, not duplicating insurance coverage, and letting your insurance company know when changes occur that might reduce your premium.

11. When an individual is refused auto insurance coverage because of a bad driving record, he or she becomes an assigned risk. Special insurance programs allow minimum insurance coverage for assigned risks, but the premiums charged for assigned-risk coverage are very high.

QUESTIONS FOR THOUGHT AND DISCUSSION

1. How much liability coverage—both for your home and your automobile—do you think is a "reasonable" amount?

2. Why have excess-liability insurance policies become more common in recent years?

3. Are you for or against no-fault insurance?

4. Do you agree with Ralph Nader that no-fault insurance is unfair to consumers because it renders those responsible for auto accidents and injuries less accountable for their actions?

5. Can you think of any reasons why you might be eligible for premium discounts when purchasing auto insurance?

THINGS TO DO

1. Go to a local property-insurance company and ask an agent to list the premiums you would pay for different types of insurance coverage (homeowners' or renters') for the home in which you are now living. Determine how much you would have to pay for maximum insurance coverage of your property.

2. Call the Insurance Information Institute's hotline given in this chapter and ask them how many states now have no-fault auto insurance laws. Have any states adopted no-fault insurance since this book was published?

3. Write to or call your state's insurance commissioner (you can find out how to reach the commissioner by calling your state's consumer protection bureau—see Consumer Issue B) and request information on your state's auto insurance laws.

APPLICATION

List the contents of your home and estimate what each of your possessions is worth as used furniture, clothing, appliances, and so forth. Make a second list of how much you believe it would cost to replace each of these items. Total each list and compare the results. Write an essay based on your findings, assessing the value of buying replacement-cost insurance.

SELECTED READINGS

▶ Cheit, R. E., and J. E. Youngwood. "How Not to Reform Insurance," *Consumers' Research Magazine,* November 1991, pp. 24–27.

▶ Hannor, K. "How to Save $1,000 on Auto Insurance." *Money,* November 1991, pp. 158–160.

▶ *The Homebuyer's Guide to HOW.* Available free from the Homeowners' Warranty Corporation, 200 L St., N.W., Washington, DC 20036.

▶ Insurance Information Institute. *Auto Insurance Issues.* New York: Insurance Information Institute, 1989.

▶ Money Management Institute. *Your Insurance Dollar.* Available for $1 from the Money Management Institute, 2700 Sanders Rd., Prospect Heights, IL 60070.

▶ Pattison, S. "Government and Auto Insurance." *Consumers' Research Magazine,* August 1991, p. 36.

▶ Waldman, Stephen. "The Insurance Mess." *Newsweek,* April 23, 1990, p. 46–53.

▶ "What's Covered with Homeowners' Insurance?" *Consumers' Research Magazine,* September 1991, pp. 24–29.

CHAPTER 21

Life Insurance and Social Security

► What are the benefits and costs of buying life insurance?

► What different types of life insurance can consumers buy?

► How much life insurance is enough?

► How may consumers investigate the financial strength of life insurance companies?

► What benefits are provided by Social Security?

We have discussed home insurance, liability insurance, automobile insurance, and medical insurance at some length. These are basically forms of protection or income security. Now we'll discuss two additional forms of protection—life insurance and Social Security.

LIFE INSURANCE AND OUR NEED FOR SECURITY

A sense of security is important for most families. In fact, psychologists contend that the average American wants a sense of security more than just about anything else in life. Some of the major hazards to *financial* security are listed here, along with the ways Americans provide for these hazards.

1. *Illness.* Health and medical insurance, savings account for emergencies, Medicare, Medicaid.
2. *Accident.* Accident insurance, savings account, state workers' compensation, Social Security, aid to the disabled, veterans' benefits.
3. *Unemployment.* Savings fund for such an emergency, unemployment compensation.
4. *Old age.* Private retirement pension plans, savings account, annuities, Social Security.
5. *Premature death.* Survivors' insurance under the Social Security Act, life insurance, workers' compensation, savings, investments.
6. *Desertion, divorce.* Savings, investments, Aid to Families with Dependent Children (AFDC).
7. *Unexpected, catastrophic expenses.* Health insurance, property insurance, liability insurance, Medicare.

The responsibility for providing family economic security may be assumed by the family, relatives of the family, charitable institutions, employers, or the government. Fifty years ago, financial security was provided primarily by the first three, but now employers and the government are assuming some responsibility for this kind of protection.

PREMATURE DEATHS

The mortality rate in the United States has been declining for many years, as it has been in most parts of the world. People are suffering from fewer fatal diseases and are living longer, as can be seen in Exhibit 21–1. Nonetheless, every year there are more than 300,000 premature deaths in the United States. In many cases, particularly when a wage earner dies, these premature deaths cause financial hardship for other members of the family. The main purpose of life insurance is to provide financial security in this event.

HISTORY OF LIFE INSURANCE

The first recorded life-insurance policy was written in June 1536 in London's Old Drury Ale House. A group of marine **underwriters** agreed to insure the life of William Gybbons for the grand sum of $2,000. This coverage was obtained for an $80 **premium.** (Unfortunately for the underwriters, Gybbons died a few days before the policy was to run out.) And so it was that life

Underwriter
The company that stands behind the face value of any insurance policy. The underwriter signs its name to an insurance policy, thereby becoming answerable for a designated loss or damage on consideration of receiving a premium payment.

Premium
The payment that must be made to the insurance company to keep an insurance policy in effect. Premiums usually are paid quarterly, semiannually, or annually.

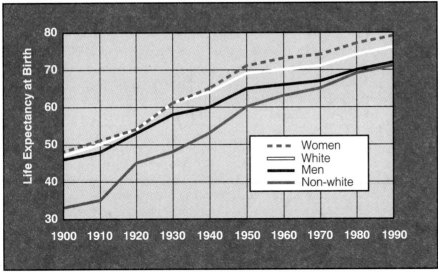

► Exhibit 21–1   Life Expectancy at Birth, 1900–1990

Source: *Historic Statistics of the United States to 1957;* and *Statistical Abstract of the United States* (Washington, DC: U.S. Government Printing Office, 1991).

insurance became a sideline for marine underwriters. Then, in 1692 the Society for the Equitable Assurance of Lives and Survivorship began issuing policies covering a person for his or her lifetime. Old Equitable, as it became known, still exists today. In North America, the first corporation to insure lives was the Presbyterian Ministers' Fund, started in Philadelphia in 1759. By 1800 there were only 160 life-insurance policies in force in the United States. Only after the Civil War did the industry begin to flourish, and since the turn of the century it has grown rapidly.

Today roughly 82 percent of all households headed by a married couple, widow, or widower, own at least some life insurance. In 1989 the average total coverage for all insured people in each household was $94,000. An average premium of $960 was paid for this coverage (roughly 25 percent of this amount was paid by employers as a fringe benefit for their employees).

THE BASIC TYPES OF LIFE INSURANCE

Although the basic principles of life insurance are simple to grasp, the various insurance programs you can purchase are many and complex. In this chapter, we outline the basic types of life insurance policies. Consumer Issue S offers some ideas to help you determine your own life insurance needs and some recommendations about the appropriate type of insurance for you.

Basically, there are two types of life insurance—term and whole life. **Whole life insurance** combines protection with a cash value, whereas **term insurance** offers pure protection. Whole life is also called *straight line, ordinary life,* or *cash-value insurance;* these are merely different names for the same type of life insurance.

Term Insurance

Premiums for term insurance, unlike those for whole life, commonly increase at the end of each term, such as every five years, if you wish to keep the same

Whole life insurance
Insurance that has both death and living benefits. That is, part of your premium is put into a type of savings account.

Term insurance
Life insurance that is for a specified term (period of time) and has only a death benefit; it is a form of pure insurance with no savings aspect.

face value on your insurance policy. The increased premium reflects the rising probability of death as age increases. Thus, it will cost you relatively little to buy term life insurance when you are 25 years old, but, by the time you are 60, your premiums will have risen dramatically. By that time, however, you probably won't want as much term insurance because your children will be well on their way to financial independence, and you will have built up other forms of financial resources for any dependents you still have. That means you can reduce the premium burden by reducing the amount of insurance carried to protect your family. An important point to note here is that term insurance is one way for a young, growing family to have more insurance at an *affordable price* than it could have with the more expensive types of insurance. This occurs at a time in the life cycle when adequate insurance is needed most, but family income is normally relatively low.

Uniform decreasing term insurance
A term insurance policy on which the premiums are uniform throughout its life, but the face value of the policy declines.

Families often choose **uniform decreasing term insurance,** which has a level premium but a decreasing face value. A similar type of policy is called a *home-protection plan*. It is decreasing term insurance that decreases at *approximately* the same rate that the outstanding amount of money owed on a house declines as payments are made on the mortgage. Thus, when a home-protection policy is taken out for a face value equal to the amount of the mortgage on the home, the home can be paid off (or the mortgage payments can be paid) with the insurance benefits if the breadwinner dies any time during the life of the mortgage.

Renewability Standard term insurance is often labeled one-year term or five-year term because those are the intervals, or terms, between premium increases. Other periods are also available. A term policy is *renewable* if the coverage can be continued at the end of each period merely by payment of the increased premium without the need for a medical examination. The renewability feature must, of necessity, add to the cost of the policy, but if you wish to preserve your insurability despite any changes in your health, you certainly would want to pay the extra costs for this feature. Term policies are commonly renewable until the policyholder reaches some age of retirement, such as 65 or 70. All coverage then stops.

In one sense, the premiums for any term policy are constant for the life of the policy, but since most term policies are written with a one-year or five-year "life," the constancy of premium is not too meaningful. The premium is truly constant throughout a long period of time only with decreasing term insurance, in which the face value falls every year.

Rider
A written attachment to an insurance policy that alters the policy to meet certain conditions, such as convertibility, double indemnity, and so on.

Convertibility Often, **riders** can be attached to term policies that give you the privilege of converting them to other than pure insurance without the necessity of a medical examination. You pay for this additional feature, however. If you have a convertible term policy, you can convert it to whole life without any problems. The main reason you might want to convert is to continue your coverage after you pass the age of 65 or 70. After converting the policy, you would pay whole life premiums based on your age at the time of conversion. Most insurance experts believe that these two features—convertibility and renewability—should be purchased. They give you much flexibility at a not inappropriate additional cost.

Exhibit 21-2 A Typical $50,000 Yearly Renewable Term Policy, Male, Age 35

YEAR	ANNUAL PREMIUM	YEAR	ANNUAL PREMIUM
1	$165.50	11	$312.50
2	172.50	12	339.00
3	181.00	13	368.00
4	192.00	14	400.00
5	204.50	15	435.00
6	219.00	16	473.50
7	235.00	17	515.50
8	252.00	18	560.50
9	270.50	19	609.50
10	290.50	20	642.50
20th Year Total	$6,838.50	Total at Age 65	$17,893.00

Exhibit 21–2 shows the costs of $50,000 of one-year renewable term insurance for a 35 year-old man. If this man keeps $50,000 of term insurance until age 65, he will pay in a total of $17,893. He will have no cash value in the policy, as he would in a whole life policy.

Whole Life Insurance

Whole life insurance accounts for a little less than half the total value of all life insurance in force in the United States. Life insurance salespersons will almost always try to sell you a whole life policy because it is more profitable for them and their company. (It has been estimated that a salesperson earns about nine times more selling the same amount of whole life than he or she does selling term insurance.)

Premiums Whole life premiums generally remain the same throughout the life of a policy. As a result, the policyholder pays more in each of the early years than is necessary to cover the company's risk in later years. Exhibit 21–3 gives an example of a $10,000 ordinary life insurance policy with an annual level premium of $222.70 for a 35-year-old man. In the first year, $205.50 of the $222.70 goes to the insurance company to cover the insurance costs, and $17.20 goes to the **cash value** of the policy for the purchaser. By the sixth year, the deposit to cash value is greater than the level annual premium and stays greater throughout the life of this particular policy. You can see in the summary of this policy that by the twentieth year—that is, when the policyholder is 50 years old—there is a total cash value in that policy of $5,608.97, after $4,454 has been paid in.

The cash value of a whole life insurance policy certainly is not the same thing as a savings account. Insurance industry people often promote whole life as an insurance policy combined with a savings plan, but it is definitely not. The cash reserve is not given to your named **beneficiary** as a separate payment; rather, it is included in the face amount of the policy. Thus, looking at Exhibit 21–3 again, let us assume you have paid in for ten years. Your total

Cash value
Applied to whole life policies only, it represents the amount of "savings" built up in the policy and available to the living policyholder, either to borrow against or to receive if the policy is canceled.

Beneficiary
The designated person or persons for any insurance policy. In a life insurance policy, the beneficiary is the person who receives the benefits when the insured dies.

$10,000 ORDINARY LIFE
Dividends* to Purchase Paid-up Additions
Annual Premium: $222.70   Male: Age 35

YEAR	DEPOSIT TO CASH VALUE	DEPOSIT TO INSURANCE	TOTAL CASH VALUE
1	$ 17.20	$205.50 –	$ 17.20
2	179.71	42.99	196.91
3	190.43	32.27	387.34
4	201.97	20.73	589.31
5	213.47	9.23	802.78
6	225.43	2.73 –	1,028.21
7	237.14	14.44 –	1,265.35
8	250.35	27.65 –	1,515.70
9	262.61	39.91 –	1,778.31
10	275.17	52.47 –	2,053.48
11	270.17	47.47 –	2,323.65
12	282.60	59.90 –	2,606.25
13	294.64	71.94 –	2,900.89
14	306.82	84.12 –	3,207.71
15	320.64	97.94 –	3,528.35
16	333.21	110.51 –	3,861.56
17	346.11	123.41 –	4,207.67
18	360.95	138.25 –	4,568.62
19	376.12	153.42 –	4,944.74
20	391.60	168.90 –	5,336.34

	SUMMARY 20TH YEAR	AT AGE 65
Total Cash Value	$5,608.97*	$10,566.83†
Total Deposits	$4,454.00	$ 6,681.00
Net Gain	$1,154.97	$ 3,885.83

*Dividends are neither estimates nor guarantees but are based on the current dividend scale.
†Includes terminal dividend.

cash value is shown to be $2,053.48. What if you die at the end of ten years? You have a $10,000 ordinary life policy, and your named beneficiary gets $10,000, not $10,000 plus your cash value of $2,053.48.

Owners of whole life policies often take comfort from the fact that their premiums are level and, therefore, represent one of the few costs that do not go up with inflation. (The real value of the policy, however, as well as the premiums, declines as the buying power of a dollar falls.) True, the cost is relatively high to begin with, but it gets no higher. The exact level of premiums that you would pay for a $10,000 ordinary life insurance policy, as represented in Exhibit 21-3, depends on your age when you buy the policy; the younger you are, the less it will be, because the company expects to collect premiums from you for many years. The older you are, the greater it is.

As we will see when we compare whole life with term insurance, whole life is relatively expensive because it is a form of financial investment as well as insurance protection. The investment feature is known as its "cash value."

In Exhibit 21–3, the cash value at the end of twenty years was in excess of $5,000; at age 65, it was actually in excess of the death benefit of the policy. You can, of course, cancel a whole life policy at any time you choose and be paid the amount of cash value it has built in. Individuals sometimes "cash in" a whole life policy at the time of their retirement when the cash value can be taken out either as a lump sum or in installments called annuities. These are the so-called **living benefits** of a whole life policy—the opposite of death benefits. The death benefit of a life insurance policy is obviously the insurance you have purchased that is payable to your beneficiary upon your death. The living benefit, on the other hand, includes the possibility of converting an ordinary policy into some sort of lump-sum payment or retirement income. In any one year, up to 60 percent of all insurance company payments are in the form of these so-called living benefits.

Note that the level premium for a whole life policy is paid throughout the life of the policyholder—unless you reach the ripe old age of, say, 95 or 100.

Living benefits
Benefits paid on a whole life insurance policy while the person is living. Living benefits include fixed and variable annuities.

Borrowing on Your Cash Value One feature of a whole life insurance policy is that you can borrow on its cash value any time you want. The interest rate on such loans is relatively favorable. If you should die while the loan is outstanding, however, the sum paid to your beneficiary is reduced by the amount of the loan. In any event, the borrowing power given to you by the cash value of a whole life insurance policy can be considered a type of cushion against financial emergencies. Note that if you ever have to drop a whole life insurance policy because you are unable to pay the premiums or because you need its cash value, you most certainly will take a loss. And, of course, you will give up the insurance protection.

When You Reach Retirement Age When you reach retirement age, you may maintain all or part of your death benefit by

1. Choosing protection for the rest of your life, but at a lower value.
2. Choosing full protection, but for a limited number of years in the future.

Or you may accept a living benefit by

3. Choosing a cash settlement that gives back whatever savings and dividends have not been used to pay off the insurance company for excessive costs it has incurred for your particular age group.
4. Choosing to convert the whole life policy into an annuity where a specified amount of income is given to you each year for a certain number of years.

Death Benefits In most life insurance policies, you specify a beneficiary who receives the death benefits of that policy. If you buy a $10,000 ordinary life policy and do not borrow any money on it, your beneficiary will receive $10,000 when you die. However, certain options can be used for settling a life insurance policy. Before you purchase any insurance policy, you should discuss the particular settlement terms that are available with the underwriter of that insurance. Generally, there are four optional settlement plans.

▶ **Plan 1:** Lump-sum payment.

▶ **Plan 2:** The face value (principal) of the insurance policy is retained by the insurance company, but a small interest payment is made to the beneficiary for a certain number of years or for life. Then the principal is paid to the children or according to the terms in the contract.

▶ **Plan 3:** The face value is paid to the beneficiary in the form of installments, either annually, semiannually, quarterly, or monthly. The company makes regular payments of equal amounts until the fund is used up. In the meantime, the company adds interest on the money remaining to be paid out. There are two types of options here. Each payment is for a specific amount where the payments are spread out over a specific time period. If each payment is made for a specific amount, then the length of time during which the payment will be made depends on the amount of the income payment, the face value of the policy, and the rate of interest guaranteed on the policy. If payments are spread out over a given time period, then the amount of each payment depends on the number of years the income is to be paid, the face value of your policy, and the rate of interest guaranteed on the policy.

▶ **Plan 4:** Regular life income is paid to the beneficiary. The insurance company guarantees a specified number of payments that will total the face value of the policy. If the beneficiary dies before the guaranteed payments have been made, the remainder goes to the estate of the beneficiary or as directed in the contract. This is sometimes called an *annuity plan*.

In sum, whole, straight, or ordinary life insurance gives you pure insurance plus forced savings and, hence, the possibility of retirement income, as can be seen in Exhibit 21–4. You can instead buy pure insurance—that is, term insurance—at a lower cost than whole life. You can invest the difference in your own saving and retirement plans and perhaps be better off (or, at least, no worse off) if you can get a higher rate of return on your savings than the insurance company offers. Let's use an example to demonstrate this idea. Suppose Fred bought a $100,000 whole life insurance policy at the age of 40. He paid annual premiums of $532 for 20 years, or a total of $10,640. The cash value of his policy when he reached 60 would be just over $10,000. If Fred could have bought a $100,000 level term policy for an average premium of $232 a year, and had invested the remaining $300 each year at a 5 percent tax-free return, he would have accumulated more than $10,400. He would be roughly $400 better off than if he had simply purchased the whole life policy.

The latest research suggests that whole life can be a sensible long-term investment for those who could otherwise expect their own investments to earn only about 4 percent *after* taxes. But if, on your investments, you can make 5 percent or more after taxes, whole life may not be the type of policy for you. For a summary of the different insurance plans, look at Exhibit 21–5.

Universal Life Insurance

A relatively new type of insurance policy, which combines some aspects of term insurance and some aspects of whole life insurance, is called *universal life*. Every payment, usually called a *contribution*, reflects two deductions made by the issuing life insurance company. The first one is a charge for term insurance protection; the second is for company expenses and profit. The

► Exhibit 21–4   How Whole Life Insurance Works to Provide Both Savings and Protection

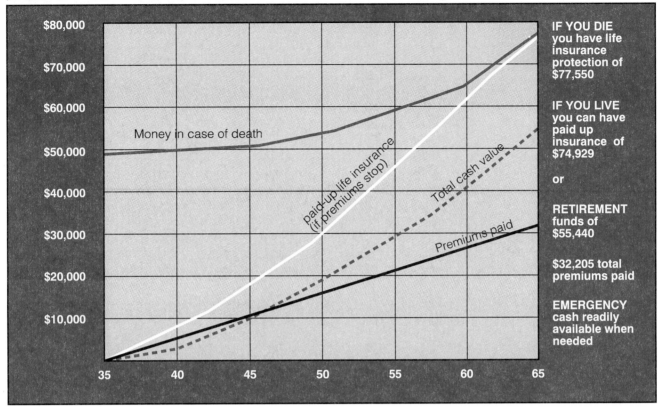

Money in case of death

paid-up life insurance (if premiums stop)

Total cash value

Premiums paid

IF YOU DIE
you have life
insurance
protection of
$77,550

IF YOU LIVE
you can have
paid up
insurance of
$74,929

or

RETIREMENT
funds of
$55,440

$32,205 total
premiums paid

EMERGENCY
cash readily
available when
needed

► Exhibit 21–5   Summary of Insurance Plans

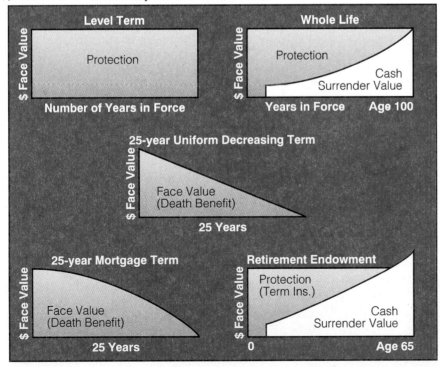

Level Term

$ Face Value

Protection

Number of Years in Force

Whole Life

$ Face Value

Protection

Cash
Surrender Value

Years in Force   Age 100

25-year Uniform Decreasing Term

$ Face Value

Face Value
(Death Benefit)

25 Years

25-year Mortgage Term

$ Face Value

Face Value
(Death Benefit)

25 Years

Retirement Endowment

$ Face Value

Protection
(Term Ins.)

Cash
Surrender Value

0   Age 65

money that remains after these deductions earns interest for the policyholder at a rate determined by the company. The interest-earning money in the policy is called the policy's *cash value*, but that term does not mean the same thing as it does for a traditional whole life insurance policy. With a universal life policy, the cash value grows at a variable interest rate rather than at a predetermined rate.

Consider Exhibit 21–6, which gives an example of a universal life policy issued by the Kemper Investor Life Insurance Company in Chicago. This particular policy, called Real Life I, offers level coverage, level premiums, and, when this example was provided by the company, a 12 percent tax-free cash accumulation.

There are two major advantages of universal life insurance over whole life insurance. The first one is a complete disclosure of the fees that the insurance companies take out for managing the policy. The other is that the interest rate earned on the cash value, at least for now, seems to be higher than for traditional whole life policies. Simply stated, universal life insurance is a term insurance package with an investment fund. As with any package arrangement, you have to ask yourself whether you can get a better deal by purchasing the components separately. In other words, you must decide whether you should buy the best term insurance policy you can find and then find the best investment.

SOME SPECIALIZED INSURANCE POLICIES

Various companies offer a number of special life policies. They include combination plans and variable life insurance policies. Every year, new ones are added and old ones modified. A qualified insurance agent could describe these to you.

Combination Plans

Some companies offer plans that combine different types of insurance, such as a family plan, family income plan, or extra protection policy.

Family Plan   This insurance plan is a combination of some term insurance and some whole life insurance. Under the family plan, every member of the

▶ Exhibit 21–6   **Kemper Investor Life Insurance Company's Real Life I $100,000 Policy**

AGE*	ANNUAL PREMIUM	CASH VALUE 10 YEARS	CASH VALUE 20 YEARS
20	$ 173	$ 805	$ 3,454
30	264	2,384	7,987
35	371	3,562	11,310
40	532	5,087	15,532
45	753	7,192	20,775
50	1,070	9,831	26,813
55	1,467	13,063	34,175
60	2,023	16,716	42,158
65	2,816	20,553	49,900

*Discount three years for women's rate.

family has some insurance; newborns are automatically covered a certain number of days after birth.

Family Income Plan   This combination term insurance and whole life insurance policy is designed to provide supplemental income to the family should the breadwinner die prematurely. In a typical 20-year family income policy plan, if the policyholder dies, his or her beneficiary might receive $10 per month for each $1,000 of the term portion of the policy during the balance of the twenty years. Then, at the end of the twentieth year, the beneficiary would receive the face value of the whole life portion of the policy, either in a lump sum or in monthly installments. There is a variation of this policy called the *family maintenance plan,* in which the monthly payments continue for a full 20-year period *after* the insured dies.

Extra Protection Policy   This policy also combines term and whole life insurance in double, triple, and even quadruple amounts. A triple protection policy, for example, gives, $2,000 of term insurance for each $1,000 of whole life insurance. The term insurance usually continues until age 60 or 65 and then expires; the whole life portion of the policy remains in force. Insurance experts point out that these policies give less protection for the extra premium dollar than the family policies previously mentioned. However, the extra protection continues for a longer time.

Modified Life Policies

Modified life plans generally are sold to newly married couples and young, single professionals just starting out. For the first three to five years, the policy is term insurance. It then converts automatically to whole life protection at a higher premium. In the trade, it is called *Mod 3* and *Mod 5.*

ADJUSTABLE LIFE INSURANCE

One of the newest insurance policies available, adjustable life, presumably offers insurance plans adjusted to each customer's needs and budget. Adjustable life differs from conventional life policies in two ways: You can switch back and forth between whole life and term coverage, and you can change the amount of insurance protection. Basically, you can increase coverage as much as you please if you can pass a medical examination or present evidence of insurability. You can adjust for inflation once every three years by adjusting your coverage and the premium, if you keep the same policy. You can also buy a guaranteed-insurability rider at an extra cost that assures you the right to buy more life insurance in the future regardless of your health.

OTHER TYPES OF LIFE INSURANCE POLICIES

In addition to life insurance that you buy as an individual, you also may be eligible for certain other types of life insurance policies that generally are offered to you at more attractive rates.

Group Insurance

Group insurance is usually term insurance written under a master policy that is issued to either a sponsoring association or an employer. Some types of group insurance are currently available through employers and various fraternal and professional organizations. Per $1,000 of protection, the cost of group insurance is generally lower than individually obtained insurance for many reasons, but primarily because of the lower selling and bookkeeping costs. The selling costs are lower because the employer or sponsoring group does all the selling; there is no commission to be paid to a selling agent. And the bookkeeping costs are lower because, again, the employer or the association may do all the bookkeeping. Generally, no medical examination is required for members of the group unless they want to take out an unusually large amount of group insurance.

Credit Life Insurance

If you take out a loan, in many cases you may be required to buy life insurance in the amount of the loan. The reason is simple: Without such insurance, if you die with part of the loan outstanding, the creditor may have trouble collecting it. But if the creditor is named the beneficiary in the life insurance policy you are required to take out as part of the loan, then the creditor is assured payment of any amount due. The average amount per policy is small, perhaps $2,000. Credit life insurance may seem inexpensive, but it isn't. It typically makes sense only for a person 50 years old or more who lives in a state with a low maximum rate, and then only if an existing insurance program is inadequate. It might, for example, be better than nothing for a person with a health problem who cannot be insured. Most consumers, however, are better off simply upgrading their basic insurance portfolio. Thus, be careful: Your creditor may, in fact, be abusing his or her right to require life insurance on your loan by demanding an overly high premium. Check to see that the rate you are actually paying is commensurate with other group policy rates. If it is not, then the difference you pay should be added to the total finance charge so you can figure out the true percentage rate of interest you are paying on the loan. Although lenders often require borrowers to buy insurance, they might not require you to purchase it through them. If their rates are higher than alternative policies, find out if you are allowed to buy your insurance from a different source.

No matter what type of life insurance you buy, you will be required to complete an application. If you fail to provide complete and accurate information on that application you may not be entitled to benefits under the policy, as illustrated by the Consumer Close-Up.

READING A LIFE INSURANCE CONTRACT

As with any major investment, you should carefully review the life insurance coverage that is provided in your contract with the insurance company (your insurance policy). Of the plethora of clauses and options that can be included in a life insurance policy, we discuss some of the major ones below.

1. *Guaranteed insurability option.* This option, sold with whole life policies, allows the policyholder to purchase additional insurance at specified ages and amounts without having to meet medical qualifications.

2. *Automatic premium loan option.* With this provision, the insurer automatically will pay any premium that is not paid when due. The premium then becomes a loan against the cash value of the policy. This option will

Honesty Is the Best Policy

A few years ago, Michael Berthiaume applied for mortgage life insurance with the Minnesota Mutual Life Insurance Company. Berthiaume wanted to make sure that if he should die, the balance due on his mortgage (about $44,000) would be covered. The insurance company did not require Berthiaume to take a physical examination for the policy, but he did have to answer questions concerning his health status on the application. One of the questions was whether the applicant had ever been treated for, or diagnosed as having, high blood pressure. Although four months earlier Berthiaume had been advised by his doctor that he had hypertension, he nonetheless answered "no" to the question. In a word, he lied.

Eight months later, Berthiaume died. When his widow submitted a claim for the mortgage insurance, however, she was denied payment. The company stated that it had no obligations under the policy because while it was investigating the claim, it discovered that Berthiaume had misrepresented his health status on the application. Under Minnesota law (and in most other states), an insurer can avoid obligations under a policy if an applicant misstates necessary information or misleads the insurance company into accepting a risk of which it is not aware. Hypertensive individuals find it difficult to obtain insurance coverage because they present a higher risk of death. When they do obtain insurance, they usually have to pay twice what other individuals do for the coverage.

Obviously, insurance companies, like other businesses, have an eye toward profits. The fewer claims they have to pay, the higher those profits, and therefore it is in their interest to investigate insurance claims carefully to see if they might uncover a problem that would allow them to avoid payment. What this means for you, the consumer, is that you must be careful not to misstate facts on an insurance application. Honesty is normally always the best policy, but especially so when it comes to insurance applications.

---

continue until a total of the automatic loans is equal to the cash value; then the policy is terminated.

3. *Convertibility.* A clause or option applied to term insurance policies that allows you to switch the policy to whole life or endowment at standard premium rates regardless of any change in your health.

4. *Accidental death or double indemnity.* An additional sum that is paid to your beneficiary if you die as the result of an accident. Because it usually doubles the face amount of the policy, it is called *double indemnity.* Most people who have evaluated insurance believe double-indemnity insurance costs more than it is worth.

5. *Incontestability.* Most policies have a clause that prohibits the company from challenging statements made in your application after two years if you should die; thus, even if you made false statements, it cannot nullify the policy after a stated period.

6. *Guaranteed renewability.* A clause typically applied to renewable term insurance, requiring that the insurance company renew the term policy for a specified number of term periods, even if there has been a significant change in the health of the insured.

7. *Settlement options.* This portion of your policy details the methods by which the death benefits can be paid to your beneficiary.

8. *Grace period.* This is the period of time that your life insurance will remain in force if your premium is overdue.

9. *Suicide.* In this clause, the insurance company stipulates what will happen should you commit suicide. The clause will limit the insurance company's liability in such a case.

10. *Misstatement of age.* This provision states that if you have given an incorrect age on your policy application, the death benefit will be adjusted to reflect your correct age.

11. *Reinstatement.* This clause describes the way in which your policy, should it lapse for any reason, can be reinstated.

CHOOSING A SOUND LIFE INSURANCE COMPANY

How would you feel if you had paid thousands of dollars into an insurance policy only to have the company fail just before you were ready to retire? Unfortunately, this is exactly what has happened with increasing frequency in recent years. The best way to avoid this problem is by carefully checking out the financial condition of insurance companies before you purchase a policy.

Money "saved" in life insurance policies is not insured by any federal government agency like the FDIC. Most states have "guaranty funds" that pay off customers of failed insurance companies for amounts up to, but not over, $100,000. When life insurance companies fail in states with guaranty funds, policyholders will receive their money, but they may be required to wait years while courts review the situation and make decisions. In 1990 Alaska, California, Colorado, Louisiana, New Jersey, Wyoming and Washington, D.C., had no guaranty funds. When insurance companies fail in these states, settlements might never come.

Although most life insurance companies are financially strong, it is worth your time to be sure that you don't choose one that isn't. Several firms rate insurance-company strength, including

Best's Insurance Reports
May be found at larger libraries or by calling
(908) 439-2200

Standard & Poors Corporation
26 Broadway
New York, NY 10004
Phone (212) 208-1592

Duff & Phels, Inc.
55 E. Monroe St.
Chicago, IL 60603
Phone (312) 263-2610

Moodys Investors Service
99 Church St.
New York, NY 10007
Phone (212) 553-0377

The Insurance Forum
P.O. Box 245
Ellettsville, IN 47429
(812) 876-6502

INVOLUNTARY BENEFIT PROGRAMS—
THE CASE OF SOCIAL SECURITY

During the depths of the Depression, the nation realized that many people had not provided for themselves in case of emergencies. It also realized that a large percentage of the elderly population unable to rely on its children for support became destitute. In an effort to prevent a recurrence of so much pain and suffering by elderly people, Congress passed the Social Security Act of 1935. By January 1940, when the first monthly benefit started, only 22,000 people received payments. Today, however, well over 90 percent of people 65 or older are receiving Social Security benefits or *could* receive them if they were not still working. If U.S. population growth continues to slow down, the average age of the population will continue to rise. Hence, the total number of people eligible for and receiving Social Security will increase as a percentage of the total population. Exhibit 21–7 shows the past and projected percentage of the population 65 and over.

We have called this section "Involuntary Benefit Programs" because you and I, with few exceptions, have no choice. If we work, we must participate in the Social Security program. Self-employed people were at one time able to avoid it, but today they must pay self-employment Social Security taxes if they do not work for someone else. If you work for someone else, your employer must file Social Security taxes for you if you earn over $50 in any quarter. Of the people earning money in the United States, those who contribute to Social Security make up fully 95 percent.

The Social Security Act provides benefits for old-age retirement, survivors, disability, and hospital insurance. It is therefore sometimes called the **OASDHI.** It is essentially an **income transfer** program, financed out of compulsory payroll taxes levied on both employers and employees: Those who are employed transfer income to those who are no longer employed. You pay for Social Security while working and receive the old-age benefits after retirement. The benefit payments usually are made to those reaching retirement age. Also, when the insured worker dies, benefits accrue to his or her survivors. Special benefits provide for disabled workers. Additionally, Social Security now provides for Medicare, which was discussed in Chapter 19.

The Social Security Act of 1935 also provided for the establishment of an unemployment insurance system. Unemployment insurance is not really a federally operated program. Rather, it is left to the states to establish and operate such programs. Although all fifty states have these programs, they vary widely in the extent and the amount of payments made. Programs are basically financed by taxes on employers; these taxes average about 2 percent of total payroll. A worker who finds himself or herself unemployed may become eligible for benefit payments. The size of these payments and the number of weeks they can be received vary from state to state.

OASDHI

Old Age, Survivors, Disability, and Hospital Insurance—the government name for Social Security insurance.

Income transfer

A transfer of income from some individuals in the economy to other individuals. This is generally done by the government. It is a transfer in the sense that no current services are rendered by the recipients. Unemployment insurance, for example, is an income transfer to unemployed individuals.

Basic Benefits of Social Security

In Consumer Issue S, you will learn where to get information with which to figure, tentatively, the benefits that you are allowed under Social Security. (The predictions must be tentative because Congress frequently changes the benefits.) Essentially, Social Security is a form of life insurance. Every time you have a child, the maximum life insurance benefit of Social Security is auto-

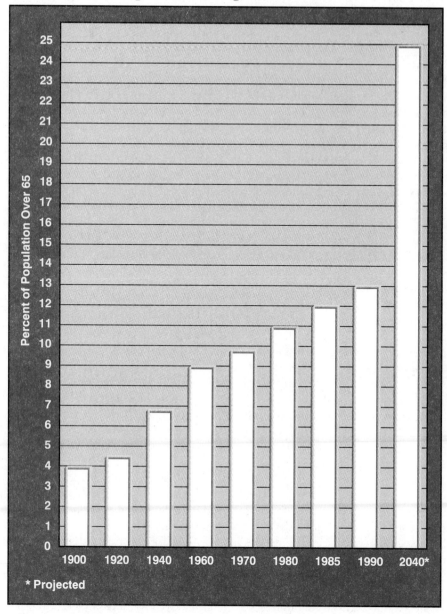

matically restored, and its term is automatically increased to a potential 21 years. Here is what you can expect from Social Security:

1. Medicare payments in the future.

2. If you should die, payments to your beneficiary.

3. Payments to you or your dependents if you are totally disabled and unable to work.

4. A retirement annuity—that is, a payment of a certain amount of money every month after you retire until you die. (This payment, however, is legislated by Congress and can be changed by Congress.)

5. If you die, a modest lump-sum payment, presumably to take care of burial expenses.

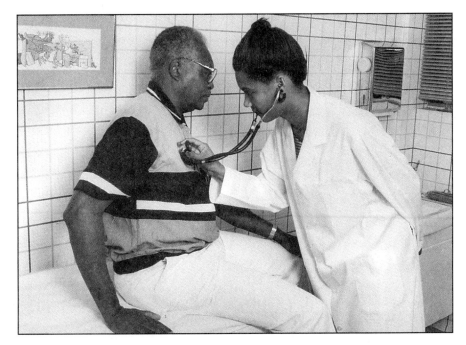

Staying fit is important to people's health no matter how old they are. However, as people grow older their need for medical care usually increases. How much assistance do you believe society owes retired Americans in paying their medical expenses? How much do you believe they should pay from their own resources?

Whenever you figure out your insurance needs, you must consult the basic coverage that you have on your Social Security. You will learn how to do that in Consumer Issue S.

How Social Security Is Paid

In theory, Social Security is supported by a tax on the employee's income that is matched by the employer. The Social Security tax is indicated on your payroll receipt as FICA—Federal Insurance Contributions Act. When this tax was first levied, it was 1 percent of earnings up to $3,000. By 1963 the percentage rate had increased to 3.625 percent, and the rate has continued to climb. In 1991 a 7.65 percent tax was placed on each employee's wages up to a maximum of $53,400 to pay for Social Security and Medicare. Income between $53,400 and $125,000 was taxed at a 2.9 percent rate for Medicare. Exhibit 21–8 shows the growth in employees' Social Security withholding rates. Employers contribute matching amounts to the amounts paid by employees. (You must realize, though, that employees pay more for the program, because their wages could be higher if the employer did not have to contribute.) Self-employed individuals, since they are effectively both the employer and the employee, pay twice what other employees contribute. In 1990 self-employed persons paid 15.3 percent (2 × 7.65 percent) of their earned income to Social Security (but got a tax credit for the employer's part).

You may recall from Chapter 9 that taxes which fall more heavily on people with lower incomes are regressive. Social Security taxes are regressive because once people's incomes exceed the maximum taxable amount, they pay no more taxes. In 1991 a person who earned $50,000 paid $3,825, or 7.65 percent in Social Security and Medicare taxes; a person who earned $70,000 paid $4,566.50, or 6.52 percent; while a person who earned $150,000 paid $6,161.50, or 4.11 percent. This is clearly a regressive tax structure.

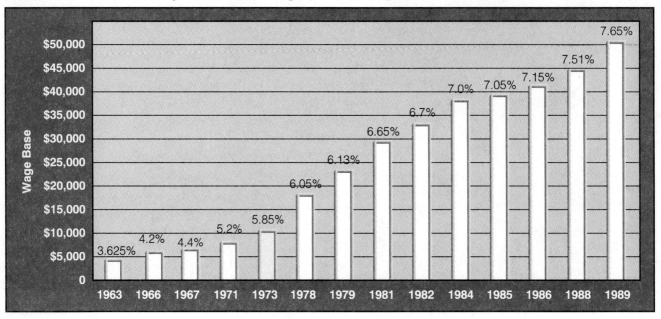

If You Work After 65, You May Not Get Paid

The Social Security Act, as it currently stands, penalizes you tremendously if you decide to work past the retirement age: Your Social Security check is reduced after you earn more than $8,880. As of 1990, if your earned income exceeds that figure, Social Security benefits are reduced $1 for every $3 above the exempt amount. "Earned" here means income that is made as a wage earner, not as dividends, interest, or pensions. If you decide to invest a lot of money, you can be making millions of dollars and still get full Social Security. But if you decide to work hard and continue getting wages, you may lose all your Social Security payments, depending on how much you earn. It is conceivable that you could work till the age of 70 and never get one penny in benefits from Social Security, even though you were forced to pay in for it your entire working life. Your decision to work after the retirement age certainly will be influenced by this highly regressive taxation system. We say "taxation system" because you are obviously taxed if, for every dollar you earn, you lose 33.3 cents in Social Security benefits. That sounds like a tax rate of 33.3 percent, does it not? (And it is in addition to taxes that you pay already, such as Social Security and income taxes.) For people between the ages of 62 and 65, the earnings limitation as of 1990 was $6,480. For people over age 70, this earnings limitation is eliminated.

This is one aspect of the Social Security program that many observers feel is unfair, because it penalizes older people for working. Also, as Professor Carolyn Shaw Bell of Wellesley College points out, the Social Security system is not insurance but, rather, a transfer. People who are working pay Social Security taxes. People who get Social Security benefits receive the income that is taxed away. Essentially, it is a subsidy by younger workers to older, retired people. There is also a transfer from those who continue to work after retirement age to their peers who do not work.

Problems with Social Security

A number of respected authorities have reached some pretty depressing conclusions about Social Security. In the first place, you have to remember that Social Security is not really an insurance policy in the sense that you are guaranteed a certain amount of money. Your dependents get that amount of money only if you die, just as with a regular insurance policy; but, if you live, you get retirement payments, the amount of which are established by Congress and based on how much money you have paid in when you were employed. Future legislators may not be as generous as past legislators, so you may find yourself with a very small retirement income if you rely only on Social Security.

There Will Always Be a Problem with Social Security

No matter what Congress does, there will always be a problem with our Social Security system. Whenever the government sets up a system that is not actuarially sound, that system eventually will be in trouble. As long as Congress continues to increase benefits, while, at the same time, the labor force grows less rapidly than the number of retirees, financial strain will plague the system. Every reform that Congress has introduced for Social Security has been designed to last 20 or 30 years. Yet, within several years, the system is in financial trouble again. You can be certain that, if you are under the age of 40, your retirement benefits from Social Security will not be as generous as they have been for those who have already retired and for those who are over the age of 40.

▶ SUMMARY

1. The major hazards to financial security are illness, accident, unemployment, old age, premature death of the person providing financial support, desertion, divorce, and unexpected catastrophic expenses.

2. Life insurance can take many forms, the most popular being term and whole life.

3. Term insurance is generally for a five-year period, after which time a higher premium must be paid to obtain the same face value in insurance because the probability of death increases as the individual becomes older.

4. Whole, straight, or ordinary life insurance involves pure protection in addition to a savings plan whereby part of your premiums are put into investments that return interest to the policyholder. At any time, a whole life policyholder has a cash value in his or her policy.

5. Whole life insurance has living benefits. You can, for example, borrow on your cash value; you can get protection for the rest of your life at retirement; you can get a cash settlement; or you can convert your whole life policy to a stream of income—called an annuity—over a certain period of time.

6. Death benefits can be paid to your beneficiaries in a lump sum equal to the face value, as interest on the face value of the insurance policy plus principal at the end of a specific period, or in installments until the face value has been paid.

7. There are several specialized life insurance policies, such as a family plan and a family income plan.

8. Social Security is a form of social insurance in the United States. It provides for living and death benefits.

9. Social Security is not an insurance policy in the normal sense of the word. Basically, contributions to Social Security are merely transfers of income from those who work to those who do not work.

10. Social Security taxes are paid both by the employer and the employee. In the economy as a whole, however, employees receive salaries that are lowered by the amount that employers must pay to Social Security. After all, that payment is a cost of hiring employees.

11. Under current law, individuals from ages 65 to 70 who work often lose benefits from Social Security because their incomes are too high. In addition, they continue to pay Social Security taxes.

▶ QUESTIONS FOR THOUGHT AND DISCUSSION

1. Who do you think should have life insurance?

2. Why would an insurance salesperson try to sell a whole life policy?

3. Why is a life insurance premium cheaper for college students than for older adults?

4. When would it be worthwhile to borrow on the cash value of a whole life insurance policy?

5. Do you know anybody who would be a good candidate for limited payment whole life insurance? Would you ever be a good candidate?

6. Why would someone choose decreasing term insurance with a constant premium rather than level term insurance with an increasing premium?

7. When do you think it would be appropriate to have a convertibility feature in your term insurance policy? That is, when do you think it would be advantageous to pay the extra price to have the option of changing your term insurance to whole life insurance?

8. Why do you think group insurance is cheaper than individually written insurance?

9. Do you think Social Security is a good deal?

▶ THINGS TO DO

1. Try to determine whether life insurance companies make a higher profit than other companies in the United States.

2. Phone several life insurance agents in your area and ask what the premium cost is of a $50,000 straight or whole life insurance policy. Is there a great variation?

3. Check newspaper ads for mail-order life insurance policies. In light of the analysis presented in this chapter, how do you interpret the claims made?

4. Select two nationally prominent politicians and compare their stands on Social Security measures. Credit your sources of information.

▶ APPLICATION

Imagine that you are of retirement age at the present. List the types and amounts of spending you believe you would need to make in order to maintain a reasonable standard of living for yourself and your spouse. Assume that Social Security will provide half of this amount. Describe the plans you should have made when you were young that would have allowed you to pay the other half of this amount from your own resources now that you have retired.

► SELECTED READINGS

► American Council of Life Insurance. *Life Insurance Fact Book*. Washington, DC: American Council of Life Insurance. Published annually.

► "Are You Really Insured?" *Business Week,* August 5, 1991, pp. 42–48.

► Belsky G. "Don't Gamble with Your Life Insurance." *Money,* July 1991, pp. 116–120.

► Dacy, Norman F. *What's Wrong With Your Life Insurance?* New York: Macmillan, 1989.

► Davis, K., and M. D. Wilcox. "Life Insurance: What to Do Now." *Kiplinger's Personal Finance Magazine,* November 1991, pp. 45–46.

► Fried, C. A. "How to Avoid Getting Stung on Your Life Insurance." *Money,* Year End 1991, pp. 129–131.

► *An Introduction to Social Security.* Available free from the Consumer Information Center, Pueblo, CO 81002.

► Lieberman T. *Life Insurance: How to Buy the Right Policy from the Right Company at the Right Price.* New York: Consumer Reports Books, 1988.

► Loeb, Marshall. "Your Insurance." *Marshall Loeb's 1992 Money Guide.* Boston: Little, Brown, 1992, pp. 539–545.

► Martz, Larry, and Rich Thomas. "Fixing Social Security." *Newsweek,* May 7, 1990, pp. 54–57.

► Schultz, Ellen E. and Karen Slater. "In Buying Insurance, Think Quality First." *The Wall Street Journal,* July 16, 1991, p. C1.

► *Social Security: How It Works for You.* Available free from the Consumer Information Center, Pueblo, CO 81002.

► *Taking a Bite out of Insurance.* Available for $11.95 from the National Insurance Consumer Organization, 121 N. Payne St., Alexandria, VA 22314.

► Thompson, Terri. "Checking Up on Life Insurers." *U.S. News & World Report,* May 28, 1990, pp. 64–68.

► Teitelbaum, R. S. "How Safe Is Your Insurance?" *Fortune,* September 9, 1991, pp. 137–138.

How to Meet Your Insurance Needs

GLOSSARY

INTEREST-ADJUSTED COST (IAC) An insurance cost index that takes account of dividends, interest, and earnings of the policy.

Before you figure out how much insurance you should buy, what type it should be, and where you should get it, first consider who should be insured in your family. You have to take into account the Social Security benefits you have coming, and that sometimes is not easy. You then have to look at the actual economic (or financial) dependency that anybody has on a particular member of a spending unit. If you are a single college student, for example, it is usually not recommended that you have any insurance at all (unless you want to use it as a forced savings mechanism or as insurance against becoming medically uninsurable later on in life). By the same token, it is usually pointless for a family to insure its children unless the children contribute a substantial amount to the family income. If one of them dies, the family's earning power generally will not fall. This is not necessarily true for a homemaker, however, who frequently contributes to the family earnings stream by employment outside the home, as well as implicitly through the value of services rendered to the family. In this case, the family may want to take out an insurance policy on the homemaker's life. The basic wage earner should, of course, be the one with the most insurance because, if he or she dies prematurely, the *spending unit* will suffer the greatest loss.

▶ SOME INSURANCE BUYING RULES

Insurance is another item competing for your consumer dollar, just as is a new bicycle, a new car, or a new house. When you make an expenditure on life insurance, you obtain a certain amount of satisfaction in knowing that your dependents will be financially secure in the event of your premature death. Note, however, that there are other possible uses of these same funds that also yield satisfaction; thus, there is no pat answer or formula that will tell you exactly how much insurance is best for you.

In determining the type and amount of insurance coverage you need, the following rules should be considered.

1. Identify the major risks that you and your family reasonably face; insure them according to the *potential* loss they can produce.
2. Insure big losses, not small ones.
3. Never buy an insurance policy until you have compared at least two companies (and perhaps more), not only on the costs but also on the terms of coverage. Use the **interest-adjusted cost** figure for comparison.
4. Limit your losses and control your risks through preventive measures.

5. *Buy* insurance; don't have it sold to you.

▶ ARE YOU UNDERINSURED?

There is a good chance that you are underinsured if anybody depends on you for even part of his or her livelihood. If, however, you live alone or are young and unmarried, or even are married but your spouse also contributes to the family kitty, then you may not need much (if any) life insurance. If you are married and have children, or a spouse who depends on you for at least part of his or her income, then you probably should have some form of life insurance. You should first realize that Social Security is the basis of all your protection needs, assuming you are covered by Social Security. You will have to find out from your local Social Security office exactly what kinds of benefits your dependents have coming in case of your death.

In this Consumer Issue we make the same assumption that you yourself should make when trying to figure out your insurance needs: Assume that you drop dead tomorrow. How much would be left to your dependents, in what form, and over what period? This is not an easy thing to figure out, so plan on spending some time at it. You may want to work it out with an insurance agent, but you can probably do it on you own.

▶ DETERMINING YOUR FUTURE SOCIAL SECURITY INCOME

The first thing you should do is obtain from the Social Security Administration a "Request for Earnings and Benefit Estimate Statement" like the one pictured in Exhibit S–1. This can be obtained from your local Social Security office or by calling the Social Security Administration at (800) 772-1213 (toll free). Three to four

---

SOCIAL SECURITY ADMINISTRATION

Form Approved
OMB No. 0960-0466 ☐ **SP**

Request for Earnings and Benefit Estimate Statement

To receive a free statement of your earnings covered by Social Security and your estimated future benefits, all you need to do is fill out this form. Please print or type your answers. When you have completed the form, fold it and mail it to us.

1. Name shown on your Social Security card:

First Name _____ Middle Initial _____

Last Name Only _____

2. Your Social Security number as shown on your card:

☐☐☐ – ☐☐ – ☐☐☐☐

3. Your date of birth _____ _____ _____
   Month   Day   Year

4. Other Social Security numbers you have used:

☐☐☐ – ☐☐ – ☐☐☐☐
☐☐☐ – ☐☐ – ☐☐☐☐

5. Your sex: ☐ Male ☐ Female

6. Other names you have used (*including a maiden name*):

_____
_____

7. Show your actual earnings for last year and your estimated earnings for this year. Include only wages and/or net self-employment income covered by Social Security.

   A. Last year's actual earnings: (*Dollars Only*)

   $ ☐☐☐☐,☐☐☐ . ☐0☐0

   B. This year's estimated earnings: (*Dollars Only*)

   $ ☐☐☐☐,☐☐☐ . ☐0☐0

8. Show the age at which you plan to retire:

   ☐☐ (*Show only one age*)

9. Below, show the average yearly amount you think you will earn between now and when you plan to retire. We will add your estimate of future earnings to those earnings already on our records to give you the best possible estimate.

   Enter a yearly average, not your total future lifetime earnings. Only show earnings covered by Social Security. Do not add cost-of-living, performance or scheduled pay increases or bonuses. The reason for this is that we estimate retirement benefits in today's dollars, but adjust them to account for average wage growth in the national economy.

   However, if you expect to earn significantly more or less in the future due to promotions, job changes, part-time work, or an absence from the work force, enter the amount in today's dollars that most closely reflects your future average yearly earnings.

   Most people should enter the same amount they are earning now (the amount in 7B).

   Future average yearly earnings: (*Dollars Only*)

   $ ☐☐☐,☐☐☐ . ☐0☐0

10. Address where you want us to send the statement.

    Name _____

    Street Address (Include Apt. No., P.O. Box, or Rural Route) _____

    City _____ State _____ Zip Code _____

11. ☐ Please check this box if you want to get your statement in Spanish instead of English.

I am asking for information about my own Social Security record or the record of a person I am authorized to represent. I understand that if I deliberately request information under false pretenses I may be guilty of a federal crime and could be fined and/or imprisoned. I authorize you to use a contractor to send the statement of earnings and benefit estimates to the person named in item 10.

Please sign your name (Do not print)
►
Signature
Date   (Area Code) Daytime Telephone No.

Form SSA-7004-SM (2-93) Destroy Prior Editions

---

weeks after you have filled out and returned this form to the Social Security Administration, you will receive in the mail a Social Security information statement containing the following facts:

1. A summary of all contributions you have made each year to Social Security. (Check this over carefully to make sure that all of your payments have been recorded.)
2. Your monthly benefit if you retire at the ages of 62, 65, or 70, respectively.

3. Survivors' benefits—the amount that your children and your spouse would receive each month following your death.
4. The amount of disability benefits per month that you and your family are entitled to.

Remember, unless you are now at retirement age, you will be able to obtain only a rough estimate. The calculations used to determine retirement benefits make certain assumptions that may or may not apply to you—regarding your health, your

average pay increases, how continuously you work, and a fixed inflation rate. In general, experts say that if you earn at or above the maximum taxable amount, you can count on Social Security to replace 22 percent of your earnings. That means, if you are currently earning $42,000 and plan to retire next year, you would receive approximately $9,240 in Social Security benefits—which would replace 22 percent of your earnings. On the other hand, if you are receiving your highest income at a current salary of $16,000 and plan to retire next year, you could expect to receive $6,300 in retirement benefits, or 40 percent of your current earnings.

Now that you have this information, you can figure out the financial condition of your family. To do this, look at Consumer Issue N in which we discuss how net-worth statements are calculated when you apply for a loan. Figuring out your net worth gives you a starting point.

You now have two major details of your financial situation in case you have dependents and die tomorrow—Social Security payments to your dependents and a net worth that is left to them. Now you must figure out a monthly income goal for a spouse and children under 18, a lump-sum education-fund goal for each child, a monthly retirement-income goal for a widow or widower starting at age 62, and a monthly income goal, if any, for a widow or widower between child-rearing and retirement. This latter is optional, depending on whether or not the family wants the widow or widower to have to work.

▶ FIGURING OUT HOW MUCH INSURANCE TO BUY

Neither you nor anyone else can estimate *exactly* how much life insurance you should buy. That depends not only on all the factors already mentioned but also on how "safe" you want to be. After all, buying insurance means that part of your income can no longer be used for other purchases. You have to decide how much you want to give up in order to be fully insured. Nonetheless, you can get a general idea of how much life insurance you need by using a method developed by financial counselors at the First National City Bank in New York (Citibank). Citibank's economists, personnel, and insurance specialists have calculated that a family can maintain its standard of living with an after-tax income of 75 percent of its current after-tax income, should the breadwinner die. Citibank believes that, if a family winds up with less than 60 percent of the pre-death level of after-tax income, its living standard will be seriously lowered. Thus, in Exhibit S–2 there are net-income-replacement columns labeled 75 percent and 60 percent. These are the target net after-tax income-replacement levels that insurance should provide. This chart basically tells you how many times your current gross salary you should own in life insurance to provide 75 or 60 percent of your current after-tax income for your family should you die. The chart assumes that your

▶ Exhibit S–2 **The Multiples of Salary Chart (for Net Income Replacement)**

To calculate the amount of life insurance needed for either net-replacement level in the chart below, multiply your present gross salary by the number under that level.

If your gross income or spouse's age falls between the figures shown, take an average between the multiples for nearest salaries and ages.

Social Security benefits will be part of both levels.

If personal liquid assets (savings, predictable inheritance, retirement plan, investment, etc.) equal one year of gross salary or less, use them as part of the fund for the small-emergency reserve and final expenses. If they equal more than one year, subtract that extra amount from the insurance needed to replace income.

People with no personal assets who can't afford the 75 percent level might try for at least 60 percent. The average family would then face some lowering in level of living but wouldn't be financially devastated.

Your Present Gross Earnings	PRESENT AGE OF SPOUSE							
	25 Years*		35 Years*		45 Years*		55 Years†	
	75%	60%	75%	60%	75%	60%	75%	60%
$ 7,500	4.0	3.0	5.5	4.0	7.5	5.5	6.5	4.5
9,000	4.0	3.0	5.5	4.0	7.5	5.5	6.5	4.5
15,000	4.5	3.0	6.5	4.5	8.0	6.0	7.0	5.5
23,500	6.5	4.5	8.0	5.5	8.5	6.5	7.5	5.5
30,000	7.5	5.0	8.0	6.0	8.5	6.5	7.0	5.5
40,000	7.5	5.0	8.0	6.0	8.0	6.0	7.0	5.5
65,000	7.5	5.5	7.5	6.0	7.5	5.0	6.5	5.0

*Assuming federal income taxes for a family of four (two children). There are four exemptions and the standard deductions. State and local taxes are disregarded.
†Assuming you have only two exemptions. (Any children are now grown.)
Reprinted by permission of First National City Bank, New York.

family will also receive Social Security benefits. In figuring out the chart, Citibank's staff assumed that insurance proceeds would be invested to produce, after inflation, a rate of return of 5 percent a year. Moreover, it is assumed that the principal from the insurance policy gradually would be eaten up, so it would disappear by the time of the surviving spouse's death.

Take an example. If your spouse is 25 years old, your gross earnings are $30,000 a year, and you wish to provide him or her with 60 percent of your after-tax income if you were to die, you need to have in force five times your gross earnings, or $150,000 worth of life insurance. This figure may seem low, but it takes into account the higher Social Security benefit that a younger spouse would obtain.

▶ WHAT TYPE OF INSURANCE SHOULD YOU BUY?

Suppose you decide you need $50,000 worth of life insurance. Which type should you purchase? Of the several life insurance plans just discussed, the most important are term, whole life and universal life. All but term insurance include some element of saving. Thus, you are not only buying pure insurance, you are also investing and getting a rate of return. Your decision whether to buy pure insurance or to buy savings will determine the payments you must make to the insurance company. The cheapest way to buy insurance is, of course, to buy term, because that way you buy only protection. If you already have a satisfactory savings program, you may not wish to save additional sums with an insurance company, since you can get a higher rate of return by going to other sources.

Consumers Union points out, as do several other research organizations, that if purchasing whole life insurance is compared with buying term and investing the difference— that is, the difference between the whole life premium and the lower term premium—the combination of term and other investments will yield a larger sum of money at the end of any period.

Insurance salespersons, however, argue persuasively that you should buy whole life, not term, insurance. They will say that whole life is a bargain, or even "free," because you eventually get back much or all of your money. Note, however, that if you die, your beneficiary will get only the face value on the policy, not the additional cash value. Salespersons use the cash-value aspect of whole life to tout its desirability over term insurance. Because term has no cash value, salespeople will tell you that buying it is "just throwing money down the drain." This "down the drain" argument ignores the fact that the term premiums are much lower than whole life premiums in the early years. For a man 25 years old, whole life premiums in the early years may cost three to four times more than term premiums.

▶ Life Insurance Sold on Campus

Insurance agents have become familiar figures on many campuses, where they sometimes contact students four to six times a year. The insurance agent approaches a premium-paying problem of the poor student by offering to finance on credit the first annual premium and even the second, with a loan to be paid off perhaps five years later. This student policyholder typically signs a policy assignment form, which makes the insurance company the first beneficiary if the student dies. Thus, the insurance company will make sure that it can collect the unpaid premium and interest. Generally, college students are advised not to buy life insurance because they generally have no dependents.

Additionally, the cost of campus life insurance is extremely high compared with policies available to the general public. If a college student has to be insured, he or she should look at a standard life insurance policy, either term or whole life.

▶ The Forced-Savings Aspect of Insurance

If you like the idea of having forced savings, then buying whole life insurance may be the way to do it. You'll feel compelled to pay the insurance premiums, and you know that part of the premium goes to a savings plan. The lower rate of return on savings left with an insurance company is compensated for by the fact that you have any savings at all, savings that you would not have had otherwise because you find it difficult, if not impossible, to save.

You do have other options. In some instances, you can have your employer credit union take out a payroll deduction every month to put in your credit union account. You can also have your employer take out a certain amount of money each month for U.S. Savings Bonds. In both instances, you will have more liquidity if you need it than if an insurance company had been doing your forced saving for you. (But if you don't trust yourself, you may prefer less liquidity.)

▶ SOME ADDITIONAL CONSIDERATIONS

A fact we have not yet mentioned about a permanent or whole life insurance policy contract is that it is essentially a piece of property and has certain characteristics that are perhaps unique. Under current law, provided that the permanent insurance plan is set up properly, it can accumulate income, tax-free: Interest on cash value is not taxable as current income. Essentially, then, you get a higher return than is actually shown in your life insurance savings plan because you are not paying a tax on the savings you are accumulating. Remember, if you have a regular savings account, you have to pay federal and sometimes state income tax on the interest earnings of that account.

Remember, too, that death benefits on ordinary or straight life insurance policies usually go to age 100; except in very rare cases, there is always going to be a death benefit.

▶ TAKE ADVANTAGE OF GROUP PLANS

Whenever you can take advantage of group term insurance plans, you probably should do so to take care of at least part of your life insurance needs. For reasons mentioned in the previous chapter, group insurance is generally cheaper than individually issued insurance (unless you happen to be significantly younger than the average age of the group).

▶ SHOPPING AROUND FOR INSURANCE

It generally is unwise to buy from the first insurance salesperson to knock on your door. Because large sums of money may be involved, look over several plans. Be aware, however, that life insurance policies are incredibly complex. Seek out a knowledgeable insurance salesperson who represents a large number of companies and who can explain clearly the benefits of each program

and the average annual costs per $1,000 of five-year renewable term insurance.

▶ Where to Find Information

A good source of information on comparative life insurance costs and coverage is *How To Save Money in Life Insurance,* a 50-page book published by the National Insurance Consumer Organization (NICO). This guide offers a wealth of information on how insurance functions, how it is sold, and what appropriate insurance costs are for people in different age groups. To order a copy, send $13.95 to NICO at 121 N. Payne St., Alexandria, VA 22314, or call (703) 549-8050.

To check the overall performance and financial stability of insurance companies, your best resource is *Best's Insurance Reports,* published buy A. M. Best Company and available in most libraries. *Best's* rates insurers from A+ all the way down to "omitted," and, although the guide isn't infallible, it is one of the best available for consumers shopping for life insurance. The National Association of Insurance Commissioners (NAIC) compiles a "watch list" that contains the names of financially troubled insurance companies— companies that you should therefore avoid. The list costs $5.00 and can be obtained by writing to The Insurance Forum, P.O. Box 245, Elletsville, IN 47429. By checking this list and *Best's Insurance Reports* before purchasing life insurance, you stand a greater chance of avoiding the plight that befalls some consumers when their insurance companies go bankrupt. Although most states[1]

1. Currently, all states but Alaska, Arkansas, California, Colorado, Louisiana, Missouri, New Jersey, Ohio, South Dakota, Tennessee, Wyoming, and the District of Columbia have such funds.

have established guaranty funds for life insurance, if you live in a state without such a fund, you may be unprotected in spite of the fact that you have paid for life insurance.

▶ Computer Information Searches

In shopping for life insurance, you can also take advantage of computerized services. One such service is offered by Insurance Information, Inc., of Methuen, Massachusetts. All you need do is call their toll-free number, (800) 472-5800, give them your age, sex, address, and health habits (including whether you're a smoker or nonsmoker), and the firm will search its computer files for the lowest-cost policies available and (for a fee of $50) send you a printout of this information. The firm guarantees that it will reduce the rates that you are now paying by $50 or refund your fee.

Another computer search firm is Select Quote Insurance Services of San Francisco, which you can call toll free at (800) 343-1985. You need pay no fee for its search services (it receives its fee from the insurance company if you decide to buy a policy on the basis of Select Quote's information).

▶ SOME WAYS TO CUT INSURANCE COSTS

1. Don't carry insurance on children. Either save the premiums or use them to buy additional term insurance for yourself.
2. Consider term as opposed to whole life insurance.
3. Some insurance companies give premium discounts for nonsmokers, nondrinkers, people with homeowner's insurance, those who exercise regularly, and so on. Find out if your insurance company offers

such discounts and take advantage of them.

4. Attempt to buy insurance on group plans through your employer or any organization of which you are a member.

5. Pay your premium annually instead of quarterly or monthly.

6. If you have a participating policy, don't let your dividends or refunds accumulate on deposit with the insurance company at a lower rate than the money could earn at a savings institution.

▶ SUMMARY

1. In deciding whom to insure, base your decision on who depends on whom and what financial stress would be undergone should an individual die prematurely.

2. Information about the basic benefits you are allowed under Social Security can be obtained from the Social Security Administration or your local Social Security office.

3. Basic insurance buying rules are to identify and insure major risks according to potential loss, insure big rather than small losses, and always compare at least two companies on costs and terms of coverage.

4. If you want a forced savings plan, you may wish to purchase whole life insurance. If you can save on your own, however, you generally should purchase lower-cost term insurance and put the difference in high (long-run) income-yielding assets, such as long-term savings certificates, the stock market, and so on.

5. Shopping for insurance requires the same skills as shopping for any other consumer product. Information is the key. You may wish to consult *Best's Insurance Reports* and other publications to compare insurance coverage and costs, as well as the financial soundness of various insurance companies. Computerized information search services are also now available for consumers.

▶ QUESTIONS FOR THOUGHT AND DISCUSSION

1. Can you think of any reason why children should have life insurance?

2. Can you think of any reason why a college student should purchase life insurance?

3. Are you underinsured?

4. Are you overinsured?

5. If you are relatively young, it is possible for you to figure out what Social Security will pay you on retirement?

6. Who should buy term insurance as opposed to whole life?

▶ THINGS TO DO

1. Try to determine whether you are overinsured or underinsured. If you are underinsured, go to the next project.

2. Call at least two (preferably three or four) insurance agents. Take the time to sit down with each of them to discuss your insurance needs. Find out what their recommendations are for an adequate amount of insurance.

3. Call Select Quote Insurance Services at (800) 343-1985. Request a printout of the lowest-cost life insurance policies available to you. Check *Best's Insurance Reports,* available in your library, for information on the firms listed on the printout. How do the firms rate, according to *Best's?*

▶ SELECTED READINGS

▶ American Council of Life Insurance. *A Consumer's Guide to Life Insurance* (latest edition). Available free from the American Council of Life Insurance, 1850 K St., N.W., Washington, DC 20006.

▶ Cohen, Charles E. "Insurance: Protecting Yourself and Your Family." *Money,* April 1989, pp. 191–92.

▶ "Inside Social Security." *Consumer Reports,* July 1991, p. 474.

▶ Kosnett, Jeff. "Life Insurance after 40." *Changing Times,* May 1989, pp. 65–70.

▶ "Life Insurance: How to Protect Your Family." *Consumer Reports,* July 1986, pp. 447–70.

▶ Loeb, Marshall. "Your Insurance." *Marshall Loeb's 1992 Money Guide.* Boston: Little, Brown, 1992 pp. 539–559.

▶ *Social Security: How It Works for You.* Available free from the Consumer Information Center, Pueblo, CO 81002.

▶ Wilson, Virginia. "Insurance: How Safe?" *Newsweek,* March 14, 1988, p. 40.

Looking to the Future

Your Retirement Years

PREVIEW

▶ What choices can I make at the present that will help assure me of satisfaction and security in my retirement years?

▶ What are the benefits of having a will?

▶ What is probate, and what problems might it cause?

▶ How may different forms of joint ownership simplify the transfer of ownership of property when a person dies?

▶ What is a trust, and what advantages do various types of trusts offer consumers?

▶ How can you protect your estate if you become incapacitated?

PLANNING FOR YOUR RETIREMENT YEARS

Providing for retirement requires consumers to use many of the skills discussed in the preceding chapters of this text. Saving and investment plans made and carried out when young can produce financial security for the latter years of life, when it may not be possible—or at least desirable—to continue working to earn money.

Needs change as we get older, too. After people retire they often make new housing choices to satisfy their changing needs and style of life. Obtaining high-quality medical care and insurance assumes growing significance. Retired people who give up their cars either out of necessity or choice need to find alternative methods of transportation. Those better off financially may take more trips or live in places with warm climates in winter months. The list of changes that may take place in our lives after we retire is very long. The people who will be best able to deal with these changes are those who have learned to evaluate their alternatives to make rational choices—not only concerning money. A certain amount (it varies per person) is essential, of course, to maintaining a fulfilling life in your retirement years. No one will argue that money is important; however, it is not enough, by itself, to make you happy. When your years of employment or raising children have ended, you are likely to find yourself with more free time to do what you want than you have had since you were a child. Having all the money you need will be of little value if you have nothing you want to do with your time. That is why we emphasize in this text the value of learning to make personally wise decisions.

The Importance of Financial Planning

You know that Americans are living longer and that more people who were part of the "baby boom" will be retiring after the year 2000. These facts mean that Social Security and other retirement programs will be asked in the future to help support a much larger number of beneficiaries from their limited resources. It is unlikely they will be able to provide the same level of benefits as they have in the past. Those who retire in the future will need to provide a larger part of their own support.

When you are young, you are likely to have a lower income than later in life. However, a budget established at this time that allocates some money to saving, investing, and paying for a reasonable amount of life insurance will set you on the road to a much more rewarding retirement, even if the amounts so allocated are small. Once you develop the habit of saving on a regular basis, saving and investing greater amounts in the future, when your income climbs, should be easier. Habits are notoriously difficult to break, and fortunately, this rule applies to good ones like saving as well as bad ones (like not saving). So now, in your youth, is the time to begin. Your retirement years will approach more quickly than you think.

Each person's financial situation is primarily his or her individual responsibility. This is true whether or not we believe that it should be the government's responsibility. The question may be a good one for debate, but the reality is that retired people will be forced to pay for a significant portion of their own support regardless of what people think is right or wrong. The government and other organizations do not have the resources to pay for all of our retirement needs. Budgeting, saving, and investing skills are valuable for all consumers, whatever their political philosophy.

Developing Other Interests

Many people have found that it is easier for them to "ease" into retirement gradually. Suppose a person has held a position of authority and responsibility in a business for many years, working 45 or 50 hours a week or even more. Simply quitting one day and staying home may leave this person without a feeling of purpose. A better choice, if it is possible, might be to work fewer hours for a period of time or to take extended vacations. This would allow the person to investigate other uses for his or her time, and to get used to finding ways to use free time.

After they retire, many people start a second career in a type of work that they find more interesting and less demanding than the occupation they previously held. Activities that were once only hobbies may become part-time jobs. The author of the text, for example, has an uncle who worked for a power company for many years. During his working years he built birdhouses for relaxation in his free time. When he retired, he increased the time he spent building them and has become quite successful selling at craft shows on weekends.

Many older people find satisfaction in helping those who are less fortunate or who are in need of friendship and guidance. Many communities have "Foster Grandparent Programs" that pair disadvantaged children with retirees. Hospitals have volunteer programs, and schools often need people to tutor students or work in libraries. There is an almost endless list of sport activities that retired people can participate in, or which they might officiate or keep records for. Retired people often help shut-ins by bringing them food or taking them to do their shopping. There is always a wide variety of ways to contribute to the welfare of your community.

Staying Active

You have probably heard the saying, "You're only as old as you feel." Although this is an exaggeration, it speaks a degree of truth as well. A lack of

People who are retired have most of the same basic needs as younger people. Among these is a need to use their time to do something that they feel is meaningful and rewarding. If you were going to retire tomorrow how would you spend your time?

activity, in mind or body, makes a person feel older. True, the type of activities possible may change as people age. Older people may not be able to play hockey or load a truck, but they can make many other contributions to the well-being of others in their family or community. Their life experiences are likely to make possible contributions of special value. Older people are often well-organized, patient, understanding, and responsible to a greater degree than the younger population.

As you approach retirement age, take time to investigate possible activities beforehand. If you think you might want to keep a vegetable garden, try a small one while you are still working. See if it is something you really enjoy. Try going back to school to take a course in photography, or philosophy, or some other topic that interests you. Instead of going away on a vacation, just stay home and pretend you are retired for a week or two and see how it goes. If you find that you can't wait to get back to work after a few days, you know you need to find more fulfilling ways to spend your time at home if you plan to be there for long hours after retirement.

Probably the best advice for newly retired people is to avoid making important changes in a hurry. Many new retirees have sold their homes and moved to Florida or Texas within weeks of leaving their jobs—and regretted their hasty decisions. Moving to new locations involves leaving old friends and making new ones. Simply finding stores where they like to shop can be a problem. Retired people who take time to evaluate their options carefully before making a decision are more likely to be satisfied with their choices. After all, time is one thing they have. They should use it.

THE DISPOSITION OF YOUR PROPERTY

Most individuals accumulate wealth throughout their lifetimes. At some point in their lives, they have more assets than liabilities; thus, their net worth is positive. For this reason, setting up wills, providing trusts, and engaging in careful estate planning are important to virtually everyone. In this chapter, we examine why it is necessary to draw up a will. Then we look at some of the more important trusts that can be created and the benefits and costs of doing so. Finally, we discuss the elements of estate planning and indicate ways in which federal and state estate taxes can be minimized.

Some specific guidelines for making out a will are offered in Consumer Issue U. Consumer Issue V looks at the final step in estate planning and the ultimate expense faced by consumers—the costs of funeral arrangements and burial.

What Is a Will and Why Should You Have One?

A **will** is a legal document through which you dispose of your property or estate. Your **estate** consists of the difference between all your assets and all your liabilities. In addition, your will gives directions for the distribution of your estate; it specifies who shall receive what and how it should be used.

Generally, a will is ineffective before the death of the writer of the will. A will can be destroyed, canceled, or modified at any time by its writer. The person who makes out the will is called a **testator** (if that person is a female, the term **testatrix** may be used instead). Thus, if a person dies leaving a will, he or she is said to have died **testate.** On the other hand, if he or she dies without a will, that person is said to have died **intestate.**

Will
A written document that allows a person to determine the disposition of his or her property at death.

Estate
The total property of whatever kind owned before the distribution of that property in accordance with the terms of a will (or, when there is no will, by the laws of inheritance in the state of domicile of the decedent).

Testator/testatrix
A person who has made a will.

Testate
To have died and left a valid will.

Intestate
To have died without a valid will.

If you should die intestate, the following things will occur, and each is an additional reason why everyone should make out at least a simple will.

1. You cannot name the person who will oversee the distribution of your estate. That person is called the **executor,** (the term **executrix** may be used for a female). Should you die without a will, the court has the authority to appoint an estate administrator, and all of your assets—should you have any after all debts are paid—will be transferred to others according to state **intestacy laws** (inheritance laws). These laws determine the order of inheritance among your legally qualified heirs. If you have no family or relatives qualified to inherit your property, the property reverts to the state (this is called *escheat*).

2. You generally cannot name a guardian for your minor children or other dependents. This is particularly critical if both you and your spouse should die at the same time.

3. You lose the ability to direct the disposal of your property in order to maximize its benefits to your heirs.

4. Your family and/or heirs will become unnecessarily involved in court procedures that could have been avoided with a valid will.

5. If you have no immediate family, persons in whom you have no particular interest (a cousin you hardly know, for example) may receive the bulk of your property.

6. The possibility of minimizing inheritance and estate taxes is eliminated.

7. Even if you have immediate family, state intestacy laws will decide which percentage of your estate each individual will receive. You may have two offspring, one of whom is immensely rich, the other abysmally poor; both may receive equal parts of your estate when you die if you do not have a will.

If you do have a will, all of these factors can be controlled. You can specify who will receive your property, how much each person or persons (or institution) will receive, when the property will be received, how the property can be safeguarded, and who will handle its disposition and act in your interests upon your death—that is, your executor.

Limitations on Disposition of Property by Will   You cannot do just anything you want in a will. For example, it is generally impossible to eliminate your spouse completely from a will. In most states, the surviving spouse can elect to take the amount granted by state statutes for intestate situations. In other words, if state law says that the surviving spouse shall receive at least one-third of the estate and the will indicates that the spouse shall receive nothing, the surviving spouse usually will get the one-third amount. In a number of situations, however, it is possible to disinherit children.

Provisions in a will that are deemed against public policy can be invalidated by the courts. For example, a provision in a person's will to spend $20 million to erect a 300-foot-high statue of that person in place of an existing house in a suburban neighborhood would certainly not be held valid, even if it didn't violate local zoning ordinances. Provisions providing for bequests of property to individuals only if they remain unmarried throughout their lifetimes usually are held invalid since marriage is considered a socially desirable institution.

A Will Disposes of Only Certain Property   A will disposes of property that is not otherwise taken care of. There may be a large amount of property

Executor/executrix
The personal representative of the person who made a will. The executor/executrix takes charge of the estate, pays the debts, and so on.

Intestacy laws
State laws determining the division of an intestate's (one who dies with no will) estate.

Probate
Proving a will before a court having jurisdiction over the administration of the estate.

in a person's estate that does not pass to heirs through disposition of the will. For example, in most cases, life-insurance proceeds automatically go to the beneficiary. If certain property is owned by two persons as joint tenants with the right of survivorship, then the survivor becomes sole owner of the property, no matter what the deceased's will states. Also, certain types of trusts (discussed below) allow you to have assets transferred upon your death to designated beneficiaries. These trust assets do not have to be disposed of, therefore, in your will.

Lawyers generally advise that, when it is possible and in your interest to do so, you transfer at least some of your property and assets in ways other than by will. This can reduce the amount of your estate disposed of by will and thus subject to probate.

What Is Probate?

Even though you have set up a will that explicitly states who should get what, how, when, and where, the will and your property must be **probated.** That is to say, it must be taken before a probate court in the appropriate jurisdiction. The court will make sure that the will has a genuine signature on it and that its execution will carry out your intent as precisely as possible. The person who has been named executor or executrix must satisfy what is usually called the *surrogate's court* in your area that all debts have been paid and that state and federal taxes also have been paid. Additionally, anyone who might have a claim on the estate has to have been notified before your will can be executed properly.

Because creditors usually have from four months to a year to make a claim, estates remain in the probate court for some time. The executor or executrix may attempt to settle federal estate taxes within nine months after your death; however, the IRS and state taxing authorities can take additional time to indicate their acceptance.

Generally, it is only after all these things are completed that the distributions can be made from your estate. Furthermore, if any provision in the will is contested, it may remain in probate for many months, if not years.

The Cost of Probate   Probate can be not only time-consuming but very expensive—depending on the value of the estate. Probating a will involves court filing fees, certification fees, and appraisal fees that can end up in the thousands of dollars. In addition, if an attorney is hired to represent the state, he or she will also charge as a fee a certain percentage (determined by state law) of the *gross* value of the estate. This means that even though the net assets of an estate (what's left after all the debts are paid) may be very few, the estate may nonetheless have to pay a substantial sum for an attorney's assistance.

Simplified Settlement Procedures   There are two major exceptions to the rule that a will must be probated. One occurs when all of the property in an estate is left to a surviving spouse. In such a case, most states allow the property to be transferred outside of probate or by a simpler and less expensive process that often doesn't even require a court appearance. Another exception is made in most states for small estates. For example, in California personal property (not real estate) worth $60,000 or less that is left by will can be transferred outside of probate by a special document called *affidavit of right*. Other states have similar laws.

Joint Ownership

If you own property jointly with another either in a joint tenancy or a tenancy by the entirety, upon your death your share of the property automatically passes to the other owner (or owners). Even if you specify otherwise in your will, your wish will be ineffective.

Joint Tenancy versus Tenancy in Common In a **joint tenancy** ownership arrangement, there are two or more owners. Each owns a percentage of an asset but not a specific part of it. Each joint owner can sell his or her share of the property without the permission of the other owner or owners. When one owner dies, however, his or her share of the property automatically is inherited by the surviving owner or owners—and probate is not involved, because the property is not disposed of by will but in accordance with property ownership law.

It is important to distinguish joint tenancy from another form of joint ownership called a tenancy in common. In **tenancy in common,** there may be two or more owners, as in a joint tenancy; however, before any owner can sell his or her share of the property, it must be partitioned. This is a legal agreement that specifies what part of the total property is owned by each individual and allows owners to sell the portions of the property they own. The most important difference between these forms of joint ownership is that when there is tenancy in common, the ownership of the deceased owner passes to his or her heirs, not to the other owners unless they are also the heirs.

Tenancy by the Entirety This type of joint ownership is available only to husbands and wives. In a **tenancy by the entirety,** neither husband nor wife can dispose of his or her share of the assets without the permission of the other. When one spouse dies, entire ownership of the property is automatically assumed by the surviving spouse.

Trusts

When planning your estate, you might consider setting up one or more trusts to benefit your heirs. Trusts can be established both during one's life or by will. Generally, a **trust** is an arrangement whereby you leave your property to an individual, a bank, or a trust company to manage for the benefit of your heirs. Most trusts are set up because there are minor children surviving a parent or parents. The funds are usually invested by the **trustee** (the designated holder of the trust) in order to support and educate the children. After a period of time designated in the will or trust agreement, the remaining assets are distributed, usually to the beneficiaries of the trust.

The trustee has two principal responsibilities: to execute his or her *fiduciary* (or trust) responsibility prudently and in good faith and to preserve the principal in the trust and invest it so that the beneficiaries receive at least a reasonable rate of return. If the beneficiaries are dissatisfied with a trustee's performance, they usually can petition a state court for a change in the trust agreement or for a change in trustees. Since the trustee is responsible for managing the assets in the trust, care must be taken in selecting the trustee. Friends or relatives obviously will take a more personal interest in your trust than will an institution. Nonetheless, a professional trust company can offer you investment competence and continuity for the life of the trust. Perhaps it

Joint tenancy
Two or more people owning a percentage, but not a specific piece, of some form of property. When one owner dies, the surviving owner(s) assumes full ownership of the property.

Tenancy in common
A form of joint ownership in which owners are not free to sell their shares in the property until it has been partitioned, and that does not provide for the automatic inheritance of the property of deceased owners by the other owners.

Tenancy by the entirety
Joint owners of property are husband and wife.

Trust
Real or personal property held or managed by one person (the trustee) for the benefit of another (the beneficiary).

Trustee
The person holding legal title to trust property.

might be best to have co-trustees—a professional company, such as a trust department of a bank, or your lawyer and a close friend or relative.

Trusts can be created for anyone's benefit, including a spouse or a charity, and are not limited to the protection of children. For example, a surviving spouse may not have the interest or ability to manage the deceased spouse's estate; therefore, a trust agreement may be the most desirable method of arranging for use of the assets. Trusts also can be established while you are still living, and these can provide at least as many benefits as a trust created at death.

Life-Insurance Trust   A life-insurance trust is administered by a bank or any other trustee but not an insurance company. The trustee is named to manage the insurance proceed after death for any heirs inexperienced in handling large sums of money.

Funded Trusts   With the funded trust, funds or assets other than life insurance can be put under the same expert management as the life insurance trust. This reduces estate administrative expenses and averts taxation. That is, taxes do not have to be paid first by a surviving spouse and then again by the children who would inherit the same funds from that person. For example, suppose Bart and Sue are married and both have significant wealth. Instead of having their wealth go to each other upon either of their deaths, it can be placed in a funded trust for their children. If Sue dies, Bart can withdraw income from the trust while he is still alive. However, because the trust is owned by the children who will receive it upon his death, it is taxed only once. This also prevents the value of Sue's estate from being added to Bart's estate and may lower the rate of the tax that must be paid on his estate when he dies.

Testamentary trust
A will or trust that bestows specific rights on specific individuals after the death of the person who created the will or trust.

Testamentary Trust   A **testamentary trust** is tailor-made. In your will, for example, you can create a testamentary trust that makes certain your property will be managed expertly and used as you desire. The trustee, usually a bank, is given broad investment powers.

Living Trust   A simple, and very flexible, way to provide for an heir is through a living *(inter vivos)* trust. Setting up such a trust requires a few legal technicalities. You specify in a document the trustee (you), the successor trustee (the person you want to take over when you die), the beneficiary or beneficiaries (those you want to receive your property upon your death), and the property in the trust—this can be real estate, securities, or anything of value, You also need to transfer title to all property to the trust's name.

The advantage of the living trust is that you have full control over it during your lifetime. You can revoke (cancel) the trust at any time, designate different beneficiaries, and so on. A further advantage is that, on your death, the successor trustee can quickly transfer the trust property to the beneficiaries. The transfer does not require a lawyer's assistance, involves no delays, and avoids the probate process.

Informal Bank Trust   Another type of trust that is relatively simple to establish is a bank account trust (sometimes called a *pay-on-death account* or a *Totten* trust). Most banks offer these types of accounts, in which the depositor names another person or persons who will become the owner or owners of the account upon the depositor's death. If you establish a bank account trust, you have full control over the account until you die—just as with a living trust. You can close the account or name different beneficiaries. Upon your death, the beneficiary to the account has nearly instant access to the money and, as with a living trust, probate is avoided.

Children's Trust   A simple and inexpensive way to provide for minor children in the event of your death is by including in your will a provision establishing a children's trust. This provision will designate the age at which you want your children to inherit property left to them and a person (trustee) to manage the assets until the children reach that age. Often, the trustee is a relative or a friend. The trustee manages the assets in accordance with your wishes as specified in your will—paying out sums for educational or living expenses, for example.

THE TAXATION OF WEALTH

In addition to income and other taxes, the federal government also imposes gift and **estate taxes.** These so-called wealth taxes are based on the value of our assets, minus our liabilities, that we transfer to others while we are alive or at our death. The tax is imposed on the donor or testator, not the recipient of the wealth. Regardless of who pays it, the imposition of the tax reduces the value of the assets transferred.

The Economic Recovery Tax Act of 1981 significantly modified gift and estate taxation in this country. The deductions and credits granted under the new law exempt all but the extremely wealthy from the tax. The same unified tax rate applies to both, gifts or estates. A unified tax simply means that the transfer of wealth, either by gift (while alive) or estate (at death), is cumulatively subject to the same tax schedule as shown in Exhibit 22–1. For instance, assume Mary gives Harry, a friend, $10,000 over the allowable donee exemption. As shown in the exhibit, the dollar amount of the unified equivalent exemption will be reduced by $10,000 for Mary. If Mary dies, her unified exemption would be $590,000 ($600,000 unified exemption minus the $10,000 in excess of the donee exemption).

As another example, suppose Wilma dies, leaving an estate of $748,890. In most cases the first $600,000 would not be taxed by the federal government because of the unified exemption of this amount. Her heirs could determine the tentative tax that would be owed to the federal government on Wilma's estate by using the table in Exhibit 22–1. The taxable part of Wilma's estate ($148,890) falls into the range between $100,000 but not over $150,000 in the left column of the table. By reading the corresponding value in the right column, we know the tentative tax will be $23,800 plus 30 percent of the $48,890 over $100,000 or $14,667. This results in a total federal tax liability of $38,467 ($23,800 + (.30 × $48,890) = $38,467). The government in the state where Wilma lived will also take a share of her estate that will vary from state to state.

Estate and Gift Tax Provisions
The following provisions are now effective for gifts made, or for estates of decedents.

Estate taxes
Taxes based on the value of the assets, minus the liabilities, of an estate when transferred to the ownership of others. These taxes are paid by the donor, if he or she is living when this transfer takes place, or by the estate, if the donor is dead.

IF THE AMOUNT TO BE TAXED IS:	THE TENTATIVE TAX IS
Not over $10,000	18% of such amount
Over $10,000 but not over $20,000	$1,800, plus 20% of the excess of such amount over $10,000.
Over $20,000 but not over $40,000	$3,800, plus 22% of the excess of such amount over $20,000.
Over $40,000 but not over $60,000	$8,200, plus 24% of the excess of such amount over $40,000.
Over $60,000 but not over $80,000	$13,000, plus 26% of the excess of such amount over $60,000.
Over $80,000 but not over $100,000	$18,200, plus 28% of the excess of such amount over $80,000.
Over $100,000 but not over $150,000	$23,800, plus 30% of the excess of such amount over $100,000.
Over $150,000 but not over $250,000	$38,800, plus 32% of the excess of such amount over $150,000.
Over $250,000 but not over $500,000	$70,800 plus 34% of the excess of such amount over $250,000.
Over $500,000 but not over $750,000	$155,800, plus 37% of the excess of such amount over $500,000.
Over $750,000 but not over $1,000,000	$248,300, plus 39% of the excess of such amount over $750,000.
Over $1,000,000 but not over $1,250,000	$345,800, plus 41% of the excess of such amount over $1,000,000.
Over $1,250,000 but not over $1,500,000	$448,300, plus 43% of the excess of such amount over $1,250,000.
Over $1,500,000 but not over $2,000,000	$555,800, plus 45% of the excess of such amount over $1,500,000.
Over $2,000,000 but not over $2,500,000	$780,800, plus 49% of the excess of such amount over $2,000,000.
Over $2,500,000	$1,025,800 plus 50% of the excess of such amount over $2,500,000.

UNIFIED CREDIT OR EXEMPTION	
Unified estate and gift tax credit	$192,800
Unified equivalent exemption from estate and gift transfers	$600,000

Marital Deduction   An unlimited marital deduction is allowed for estate and gift tax purposes. In other words, an estate that passes entirely to a surviving spouse is effectively exempt from transfer tax liability regardless of the size of the estate.

Annual Gift-Tax Exclusion   The annual gift-tax exclusion is now $10,000 per donee. An unlimited exclusion for amounts paid for the benefit of a donee for medical expenses and school tuition is also provided.

State Inheritance and Estate Taxes

Inheritance tax

A tax assessed by the federal government or the state government (or both) on a certain portion of an estate upon the death of its owner.

An **inheritance tax** is paid by those who receive the property; an estate tax is paid by the estate. Most states impose an inheritance tax, but some impose an estate tax instead. A few impose both. The state inheritance tax (or estate tax, if that is the case) usually is set at a lower rate than the federal estate tax. Note, though, that state exemptions usually are smaller than federal exemptions. Thus, the actual state tax due can be, and often is, considerably higher than the federal tax due.

State inheritance taxes are based on the value of the assets inherited by the individual. They are owed to the state in which the inherited assets are located rather than the state in which the person inheriting them lives. In many cases, the state tax varies not only with the value of the assets but also with the relationship of the recipient to the deceased.

The Pick-Up Tax

Most states have an added estate tax, which usually is called a *pick-up tax*. This tax is designed to ensure that an amount at least equal to the maximum allowable federal-estate-tax credit is charged. This tax does not, however, increase the *total* death taxes paid; it applies only when the amount due from other state death taxes is less than the allowable federal estate credit.

WHAT IF YOU BECOME INCAPACITATED?

A major estate-planning consideration is the possibility that you might at some point become incapable—through accident or illness—of making decisions yourself. Who will make decisions for you, should such a situation arise? The executor of your will can't, because he or she is authorized only to make decisions for you on your death. Even if you give a person power of attorney (the power to take over your legal affairs), that person retains such power only as long as you have the competence to give it.

Durable Power of Attorney

One way to make sure that someone will be able to make decisions for you should you become unable to do so is by giving to a person of your choice **durable power of attorney.** A durable power of attorney authorizes another to act for you—write checks, collect insurance proceeds, and otherwise manage your affairs, including health care—when you are incapacitated. Spouses often give each other durable power of attorney and, if they are advanced in age, often give a second such power of attorney to an older child.

Durable power of attorney
A document that specifically assigns the power to another person to make decisions for you should you become incapable of making your own.

Living Wills

A similar power is created by what is called a **living will.** A living will is not a will in the usual sense—that is, it doesn't appoint an estate representative, dispose of property, establish trusts, and so on. Rather, it allows you to control the methods of medical treatment that may be used after a serious accident or illness. Through a living will, you can designate whether you do or do not want certain life-saving procedures to be undertaken in cases where the treatment cannot offer a reasonable quality of life.

Forty states and the District of Columbia now have so-called death-with-dignity statutes authorizing living wills. To obtain a copy of a living will, including a durable power of attorney, you can write to Choice in Dying, 200 Varick St., New York, NY 10014, or call (212) 366-5540. To increase the chances that your living will will be followed, have it signed by two nonrelated adult witnesses and notarized. You should give your attorney, your doctor, and a friend or family member each a copy of the will also, and, if you are hospitalized, you can ask that a copy of the will be placed with your medical chart.

Living will
A document that grants specific authority to a person or persons to discontinue the artificial prolongation of life; now allowed in 40 states plus the District of Columbia.

A WORD ABOUT ORGAN DONATION

Many organs and tissues of the body can be used for medical transplants. In most cases, however, they must be available immediately after death to be useful. Kidneys, for example, have to be transplanted within 30 hours of the death of the donor, and corneas must be received within six hours for successful transplantation. Because of this, a will is *not* the place to inform others of your wish to donate organs to save the lives of others.

If you wish to be an organ donor, you must obtain a Uniform Donor Card that conforms to the Uniform Anatomical Gift Act. These donor cards are available at your local Department of Motor Vehicles and numerous health-care centers. You can also obtain one, and further information about organ donation, by calling toll-free 1-800-24-DONOR.

Make your wishes known to your family and friends, and carry your card with you at all times.

1. Virtually everyone with any assets should have a will prepared; otherwise a person will die intestate.

2. When you die intestate, you have no control over who oversees the distribution of your estate, who will be the guardian for minor children if your spouse is no longer living, or who will get what percentage of your estate.

3. A will allows you to designate who gets your property, how much each person or institution gets, when the property will be received, how the property can be safeguarded, and who will handle its disposition.

4. Certain types of property are not disposed of by will. Insurance proceeds, for example, automatically go to the stated beneficiary upon the death of the policyholder. Property jointly owned in a joint tenancy or tenancy by the entirety passes automatically to the other owner (or owners) upon the death of an owner (even if the owner's will specifies otherwise).

5. A will must be probated—that is, taken to the appropriate court to demonstrate that all debts and taxes have been paid and that the will is valid.

6. Probate takes from four months to a year for relatively simple estates and wills and longer for more complicated and/or contested wills.

7. Joint ownership of property can assume the following forms: joint tenancy, tenancy in common, and tenancy by the entirety. Unlike in a joint tenancy or a tenancy by the entirety, property held in a tenancy in common passes to each owner's heirs upon the owner's death and not to the other owner or owners (unless he or they are the deceased owner's heirs).

8. Trusts can be created to allow at least part of one's estate to pass to your heirs outside of probate.

9. The trustee has two principal responsibilities: to execute his or her trust responsibility in good faith, and to preserve the principal in the trust and invest that principal wisely.

10. There are numerous types of trusts, including life-insurance trusts, funded trusts, testamentary trusts, living trusts, informal bank trusts, and children's trusts.

11. The Economic Recovery Tax Act of 1981 greatly reduced and simplified the taxation of estates. All estate and gift taxes are now unified, and there are large credits for married individuals.

12. In addition to federal estate taxes, state inheritance and estate taxes must be paid in certain states.

13. A durable power of attorney authorizes another to make decisions for you should you become incapable of making your own. A living will is a document that allows you to specify what medical procedures, such as life-sustaining measures, you want (or don't want) to be undertaken when you are seriously ill, if the measures do not offer a reasonable quality of life. Forty states plus the District of Columbia have passed death-with-dignity statutes that recognize the legitimacy of such wills.

14. Because organ donation should be effected immediately after death, a will is not the place to specify such a wish. Rather, you should carry an organ-donor card with you at all times and make sure your family and friends know of your wishes in this respect.

1. What are the goals of estate planning?
2. Explain the major purposes of a will.
3. Why is it necessary to probate wills, especially since it is such a time-consuming and often expensive process?
4. Can you imagine any circumstances in which it would be more rational *not* to write a will?

1. Write to Concern for Dying at the address given in this chapter (or call them) and request a copy of the forms they recommend using to create a durable power of attorney and a living will. Study the forms carefully and determine whether these are options that you might want to consider.
2. If you have a friend who is an attorney, ask him or her about the inheritance laws (intestacy laws) in your state. What is the order of inheritance among relatives?
3. Visit the court in your area that probates wills (you can learn which court does this by calling your county courthouse offices, listed under your county's name in the White Pages of the telephone book). Find out from the court clerk what kinds of fees are required in probating a will, how long it takes, and other information.

As more people live longer, a larger proportion of elderly Americans will exhaust their personal savings. In cases where this happens, do you believe the children of these people should be expected to bear the cost of supporting their parents? Consider your own parents. What responsibilities (financial and otherwise) do you feel toward them? To what extent would you be willing to help them if they were in need? These are questions that the majority of Americans will eventually be forced to answer.

▶ Clifford, Denis. *The Power of Attorney Book*. 2d ed. Berkeley: Nolo Press, 1987.
▶ Dunn, D. H. "First Things First: A Last Will and Testament." *Business Week*, December 9, 1991, pp. 108–109.
▶ "Estate Plans Compared." *Modern Maturity*, August–September 1991, p. 49.
▶ Frelincher, Morton. *Estate Planning Handbook—with Forms*. Englewood Cliffs, NJ: Prentice-Hall (latest edition).
▶ Loeb, Marshall. "Your Estate." *Marshall Loeb's 1992 Money Guide*. Boston: Little, Brown, 1992, pp. 597—613.
▶ Shekerjian, Denise G. *Competent Counsel: Working with Lawyers*. New York: Dodd, Mead, 1985.
▶ Szabo, J. C. "Don't Put Off Estate Planning." *Nation's Business*, December 1991, pp. 34–35.

Choosing a Lawyer

GLOSSARY

GENERALIST   a lawyer who does not practice in a specialized field of law but who is qualified to provide legal advice in most normal situations.

NONLEGAL PROFESSIONAL   a person who is not a lawyer but who is qualified to provide legal advice about specific situations.

Most consumers have heard stories about lawyers who charge $200 or more an hour and drag cases out for twice as long as necessary to inflate their bills. Rumors of lawyers receiving enormous bonuses and maintaining opulent lifestyles are common. There may be individual cases where such stories are true, but most lawyers earn their fees by providing honest value and a necessary service.

There are many situations in which consumers need the services of a lawyer to protect their rights. There are other circumstances, however, that involve the law but do not require the services of a lawyer. Consumers can often receive legal information and guidance from other sources at a fraction of the cost of hiring a lawyer.

▶ OBTAINING HELP FROM NONLEGAL PROFESSIONALS

Accountants are probably the most common **nonlegal professionals** who serve as a source of information for consumers who need legal advice but not a lawyer. Certified public accountants and professional financial advisors are often qualified to provide information about tax laws and accounting methods that can solve many financial and legal questions consumers have. Most accounting firms charge roughly half as much as qualified tax attorneys for similar services. This does not mean consumers should never consider using a lawyer when they have financial problems. It does mean they can save money by using other professionals for help that does not require a lawyer.

Real estate agents are not lawyers but are often able to explain the legal requirements of real estate transactions. They are generally qualified to provide basic information about title searches, zoning ordinances, easements, leases, or registering deeds that can save prospective buyers hundreds or even thousands of dollars in legal fees. Ultimately, when a consumer buys or sells a home, a lawyer will probably be needed to finalize the deal, but much of the initial work can be performed by nonlegal professionals.

Bankers are also qualified to provide certain types of financial information. Most banks maintain entire departments that are devoted to trust and estate planning. Although banks will charge a fee for their services and may require legal consultations in some matters, the cost of estate planning through banks is likely to be less than the cost of using only a lawyer. For consumers who have specialized needs, however, the bank may not have sufficiently qualified personnel. In such cases, consumers need to seek help from a tax lawyer. There is little sense in saving a few hundred dollars in legal fees if it results in paying the government thousands more in taxes.

▶ SOURCES OF LOW-COST LEGAL ADVICE

There are sources of legal information available that consumers may use at little or no cost. When people feel, for example, that their civil rights have been violated, they can ask for assistance from the American Civil Liberties Union, the National Organization of Women, the National Association for the Advancement of Colored People, or from the federal government's Equal Employment Opportunity Office. Most states also maintain departments that can help people protect their civil rights. There is, of course, no guarantee that these organizations will choose to support a particular case, but people have little to lose from asking.

When people believe they have been harmed by a fraudulent business practice or by a defective and dangerous product, they can contact either the Federal Trade Commission or the Consumer Products Safety Commission. Again, there is no guarantee that these agencies will help individuals receive satisfaction, but people may as well ask.

Free legal aid may also be available from state family services agencies, insurance commissions, divisions of employment, or health and human services departments. The point to remember is that consumers may not need to hire a lawyer when they have a legal problem. It often pays to investigate other alternatives.

WHEN YOU NEED A LAWYER

The best time to choose a lawyer is before you need one. It is better to avoid being placed in the situation of needing to choose a lawyer today to represent you in court tomorrow. Consumers should use the same process to select lawyers that they would use to select any other important purchase, for they are purchasing a service that may be expensive both in cost and in the impact it may have on their lives and financial well-being. No one is likely to make the best possible choice hiring a lawyer in a hurry.

A good way to start is to ask yourself what type of services you expect an attorney to provide. People who lead a simple life with few legal complications may need to employ only a **generalist** who is able to draw up a will, or help complete the purchase or sale of a home. However, people who are wealthy, run a complex business, intend to sue someone, or are involved in complicated disputes with the IRS need to hire specialists.

CHOOSING A SPECIFIC LAWYER OR LAW FIRM

The actual selection of a specific lawyer or legal firm may be accomplished through a series of steps. It is often best to begin by asking friends and relatives whom you respect for recommendations. This will provide you with insight as to a particular lawyer's ability and character, and knowing he or she was recommended may cause the lawyer to take a greater interest in you. Few lawyers would jeopardize an existing relationship with a customer by providing unsatisfactory service to a friend or relative of that person.

Another common source of advice is from other professionals you em-

ploy. If you have an established relationship with an accountant, this person might be able to recommend a lawyer who can provide specialized legal advice required by your financial situation. Real estate agents are often able to recommend lawyers. However, the fact that a lawyer has been recommended to you by someone you trust doesn't mean you shouldn't evaluate him or her and the services offered for yourself.

Directories that list lawyers and their qualifications may be helpful. The best known is the *Martindale-Hubbell Law Directory,* available at many larger libraries. This directory rates lawyers based on information solicited from other lawyers and provides information about each lawyer's law school degree, professional associations, fields of practice, and honors. It probably is not wise to blindly accept what this, or any directory has to say about individual lawyers, but it is a good place to begin an investigation.

When choosing a lawyer, consider the size of a legal firm and the length of time the firm or an individual lawyer has been in practice. New lawyers who are out on their own for the first time are not necessarily bad lawyers. Everyone was new once; however, new lawyers will not have had time to develop the relationships and understanding of the legal system that can make the difference between winning and losing a case. Large firms are more likely to have lawyers who can share their expertise to solve more complicated legal matters. On the other hand, large, established legal firms are likely to charge higher fees for simple legal services that could be provided equally well by smaller organizations. Large firms may also act more slowly or be less sensitive to the wishes of a client with limited

needs who will generate smaller rather than larger fees.

MEETING YOUR PROSPECTIVE LAWYER

When you have identified a firm and a specific lawyer you believe you might want to employ, your next step is to make an appointment to meet this person to discuss your legal needs. The purpose of this meeting is often more to develop a personal relationship with the lawyer than to resolve a specific legal problem. It is important for people to feel lawyers they hire will responsibly protect their interests. A woman involved in a divorce, for example, would probably not want to employ a male lawyer who she believed had sexist attitudes.

There are a number of questions consumers should ask at their initial meeting with a lawyer.

1. *What are your areas of expertise?* Assure yourself that your prospective lawyer is qualified to provide you with the services you are likely to need. There is no reason to hire a lawyer who specializes in divorce if you need help running a business.
2. *What is your availability?* Good lawyers tend to be busy. A lawyer who is already overcommitted is not a good choice if you expect to need frequent and lengthy consultations.
3. *What fees will be charged for standard services?* There is, of course, no way to foretell the future; however, a lawyer should be willing to explain how billing will be computed for standard services.
4. *Will you sign an agreement or provide a written statement that outlines your fees and the services they will purchase?* Lawyers are often hesitant to put such agreements in writing, but without them clients are often left to their lawyer's mercy.

Once a service has been provided and billed, clients must pay that amount, even if it seems unreasonable, unless they have a contractual agreement on which they can base their refusal or are willing to hire another lawyer and go to court—where they may lose.

▶ What to Bring with You to the Meeting

Consumers can save time and money by anticipating information and documents that their lawyers will need. Whether you need help with your business, an estate, or an adoption, bringing documents the lawyer is likely to want to see to your initial meeting should speed the legal process. Moreover, having such information with you can reduce the number of meetings you will need to have, the amount of time these meetings will take, and consequently the cost of your legal consultation.

In addition to information and documents, consumers who have a specific legal objective for meeting with a lawyer will benefit from preparing questions they need answered. List these questions in a logical sequence and leave space under each question to summarize the lawyer's answers. Your personal notes are important because although you may expect a lawyer to provide you with a written letter or brief that includes specific information you have requested, it will not include every comment made during an interview or your impression of what was said.

▶ WHAT DETERMINES A LAWYER'S FEES?

Many factors contribute to a lawyer's, or law firm's, determination of fees that are charged for services rendered. Obviously, the complexity of a case and the amount of time it will require is a primary consideration. Related factors include the lawyer's existing workload and the length of time that is available before the work must be completed. The more pressure there is to finish a case quickly, the more a customer can expect to be charged.

An attorney's reputation and experience also have a direct bearing on the fee. A consumer who hires a nationally famous lawyer should expect to pay more than one who hires a recent law school graduate. Lawyers are more likely to charge lower fees when they believe a lasting relationship has been established that will generate future income. In some cases a client's financial situation will affect what a lawyer charges as well. A final, and often important consideration, is the lawyer's overhead, or cost of doing business. If a law firm maintains a large, professionally decorated office in an expensive high-rise building, it will need to earn the money from its clients to pay for the office. There is no reason to be put off by a lawyer who has a well-decorated office, but there is no reason to be impressed, either. The important question to consider when choosing a lawyer is, "What will this lawyer be able to do for me?" not, "Is his or her office impressive?" In the early 1990s the least a consumer could expect to pay for a qualified lawyer's services in most parts of the United States was roughly $70 an hour.

▶ Different Ways Fees are Billed

There are a number of common methods of billing used by lawyers and legal firms.

1. *A flat fee, in which a specific amount is charged for each particular service.* This allows clients to know how much they will be charged before a service is rendered, but gives lawyers little incentive to "go the distance" to provide the extra work that may win a case or successfully resolve a problem.

2. *An hourly rate in which a specific amount is charged for each hour a lawyer works on a legal problem.* This is a common method of setting fees for nonstandard services when a lawyer cannot be sure how long a case will take to complete. Consumers who agree to this type of arrangement should ask for a written *cap,* or a limit on the number of hours a lawyer may put in on a case without client approval. Without such a cap, it is possible for legal fees to grow rapidly to an amount that is far more than a client expected to pay.

3. *A contingency fee, meaning a share of any settlement that is paid to the lawyer.* In accident cases many lawyers charge one-third of any judgment regardless of the size of that judgment. Lawyers will agree to this type of fee only when they are reasonably sure that a significant judgment will be made. It obviously can be used only in cases where a financial settlement is expected.

4. *A fee-plus-cost agreement that allows lawyers to bill clients for the costs they pay for researching and preparing a case in addition to their regular legal fee.* Consumers need to be very careful when they agree to this type of arrangement. They need to know how the costs of a case will be determined. There have been situations where lawyers have charged $50 an hour for the services of a legal assistant who was paid $10 to $20 an hour for his or her work. This arrangement provides lawyers with an incentive to have unnecessary work done by assistants to increase the size of their own income.

If consumers feel a lawyer's fees are excessive, they can try to negotiate lower fees. They may also choose to employ a different attorney who charges less. Whatever they do, they must do it before services have been rendered. The time to discuss a lawyer's fees is before a bill has been charged.

► SUMMARY

1. Although there are many situations in which consumers need to employ a lawyer, they should recognize that legal advice is often available from other, less expensive sources that include accountants, real estate agents, and banks.

2. There are many sources of free or low-cost legal assistance that can be used in some situations. Consumers have no guarantee that these sources will take on the responsibility of their particular cases, but there is no reason not to ask.

3. Lawyers should be chosen before a consumer has the immediate need for a lawyer's services. A series of steps may be used to select a particular lawyer or law firm that includes asking friends for recommendations, making inquiries with professionals, and consulting directories of lawyers. Consumers should also consider the size and reputation of the firm a lawyer works for.

4. When consumers identify a lawyer they think they might like to employ, they should arrange an interview that will help them learn about the lawyer's personality and character. At this interview, clients

should ask the lawyer about his or her areas of expertise, availability, fee structure, and if a written agreement can be signed concerning this fee structure. Consumers can speed the legal process by bringing relevant documents and information with them to this meeting.

5. The fees lawyers charge depend on the complexity of the cases being considered, their work load, their experience and reputation, and the overhead costs they must pay for their office and assistance.

6. Common billing methods used by lawyers include flat fees for specific services, hourly rates, contingency fees, and fee-plus-cost agreements. Agreements for how any fee will be charged must be made before services are rendered and billings are made. If this is not done, clients will often be in the position of being forced to pay whatever their lawyer bills, even if it seems unreasonable.

► QUESTIONS FOR THOUGHT AND DISCUSSION

1. Why are lawyers a necessary part of any effective legal system?

2. How much do you believe a qualified lawyer should be paid for an hour of labor? Explain the reasons for your answer.

3. If you were permanently disabled as the result of an accident, would you accept a contingency agreement that would pay your lawyer one-third of any settlement that you receive? Explain the costs and benefits of such an agreement in your answer.

4. Would you consider hiring a relative to be your lawyer? Explain the reasons for your answer.

► THINGS TO DO

1. Go to your library and investigate local lawyers in the *Martindale-Hubbell Law Directory*. Identify lawyers who you would and would not consider hiring. Explain your choices.

2. Look through your local newspaper for advertisements placed by lawyers or legal firms. Evaluate these advertisements in terms of the quality of the information they provide to consumers. Do you believe allowing lawyers to advertise is a good idea? Explain the reasons for your answer.

3. Attend a trial in a local court. Evaluate the attorneys. What skills did they demonstrate that typical consumers do not have? Do you believe the attorneys served their clients well? Explain the reasons for your answers.

► SELECTED READINGS

► Galen, M. "So Many Lawyers, So Little Opportunity." *Business Week*, August 26, 1991, p. 31.

► *How to Choose and Use a Lawyer*, available from the Office of Consumer Affairs, 1009 Premier Bldg., 1725 I St. N.W., Washington, DC 20201.

► Johnson, J. "Do We Have Too Many Lawyers?" *Time*, August 26, 1991, pp. 47–49.

► Mallozzi, A. C. "When (and How) to Fire Your Lawyer." *Good Housekeeping*, July 1991, p. 173.

► *You Don't Always Need a Lawyer*. New York: Consumer Report Books, 1989.

How to Make Out Your Will

For better or worse, we have no way of knowing how long each of us will live. That doesn't mean, though, that we can't plan rationally for possible eventualities. When you reach your state's legal age and if you have many assets, you should make out a will.

▶ THE COMPOSITION OF A WILL

While each will is different, most have at least five principal sections:

1. The opening recitation.
2. The dispositive clauses.
3. The administrative clauses.
4. A testamonium clause.
5. An attestation clause.

▶ Opening Recitation

This part of a will indicates who you are, where you live, and that you are of sound mind and competent to make a will. In addition, this section may revoke all previous wills, will indicate that all debts and funeral expenses should be paid, and sometimes give instructions as to how you should be buried.

▶ Dispositive Clauses

This section indicates who should get what. In other words, it indicates **legacies,** of which there are four types: specific, general, demonstrative, and residuary.

1. *Specific legacy.* A particular piece of property in the estate is given to a particular person or institution; for example, you give your dog to your daughter.
2. *General legacy.* You give a specific amount of money to an individual or institution. Such a cash bequest is paid out of the general assets of the estate.
3. *Demonstrative legacy.* A specific amount of money is bequeathed, along with the source of its payment; for example, $5,000 a year will go to the deceased's mother to be paid out of royalties on books the deceased has written.
4. *Residuary legacy.* This bequest is payable out of the remainder of the estate after everything else has been paid, including the preceding three types of legacies and all debts and administrative expenses.

▶ Administrative Clauses

The section of the will containing **administrative clauses** sets up the machinery for making sure your instructions are followed. In this section, you name your executors and the guardians for any minor children you have.

▶ Testamonium Clause

The **testamonium clause** concludes the will and indicates that you are signing your name to approve it. The will should not, however, be signed unless witnesses are present. An unwitnessed will may be no better than a blank piece of paper.

▶ Attestation Clause

The **attestation clause** is signed by witnesses. It indicates that they know you signed the will of your own free will and were of sound mind when you did it. Witnesses must sign in the presence of each other, as well as in your presence.

▶ THE IMPORTANT JOB OF THE EXECUTOR

In your will, you must indicate who shall carry out your instructions. These persons or institutions are called your *executors*. Choosing an executor is a difficult task. You must be able to trust that person or institution to take a personal interest in seeing that your estate is properly handled after your death. Many states have limitations on who can be an executor. For example, Florida requires that the person either be a blood relative or a resident of the state of Florida; if you live in Florida, you could not name as executor for your estate a close friend who lived in California.

▶ The Executor's Duties

It would be impossible to indicate all the duties the executor must perform, but here are some.

1. Managing the estate until it is settled, including
   a. Collecting debts due the estate.
   b. Managing real estate and ar-

ranging for maintenance and repairs.

c. Registering securities in the name of the estate.

d. Collecting insurance proceeds.

e. Running the family business, if necessary.

f. Arranging for the family's support during probate.

g. Properly insuring assets.

2. Collecting all assets and necessary records, including

a. Locating the will, insurance policies, real estate papers, car registrations, and birth certificates.

b. Filing claims for pension, Social Security, profit sharing, and veterans' benefits.

c. Taking possession of bank accounts, real estate, personal effects, and safe-deposit boxes.

d. Obtaining names, addresses, and Social Security numbers of all heirs.

e. Making an inventory of all assets.

f. Setting up records and books.

3. Determining the estate's obligations, including

a. Determining which claims are legally due.

b. Obtaining receipts for all claims paid.

c. Checking on mortgages and other loans.

4. Computing and then paying all death taxes due, which requires

a. Selecting the most beneficial tax alternatives.

b. Deciding which assets to sell to provide necessary funds.

c. Paying taxes on time to avoid penalties.

d. Opposing what you think are unfair evaluations, established by government taxing authorities.

5. Computing beneficiaries' shares and then distributing the estate, which involves

a. Determining who gets particular items and settling family disputes.

b. Transferring titles to real estate and other property.

c. Selling off assets to pay cash legacies.

d. Paying final estate costs.

e. Preparing accountings for the court's approval.

Given the amount of work in giving effect to the provisions of a will, you would hope that the executor would take a personal interest in the situation. A friend or relative might, but such a person might lack the necessary financial training to do so properly. That's why some people name a close relative or personal friend as one coexecutor and name a professional trust company as another coexecutor.

▶ AVOIDING COMMON MISTAKES

Lawyers who handle estates and wills frequently encounter a number of related mistakes. Here are some of these mistakes and suggestions for avoiding them.

▶ Writing Your Will Yourself

Handwritten wills (officially called *holographic wills*) are legal in most states. Nonetheless, it is often difficult to establish their validity. Oral wills are generally accepted only during combat, although some states recognize oral wills made during a final illness.

Many books and kits are sold that tell you how to write your own will so that it is as legal as one prepared by an attorney. One example is the *Simple Will Book*, by Denis Clifford, published by Nolo Press of Berkeley, California. If you have a simple estate and wishes for how it should be distributed, do-it-yourself wills can save you a lawyer's fee; how-

ever, if you have a substantial estate, or if you wish a complex distribution, you should pay a qualified attorney to prepare your will.

▶ Disinheritance

If you desire to disinherit a particular family member (where it is possible to do so), you must state this explicitly in your will. Otherwise, the disinherited person may be able to persuade a court that you were not competent to make the will. You might want to write something like the following:

> After careful thought and reflection, I have decided and hence determined that it is better not to include a bequest to my niece, Martha.

▶ Misunderstanding State Requirements

Each state has different requirements for a valid will. When you die, your permanent residence determines which state's laws apply. If you retire to California, make sure that the will you made in Minnesota is valid.

▶ Not Keeping Your Will Up to Date

In many states, a will becomes invalid if it was drawn up before you either married or had children. Any change in marital status or family size should dictate that a new will is in order, with new specifications about dividing your estate.

▶ Not Reappraising Your Executor Regularly

What if you named as an executor a person who since has become mentally incompetent? What if you named a person who has since died? It will take much longer than usual to wind up an estate when such an event occurs. In any case, it is generally wise to name an alternate executor in case the first person you chose cannot or will not serve.

▶ Not Specifying What Happens If an Heir Dies Before You Do or Simultaneously

Air and automotive travel have increased the likelihood that several members of the same family may die in the same accident. If this happens, it is necessary that a second or even third beneficiary be listed in the will in case the previous one or ones are already dead. You might put a *delay clause* in all insurance policies and in the will; it would specify that the first listed beneficiary must survive you by at least 30 days, or the money will go to other heirs on the list.

▶ Omitting Too Much

Essentially, a will should dispose of the entire estate. In other words, wills should have a clause directing the disposal of residue and remainder.

▶ WHAT IF YOU WANT TO CHANGE YOUR WILL?

A will is not a final document (unless, of course, you die). While you are living, you may change your will as often as necessary to reflect changed circumstances and changed wishes on your part. As mentioned above, it is sometimes necessary to draft a new will if an old one was prepared before you married, had children, and so on.

If you do create a new will, it is important that you specify in the new will that it revokes all previously made wills. This is because a new will does not automatically invalidate an old one. Often, if you want to add a provision to your will or make a change or two, these

changes can be effected by drawing up a **codicil** to your existing will. The codicil is signed and witnessed, just as your will is, and becomes a part of your will. Creating a codicil to an existing will is much simpler (and therefore less expensive) than writing an entirely new will.

▶ A LETTER OF LAST INSTRUCTION

In addition to your will, you should have a separate *letter of last instruction*. The letter, which is opened at your death, should contain the following information.

1. The location of your will.
2. Instructions about your burial.
3. The location of all relevant documents, such as your Social Security card, marriage certificate, and birth certificate.
4. The location of all safe-deposit boxes.
5. A list of your life insurance policies and where they are located.
6. Pension statements.
7. A list of all stocks and bonds, real and other property, and bank accounts and their locations.
8. Any instructions concerning a business in which you might have been engaged.
9. A statement of reasons for not giving part of your estate to someone who normally would be expected to receive it.

A letter of last instruction is not a legal document. It does not replace a will and should not be considered a substitute for a valid will.

▶ WHERE SHOULD YOU PUT YOUR WILL?

A will should be readily available upon the death of its maker. Therefore, once your will has been writ-

ten, you should do at least one of the following:

1. Leave the original copy of the will with the attorney who drew it up. The attorney then will put it in a safe-deposit box in his or her law offices or in a financial institution.
2. You can keep the original copy of the will in your own safe-deposit box in a financial institution. Many experts object to this arrangement, however, because a court order may be necessary for the box to be opened after your death.
3. Some financial experts suggest that the husband's will be put in the wife's safe-deposit box and the wife's will be put in the husband's safe-deposit box.
4. Others recommend that you purchase a fireproof safe for your home in which to keep your will and other important documents.
5. If a professional trust company or financial institution has been named as an executor of the estate, that institution may keep the original copy of the will.

▶ SUMMARY

1. Wills generally have at least five principal sections: the opening recitation, the dispositive clauses, the administrative clauses, a testimonium clause, and an attestation clause.
2. In your will, you must indicate who your executor will be. That person will carry out all instructions left by you regarding the settlement of your estate. In effect, the executor stands in your shoes until the estate is settled.
3. The primary functions of the executor are to manage the estate until it is settled, to collect all assets and necessary records concerning the estate, to determine and pay all debts of the estate, to compute and pay

death taxes due, and to compute the beneficiaries' shares of the estate and then distribute the assets of your estate accordingly.

4. To avoid problems for your heirs, it is advisable not to write your will yourself (in handwriting), to phrase carefully any disinheritance clause, to know state requirements for a valid will, to keep your will up to date, to reappraise your executor regularly, to specify what you want to happen if an heir dies before you or simultaneously, and to include provisions for the disposal of all of your estate.

5. To change your will, you can either create an entirely new will and specify that it replaces your existing will or create a codicil to your will. A codicil changes only a specified portion of your will or adds another clause to your will; the same requirements are necessary for codicils (witnesses and so on) as for wills.

6. In addition to your will, you should have a separate letter of last instruction to be opened at your death. The letter should indicate the location of your will and all other important documents and include instructions for your burial.

7. For safekeeping and to make sure that it is readily available at your death, you can leave your will with your attorney, in your own safe-deposit box (although this may create difficulties if in your state a court order or other formalities will be required to open your box after your death), in your spouse's safe-deposit box, in a fireproof box or safe in your home, or with a professional trust company or financial institution if such has been named as executor of the estate.

▶ **QUESTIONS FOR THOUGHT AND DISCUSSION**

1. Cornelius Vanderbilt's grandson once said that inherited wealth results in "certain . . . death to ambition." Do you agree?

2. If you were a multimillionaire, would you give half of your wealth to charity—as approximately half of the multimillionaires surveyed recently by *Fortune* magazine plan to do?

3. Do you perceive any conflict between inherited wealth and the democratic ideal that all persons are created equal?

4. At what age do you think one should create a will?

▶ **THINGS TO DO**

1. If your parents have a will, ask them if you can look at it and discuss its provisions with them. See if you can determine which provision or provisions make up the types of clauses (dispositive clauses, administrative clauses, and so on) discussed in this issue.

2. Imagine that you have an estate worth $1 million, a spouse, and two minor children. Based on what you have learned from Chapter 22 and this Consumer Issue, how would you plan to transfer your estate upon your death? In listing the possibilities, include gifts that you might make, trusts that you could establish, and so on.

3. Write your will.

▶ **SELECTED READINGS**

▶ Barrett, W. P. "IBM Esq." *Forbes,* July 22, 1991, p. 308.

▶ Biggs, Don. "Preparing Your Own Will." *How to Avoid Lawyers.* New York: Garland Publishing, 1985, Chs. 51–59.

▶ Clarkson, Kenneth W., et al. "Wills, Trusts, and Estates." *West's Business Law.* 4th ed. St. Paul, MN: West, 1989, Ch. 56.

▶ Frelincher, Morton, *Estate Planning Handbook—with Forms.* Englewood Cliffs, NJ: Prentice-Hall (latest edition).

▶ Loeb, Marshall. "Wills: Drafting Your Most Important Document." *Marshall Loeb's 1989 Money Guide.* Boston: Little, Brown, 1988, pp. 537–41.

▶ Winter, Annette. "What Should I Do?" *Modern Maturity,* October–November 1988, pp. 8–11.

▶ Yakal, K. "Will Builder." *Compute,* September 1991, p. 130.

Providing for the Ultimate Expense

It is possible to make, while you are living, fairly specific arrangements for your funeral and the way in which you want your body disposed of when you die. In today's world, the possibilities seem almost limitless—from mummification of your body (which the Summum Company of Salt Lake City will do for a current price of $7,700) to "drive-through visitation" at a funeral home (where your remains can be viewed by family and friends at a drive-up TV terminal).

Whatever you decide, it is prudent to remember that not you, but somebody else, will be charged with the task of either carrying out your instructions or, if you haven't specified any details, determining what type of funeral service and body disposal is appropriate. Usually, this task devolves upon the ones you love the most and at a time when they are least prepared to make rational consumer decisions.

This Consumer Issue offers some guidelines both for arranging funeral services for others and for prearranging your own funeral. We first discuss why the consumer is at a disadvantage when it comes to making funeral arrangements.

▶ THE CONSUMER IS AT A DISADVANTAGE

When arranging for funeral services, the consumer is often at a great disadvantage because of the following facts.

1. *Lack of knowledge.* The consumer usually has no idea how much funerals cost or what cost alternatives are available, because there is relatively little advertising in the funeral business.

2. *Lack of experience.* Clearly, most consumers lack experience in taking care of funeral arrangements for a loved one. This lack of experience means that a naive consumer can be victimized by an unscrupulous funeral director.

3. *Emotional state.* When a loved one dies, it is difficult to be rational about what is an appropriate funeral service, Again, some unscrupulous funeral directors will play on the emotional state of grieving relatives.

▶ What You Must Do When Arranging for a Funeral

1. Take care of the immediate needs of the bereaved.

2. Contact the funeral director and the clergyperson preferred by the family.

3. Notify the attorney who administered the affairs of the deceased.

4. Secure personal data and any special requests or instructions of the deceased affecting the funeral services; contact the local newspaper for the obituary.

5. Make the necessary arrangement with a cemetery.

6. Cooperate with the funeral director and the attorney in securing forms for filing claims with insurance companies, banks, fraternal groups, veterans or military organizations, government offices, and others.

▶ KEEPING FUNERAL COSTS UNDER CONTROL

For understandable reasons, many people underplay the cost factor when arranging a funeral. But funerals are costly and, for most consumers, represent the third-largest expenditure they will make—next to housing and automobiles. Today, the cost of a funeral ranges from $3,500 to $8,000 or more. Exhibit V–1 illustrates how average funeral costs have increased in recent years.

▶ The Funeral Rule

To enable consumers to compare more readily the prices of different funeral providers, the Federal Trade Commission has developed a set of regulations, collectively referred to as the Funeral Rule, pertaining to the funeral industry. The Funeral Rule, which became effective April 30, 1984, requires that all funeral-service providers make available to consumers an itemized list of their goods and services and the cost for each. If you go in person to a funeral home, such a list must be provided to you at your request, and the list must include all lower-cost alternatives whenever such are available. The Funeral Rule also requires that funeral providers give price information on the telephone to consumers, if requested, and answer any reasonable questions.

The Funeral Rule of 1984 makes it much easier for consumers to control the costs of funerals and to pick and choose the goods and services they want—apart, of course, from those required by law.

When the Funeral Rule was enacted in 1984, the FTC promised to review it after four years to decide whether to retain it, repeal it, or modify it. FTC hearings held in 1988 and 1989 resulted in no significant changes in the Funeral Rule.

As might be expected, those involved in the funeral industry, such as the National Funeral Directors Association, oppose the continuance of

▶ Exhibit V–1 Average Funeral Costs, 1983–1988

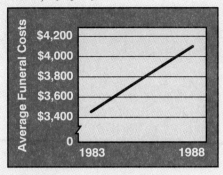

Source: Federated Funeral Directors of America.

the rule. Consumers, however, have largely benefitted by the rule. If you would like to express your view of the Funeral Rule to the FTC, write to Henry B. Cabell, Presiding Hearing Officer, Federal Trade Commission, Washington, D.C. 20580. For more information, you can call the FTC at (202) 326-3642.

▶ Funeral Expenses

Once you have decided on a funeral director, obtain a written statement of the charges for the funeral arrangements. The statement should contain the following:

1. Services, including merchandise selected, and the total price.
2. The supplemental items of service or merchandise requested and the price of each item.
3. The terms of payment.
4. The items for which the funeral director will advance cash, such as flowers, long-distance calls, and so on.

Funeral directors often quote a single amount for standard services. These include the casket and the use of the funeral home facilities and a hearse. However, they do not include the cemetery plot (which could have been chosen earlier), the burial or cremation fees, and such

items as flowers, obituary notices, and the clergyperson's honorarium.

In addition to the type of funeral service, you will have to decide on whether an earth burial or cremation is appropriate or desirable. If you choose the former, you will need to decide on the following three items: casket, cemetery space, and grave container and marker. Although cremation can often be a less costly alternative to earth burial, this isn't always the case. In some states, such as South Dakota, there is only one crematorium serving the entire state, and transportation costs make cremation more expensive than in more densely populated states. Thus, the relative costs of earth burial and cremation can vary widely from area to area. Strangely, several states require a casket even though the family has decided that the loved one will be cremated. Even in states where it is not required by law, a funeral director may nonetheless tell the consumer that a casket is necessary. This must be verified ahead of time.

Exhibit V–2 indicates how much the separate goods and services provided by funeral homes cost. Exhibit V–3 offers a glossary of terms that you will want to be familiar with should you need to arrange for a funeral service and burial (or cremation).

▶ Where to Go for Help

If you need help in determining what amount you should spend for a funeral, you can call Learning Resource Center, National Funeral Directors Association, 11121 W. Oklahoma Ave., Milwaukee, WI 53227 (414) 541-2500. You will be informed of the current cost ranges for funeral services and various goods and services provided by funeral homes, information that can help you make your decision. If you

▶ Exhibit V–2 Itemized Funeral Costs

Item/Service	Cost
Casket	$300 to $12,000
Hearse	$90 to $190
Limousines	$50 to $190/hr.
Funeral home staff	$500 to $1,000
Embalming	$150 to $250
Other preparations of the remains[1]	$50 to $90
Use of funeral home for a service	$125 to $250
Use of funeral home for visitation	$150 to $275
Cremation[2]	$600 to $1,100

1. Dressing the body, putting it in the casket, hairdressing, cosmetology, etc.
2. Does not include funeral services, special container for cremated remains.

Source: Federated Funeral Directors of America.

wish to make a complaint about funeral goods or services, there are several organizations to which you can turn.

1. Your state's attorney general's office or other state and local consumer groups (see Consumer Issue B).
2. The funeral licensing board in your state. Forty-seven states have such licensing boards that you can contact for information or help. Alternatively, you can write or call the following association, which represents all 47 licensing boards at the national level:

Conference of Funeral Service
Examining Boards
2404 Washington Blvd.,
Suite 1000
Ogden, UT 84401
(801) 392-7771

3. The Funeral Service Consumer Action Program (ThanaCap), a consumer mediation group sponsored

▶ Exhibit V–3   **Glossary for Funeral Services**

Casket   A coffin or box of any material that holds the deceased.

Columbarium   A building or wall for above-ground accommodation of cremated remains.

Cremation   The reduction of human remains by means of heat. The remains are commonly called ashes and weigh between six and eight pounds.

Crematorium   An establishment in which cremation takes place.

Crypt   A concrete chamber in a mausoleum into which a casket is placed. The chamber is slightly larger than the casket.

Disposition   Final placement or disposal of a dead person.

Double-depth grave   One grave space that accommodates two caskets, one on top of the other.

Embalming   Temporary preservation of the deceased by means of chemicals.

Entombment   Opening and closing of a crypt, including the placement and sealing of a casket within.

Grave liner   A concrete container into which a casket or urn is placed for ground burial. Its function is to prevent the ground from settling.

Honorarium   Payment (as to the clergy) for professional services.

Inurnment   The opening and closing of a niche, including the placement and sealing of an urn within.

Mausoleum   A building or wall for above-ground accommodation of a casket.

Niche   A chamber in a columbarium into which an urn is placed.

Opening and closing   Preparing a grave space for ground burial—that is, digging a grave, placing a casket or urn within, and covering it over.

Side-by-side grave   A double or companion grave space that accommodates two caskets adjacently.

Urn   A container for cremated remains.

Urn garden   An area in a cemetery for ground burial of cremated remains.

Vault   An elaborate container into which a casket is placed for ground burial. It serves to prevent ground settling and also helps slow the deterioration of the casket.

Source: *The Price of Death.* Consumer Survey Handbook 3. Seattle Regional Office, Federal Trade Commission.

---

by the National Funeral Directors Association. ThanaCap can be reached at:

> Consumer Assistance Program
> 2250 E. Devon Ave., Suite 250
> Des Plaines, IL 60018
> (800) 662-7666

▶ PREARRANGEMENTS

Donation of the body to a medical school (either before or after a memorial ceremony) is an obviously less costly (and, for many, a more purposeful) means of disposition. If you wish to become such a donor, you must let your loved ones know so that the appropriate steps can be taken upon your death (see Chapter 22).

▶ Prearranging Your Funeral

It is also possible to prearrange your own funeral. This saves not only on costs but also spares others certain

difficulties when arranging your funeral. Several funeral and memorial societies offer lifetime membership for you and your family for a one-time fee of between $20 and $40. There are currently nearly 200 of these societies in the United States, one of which may be located in your city or area. According to the Continental Association of Funeral and Memorial Societies, consumers can save up to 50 percent in funeral costs by joining a memorial society, regardless of the type of funeral arrangement desired.

▶ Prefinancing

Notice that there is a difference between prearrangement and prefinancing. You can prearrange all types of funeral services, but you don't necessarily have to use prefinancing. Indeed, you must be care-

ful of prefinancing plans, because implicitly you are allowing a funeral-home owner or director to keep your money, interest-free, until you die or until a loved one for whom you are prefinancing a burial plan dies.

Many books have been written about planning funerals and dealing with their expenses; the list of such books is far too extensive to include in this text. One of the best is *The American Way of Death,* by Jessica Medford. You will be able to find a wide selection of others in your public library.

▶ SUMMARY

1. Consumers are normally at a disadvantage when making funeral arrangements owing to lack of knowledge, lack of experience, and their emotional state at the time it is

necessary to make these kinds of decisions.

2. If someone you love dies and you must arrange for the funeral, first take care of the immediate needs of the bereaved. Then contact the funeral director and clergyperson preferred by the family and the attorney or other person handling the affairs of the deceased. Make sure that you learn what provisions the deceased made concerning funeral arrangements also. Contact the local newspaper for the obituary, make arrangements with a cemetery or crematorium, and follow through on funeral arrangements with the funeral home.

3. Funerals represent the third-largest expenditure that most consumers incur. Today, the average funeral costs more than $4,000.

4. The Federal Trade Commission's Funeral Rule of 1984 aids consumers by requiring funeral-service providers to make available to consumers an itemized list of their goods and services and the costs of each.

5. In addition to the type of funeral service, the decision on whether earth burial or cremation is appropriate for the deceased must be made. With some exceptions, cremation is far less costly than burial.

6. If you need information or have a complaint concerning funeral goods or services, organizations to contact include your state's attorney general's office, the funeral licensing board in your state, and the Funeral Service Consumer Action Program.

7. Prearranging your funeral can save on costs as well as spare others certain difficulties in arranging a funeral for you after you die. Prefinancing your funeral is also possible, but you must use caution with prefinancing plans.

▶ QUESTIONS FOR THOUGHT AND DISCUSSION

1. When it comes to funeral arrangements and planning, do you think most consumers are as rational as they are when making other types of financial arrangements?

2. When you die, would you prefer to have your body buried, cremated, or donated to a medical school or organization for research purposes? Is the relative cost of each of these forms of body disposal a factor in your decision?

3. Do you think it is important to specify, either in your will or in some other way, what kind of funeral service you want and how you want your body disposed of? Why or why not?

4. To what extent are cultural customs and taboos operative in the way we handle death in America?

5. How can you explain the fact that only a minority of Americans (currently about 17 percent) prefer cremation to burial, in spite of the fact that cremation is a simpler and less expensive undertaking?

▶ THINGS TO DO

1. Visit or call a local funeral home and ask for an itemized list of funeral goods and services and their respective costs. Find out what a typical funeral would cost and what goods and services it would include.

2. Write to the Federal Trade Commission at the address given in this issue and ask about the current status of the Funeral Rule.

3. Ask every member of your immediate family if he or she would prefer cremation or burial. If reasons are offered for a preference, evaluate whether those reasons are based on subjective assumptions (involving feelings, intuitions, and the like) or objective considerations (relative costs, for example).

▶ SELECTED READINGS

▶ Berns, David L. "Don't Wait Till Death to Plan a Funeral." *USA Today,* February 20, 1989, p. 3B.

▶ Burton, Brian. "Growth of the Chains." *MacLeans,* April 4, 1988, p. 29.

▶ *Consumer Guide to the FTC Funeral Rule.* Available free from the Federal Trade Commission, 6th St. and Pennsylvania Ave., N.W., Washington, DC 20580.

▶ "FTC Hearings Will Decide Fate of the 'Funeral Rule.' " *AARP News Bulletin,* October 1988, p. 5.

▶ Landis, David. "Cemeteries Struggle to Stay Alive." *USA Today,* January 9, 1989, p. 1B.

▶ "Prepaid Funerals: Not the Way to Go." *Consumer Reports,* February 1986, p. 75.

▶ *Prepaying Your Funeral: Some Questions to Ask.* Available free from American Association of Retired Persons, 1909 K St., N.W., Washington, DC 20049.

▶ *Tips on Planning a Funeral.* Available for $1 from the Council of Better Business Bureaus, Department 023, Washington, DC 20042.

▶ Wilkerson, Isabel. "New Funeral Option for Those in a Rush." *New York Times,* February 23, 1989, p. 10.

Consumers in a Changing World

PREVIEW

▶ How have technological changes affected decisions consumers make?

▶ What steps can consumers take to help them keep up with changing technology?

▶ What problems do consumers face because of new technology in the computer age?

▶ How has consumers' right to privacy been affected by changing technology?

▶ What changes in technology are consumers likely to experience in the future?

The day-to-day existence of today's consumers is incredibly more complex than that of our ancestors. When the United States was young, life was hard, but it does not appear to have been as complicated as it is today. For many people it was do-or-die, eke out a bare existence tilling the soil or starve to death. At the time of the American Revolution, more than 90 percent of the population earned their living through agriculture. One of the most complicated aspects of life was coping with the weather. Of course, all of the common problems that involve human relationships existed then as they do now, or as they will in the future. But as consumers and producers, Americans had fewer choices to make, and many of their choices were relatively simple compared to the decisions of today.

As we prepare to enter the 21st century, the number and variety of products available seem to approach infinity. Our technology is changing so rapidly that we may find it impossible to know from one minute to the next what our best consumer choices are. Some observers believe that the development of new products and their increasingly complex technological nature is causing some consumers to suffer from what might be called *decision overload.* If people feel overwhelmed by the complexity of their lives and the decisions they must make, they may stop trying to make rational choices. They might in effect say, "I can't figure out what's happening no matter how hard I try, so what's the point in trying? I'll just do whatever I feel like doing and let the pieces fall where they may." Although such an attitude may be understandable, it will almost certainly harm people who hold it. To be sure, the complexity of present-day consumer decisions has added to the difficulty of making rational choices, but we should never give up trying to make the best decisions possible to protect the quality of our lives.

THE EVER-CHANGING PRODUCT LANDSCAPE

When Henry Ford introduced the Model-T Ford in the first decade of this century, he let people choose any color they wanted, "provided that it was black." Indeed, there was no choice if you wanted to buy one of his cars. Whatever features it had when it came off the assembly line, you bought. Times have changed. Today the options available on a new Lincoln Town Car make possible more than 70,000 different combinations. This example illustrates the amazing complexity in consumer choice that has been introduced into our lives, not only because of the sheer number of products we are offered, but also because of the variety of choices available within each product category. Today's consumer can go into any shopping mall and face an array of choices for his or her consumer spending that boggles the mind. The simple life consumers had in the past no longer exists for anyone who wants to take advantage of the opportunities offered in our economic system. Of course, consumers could preserve a simple lifestyle by becoming hermits in Alaska and living off the land. However, for most this is not a realistic alternative.

TECHNOLOGICAL OBSOLESCENCE

Consumers often feel a sense of frustration when they need to replace a worn-out product they own. Imagine the problems you would face making consumer choices if you had not kept up with changes in technology. Further, imagine that the television set you bought in 1980 has died. You have not studied or even thought about features offered by televisions in over a decade. Your old TV worked well, now it is dead and you just want to replace it. When you visit the appliance store where you bought your old TV, you are in for a big surprise. It isn't easy to buy a simple TV set any more. Most have electronic tuning, remote controls, automatic color, and signal tracking. You can buy TVs that have screens from three inches to four feet across. Many televisions have controls that operate a VCR as well. The list of options you can purchase on a television goes on and on. Almost all the knowledge you thought you had of televisions is out of date. You are forced to start over, investigating your consumer choice from "ground zero." What's more, in a few more years, when you need to buy your next television, you will be faced with the same problem again, thanks to changing technology.

Consumers today are faced with **technological obsolescence** that makes many products outdated almost as soon as they buy them. The best example of this is probably found in the market for personal computers. When these products were first introduced in the 1970s they cost $3,000 or more, had limited capabilities, and the programs they ran were often not user-friendly. In the 20 years since then, technological developments have progressed at a rate that almost guarantees that a personal computer is already out-of-date when it is first unpacked from its shipping crate. It was possible to buy a computer system in 1993 that had a 100-megabyte hard disk, 640 K of random access memory, a high-resolution monitor, and several software packages already installed for little more than $1,000. Furthermore, there was general agreement among those "in the know" about computer research that the pace of change was accelerating. Consequently, many consumers who buy computers cannot hope to fully understand the product they purchase, its capabilities, or whether they are making the best choice for their needs.

This same phenomenon can be seen in other consumer products. When compact disc (CD) players were introduced not too many years ago by the Sony Corporation of Japan, they cost around $1,000. Currently, you can buy a CD player to add on to your existing stereo system for as little as $69. (This price may have come down further by the time you read this text.) Similar events occurred with videocassette recorders (VCRs). Not only are current models cheaper, but they are also of better quality than those that were first introduced.

What should you do? Should you plan on continually upgrading your electronic and video equipment? Should you put off buying equipment until new advancements are perfected, or until prices come down? How much should you care? What is the value of your time that you use to try to keep up with technological change? These are all questions that may swirl through your mind and disturb your sleep.

Technological obsolescence
The process of a product becoming obsolete due to technological advances. This problem is particularly notable in the high-tech electronics industry, in which the rapid development of new, state-of-the-art products significantly diminishes the utility and value of previously marketed models.

FACING THE DEPRECIATION PROBLEM

With such rapid advances in technology, consumer products—particularly cameras, video equipment, computers, and other electronic products—lose their value in the marketplace rapidly once they are purchased. This kind of depreciation is, in many respects, not due to wear and tear or consumer use. The normal depreciation of an automobile or a bicycle can be attributed to consumer use. Things do wear out, but in today's rapidly changing technological world, many products have depreciated in the marketplace even when they are still in perfect working order. Indeed, a five-year-old computer that was never taken from its box will have little resale value today because it is out-of-date. This problem is not necessarily the result of manufacturers planning to create products that rapidly become obsolete (although they might in some cases). It is more likely the result of consumers wanting to keep up with the newest technological advances and their refusal to purchase outdated products.

For example, current models of CD players have what is called *oversampling* and better error-correction systems that result in better-quality sound compared with older systems. VCRs today have simplified programming systems, digital video reduction systems for removal of "snow," faster fast-forwarding and rewinding capabilities, more refined slow-motion and other special-effects systems, and so on, than do older VCRs. It's no wonder·that, if you have an older model, maybe even one that you kept in the closet and never used, you won't find anyone who wants to buy it for even a small fraction of what you paid for it, say, five years ago.

There are at least two aspects to rapid technological advances in our economy that you should keep in mind when you make consumer choices: (1) improved models of consumer products are likely to become available at the same price as older models, or the same product should fall in price as better models become available; and (2) you should expect rapid depreciation in the market value of any technologically based consumer product. This means you as a consumer must choose between buying better and cheaper products in the future, or purchasing today more expensive and often less sophisticated products that will depreciate in value.

OBTAINING INFORMATION ISN'T ALWAYS EASY

When there are seemingly hundreds of models and brands of VCRs or microwave ovens from which to choose, how can the average consumer find information on each of these models and make a rational purchasing decision? Obviously, living in a technological world as we do, the more information we are able to gather and consider, the more likely we are to make good consumer choices. But we don't always have the time or the ability to gather and evaluate information. Therefore, we often rely on the guidance of others who we hope have better or more complete knowledge than we possess. Consumers often rely on specialists—people who make it their business to know about products—and who are often willing to sell us their information for a price.

Who are these specialists, and how should consumers find them? An obvious source of information is the retail outlet in the form of promotional materials and instruction booklets provided by manufacturers. Salespeople may be able to provide additional technical explanations. Consumers, however, need to remember that the people who provide this source of information have an interest in selling products whether or not they are the best choice a consumer could make. Consumers need to find additional sources of information that are more neutral in perspective.

There are consumer-oriented publications that provide information and often specific recommendations for many types of products. *Consumer Reports,* and *Consumers' Research Magazine,* provide detailed information about many goods and services. There are other publications that may help consumers. Many magazines, for example, concentrate on reporting new developments in computer technology. Other trade journals deal with woodworking, cooking, cleaning, and home decorating. A few of these publications are financed by the industries they report on and therefore are not likely to say anything negative about these firms' products. This does not mean such publications contain lies and are of no value. It does mean consumers should realize that they may not provide a balanced report.

Although many consumers may not think of word-of-mouth as being a good source of information about complex products, it is often useful. Listening to what other consumers have to say about specific brands of products may tell you which ones to avoid, if nothing else. Another important type of information you are likely to be able to learn from other consumers is the quality of service offered by specific retail outlets. Remember, when you buy a product like a VCR, you are also buying the willingness of the store and manufacturer to stand behind the product's warranty. If you hear stories about a retailer refusing to service products or fulfill the terms of a contract cheerfully, that is a store you might choose to avoid. Even if a consumer you talk to doesn't understand how a product works, he or she can usually tell you if it works, and whether it has been properly serviced. Like any other source of information, we should evaluate what we hear from other consumers in relation to what we know of them and the knowledge that we have gained from other sources about the product in question.

One alternative consumers may choose when they purchase products they know little about is to buy a nationally advertised brand-name product. Although such products are usually not the least expensive or might not even have the highest quality, consumers can be reasonably sure that at least such goods are not of low quality and that there is a warranty and the reputation of a large firm behind them.

> One rule of thumb about brand-new products is, wait. Products that have just been introduced are almost always the most expensive they will ever be, and almost always have the most defects they will ever have.

THE TRADEOFFS IN BUYING NEW PRODUCTS

Are there special dangers in buying brand-new products that have never been on the market before? This situation poses a special problem. You cannot get information from trade journals or consumer publications—or even by word of mouth—because the product is too new for anyone to have much experience in using it. One rule of thumb about brand-new products is, wait. Products that have just been introduced are almost always the most expensive they will ever be, and almost always have the most defects they will ever have during their product life. It is almost always better to wait a while before buying such new products.

Notice the word "almost" in the previous sentence. The fact that a product is new and expensive should not prevent consumers from buying it if it provides a benefit they really need. Consumers who, for example, are diabetic must take medication when the sugar level in their blood is not in balance. In the 1980s new home-testing devices were marketed that made testing sugar levels in blood quick and easy. For these people, it was worth paying a high price to have such a product even if it had minor defects. The same was true of professional accountants who paid more than a hundred dollars for the first hand-held electronic calculators that became available in the early 1970s. They were expensive and had limited capabilities, but they were so much better than other calculators sold at that time that they were purchased as quickly as stores could put them on their shelves.

The rule to remember when considering brand-new products is always to study the tradeoff between the benefits and costs of buying now or later. If you "just have to have it now" and can afford the product, go ahead and buy it. But realize that you could probably pay less for a better model if you wait.

WATCH OUT FOR HAZARDS

One problem with new products, and even some older ones, is that consumers may face hazards in using them that even the manufacturers do not know about. For example, there is a growing body of evidence that many people suffer adverse effects from using computers—specifically, from looking at the green or amber writing on a computer screen for long periods of time, sitting in the same position for hours, and using the same muscles over and over to strike the computer's keys. Users have reported side effects that include eyestrain, mental confusion, and muscle cramps. Many firms are adding antiglare surfaces to monitor screens, changing the viewing angle, and requiring employees who use computers to look away from their work and rest their hands and arms briefly at regular intervals.

Other types of problems have been associated with common consumer goods like microwave ovens, television sets, chemicals in household cleaners, lawn fertilizers, and many other products. The fact that problems have been encountered among people who use some consumer products does not mean you should avoid using new products. It does mean that you should make an effort to be aware of news about such products. By reading your newspaper and national publications, you should be able to stay informed of any serious problems.

Remember, in every situation that requires a consumer decision, you have the final choice. Even if your only choice is to refuse to use a product, it is

Many consumers buy new products without considering possible hazards to their health. Spending many hours each day working at a computer, for example, has been shown to cause health problems that include muscle cramps, blurred vision, and nerve damage. As in most types of physical activity, using a computer in moderation is probably the best choice for consumers to make.

still your choice to make. When new products are introduced, the determination of whether or not they are successful is made by consumers. Marketing and advertising efforts can hope to persuade, but they cannot command the still-sovereign consumer.

THE CONSUMER IN A COMPUTER AGE

We all know how radically our lives have been changed by the explosion of computer technology in our society. Consider one specific example. When the author of this text attended college (not so many years ago) registration for classes seemed like a special level of hell in Dante's *Inferno*. Thousands of students raced among hundreds of tables in the school gymnasium searching for class cards that would not result in conflicts between required courses. The sound of a thousand pencils scratching in unison filled the air as students completed endless forms in triplicate by hand. All the while, there was an undertone of vague mutterings and often profane oaths. Registration could take six or more hours. When finished, students were not always sure what they had signed up for, and there was always "add-drop day" to look forward to.

Today you are probably able to register for classes in less than an hour, and most of the work is completed by a computer. You may not be able to get every class you want, but at least you find out quickly what is available and without having to complete endless forms. Students should appreciate how much easier almost every aspect of education has been made by computers. Computers have made our lives richer and have freed us from much time-consuming paperwork. However, there are serious problems associated with this technology that consumers need to protect themselves from.

Potential Dangers of Technology in a Computer Age

Our workplace, our homes, and our consumer transactions have all been transformed by the rapid development of computer technology. These changes of the last two decades have in turn created new kinds of problems with which consumers must cope.

Computers and Consumer Rights

One of the problem consumers face in the computer age is that traditional laws were not written to deal with the unique problems computers have presented. This often means that, until new legislation is passed, consumers are uncertain of their rights with regard to computerized transactions. For example, electronic fund transfers and the use of automated teller machines existed for a number of years before the Electronic Fund Transfer Act (EFTA) of 1980 was passed to regulate these transactions. This meant that for several years there was no clear-cut list of rights that applied to consumers of electronic banking services. There was no standard for judging when a bank was liable for an error in a computerized transaction or when it was not.

The EFTA was a boon to consumers, but it—and other recent consumer protection legislation—will not always benefit us if we fail to learn what our rights and responsibilities are under the laws. For example, what if your access card (debit card) is stolen or lost and used by another person who withdraws $2,000 from your checking account? In such a situation, it is important to know that if you report the theft or loss of your card to the bank within two days,

> Computers have made our lives richer and have freed us from much time-consuming paperwork. However, there are serious problems associated with this technology that consumers need to protect themselves from.

your liability is only $50. But if you fail to report the theft within two days, you will be liable for $500 of the stolen funds. This means that, as consumers, our lives are complicated not only by the uncertainties involved in new types of computerized transactions, but also by the need to learn of our rights and responsibilities under new legislation regulating these transactions. Consider the Consumer Close-Up in this chapter for a specific example of why laws need to keep up with new technology.

Computer Misinformation

Today every consumer faces the potential problem of having to deal with computer errors—or more accurately, with human errors that result in incorrect information being stored and then distributed from computer data files. There are many times when a simple phone call can remedy this type of problem. For some consumers, however, a seemingly endless amount of time is spent in trying to have such errors corrected. A man in Atlanta, Georgia, for example, who tried to borrow money was denied credit time after time. Finally, he found that his credit record stated that he had been involved in a lawsuit, had bad debts, had gone bankrupt, and had skipped town. In fact, he had a business, had lived in the same house for 12 years, was not involved in a lawsuit, had no bad debts, and had never filed for bankruptcy. Six years later, after he and his lawyers had talked to the credit-reporting agency that had furnished the incorrect information, and after letters had been sent to the Justice Department, the Federal Trade Commission, and the president of the United States, he finally was told that the incorrect information had been removed from his file. Later the same year when he applied for credit cards from Standard Oil and Sears, he was again denied credit because the same incorrect information had again been placed in his file by the credit-reporting agency. This, to be sure, is an extreme example, but computer misinformation is one of the problems with which consumers are forced to cope. The results of such situations can range from being a minor annoyance to doing major damage to one's reputation and credibility.

You might wonder how a credit-reporting firm could place incorrect information in a person's file in the first place. And once the firm was made aware of its mistake, why there would be so much trouble removing the information and then preventing it from being placed there again? The answers to these questions can be found in the way that new technology, and more specifically, computers, have been used by credit-reporting firms.

From a credit-reporting firm's point of view, the great advantage of using computers to maintain files is that this allows them to employ fewer workers at lower wages, workers who need not be highly skilled just to input information. Such workers often accept without question most information about individual consumers supplied by businesses and banks no matter how absurd or unlikely it may seem. Indeed, the people who place this information in consumers' files are not responsible for, nor are they qualified to, check the accuracy of the information they enter into the computer.

Suppose two consumers had the same name (not an uncommon event) or they had similar social security numbers, resulting in information about one (who did not pay bills) being placed incorrectly in the file of the other (who paid every bill on time). Soon the person who had a spotless credit history would be refused credit because of the mistake. He or she could complain, and the information would be removed from the file, ending the problem. Right? Wrong! Until recently credit bureaus tried to force individual consumers

ATMs and Computer Crime

We have been told that computers don't make mistakes. So if a computer says you used an ATM to withdraw $100 from your checking account, you must have done it. Right? Well, maybe not. Whenever a new type of technology comes along, it seems to open up new ways for dishonest people to commit crimes.

In 1989 Mark Koenig and four other employees of GTE Corporation were charged with trying to steal as much as $14 million with forged ATM cards. The prosecution claimed that the gang intercepted the personal ATM identification numbers of Bank of America customers from GTE telephone lines. They were accused of then making up 5,500 fake ATM cards from magnetic tape and cardboard. Their plan was to use the cards at different ATMs across the eastern United States in a single weekend. According to Secret Service officers, the plan would have worked if an anonymous tip hadn't given the plot away.

In another case someone used a Security Pacific National Bank Master Card to tap into a customer's private accounts to withdraw $237,000. After the crime was detected, the bank replaced the customer's funds. Bank officials admitted that whoever did this had to be a bank insider to have access to the information that would allow him or her to accomplish this theft.

Although banks are trying to tighten up on their internal security, there is no way to be sure that every employee will be totally honest. Methods have been developed to combat this type of crime, but the new technology is expensive. Identix, Inc., of Sunnyvale, California, is working on a device that reads customer fingerprints. Another firm is promoting the idea of using voice prints to identify customers. A difficulty of both of these methods is that they would require different cards for each individual. You could not allow your spouse or child to use your card if you wanted to. Using the new technology would require replacement of existing ATM machines—an expense banks would rather avoid. Regardless of how banks choose to fight the problem of computer crime at ATMs, you should be sure to keep records of all your transactions and check your statements carefully to avoid becoming a victim of computer crime. This type of crime is not likely to be stopped anytime soon.

to find firms that had provided incorrect information and force the firm to file new corrected reports with the credit bureau. The most probable reason for this policy was that it was less expensive for that credit bureau to have someone else do the work. Even when such corrections were filed, they would not necessarily end the consumer's problems.

Suppose that in the meantime the credit bureau sold its information, including the mistake, to other credit bureaus. Although the original credit bureau might remove the erroneous information from the file once, it could reappear six months later when the bureau buys information back from the other bureaus it sold to in the past. The same, exact mistaken information could again stop the person with a good credit history from being able to receive credit. The process of correcting this mistake could start all over again. This problem is caused by credit bureaus employing people unqualified to check the accuracy of information in consumer files. The ease with which information (be it right or wrong) can be transferred has increased the probability of such mistakes.

You learned about the Fair Credit Reporting Act in Chapter 16. This law gives people the right to be told which credit bureau supplied the information that caused them to be turned down for credit. They also have the right to a free copy of their file at that credit bureau if they ask for it within 60 days of the credit denial. Many states have taken actions that have been intended to further protect consumers. In 1991 the states of Texas, California, Alabama, Idaho, Michigan, and New York joined together to sue TRW, one of the three largest credit reporting services, charging "fraudulent and illegal practices." Apparently in an attempt to protect its public image, and perhaps to forestall further government action, TRW announced on October 14, 1991, that it would provide consumers who asked with free copies of their credit files once a year. Although the problem of incorrect credit reporting seems to be less than it once was, the existence of this problem points out the danger in relying too heavily on computers that do what we tell them, but do not think and have no judgment. Many recent laws and decisions would not have been necessary without the technological advancements that made our computer society possible.

THE NEW WORLD OF MARKETING

Although many consumers may not be aware of it, our computerized society has allowed advertisers, politicians, charity-seeking organizations, and numerous other groups to better target their audiences. So much data are now available on the American population, and computers are so powerful, that it is possible to direct an advertising campaign almost down to the level of an individual family. For example, campaigning by politicians is now very finely tuned: laser-printed letters in a candidate's handwriting can be individually sent to a targeted group of voters, who are addressed by name. The letter will vary depending on the voter's age, profession, and any number of other factors. A doctor and a lawyer and a fly fisherman will each receive a different, personalized letter.

Although you won't yet be receiving this kind of letter to sell you soap, manufacturers of consumer products have better demographic information than ever before, thanks to the computer, and they are beginning to use it in their marketing strategies. From agencies that specialize in collecting and analyzing such information, manufacturers can better determine which consumer groups are most likely to respond favorably to advertisements—on TV or through the mails—of particular products. This allows them to focus their marketing campaigns more sharply on a specifically targeted audience. They may advertise in one city differently from the way they advertise in another city because they have information about the demographic differences of those two cities. An automobile manufacturer, for example, may push the safety record of its car in a medium-sized town in the Midwest but stress the zero-to-60 mph elapsed time of the auto in its Los Angeles marketing campaign.

What does this mean for you, the consumer? It means two things: On the one hand, you will be more likely to receive information on products that interest you. On the other hand, you may be more vulnerable to slick advertising techniques. *Caveat emptor.*

TECHNOLOGY AND PRIVACY

Virtually all institutions with which you have dealings obtain information about you and store that information in their computer files. For most of us, this raises some questions. In particular, what institutions or agencies have what kind of information about our private lives? And what are our rights in terms of verifying the accuracy of this information and in controlling others' access to it?

The Right to Privacy

The U.S. Constitution does not specifically provide for the right to privacy, but the Supreme Court has recognized that such a right is implied under various constitutional provisions and has held that an individual's privacy should be protected against government intrusion. Although the government can legally collect data on private individuals, it can assemble and use only those data in which it has a legitimate interest—and for which it provides adequate safeguards against abuse.

To ensure that our right to privacy is not abused, Congress has enacted numerous laws. These laws, which are listed and briefly described in Exhibit 23–1, basically regulate the use and dispersal of personal information collected by government and private organizations. Generally, they provide that indi-

▶ Exhibit 23–1 **Federal Legislation Relating to Privacy**

TITLE	PROVISIONS CONCERNING PRIVACY
Freedom of Information Act (1966)	Provides that individuals have a right to obtain access to information about them collected in government files.
Fair Credit Reporting Act (1970)	Provides that consumers have the right to be informed of the nature and scope of a credit investigation, the kind of information that is being compiled, and the names of the firms or individuals who will be receiving the report.
Crime Control Act (1973)	Safeguards the confidentiality of information amassed for certain state criminal systems.
Family Educational Rights and Privacy Act (1974)	Limits access to computer-stored records of education-related evaluations and grades in private and public colleges and universities.
Privacy Act (1974)	Protects the privacy of individuals about whom the federal government has information. Specifically, the act provides that: 1. Agencies originating, using, disclosing, or otherwise manipulating personal information must ensure the reliability of the information and provide safeguards against its misuse. 2. Information compiled for one purpose cannot be used for another without the concerned individual's permission. 3. Individuals must be able to find out what data concerning them are being compiled and how the data will be used. 4. Individuals must be given a means through which to correct inaccurate data.
Tax Reform Act (1976)	Preserves the privacy of personal financial information.
Right to Financial Privacy Act (1978)	Prohibits financial institutions from providing the federal government with access to a customer's records unless the customer authorizes the disclosure.
Electronic Fund Transfer Act (1980)	Requires financial institutions to notify an individual if a third party gains access to the individual's account.
Counterfeit Access Device and Computer Fraud and Abuse Act (1984)	Prohibits use of a computer without authorization to retrieve data in a financial institution's or consumer reporting agency's files.
Cable Communications Policy Act (1984)	Regulates access to information collected by cable service operators on subscribers to cable services.
Electronic Communications Privacy Act (1986)	Prohibits the interception of information communicated by electronic means.

Census Bureau

The Census Bureau collects data every ten years on the U.S. population. Information collected includes the age, address, sex, ethnic origin or race, marital status, income, and place of employment of every person living in every household.

Federal Bureau of Investigation (FBI)

The FBI has a file on anyone who has ever been employed by the federal government, been in the military, or attempted to obtain a security clearance. The FBI also keeps files on some other individuals—for example, those who subscribe to publications by, contribute to, or are a member of certain organizations and causes.

Social Security Administration (SSA)

If you have ever been an employee and received wages, the Social Security Administration will have a record of it. In other words, your entire employment record— where you have worked and when—is contained within these records. Additionally, the Social Security Administration has information concerning the income, indebtedness, marital status, medical history, and household arrangements of anyone who has applied for Social Security benefits, Medicare or Medicaid, or Aid to Families with Dependent Children (AFDC).

Internal Revenue Service (IRS)

The IRS has information concerning age, sex, marital status, and all sources of income—jobs, checkable and savings accounts, investments, and so on.

Veterans Administration (VA)

The VA contains information in its files of all persons who have served in the military. This includes not only military records but also information concerning jobs held, medical histories, education, and residences prior to entering the service. Additional information will be entered if a veteran is receiving service-related benefits, such as a VA mortgage loan, educational assistance, or medical care.

Federal Housing Administration (FHA)

Has information on all persons applying for federal housing assistance.

Selective Service System

Has information on draft registration.

Defense Department

Has information on anyone who has sought a security clearance.

Securities and Exchange Commission (SEC)

Has information on anyone involved in the sale of securities.

---

viduals have a right to obtain access to, and verify the accuracy of, information about them in any government files and a right to know when such information is requested or used by a third party.

What the Government Knows About You

Exhibit 23–2 gives you an idea of the kind of data collected by the government on individual Americans. Keep in mind that this is only a partial list. For example, any time you apply for a license of any kind from the state or federal government, a file containing information about you is created.

Can you find out whether a government agency—the FBI, for example— has a file on you? Or whether the personal information about you stored in any other government file is accurate? Yes, you can. Under the Freedom of Information Act and the Privacy Act (see Exhibit 23–1) you have a right to gain access to any information about you that has been collected by the government, with certain exceptions that relate to confidentiality or national security. To obtain a copy of such information, all you need to do is write to the government agency and state that "under the provisions of the Privacy Act of 1974, 5 U.S.C. Section 522a, I hereby request all information concerning myself in your files." Send your letter to the relevant agency and to the attention of "Freedom of Information/Privacy Acts Office"—every agency has one. Be sure to include relevant information that will help government personnel to locate the file.

If you need to obtain information concerning your earning record—it may one day be very important to you that this information is accurate—you can write directly to the Social Security Administration. The way to obtain the appropriate form to use for this request was discussed in Consumer Issue S.

Private Organizations

In addition to the government agencies and departments listed in Exhibit 23–2, numerous other institutions maintain files of information on consumers. For example, when you attended elementary and high school, records were kept of your grades, health, and possibly of your behavior. In 40 states it is legal for such information to be released to people other than your parents, colleges, other schools, or government personnel.

Banks keep records of your financial transactions—your deposits, withdrawals, and so on. In 41 states it is legal for banks to release such information to people other than the bank customer. In all states this information may be requested by the FBI or IRS; however, these agencies must comply with procedural rules before gaining access to such information.

Medical information is collected and stored whenever you see your doctor or visit a hospital. Such information is confidential—in 35 states it is illegal even for the patient to have access to it. Insurance companies maintain similar files concerning their policyholders' health and medical treatments.

Remember, this is just a partial list of the kinds of institutions that might have personal information concerning you, your family, your income, your debts, and so on. If you have ever applied for insurance, data concerning you will have been added to the insurance company's computer network. If you have ever bought a car on credit, you are the subject of yet another computer file. And so on. The point is, even though we have a right to privacy, our lives are no longer really that private. Given today's technology, any person—and particularly, the government—can assemble a lot of information about any given individual in as little as an hour's time.

> Given today's technology, any person—and particularly, the government—can assemble a lot of information about any given individual in as little as an hour's time.

NEW TECHNOLOGY SHAPES YOUR FUTURE

You, and every other American, must learn to live in a world of changing technology. Products we take for granted today would have astounded your parents when they were young. You have acquired many technical skills just by living in our world. You probably know how to operate a microwave oven, run a VCR, and use an electronic calculator. Devices that scan product codes in grocery stores, check your individual account when you use a credit card to buy a product in a department store, or allow you to withdraw money from your bank account using a machine are no longer considered anything special. At work you might use a computer to automatically print hundreds of individualized letters, or an electronic device to measure the thickness of a piece of metal with a laser beam. All of these innovations have taken place within your lifetime.

When people look for work today, they are likely to find few job openings that offer much more than the minimum wage for untrained workers. To advance beyond the level of clerk or dishwasher, people need more than a high school diploma—they need some form of specialized training. People often can't even repair a car anymore without knowing how to use computer equipment. Having a strong back and willing hands assures you of almost nothing in today's world. But if you know how to repair computers or VCRs, you should earn a good living wherever you choose to reside.

If your life has seen so much technological change, can you imagine what is likely to happen during your children's lifetime? In July 1991, IBM announced that it had succeeded in manipulating single atoms of silicon. This ability is expected eventually to lead to the construction of super-powerful computers little larger than a typewriter. The time of cash purchases may be rapidly coming to an end. In the not-too-distant future most stores may become wired into the banking system so that our purchases will immediately be charged to our bank accounts when we make purchases, even as they are now on a limited basis. Stores may become unwilling to accept cash that involves risks and complicates their operations.

Every sign points to more automation and technology in our schools. Interactive computer programs already allow students in effect to discuss problems with computers. Television satellite linkups promise to allow students to watch courts make decisions, Congress debate issues, and markets function. It is now possible to store the entire 28 volumes of an encyclopedia on one laser disk. In the future we will be able to use vast library holdings stored on laser disks in central locations that can be accessed by computers.

Automobiles will become more fuel-efficient and probably be more electronically controlled. There are already on-board computers in many cars that monitor their functions. It is possible that driving on major highways may become automated and controlled by computers. The list of technological innovations that we and our children will face seems endless.

For the typical consumer, technological advancements will require a constant learning process. To make responsible decisions, consumers need to understand products they purchase and use. If consumers do not make an effort to keep up with the times, they will find it progressively more difficult to make consumer decisions that maximize the satisfaction they receive from the money they have to spend. Being a responsible consumer means committing oneself to a life of learning.

▶ SUMMARY

1. High-tech products present special problems for today's consumers. These problems include technological obsolescence, rapid depreciation, product complexity, difficulty of obtaining relevant information on new products, and possibly hazardous side effects of using many technologically advanced consumer products.

2. Consumers now face more complicated decision-making tasks than consumers did in an earlier America. This is due to the increased number and complexity of products available to consumers today.

3. One of the problems of the computer age is that traditional laws often do not cover the unique kinds of problems that arise in our computerized society. There is often a lag between the development of new computer applications and the creation of new laws (or the extension of existing laws) to cover them. During this period of time, the rights and responsibilities of

participants in transactions that involve computers or other new types of technology are unclear.

4. Although the explosion of computer applications in our society has aided us in many ways, it has also created many problems for consumers. One of these is a result of the ease with which information may be stored and distributed with computers. Many people have been denied credit because of incorrect information provided by credit bureaus. It has often proven difficult for consumers to have such information removed from, and kept off, their credit histories because the computers that store and share information have no ability to distinguish between true, false, or unlikely information.

5. With the aid of computers, manufacturers and marketing specialists can now obtain more accurate demographic information. Such information allows them to target their audiences and more finely tune advertising for their products.

6. A problem of increasing concern to many consumers is the extent to which the computerization of society is affecting our right to privacy. Private institutions, as well as numerous government agencies, have computer files containing personal information about individuals. The federal government has enacted numerous laws to help ensure that our right to privacy is not abused by the unauthorized use of private information contained in business or government computer files.

7. Although technology has led to the new types of consumer problems, it has also helped to simplify our lives. Ultimately, technology responds to the profit incentives that our economy is based on. Consumers have the ultimate decision in choosing whether to buy many types of products that involve new technology. In many ways the American consumer remains sovereign.

▶ QUESTIONS FOR THOUGHT AND DISCUSSION

1. In what ways have technological innovations affected your life in the past ten years?

2. What changes do you believe advancements in computer technology will bring about in our economy in the next ten years?

3. In your opinion, what is the most important tradeoff consumers have made to obtain the benefits of improved technology?

4. One of the consequences of new technology is that many transactions have become very impersonal (such as doing banking through ATMs). In your opinion, is it possible—or even desirable—to maintain a "personal touch" in our computerized society? Explain the reasons for your answer.

5. Assume for the moment that you have the choice of living in any era in history. Which time would you choose? What factors—health, available products, and so on—would figure most prominently in your decision?

▶ THINGS TO DO

1. Assume that you wish to purchase a new or used personal computer. Make a list of steps you would take before making your final decision.

2. Write to a government agency that you think may have information concerning you in its files. Use the method described in this chapter to complete your letter.

3. Discuss changes in the lives of typical American consumers with a person who is substantially older than you. How does this person feel about new types of technology he or she must deal with? Has technology made this person's life better or worse? Make a list of similarities and differences between your perception of new technology and those of the person you interview.

▶ APPLICATION

Examine a copy of *Popular Mechanics* that is ten or more years old at your library. Make a list of technological advances the magazine accurately predicted. Discuss how these advancements have changed the lives of American consumers. Complete a similar assignment with a current issue of this magazine using predictions it makes about the future. How will these advancements affect consumers if they do take place? How does your research demonstrate the need consumers have to keep up with changing technology?

▶ SELECTED READINGS

▶ *A Citizen's Guide to Using the Freedom of Information Act and the Privacy Act of 1974 to Request Government Records.* Washington, DC: U.S. Government Printing Office, 1987.

▶ Buckley, Jerry. "How Doctors Decide Who Shall Live, Who Shall Die." *U.S. News & World Report,* January 22, 1990, pp. 50–58.

▶ Clarkson, Kenneth W., et al. *West's Business Law.* 4th ed. St. Paul, MN: West, 1989, Chs. 28 and 55.

▶ "Communications Computers and Networks." *Scientific American,* September 1991, pp. 62–69.

▶ Freudenheim, Milt. "Insurance vs. Doctors: A Software Battleground." *New York Times,* November 15, 1989, p. 37.

▶ Hadlock. P. "High Technology Employment: Another View." *Monthly Labor Review,* July 1991, pp. 26–30.

▶ Miller, Michael W. "Data Mills Delve Deep to Find Information about U.S. Consumers." *The Wall Street Journal,* March 14, 1991, p. A1.

▶ Reid, P. P. "The Globalization of Technology." *Issues in Science and Technology,* Summer 1991, pp. 92–93.

▶ Quint, Michael. "Banking's High-Tech Pursuit of Retail Customers." *New York Times,* December 31, 1989, pp. 1, 8.

▶ "Taking It Personally." *The Wall Street Journal,* October 21, 1991. Special section on technology.

▶ "You Can Look It Up—On a Disk." *U.S. News & World Report,* November 19, 1990, p. 73–75.

▶ Weaver, P. "When You Use Your Phone Card, Look Out for 'PIN Peepers.' " *Nation's Business,* September 1991, p. 67.

Glossary of Terms

Abstract A short history of title to land; a document listing all records relating to a given parcel of land.

Acceleration clause A clause contained in numerous credit agreements whereby, if one payment is missed, the entire unpaid balance becomes due, or the due date is accelerated to the immediate future.

Add-on clause A clause in an installment contract that makes your earlier purchases from that source security for the new purchase.

Administrative clauses Those clauses in a will that ensure that the instructions are carried out.

Age/earnings profile The profile of how earnings change with your age. When you're young and just starting out, your earnings are low; as you get older, your earnings increase because you become more productive and work longer hours; finally, your earnings start to decrease.

Amortization schedule A table showing the amount of monthly payments due on a long-term loan, such as a mortgage; it indicates the exact amounts going toward interest and principal.

Anesthesiologist A doctor who specializes in administering anesthesia to patients before surgery.

Annual percentage rate (APR) The annual interest cost of consumer credit.

Annual percentage yield (APY) The standard annualized return on a savings deposit that all savings institutions must provide to depositors under the Truth in Savings Act of 1993.

Antitrust laws Laws designed to prevent business monopolies. Antitrust laws are part of government antitrust policies that are aimed at establishing and maintaining competition in the business world to assure consumers of fair prices and goods of adequate quality.

Asset Something of value that is owned by an individual, a business, or by the government.

Assigned risk A person seeking automobile insurance who has been refused coverage. That person is assigned to an insurance company that is a member of the assigned-risk pool in the person's state.

Attestation clauses The clauses that witnesses sign to validate a will.

Automated teller machine (ATM) An electronic customer-bank communication terminal that, when activated by an access card and a personal identification number, can conduct routine banking transactions.

Bait and switch A selling technique that involves advertising a product at a very attractive price (the "bait"); then informing the consumer, once he or she is in the store, that the advertised product either is not available, is of poor quality, or is not what the

533

consumer "really wants"; and, finally, promoting a more expensive item (the "switch").

Balance of trade   The relationship between the value of a country's imports and exports: if exports have a greater value it has a positive balance of trade: if its imports have a greater value it has a negative balance of trade.

Bankruptcy   The state of having come under the provisions of the law that entitles a person's creditors to have that person's estate administered for their benefit.

Basic form policy   A homeowners' insurance policy that covers 11 risks.

Bed-and-breakfast   A business run by an individual who rents rooms in his or her home and provides breakfasts to travelers.

Beneficiary   The designated person or persons for any insurance policy. In a life insurance policy, the beneficiary is the person who receives the benefits when the insured dies.

Bond   A type of debt that a business or a government issues to investors. A bond represents a promise to pay a certain amount of money (called interest) each year. At the end of a specified amount of time, the principal on the bond is repaid to the bondholder.

Brand loyalty   A willingness by consumers to purchase a particular brand of product without seriously considering alternative brands.

Broad form policy   A homeowners' policy that covers 18 risks.

Bushing   Adding unordered accessories to a product to increase its price.

Capitalism   An economic system based on private ownership of the means of production and on a demand and supply market. This system emphasizes the absence of government restraints on ownership, production and trade.

Capital gain   An increase in the value of something you own. Generally, you experience a capital gain when you sell something you own, such as a house or a stock. You compute your capital gain by subtracting the price you paid for whatever you are selling from the price you receive when you sell it.

Capital loss   The difference between the buying and the selling price of something you own when the selling price is lower than the buying price.

Cashier's check   A check drawn on the bank by its own order to a designated person or institution. A cashier's check is paid for before it is obtained.

Cash value   Applied to whole life policies only, it represents the amount of "savings" built up in the policy and available to the living policyholder, either to borrow against or to receive if the policy is canceled.

Cease-and-desist order   An administrative or judicial order commanding a business firm to cease conducting the activities that the agency or a court has deemed to be "unfair or deceptive acts or practices."

Certificate of deposit   A federally insured deposit that cannot be cashed in before a specified time without paying an interest-reduction penalty.

Certified check   A check the bank has certified, indicating that sufficient funds are available to cover it when it is cashed.

Chlorofluorocarbons (CFCs)   A family of chemicals that are associated with the depletion of ozone in the earth's upper atmosphere.

Codicil   A written supplement to, or modification of, a will. Codicils must be executed with the same formalities as a will.

Collateral   The backing that people often must put up to obtain a loan. Whatever is placed as collateral for a loan can be sold to repay that loan if the debtor cannot pay it off as specified in the loan agreement. For example, the collateral for a new-car loan is generally the new car itself. If the finance company does not get paid for its car loan, it can then repossess the car and sell it to recover the amount of the loan.

Common law The unwritten system of law governing people's rights and duties, based on custom and fixed principles of justice. Common law is the foundation of both the English and U.S. legal systems (excluding Louisiana, where law is based on the Napoleonic Code).

Common stock A unit of ownership that has a legal claim to the profits of a company. For each share owned, the common-stock owner generally has the right to one vote on such questions as merging with another company or electing a new board of directors.

Comparative advertising Advertising that makes comparisons between a product and specific competing products.

Comparison shopping Comparison shopping is acquiring and comparing information about different sellers and different products in order to find the best price for products of substantially the same quality.

Compound interest When interest is paid on interest that has already been earned on a deposit or a loan.

Comprehensive form policy A homeowners' policy that covers all risks except, usually, flood, war, and nuclear attack.

Condominium An apartment house or complex in which each living unit is individually owned. Each owner receives a deed allowing him or her to sell, mortgage, or exchange the unit independently of the owners of the other units in the building. Title to a condominium also gives the purchaser shared ownership rights in common areas.

Conspicuous consumption Consumption of goods more for their ability to impress others than for the inherent satisfaction they yield.

Consumers Individuals who purchase (or are given), use, maintain, and dispose of products and services in their final form in an attempt to achieve the highest level of satisfaction possible with their income limitation.

Consumer durable goods Consumer goods with a lifetime that exceeds one year—for example, washers, dryers, refrigerators, and stereos.

Consumer price index (CPI) A price index based on a fixed representative market basket of about 400 goods and services purchased in 85 urban areas.

Consumer redress The right of consumers to seek and obtain satisfaction for damages incurred through the use of a product or a service: protection after the fact.

Consumer sovereignty A situation in which consumers ultimately decide which products and styles will survive in the marketplace; that is, producers do not dictate consumer tastes.

Cooling-off period A specific amount of time in which a consumer has the right to reconsider and back out of a transaction.

Cooperative An apartment building or complex in which each owner owns a proportionate share of a nonprofit corporation that holds title or a legal right to use the building.

Cost/benefit analysis A way to reach decisions in which all the costs are added up, as well as all the benefits. If benefits minus costs are greater than zero, then a net benefit exists and the decision should be positive. Alternatively, if benefits minus costs are less than zero, then a net cost exists and the decision should be positive.

Counteradvertising New advertising that is undertaken pursuant to a Federal Trade Commission order for the purpose of correcting earlier false claims made about a product.

Counting calories Keeping track of the calories you consume in your food versus the calories you expend by various activities. If you eat more calories than you expend, you will gain weight; if you expend more calories than you eat, you will lose weight.

Debit card A plastic card similar to a credit card that allows a consumer to use a computerized banking system.

Deductible The amount of out-of-pocket expenses that must be paid before the insurance company will start paying.

Deduction Different types of expenses taxpayers may subtract from their income before figuring their tax liability.

Defensive advertising Advertising intended to rebut claims made by competing firms about a firm's product or business practices.

Demand The quantity of a product that will be sold at each possible price.

Depository institution Any institution that can accept deposits; commercial banks, savings and loan associations, mutual savings banks, brokerage houses, and credit unions are depository institutions.

Depreciation A reduction or loss in value that occurs as a result of wear and age.

Diet or dietetic foods Low-calorie or reduced-calorie food, or food intended for a special dietary purpose—for example, low-sodium diets.

Discount points Additional charges added to a mortgage that effectively raise the rate of interest you pay.

Discretionary spending Spending for goods and services that are not necessities.

Durable power of attorney A document that specifically assigns the power to another person to make decisions for you should you become incapable of making your own.

Earnest money Sometimes called a deposit on a contract or an offer to purchase a house. It is the amount of money you put up to show that you are serious about the offer you are making to buy a house. Generally you sign an earnest agreement, or a contract that specifies the purchase price you are willing to pay for the house in question. If the owner selling the house signs, then you are committed to purchase the house; if you back down, you could lose the entire earnest money.

Economic system A set of understandings that governs the production and distribution of goods and services that satisfy human wants.

Electronic fund transfer A transfer of funds with the use of an electronic terminal, a telephone, a computer, or magnetic tape.

Electronic fund transfer systems (EFTS) Systems used to transfer funds electronically.

Energy budget A record of a family's energy-consumption expenses, which is formulated to make family members more conscious of the kilowatt hours used during a given time period and to limit those hours to reduce energy costs.

Energy labels Labels attached to new appliances that inform purchasers of the amount of energy each labeled appliance will require. Energy labeling of major appliances is mandated by the Energy Policy and Conservation Act of 1975.

Engel's law A proposition, first made by Ernst Engel, that states that as a family's income rises, the proportion spent on food falls.

Equilibrium price A price at which the quantity of a good or service demanded is exactly equal to the quantity that is supplied.

Equity   A legal claim to the profits of a company. This is another name for stock, generally called common stock.

Estate   The total property of whatever kind owned before the distribution of that property in accordance with the terms of a will (or, when there is no will, by the laws of inheritance in the state of domicile of the decedent).

Estate taxes   Taxes based on the value of the assets, minus the liabilities, of an estate when transferred to the ownership of others. These taxes are paid by the donor, if he or she is living when this transfer takes place, or by the estate, if the donor is dead.

Ethical behavior   Behavior that is directed by moral principles and values; determining what is "right" in a given situation and acting in accordance with that determination.

Ethical investing   Investing in corporations that are deemed to be socially responsible according to a given set of ethical criteria.

Ethical shopping   Purchasing products manufactured by socially responsible business firms and refusing to purchase products manufactured by firms whose ethical behavior is perceived to be reprehensible.

Excise tax   A tax that is collected from the manufacturer of a product.

Executor/executrix   The personal representative of the person who made a will. The executor/executrix takes charge of the estate, pays the debts, and so on.

Exemption   An amount of income that may be subtracted from income for each person a taxpayer supports.

Filing status   The family situation under which taxes are filed: single, married filing jointly, head of household, etc.

Finance charge   The total costs you pay for credit, including interest charges, possible credit-insurance premium costs and appraisal fees, and other service charges.

Fixed expenses   Expenses that occur at specific times and cannot be altered. Once a house is purchased or rented, a house payment is considered a fixed expense; so is a car payment.

Flexible expenses   Expenses that can be changed in the short run. The amount of money you spend on food can be considered a flexible expense because you can buy higher- or lower-quality food than you now are buying. These are also known as variable expenses.

Float time   The time between the issuance of a check and the deduction of the amount of the check from the drawer's account.

Fraud   Making a false statement of a past or existing fact with knowledge of its falsity, or with reckless indifference as to its truth, with the intent to cause someone to give up property or a right that has value.

Free rider problem   When individuals attempt to receive benefits from a good or service without paying their appropriate share.

Garnishment   (wage attachment) A court-ordered withholding of part of wages, the proceeds of which are used to satisfy unpaid debts.

Generalist   A lawyer who does not practice in a specialized field of law but who is qualified to provide legal advice in most normal situations.

General practitioner   A doctor who has a family practice rather than a specialized practice.

Generic drugs Non-name-brand medicines that are often sold at much lower prices than the same name-brand products.

Goods Tangible objects that have the ability to satisfy human wants.

Greenhouse effect The gradual warming of the earth's atmosphere, primarily as a result of the release of carbon dioxide from the burning of fossil fuels.

Hardware Computer equipment, including the computer itself and all input and output peripherals.

Health maintenance organization (HMO) A type of insurance plan in which members pay a flat fee in return for all medical services, provided they are administered by participating doctors and hospitals.

High-balling When an artificially high value offered for a product that is traded in is made up for by inflating the price of the new product.

Home energy audit A thorough check of your home to evaluate how much energy is being wasted. A home-energy auditor will recommend energy-saving steps you can take to reduce fuel and electric bills. Most public utilities offer this service free.

Hospice An organization that helps the families of terminally ill patients.

Human capital The skills and abilities humans have that allow them to produce goods and services from other productive resources.

Imperfect competition A market condition in which individual businesses have some power to set the price and quality of their products.

Implied warranty of fitness An implicit warranty of fitness for a particular purpose, meaning that the seller guarantees the product for the specific purpose for which a buyer will use the goods, when the seller is offering his or her skill and judgment as to suitable selection of the right products.

Implied warranty of merchantability An implicit promise by the seller that an item is reasonably fit for the general purpose for which it is sold.

Income transfer A transfer of income from some individuals in the economy to other individuals. This is generally done by the government. It is a transfer in the sense that no current services are rendered by the recipients. Unemployment insurance, for example, is an income transfer to unemployed individuals.

Individual retirement account (IRA) An investment account on which the earnings are not taxed until funds are withdrawn from the account, usually at retirement. IRA contributions may also be tax-deductible, depending on one's income level.

Inflation A sustained rise in the weighted average of all prices.

Informative advertising Advertising that simply informs.

Inheritance tax A tax assessed by the federal government or the state government (or both) on a certain portion of an estate upon the death of its owner.

Injunction A legal order requiring that an activity be stopped, corrected, or undertaken.

Inpatient services Services rendered to an individual by doctors and/or a hospital while the patient remains in the hospital for at least one night.

Inside information Information about a company's financial situation that is obtained before the public obtains it. True inside information is usually known only by corporate officials or other insiders.

Insurable interest Something of value that is to be insured.

Insurable risk   An insurer's understanding of the risk of insuring a particular object or condition.

Interactions   Reactions between drugs that sometimes can be life threatening.

Interest-adjusted cost (IAC)   An insurance cost index that takes account of dividends, interest, and earnings of the policy.

Interest   The cost of using someone else's money.

Intestacy laws   State laws determining the division of an intestate's (one who dies with no will) estate.

Intestate   To have died without a valid will.

Investment   Giving up something of value at the present to be able to receive something else of greater value in the future.

Joint tenancy   Two or more people owning a percentage, but not a specific piece, of some form of property. When one owner dies, the surviving owner(s) assumes full ownership of the property.

Keogh plans   A retirement program designed for self-employed persons by which a certain percentage of their income can be sheltered from taxation. As with IRAs, interest earnings are not taxed until withdrawal.

Law of demand   A basic economic principle that states that as the price of goods or services rises, the quantity of those goods and services demanded will fall. Conversely, as the price falls, the quantity demanded will rise.

Law of supply   A basic economic principle that states that as the price of goods or services rises, the quantity of those goods and services supplied will increase. Conversely, as the price falls the quantity supplied will also decline.

Lease   A contract by which one conveys real estate for a specified period of time and usually for a specified rent; and the act of such conveyance or the term for which it is made.

Legacy   A gift of property by will, usually a specific gift to a specific person.

Liability   Something for which you are liable or responsible according to law or equity, especially pecuniary debts or obligations.

Lien   A claim placed on the property of another as security for some debt or charge.

Light, lite, or reduced calorie   Foods that contain one-third fewer calories per serving than comparable unmodified food products. If the word "light" is used to describe a food's appearance the label must state that the word is being used in this way.

Liquid asset   An asset that can be easily turned into cash.

Litigants   Those people involved in a lawsuit, that is, in the process of litigation.

Living benefits   Benefits paid on a whole life insurance policy while the person is living. Living benefits include fixed and variable annuities.

Living will   A document that grants specific authority to a person or persons to discontinue the artificial prolongation of life; now allowed in 40 states plus the District of Columbia.

Loopholes   Legal methods of reducing tax liabilities.

Low-balling   Offering to sell a product at a low price in a telephone conversation and then increasing the price when the consumer visits the firm to purchase the product.

Low calorie   Foods that contain no more than 40 calories per 100 gram (3.5 ounce) serving.

Low in saturated fat   Foods that have 1 gram or less of saturated fat per serving and in which no more than 15 percent of the calories come from saturated fat.

Luxury good   A good whose purchase increases more than in proportion to increases in income. Jewelry, gourmet foods, and sports cars usually fall into this category.

Marginal tax rate   The share of the next dollar earned that must be paid in taxes.

Market   The sum of all transactions that take place between buyers and sellers of a particular type of product.

Market economy   An economy that is characterized by exchanges in markets that are controlled by the forces of demand and supply.

Market power   The ability of producers to change price and/or quality without substantially losing sales.

Money income   The total amount of actual dollars you receive per week, per month, or per year.

Money market deposit account (MMDA)   A checkable account on which a depository institution can pay a market-determined interest rate.

Money price   The price that we observe today in terms of today's dollars. Also called the absolute, nominal, or current price.

Monopoly   The only producer of a product that has no substitutes.

Mortgage   A loan obtained for the purpose of purchasing land or buildings, in which the property is pledged as security.

Municipal bonds   Bonds sold by government entities, such as cities. The distinguishing feature of these bonds is that the interest income from them is nontaxable.

Mutual fund   A fund that purchases the stocks of other companies. If you buy a share in a mutual fund, you are, in essence, buying shares in all the companies in which the mutual fund invests. The only business of a mutual fund is buying other companies' stocks.

Negotiable order of withdrawal (NOW)   The equivalent of a check covered by a special type of interest-earning account.

Net worth   The difference between the value of your assets and your liabilities—that is, what you are actually worth.

Nonlegal professional   A person who is not a lawyer but who is qualified to provide legal advice about specific situations.

No-fault auto insurance   A system of auto insurance whereby, no matter who is at fault, the individual is paid by his or her insurance company for a certain amount of medical costs and for the damage to the car.

OASDHI   Old Age, Survivors, Disability, and Hospital Insurance—the government name for Social Security insurance.

Opportunity cost   The value of a second-best choice that is given up when a first choice is taken.

Outpatient services The services of doctors and/or hospitals that do not require the individual to remain as a registered patient in the hospital.

Parkinson's law Work will expand to fit the time allotted for it.

Perfect competition A market condition in which many businesses offer the same product for sale to many customers at the same price.

Personal identification number (PIN) A number given to the holder of a debit card that is used to conduct financial transactions in electronic fund transfer systems. Typically, the card will not provide access to a system without the number, which is meant to be kept secret to inhibit unauthorized use of the card.

Persuasive advertising Advertising intended to associate a specific product with a certain lifestyle or image in the minds of consumers.

Plaintiff One who initiates a lawsuit.

Point-of-sale system An electronic customer-merchant-bank communication terminal that, when activated by a debit card and a personal identification number (PIN), can debit the customer's account to cover a purchase from the merchant.

Preferred provider organization (PPO) A type of insurance plan similar to an HMO but more flexible. In a PPO members are allowed to choose the services of non-PPO medical providers in return for a higher copayment or deductible.

Preferred stock A unit of ownership in a corporation; each share entitles the owner to a fixed dividend that the corporation must pay before it pays any dividends to common stockholders; owners have call on the firm's assets before common stockholders if the firm fails, but have no vote in choosing the firm's board of directors.

Premium The payment that must be made to the insurance company to keep an insurance policy in effect. Premiums usually are paid quarterly, semiannually, or annually.

Prepayment privileges In a mortgage loan with prepayment privileges, you can prepay your loan before the maturity date and not have to pay a penalty.

Preventive medicine Medical procedures carried out with the intention of preventing people from becoming ill.

Principal A capital sum that is distinguished from interest; it is the original amount deposited or loaned.

Private costs The costs that are incurred by an individual and no one else. The private costs of driving a car, for example, include depreciation, gas, insurance, and so on.

Probate Proving a will before a court having jurisdiction over the administration of the estate.

Productive resources Raw materials, tools, and labor that may be used to produce other goods or services that have the ability to satisfy human wants.

Profit The difference between the total amount of money income received from selling a good or a service and the total cost of providing that good or service.

Progressive taxation A taxing system in which the greater your income is, the greater the share of that income you will pay in tax.

Proportional taxation A taxing system in which all people pay the same share of their income in tax.

Pro rata Proportionately; that is, according to some exactly calculable factor.

Psychic income The satisfaction derived from a work situation or occupation; non-monetary rewards from doing a particular job.

Pyramid scheme   An illegal sales plan through which people collect fees and a share of income earned from sales made by other individuals they recruit into the program.

Rational consumer decision making   Making consumer decisions that maximize the satisfaction you can obtain from your time and money resources and that assist you in attaining life-long, as well as short-term, goals.

Real values   Dollar values that have been adjusted for inflation.

Recommended dietary allowances (RDAs)   A system devised by the National Academy of Sciences in which a specified daily intake of particular vitamins and nutrients is given for infants, children, males, and females, as well as pregnant and lactating women. Not to be confused with U.S. recommended daily allowances.

Reduced sodium   Foods that contain no more than half the sodium of an identified comparison food.

Regressive taxation   A taxing system in which the greater your income is, the smaller the percent of that income you will pay in tax.

Regulation E   The set of rules issued by the Federal Reserve Board to protect users of electronic banking services.

Relative price   The price of a commodity expressed in terms of the price of another commodity or the (weighted) average price of all other commodities.

Residence contents broad form policy   A renters' insurance policy that covers possessions against 18 risks. It includes additional living expenses and liability coverage in case someone is injured in the apartment or house you are renting.

Resume   A brief summary of your education, training, and other achievements that you give to a prospective employer.

Rider   A written attachment to an insurance policy that alters the policy to meet certain conditions, such as convertibility, double indemnity, and so on.

Right of rescission   The right to cancel a contract or an agreement that has been signed. For example, if you sign an agreement to buy a set of encyclopedias from a door-to-door salesperson, you have the right to cancel the agreement within a three-day period in some states.

Saving   The act of not consuming or not spending your money income to obtain current satisfaction.

Scarcity   A term used to describe the condition in which we are unable to provide enough products to satisfy all people's needs and wants because of our limited resources.

Services   Intangible actions that have the ability to satisfy human wants.

Service contract   For an annual fee, the appliance owner receives a contract allowing for all repairs to be made without further payments.

Service flow   The flow of benefits received from an item that has been purchased or made. Consumer durables generally give a service flow that lasts over a period of time. For example, the service flow from a VCR may be a certain amount of satisfaction received from it every year for five years.

Socialist economic system   An economic system in which there is group (most often government) ownership of productive resources and control over the distribution of goods and services.

Social costs   The costs that society bears for an action. For example, the social costs of driving a car include any pollution or congestion caused by that automobile.

Software   Programs that direct the computer in problem solving and other tasks. Software programs are packaged in the form of cassette tapes, cartridges, or diskettes.

Specialization   The concentration of efforts on one area of production with the aim of having a comparative advantage in the marketplace. Students specialize when they major in a certain subject at college, thus allowing them to have a comparative advantage in the job market later—assuming there is a demand for their specialized knowledge.

Standard deduction   An amount all taxpayers are allowed to subtract from their income before figuring their tax liability. The amount varies depending on the taxpayer's filing status.

Stock market   An organized market where shares of ownership in businesses are traded. These shares generally are called stocks. The largest stock market in the United States is the New York Stock Exchange.

Stop-payment order   An order to one's bank not to honor a particular check when it is presented for payment.

Super NOW account   A checking-type account available in most commercial banks in which market rates of interest are paid, provided that a minimum balance (originally $2,500) is maintained in the account.

Supply   The quantity of a product businesses are willing to offer for sale at each possible price.

Tax exempt   An investment that yields income that is not taxed. Generally, tax exempts are municipal bonds with an interest rate that is not taxed by the U.S. government.

Technological obsolescence   The process of a product becoming obsolete due to technological advances. This problem is particularly notable in the high-tech electronics industry, in which the rapid development of new, state-of-the-art products significantly diminishes the utility and value of previously marketed models.

Tenancy by the entirety   Joint owners of property are husband and wife.

Tenancy in common   A form of joint ownership in which owners are not free to sell their shares in the property until it has been partitioned, and that does not provide for the automatic inheritance of the property of deceased owners by the other owners.

Term insurance   Life insurance that is for a specified term (period of time) and has only a death benefit; it is a form of pure insurance with no savings aspect.

Testamentary trust   A will or trust that bestows specific rights on specific individuals after the death of the person who created the will or trust.

Testamonium clause   The concluding clause of a will that indicates you are signing your name to approve it.

Testate   To have died and left a valid will.

Testator/testatrix   A person who has made a will.

Third market   A network of traders who bypass the major stock exchanges.

Time deposit   Deposits that in principle cannot be withdrawn until the end of a specific period of time. This right of a bank, however, is not generally exercised.

Time-sharing plan   An agreement through which consumers purchase the right to use a vacation facility for a specified period of time each year.

Title   The physical representation of your legal ownership of a house. The title is sometimes called the deed.

Title insurance Insurance that you pay for when you buy a house so you can be assured that the title, or legal ownership, to the house is free and clear.

Townhouse A house that shares common sidewalls with other, similar houses.

Tradeoff A term relating to opportunity cost. To get a desired economic good, it is necessary to trade off some other desired economic good whenever we are in a world of scarcity. A tradeoff involves a sacrifice, then, that must be made to obtain something.

Transaction costs All the costs associated with completing an exchange beyond the price of the product that is purchased.

Traveler's check A check purchased from a financial institution and signed by the purchaser at the time it is purchased. The check can be used as cash upon a second signature by the purchaser. It has the characteristics of a cashier's check.

True-name fraud When a person uses another individual's identity to obtain and use credit cards issued in the other person's name.

Trust Real or personal property held or managed by one person (the trustee) for the benefit of another (the beneficiary).

Trustee The person holding legal title to trust property.

Umbrella policy A type of supplemental insurance policy that can extend normal liability limits to $1 million or more for a relatively small premium.

Underwriter The company that stands behind the face value of any insurance policy. The underwriter signs its name to an insurance policy, thereby becoming answerable for a designated loss or damage on consideration of receiving a premium payment.

Uniform decreasing term insurance A term insurance policy on which the premiums are uniform throughout its life, but the face value of the policy declines.

U.S. recommended daily allowances (U.S. RDAs) Related to recommended dietary allowances but in a simplified form. The U.S. RDAs are the maximum amount of each nutrient needed for four broad categories of the population.

Values Fundamental concepts or high-level preferences that regulate our behavior. High-level values determine lower-level tastes and preferences that affect our everyday lives.

Voluntary exchange Transactions completed through the free will of those involved.

Warranty of habitability An implied warranty made by a landlord to a tenant that leased or rented residential premises are in a condition that is safe and suitable for human habitation.

Whole life insurance Insurance that has both death and living benefits. That is, part of your premium is put into a type of savings account.

Will A written document that allows a person to determine the disposition of his or her property at death.

W-2 form The form used by employers to report employee income and withholding to the employee and the government.

Zero deductible In the collision part of an automobile insurance policy, the provision that the insured pays nothing for any repair to damage on the car due to an accident that is the fault of the insured. Zero deductible is, of course, more expensive than a $100 or $200 deductible policy.

Index

Tenancy by the entirety, 497
Tenancy in common, 497
Term insurance, 463–465
Testamentary trust, 498
Testate, 494
Testator/testatrix, 494
Textile Fiber Products Identification Act, 29, 239
Third market, 405, 408
Time deposits, 378–380
    disadvantages of, 379
    reasons for, 379
    variety of, 379–380
Time management, 70–72
    list making and, 72
    Parkinson's Law, 71–72
    planning, 72
    rewards and, 72
Time-sharing plan, 170, 171
Title, 255
Title insurance, 255
TOPS, 224
Townhouse, 257
Toy Safety Act, 29
Tradeoff, 6
Transaction costs, 63
Transaction plan, 325
Traveler's check, 328
Treasury securities, 383
True-name fraud, 122, 123
Trustee, 497
Trusts, 496, 497–499
Truth-in-Lending Act, 29, 352–354, 355, 361
Truth in Savings Act, 380

U. S. Department of Agriculture (USDA),
    grades on food, 201, 203
U. S. Postal Service, 52, 53, 100
U. S. Recommended Daily Allowances (RDA),
    206–207
U. S. Savings Bonds, 381–382
Umbrella policy, 447
Underwood-Simmons Tariff Act, 181
Underwriter, 462
Uniform Commercial Code, 41
Uniform decreasing term insurance, 464

Universal life insurance, 468–470
Unsafe at Any Speed (Nader), 31, 300

Vacations, 170–174
    advantages of special vacation plans, 316
    cutting costs, 172
    growth in, 170
    state and national parks, 173–174
Value clarification, 65–66
Value pattern, 229
Values, 64–67
    clothing and, 229
    customs and, 64–65
    defined, 64
    formation of, 64–65
    goals and, 66–67
Veterans' Reemployment Rights Act, 143
Veterans Administration (VA),
    mortgage loans by, 260–261
Voluntary exchange, 7

W-2 form, 185
Wages:
    age/earnings profile, 135–136, 138
    ages and, 138
    different occupations and, 137–139
    education and, 134–135
    inflation and, 144
    legislation and, 142–143
    women and, 140–141
Walsh-Healey Act, 143
Warranties, 40–42
    for appliances, 289
    of brand-name products, 94–95
    express, 41
    full, 40–41
    implied, 41–42
    limited, 40–41
    loans for, 311–313
    Magnuson-Moss Warranty Act and, 40
    new home, 450
    for used automobiles, 311
Warranty of habitability, 268, 271
Washington, George, 346
Weight-loss products, fraud and, 113
Whole life insurance, 463, 465–468

Wholesome Meat Act, 29
Weight Watchers, 224
Wills:
    administrative clauses of, 508
    attestation clause, 508
    avoiding mistakes in, 509–510
    changing, 510
    codicil for, 508, 510
    defined, 494
    disinheritance and, 509
    dispositive clause of, 508
    executor of, 508–509
    how to make out, 508–510
    joint ownership and, 497
    joint tenancy, 497
    legacy and, 508
    letter of last instruction and, 510
    limitations on disposition of property and,
        495–496
    living, 501
    organ donation and, 501–502
    probate of, 496
    tenancy by the entirety, 497
    tenancy in common, 497
    testamonium clause of, 508
    trusts and, 496, 497–499
    wealth taxation and, 499–501
    where to keep, 510
    why make out, 495
Wilson, Woodrow, 322
Wilson-Gorman Tariff Act, 181
Women:
    as participants in workplace, 140–141
    wages of, compared to men, 135, 138, 141
Wood-burning stoves, 296–297
Wool Products Labeling Act, 29, 238–239
Worker Adjustment and Retraining Notification
    Act, 143
Workplace, environmental concerns, 77
Wraparound mortgage, 263
Writ of execution, 56

Your Money's Worth (Chase), 31

Zero-coupon bonds, 409
Zero deductible, 453

Credits